THE OXFORD HANDBOOK OF
CHRISTMAS

THE OXFORD HANDBOOK OF
CHRISTMAS

Edited by
TIMOTHY LARSEN

Great Clarendon Street, Oxford, OX2 6DP,
United Kingdom

Oxford University Press is a department of the University of Oxford.
It furthers the University's objective of excellence in research, scholarship,
and education by publishing worldwide. Oxford is a registered trade mark of
Oxford University Press in the UK and in certain other countries

© Oxford University Press 2020

The moral rights of the authors have been asserted

First Edition published in 2020

Impression: 1

All rights reserved. No part of this publication may be reproduced, stored in
a retrieval system, or transmitted, in any form or by any means, without the
prior permission in writing of Oxford University Press, or as expressly permitted
by law, by licence or under terms agreed with the appropriate reprographics
rights organization. Enquiries concerning reproduction outside the scope of the
above should be sent to the Rights Department, Oxford University Press, at the
address above

You must not circulate this work in any other form
and you must impose this same condition on any acquirer

Published in the United States of America by Oxford University Press
198 Madison Avenue, New York, NY 10016, United States of America

British Library Cataloguing in Publication Data

Data available

Library of Congress Control Number: 2020937120

ISBN 978-0-19-883146-4

Printed and bound by
CPI Group (UK) Ltd, Croydon, CR0 4YY

Links to third party websites are provided by Oxford in good faith and
for information only. Oxford disclaims any responsibility for the materials
contained in any third party website referenced in this work.

For Tom Perridge
With ongoing gratitude. Nadolig Llawen.

Contents

List of Illustrations	xi
List of Contributors	xiii
A Note on the Cover Image	xxi

PART I HISTORY

1. The Dating of Christmas: The Early Church — 3
   PAUL F. BRADSHAW

2. The Middle Ages — 15
   KATI IHNAT

3. The Reformation and Early Modern Periods — 27
   KATRINA JENNIE-LOU WHEELER

4. The Nineteenth Century — 35
   TIMOTHY LARSEN

5. The Twentieth and Twenty-First Centuries — 51
   CHRISTOPHER FERGUSON

PART II THEOLOGY

6. The Old Testament — 67
   JOHN BARTON

7. The New Testament — 77
   MARKUS BOCKMUEHL AND EVANGELINE KOZITZA

8. Jesus Christ and the Incarnation — 90
   KATHERINE SONDEREGGER

9. The Blessed Virgin Mary and the Virgin Birth — 102
   KATHERINE G. SCHMIDT

PART III WORSHIPPING COMMUNITIES

10. Roman Catholicism 113
    ANNE McGOWAN

11. Eastern Orthodoxy 126
    MARY B. CUNNINGHAM

12. Lutheranism 141
    KIRSI STJERNA

13. Anglicanism 153
    MARTYN PERCY

14. Reformed and Dissenting Protestants 167
    ANDREW R. HOLMES

PART IV THE NATIVITY STORY

15. The Holy Family 185
    HOLLY TAYLOR COOLMAN

16. Gabriel and the Angels 192
    DAVID LYLE JEFFREY

17. Bethlehem and the Census 203
    LEROY A. HUIZENGA

18. The Magi and the Star 213
    D. H. WILLIAMS

19. The Inn, the Manger, the Swaddling Cloths, the Shepherds, and the Animals 224
    JODY VACCARO LEWIS

PART V TRADITIONS

20. The Winter Solstice and other Celebrations of the Season 239
    DANIEL GIFFORD

21. St Nicholas to Santa Claus 252
    ADAM C. ENGLISH

22. Trees and Decorations   265
DAVID BERTAINA

23. Gifts and Charity   277
ELLEN M. LITWICKI

24. Children and Childhood   288
MARCIA J. BUNGE

25. Food and Drink   297
PAUL FREEDMAN

PART VI THE ARTS

26. Carols and Music to 1900   311
TOVA LEIGH-CHOATE

27. Carols and Music since 1900   329
TODD DECKER

28. Paintings   346
BARBARA VON BARGHAHN

29. Plays   371
FRANCES CLEMSON

30. Poetry   384
EMMA MASON

31. Fiction   397
NATALIE MCKNIGHT

32. Film and Television   411
MARK CONNELLY

PART VII AROUND THE WORLD

33. Bethlehem and the Middle East   423
ELIZABETH MONIER

34. Catholic Europe   433
NADINE CRETIN

35. Germany and Scandinavia — 445
    JOE PERRY

36. Russia — 463
    FRANCESCA SILANO

37. The United Kingdom — 475
    MARTIN JOHNES

38. The United States — 489
    DANIEL VACA

39. Africa — 500
    JOEL CABRITA

40. Asia — 511
    JOSEPH TSE-HEI LEE

41. Latin America and the Caribbean — 522
    DAVID THOMAS ORIQUE, O.P.

PART VIII THE STATE AND SOCIETY

42. Public Holidays and the Law — 537
    RICHARD W. GARNETT AND JACKSON C. BLAIS

43. Commercialism and Consumerism — 549
    JOHN SCHMALZBAUER

44. Secularity — 560
    DAVID NASH

45. Culture Wars — 570
    GERRY BOWLER

    Epilogue: The Many True Meanings of Christmas — 581
    TIMOTHY LARSEN

Index — 585

List of Illustrations

11.1 Icon of the Nativity of Christ by Onufri, 16th century, National Museum of Medieval Art, Korce, Albania © PRISMA ARCHIVO/Alamy Stock Photo.   133

28.1 FRA FILIPPO LIPPI, The Murate Annunciation Altarpiece (tempera on poplar), 1443–45 (203 × 186 cm: 79.9 × 73"), Munich Alte Pinakothek 1072. © PRISMA ARCHIVO/Alamy Stock Photo.   347

28.2 KONRAD WITZ, The Counsel of Salvation and the Visitation, left wing of a dispersed Redemption Altarpiece (tempera on fir), ca. 1445, (135.3 × 164 cm: 53.3 × 64.6"), Berlin, Gemäldegalerie, Staatliche Museen Preußischer Kulturbesitz, Basel, Alte Pinakothek (Photo: Jörg P. Anders, No. 1673, 1910 donated by F. Kleinberger, Paris). © Peter Horree/Alamy Stock Photo.   349

28.3 PIETER BRUEGHEL THE ELDER, The Census at Bethlehem, S&D 1566, oil on panel (116 × 164.5 cm: 45.7 × 64.8"), Brussels, Musées Royaux des Beaux-Arts 3637. © Art Collection 2/Alamy Stock Photo.   350

28.4 ROBERT CAMPIN, The Nativity of Christ, oil on panel (84.1 × 69.9: 33.1 × 27.5"), ca. 1425–30, Dijon, Musée des Beaux-Arts 150. © classicpaintings/Alamy Stock Photo.   352

28.5 GEORGES DE LA TOUR, The Adoration of the Shepherds, ca. 1644, oil on canvas (107 × 137 cm: 42 × 54"), Paris, Louvre Museum R.F. 2555. © Peter Horree/Alamy Stock Photo.   354

28.6 JACOB CORNELISZ VAN OOSTSANEN, The Circumcision of Christ, 1517, oil and fabric on panel (109.2 × 60.5: 43 × 23.8), monogram and date bottom centre, Gift of the Samuel H. Kress Foundation, Portland Art Museum, Oregon 61.59.   356

28.7 GERBRAND VAN DEN EECKHOUT, Simeon in the Temple (The Presentation of Christ in the Temple), S&D 1672, oil on canvas (84.5 × 105.1 cm: 33.3 × 41.4"), Collection Thomas S. Kaplan and Daphne Recanati Kaplan, (cur.) Arthur Wheelock. The Leiden Collection GE-100.   358

28.8 PETER PAUL RUBENS, The Adoration of the Magi, 1624, oil on panel (447 × 336 cm: 14'81/8 × 11'43/10"), Antwerp, Koninklijk Museum voor Schone Kunsten, 194612. © ICP/incamerastock/Alamy Stock Photo.   360

28.9 DANIELE CRESPI, Joseph's Dream, 1620–1630, oil on canvas (297 × 203 cm: 116.9 × 79.9"), Vienna, Kunsthistorisches Museum GG 271. © Dipper Historic/Alamy Stock Photo. 362

28.10 JOACHIM PATINER, Rest during the Flight into Egypt, 1518–1520, oil on panel (121 × 177 cm: 47.6 × 69.6"), Madrid, Museo del Prado P001611. © Javier Larrea, agefotostock/Alamy Stock Photo. 364

28.11 NICOLAS POUSSIN, The Return of the Holy Family from Egypt, ca. 1627, oil on canvas (134 × 99 cm: 52 3/4 × 39"), Cleveland Museum of Art, Gift of the Hanna Fund 1953.156. © ICP/incamerastock/Alamy Stock Photo. 366

28.12 BARTOLOMÉ ESTÉBAN MURILLO, The Holy Family with the Infant St. John the Baptist, 1655–1660, oil on canvas (156 × 126 cm: 61.4 × 49.6), Budapest, Szépmüvészeti Múzeum, 779. © Mariano Garcia/Alamy Stock Photo. 368

List of Contributors

John Barton was Oriel and Laing Professor of the Interpretation of Holy Scripture at the University of Oxford, 1991–2014, and is now a Senior Research Fellow of Campion Hall, Oxford. He is a Fellow of the British Academy. His most recent book *is A History of the Bible: The Book and Its Faiths*, London: Allen Lane, 2019.

David Bertaina is Professor of History at the University of Illinois at Springfield. He researches religious history, including Christian–Muslim encounters and the development of the Christmas feast in the Christian East. Bertaina has published *Christian-Muslim Dialogues* (2011) and co-edited *Heirs of the Apostles: Studies on Arabic Christianity in Honor of Sidney H. Griffith* (2019), and he also teaches a course on the History of Christmas.

Jackson C. Blais is a recent graduate of the Notre Dame Law School where he served as the Executive Note Editor on the *Notre Dame Law Review* and a Brief Writer for the Moot Court Board. He currently works as a law clerk for the United States District Court for the Middle District of North Carolina.

Markus Bockmuehl is the Dean Ireland's Professor in the Exegesis of Holy Scripture at the University of Oxford and a Fellow of Keble College. Among his authored books are *Seeing the Word: Refocusing New Testament Study* (2006), *Simon Peter in Scripture and Memory* (2012), and *Ancient Apocryphal Gospels* (2017).

Gerry Bowler is a Canadian historian and a Senior Fellow of the Frontier Centre for Public Policy. His works include *The World Encyclopedia of Christmas* (2000), *Santa Claus: A Biography* (2005), *Christmas in the Crosshairs* (2016), and *The World's Greatest Christmas Stories* (2018).

Paul F. Bradshaw is Emeritus Professor of Liturgy at the University of Notre Dame, a former President of the North American Academy of Liturgy and of the international association Societas Liturgica, and from 1987 to 2005 editor-in-chief of the scholarly journal, *Studia Liturgica*. He has written or edited more than thirty books, together with over 130 essays or articles in periodicals.

Marcia J. Bunge is Professor of Religion and the Bernhardson Distinguished Chair of Lutheran Studies at Gustavus Adolphus College (St. Peter, Minnesota) and Extraordinary Research Professor at NW University (South Africa). She has published numerous articles and five books on conceptions of childhood in world religions, including

The Child in Christian Thought (2001), *The Child in the Bible* (2008), and *Children, Adults, and Shared Responsibilities: Jewish, Christian, and Muslim Perspectives* (2012).

Joel Cabrita is Assistant Professor of African History at Stanford University. She has held previous positions at the University of Cambridge and SOAS, University of London. Her books include *The People's Zion: Southern Africa, the United States and a Transatlantic Faith Healing Movement* (2018); *Religion, Media and Marginality in Africa* (2018); *Relocating World Christianities* (2017), and *Text and Authority in the South African Nazaretha Church* (2014).

Frances Clemson is Assistant Professor in Theology and Ministry at Durham University, UK. She is the author of a forthcoming book on theology and drama in the work of Dorothy L. Sayers, and has written chapters on drama in the edited collection *Peacebuilding and the Arts* (2020), and on theologies of time and tradition in *Thinking Again About Marriage: Key Theological Questions* (2016).

Mark Connelly is Professor of Modern British History at the University of Kent. His main research and teaching interests focus on war, commemoration, and popular culture, including the celebration of Christmas in Britain and the British Empire. His publications include, *Christmas. A Social History* (new edition, 2012), and the edited collection, *Christmas at the Movies: Images of Christmas in American, British and European Cinema* (2000).

Holly Taylor Coolman is Assistant Professor of Theology, Providence College. She has written on the law in the thought of Aquinas and the family, particularly adoption.

Nadine Cretin is a historian who specializes in religious anthropology in Europe (PhD, EHESS, Paris). She is a member of the *Société d'Ethnologie Française*, and has written twelve books about the history of festivities, most notably about Christmas, the most fascinating and complex of them all.

Mary B. Cunningham is Honorary Associate Professor of Historical Theology at the University of Nottingham. She has published books and articles in the fields of Byzantine homiletics, the Virgin Mary, Byzantine theology, and church history. Recent publications include *Gateway of Life: Orthodox Thinking on the Mother of God* (2015) and (with T. Arentzen), *The Reception of the Virgin in Byzantium: Marian Narratives in Texts and Images* (2019).

Todd Decker is the Paul Tietjens Professor of Music at Washington University in St. Louis. The author of four books and numerous articles on American popular music and media, he has presented at the Library of Congress, London's Victoria and Albert Museum, and Labex-Arts H2H in Paris. Decker edits the journal, *American Music*.

Adam C. English serves as Chair of the Department of Christian Studies and as Professor of Christian Theology and Philosophy at Campbell University, North Carolina. He is author of *The Saint Who Would Be Santa Claus* (Baylor University Press, 2012) and *Christmas: Theological Anticipations* (Cascade, 2016).

Christopher Ferguson is Associate Professor of History at Auburn University. He is the author of *An Artisan Intellectual: James Carter and the Rise of Modern Britain, 1792–1853* (2016).

Paul Freedman is Professor of Medieval History at Yale University where he has taught since 1997. His doctoral degree was awarded in 1978 by UC Berkeley. His interests are in the Middle Ages and in the history of food and cuisine. His book, *Ten Restaurants that Changed America*, was published in 2016, and a more general work on American food history, *American Cuisine and How It Got This Way* appeared in 2019.

Richard W. Garnett is Paul J. Schierl/Fort Howard Corporation Professor of Law, Concurrent Professor of Political Science, and Founding Director of the Notre Dame Program on Church, State and Society at the University of Notre Dame. He teaches and writes in the areas of Criminal Law and Constitutional Law, with an emphasis on the freedoms of speech and religion. He has published extensively on questions relating to religious freedoms and church–state relations. His current book project is titled *Two There Are: Understanding the Separation of Church and State*.

Daniel Gifford has a career that spans both academia and public history, including several years with the Smithsonian Institution. He teaches at multiple universities in the Louisville, Kentucky area, focusing his courses on American popular and visual culture, as well as museum studies. His book, *American Holiday Postcards 1905–1915: Imagery and Context* (McFarland Press, 2013), examines deep divides at the height of the Progressive Era as expressed through holidays and holiday imagery.

Andrew R. Holmes is Reader in History in the School of History, Anthropology, Philosophy, and Politics at Queen's University Belfast. He is the author of *The Shaping of Ulster Presbyterian Belief and Practice, 1770–1840* (OUP 2006) and *The Irish Presbyterian Mind: Conservative Theology, Evangelical Experience, and Modern Criticism 1830–1930* (OUP 2018).

Leroy A. Huizenga is the Administrative Chair of Arts and Letters and Associate Professor of Theology at the University of Mary in Bismarck, North Dakota. He is the author of *The New Isaac: Tradition and Intertextuality in the Gospel of Matthew* (2012) and *Loosing the Lion: Proclaiming the Gospel of Mark* (2017).

Kati Ihnat is Assistant Professor of Medieval History at the Radboud University Nijmegen. Her book, *Mother of Mercy, Bane of the Jews: Devotion to the Virgin Mary in Anglo-Norman England*, reflects her wider interest in religious life and practice in medieval Europe, now focusing increasingly on early medieval Spain.

David Lyle Jeffrey is Distinguished Senior Fellow of Baylor University's Institute for Studies in Religion, Emeritus Distinguished Professor of Literature and the Humanities at Baylor, and Guest Professor, Peking University in Beijing. He is the author of a theological commentary on Luke (2012), *In the Beauty of Holiness: Art and the Bible in Western Culture* (2017), and *Scripture and the English Poetic Imagination* (2019).

Martin Johnes is Professor of Modern History at Swansea University (Wales) where he teaches and researches the histories of British popular culture and modern Wales. His books include *Christmas and the British: A Modern History* (2016), *Wales: England's Colony?* (2019), and *Wales since 1939* (2012).

Evangeline Kozitza is in the final stages of her D.Phil. in New Testament Studies at the University of Oxford. Her doctoral dissertation offers a fresh reading of the Matthean and Lukan infancy narratives through the lenses of visuality, aurality, and reception history.

Timothy Larsen is McManis Professor of Christian Thought, Wheaton College, and an Honorary Fellow, School of Divinity, University of Edinburgh. He has been a Visiting Fellow at Trinity College, Cambridge, and All Souls College, Oxford. His books include *Crisis of Doubt: Honest Faith in Nineteenth-Century England* (2006); *A People of One Book: The Bible and the Victorians* (2011); *The Slain God: Anthropologists and the Christian Faith* (2014); and *John Stuart Mill: A Secular Life* (2018).

Tova Leigh-Choate (Ph.D., Yale, 2009) is a cultural historian specializing in the intersections of sacred music and liturgy with other forms of commemoration in the Middle Ages and beyond, from hagiography to iconography to food. Her current book project, a study of music, memory, and the miraculous at Abbot Suger's Saint-Denis, was supported by a twelve-month fellowship from the National Endowment for the Humanities. She has also contributed to Brill's *Companion to Hildegard of Bingen* (2014).

Joseph Tse-Hei Lee is Professor of History at Pace University, New York. His research focuses on faith and politics in China. He is the author of *The Bible and the Gun: Christianity in South China, 1860–1900* (New York: 2003), and *Context and Vision: Visualizing Chinese–Western Cultural Encounters in Chaoshan* (with Christie Chui-Shan Chow, Beijing: 2017).

Jody Vaccaro Lewis is Assistant Professor of Sacred Scripture and Patrology at the Pontifical Faculty of the Immaculate Conception at the Dominican House of Studies in Washington, D.C. She works in the areas of the history of Christian exegesis, early Christian biography, and women, marriage, and family in early Christianity.

Ellen M. Litwicki is Professor Emerita of History at the State University of New York at Fredonia, and a former Fulbright Scholar at the University of Szeged (Hungary). Her publications include *America's Public Holidays 1865–1920* (2000) and articles on American holidays and gift giving.

Emma Mason is Professor and Head of English and Comparative Literary Studies at the University of Warwick. She has written widely on religion and poetry, and with Mark Knight is general editor of Bloomsbury's New Directions in Religion and Literature series. Her most recent book is *Christina Rossetti: Poetry, Ecology, Faith* (Oxford University Press, 2018).

Anne McGowan is Assistant Professor of Liturgy at Catholic Theological Union in Chicago. She is the author of *Eucharistic Epicleses, Ancient and Modern* (2014) and co-author (with Paul Bradshaw) of *The Pilgrimage of Egeria: A New Translation of the Itinerarium Egeriae with Introduction and Commentary* (2018).

Natalie McKnight is Professor of Humanities and Dean of the College of General Studies at Boston University. She has published several books and numerous articles and book chapters on Victorian fiction and is currently President of the Dickens Society and Co-Editor of *Dickens Studies Annual*.

Elizabeth Monier is an Early Career Fellow in Middle Eastern Studies, Department of Middle Eastern Studies, University of Cambridge, supported by the Leverhulme Foundation and the Isaac Newton Trust.

David Nash is Professor of History at Oxford Brookes University. He has researched the history of atheism, secularism, and blasphemy in Britain for thirty-five years. He has also advised the British and Irish governments, the European Commission, and the United Nations on the history of blasphemy repeal. His books include *Secularism, Art and Freedom* (1992), *Blasphemy in Modern Britain 1789 to the Present* (1999), *Blasphemy in the Christian World* (2007), and *Christian Ideals in British Culture: Stories of Belief in Twentieth Century Britain* (2013).

David Thomas Orique, O.P., is Associate Professor of Colonial and Modern Latin American as well as Iberian Atlantic World History, and the Director of Latin American and Latina/o Studies at Providence College. His publications include being the author of *To Heaven or to Hell: Bartolomé de Las Casas's Confesionario* (2018), and the editor for the *Oxford Handbook of Latin American Christianity* (2019) and *Bartolomé de las Casas, O.P.: History, Philosophy, and Theology in the Age of European Expansion* (2019).

Martyn Percy was appointed as the Dean of Christ Church, Oxford, in 2014. Previously, he has served as the Principal of Ripon College, Cuddesdon, and as the founding Director of the Lincoln Theological institute. Percy writes on Christianity in contemporary culture and on modern ecclesiology. His work is the subject of a significant book edited by Ian Markham and Joshua Daniels—*Reasonable Radical? Reading the Writings of Martyn Percy* (2018).

Joe Perry is Associate Professor of Modern European and German History at Georgia State University. His book *Christmas in Germany: A Cultural History*, appeared in 2010. He is currently writing a second book about techno music, the Berlin Love Parade, and the political culture of urban development in contemporary Germany.

John Schmalzbauer teaches courses on religion and media, spirituality and health, and North American religion in the Department of Religious Studies at Missouri State University, where he holds the Blanche Gorman Strong Chair in Protestant Studies. He is the author of *The Resilience of Religion in American Higher Education* (with historian Kathleen Mahoney), and *People of Faith: Religious Conviction in American Journalism and Higher Education.*

Katherine G. Schmidt is Assistant Professor of Theology and Religious Studies at Molloy College (New York). Her interests include theology and culture, specifically in the American Catholic context. Her forthcoming book, published with Lexington, is titled *Virtual Communion: A Theology of the Internet and the Catholic Sacramental Imagination.*

Francesca Silano is Visiting Assistant Professor and Teaching Fellow at Miami University and the Havighurst Center for Russian and Post-Soviet Studies. She specializes in the history of the Russian Orthodox Church in the late-imperial and early-revolutionary eras. She has written articles for *Revolutionary Russia* and *Kritika*, and is a co-editor of the forthcoming volume, *Religion and the Russian Revolution of 1917: Conflicts, Encounters, and Transformations.*

Katherine Sonderegger is the William Meade Professor of Systematic Theology at Virginia Theological Seminary, and a priest of the Episcopal Church. She is writing a multi-volume Systematic Theology, volume 1 of which appeared in 2015.

Kirsi Stjerna is the First Lutheran, Los Angeles/Southwest Synod Professor of Lutheran History and Theology at Pacific Lutheran Theological Seminary in Berkeley of California Lutheran University. She serves in the Core Doctoral Faculty for the Graduate Theological Union, Berkeley, and is a Docent at Helsinki University, Finland. Her publications include *Women and the Reformation*, *Martin Luther, the Bible, and the Jewish People* (with Brooks Schramm), and *The Annotated Luther*, for which she serves as the co-general editor, volume editor, and a contributor.

Daniel Vaca is the Robert Gale Noyes Assistant Professor of Humanities at Brown University, where he teaches courses on American religious history and culture in the Department of Religious Studies. In addition to teaching a course on the history of Christmas in America, Vaca focuses his research and teaching especially on cultures of business and media. His most recent publications explore how evangelical Christianity took shape in the twentieth-century United States through the initiative of commercial media industries.

Barbara von Barghahn, George Washington University Professor of Art History (in Northern Europe, Spain, Portugal, and Colonial America), is author of several publications about sacred art and royal patronage. A recipient of the Order of Henrique the Navigator, her most recent book is *Jan van Eyck and Portugal's 'Illustrious Generation'*.

Katrina Jennie-Lou Wheeler is a PhD Candidate in History at The Graduate Center, CUNY, and was a member of the sixth cohort of the Lilly Graduate Fellows Program and a Doctoral Dissertation Student Fellow with the Committee for the Study of

Religion at the Graduate Center, CUNY. She holds an MPhil and an MA in History from the Graduate Center and an MA in the History of Christianity from Wheaton College.

D. H. Williams is currently Professor of Patristics and Historical Theology in the Departments of Religion and Classics at Baylor University. His most recent book is *Defending and Defining the Faith: An Introduction to Early Christian Apologetics* (Oxford University Press, 2020).

A Note on the Cover Image

William Kurelek, A Regina Construction Site Christmas (1975)

In classic Orthodox icons of the Nativity, Joseph is off standing in the corner, looking a bit grumpy. In the plans for the salvation of the world, after all, he had been deliberately left out. The shaft of light descending on the Christ Child in such icons reminds viewers that this baby's father is not Joseph, but God. The Canadian Catholic artist William Kurelek (1927–1977) gives us a modern rendition of this scene in *A Regina Construction Site Christmas* (1975), now in the Howard and Roberta Ahmanson collection. Like great Renaissance paintings such as Rogier van der Weyden's *Pierre Bladelin Triptych*, Kurelek dares to depict the Holy Family in the present, in this case a trailer in Saskatchewan. But like the Orthodox icons, Joseph is again sidelined, warming his hands by a fire. Proof of paternity—the confirming shaft of light from the heavens—is in this case a construction beam. A blue-collar Joseph seems to be relating to his companion something like, 'Honestly, I had nothing to do with it.' Perhaps his interlocutor can be understood as Christians who, in Kurelek's day, still thought the faith could get along without the Virgin birth, or maybe as modern sceptics who go the next step and give up faith altogether. Still, Joseph seems almost to have convinced his companion, his radiance coming dangerously close to the other's face. Halos, Kurelek seems to be suggesting, are contagious.

Matthew J. Milliner
Associate Professor of Art History, Wheaton College

PART I
HISTORY

CHAPTER 1

THE DATING OF CHRISTMAS
the early church

PAUL F. BRADSHAW

ALTHOUGH the Gospel of Matthew showed interest in the *place* of Christ's Nativity—because Bethlehem fulfilled the prophecy of Micah (Matthew 2:1–6; cf. Micah 5:1)—and the Gospel of Luke made it possible for others to try to estimate the *year* when it took place—from the statement that John the Baptist began his ministry 'in the fifteenth year of the reign of Tiberius Caesar' (Luke 3:1–2) when Jesus was 'about thirty years of age' (Luke 3:23)—none of the New Testament writings record the precise *date* of his birth. The lack of concern about this historical fact is easy to understand when one recalls that the first Christians expected the 'end of the age' to arrive imminently and Christ to return to establish God's Kingdom on Earth in all its fullness. Knowledge of such matters would have little significance in the age to come.

It is more than a century later, therefore, after that expected event had manifestly not so far taken place, when we encounter the first evidence of various attempts by Christians to work out when Christ might have been born. Clement of Alexandria, writing about 200 CE, reports:

> And there are those who have determined not only the year of our Lord's birth, but also the day; and they say that it took place in the twenty-eighth year of Augustus, and in the twenty-fifth day of Pachon [20 May]. And the followers of Basilides hold the day of his baptism as a festival, spending the night before in readings. And they say that it was the fifteenth year of Tiberius Caesar, the fifteenth day of the month Tubi [10 January]; and some that it was the eleventh of the same month [6 January]. And treating of his passion, with very great accuracy, some say that it took place in the sixteenth year of Tiberius, on the twenty-fifth of Phamenoth; and others the twenty-fifth of Pharmuthi and others say that on the nineteenth of Pharmuthi the Saviour suffered. Further, others say that He was born on the twenty-fourth or twenty-fifth of Pharmuthi [19 or 20 April].   (Clement 2004: 333)

This statement reveals that estimates were being made not only of the date of Christ's death but also of his birth, and furthermore that quite differing conclusions were being reached on these questions. Except among the Basilidian sect, however, who believed that Jesus became the Son of God at his baptism and so marked the presumed date of that event liturgically, there is no sign of any observance accompanying any of the other dates at this time. Even half a century later, Clement's compatriot Origen (c.184–c.253) does not mention any such occasion in a list of festivals (*Contra Celsum* 8.22). However, at some unknown point after that, Christians both in Egypt and throughout the eastern Mediterranean area, and perhaps beyond, did begin to celebrate a festival on 6 January, like the Basilidians, which was known as Epiphany (meaning 'manifestation' in Greek) or Theophany ('appearance of God').

Two Theories

Among modern scholars there have been two principal schools of thought in the attempt to explain why this date—and later 25 December—had been chosen as festivals by the early Christians. One has been dubbed the '*History of Religions*' *hypothesis*, first developed substantially by Usener (1889) and adopted by many scholars thereafter, most notably Botte (1932). It claims that those festivals were influenced by—or intended to supplant—pagan feast days that were being celebrated on those particular dates. In the case of 6 January, it was alleged that according to the calendar in use at the time of Amenemhet I, in 1996 BCE the winter solstice in Egypt had been celebrated on the equivalent of that day (Norden 1924). Furthermore, Epiphanius of Salamis (315–403) described a festival in honour of the birth of the god Aeo, born to the virgin Core, that according to him took place on 6 January:

> At Alexandria, in the Coreum, as they call it, there is a very large temple the shrine of Core. They stay up all night singing hymns to the idol with a flute accompaniment. And when they have concluded their nightlong vigil torchbearers descend into an underground shrine after cockcrow and bring up a wooden image which is seated naked [on] a litter. It has a sign of the cross inlaid with gold on its forehead, two other such signs, [one] actually [on each of] its two knees—altogether five signs with a gold impress. And they carry the image itself seven times round the innermost shrine with flutes, tambourines and hymns, hold a feast, and take it back down to its place underground. And when you ask them what this mystery means they reply that today at this hour Core—that is, the virgin—gave birth to Aeo.   (Williams 1994: 50–1)

Epiphanius went on to claim that the same celebration took place in the cities of Petra and of Elusa in Arabia. The parallels between this virgin birth and that of Jesus seem to suggest the reason why the Christian festival that emerged on 6 January celebrated the birth as well as the baptism of Jesus, both constituting manifestations of divinity (see, for example, John Cassian, *Conferences* 10.2).

Unfortunately for the History of Religions hypothesis, however, after sixty years of dominance, Talley convincingly demonstrated that its theory about the winter solstice was based upon a fundamental miscalculation: 'there is no such calendar, nor is there any meaningful basis for the association of the Julian date, January 6, with any festival connected with the winter solstice in the twentieth century before Christ' (Talley 1986: 111). Doubts have even been expressed by some about the reliability of the testimony of Epiphanius concerning a pagan Egyptian festival on 6 January, on the grounds that he was not an Egyptian, that the feast he described was of Hellenistic and not Egyptian origin, and that his detailed account lacks any other contemporary witness. Talley concluded: 'When all is said and done, from all of the evidence we have considered for a pagan background to Epiphany, nothing points definitely to a widespread festival on January 6' (Talley 1986: 117).

The alternative school of thought, known as the *Calculation (or Computation) hypothesis*, emerged at the same time as Usener's work. This title did not refer to calculation in a modern scientific sense, but to symbolic number systems that flourished widely in the ancient world. Duchesne asserted that in antiquity Christ must have been believed to have lived for a whole number of years, because those systems did not allow the imperfection of fractions (Duchesne 1889: 247–54) Thus, he argued, Christians in Asia Minor who adopted 6 April (14 Artemisios) in the Julian calendar as the equivalent to the Jewish date of the Passover, 14 Nisan, would not only have celebrated it as the date of Christ's death but also viewed it as the date of his conception, with the result that exactly nine months later, 6 January would have marked the date of his birth. The weakness of the theory was that Duchesne was unable to produce any firm evidence in support of it.

An attempt was later made by Strobel (1962) to strengthen the case by pointing to rabbinic belief that the patriarchs had lived for an exact number of years, but this still failed to provide any more testimony as to why the dates of death and conception rather than birth might have been thought to have been identical in the case of Christ. Although Talley tried to bolster his argument with further rabbinic witness, the majority of scholars were still not sufficiently convinced to abandon their preference for the History of Religions hypothesis (Talley 1986: 81–3).

The Spread of Epiphany

Regardless of the uncertainty about its ultimate origin, what is sure is that the feast of Epiphany spread widely throughout the ancient Christian world. For *Syria*, we have the evidence of the Syriac hymns written by the fourth-century Ephrem, twenty-eight of which focus on the celebration of Christ's Nativity on 6 January. At the same time they weave in references to other themes of the manifestation of Christ associated with the feast, primarily his baptism but also the visit of the Magi to the infant Jesus (Matthew 2:1–12) and the miracle at Cana (John 2:1–11; see v. 11, 'manifested his glory'), which we shall find become associated with this day in other places too. This extract from Hymn 23 well illustrates the juxtaposition of birth and baptism:

Blessed is your birth that stirred up the universe! . . .
[Too] small for You is the earth's lap,
but large enough for You is Mary's lap. He dwelt in a lap, and He healed by the hem [of his garment].
He was wrapped [in] swaddling clothes in baseness, but they offered Him gifts.
He put on the garments of you, and helps emerged from them.
He put on the water of baptism, and rays flashed out from it.
With his humiliations [came] His exaltations. Blessed is He who joins His glory to His suffering! . . .
Great One Who became a baby, by Your birth again You begot me.
Pure One who was baptized, let your washing wash us of impurity.
Living One Who was embalmed, let us obtain life by Your death.
(McVey 1989: 189–90)

Winkler (1994) argued in some detail that a fundamental theme of Epiphany in this region was the appearance of fire or light at the baptism of Jesus, reflected in this hymn by the words 'rays flashed out from it' and also by the name given to the feast in Syriac, *Denha*, 'dawn of the light'. We should also recall that in early sources Christian baptism was understood as illumination. Thus, Justin Martyr in the middle of the second century declares that 'this washing is called illumination, because they who learn these things are illuminated in their understandings' (*First Apology* 61); in one of the accounts of baptisms in the third-century Syrian *Acts of Thomas*, 'when they had been sealed, a youth appeared to them carrying a lighted lamp, so that even the lamps became faint by the approach of its light' (Attridge 2010: 35); and at least from the fourth century onwards in the East those about to be baptized were termed *photizomenoi*, 'those being enlightened'.

Our earliest evidence for Epiphany in *Jerusalem* comes from the late-fourth-century account of the liturgical practices of that city forming part of the *Itinerarium Egeriae* (McGowan and Bradshaw 2018). Unfortunately, there is a break in the manuscript at this point, and the narrative resumes with the whole church community apparently returning from Bethlehem during the early hours of 6 January in order to celebrate the feast in the major church of the city. The festivities continue for a further seven days after that with a Eucharist each day, mostly in different churches in and around Jerusalem. Our knowledge is supplemented by an early-fifth-century lectionary, which provides the readings used at these services, together with directions as to the place of each celebration (Renoux 1969–71). It confirms what we might have suspected from the visit to Bethlehem recorded by Egeria, that the feast is focused exclusively on the Nativity of Jesus with no trace of any reference to his baptism, in contrast to churches elsewhere. This is not particularly surprising, given the close proximity to Jerusalem of the places associated with the Nativity story in comparison with the distance from the presumed location of Christ's baptism. The celebration began on the evening of 5 January with a brief liturgy at what is described as 'the place of the shepherds', with Luke 2:8–20 (the account of the appearance of the angels to the shepherds) being read there. Then Matthew 1:18–25 (the account of the birth of Jesus) was read in the cave where it was believed Jesus had been born, followed by a nocturnal vigil and Eucharist celebrated in the middle of the night in the Bethlehem church itself, for which the readings were Titus 2:11–15 and Matthew 2:1–12 (the visit of the Magi). The readings at the Eucharist that was held on the return to Jerusalem on 6 January were again Titus 2:11–15 and Matthew 1:18–25, which seems to suggest that this liturgy had been the original celebration of the feast, especially as Matthew 2:1–12 was used on the following day, with the visit to Bethlehem being a later addition.

For *Cappadocia* and *Constantinople*, we have rather less information as to their practices at an early date. A sermon preached by Gregory of Nazianzus on 6 January 380 CE in Constantinople, however, urged people to be baptized then and not wait until one of the greater feasts of the year. This implies that the theme of the baptism of Jesus on this day may have been long established, as does the use as the Greek name for the occasion in Cappadocia *Ta Phota*, 'The (festival of) Lights', paralleling the Syriac *Denha* we noted earlier (Comings 2005: 61–94).

There are also signs that the festival of 6 January may have spread even further afield and been known in at least some places in the West before 25 December was established there. As we shall discuss later, Connell (1999) argued that some passages in the writings of Ambrose of Milan (*c.*340–397) pointed to 6 January having been celebrated as Christ's Nativity in Milan in the 350s. Furthermore, Chromatius, bishop of Aquileia in northern Italy (388–407), in a sermon for Epiphany clearly demonstrated that the theme of that day was the baptism of Christ, as in the East, and not the visit of the Magi, which became the theme later in the West. This is another possible sign of the existence of a tradition there that predated the adoption of 25 December as the feast of the Nativity (Connell 2006: 173–6).

25 December

So far no mention has been made of Rome or North Africa. That is because there is no evidence for the feast of 6 January having been adopted by Christians there in early times. This is not surprising because both churches tended to be conservative, following similar liturgical traditions to one another but differing from the rest of the ancient Christian world. It appears therefore that there was no festival celebrating Christ's birth in these regions until the fourth century, and when one was instituted, it was on 25 December.

The earliest quite firm evidence for the Christian celebration of the Nativity on this date occurs in what is known as the Philocalian Calendar or Chronograph of 354 CE, a collection of both civil and religious chronologies. Among these are lists of consuls of the city of Rome up to 354, of Roman bishops from 255 to 352 arranged on an annual cycle in the order of the dates on which they died, and of the anniversaries of Roman martyrs similarly organized. The list of martyrs actually begins with the notation of the birth of Christ on 25 December, while the list of consuls includes not just this date, but that it was on a Friday, the fifteenth day of the new moon—although some scholars have raised doubts about the authenticity of this latter entry. Questions could also be asked about the congruity of the inclusion within a listing of the *deaths* of martyrs of the *birth* of Christ, and also of another entry, 'the birth of the Chair of Peter' on 22 February. However, because the list of bishops ends with the two most recent ones being out of their calendrical sequence, it has generally been agreed by liturgical scholars that this list was originally compiled in the year 336, prior to the time of these two bishops. Perhaps a little more surprisingly, those scholars have accepted that the record of the date of Christ's birth was part of the original stratum of the list of martyrs, and therefore was being celebrated as a festival in the city by that time (Roll 1995: 83–6).

It was over the reason for the choice of this date that the two competing schools of thought among modern scholars mentioned earlier had originally focused, with their application to the origin of Epiphany being a secondary consequence of that debate. The proponents of the History of Religions hypothesis based their case on two principal points. First, 25 December was the official date of the winter solstice in the Roman Empire until the Julian calendar was adjusted by the Council of Nicaea in 325 to the true date of 21 December. Second, the Emperor Aurelian had revived the cult of Sol Invictus, 'the invincible sun', proclaiming Sol as the sole divine protector of the empire and of the emperor in 274 and creating an annual festival, *Dies natalis Solis Invicti*, 'Birthday of the Invincible Sun', at the time of that winter solstice. Thus, they argued, the establishment of the Christian feast on that day was in order to act as a counter-attraction to those pagan festivities (Roll 1995: 65, 113–14, 127–49).

We have seen that the supporters of the Calculation hypothesis pointed to Christians in Asia Minor having adopted 6 April as the local equivalent of the Jewish Passover on 14 Nisan and hence also as the date of Christ's death and conception, resulting in a birthdate of 6 January. They also cited ancient Western sources that had done the same with the Julian calendar and produced a date of 25 March, which would have resulted in a date for the Nativity of 25 December (Roll 1995: 87–94). Foremost among these sources were third-century paschal tables inscribed on the sides of the base of a statue discovered in Rome in the sixteenth century. These set out the date of the paschal full moon for each year of a sixteen-year cycle together with the corresponding date of Easter for 112 years beginning from 222. Among eight marginal notes on the dates of biblical Passovers was one that indicated that the 'genesis' of Christ was on the Passover of 2 April, 2 BCE, and another that his death was on 25 March, 29 CE (Mosshammer 2008: 117–25). There was inevitably some debate among scholars as to whether 'genesis' here meant his birth or his conception. If it were the latter, that would have put his birth about nine months later. In general, however, the supporters of the hypothesis focused on the 25 March date alone, arguing for the conception on the same date and hence birth on 25 December.

The statue itself was presumed to be of a certain Hippolytus, because on the back of the base was a list of works, most of which were known to be by him (although archaeological research has subsequently established that the figure was originally of a female that had later been adapted to a male form). Another work by Hippolytus not included in the list on the statue, a commentary on the Book of Daniel, gave the date of the birth of Christ as Wednesday, 25 December in the forty-second year of Augustus, 5,500 years after the creation of Adam (4.23). However, this passage, with all its manuscript variants, is normally regarded as a later interpolation (Roll 1995: 80–1).

The value of other early sources of evidence was disputed between the proponents of the two theories. Thus, an anonymous work, *De Pascha computus*, once wrongly ascribed to Cyprian of Carthage (c.200–258) but can be reliably dated to 243 CE, uses both traditional chronology and symbolic number systems to associate the birth of Christ with the anniversary of creation, which it locates on the spring equinox, 25 March. It claims that Christ was born on the anniversary of the creation of the sun on the fourth day of creation, that is, 28 March. Although this particular date was not taken up in later sources, those promoting the Calculation hypothesis could claim that this early use of symbolic numbers gave some support to their case. On the other hand, supporters of the History of Religions hypothesis could point out that the fact that a link was being made between Christ's birth and the equinox and also that solar symbolism was already being applied to the person of Christ at this early date lent further credence to their cause (Roll 1995: 81–3). While it is certainly true that both of these features were to become aspects of later Patristic thought, neither of them settles the question as to whether 25 December was originally chosen for that reason.

Further debate ensued from the publication, in an appendix to Botte's landmark 1932 study, of an edition of another anonymous work, *De solstitiis et aequinoctiis*, once again formerly wrongly attributed, this time to John Chrysostom (c.349–407). It probably dates from the early fourth century and comes from North Africa (although a Syrian background for the author has also been proposed). It ascribes the conception of John the Baptist to the autumn equinox, his birth nine months later to the summer solstice, the conception of Jesus to the spring equinox (with John's mother Elizabeth being visited by Mary shortly afterwards when she was six months pregnant: see Luke 1:26, 36, 39ff.), and his birth nine months later to the winter solstice. This use of the cardinal points of the solar calendar was hailed by the advocates of the History of Religions hypothesis as supportive of their cause.

However, as this tractate also associated the date of Christ's conception with that of his death, it was naturally seized upon by those supporting the Calculation hypothesis as evidence in favour of their position (Roll 1995: 97–9). This apparently sole ancient source for the association of the two dates was the primary basis of an attempt by Engberding (1952) to resurrect the Calculation hypothesis after Botte's powerful 1932 defence of the opposing theory. In a review of Engberding, Botte (1955) criticized the assumption that the composition of *De solstitiis* had been prior to the establishment of the Christmas festival rather than being a later rationale for it, and emphasized the Syrian origin of the work, as Syria did not adopt 25 December until the late fourth century.

Talley gave the Calculation hypothesis a boost by a detailed reiteration and expansion of the arguments made by earlier scholars, including the point that in a sermon on Epiphany, Augustine of Hippo (354–430) had said that the heretical Donatists had never wished to celebrate that feast 'with us' (Talley 1986: 86–7, 92–6). Talley argued that because Augustine did not say anything like that in relation to the Donatists and Christmas, it seemed likely that they did celebrate that particular festival, and thus Christmas would have ante-dated the Donatist schism in 311, which was long before Christians were likely to have been influenced by pagan feast days. Moreover, Christmas could have originated in North Africa rather than Rome. His conclusions have been challenged by Connell on the basis that they rely entirely on the absence of contrary evidence rather than any positive piece of data (Connell 2006: 110–12).

This is where the debate between the supporters of the two rival hypotheses stood until very recently, with neither side able to produce convincing arguments to sway the other. As Roll observed, Germanic and Romance-language scholars on the whole have tended to lean in the direction of the History of Religions theory, while Anglo-Saxon writers display somewhat more sympathy for the Calculation hypothesis (Roll 1995: 148). However, two recent contributions might help to tip the balance. Hijmans (2003) showed that the evidence for the existence of a festival of Sol Invictus on 25 December is actually very tenuous; and indeed that it may have been the apostate Roman Emperor Julian, in his desire to promote traditional pagan religion, who was the first to assert in 362 that the Christian observance was based on an ancient sun festival! Since the festival of Sol Invictus has been the main premise on which the History of Religions hypothesis had been built, it robs that theory of much of the strength it previously had been thought to possess.

Second, Schmidt (2015) argued from a detailed study of the use of the word 'genesis' among contemporaries of Hippolytus that, when referring to a person, it meant 'conception' and not 'birth', and that Hippolytus in his work known as *Chronicon* appears to place the birth of Christ exactly nine months after the anniversary of the creation of the world, which he located on 25 March. While Schmidt admitted that his arguments cannot be regarded as conclusive, they do seem to make the assumptions of the Calculation hypothesis appear rather less improbable than they have previously been regarded by many.

The Spread of Christmas

Whatever lay behind the adoption of 25 December at Rome as the feast of Christ's birth—whether reaction to pagan festivities or the result of the convoluted number symbolism—its observance did not spread as rapidly to other parts of the ancient Christian world as has often been supposed. Indeed, why would other churches want to add another Nativity festival to their calendars when they already had one on 6 January?

The earliest evidence for the existence of Christmas on 25 December outside Rome is a sermon delivered at the feast by Optatus, bishop of Milevis in North Africa, probably around 361–3 (Roll 1995: 195–6). It is not surprising that North Africa should be the first to adopt it from Rome, given the close relationship in liturgical tradition that existed between those two churches that was mentioned earlier. The sermon spoke of the Nativity of Christ as being a *sacramentum*, thus bestowing on it a greater status than Augustine would grant to it at the end of the century, when he distinguished Christmas as a mere commemoration (*memoria*) from Easter as a *sacramentum*: 'A celebration of something is a sacrament only when the commemoration of the event becomes such that it is understood also to signify something that is to be received as sacred' (*Ep.* 55.2). On the other hand, Optatus' vocabulary is in line with that of Pope Leo the Great at Rome in the fifth century (Roll 1995: 212–14).

Because of its relative geographical proximity to Rome one might have expected Christmas also to have spread to northern Italy quite quickly, but the evidence for this is not very strong. A passage in Ambrose of Milan's *De virginitate*, written in 378, recalled the occasion over twenty years earlier (in 353 or 354) when his sister Marcellina dedicated herself to virginity before Liberius, bishop of Rome. Ambrose said that this had taken place 'on the birthday of the Saviour', and then quoted what he claimed was an extract from the sermon of Liberius on that day that referred to the miracle at Cana and the feeding of the multitude. Because both these themes came to be associated with the Epiphany, some scholars in the early twentieth century cited this passage as evidence that Epiphany had been celebrated at Rome as the feast of Christ's birth prior to the adoption of 25 December. In response, Michels (1923) advanced an alternative explanation that Ambrose's recollection had been shaped by the practice in Milan in his own day, where 6 January rather than 25 December was still being observed as the birth of Christ.

Michels' explanation has also been supported more recently by Connell (1999), who added the further consideration that while Christmas is never mentioned in Ambrose's commentary on Luke 2:43–4, surprisingly the Magi from Matthew's Gospel, normally associated with 6 January, do feature prominently in it. Connell also argued that the themes in Ambrose's hymn *Illuminans Altissimus* similarly pointed to the observance of 6 January rather than 25 December. Roll, however, maintained that several other hymns composed by Ambrose implied the existence of the 25 December feast at Milan in his day, especially *Intende qui regis Israel*, which was cited by Pope Celestine in 430 as having been ordered to be sung at Christmas by Ambrose (Roll 1995: 200–3). On the other hand, if Connell is right, it means that the earliest sure mention of the celebration of 25 December anywhere in northern Italy comes from Filastrius of Brescia around 383, nearly fifty years after the first evidence for it at Rome. As for the spread of 25 December further westwards, sources from Spain that have been cited to show the existence of Christmas there in the 380s have rightly been challenged as being inconclusive: we simply cannot say when it was first celebrated there (Connell 1999: 155–7).

The earliest references to the adoption of 25 December in Eastern churches do come from the 380s, although scholars dispute whether the feast had only just spread there or whether it had been in existence for some time but unmentioned. Thus, several sermons by John Chrysostom from 386 seem to imply that it was a recent development in Antioch, one of them stating that it had been known for less than ten years. Some scholars assert that it had been celebrated there for the whole of that time, while others argue that it was a new arrival in that very year because Chrysostom's Pentecost sermon earlier in that year had mentioned the existence of only three festivals—Theophany (Epiphany), Pascha, and Pentecost—and described the first of these as being the one on which 'God has appeared on earth and lived with humans'. Similarly, sermons by Gregory of Nazianzus preached at Constantinople in 380–1 indicate that 25 December was already being observed there at that time, but whether the feast had been newly introduced by him or had existed for some years before has again been disputed. It depends whether Gregory's designation of himself as 'exarchos' of Christmas in Constantinople means 'originator' of the feast there or simply the one who presided over it (Talley 1986: 135–8).

Although the celebration of 25 December also seems to have been adopted in Cappadocia at about the same period, this was not the case everywhere else in the East. The early-fifth-century Armenian lectionary from Jerusalem still places the celebration of Christ's Nativity on 6 January, and it was only later in the century that 25 December was added to the calendar, both in Jerusalem and in Egypt. The Armenian Church itself never adopted it (Talley 1986: 138–41). Connell suggested that the apparent delay in and resistance to the widespread adoption of the Roman celebration of Christmas in other churches may have been because the narrative of the vulnerable infant in a manger would not have helped promote the high Christology of the Son as 'one in being with the Father' but rather have been more congenial to the subordinationist Arian cause (Connell 2006: 101–3).

The Eastern churches that did adopt the observance of Christ's Nativity on 25 December did not abandon the festival on 6 January: it became instead primarily focused on the baptism of Christ, which had already been an element in its celebration along with the birth in some of the earlier Eastern traditions. On the other hand, this did not happen at Rome when it later adopted Epiphany, nor in the other Western churches as they took their lead from Rome. Here Epiphany became a commemoration of the visit of the Magi, and although some places made reference to other Epiphany themes, in particular the baptism of Christ and the miracle at Cana, there was never a festival of the baptism of Christ as such in the Roman tradition itself until modern times. But that tradition did absorb one element from the East. When the basilica of St Mary Major was built at Rome in the early fifth century, it included a subterranean chapel that symbolized the cave of the Nativity. As a result, the annual visit on the evening of 5 January at Bethlehem to what was thought to be the place where the angels had appeared to the shepherds was imitated in that church as a Midnight Mass, with the Gospel reading being the Nativity story from Luke 2. This was celebrated in addition to the Eucharist on Christmas Day itself, where the Gospel reading focused on the more theologically profound theme of the Incarnation of the pre-existent Son of

God in John 1 ('And the Word was made flesh'). In time, this practice was adopted throughout the West and continues to the present.

References and Further Reading

Attridge, Harold W. (2010). *The Acts of Thomas*. Salem, OR: Polebridge Press.
Botte, Bernard (1932). *Les origines de la Noël et de l'Épiphanie*. Louvain: Mont César.
Botte, Bernard (1955). 'Review of Engberding (1952)', *Bulletin de Théologie ancienne et médiévale*, 7: 198–9.
Bradshaw, Paul F. and Johnson, Maxwell E. (2011). *The Origins of Feasts, Fasts, and Seasons in Early Christianity*. London: SPCK/Collegeville: Liturgical Press.
Clement of Alexandria (2004). 'The Stromata, or Miscellanies', in Alexander Roberts and James Donaldson (eds), *Ante-Nicene Fathers*. Peabody, Massachusetts: Hendrickson Publishers, 2: 299–567.
Comings, Jill Burnett (2005). *Aspects of the Liturgical Year in Cappadocia (325–430)*. New York: Lang.
Connell, Martin F. (1999). 'Did Ambrose's Sister Become a Virgin on December 25 or January 6? The Earliest Western Evidence for Christmas and Epiphany outside Rome', *Studia Liturgica*, 29: 145–58.
Connell, Martin F. (2006). *Eternity Today: On the Liturgical Year*, Volume 1. New York/London: Continuum.
Duchesne, Louis (1889). *Origines du culte chrétien*. Paris: Thorin.
Engberding, Hieronymous (1952). 'Der 25. Dezember als Tag der Feier der Geburt des Herrn', *Archiv für Liturgiewissenschaft*, 2: 25–43.
Hijmans, Steven (2003). 'Sol Invictus, the Winter Solstice, and the Origins of Christmas', *Mouseion*, 47: 377–98.
Kelly, Joseph F. (2004). *The Origins of Christmas*. Collegeville: Liturgical Press. Revised edition, 2014.
McGowan, Anne and Bradshaw, Paul F. (2018). *The Pilgrimage of Egeria*. Collegeville, MN: Liturgical Press.
McVey, Kathleen E. (1989). *Ephrem the Syrian: Hymns*. New York: Paulist Press.
Michels, Thomas (1923). 'Noch einmal die Ansprache des Papstes Liberius bei Ambrosius, de virg. III 1,1ff', *Jahrbuch für Liturgiewissenschaft*, 3: 105–8.
Mosshammer, Alden A. (2008). *The Easter Computus and the Origins of the Christian Era*. Oxford/New York: Oxford University Press.
Norden, Eduard (1924). *Die Geburt des Kindes*. Leipzig: Teubner.
Renoux, Athanase (Charles) (1969–71). *Le Codex Arménien Jérusalem 121*, Patrologia Orientalis 35.1, 36.2. Turnhout: Brepols.
Roll, Susan K. (1995). *Toward the Origins of Christmas*. Kampen: Kok Pharos.
Schmidt, Thomas C. (2015). 'Calculating December 25 as the Birth of Jesus in Hippolytus' *Canon* and *Chronicon*', *Vigiliae Christianae*, 69: 542–63.
Strobel, August (1962). 'Jahrespunkt-Spekulation und frühchristliches Festjahr', *Theologische Literaturzeitung*, 87/3: 183–94.
Talley, Thomas J. (1986). *The Origins of the Liturgical Year*. Collegeville, MN: Liturgical Press.
Usener, Hermann (1889). *Das Weihnachtsfest*. Bonn: Cohen.

Williams, Frank (1994). *The Panarion of Epiphanius of Salamis: Books II and III*. Leiden: Brill.

Winkler, Gabriele (1994). 'Die Licht-Erscheinung bie der Taufe Jesu und der Ursprung des Epiphanie-festes', *Oriens Christianus*, 78: 177–229; English translation: 'The Appearance of the Light at the Baptism of Jesus and the Origins of the Feast of Epiphany', in Maxwell E. Johnson (ed.) (2000). *Between Memory and Hope*. Collegeville, MN: Liturgical Press, 2000, 291–348.

CHAPTER 2

THE MIDDLE AGES

KATI IHNAT

When in 1207 Pope Innocent III decried the 'theatrical entertainments', 'masked shows', 'scandalous stupidities', and 'obscene revelries' performed in churches during the Christmas season—in a letter that would make its way into canon law—he revealed something of the nature of Christmas as celebrated in many parts of medieval Europe (Tydeman 2001: 114). The traditional time of merry-making around the winter solstice had become by the High Middle Ages, Christmas, one of the principal feasts of the Christian year, observed with special fervour in northern areas, where it brought relief from the long months of darkness. The celebration extended over twelve days—sometimes more—of activities, and was preceded by a long period of fasting, Advent. Christmas was commemorated in the liturgy as the return of the light and the culmination of human history in the Incarnation. The feast marking the birth of Jesus increasingly became a time to remember the Messiah as a little baby, wrapped in swaddling, and tended by his loving mother. Special customs, such as the crèche, emerged to remind believers of Christ's humanity and poverty.

Moreover, the days following Christmas were dedicated to the clergy; each order of clergy had its own special day, during which it took charge of much of the liturgy. But this did not make Christmas an overly official affair. In the High Middle Ages, we witness the Christmas season as a period of carnivalesque revelry, when, both within the church and without, the commemoration of Christ's birth was an opportunity for merriment. Rich traditions of feasting, mumming, and general high spirits were supplemented by extravagant liturgical celebrations that expressed a spirit of inversion—as God was made flesh—in celebrations such as the Feast of Fools and Boy Bishop. Elaborate liturgical dramas also emerged in this period, and biblical events were dramatized in sophisticated ways, allowing lay people and clerics alike the chance to rejoice in the reversal of roles that the birth of God in human form represented. Our most abundant source-base concerns ecclesiastical traditions, and this chapter will focus particularly on the important developments in this domain during the twelfth to fourteenth centuries in western Europe. Drawing especially from liturgical and homiletic sources, I will show the shared customs but also tensions between the lay and clerical celebration of Christmas, a focal point of Christian worship and a time for release.

The Nativity of Christ was celebrated in medieval Europe on 25 December as one of the major feasts of the calendar year, unlike Byzantium, where the feast of the Epiphany (6 January) took precedence. Christmas was not celebrated as a one-day affair, however, but rather as an entire season that extended up to the feast of the Purification of Mary (2 February) (Beleth 1976: 133). Christmas Day was also preceded by Advent, whose length could vary between four and six weeks, depending on region and century, but which generally began on the Sunday following the feast of St Andrew (30 November). Dominated by the themes of prophecy and genealogy, Advent was commemorated as a time of preparation for the Messiah's arrival. The sense of anticipation was reflected in the liturgical readings from the books of the prophets, particularly Isaiah. Throughout the Advent season, special attention was given also to the Virgin Mary, so that the entire season was to be celebrated in her honour, according to the liturgical commentator, John Beleth (fl. ca. 1160) (Beleth 1976: 119). The prophetic texts cited were those which foretold the Virgin Birth (e.g. Isaiah 7:14, Isaiah 11:1, Ezekiel 44:1–2, Numbers 17:8, Judges 6:37–40); chants and sermons were peppered with images of flowering rods, impregnable fortresses, and dewy fleeces. Advent was not purely a time for rejoicing, however: it was a solemn time during which the *Gloria in excelsis*, *Te Deum laudamus*, and *Ite missa est* were omitted from the liturgy in recognition that the coming of Christ at his Nativity pointed to his Second Coming, meaning that the joy and gladness of the Advent season were tempered by the bitterness of future judgement (de Voragine 2012: 4–12). As a result, fasting was to be observed and charity given to the poor as a means for each Christian to prepare (Beleth 1976: 122), particularly during the Ember Days (Wednesdays, Fridays, and Saturdays). As with other periods of fasting, no weddings were to be celebrated, and marital relations were off. Complaints about peasants engaging in drinking bouts (Beleth 1976: 121), while potentially reflecting common stereotypes, could nevertheless indicate that it was hard to prevent the festive nature of Christmas from spilling over into the weeks before.

The time of rejoicing returned at Christmas itself. To mark its importance, the day was preceded by a full-day liturgical commemoration complete with Mass: the Christmas Vigil. From approximately the fifth century, Christmas Day was celebrated with three Masses, the first at midnight (known by its introit, *Dixit Dominus*), the second at dawn (*Lux fulgebit*), and the third mid-morning (*Puer natus est nobis*), interspersed with the offices of matins, lauds, and terce, much of which the laity was expected to attend. (Young 1912: 352) The Midnight Mass was thought to mark the moment of Christ's birth, giving rise to the Old English word *Cristes Maessan*—first attested in 1038—from which our modern-day 'Christmas' derives (Hutton 1996: 6). The thirteenth-century liturgical commentator William Durandus explained that each Mass symbolized a period of history: before the law (when humanity was still in the dark), under the law (when humanity had the law and prophets, but not full knowledge of God), and in the time of grace (when humanity had full knowledge of God through Christ) (Durandus 1859: 419). Special actions performed during the liturgy coincided with the themes of the Mass. Three loaves of bread (one black, one grey, and one red) were placed on the altar at matins in some places, and removed one by one at each nocturn, to signify the three ages (Beleth 1976: 127–8). At the third nocturn of matins, the candles were lit in the church to commemorate Christ bringing the Church out of the darkness of hell (Beleth 1976: 128). The theme of light was central to many sermons and homilies. Christ as the light of day, coming to illuminate the world, was linked to the winter solstice, when 'the nights began to be shorter, while the days became longer' (Augustine 1952: 102). The time of day was also relevant; the lesson for the Midnight Mass (Isaiah 9:2–7) and the introit of the dawn mass (*Lux fulgebit*) refer to the coming of the light. To recognize the new life ushered in by this day, the *Gloria* and other suppressed chants were restored, and the psalms chanted emphasized great rejoicing (e.g. Psalm 47, 94, 95, 97).

For medieval theologians, the joy of Christmas lay in its celebration of the Incarnation: God's taking human form for the salvation of humanity. In the seventh century, Isidore of Seville explained Christmas' importance in terms of John 1:14, the Gospel reading for the Third Mass: 'the Word became flesh even though, taking on flesh, he was not changed in the flesh. For he took on humanity; he did not lose divinity. The same one is God and the same one is human' (Isidore 2008: 49). For Isidore, as for other commentators, Christmas was also the culmination of the entire history of humanity, starting with the fall of Adam and Eve, through the subsequent growth of evil in the world, and ending with God sending his Son to set things right (e.g. Hrabanus 1841: PL 107:343). The arrival of the Word as a baby unable to speak (*verbum infans*) was a widely acknowledged paradox. We see this in a patristic sermon found in Alan of Farfa's homiliary, where Jesus is described as 'unspeakably wise...wisely speechless; filling the world, he lies in a manger; guiding the stars, he nurses at his mother's bosom; he is both great in the nature of God, and small in the form of the servant' (Augustine 1952: 85).

While such seeming incongruities played a role early on in the commemoration of Christmas, the eleventh century saw a significant shift in emphasis from celebrating the all-powerful Christ to the man Jesus. In Christmas sermons, this led to an increased focus on the human baby in the manger, building from the text of Isaiah 9:6, which served as the Introit of the Third Mass: *For a child is born to us*. The eleventh-century reformer Peter Damian wondered at 'the little infant who is tightly bound in a child's swaddling clothes by his mother...the immense one who, with his father, governs the rights of all things' (Dzon 2017: 6). Sermons by the Cistercian abbot Bernard of Clairvaux insist particularly on the fragility and helplessness of the babe, key elements of human nature in his view (Foulon 2003: 221). Christ was born in the most difficult of settings: in winter, at night, from a mother so poor she could hardly clothe him, and in a manger for lack of a better crib (Foulon 2003: 225). Growing interest in the apocryphal works that describe Christ's childhood (e.g. Gospel of Pseudo-Matthew, Infancy Gospel of Thomas) drew additional attention to the birth of Christ as a very human, if remarkable, boy. Such works also added elements to the Nativity narrative not found in the Gospels, for example the presence of ox and ass in the manger (from Isaiah 1:2—*The ox knoweth his owner, and the ass his master's crib*) and midwives who attest to the virgin birth. These images became ubiquitous in depictions of the Nativity all over medieval Europe (Comet 2003: 207–10). Within these artworks, Jesus became recognizable as a baby instead of a tiny man, something that was still not frequent before the fourteenth century (Martindale 1994: 206).

Representations of the Nativity bring us to a turning point in the celebration of Christmas, as imagined by modern scholars: Francis of Assisi's invention of the crèche—a figural staging of the Christmas scene. In 1223, at the village of Greccio, Francis is said to have prepared a tableau complete with manger, hay, and animals, over which the Christmas Mass was said (Thomas of Celano 1999: 254–7). Modern interpretations of this scene have varied, some arguing that Francis was inspired by the papal Midnight Mass celebrated at Santa Maria Maggiore in Rome at the 'manger altar', which stood over the relics of Christ's crib (de la Roncière 2003). Others maintain that the widespread use of cribs as props in liturgical dramas explains Francis' act as part of a wider dramatic tradition (Gougaud 1922). It remains unclear whether Francis' re-enactment included an effigy of the baby Jesus, but a particularly devout man, John, is said to have seen a little baby lying asleep in the manger waken as Francis preached and bleated the words 'babe of Bethlehem'. This account is thought to have influenced the spread of dolls of the baby Jesus together with elaborate cribs (*jésueaux*) for display and use during Christmas celebrations, starting in the fourteenth century and associated especially with female religious communities (LeZotte 2011).

Francis' special love of Christmas was described in his biographies and seems to have been connected with the ideal of poverty he promoted by personal example. He allegedly spent Christmas sitting on the floor to honour Christ's humble beginnings. Similarly, his follower Clare of Assisi encouraged her fellow nuns to wear only shabby clothes 'out of love of the most holy and beloved Child wrapped in poor swaddling clothes' (Dzon 2017: 71). Christ's taking on the form of the servant (Philippians 2:7)—a common trope in Christmas sermons—was therefore thought to provide not just hope for the poor, but glorification of poverty, a state actively chosen by reforming movements like the Franciscans and the Cistercians before them (Foulon 2003: 226). The message became more universal in one twelfth-century sermon delivered in Canterbury, where the Nativity story was meant to inspire the congregation to take in weary pilgrims present for the celebration of Christmas in the cathedral (Honorius 1841: PL 172:816). Commemoration of the baby's birth also often included forewarnings of his Passion, and Christmas devotional texts, sermons, hymns, and lyrics play with the paradox of the 'child born to a crown of thorn' and 'the cradle that is also a bier' (Kenney 2012). The Canterbury sermon just mentioned compares the new splendour of the solstice sun to Christ as the sun of justice, the red halo surrounding it (a meteorological phenomenon caused by ice crystals) pointing to the blood Christ would shed (Honorius 1841: PL 172:816). Such a collapse of time—where one moment in biblical history is superimposed on another in the liturgy—tied the major celebrations together, while ultimately presaging the Second Coming.

Central to the Incarnation and to the interest in Christ's humanity was his mother, Mary—hence many Christmas sermons marvel at the miracle of Christ's conception and birth from a virgin who crucially remained a virgin throughout her life. Just as Mary was a virgin, so too was the Church, and many sermons make the comparison while also declaring Christmas to mark the very birth of the Church (e.g. Leo I 1841: PL 54:213). While the Church was glorified on this day, the Synagogue was supposedly abandoned by Christ for his new bride. A number of medieval sermons take this to mean that the Jews themselves were condemned, since contemporary Jews refused to accept that God was made flesh of a virgin, unlike the ox and ass in the manger, thought to represent those Jews and Gentiles who came to honour Christ (e.g. Leo I 1841: PL 54:228; Bede 1843: 339–40). Alongside liturgical praise as Mother of God, Mary increasingly received attention as the human, doting mother of the little baby in the manger. The Franciscan devotional manual, *Meditationes Vitae Christi,* highlighted the paradox of divine motherhood while encouraging Christians to picture the deep bond between mother and child in their mind's eye:

> See with what reverence and care and with what fear she handled him whom she knew to be her God; and how with bended knee she took him and placed him in the cradle; with what joy and confidence and motherly authority she embraced him, kissed him, hugged him and delighted in him whom she knew to be her son.
> (de Caulibus 2000: 37)

Such devotional materials are thought to have inspired female mystics, for example, Birgitta of Sweden, who experienced detailed visions of Mary's careful ministerings of her shivering newborn son, or the thirteenth-century Marie of Oignies, who went so far as to imagine herself nursing the Christ child in bed (Dzon and Kenney, 2012: 40; 192–200).

Christmas also provided the opportunity to meditate on the Gospel narrative. In one well-known homily, a lengthy dialogue between a sceptical Joseph and Gabriel addresses Mary's mysterious pregnancy (PL 39:2107–10), no doubt answering questions many in the congregation would themselves have had. Interest in the more mundane details of the Holy Family resulted also in a greater role for Joseph, who, starting in the fifteenth century, became increasingly active and present in depictions of the Nativity and less the glum, ageing man on the margins he had previously been (Comet 2003: 208–9). Depictions of the Magi arriving at the manger also changed over the centuries, as they evolved from European-style kings (as in the tenth-century Anglo-Saxon Benedictional of Aethelwold) to ethnically diverse monarchs with exotic entourages (as in Hans Memling's fifteenth-century Adoration panel).

Christmas was believed to be a time of miracles. Many wondrous signs marked the event, according to the well-known preaching tool, the *Golden Legend* (de Voragine

2012: 38). A sermon by the Franciscan theologian Bonaventure lists the twelve miracles that are thought to have taken place at the moment of Christ's birth, including a spring of oil sprouting up in Rome and the spontaneous speaking of animals in Judaea (Bonaventure 1901: 122–3). The miracle of the talking animals was thought to be reproduced each year; a twelfth-century sermon claims it was a popular understanding that brute animals would speak with human voices on this night (Honorius 1841: PL 172:816). Another English belief was that grain that had been placed outside on Christmas Eve would be sprinkled with heavenly dew (from the Vigil chant, *Rorate caeli*), and bread made of this grain could cure illness (Gervase of Tilbury 2002). Plants were thought to miraculously flower, and many churches in England were decorated with seasonal plants, such as holly and ivy, as we can see from parish accounts (Hutton 1996: 34). The devil often made an appearance too, only to be rebuffed, as he was at the French reform abbey of Cluny, where he was witnessed trying to squeeze into the chapter house; that he was too fat revealed his gluttony compared to the monks' sobriety (de Voragine 2012: 42). Perhaps unsurprisingly, visions of the Christ Child often occurred at Christmas. Late-medieval Dominican nuns recorded many visions, for example Margreth Flastrerin, who saw the Christ Child descend from the altar at Christmas, dressed in silk robes, and come to her in the choir, where she held and played with him until the end of Mass. In another account from the abbey of Adelhausen, a heavily pregnant Mary was seen entering the choir at compline, only to reappear the next morning carrying a baby in her arms, whom she presented to the sisters (Kieckhefer 2012: 179).

Following Christmas Day, medieval Christians entered Christmastide, or the Twelve Days of Christmas. Of these days, the first three took on special importance. December 26, commemorating St Stephen, December 27, John the Evangelist, and 28 December, the Holy Innocents, are described by John Beleth as a *tripudia,* a term that connotes dancing and music, meaning that some of the chants performed on those days may have been accompanied by dance (Hiley 1993: 40). In many European churches, each day also came to be associated with a particular order of cleric: deacons with the 26th, priests with the 27th and choirboys fittingly with the 28th. On these days, the respective clerics were given special responsibilities in leading the liturgical celebration, for example choosing liturgical elements, performing much of the office while seated in the high stalls, carrying liturgical objects such as crosses and censers, holding the book for the officiating priest, and in some cases even delivering the sermon.

Although the feast of the Innocents was meant to be a solemn occasion in memory of the children martyred by Herod, the feast took on a particularly festive atmosphere. A tradition celebrated in many northern churches involved the election of a Boy Bishop by his fellow acolytes. In a carnivalesque role-reversal, the little bishop carried the insignia of office (e.g. mitre, ring, and staff), acting in all ways like an actual bishop, including blessing the people and distributing wine. At the Mass of the Boy Bishop in Padua, a spear was thrown into the congregation presumably by someone playing Herod, and armed soldiers ran through the nave, as the Holy Family—complete with live ass—walked through at the same time. Multiple repetitions of the verse of the

Magnificat that reads, 'He hath put down the mighty from their seat, and hath exalted the humble and meek', referred playfully to the boys taking over, but also to the triumph of the Innocents. But despite the seeming irreverence represented by these traditions, the liturgy was carried out very much as usual, in what Susan Boynton has called 'highly controlled liturgical play' (Boynton 2002: 73).

A little more licence seems to have been taken by another group of clerics who had charge of the liturgical proceedings on 1 January. By the eighth century, this day marked the celebration of Christ's circumcision, and, in many places, came to be associated with the subdeacons (in others, it was 6 or 13 January). Although the tradition's precise beginnings are unknown, the mid-twelfth century saw the day referred to for the first time as the Feast of Fools, or variably as the Feast of the Ass or Feast of the Staff, after the cantor's staff seized by the elected master of fools (Beleth 1976: 133). The feast was celebrated mainly in northern French cathedrals, with notable examples at Sens, Beauvais, and Laon, but also in Santiago de Compostela and various parts of England. Initially, there seems to have been no prescribed office for the day (Beleth 1976: 134), and it has long been thought to have involved raucous misbehaviour on the part of the clergy, including drinking bouts, bloodshed, and subversive mockery in the very liturgy, based largely on surviving condemnations (Chambers 1903: I, 274–419). In mid-twelfth-century Paris, the canon Richard of St Victor in Paris decried that around the New Year 'fortune tellings, divinations, deceptions and feigned madnesses' invaded the church, and other accounts tell of the unusual pealing of bells, strange lights, and the performance of rhythmic poetry and impersonations during the service (Fassler 1992: 73, 78). By the fifteenth century, accusations ranged from cross-dressing, leaping through the church, playing dice, eating black pudding at the altar, and censing with old shoes (Harris 2011: 1–2).

Instead of trying to ban the Feast of Fools outright, many churches sought to reform it, as Odo of Sully did in Paris by creating an elaborate office of the Circumcision. They nevertheless retained the jovial nature of the day, infusing the often extravagant liturgy with a sense of fun. New genres of chant were composed, including the *conductus* and *versus*, which included moments of prescribed laughter, comic repetitions, and references to drinking. Perhaps the most famous conductus is *Orientibus partibus*, otherwise known as 'the prose of the ass', performed at Beauvais, Sens, and Bourges. It was sung while an actual ass was led into the church and included a lively refrain in French goading the ass on: 'hez hez sire asne hez' (Harris 2011: 76–7). But these elements suggest nothing more than that commemoration of the Circumcision was made more orthodox while remaining a lively occasion, as general widespread support for the Feast of Fools suggests.

Scholars have recently argued that the Feast of Fools was not reformed to curb wild behaviour in churches, but was rather a new observance created as a counter-weight to the secular festivities around the New Year, celebrated on 1 January in many parts of Europe as heir to the Roman Kalends. According to Max Harris, it was secular Kalends traditions that were criticized when reference was made to cross-dressing, masquerading through town, wearing floral wreaths, and generally dissolute behaviour. Certainly, feasting and merriment were common; Christmas was often celebrated as the carnival season in areas where the pre-Lenten Carnival did not play such an important role, as in England (Harris 2006: 104). In accordance with the December liberty tradition, the rich were meant to feed the poor, and manorial court records show that households provided a feast for all those working the land (Hutton 1996: 10) Mumming is recorded in penitentials as early as the seventh century, pointing to people 'doing the stag' or going from house to house in animal masks, likely receiving some form of hospitality at each (Harris 2011: 21). Even the boys of the Schola Cantorum in Rome enacted the stag tradition (Harris 2011: 37). In thirteenth-century Paris, youths, most likely university students, were said to blacken their faces with coal dust and engage in boisterous behaviour. Later in the same century, these anarchic revelries became formalized in *compagnies de jeunesse*, organized youth groups which staged masquerades on the Feast of Fools and were regulated by the civic authorities. They too elected a king, bishop, or abbot for the Twelve Days of Christmas, and processed through the streets in disguise (Harris 2011: 169). Dancing was another staple of the celebrations, and included both clergy and laity. At the cathedral in the French town of Nîmes, a large circle dance in the nave marked the festivities on Christmas Day accompanied by musical instruments (Harris 2011: 160). Held at some point during the Christmas season, a ball game was played within the precincts of a number of French churches by bishop and clergy with laity in attendance, most likely a song and dance with a ball rather than a full-on football match (Harris 2011: 54–62). The difficulty in distinguishing between clergy and laity in these activities suggests that we should probably not imagine these as completely separate spheres, and that both groups participated in Kalends and Feast of Fools traditions.

Attempts to reform the wilder elements of Christmastide celebrations while allowing these elements some purchase, can be seen in the liturgical drama developed in the High Middle Ages. Again northern French cathedrals led the way, as reformers, such as the bishop William of Auxerre, sought to exchange games/performances (*ludi*) which were considered against the faith for those that were not (cf. Fassler 1992: 77). Their solution was to put on elaborate plays that educated as much as they delighted; these were performed exegesis, the sung texts of the plays dramatizing the new learning developed in cathedral schools and the nascent universities. The first were small Nativity plays (*Officium pastorum*, or 'Office of the Shepherds'), performed on Christmas Day, which developed from a trope of the Introit of the Third Mass: *Quem queritis in presepe, pastores, dicite?* ('Whom do you seek in the manger, shepherds, do tell?') (Young 1922). As of the eleventh century, clerics increasingly sang the verses to each other in dialogue form, taking on the roles of shepherds and angels, leading to full-scale dramatic re-enactments of the Nativity story. Another play performed on the Christmas Vigil as a culmination of Advent themes, is the *Ordo Prophetarum* or Prophets' Play. Based on the Advent sermon, *Vos inquam convenio*, the play features a series of Old and New Testament prophets, and some pagan voices, who foretell Christ's birth. In one late-twelfth-century version from Laon, rubrics at the beginning of the play describe each character in costume, including a pregnant Elizabeth, a madly acting Erythraean Sybil, and the stage prop of Balaam's talking ass voiced by a boy (Young 1933: II, 145).

On the day of the Holy Innocents, the *Ordo Rachelis* ('Play of Rachel') or *Interfectio puerorum* ('Killing of the Boys'), re-enacted the massacre of the Innocents, ending with the prophesied weeping of Rachel in Jeremiah 31:15/Matthew 2:17–18. This play may have been inspired by the Herod games played in Germany and Italy, where clerics impersonating Herod and his soldiers would storm the church and beat people with bladders, as happened in Padua. Unsurprisingly, the Feast of Fools came to feature its own play, the *Danielis Ludus* ('Play of Daniel') performed at Beauvais. Here, the book of Daniel was re-enacted with special effects to reproduce the writing on the wall and the lions' den. The relevance of Daniel's story can be understood in light of attempts to reform the wilder aspects of the Feast of Fools (or Kalends) celebrations with a play extolling a sober young cleric (Daniel) and excoriating the drunken revelries of the Babylonian court. A similarly themed play, the *Ordo Joseph*, staged the Old Testament story of Joseph at Laon on the Feast of Fools celebrated there on 6 January. As Margot Fassler has explained it, such plays channelled the carnivalesque energy of the Feast of Fools into a respectable if still joyous articulation (Fassler 1992).

The last day on which dramas are known to have been performed coincided with the last day of the Christmas season, Epiphany (6 January), on which lengthy *Officii Stellae* ('Plays of the Star') were performed retelling the arrival of the Magi. The concentration of so much high medieval religious drama in the Christmas season is revealing of the sumptuous way in which this time of year was celebrated, particularly in the large churches of Europe: a feast for every sense.

The rich tradition of liturgical drama provides a fitting end point for this brief discussion of the Christmas season as celebrated in Western Europe in the High Middle Ages. Although Christmas festivities extended far back into late Antiquity as heirs to Kalends traditions, the twelfth to fourteenth centuries saw these festivities move into the sphere of the church in new ways. Instated under a reforming impulse, the introduction of liturgies for the Feast of Fools and liturgical drama preserved the joyfulness of the season if dispensing with some of its more extreme ribaldry. During Christmas, the stage was set, literally, to showcase the extravagant musical and intellectual developments of the period, mixing 'the sacred and the secular, the serious and the comic' (Fassler 1992: 99). These traditions were also tied to the growing sensibility to Christ's humanity, as seen in the popularization of the manger as devotional object. Care should be taken not to make too clear a separation between clerical and lay spheres in the celebration of Christmas. Both groups mingled, clerics cavorting in the Kalends activities as lay people attended church for lavish services and moving sermons. Late medieval reformers attempted to curb some of these practices. The Council of Basel in 1435 banned liturgical drama and extra-liturgical activity in churches, and by the early sixteenth century, many such customs had been suppressed. But the fact remains that the musical and artistic advances made in a period of significant cultural flourishing infused the celebration of Christmas, turning it into a joyous occasion of sanctioned (and unsanctioned) celebration to rival Carnival itself.

References and Further Reading

Anon. (1975). *The Ordinal of the Papal Court from Innocent III to Boniface VIII and Related Documents*, Stephen van Dijk (ed.), Spicilegium Friburgense 22. Fribourg: The University Press.

Arlt, Wulf (2000). 'The Office for the Feast of the Circumcision from Le Puy', in Margot Fassler and Rebecca A. Baltzer (eds.), *The Divine Office in the Latin Middle Ages*. Oxford: Oxford University Press: 324–33.

Augustine (1952). *Sermons for Christmas and Epiphany*, trans. J. Quasten and J. Plumpe, Ancient Christian Writers 15. Washington DC: Paulist Press.

Bede (1843). *Complete Works*, ed. John Allen Giles. London: Whitaker. Vol. 5.

Beleth, Johannes (1976). *Summa de Ecclesiasticis Officiis*, ed. Heribert Douteil. CCCM 46A. Turnhout: Brepols.

Beer, Manuela et al. (2014). *Die Heiligen Drei Könige. Mythos, Kunst und Kult. Katalog zur Ausstellung im Museum Schnütgen, Köln, 25. Oktober 2014-25. Januar 2015*. Hirmer: Munich.

Bonaventure (1901). *Opera Omnia*, ed. David Fleming. Florence: Typographia Collegii S. Bonaventurae. Vol. 9.

Boynton, Susan (1998). 'Performative Exegesis in the Fleury Interfectio Puerorum', *Viator*, 29: 39–64.

Boynton, Susan (2002). 'Work and Play in Sacred Music and its Social Context, c. 1050–1250', in R. N. Swanson (ed.), *The Use and Abuse of Time in Christian History. Studies in Church History* 37. Woodbridge: Boydell Press: 57–79.

Johannes de Caulibus (2000). *Meditations on the Life of Christ*, trans. Francis X. Taney. Asheville: Pegasus Press.

Chambers, E. K. (1903). *The Medieval Stage*. 2 Vols. Oxford: Oxford University Press.

Comet, Georges (2003). 'L'iconographie de la Nativité à l'époque médiévale', in Gilles Dorival and Jean-Paul Boyer (eds.), *La Nativité et le temps de Noël. Antiquité et Moyen Age*. Aix-en-Provence: Publications de l'Université de Provence: 203–11.

Dahhaoui, Yann (2005). 'Enfant-évêque et fête des fous: un loisir ritualisé pour jeunes clercs?' in *Temps libre et loisirs du 14e au 20e siècle. Freizeit und Vergnügen vom 14. bis zum 20. Jahrhundert*. Zürich: Chronos (Société suisse d'histoire économique et sociale): 33–46.

Dahhaoui, Yann (2007-2008). 'Entre *ludus* et *ludibrium*. Attitudes de l'Église médiévale à l'égard de l'évêque des Innocents,' *Ludica* 13–14:183–98.

Dudley, Martin R. (1994). '*Natalis Innocentum*: The Holy Innocents in Liturgy and Drama', in Diana Wood (ed.), *The Church and Childhood. Studies in Church History* 31. Oxford: Blackwell: 233–42.

Durandus, William (1859). *Rationale Divinorum Officiorum*. J. Dura (ed.). Naples.

Dzon, Mary (2017). *The Quest for the Christ Child in the Later Middle Ages*. Philadelphia: University of Pennsylvania Press.

Dzon, Mary and Theresa Kenney (2012). 'Introduction', in Mary Dzon and Theresa Kenney (eds.), *The Christ Child in Medieval Culture: Alpha es et O!* Toronto: University of Toronto Press, xiii–xxii.

Fassler, Margot (1992). 'The Feast of Fools and *Danielis ludus*: Popular Tradition in a Medieval Cathedral Play', in Thomas Forrest Kelly (ed.), *Plainsong in the Age of Polyphony*. Cambridge: Cambridge University Press: 65–99.

Fassler, Margot (2000a). 'Mary's Nativity, Fulbert of Chartres and the Stirps Jesse: Liturgical Innovation circa 1000 and its Afterlife', *Speculum*, 75: 389–434.

Fassler, Margot (2000b). 'Sermons, Sacramentaries, and Early Sources for the Office in the Latin West: The Example of Advent', in Margot Fassler and Ruth A. Baltzer (eds.), *The Divine Office in the Latin Middle Ages*. Oxford: Oxford University Press: 15–47.

Fassler, Margot (2009). *The Virgin of Chartres: Making History through Liturgy and the Arts*. New Haven: Yale University Press.

Foulon, Jean-Hervé (2003). 'La Nativité dans la prédication de saint Bernard, abbé de Clairvaux', in Gilles Dorival and Jean-Paul Boyer (eds.), *La Nativité et le temps de Noël. Antiquité et Moyen Âge*. Aix-en-Provence: Publications de l'Université de Provence: 213–229.

Gervase of Tilbury (2002). *Otia Imperialia: Recreation of an Emperor*, trans. S. E. Banks and J. W. Binns. Oxford: Oxford University Press.

Gougaud, L. (1922). 'La crèche de Noël avant St. François d'Assise', *Revue des Sciences Religieuses*, 2: 26–34.

Grégoire, Réginald (1966). *Les homéliaires du Moyen Âge. Inventaire et analyse des manuscrits*. Rerum ecclesiasticarum documenta, Serie maior. Fontes VI. Rome: Herder.

Harper, John (1991). *The Forms and Order of Western Liturgy from the Tenth to the Eighteenth Century: A Historical Introduction and Guide for Students and Musicians*. Oxford: Clarendon Press.

Harris, Max (2006). 'Claiming Pagan Origins for Carnival: Bacchanalia, Saturnalia and Kalends', *European Medieval Drama*, 10: 57–107.

Harris, Max (2009). 'A Rough and Holy Liturgy: A Reassessment of the Feast of Fools', in Katja Gvozdeva and Werner Röcke (eds.), *Risus Sacer—Sacrum Risibile: Interaktionsfelder von Sakralität und Gelächter im kulturellen und historischen Wandel*. Bern: Peter Lang: 77–100.

Harris, Max (2011). *Sacred Folly: A New History of the Feast of Fools*. Ithaca: Cornell University Press.

Hiley, David (1993). *Western Plainchant. A Handbook*. Oxford: Clarendon Press.

Honorius Augustodunensis (1841–64). *Speculum Ecclesiae*. J.-P. Migne (ed.), *Patrologia Latina*, vol. 172, cols. 807–1107.

Hrabanus Maurus (1841–64). *Liber de sacris ordinibus, sacramentis divinis, et vestimentis sacerdotalibus ad Thiotmarum*, J.-P. Migne (ed.), *Patrologia Latina*, vol. 112, cols. 1165–92.

Hutton, Ronald (1996). *The Stations of the Sun: A History of the Ritual Year in Britain*. Oxford: Oxford University Press.

Isidore of Seville (2008). *De Ecclesiasticis Officiis*, trans. Thomas Knoebel. Ancient Christian Writers 61. New York: Newman Press.

Kenney, Theresa (2012), 'The Manger as Calvary and Altar in the Middle English Nativity Lyric', in Mary Dzon and Theresa Kenney (eds.), *The Christ Child in Medieval Culture: Alpha es et O!* Toronto: University of Toronto Press: 29–65.

Kieckhefer, Richard (2012), '*Ihesus ist unser!* The Christ Child in the German Sister Books', in Mary Dzon and Theresa Kenney (eds.), *The Christ Child in Medieval Culture: Alpha es et O!* Toronto: University of Toronto Press: 167–98.

Lagueux, Robert (2009). 'Sermons, Exegesis and Performance: The Laon *Ordo Prophetarum* and the Meaning of Advent', *Comparative Drama*, 43, no. 2: 197–220.

Leo I (1841–64). *Sermones in Nativitate Domini*. J.-P. Migne (ed.), *Patrologia Latina*, Vol. 54, cols. 190–234.

LeZotte, Annette (2011). 'Cradling Power: Female Devotions and Early Medieval Jésueaux', in Sarah Blick and Laura Gelfland (eds.), *Push Me, Pull You: Imaginative, Emotional Physical and Spatial Interaction in Late Medieval and Renaissance Art*, Vol. 2. Leiden: Brill: 59–84.

Marcus, Leah S. (2012). 'The Christ Child as Sacrifice: A Medieval Tradition and the English Cycle Plays', in Mary Dzon and Theresa Kenney (eds.), *The Christ Child in Medieval Culture: Alpha es et O!* Toronto: University of Toronto Press: 3–28.

Marsicano, Vincent (1982). 'Adaptations of the Pseudo-Augustine *Sermon against the Jews* in the *Benediktbeuern Christmas Play* and the *Frankfurt Passion Play*', *Colloquia Germanica*, 15: 59–65.

Martindale, Andrew (1994). 'The Child in the Picture: A Medieval Perspective,' in Diana Wood (ed.), *The Church and Childhood. Studies in Church History* 31. Oxford: Blackwell: 197–232.

de la Roncière, Charles (2003). 'La Nativité dans la dévotion de saint François d'Assise', in Gilles Dorival and Jean-Paul Boyer (eds.), *La Nativité et le temps de Noël. Antiquité et Moyen Age*. Aix-en-Provence: Publications de l'Université de Provence: 231–43.

Shahar, Shulamith (1994). 'The Boy Bishop's Feast: A Case-study in Church Attitudes towards Children in the High and Late Middle Ages,' in Diana Wood (ed.), *The Church and Childhood. Studies in Church History* 31. Oxford: Blackwell: 243–60.

Thomas of Celano (1999). 'First Life of Francis of Assisi', in R. J. Armstrong, J. A. Wayne Hellman, and W. J. Short (trans.), *Francis of Assisi. The Saint: Early Documents*. New York: New City Press. Vol. I

Tydeman, William, trans. (2001). *The Medieval European Stage, 500–1500*. Cambridge: Cambridge University Press.

Jacobus de Voragine (2012). *The Golden Legend: Readings on the Saints,* trans. William Granger Ryan (trans.). Princeton NJ: Princeton University Press.

Young, Karl (1912). Officium Pastorum: *A Study of the Dramatic Developments within the Liturgy of Christmas*. Madison: Wisconsin Academy of Sciences, Arts and Letters.

Young, Karl (1933). *The Drama of the Medieval Church*, 2 Vols. London and Oxford: Oxford University Press.

CHAPTER 3

THE REFORMATION AND EARLY MODERN PERIODS

KATRINA JENNIE-LOU WHEELER

A common narrative of Christmas observance during the Reformation and into the early modern period claims that Protestantism decimated the celebration of Christmas, and the holiday was only subsequently revived in the nineteenth century thanks to the work of Charles Dickens, Washington Irving, and Victoria and Albert in popularizing it again. While this claim has been challenged by historians, some of whom call it 'cliché' and 'commonplace', books and articles on the early modern history of Christmas still grapple with assessing its validity (Restad 1995: vii). As we will see, there is much evidence to show that bans on Christmas in the anglophone world were rarely long lived while in other Western countries, Christmas celebrations continued in force. And many historians have noted that while Dickens did much to popularize Christmas, he did not invent the traditions and observances contained in *A Christmas Carol* out of whole cloth. Rather, he reflected a familiar image of Christmas festivity, helping to shape the traditions but not invent them (Wernecke 1959: 14; Connelly 1999: 3). These traditions were not new in the nineteenth century, however much they may have been revived and renewed in cultural practice.

This chapter will explore the ways that leaders of the sixteenth-century Protestant Reformation and subsequent Protestant groups treated Christmas celebrations in Europe and America. It will also look briefly at early modern Catholic Christmas traditions that continued during this period to show that the cliché of a waning Christmas is a fairly narrow and anglo-centric historical view, prioritizing more radical forms of Protestantism and dismissing the many Christians around the Western world who remained faithful celebrants of the Nativity of Christ. Finally, it will also point out several elements of Christmas observance that became iconic in the nineteenth century but were rooted in or grew in importance during the sixteenth to eighteenth centuries.

The claim of a waning Christmas is rooted in the late sixteenth and early seventeenth centuries, as more radical Protestants reacted against Catholic ceremonies to the point of removing all religious festivals from their calendars. While this is not the whole story, it is an important aspect of how Christmas fared through the early modern period and should be examined. As we will see later in this chapter, the early Reformers in Germany and England did not abandon Christmas, though they were intent on reforming some of the popular methods of observing the holiday. But some Protestants wanted to be rid of Christmas celebrations entirely as a part of their larger programme of 'purifying' their religion and removing the 'superstitious' practices that they did not believe to have any biblical basis. (On the note of superstition, they might not have been so far off: one popular belief in many countries was that animals could speak on Christmas Eve, bringing misfortune to any humans who heard what they had to say, which was often a prediction of the eavesdropper's impending demise (Lebrun 1983: 50)). Often, these Protestants are referred to as Calvinist, though John Calvin himself did not formally condemn Christmas, and it is more accurate to refer to them as Reformed, as they also come from reform movements led by John Knox and Ulrich Zwingli. Furthermore, it was only some Reformed Protestants who banned the holiday. In the 1560s, we see two opposing decisions made by Reformed Churches. While in the Swiss cantons, the Second Helvetic Confession of 1562 upheld Christ-themed feast days, including Christmas, in 1560, the Scottish Kirk (Protestant Church) marked all holy days as 'abominations' that were not from Scripture (Bowler 2017: 25–6). In the Kirk's *First Book of Discipline,* they focused on Christmas as one of the 'holy dayis of certane Sanctis commandit by man, such as be all those that the Papistis have invented' (Nothaft 2011: 504). This more radical stance against Christmas in Scotland stood apart in its own time and also presaged the famous anti-Christmas actions of seventeenth-century Puritans in both England and its colonies in the New World.

The Puritans, often called the 'hotter sort of Protestants', were those in the Church of England who believed even more radical reforms were necessary. Their crusade against Christmas was carried out in both England and the New England colonies. After the establishment of the Puritan Commonwealth, the English Parliament wrote in 1647, 'be it ordained, by the Lords and Commons in Parliament assembled, that the Feast of the Nativity of Christ, and all other festival days commonly called Holy-days, be no longer observed within this kingdom of England' (Bowler 2017: 32). Ministers were even threatened with imprisonment if they preached special sermons to commemorate the Nativity on 25 December (Restad 1995: 7–8). But even under this ban, the government was hard pressed to enforce the laws, and resistance ranged from the quiet continuation of celebrations to riots until the law was overturned in 1660 with the Restoration (Stevens 1979: 118). More successful was the ban in Scotland already mentioned, which minimized Christmas in that country until the twentieth century. Puritan colonists in New England, intent on building their 'city on a hill' banned Christmas celebrations. In 1620, Governor William Bradford insisted that 25 December be a workday for the nascent colony, just as any other day. The following year, when the growing colony counted Anglicans among their number, they refused to work on Christmas, sparking a disagreement with Bradford, who at least insisted that they not be allowed to have revelry while their neighbours worked. By 1659, it was forbidden in Massachusetts to celebrate Christmas with feasting or even to take the day off work (Stevens 1979: 121–2). This ban on Christmas lasted within the colony until Charles II and the Restoration government in England threatened in 1681 to revoke their charter if they did not follow the oft-repeated injunction to remove the anti-Christmas laws from the books (Nissenbaum 1996: 18). To better understand why these bans against Christmas were so important to the Puritans, we can look at two aspects of their belief about what made their religion 'pure' and reformed: a clear scriptural command for their religious practices (orthodoxy of their beliefs) and a manner of life that was holy and above reproach (orthopraxy in their actions).

One of the complaints against celebrating Christmas was that celebrating any day as holier than another was not a practice based in Scripture. The only day that Christians were commanded to keep especially holy was the Sabbath. While Christmas was especially named in the Puritan Parliamentary ban, it is important to recognize that it sits alongside 'all other festival days'. Protestants who rejected or downplayed it did so as a larger project of reducing the Catholic focus on the saints. Christmas was one of many winter festivals honouring the saints in the Catholic calendar that were celebrated to varying degrees around the Western world. These holy days had several areas of overlap in the ways that they were observed, often including special masses, feasts, and almsgiving. Gift-giving was frequently a part of their observation, and this practice often was accompanied by tales of fantastical visitors who brought the gifts to good children. Rejection of the 25 December feast of the Nativity is situated in the context of the rejection of a whole host of saints' days taking place in the autumn and winter. When we recognize that these included feasts on 11 November (St Martin), 25 November (St Catherine), 30 November (St Andrew), 1 December (St Eligius), 4 December (St Barbara), 6 December (St Nicholas), 13 December (St Lucia), 21 December (St Thomas), 26 December (St Stephen), 27 December (St John the Evangelist), 28 December (Feast of Holy Innocents), and 6 January (Epiphany or Kings' Day), it no longer seems a singular attack on celebrations of the birth of Christ. It truly was 'one feast among many feasts', and these feasts seemed to be unnecessary, distracting, or even harmful to what they considered 'pure' religion (Lebrun 1983: 34–7).

Besides not having any biblical commandment to celebrate Christ's birth, Puritans also noted that the early Church did not mark the date of the Nativity on 25 December, or indeed at all. This was true, as early Christians did not celebrate births in general, and Christ's birth was not recognized as a holy day until the fourth century (Restad 1995: 3-4, 7). Several Reformed theologians throughout the sixteenth and early seventeenth centuries argued against the historicity of 25 Christmas as the actual birth date of Christ. In 1593, Swiss theologian Rudolph Hospinian wrote to debunk the Catholic calendar entirely, including Christmas. He went on to claim that choosing 25 December for the celebration of Christ's Nativity was only a tactic to co-opt the Roman festival of Saturnalia, a celebratory season that shared many common winter festival elements with Christmas, such as bringing greenery indoors, feasting, and giving gifts. In 1598, Joseph Scaliger worked out a more elaborate method of finding the date of Christ's birth that would likewise disprove 25 December in favour of a date in the spring. These arguments were acknowledged even by those who defended celebrations of Christmas, including George Palmer, author of the *Lawfulness of the Celebration of Christs Birth-day* (Nothaft 2011: 515–19). For those who discouraged Christmas celebrations, however, undermining the date itself as having pagan origins was one way to bolster their argument against celebrating the Nativity at all.

Another complaint against Christmas was that its excessive celebration only encouraged debauchery, quite the opposite of a holy celebration to honour Christ and express religious piety. Puritans voiced their disapproval of traditional revelry from the Middle Ages that included cross-dressing, social inversion, heavy drinking, and aggressive begging. In the sixteenth century, Hugh Latimer argued 'men dishonour Christ more in the twelve days of Christmas, than in all the twelve months besides' (Nissenbaum 1996: 7). Combining both the complaint against unruly celebration and the belief that it was wrong to have any festival days that are set apart from other days, Philip Stubbes reasoned, in his *Anatomie of Abuses* of 1583, 'the holier the time is (if one time were holier than an other, as it is not), the holier ought their exercises to bee' (Miles 1976: 84). The same concern that Christmas became a time of increased debauchery carried on into the seventeenth century, where in a tract from 1656, Hezekiah Woodward claimed that 'no thing more hindereth the Gospel work all the year long, than doth the observation of that Idol Day once in a year' (Stevens 1979: 118). In the late seventeenth century and into the early eighteenth, both Increase Mather and his son Cotton Mather complained that Christmas was neither biblical nor holy, full of 'corrupt' revelry (Restad 1995: 14–15). Cotton's concession that it was possible to observe Christmas in a holy way, focusing on charity and love to honour the Lord's birth, represents a later generation of Puritans willing to compromise on the strict banning of the holiday, as Increase still recommended (Nissenbaum 1996: 26). While attitudes may have become more irenic in the latter part of the early modern period, the same concerns against Christmas as a time of excess remained in the Puritan community. These concerns did continue to characterize some attitudes towards Christmas into the eighteenth century, even among those who did not descend from the seventeenth-century Puritans. American almanac-makers, including Nathanael Ames and Benjamin Franklin, while not rejecting a celebration of Christmas, encouraged sobriety and temperance in its celebration (Nissenbaum 1996: 27).

This story of legal impediments and clerical warnings against celebrating Christmas is an important aspect of early-modern Christianity, but it is only one narrative from one particular branch of Christianity, while other Christian communities continued celebrating Christmas. In contrast to the Puritan ban of Christmas, other Christians in the Americas continued to observe Christmas in the sixteenth and seventeenth centuries. For example, Spanish Catholics celebrated the Christmas Midnight Mass in Saint Augustine, Florida, in 1565 at the *Nombre de Dios* mission, while French Catholics did the same in New Orleans, St. Croix, Maine, and Texas into the seventeenth century (Gulevich 2000: 11; Stevens 1979: 125; Restad 1995: 9). Anglicans celebrated in 1607 at Jamestown, John Smith asserting 'wherever an Englishman may be, and in whatever part of the world, he must keep Christmas with feasting and merriment!' (Stevens 1979: 121). Southern colonists in Virginia, Maryland, and North and South Carolina also celebrated the festival with traditions such as singing carols and burning Yule logs, sometimes celebrating for the entire twelve-day season (Gulevich 2000: 13; Stevens 1979: 123). The Dutch, German, and other settlers in New Amsterdam celebrated Christmas in a variety of different ways, eventually contributing to the modern celebrations of Christmas with elements drawn from around the Western world (Restad 1995: 9). This cultural variety continued, and the methods of celebration continued into the early Republic, where it was popular for a time to reject all British holidays, eventually leading to an American focus on fewer holidays in general, such as Christmas, New Year's, and Thanksgiving (Restad 1995: 21, 25).

Likewise, in England Christmas remained an important holiday for the Protestants who rejected the strictures of the Puritans, one especially focusing on the practice of hospitality expressed through feasting, gift-giving, and wassailing. While Protestants in the Church of England wished to reform celebratory practices, as they wished to reform other aspects of religious life, they did not go so far as to call for the abolition of the Christmas holiday (Jensen 2012: 215). The Tudor Court was known for its Christmas celebrations from the reign of King Henry VIII to that of Elizabeth I (Bowler 2017: 27). However, the specific festival celebrations varied, reflecting the changing religious priorities of the Tudor kings and queens and either their rejection or embrace of Catholicism. For example, Henry VIII banned the practice of electing a boy to play bishop for the feast of Innocents on 28 December, and while Mary reinstated it after him, it was finally abolished under Elizabeth I (Stevens 1979: 62). The royals set the tone for hospitality and celebration in the Christmas season and likewise expected the nobles to do so for their vassals. In fact, Elizabeth requested in the 1590s that the nobles be at home on their estates to show proper Christmas hospitality to others, rather than spending the holiday at court (Connelly 1999: 23, 25; Jensen 2012: 215). Christmas continued to be popular in the Stuart Court as well, with James I's accession to the throne, and he continued the enjoinders to the nobles to be at home, offering Christmas hospitality, and encouraged revelry at court, including the writing and performance of Ben Jonson's *Christmas, His Masque*, which defended the holiday in 1616 against Puritan complaints (Jensen 2012: 216; Bowler 2017: 29–30). In his role as James VI of Scotland, he also combatted the Scottish ban on Christmas with the Five Articles of Perth in 1618 (Bowler 2017: 30). The status of Christmas also reflected the changing religious priorities of the English government. The Anglican Convocation of 1562 officially upheld the Church calendar as it stood in the Catholic Church, though this decision was to be overturned by the Puritan Commonwealth (Restad 1995: 7). As we can see, in the early modern anglophone context, the Puritan attacks on Christmas did not go unanswered and their opinions against Christmas were not the only ones, nor were they in the majority.

In other parts of the western world, the Reformation did bring some changes to the ways that Christmas was observed, but it did not nearly have the same negative effect as the bans in Scotland, England, or the New World. In Protestant Germany, some Christmas celebrations were adjusted, rather than discouraged entirely. One such practice was the traditional practice of children expecting gifts from the figure of

Saint Nicholas; Reformers instead introduced the figure of the Christ Child (*Kristkindl*) as the gift-giver, a character who soon began to be depicted by a young woman with blonde hair rather than an infant boy. Removing Saint Nicholas from the popular gift-giving winter celebrations was a casualty of Protestant de-emphasis of the saints. Instead, families were encouraged to teach their children that Christ was the provider of all good things, even holiday gifts (Stevens 1979: 80). In fact, the Protestant leaders discouraged gift-giving on Saint Nicholas's Day (6 December), and encouraged gifts from the *Kristkindl* on Christmas Eve (Forbes 2007: 78). This was only the case in northern Germany, however, where Lutheranism grew, while in southern Germany and in Austria, Saint Nicholas's Day remained popular among Catholics (Lebrun 1983: 56). Even among the Protestants, the old traditions were slow to change. Into the seventeenth century, a Lutheran pastor continued to decry attributing gift-giving to Saint Nicholas, as 'a bad custom, because it points children to the saint, while yet we know that not Saint Nicholas but the holy Christ-Child gives us all good things for body and soul' (Miles 1976: 230). While this indicates the difficulty that Protestant clergy had in changing traditional holiday celebrations amongst their parishioners, it illustrates an important point. Instead of discouraging any religious festivals, as happened in the Scottish or the Puritan context, in Germany, Protestant leaders encouraged celebrations of Christmas as a way to focus on Christ in the holiday season. This was their way of trying to direct Christians away from the many celebrations of saints, including Saint Nicholas, and towards the figure of Christ above all.

Many familiar elements of modern Christmas festivities, supposedly developed in the nineteenth century, originated or grew in the early modern period. Diaries from the mid-1700s by Reverend James Woodforde reveal the strength of Christmas traditions in England, detailing the use of holly, carols, and feasts (Connelly 1999: 3). A popular legend holds that the sixteenth-century Reformer Martin Luther brought the first Christmas trees indoors, although this has little historical evidence. The legend claims that Luther was inspired by the trees and the stars that he saw while walking outside and wanted to bring them indoors, adorning the boughs with lit candles to represent the light of Christ (Auld 1968: 146). Whether or not the sixteenth-century reformer actually originated Christmas trees, a verified historical reference to Christmas trees appeared in the early seventeenth century, in what was at the time an imperial free city in the Holy Roman Empire, Strasbourg [*Straßburg* in the then-current German spelling] (Miles 1976: 265). By the 1640s, the popularity of Christmas trees was growing, to the point that Dr Johann Dannhauer, a Catholic preacher at the Strasbourg Cathedral, spoke out against the practice of decorating trees for Christmas, arguing instead that pointing to Christ as the 'spiritual cedar-tree' was a more useful lesson for children's spiritual growth (Stevens 1979: 95–6; Auld 1968: 147). Though the nineteenth century witnessed a growth in the popularity of Christmas trees, especially after Queen Victoria and Prince Albert brought them to the English court, they were already becoming very popular in Germany throughout the early modern period.

Catholic countries continued celebrations of Christmas during the early modern period, even if the clergy sometimes complained of excesses in the festivities, and there we find many more Christmas practices familiar to modern revellers. The practice of burning the Yule log also continued in some countries, including in France, where burning the *bûche de noël* remained a standard custom into the seventeenth century (Lebrun 1983: 44). The ceremony of lighting the Yule log often included anointing it with wine or sprinkling breadcrumbs on top of it, both symbolic of ancient ceremonies for fertility and of Christian eucharistic rites (Miles 1976: 255). Fabricated Nativity scenes were popular expressions of Christmas cheer in several countries, especially in Italy. In Naples, for example, these impressive *presepios* reached their height of popularity and artistic sophistication in the eighteenth century, including elaborate ornamentation of the wooden and terracotta figurines with expensive fabrics and jewels (Stevens 1979: 64). Living nativities, originated by Saint Francis of Assisi in the thirteenth century, cropped up in Marseille as late as 1775 and returned to popularity in southern France after a brief pause during the French Revolution (Lebrun 1983: 47). During the French Revolution, a period of dechristianization led to suspension of the Christmas holiday in many parts of the country in 1793, though many communities across France resisted the change in their seasonal rhythms of life, and the official removal of Catholic holy days from the French Republican calendar was reversed by 1805 (Bowler 2017: 42).

Catholics and Protestants contributed to the growth of Christmas music throughout the early modern period in Europe and the Americas. From the fifteenth through to the nineteenth centuries, Catholic Germany and Austria saw a growth of 'realistic' Christmas songs telling the stories of the manger scene and the activities of the Holy Family (Miles 1976: 45). In France, Christmas carols (*Noëls*) became popular and were sold in collections by *colporteurs* in the fifteenth and sixteenth centuries. They continued to be written into the seventeenth century as well, with the first known composer identified in Avignon, and grew to their height of popularity in the eighteenth century (Lebrun 1983: 67). French carols often drew the singer into the Christmas story, placing them into the cast of characters (Miles 1976: 61). The fifteenth century also witnessed a large collection of Christmas carols growing in England as well. They grew to their height in England through the fifteenth and early sixteenth centuries, waned in the later sixteenth century, but continued to be written throughout the seventeenth and eighteenth centuries as well (Miles 1976: 55, 76–7). In late-sixteenth- and early-seventeenth-century England, carols were mainly kept alive through Catholic traditions and collections, rather than Protestant (Jensen 2012: 213). Protestant hymn traditions in Germany also yielded many Christmas songs, from Luther in the sixteenth century to Paul Gerhardt in the seventeenth century, and of course Bach's famous Christmas Oratorio written in the 1730s (Miles 1976: 70, 73). Even in New England, by the 1750s, churches had shifted from using only Psalms in their services to including Christmas hymns in their printed songbooks (Nissenbaum 1996: 33). Songs were a powerful way to draw communities together in celebrating the holiday, whether they were strongly religious in nature and sung in churches or whether they were popularized and sung at home or in public merry-making.

In the early modern period, Christmas celebrations did not look the same as they do today, and many religious and cultural practices varied from country to country as well as between religious communities. The Protestant Reformation contributed to change and development in the way that Christmas was celebrated, whether by emphasizing Christmas in order to draw attention away from other saints' days, or by reforming traditional methods of celebration to make them less rowdy and more holy. In some areas, primarily English-speaking areas, long-term effects of the Reformation resulted in laws against Christmas celebration. But in the end, that was one part of a multifaceted story of the many different ways Christmas was kept, changed, or banned in the Western world during the early modern period.

REFERENCES AND FURTHER READING

Auld, William Muir (1968). *Christmas Traditions*. Detroit: Gale Research Co.
Bowler, Gerry (2017). *Christmas in the Crosshairs: Two Thousand Years of Denouncing and Defending the World's Most Celebrated Holiday*. New York: Oxford University Press.
Connelly, Mark (1999). *Christmas: A Social History*. London: I.B. Tauris Publishers.
Forbes, Bruce David (2007). *Christmas: A Candid History*. Berkeley: University of California Press.
Gulevich, Tanya (2000). *Encyclopedia of Christmas*. Detroit: Omnigraphics.
Jensen, Phebe (2012). "'Honest Mirth & Merriment': Christmas and Catholicism in Early Modern England," in Lowell Gallagher (ed.), *Redrawing the Map of Early Modern English Catholicism*. Toronto: University of Toronto Press: 213–244.
Lebrun, Françoise (1983). *Le Livre de Noël*. Paris: Editions Robert Laffont.
McGreevy, Patrick (1990). 'Place in the American Christmas', *Geographical Review*, 80, no. 1: 32–42.
Miles, Clement A. (1976). *Christmas Customs and Traditions, Their History and Significance*. New York: Dover Publications.
Miller, Daniel (ed.) (1993). *Unwrapping Christmas*. Oxford: Clarendon Press.
Nissenbaum, Stephen (1996). *The Battle for Christmas*. 1st ed. New York: Alfred A. Knopf.
Nothaft, Carl Philipp Emanuel (2011). "From Sukkot to Saturnalia: The Attack on Christmas in Sixteenth-Century Chronological Scholarship", *Journal of the History of Ideas*, 72, no. 4: 503–22.
Restad, Penne L. (1995). *Christmas in America: A History*. New York: Oxford University Press.
Stevens, Patricia Bunning (1979). *Merry Christmas!: A History of the Holiday*. New York: Macmillan.
Wernecke, Herbert H. (1959). *Christmas Customs Around the World*. Philadelphia: Westminster Press.
Wernecke, Herbert H. (ed.) (1962). *Celebrating Christmas Around the World*. Philadelphia: Westminster Press.

CHAPTER 4

THE NINETEENTH CENTURY

TIMOTHY LARSEN

In the feature film, *The Man Who Invented Christmas* (2017), a character gives voice to the supposed truth that the holiday was wasting away in the decades before the publication of *A Christmas Carol* (1843): 'Does anyone celebrate it anymore?' In the book on which the film was based, the English Christmas in the first decades of the nineteenth century is described as 'a down-trodden holiday', 'a second-tier holiday', and 'a relatively minor affair' (Standiford 2008: 5, 104, 180). While these are popular sources, they illustrate the persistence of this overblown impression. Indeed, a scholarly source published in 1993 went so far as to make this unmeasured assertion: 'Christmas celebrations were dying out in Europe and America before Charles Dickens's 1843 publication' (Belk 1993: 85). Christmas was both transformed and greatly expanded over the course of the Victorian age. Nevertheless, it was already a major, thriving holiday in England even in the early decades of the nineteenth century.

Not all scholars have accepted the view that Christmas was becoming moribund, but those who do have repeatedly used one particular piece of evidence to prove the point. In 1986, J. M. Golby and A. W. Purdue wrote, 'Christmas, in the first decades of the nineteenth century, was neither a major event in the calendar nor a popular festival...in twenty of the years between 1790 and 1835 *The Times* did not mention Christmas at all' (Golby 1986: 40). In 2008, for instance, a scholar evoked this exact same claim (Storey 2008: 19). Even the superb scholar Ronald Hutton echoed it: 'In twenty of the years between 1790 and 1835 *The Times* did not mention the festival, and it never referred to it with enthusiasm' (Hutton 1996: 112). There are, however, several problems with using this evidence to establish the wider thesis. First, newspapers were shorter in those days: tellingly, *The Times* was only four pages throughout this entire date range, but doubled to eight pages in the year immediately following (1836). Second, newspapers then were less likely to refer to features of life that are so common that they can be taken for granted. (Imagine arguing that schoolchildren in this period were less enthusiastic about getting out for the summer holidays because

The Times often failed to mention it!) Third, in order to prove that Christmas was a 'second-tier holiday' one would also need to offer evidence that *The Times* spoke more often and with greater ardour about Easter, New Year's, St Valentine's, Guy Fawkes, or whatever holidays one was reserving for the first tier. That has never been done by any of these scholars. Most of all, however, this oft-repeated claim is simply wrong. *The Times*, in fact, never failed to mention Christmas in a single year from 1790 to 1835. From 1817 onwards, Christmas is referred to over 125 times every year (for ten of those years, it was over 200 times; in 1829, the total was 308). As to enthusiasm, in an article titled 'Christmas' in the 25 December 1822 issue, *The Times* exhorted everyone to celebrate the festival with gaiety, generosity, decorations of holly and berries, wassail bowls, mirth without limit, and, in general, 'all the merriments of Christmas'. The feast of Christ's Nativity was observed by a much smaller percentage of the population north of Hadrian's Wall—where Hogmanay was the most popular holiday in those decades— but even Scottish newspapers tended to comment on Christmas annually. In the year before *A Christmas Carol* was published, the *Perthshire Advertiser* accepted that Presbyterian Scotland stood apart from the religious observances of Christmas undertaken in 'the English and Romish Churches'. Nevertheless, it also assumed that even Calvinist Scots were keeping Christmas as 'a season of merry-making' (complete with mistletoe), and it exhorted them to uphold the custom of charity to the poor as well (Anon. 1842: 2). The narrower claim that *A Christmas Carol* revived a dying festival does not even make internal sense: the entire story emphasizes that, with the sole exception of Scrooge, everyone is already enthusiastically celebrating Christmas. This sour, old miser is being continually greeted with 'Merry Christmas', and other Yuletide activities assault him in an ongoing barrage: carolling, charity fundraising, an invitation to a holiday party, and so on. On Christmas Day, Scrooge sees people 'flocking through the streets in their best clothes' on their way to 'church and chapel' (Dickens 2003: 76–7). Likewise in *The Pickwick Papers*, in a passage written in 1836 and set in 1827, Dickens portrays a season of general merriment—including holly, mince pies, mistletoe, games, storytelling, and much more. The Christmas carol sung in that novel even pronounces the feast of Christ's Nativity to be 'the King of the Seasons all!' The Christmas chapters in Washington Irving's *Sketch Book* were first published in 1820. Although that account is remembered for its nostalgic emphasis on past customs, it is nevertheless framed with a portrait of the 'universal festivity and social enjoyment' in Christmas present (Irving 1876: 39). In addition to Sundays, the Factory Act of 1833 only gave child labourers the right to two other days off in the entire year: Good Friday and Christmas. Even in the first decades of the century, Christmas was widely observed as one of the greatest days for feasting in the annual cycle. For many, it was the greatest.

While therefore keeping continuities in mind, this chapter will present some of the ways that Christmas changed and expanded over the nineteenth century. It will wander around some to various countries geographically, including Germany. Its primary focus, however, will be on English-speaking countries as so much of what makes the modern Christmas the celebration that it is results from their innovations and transformation of the festival. One of the major threads offered here is an underexplored but vital component of this story: the growing acceptance of Christmas by Reformed and Dissenting Protestants. As the contrast between England and Scotland has already indicated, the merging of these additional, Protestant streams into the already existing currents of holidaymaking caused Christmas to leave the nineteenth century as a far mightier river. The Society of Friends was one of the Protestant bodies that most strongly objected to Christmas. This stance was articulated in an article by John Bellows, 'Why I Ought Not To Keep "Christmas"', written in 1879, but often reprinted in Quaker periodicals, even into the twentieth century. Bellows argued that Friends had a duty to refrain from feasting and to keep their businesses open on December 25. To do otherwise would be to further superstition, idolatry, and apostasy—and even, he hinted darkly, the cause of the Antichrist. The Society of Friends, however, was numerically small. The significant forces of opposition to Christmas came from the Presbyterians, Congregationalists, and Baptists. These denominations had enough local autonomy that their witness on this matter was not uniform. Still, some at least asserted that all their co-religionists also repudiated the holiday. Daniel Dana, a Presbyterian minister in Massachusetts, claimed in 1816: 'If the sanctity of Christmas cannot be supported by the Scriptures, the question, one would think, is decided. Protestants acknowledge no other rule of faith and practice....The same is the opinion of Presbyterians at large, and of the generality of Christians, except Episcopalians, throughout the United States. The same opinion prevails almost universally among the Scotch' (Dana 1816: 10, 36). A minister in New Jersey, Cortlandt Van Rensselaer, writing in 1842, assumed that he was speaking for all Presbyterians when he rejected Christmas as unbiblical. Rather, he insisted, the holiday was a popish plot from a corrupt age: a *'human innovation leading on human depravity to greater depravity'* (Van Rensselaer 1842: 5). Especially in the early decades of the century, many Congregationalists and Baptists agreed. The Congregational minister Jonathan Blanchard, for example, although he lived to 1892, rejected Christmas on principle to the last. He was president of Wheaton College in Illinois, and as late as 1864 he was still insisting that the term break not come until after December 25. Even in 1880, the college newspaper was still trying to shore up the old view:

> Christmas is coming. The observance of the day is on the increase, but it does not follow that its observance is desirable....Christians are nowhere commanded to commemorate the supposed day on which our Lord took upon Him the form of fallen man but they are rather to commemorate His death and resurrection, when He took upon Him his glorified body.   (Anon. 1880: 7)

As we all know, however, Christmas is hard to escape. In a steadily expanding number of places, it was a public holiday. Businesses closed. Families gathered. Presbyterians in New Zealand, for instance, used the opportunity to meet with their relations. Especially as the century wore on, only a very small minority of Reformed and Dissenting Protestants objected to feasting on December 25—or even traditions such as holly decorations. By 1874, the Quaker statesman John Bright was keeping at home what he described as an 'old-fashioned' Christmas. Thus, the situation became more and more blurred. This is delightfully evoked in a story by Harriet Beecher Stowe that draws autobiographically on her own childhood in Connecticut in the 1810s and 20s. A little girl called Dolly is the daughter of a minister (presumably Presbyterian) who preaches against Christmas and does not allow his family to observe it. The fun of the story is that this prohibition does not really matter: it is overwhelmed by the Yuletide. As everyone else is celebrating Christmas, Dolly gets to as well—her maternal grandparents send her gifts, a neighbour gives her treats. She even sneaks into the Episcopal church for its Christmas Eve service. By 1867, the Congregational minister R. W. Dale reported that the social side of the holiday had swept all before it: 'Here in England we all keep Christmas—Romanists and Protestants, Churchmen and Dissenters, Wesleyans and Baptists. I have a strong suspicion that even the members of the Society of Friends eat roast-beef and set fire to their plum-puddings on the twenty-fifth of December' (Dale 1867: 238–9). An 1870 article, 'Christmas in Scotland', claimed that even the land of the Covenanters was capitulating:

> Christmas dinners, Christmas shows, Christmas boxes, Christmas trees, Christmas cards, and so forth, are fast coming in vogue amongst all classes. Shop-windows in the towns are duly decorated with holly at the festive season.... Such signs warrant the impression that, despite all ecclesiastical antagonism, Scotland will in course of time assimilate somewhat to her southern sister in paying honour to the great Christian festival.   (Roscoe 1870: 319)

Good Calvinist men and women, rejoice!

The crucial difference was that these denominations generally did not offer a Christmas worship service. Still, even that line could become fuzzy. The public holiday was a convenient occasion for congregational as well as family gatherings. It became a popular day for the inaugural service of a new congregation. Christmas 1828 (a Thursday) was marked by worship services to open a General Baptist chapel in Loughborough, England (Anon. 1828: 2). After such an occasion, Baptists as well as Anglicans could discuss the sermon that they had heard on December 25—making the distinction between observing a holy day with public worship and using a holiday for public worship a subtle one. The practice was sufficiently congenial that this Baptist congregation began to gather on Christmas for a tea meeting in support of its charitable work. The biggest wedge by far, however, was the Sunday schools and children's ministry. As the century progressed, it became highly popular for Sunday schools to gather on the holiday for a special event or to have some kind of Christmas party or programme. This was true across the major denominations. An eminent Protestant Episcopal clergyman in Boston, Phillips Brooks, wrote the Christmas carol, 'O little town of Bethlehem' for the 1868 Christmas programme of his church's Sunday school. For Reformed and Dissenting congregations, however, such occasions were a major stepping-stone toward celebrating Christmas. Moreover, these events could be indistinguishable from a Christmas worship service. The Congregational minister

James Sherman preached a sermon for 'young persons' at Surrey Chapel, London, on Christmas 1837 (a Monday). Not only did he choose for his text the most traditional passage possible (Luke 2), but he even recommended observing Christmas: 'Let us therefore pray, that a day set apart by the general consent of the Christian Church to commemorate the Nativity of our blessed Saviour, may be kept by us as a holy day—a joyful day—a thanksgiving day—a day of spiritual feasting and gladness' (Sherman 1837: 4). Alexander Fletcher, despite being both Scottish and Presbyterian, became famous for his annual Christmas sermon to thousands of children gathered together from a variety of London Sunday schools. He began this practice in 1816 or soon thereafter. In one of these, Christmas 1854 (a Monday), he even reflected that they could learn from Catholics to attend more to the Virgin Mary:

> How thankful Mary was! We do not say so much about the Virgin Mary as at the chapel opposite. Perhaps we do not think enough about her; of her wonderful humility, her wonderful holiness, and her wonderful gift of prayer. "My soul doth magnify the Lord." (Luke 1) How beautiful! (Fletcher 1855: 13)

The report in the *Blackburn Standard* on Christmas 1838 (a Tuesday) was overwhelmingly a list of Sunday school events and Nonconformist tea parties. The Independent Chapel had around 600 people at its event, both adults and 'scholars'. These Congregationalists called it a 'tea party', but there was an address by the minister and 'appropriate hymns were also sung', once again indicating that what was officially a social event could serve pretty well for a Christmas worship service (Anon. 1839: 2).

For some, even such efforts were not enough. Christmas worship services were very popular with Catholics, Anglicans, and Lutherans. Even when it fell on a weekday, in many churches Christmas would gather the largest, or one of the largest, congregations of the entire year. Scrooge went to church on Christmas—as does most everyone in Anthony Trollope's Christmas stories. The Congregational minister C. M. Davies made a concerted effort to attend as many Anglican worship services as possible in London on Christmas 1871 (a Monday). He found everywhere that the churches were putting on numerous services—and they were all packed. Davies observed that evening services were not held because there was a general feeling that this time should be allotted to 'social festivity'. St Mary Magdalene's, Paddington, was a church that was only a few years old at that time, and Davies treats it as typical rather than exceptional. It offered seven services on Christmas (while still being careful not to intrude into the evening), including six Eucharist services: 5 a.m., 6 a.m., 7 a.m., 8:30 a.m., 10:30 a.m., and 11:45 a.m. Moreover, the church 'was crowded in every part' (Davies 1873: 354–5). Davies was doing journalistic research, but there are numerous reports from across the English-speaking world of Reformed and Dissenting Protestants, even ministers, sneaking off to another denomination to attend a Christmas service. In the 1868 account of Midnight Mass at St Patrick's Catholic cathedral in Auckland, the reporter not only emphasized the large attendance (around 800 people), but also made a point of observing that they were 'persons of all denominations' (Clarke 2007: 31).

Thus the next step was for these Reformed and Dissenting congregations to begin offering Christmas services themselves, if for no other reason than so as not to be at a competitive disadvantage. In Stowe's story, the minister's wife warns her husband that if he does not get over his objections: 'I shouldn't wonder if this other church should draw very seriously on your congregation; but I don't want it to begin by taking away our own children.' When the First Congregational Church of Rockford, Illinois, decided to celebrate Christmas in 1864, it explained bluntly: 'Our Episcopal and Methodist friends make so much of this holiday that others must follow suit' (Richards 1934: 115). In Catholic Dublin, a Presbyterian congregation in the Synod of Ulster found it desirable to have an annual Christmas service already beginning in 1798 (Holmes 2006: 92–3). In Boston, a concerted attempt was made in 1818 to turn December 25 into a day of worship rather than business, with three Congregational churches readily joining in. The Baptist minister C. H. Spurgeon was the most popular preacher of the Victorian age. Despite his devotion to the Puritans, as a 17-year-old interim pastor at Waterbeach near Cambridge he held services on Christmas 1841 (a Thursday): 'I preached twice on Christmas to crammed congregations, and again on Sunday quite as full' (Spurgeon 1897: I: 59). There were early-adopters and hold-outs, but a lot more congregations from the major Reformed and Dissenting denominations were offering Christmas services from the 1860s onwards—and very few of those who were not, still believed that some principle was at stake.

Scholars have also rightly noted the influence of another religious force: the rise of Tractarianism (the Oxford Movement), Anglo-Catholicism, and ritualism. The effect of these intertwined movements arising within Anglicanism was to move their followers closer to some of the practices of the Roman Catholic Church. John Keble's *The Christian Year* (1827), which was popular even with many non-Anglicans, helped to emphasize observing the feasts and fasts of the Church. The Victorian period saw a craze for adding ever more evergreens and other decorations to the interior of churches for the feast of Christ's Nativity. Especially towards the end of the century, some Protestants began adopting Catholic practices such as Midnight Mass and a crib or manger scene. Admittedly, the Tractarians did not always get their way. From a strict, liturgical point of view, Advent should be a time of self-denial and sombre reflection, including on the Second Coming of Christ. In the *Tracts for the Times* that gave the movement its name, John Henry Newman contributed 'Advent Sermons on Antichrist'. One of these sermons ends:

> Men now give fair names to sins and sinners; but then all the citizens of Babylon will appear in their true colours, as the word of God exhibits them, 'as dogs, and sorcerers, and whoremongers, and murderers, and idolaters, and lovers and makers of lies.'

Merry Christmas! While that particular tradition was not destined to become popular, even low-church Protestants were often pulled in more liturgical directions when it came to celebrating the birth of their Saviour.

A distinct but related factor was a theological trend toward emphasizing the doctrine of the Incarnation. Boyd Hilton has argued convincingly that the first half of the nineteenth century was part of the 'Age of Atonement', but the second half was the Age of the Incarnation. This doctrinal shift was a strong current among Anglo-Catholics. Their manifesto volume, *Lux Mundi* (1889), actually conceptualized the entire Christian faith as 'the religion of the Incarnation'. One essay even speculated that God would have still become incarnate even if there had been no Fall, thus making the atonement merely a contingent reality while the Incarnation is an inevitable and essential one. Many varieties of Christians shared in this theological development. Influential Broad Church, liberal, and modernist Anglicans found their way to making the Incarnation central through their growing commitment to Hegelian forms of thought or their desire to give theological grounding to Christian Socialism. Evangelicals and Dissenters also drew closer to the manger. In *The Old Evangelicalism and the New* (1889), the evangelical Congregational minister R. W. Dale observed that even for his co-religionists the Age of Atonement was over:

> I do not mean that the Death of Christ for the sins of men is denied by Modern Evangelicals—if it were denied they would cease to be Evangelicals—but it is practically relegated by many to a secondary position. The Incarnation, with all that it reveals concerning God, man, and the universe, concerning this life and the life to come, stands first; with the early Evangelicals the Death of Christ for human sin stood first. (Dale 1889: 49)

The older view naturally lent more theological weight to Good Friday and Easter Sunday. In other words, another factor in the exaltation of Christmas to the pre-eminent place in the nineteenth century is that the doctrine it celebrates had also risen for many to the supreme position in Christian thought.

A well-known feature of Christmas in the nineteenth century is the emergence and ascendency of Santa Claus. What has not been appreciated, however, is that this was the result of a concerted campaign by a range of Christians. If you view it as a conspiracy, it was a Christian conspiracy. St Nicholas as a magical gift bearer was introduced into the consciousness of the English-speaking world by a group of High Church Episcopalians in New York. The most important of these was Washington Irving, who sprinkled into his fanciful history of the Dutch in New York accounts of St Nicholas flying around in his wagon and coming down chimneys to deliver presents. Charles W. Jones went so far as to claim: 'Santa Claus was *made* by Washington Irving' (Jones 1954: 376). That level of credit, however, is usually given to another New Yorker who was presumably influenced by Irving, Clement Clarke Moore. In 1822, Moore wrote one of the most oft-reprinted poems by an American, 'A Visit from St. Nicholas' ('Twas the Night Before Christmas).[1] In it, St Nicholas is a jolly, rotund figure dressed

---

[1] The present author is confident that Moore was the author of this poem, but see chapter 22 for the claim that it was Henry Livingston.

in fur who drives a sleigh pulled by reindeer and who spreads Christmas cheer by surreptitiously coming down chimneys to fill stockings with toys. Moore was a devout Episcopalian. His father had been bishop of New York, and Moore himself taught 'Biblical learning and interpretation of the Scriptures' at General Theological Seminary (Patterson 1956: 79). His publications included one attacking Thomas Jefferson for having an insufficiently reverent attitude toward the Bible. The good news of this gift bearer spread, and it was enthusiastically propagated by innumerable Christians. People today often think of seeing Santa Claus in a department store, but that practice did not begin until the last dozen years of the century and was confined to cities and large towns. Most children in the nineteenth century who saw Santa Claus in person met him at their church's Sunday school. This was so much the case that if one wanted to dress up like Santa the way to acquire your costume was to order it through a religious supplies company. To continue to keep an eye on Reformed and Dissenting Protestants, in 1886 in Sioux Falls, South Dakota, boys and girls were welcomed to both 'Santa Clausville' (sponsored by the Congregationalists) and the 'Gathering of the Nations to Meet Santa Claus' (Presbyterians) (Bowler 2005: 89). By the end of the century, children did not even need to go to a Sunday school event or a department store to see Santa: they could just encounter him as they walked across town because one of the most theologically conservative of evangelical denominations, the Salvation Army, had started populating street corners with Santa raising money to help the poor. In 1897, Francis Church wrote his famous editorial, commonly known by its line, 'Yes, Virginia, there is a Santa Claus.' Church was the religion editor for *The Sun* (New York City), the son of a Baptist minister, and an Episcopalian. At his death, the paper did not mention his celebrated answer to the question, 'Is There A Santa Claus?', but it did run 'A Clergyman's Tribute to Francis P. Church' which emphasized his personal Christian faith (Duryee 1906: 6). In the nineteenth century, if one were to sneak a peek under a Santa beard, one would usually encounter a devoutly Christian countenance.

Why was this so? At least part of the answer is that Santa Claus was a welcome vehicle for expressing the Christian ideal for giving. Jesus instructed his followers to use secrecy: 'But when though does alms, let not thy left hand know what thy right hand doeth: That thine alms may be in secret' (Matthew 6:3-4 AV). St Nicholas was so popular in the medieval period primarily for one act of his: giving money anonymously (by throwing it through a window into their house at night) so that three poor girls could have a dowry. In the twelfth century, some French nuns hit upon the pious and happy idea of secretly leaving presents for poor children in the name of St Nicholas. In later centuries, Europeans credited a variety of other such gift bearers. Moore's depiction of St Nicholas—who was soon going by the name of Santa Claus—was the one that best captured the popular imagination in America, and which would go on to sweep many other countries before it. Before they were introduced to Santa Claus, we can sometimes almost sense that Christians felt his absence. The Scottish author George MacDonald, for instance, was given to filling his stories with Christian teaching, and even to writing sermons. Word of Santa Claus did not spread widely in Britain until the 1870s. In 1864, MacDonald published 'My Uncle Peter', a story about a generous Christian man. He would find out that people were in need and then send them money or gifts anonymously with the attached note saying only, '*With Christmas Day's compliments*' (MacDonald 1864: 197; Larsen 2018). One senses that both Uncle Peter and George MacDonald would have found it great fun to write instead, '*From Father Christmas*', had they known of such a possibility. (Britons often continued to use the pre-existing title, Father Christmas, while applying to this figure the traits that had been revealed in accounts of Santa Claus.) Not only does crediting Santa allow for giving secretly, as Christ counselled, but it also takes away the patronizing tone of the better off giving to the needy and replaces it with lighthearted charm and brotherly mischievousness. Such a service is invaluable. It is hardly surprising that by 1885 there was a Santa Claus Society in London for distributing gifts to the poor: to give in a Christian manner, is to be a secret Santa. And it is deeply within the spirit of Christianity to give to your children in such a generous and enchanting way that it not only greatly enhances the delight but also eradicates all the usual worries about whether or not father and mother can afford it. In short, from a Christian point of view, if Santa Claus did not exist it would have been desirable to invent him.

Along with Santa Claus, the nineteenth century brought the widespread adoption of the Christmas tree. German Protestants rightly take credit for this pleasant custom. Ernst T. A. Hoffman's *The Nutcracker and the Mouse-King* (1816) set a scene of domestic delight by first describing the tree:

> The large Christmas tree in the center was laden with gold and silver apples, and like birds and blossoms, sugar almonds and bright bonbons and other pretty cakes came forth from the branches. The most wonderful thing about the tree, however, was the hundreds of lights that sparkled like stars, and the tree seemed to invite them in a most friendly fashion to come and pluck its buds and fruits. Around the tree everything shone in bright and superb colors. (Hoffman 1930: 13)

In the 1830s, this custom spread to Norway and other Lutheran countries. In December 1844, the Danish writer Hans Christian Andersen even published a short story about the life of a Christmas tree. Meanwhile, the tree was also on the rise in America. There is an 1812 depiction of a Christmas tree from Germantown, Pennsylvania, but the 1830s are the crucial decade for its spread in America. As a widespread trend, it came later in Britain. A popular illustration of Queen Victoria, her German husband, Prince Albert, and their children, around a Christmas tree in 1848 is credited with awakening more general interest in that nation. When Dickens wrote 'A Christmas Tree' for a December 1850 issue of *Household Words*, he was still referring to it as 'German' (Dickens 2003: 231). Later in the century, Germans added another association: they became the major producer of glass Christmas tree ornaments. For those who could afford one, a Christmas tree was often seen as an essential part of celebrating Christmas for German Protestants. The great efforts that were made to import *tannenbaum* to the German frontline trenches during the First World War are indicative of how indispensable they were perceived to be. Hans Christian Andersen's Christmas tree was indeed a fir, but adjustments had to be made in other climates. Already in 1857 came the first reference to the pohutukawa as the New Zealand Christmas tree (because it was often in bloom around Christmastide, and thus was a pleasant blend of green leaves with red flowers) (Lineham 2016: 163). As with Santa Claus, many children in nineteenth-century America first saw a Christmas tree at a Sunday school event.

One of the most important trends in the nineteenth century was the domestication of Christmas. Older customs were often communal ones in the open air. These could include begging rituals and obnoxious music. Irving's 'good old Christmas song' proclaims:

> Now Christmas is come,
> Let us beat up the drum,
> And call all our neighbours together.   (Irving 1867: 64–5)

In the long run, such ways could not survive the forces of industrialization and urbanization. Stephen Nissenbaum has argued lucidly that these older rites served to blow off steam in traditional communities, but were experienced as more menacing and intolerable by prosperous people in urban areas who no longer knew or trusted those from the lower orders. Once again, Germans led the way. When S. T. Coleridge wrote an account of his experience of Christmas 1798 at Ratzeburg, it is telling that he titled it, 'Christmas Within Doors in the North of Germany' (Coleridge 1818: II: 320–5). It is as if Coleridge is reporting that the focus of the German Christmas is the home. In his *Christmas Eve: A Dialogue* (1806), the German theologian Friedrich Schleiermacher went to great lengths to signal that Christmas should be centred on the home, even striking a related note that would also triumph in the nineteenth century: 'Christmas is very specially the children's festival' (Schleiermacher 1890: 7). When the German Charles Follen immigrated to America in 1827, he expressed his disappointment that, unlike in his homeland, there were 'no feasts for the children' (Nissenbaum 1998: 208). Follen needed only to wait for the shift to reach his adopted country. By 1868, Louisa May Alcott could confidently classify Christmas as one of the 'home-festivals' (Alcott 1880: 20). Dispersed families reuniting for the holiday was a long-standing ideal. Even in 1820, Irving extolled Christmas as 'the season for gathering together of family connections…of calling back the children of a family who have launched forth in life…once more to assemble about the paternal hearth' (Irving 1876: 4–5). That, however, was only a realistic as well as idealistic standard for those elite families that possessed the required money and leisure. With the rise of railway travel and employers giving more than just one day off, this goal could be achieved by a wider circle. The countervailing reality was that many people were household servants and therefore their time was not their own even on December 25, perhaps especially not on that day. They experienced the domestic Christmas only to the extent that their employers made them feel like they were part of their families. The rise of Santa Claus—who visits the home—and the Christmas tree in the home, as well as the new emphasis on children, all reinforced the domestication of Christmas.

Supporting Nissenbaum's analysis, one can see the communal Christmas living on longer in more close-knit societies. In Virginia, traditions of large foxhunts and roaming from house to house continued longer. In Britain, some working-class communities still wanted to attend sporting events on December 25 into the twentieth century, before they too eventually capitulated to the cult of home. Throughout the nineteenth century, some Maori Christians would keep Christmas with large, outdoor feasts. A report in the *New Zealander* (30 December 1857) has Chief Patuone of Waiwharariki, North Shore, hosting around 530 people from eight different tribes: 'Divine Service having been performed by Heta, a native teacher'. The growing conviction that the holiday was primarily a home festival caused many Reformed and Dissenting Protestants to abandon their experiments with Christmas worship services. Instead, they usually just held a Christmas-themed service on the Sunday closest to December 25. This became C. H. Spurgeon's practice as a settled pastor in London. (Spurgeon 1884) Christmas Eve services were also popular. Edward Benson, then bishop of Truro, introduced in 1878 the Lessons and Carols service which would also win widespread appreciation. Many beloved Christmas carols were written in the nineteenth century. In 1818, an Austrian Catholic priest, Josef Mohr, wrote the lyrics for *Stille Nacht* (Silent Night). Whether or not they went to church on December 25, for many people Christmas was no longer primarily an open-air event, nor an ecclesial event, but a domestic one. It would be a mistake, however, to equate domestication with secularization. Passover is primarily a domestic holiday, but that does not make it a secular one. Rather than categorizing things as inherently religious or secular, it is more often the case that the devout often experience things that are not intrinsically religious devotionally, while the secular are impervious to the devotional aspects even of explicitly religious matters. Certainly, the domestic Christmas was more aligned with Christian sentiment than a certain kind of older, communal Christmas marked by gambling, drunkenness, and public rowdiness. Schleiermacher was so committed to portraying Christmas as centred in the home that he even had his characters unmoved by the church service. Nevertheless, he saw this domestic festival as Christian, holy, and devotionally powerful. He even went so far as to have a minister perform the sacrament of baptism in the home to underline the profound sacredness of the occasion. Drawing on Christ's words of consecration for the Eucharist, Dickens insisted that even a Christmas tree brought sacramental grace: 'I hear a whisper going through the leaves. "This, in commemoration of the law of love and kindness, mercy and compassion. This, in remembrance of Me!"' (Dickens 2003: 247) In 1889, the *New Zealand Herald* expressed well the ideal of Christmas as a sacred, domestic festival: 'As is customary in all English communities the holiday of Christmas Day will be chiefly observed as a day of devotion...according to which the scattered members of a family gather round the paternal table, and observe the day for the most part as a religious festival' (Connelly 1999: 116).

Some of the older Christmas traditions were therefore domesticated as well. Another Victorian innovation was the Christmas cracker and it can be seen as a family-friendly, household echo of the rowdy, old public Christmas that sometimes involved fireworks and gunfire. Children could be set loose to romp around the house as little lords of misrule. Antiquarians relished accounts of Christmases of old at which kings and queens had a play performed for their numerous guests. In yet another domestication, in *Little Women* (1868) the girls put on a little play in their home. As the holiday moved from communal celebration with neighbours to a domestic celebration with family, this left a void regarding how to acknowledge the day in one's wider social circle. One way that emerged to meet that need was with the Christmas card. For more than six decades now, it has been thought that the first Christmas card for general sale was the one designed by J. C. Horsley at the prompting of Henry Cole in 1843. (Buday 1964) The research for this chapter, however, has uncovered evidence of one fourteen years earlier. On 7 December 1829, the *Hampshire Chronicle* reported: 'We learn that the "Olde Winchester" Christmas and New Year's Greetings, designed by Mr. A. Clements, of Northgate Studio, are receiving a most cordial welcome from Christmas card buyers, sales already nearing the 2000 mark. Large numbers have been sent abroad to friends interested in Winchester.' (Anon. 1829: 6) Nevertheless, even the 1843 card did not produce an immediate trend. Publishers tried again in the 1860s and Christmas cards took off in the decades that followed. By 1882, a postal worker in Washington DC was becoming resigned to the new normal: 'I thought last year would be the end of the Christmas card mania, but I don't think so now' (Restad 1995: 117–18). By that time, most Christmas cards were being made in Germany. Significant decreases in the cost of postage helped the trend along. If whom one was with for most of Christmas Day had shrunk down to the family circle, the Christmas card allowed one to include numerous friends and acquaintances in one's celebration of the season. By 1895, it was reported that Queen Victoria was sending out thousands of Christmas cards every year. For the tighter circle of close friends and relations, one could send a gift. The nineteenth century also saw a move from sending gifts at New Year's to sending them for Christmas. This was less of a stark shift than it is sometimes made out to be. New Year's is, after all, one of the twelve days of Christmas—and gifts given on January 1 were sometimes called Christmas gifts. Santa Claus himself sometimes even made his mysterious visit on New Year's Eve. On this front, Queen Victoria was not an early adopter: she entered the twentieth century still keeping to the old custom of New Year's gifts. The growing abundance and availability of mass-produced goods turned shopping into another major feature of the holiday season.

Many of the standard ways of describing aspects of Christmas—though all convene truth—have become so overdone that they now sometimes obscure rather than just illuminate: pagan, secular, invention of tradition, sentimentality, consumerism, commercialism, and so on. One of these is nostalgia. Of course, there is a nostalgic element in how many people approach Christmas. Nevertheless, other realities are often misguidedly subsumed under this label. True nostalgia is rooted in the belief that the past was better than the present. Its purest form is a wish to be living in former times. The Squire in Irving's *Sketch Book* is a genuine specimen: 'He even regrets sometimes that he had not been born a few centuries earlier' (Irving 1876: 45). The evocation of Christmas past, however, can be rooted in a human delight in tradition, in a desire to be reassured that change is tempered by continuity, in antiquarian enthusiasms, and in a longing to make connections across time. The more discontinuity one is currently experiencing, the more meaningful traditions can become. Hence the ideal of having 'an old-fashioned' Christmas. Out on an extreme sledging expedition in the Antarctic on Christmas 1902, Ernest Shackleton triumphantly produced a Christmas pudding he had hidden away in a sock. Every Christmas has such moments when a connection with what endures over time makes the present more endurable. If traditions sometimes need to be invented to decrease the sense of queasiness that comes with too much change, so be it. A character in Schleiermacher's *Christmas Eve* speaks for many when he pronounces: 'This institution, then, we will maintain as it has been handed down to us... To me at least, even its smallest details are full of significance.' It is no contradiction that the same text declares the holiday to have an orientation towards the future as well: 'such happy events bring home to us in a vivid manner at present the joys of the future', 'the festival itself is the proclamation of a new life for the world', it therefore has 'the present, the past, and the future entwined in it' (Schleiermacher 1890: 60, 11–12). *A Christmas Carol* is very much about changing the future.

Which brings us back to the claim that Dickens invented the modern Christmas. The Christmas past that the Victorians delighted to recall was the one of great medieval halls. The erstwhile shoemaker Thomas Cooper witnessed so much suffering during the Hungry Forties that be became a militant Chartist and was found guilty of seditious conspiracy. In prison, he wrote a long poem with a suitably bitter theme, *The Purgatory of the Suicides* (1845). His next book-length poem, however, was *The Baron's Yule Feast* (1846), a work overflowing with every medieval, Christmas detail imaginable— mummers and minstrels, a Lord of Misrule and an Abbot of Unreason, a yule log and snow, mistletoe and 'wreaths of bright holly and ivy', plum puddings and mince pies, a wassailing bowl, a boar's head, and mouthwatering lists of drinks and dishes from 'jolly ale' to swan. Rather than an attack on aristocracy, it was an attempt to evoke the baronial generosity of Old Christmas as a way of rousing his fellow Victorians to acts of charity:

> O that my simple lay might tend
> To kindle some remorse
> In your oppressors' souls, and bend
> Their wills a cheerful help to lend
> And lighten Labour's curse!   (Cooper 1846: 63)

Dickens's great achievement, by contrast, was to place Christmas charity in a modern, urban setting. He translated the old Christmas ideal to an industrialized world and brought home its responsibilities to the middle classes and those who had made their fortunes in business. The world was changing, rearranging, did that mean that Christmas changes too? Yes, and Dickens helped with the transition. Christmas was not dying out; people were still feasting. That was not enough, however. Christmas was always also about charity, generosity, and the binding together of the social classes.

As the theologian F. D. Maurice observed in a sermon he preached on Christmas 1839, a holiday that was no more than a self-indulgent feast was not satisfactory: 'If we care about nothing but ourselves, we shall not be merry at Christmas time, or at any other time' (Maurice 1892: 13). Dickens inspired modern people to find some way to help people in need at Christmastime. Jane Carlyle read an advance copy of *A Christmas Carol* given to her and her husband, Thomas Carlyle, by Dickens himself. She was immediately convicted by it. Her response was to renew her relationship with a poor governess who she had come to find annoying but whom she realized was socially isolated and in need of her support.

With the vast majority of Reformed and Dissenting Protestants now enthusiastically on board, a domestic focus on family and children, Santa Claus, Christmas trees, shopping, new carols, Christmas cards, a renewed commitment to generosity and charity in a modern context, and more, Christmas reached the end of the nineteenth century significantly bigger and stronger than it was at its start. It could be said of people in the late nineteenth century that they knew how to keep Christmas well, if any moment in history ever possessed the knowledge.

REFERENCES AND FURTHER READING

Alcott, Louisa May (1880). *Little Women*. Boston: Roberts Brothers.
Anon. (1828). 'Loughborough', *Leicester Herald*, 31 December: 2.
Anon. (1829). 'A Cordial Welcome', *Hampshire Chronicle*, 7 December: 6.
Anon. (1839). 'Christmas Day', *Blackburn Standard*, 2 January: 2.
Anon. (1842). *Perthshire Advertiser*, 29 December: 2.
Anon. (1857). 'Maori Christmas Feast', *New Zealander*, 30 December: 3.
Anon. (1880). 'Christmas is Coming', *Record* (Wheaton College, Illinois), 6, no. 3, December: 7.
Armstrong, Neil (2010). *Christmas in Nineteenth-Century England*. Manchester: Manchester University Press.
Armstrong, Neil (2011). 'The Christmas Season and the Protestant Churches in England, c. 1870–1914', *Journal of Ecclesiastical History*, 62, no. 4, October: 744–762.
Belk, Russell (1993). 'Materialism and the Making of the Modern American Christmas', in Daniel Miller (ed.), *Unwrapping Christmas*. Oxford: Clarendon Press: 75–104.
Bellows, John (1881). 'Why I Ought Not To Keep "Christmas"', *British Friend* (1st Day, 2nd Month 1881): 42–3.
Bowler, Gerry (2005). *Santa Claus: A Biography*. Toronto: McClelland & Stewart.
Brunner, Bernd (2012). *Inventing the Christmas Tree*, trans. Benjamin A. Smith. New Haven: Yale University Press, 2012.
Buday, George (1964). *The History of the Christmas Card*. London: Spring Books.
Clarke, Alison (2007). *Holiday Seasons: Christmas, New Year and Easter in Nineteenth-Century New Zealand*. Auckland: Auckland University Press.
Coleridge, S. T. (1818). *The Friend: A Series of Essays*. 3 vols. London: Rest Fenner.
Connelly, Mark (1999). *Christmas: A Social History*. London: I. B. Tauris.
Cooper, Thomas (1846). *The Baron's Yule Feast: A Christmas-Rhyme*. London: Jeremiah How.
Dale, R. W. (1867). *Week-Day Sermons*, London: Hodder and Stoughton.

Dale, R. W. (1889). *The Old Evangelicalism and the New*. London: Hodder and Stoughton.
[Dana, Daniel] (1816). *The Controversy between the 'Inquirer' and 'Philo' on Christmas, as published in the Newburyport Herald*. Newburyport, Massachusetts: William B. Allen.
[Davies, C. M.] (1873). *Orthodox London: Phases of Religious Life in the Church of England*. London: Tinsley Brothers.
Dickens, Charles (2003). *A Christmas Carol and Other Christmas Writings*. London: Penguin Classics.
Duryee, J. R. (1906). 'A Clergyman's Tribute to Francis P. Church', *Sun*, 15 April: 6.
English, Adam C. (2012). *The Saint Who Would Be Santa Claus: The True Life and Trials of Nicholas of Myra*. Waco: Baylor University Press.
Fletcher, Alexander (1855). *The Annual Christmas-Day Sermon to upwards of five thousand children, at Finsbury Chapel, London. Preached on Christmas-Day, 1854*. London: Ward & Co.
Golby, J. M. and Purdue, A. W. (1986). *The Making of the Modern Christmas*. Athens: University of Georgia Press.
Gore, Charles (ed.) (1889). *Lux Mundi: A series of studies in the Religion of the Incarnation*. London: John Murray.
Hilton, Boyd (1988). *The Age of Atonement: The Influence of Evangelicalism on Social and Economic Thought, 1795–1865*. Oxford: Clarendon Press.
Hoffman, Ernst T. A. (1930). *The Nutcracker and the Mouse-King*, trans. Louise F. Encking. Chicago: Albert Whitman.
Holmes, Andrew R. (2006). *The Shaping of Ulster Presbyterian Belief and Practice, 1770–1840*. New York: Oxford University Press.
Hutton, Ronald (1996). *The Stations of the Sun: A History of the Ritual Year in Britain*. Oxford: Oxford University Press, 1996.
Irving, Washington (1876). *Old Christmas: From the Sketch Book*. London: Macmillan.
Jones, Charles W. (1954). 'Knickerbocker Santa Claus', *The New-York Historical Society Quarterly*, 38, no. 4, October: 357–383.
Larsen, Timothy (2018). *George MacDonald in the Age of Miracles: Incarnation, Doubt, and Reenchantment*. Downers Grove, IL: IVP Academic.
Lineham, Peter (2016). 'The New Zealand Christmas and the Interweaving of Culture and Religion', in Geoffrey Troughton and Stuart Lange (eds.), *Sacred Histories in Secular New Zealand*. Wellington: Victoria University Press: 154–170.
MacDonald, George (1864). *Adela Cathcart*. London: Sampson Low, Marston & Company.
Maurice, Frederick Denison (1892). *Christmas Day and other sermons*. London: Macmillan and Co.
Moore, Tara (2009). *Victorian Christmas in Print Culture*. New York: Palgrave Macmillan.
Nissenbaum, Stephen (1998). *The Battle for Christmas*. New York: Alfred A. Knopf.
Patterson, Samuel White (1956). *The Poet of Christmas Eve: A Life of Clement Clarke Moore, 1779–1863*. New York: Morehouse-Gorham.
Perry, Joe (2014). *Christmas in Germany*. Chapel Hill: University of North Carolina Press.
Pimlott, J. A. R. (1978). *The Englishman's Christmas: A Social History*. Hassocks, Sussex: Harvester Press, 1978.
Restad, Penne L. (1995). *Christmas in America: A History*. New York: Oxford University Press.
Richards, Katharine Lambert (1934). *How Christmas Came to the Sunday-Schools: The observance of Christmas in Protestant church schools of the United States, an historical study*. New York: Dodd, Mead & Company.

Roscoe, Edmund S. (1870). 'Christmas in Scotland', *Belgravia*, X: 311–319.

Schleiermacher, Friedrich (1890). *Christmas Eve: A Dialogue on the Celebration of Christmas*, trans. W. Hastie, Edinburgh: T. & T. Clark.

Schmidt, Leigh Eric (1995). *Consumer Rites: The Buying and Selling of American Holidays*. Princeton: Princeton University Press.

Sherman, James (1837). *The Angels' Song: a sermon preached to young persons, at Surrey Chapel, December 25, 1837*. London: Hamilton, Adams, & Co.

Spurgeon, C. H. (1884). *Twelve Christmas Sermons*. New York: Fleming Revell.

Spurgeon, C. H. (1897). *Autobiography*. 4 vols. London: Passmore and Alabaster.

Standiford, Les (2008). *The Man Who Invented Christmas*. New York: Crown Publishers.

Storey, John (2008). 'The Invention of the English Christmas', in Sheila Whiteley (ed.), *Christmas, Ideology and Popular Culture*. Edinburgh: Edinburgh University Press: 17–31.

Stowe, Harriet Beecher (1884). *Poganuc People*. Boston: Houghton, Mifflin and Company.

[Van Rensselaer, Cortlandt] (1842). *Man's Feasts and Fasts in God's Church. A New Year's Gift; being a review of 'The Rector's Christmas Offering'*. Burlington: J. I. Powell.

CHAPTER 5

THE TWENTIETH AND TWENTY-FIRST CENTURIES

CHRISTOPHER FERGUSON

In 1963, my mother received a Christmas gift from a childhood friend. The gift was a book: *Christmas Around the World* (1961). The book was a thin, hardback volume, with a painting of a Nativity scene on the front, and a reproduction of a stained-glass window on the back. Inside, monochrome pages of yellow or blue, embellished with large black and white illustrations, described the Christmas traditions of thirty-two different cultures around the world, including those of Austria, Denmark, Mexico, Poland, Serbia, and the Philippines.

My mother loved this book. When I was old enough, she read it to me, and I came to love it too. We read it before bed in the weeks leading up to Christmas, a different country each night, from when I was 7 years old until I was in my early teens. Rereading it together became one of our annual Advent rituals. When my mother died in 2014, the book passed to me, and I have now started to read it with my daughter, and I also hope to read it with my son once he is old enough.

While researching the history of Christmas, however, I have come to appreciate this book in a new way, seeing it as a sort of prism, refracting the varied hues of the holiday's broader history. Thus, here this book will be used as a recurring point of reference, with its contents, its insights and imperfections, its gaps and silences, and its history as a specific object that was produced, exchanged, cherished, and used, all serving as the means for exploring a number of aspects of the history of Christmas during the immediate past and present centuries.

Let us begin with the title of the book itself: *Christmas Around the World*. As it rightly proclaims, during the twentieth century Christmas became a truly global holiday. It literally was celebrated 'around the world' to an extent that was unprecedented in earlier eras, with observances occurring on every continent, including Antarctica, where it initially was celebrated by the members of scientific expeditions during the twentieth century. These were later joined in the twenty-first century by the participants in special 'polar voyages' organized by a number of luxury cruise lines to allow passengers to celebrate 'Christmas in Antarctica', where—in the words of the company Swoop Antarctica—'a White Christmas is guaranteed'.

The global expansion of Christmas was nevertheless far from all encompassing. The coverage of *Christmas Around the World* reflected the holiday's uneven global development. Of its thirty-two entries, twenty-four described the customs of European countries, while only two each were dedicated to cultures in North America, South America, Asia, and the Middle East, with no mention of Africa whatsoever. Of course, this skewed focus partly reflected the perspective and biases of the volume's editor, Van B. Hooper, a white American, viewing the world from the vantage point of 1960s Milwaukee, Wisconsin. However, it was also indicative of the fact that in the twentieth century the largest and most influential observances of Christmas continued to be centred in the countries of Europe, and in those regions settled by large numbers of Europeans in North and South America and Oceana. The ancestors of these same Europeans and European settlers had likewise played a leading role in contributing to the holiday's expansion into other parts of the world.

The holiday's global spread in the twentieth century may be attributed to a number of factors. First, as Timothy Larsen has demonstrated in the preceding chapter, by the end of the nineteenth century the holiday had become a cross-denominational phenomenon, observed by most practising Christians, with the exception, mostly, of a few non-Trinitarian groups such as the Jehovah's Witnesses or Seventh Day Adventists. During the same century, however, the holiday had also evolved separate, secular customs in Europe and the United States. In particular, Christmas had become associated with specific cultural traditions as part of the development of nationalist ideologies.

Joe Perry notes, for example, how over the course of the nineteenth century a number of elements—including the decorating of fir trees, the singing of specific carols, outdoor Christmas markets, and a particular 'Christmas mood' (*Weihnachtsstimmung*) of warmth, joy, and nostalgia—all came to be identified with the concept of a distinctly 'German Christmas', despite the fact that no German country existed until 1871 (Perry 2010: 3–7). Once German unification was achieved by the policies of the Prussian state, this same supposedly 'uniquely German permutation' of the holiday was further promoted, popularized, and standardized through private initiatives and government policies alike, as a means of uniting a newly invented polity 'divided by region, class, and confession' (Perry 2010: 54).

During the same years, other European nationalities also sought to identify and codify their own, distinct Christmas traditions as part of their larger struggles for national identification, independence, and unification. The 'English Christmas', for example, came to be associated with carolling, the hanging of greenery, the telling of ghost stories, Christmas pantomimes, and the exchange of Christmas cards, and other European cultures developed a similar sense of their own distinctive 'national' Christmas customs during the same years (Connelly 1999). For this reason, by the end of the nineteenth century, Christmas had become very important to most Europeans for both religious and non-religious reasons.

It was not just that Christians and Europeans came to embrace Christmas to a heightened extent over the course of the nineteenth century, however, but that they also exposed the rest of the world to these beliefs and practices during the same historical moment. Over the course of the century, industrialization and imperial competition together accelerated Western encounters with the non-Western world, with European products and peoples (merchants, migrants, missionaries, and militaries) pouring out of Europe in revolutionary volumes. When the representatives of European nationalities settled in other corners of the world, they brought their Christmas customs with them and clung to them as a means of preserving their cultural identities in foreign lands. The agents of European imperial governments did much the same, albeit in their case as a means of preserving their sense of difference and superiority over the Africans and Asians they governed as part of their nation's colonial empires.

As a result, during the nineteenth century, local Christmas traditions became nationalized, and then globalized, as a result of trade, migration, settlement, and imperial conquest. These patterns continued and intensified during the subsequent century, facilitated, for example, by new developments in media and communications—cheap print, radio, film, television, and ultimately the World Wide Web—all of which increased the ease with which people around the world could learn about, and potentially adopt, foreign holiday customs. The fact that churches around the world in the twenty-first century frequently observe the holiday by holding services of 'Nine Lessons and Carols', exemplifies the international expansion of what was once an exclusively English-Anglican practice, first revived at King's College, Cambridge, after World War I. Over the course of the century, this distinctly local tradition evolved into a non-denominational, international service form, popularized by radio (and later television) broadcasts and recordings of the service at King's that first became available internationally in the late 1930s.

The deployment of large numbers of American soldiers overseas during the world wars and the Cold War also played a very important role in contributing to Christmas's further globalization. The celebration of the holiday in Japan was inspired almost entirely by Japanese observations of Christmas celebrations among occupying US forces during the immediate postwar years (Forbes 2007: 52). The economic dominance of the United States during the second half of the century also helped to popularize and standardize a range of Christmas customs on a global level, including the use of electric Christmas lights for both interior and exterior displays—something many Europeans, for example, continue to view as very 'American' today, despite their widespread use in Europe since the 1960s (Brunner 2012: 72). The most pronounced manifestation of America's commercial influence over global Christmas customs, however, probably was the emergence of an increasingly uniform, international representation of Santa Claus as jolly, portly, rosy-cheeked, and dressed all in red, facilitated in no small part by the annual illustrations Haddon Sandblom designed for the Coca-Cola company depicting the celebrated gift-bringer between 1931 and 1964 (Forbes 2007: 92–3).

Of course, the proliferation and diversification of Christmas traditions around the world was further intensified by the fact that by the middle of the twentieth century Americans were themselves celebrating Christmas by employing a hybrid of customs adopted from the wide range of national groups that had immigrated to the country during the previous century. By the early 1900s, the decoration of a Christmas tree already had become as much an iconic component of the 'American' as the 'German' Christmas, with the first 'National Christmas Tree' appearing on the White House lawn in 1923 (Brunner 2012: 56, 60).

The editor of *Christmas Around the World* asserted that responding to this proliferation and amalgamation of foreign Christmas traditions in America represented the primary motivation informing the book's compilation, noting that in the contemporary United States, 'from the four quarters of the globe, our ancestors brought with them the Christmas traditions of their native lands, customs which have become an integral part of the Christmas observance in various parts of our country today' (Hooper 1961: 1). From the nineteenth century up to the present day, the ancestors of Norwegian immigrants in Minnesota continue to eat lutefisk and open family gifts on Christmas Eve, while their Swedish neighbours observe St. Lucia Day on December 13 (Hooper 1961: 21, 30). The ancestors of Irish immigrants in America and Australia likewise still place candles in the windows of their houses to ensure that 'no couple seeking shelter for a Baby who is the son of God will be homeless' (Hooper 1961: 16).

In similar fashion, the annual college report of King's College, Cambridge, could note with pleasure in 1936 that their service of Nine Lessons and Carols had been broadcast to audiences on 'every continent', not only because by this time considerable numbers of former Britons had settled in Canada, Australia, New Zealand, and South Africa, but also because the British state continued to preside over a global empire encompassing roughly a quarter of the inhabited world (Day 2018: 3). Indeed, the transposition of Northern European Christmas traditions to different climates as a result of colonial conquest and settlement produced some striking juxtapositions, perhaps best exemplified by the contemporary Australian Christmas, where one finds homes adorned with spruce needles *and* palm leaves, backyard barbeques serving Christmas puddings, and surfers wearing Santa hats (Brunner 2012: 75).

The evolution of Christmas as a holiday that was observed with simultaneous, overlapping religious and non-religious elements was both a cause and a consequence of the holiday's global spread during the twentieth century. One result of this continued process of expansion (itself accompanied by additional patterns of adaptation and hybridization), was that by the end of the century, the world was really celebrating two 'Christmases'—'a cultural Christmas, and a religious or Christian Christmas' in the words of Bruce David Forbes (Forbes 2007: 142). (Of course, as he notes, many people observed—and continue to observe—both versions of the holiday simultaneously.) This two-pronged evolution, nevertheless, ensured that the meaning of Christmas was repeatedly contested during the twentieth century. Indeed, as Gerry Bowler argues, when in the early 2000s conservative commentators like Bill O'Reilly claimed that there was a 'War on Christmas' being waged in the United States, they had hardly discovered a novel phenomenon, but instead were merely the latest group to identify the holiday as a cultural battleground (Bowler 2017: 230–2).

The twentieth century was notable, among other things, for pronounced political conflicts, producing both violent revolutions and some of the most destructive wars in human history. The signature importance of the annual holiday in Western religious and national cultures ensured that during the twentieth century observances of Christmas frequently were shaped by the larger political or wartime contexts in which they unfolded, influencing the way the holiday was (or was not) celebrated and remembered afterwards.

During the world wars, for example, civilians and soldiers frequently demonstrated a stubborn determination to mark the holiday, regardless of shortages, dangers, and other wartime miseries. British civilians carefully saved their ration cards to ensure they would still be able to have their traditional large Christmas dinners (Johnes 2016: 99), while German civilians, unable to obtain fir trees, fashioned ersatz Christmas trees from broom handles by drilling holes in them and filling these with whatever greenery they could acquire (Brunner 2012: 66). In World War I, both British and German soldiers also created improvised Christmas trees in their trenches out of scrap wood, branches, and other items they acquired from the trenches or No Man's Land (Weintraub 2001: 14–15). In 1917, one British soldier wrote home claiming that on Christmas Day the soldiers had endeavoured 'to go through the old routine no matter what was happening' (Johnes 2016: 73). During the next war, British soldiers likewise organized services of Nine Lessons and Carols in POW camps (Day 2018: 4), while in Germany in 1944, Berlin hospital workers gathered around a small Christmas tree to celebrate the holiday in an air-raid bunker (Perry 2010: 233).

The wars likewise left behind permanent Christmas associations in the minds of those who had experienced the holiday during wartime. A Polish woman, Wanda Pomykalski, noted that she could never hear certain carols in later life, without recalling how her eyes had filled with tears when she had sung them with fellow Polish political prisoners on a freezing Soviet train on Christmas Eve in 1939 (Pomykalski 1994: 8). The British intelligence officer Gerald Pawle claimed that the 'the most unusual Christmas' he ever experienced was spent celebrating the holiday with Winston Churchill in a Tunisian villa in 1943, where 'one could not remotely imagine a seasonal snowfall', but where there was, nonetheless, 'turkey and Christmas pudding', and where he was 'reproached' by Mrs Churchill 'for not attending morning service' in the villa's temporary chapel (Pawle 1973: 481–4). Pawle remembered being particularly surprised by Churchill greeting him personally and remarking that he had 'asked you here today... because I thought you might have a more agreeable Christmas with me' (Pawle 1973: 483).

Churchill's statement was indicative of the larger importance national leaders during both world wars placed on ensuring their citizens, and especially their soldiers, had a 'happy' Christmas. During the wars, governments and civilian organizations arranged to send holiday gifts to soldiers. In World War I, 'Christmas packages' donated for soldiers at the front from German civilians across the country included items like pocket knives, flashlights, games, chocolates, marzipan, cognac, and cigars (Perry 2010: 123). Among the most iconic of such wartime gifts were the Princess Mary Gift Boxes given to all British soldiers in Christmas 1914, whose contents were carefully differentiated for 'smokers' and 'non-smokers', but all of which included a Christmas card and a photograph of the princess (Wakefield 2006: 4–5).

Governments made similar efforts to ensure the comfort of their own civilian populations during the wars, seeing this as a vital means of maintaining morale on the home front, and this was sometimes done at a terrible cost to other civilians among occupied populations. In one particularly horrifying instance, Heinrich Himmler arranged to provide Christmas gifts for German nationals resettled as 'colonists' in Poland from clothing and other items confiscated from Jews murdered at the Auschwitz death camp (Bowler 2017: 103).

Efforts made by governments to provide some modicum of 'Christmas cheer' during the wars also demonstrate how the experience of these wars came to be inflected by the return of the annual Christmas holiday, sometimes shaping wartime events and outcomes in unpredictable ways. Perry argues, for example, that during World War II the 'conjuncture of Christmas 1942 and the defeat at the Battle of Stalingrad' intensified the psychic impact the defeat exerted over the morale of the German population on the Home Front (Perry 2010: 231). A similar argument might be made about the psychic importance the 1944 German Ardennes offensive ('The Battle of the Bulge') came to occupy among American soldiers and civilians during and after the war, with the Christmastime battle even providing the opening scene for Irving Berlin's popular holiday film, *White Christmas* (1954).

Perhaps the most notorious manifestation of the holiday in the history of twentieth-century warfare, however, was the 1914 Christmas Truce. Beginning on the night of December 24, along the Western Front soldiers began lighting often-improvised Christmas trees and exchanging greetings and carols. On Christmas Day, multiple instances of fraternization were recorded, especially between the Germans and the British, in which gifts of food, alcohol, cigarettes, and souvenirs were exchanged, soldiers worked together to bury the dead, and impromptu soccer matches were held in No Man's Land (Weintraub 2001). The extent of the truce should not be exaggerated. French and Belgian troops were far less likely to feel any sense of affinity with the German soldiers opposite them (given the latter were occupying Belgian and French soil), and even in some British sectors, German soldiers erected Christmas trees, only to have them immediately shot to pieces by the soldiers on the opposing side (Weintraub 2001: 24). Nevertheless, incidents of fraternization on Christmas Day in 1914 were widespread enough for the leaders of both the armies of the Allies and the Central Powers to take steps to ensure that no further Christmas truces occurred during the war (Weintraub 2001: 170). Despite their efforts, the 1914 Truce became an iconic moment in the larger history of the war, the subject of scholarly histories, children's books, plays, poems, popular songs, films, and even the Pulitzer-Prize winning opera, *Silent Night* (2011). In 2013, the opera's librettist Mark Campbell explained the enduring fascination of the truce as arising from the realization that war becomes unsustainable 'when you come to know your enemy as a person' (Francis 2013), and in this instance it was the arrival of the Christmas holiday that made this realization possible.

Campbell's observation about the historical importance of the 1914 Christmas Truce is indicative of the way in which the enormous importance of the Christmas holiday ensured that it frequently became an arena in which larger political conflicts played out. The 1950s United States, for example, witnessed a massive expansion in domestic Christmas tree ornament manufacturing, as the Cold War context no longer allowed Americans to purchase their ornaments from Polish, East German, and Czechoslovakian manufacturers, because these were now located in 'Soviet dominated lands' (Brunner 2012: 74).

The treatment of the Christmas customs of the United States in *Christmas Around the World*, also subtly hinted at the Cold War context in which it was published, noting that, 'At Christmas time in the United States, all customs and religions stand on a common ground...clearly reveal[ing] the message of the angels of, "Peace on earth and good will to all men"' (Hooper 1961: 17–18). It likewise makes no reference to the existence of the Soviet Union, instead including a brief entry on Russia, beginning with the observation, 'Many of Russia's traditions have been lost and forgotten' (Hooper 1961: 26). The American reader in the 1960s required no further explanation of why this was the case. Since 1917, Russia had been a communist country, and references to the avowedly atheist ('godless') stance of the government of the Soviet Union routinely inflected American political rhetoric during the Cold War, which many came to view not only as a war between rival political and socio-economic systems, but also between religion and secularism (Wallace 2013).

Similar ideas informed the Christmastime policies of the government of West Germany, which employed the holiday as a means of defining their state as the only Germany in which the 'true' German Christmas continued to be observed. Konrad Adenauer, for example, urged West Germans in a 1959 speech to remember their fellow Germans in the East, 'who live in slavery [and] are not allowed to celebrate Holy Eve as we do' (Perry 2010: 246). After the Berlin Wall was erected in 1961, the West German government regularly erected Christmas trees along it, as well as at other prominent locations along the East/West border, effectively weaponizing the most iconic German Christmas custom for political purposes as a means of reminding those Germans in the East of the freedoms they lacked under communism (Perry 2010: 247). During the same years, however, the government of East Germany also employed the holiday for political ends, promoting Christmas as a holiday of universal plenty, and as a 'celebration of peace'—a peace made possible exclusively by 'state socialism' (Perry 2010: 258).

The official atheist stance of the government of the Soviet Union allowed for no similar attempts to co-opt the Christmas holiday for political purposes. Instead, there was officially no Christmas in the Soviet Union, the holiday being outlawed under Lenin almost immediately after the Bolshevik seizure of power, and replaced by the Soviet New Year festival (*elka*). Thereafter, the Soviet state's stance toward the holiday varied in accordance with the larger ebb and flow of the party's commitment to the promotion of atheism among the Soviet populace, with those who celebrated the holiday being actively persecuted in the 1920s and 1930s, openly tolerated during the Second World War in the name of promoting national unity, and grudgingly allowed to continue in a quasi-underground state in the decades after the war (Rolf 2013: 76, 146; Miner 2003: 87).

In addition, celebrations of the Soviet New Year continued to involve the erection of *elka* trees, the giving of gifts to children from 'Grandfather Frost', and the exchange of 'New Year's cards', all of which betrayed a striking affinity to many of the Christmas customs of both prerevolutionary Russia and those of many Europeans and Americans during the Cold War. Thus, the British anthropologist Christel Lane observed in the 1980s that in the Soviet Union, 'The New Year is celebrated in the home in much the same way as Christmas is in an English family without strong Christian commitments' (Lane 1981: 137–8). After the fall of communism, many of these same customs continued to be associated with the New Year, having been effectively severed from association with the Christmas holiday under the Soviets, while the open observance of Christmas in Russia after communism took on a much more overtly religious character, as a result of its years of being celebrated 'underground' (Bowler 2017: 90; Rolf 2013: 194).

Christmas also posed problems for the century's other 'totalitarian' regimes. The association of specific Christmas practices with specific national cultures, for example, made them problematic in the eyes of leaders like Francisco Franco and Benito Mussolini, both of whom opposed the use of the Christmas tree, as a 'German' cultural import that threatened the purity of their own nation's cultures (Brunner 2012: 74). For the Nazis, 'German' Christmas trees posed less of a problem (so long as they were decorated with pagan symbols, black suns, and swastikas) (Brunner 2012: 73). Their problems lay with Christmas's Judaeo-Christian origins and images, which they sought to replace with exclusive references to the holiday as a cultural celebration of the German 'people's community' (*Volksgemeinschaft*), and endeavoured to eliminate with uneven success through scripted school productions, mandatory charity campaigns, refashioned lyrics for popular carols, family advice manuals, the promotion of traditional, handmade 'German' Christmas gifts, and radio broadcasts (Perry 2010: 193–215).

Yet as Bowler and other scholars observe, many of the conflicts Christmas generated in the twentieth century played out in a less dramatic fashion, unfolding, not in the policies of specific national governments, but in the day-to-day social and emotional lives of communities, families, and individuals. Again, the holiday's global expansion and pronounced importance in a large range of people's lives played an important part in helping to create these conflicts, not the least because people had come to celebrate the holiday for a range of secular or religious reasons (or some mixture of both).

One prominent source of conflict involved questions of whether Christmas customs were changing or staying the same. During the nineteenth century, nationalist promoters had sought to justify the authenticity of their distinct national Christmas traditions by invoking the past, claiming to describe ancient, 'timeless' customs. In many respects, the anonymous authors of *Christmas Around the World* continued to portray holiday traditions in this fashion in the 1960s. Despite the editor's assertion that the book's purpose was to understand the varied customs that had contributed to the celebration of Christmas in America 'in their original form' (Hooper 1961: 1), the heavy use of the present tense throughout the majority of the individual descriptions implied the very opposite—that Christmas traditions involved unchanging patterns of observance between past and present. The section on Greece, for example, describes how, 'Remembering a custom of long ago, Greek mothers again make their famous fried cakes, while the little children watch in wide-eyed wonder, listening to the stories and old folk legends' (Hooper 1961: 14). Reading these descriptions, one gets the sense that at Christmas, people around the world entered a trans-generational cultural space untouched by the passage of time. In fact, since 1944, Ideals Publishing, the company responsible for producing *Christmas Around the World*, has been associated primarily with the publication of annual Christmas magazines consisting of a 'classic collection of all things Christmas', including, 'poetry, essays, quotations, and recipes', all 'carefully chosen' under the guiding assumption (in the words of the editor of the 2017 edition), that the 'values celebrated in its pages are unchanged', and that 'loyal readers' continue to seek out the publication for the same reasons 'each year . . . since 1944' (Rumbaugh 2017).

Now and in the 1960s, the claims of the authors of publications like *Christmas Ideals* and *Christmas Around the World* ignore the fact that Christmas customs have never been static. They were (and are) far from 'timeless'—and were already so in the 1960s, many having been rediscovered, refashioned, or invented entirely during the nineteenth century. Nor did they acknowledge the fact that many of these customs had continued to evolve over the course of the twentieth century. The reader of *Christmas Around the World*, for example, learns that in England on Christmas Eve 'the yule log is brought inside and placed in the big fireplace' (Hooper 1961: 10), despite the fact that the tradition of burning Yule logs had almost entirely disappeared from England more than thirty years previously, largely due to the increased rarity of fireplaces large enough to accommodate them (Johnes 2016: 110).

The very same claims, however, illustrate the powerful appeal of Christmas as a supposedly 'timeless' entity, and the profound desire to keep it so. The recorded practices of individuals and families demonstrate the influence of such desires. During the first half of the twentieth century, for example, the Berlin couple Anna and Richard Wagner took the same photo every year in front of their Christmas tree. The resulting impression yielded by the photographic series, Brunner notes, is of a couple that 'got older, but the trees and their decorations stayed the same, almost down to the branch' (Brunner 2012: 66). Indeed, he likewise rightly observes that, although 'thick books could be filled with the countless little things that have hung from Christmas trees', those of any given family often exhibited very little difference from year to year, as ornament collections were reused by choice, and often even handed down between generations, demonstrating in a striking fashion how while local, national, or even global Christmas traditions may have been changing during the twentieth century, those within families often managed to achieve a remarkable degree of continuity (Brunner 2012: 64–6).

Considerable differences likewise existed between individual families' Christmas customs, and those of the broader local or national culture of which they were a part. This could also provoke anxiety and conflict, especially if for many people, as Daniel Miller shrewdly observes, 'Christmas may [have been] everywhere, but the only true Christmas [was] within one's own home' (Miller 1993: 30). As the century progressed, many Christians particularly began to worry about Christmas's secular elements. The editor of *Christmas Around the World* already stressed in the 1960s the importance of remembering that regardless of their individual origins, 'running through' every Christmas tradition 'in word and song, is the recognition of the greatest of all holy days...the birth of Jesus Christ' (Hooper 1961: 1). For many Christians, however, the problem was that this increasingly no longer seemed to be the case—that the holiday's enormous popularity and global expansion now threatened to undermine its character as a Christian festival.

Given such concerns, it is unsurprising that the editor of *Christmas Around the World* did not include a section devoted to Christmas observances in Japan. In the 1960s, the vast majority of Japanese did not practise any form of Christianity, nor do all but a tiny minority today. However, since the 1950s, the majority of Japanese have celebrated Christmas (*Kurisumasu*), but as a festival with very different associations. As the anthropologists Brian Moeran and Lise Skov note, when Christmas developed in Japan after World War II, it emerged purely as a festival of 'consumerism', focused on 'youth, couples and exclusivity', and thus it 'bears hardly any resemblance to Christmas in Europe or America' (Moeran and Skov 1993: 108). Indeed, by the 1990s, for young Japanese couples, Christmas Eve had become the ultimate 'date night'. Thus, when the words 'Silent Night' appeared in Christmas advertising campaigns, it was being employed by marketers with decidedly different, often erotically charged, overtones (example: 'Silent Night's Sweet Message for Him'), as the means of promoting bottles of champagne or boxes of fancy chocolates (Moeran and Skov 1993: 106).

Anxieties about the secularization of the Christmas holiday, however, were often rooted much closer to home—in the schools, shops, and streets of Western cities and towns. Furthermore, as Forbes notes, these worries themselves were far from universal in character, with some believers worrying that 'society's Christmas' was not 'Christian enough' (with the resulting demands to 'Keep Christ in Christmas'), while for others the source of conflict emerged out of an inability to assess whether one's *own* family's Christmas observances were 'Christian enough' (Forbes 2007: 140).

In adopting Christmas as an exclusively 'consumer festival', the Japanese were in some respects merely foregrounding what had become an increasingly prominent aspect of the holiday's celebration in Europe and the United States and thus occupied an equally prominent place in concerns about the holiday's (supposedly) increasing secular tendencies: commercialization (Schmidt 1995). Ironically, Ideals Publishing was itself one manifestation of this trend, having initially developed as a company marketing nostalgic Christmas magazines to American readers. The last six pages of *Christmas Around the World* were dedicated to a full-colour catalogue of other Christmas-related publications offered by the company, with instructions on how they could be ordered by mail (Hooper 1961: 36–42).

Arguably, there was no greater contributing factor to the anxieties of Western Christians about the secularization of Christmas during the twentieth century, than the holiday's seemingly ever more rampant materialism. The Ideal company's publications thus exhibited one of the inherent paradoxes of Christian ambivalence toward Christmas commercialization: the fact that publishers and manufacturers actively contributed to the process of commercializing Christmas by producing products that sought to help the religious avoid the secularizing tendencies of Christmas commercialism. In Great Britain, for example, the vast majority of Christmas cards at the beginning of the twentieth century were notable for having little or no religious content. As the century progressed, however, more cards with overtly religious messages began to appear, as fears of secularization increased, and manufacturers stepped in to capitalize on this rising anxiety (Johnes 2016: 78).

Furthermore, for all that creeping commercialization frequently featured in private and public handwringing about the holiday, it is also clear that few people actively resisted Christmas's rising commercialization. Indeed, a far greater number embraced the holiday's consumerism, purchasing larger numbers of gifts and more elaborate decorations as the century progressed. Yet, as Martin Johnes notes, while the commercial activity of the weeks leading up to Christmas Day steadily intensified over the century, Christmas Day itself remained arguably one of the days that was dedicated *the least* to commerce in the annual calendar (Johnes 2016: 38). Throughout the twentieth century, most stores were closed on Christmas Day. Indeed, nothing better illustrates Johnes's assertion than the fact that even in the hyper-consumerist United States of 2018, while nearly every major retailer—including Walmart, Target, Macy's, and Kohls—extended their annual 'Black Friday' sales backwards into the evening of the preceding Thanksgiving Day, all of these same stores were closed for the entirety of Christmas Day, along with most other American businesses. Though in the present century, online shopping may have begun to move consumers and retailers away from the tradition of observing Christmas as a day 'without commerce', the persistence of this pattern during the twentieth century nevertheless existed in sharp distinction to the parallel expansion of Christmas commercialism during the same years.

All this suggests that expressions of anxiety about the holiday's commercialization themselves arguably became another Christmas custom in the twentieth century, one annually expressed by ambivalent minorities, while largely ignored by much of the rest of the populace as they gleefully went about another year's Christmas shopping. It likewise suggests that at least some of the conflicts regarding changes in Christmas customs arose either because many people actively embraced these changes or were oblivious to them. Indeed, where the holiday was concerned, continuity could often seem as pronounced as change, for both good or ill.

If the editor of *Christmas Around the World* got one thing right, it was in emphasizing that Christmas was a holiday celebrated by the family, a time when 'we gather about the fire' as multiple generations, 'with our loved ones' (Hooper 1961: 1). Writing in the 1990s, Miller heartily agreed, arguing that, 'All interpretations of Christmas acknowledge the central image of the family in its celebrations' (Miller 1993: 11). Yet families are not always functional, and family Christmases are not always pleasurable.

The central role of the family in the Christmas festival throughout the century, therefore, could provoke as much conflict within the individual family unit, as it produced within the larger civic families of cities and nations. This was especially the case where holiday responsibilities were not distributed evenly among the family members, with the result that one person's celebration became another person's burden.

As early as 1954, the American scholar James Barnett noted that the American family Christmas was 'largely controlled by women'—that 'women buy and prepare most of the gifts for the occasion as well as provide holiday food and delicacies', and he posited that women's domination of 'our most important national festival' might offer some form of 'symbolic compensation for accepting the disadvantages of their social role' (Barnett 1954: 64–5). Much the same might have been said of many European women at that time. As the century progressed, and more women overcame these 'social disadvantages', above all by taking on economic roles outside the home, their families' (much less society's) expectations of them at the Christmas holidays did not evolve to the same degree, with the result that by the end of the century, many women felt increasingly frustrated and resentful at the holidays, resulting in heightened marital and family tensions (Johnes 2016: 55–63). The continued assumptions of both many men *and* women in Europe and the United States that it is women's primary responsibility to shop, decorate, and cook for the holiday, therefore, arguably demonstrates that in some cases Christmas generated conflict, not only when the holiday's customs changed, but also when changes failed to occur.

Furthermore, within the realm of ordinary people's Christmas practices, changes often unfolded within the context of broader continuities. In the United States and Great Britain, the importance of a family meal—prepared and eaten at home—remained a paramount component of both countries' holiday observances. Yet, what was actually eaten at these meals evolved over time. At the beginning of the century, most Britons dined on beef. The importation of cheap turkeys from Canada in the 1930s, however, caused many British families to switch to turkey, and by the 1970s turkey had become 'ingrained' as the national Christmas dish. In 1997, three-quarters of Britons reported eating turkey on Christmas Day (Johnes 2016: 97). In the same way, the gifts individuals purchased for each other changed from year to year, but the sacrifices of time and money made to ensure that one's friends and loved ones received 'just the right gift' remained remarkably steady throughout the century. The money and time lavished on the selection, purchase, and wrapping of gifts for children was especially true in this regard. A Bolton shopkeeper remarked in the 1930s, 'Money may be short but it is always found at Christmas', and this was especially so when it was needed to buy gifts for children and other loved ones, even if it meant going into debt (Johnes 2016: 21–3).

Despite the resiliency of some families' Christmas traditions, the fact that Christmas could, and did, seem to change out in the wider world, became an oft-cited cause for ambivalence among ordinary Americans and Europeans. Indeed, much like the annual anxieties expressed about commercialization, Johnes argues that during the twentieth century discussions of how Christmas was 'better' in the past themselves became another Christmas tradition, providing a leitmotif for public discussion of the holiday for much of the century, and likewise demonstrating the way the holiday 'encouraged contemplation and reflection' among ordinary people around their tables and firesides (Johnes 2016: 113).

Thus, what are we to conclude about the place of Christmas in the conflict-ridden history of the twentieth century? Rather than return to the pages of *Christmas Around the World*, I would argue that a better sense of the meaning of the history of Christmas might be offered by another volume, Shirley Hughes's children's book, *Lucy and Tom's Christmas* (1981). In the book, Lucy and Tom eagerly await the coming holiday. They help to decorate their home, they purchase or make presents for family members, and they 'talk a lot about the presents they hope they're going to get for Christmas.' On Christmas Eve they are '*far* too excited to go to sleep...But somehow they do.' Christmas morning finally arrives. They discover their gifts from Santa Claus, they play with them, they wake up their parents, attend church, and eat a dinner of 'delicious things' with visiting relatives. The day is not perfect. Tom, for example, 'gets very excited about his presents and rather cross', and has to go for a walk with his grandfather to settle down, before returning home to play games with the rest of the family by the lighted Christmas tree (Hughes 1981).

The genius of Hughes's book lies in the way it manages to link the mundane with the wondrous, excitement with exhaustion, and the local with the national and universal elements that informed so many ordinary European and American Christmas observances in the twentieth century. Lucy and Tom clearly inhabit England. They mail their letters to Santa up their chimney, but hang their stockings on the ends of their beds, as opposed to over the fireplace. They eat Christmas pudding. They play with 'Christmas Crackers' after dinner. Yet, much of their holiday experience feels enormously familiar, and would have felt so for a large number of Europeans and Americans, not only in the 1980s, but across the whole of the twentieth century. The enormous sense of anticipation, the gathering with family, the joy and excitement, and the occasional crossness all played a role in the annual observance of the Christmas festival. It is these emotional associations, as much as those provided by religion, politics, nation, or tradition, that have helped to cement Christmas to a central position in the calendars of countless inhabitants of the modern world. This same emotional investment ensures that Christmas likely will continue to be a contested battleground for the analyses of social critics and historians, but also a source of countless treasured memories and unrecorded pleasures for many individuals, as the twenty-first century continues to unfold.

References and Further Reading

Barnett, James H. (1954). *The American Christmas: A Study in National Culture*. New York: Macmillan.

Bowler, Gerry (2017). *Christmas in the Crosshairs: Two Thousand Years of Denouncing and Defending the World's Most Celebrated Holiday*. Oxford: Oxford University Press.

Brunner, Bernd (2012). *Inventing the Christmas Tree*, trans. Benjamin A. Smith. New Haven: Yale University Press.

Connelly, Mark (1999). *Christmas: A Social History*. London: I. B. Tauris.

Day, Timothy (2018). *I Saw Eternity the Other Night: King's College, Cambridge, and an English Singing Style*. London: Allen Lane.

Forbes, Bruce David (2007). *Christmas: A Candid History*. Berkeley: University of California Press.

Francis, Naila (2013). '*Silent Night* Librettist Mark Campbell: Bored at the Opera', *Burlington County Times*, 6 February.

Hooper, Van B. (1961). *Christmas Around the World*. Milwaukee: Ideals Publishing Company.

Hughes, Shirley (1981). *Lucy and Tom's Christmas*. London: Victor Gollancz.

Johnes, Martin (2016). *Christmas and the British: A Modern History*. London: Bloomsbury.

Lane, Christel (1981). *The Rites of Rulers: Ritual in Industrial Society—The Soviet Case*. Cambridge: Cambridge University Press.

Miller, Daniel (1993). 'A Theory of Christmas' in Miller (ed.), *Unwrapping Christmas*. Oxford: Oxford University Press: 3–37.

Miller, Daniel (1993), ed. *Unwrapping Christmas*. Oxford: Clarendon Press.

Miner, Steven Merritt (2003). *Stalin's Holy War: Religion, Nationalism, and Alliance Politics, 1941–1945*. Chapel Hill: University of North Carolina Press.

Moeran, Brian and Lise Skov (1993). 'Cinderella Christmas: Kitsch, Consumerism and Youth in Japan', in Miller (ed.), *Unwrapping Christmas*. Oxford: Oxford University Press, 105–33.

Pawle, Gerald (1973). 'Christmas with Churchill', *Blackwoods Magazine*, 314, no. 1898, December: 481–5.

Perry, Joe (2010). *Christmas in Germany: A Cultural History*. Chapel Hill: University of North Carolina Press.

Pomykalski, Wanda (1994). 'Christmas 1939: A Memoir of World War II', *Minerva*, 12, no. 1, March: 1–24.

Rolf, Malte (2013). *Soviet Mass Festivals, 1917–1991*, trans. Cynthia Klohr. Pittsburgh: University of Pittsburgh Press, 2013.

Rumbaugh, Melinda L. R. (2017). *Christmas Ideals 2017*. Nashville: Ideals Publishing, 2017.

Schmidt, Leigh Eric (1995). *Consumer Rites: The Buying and Selling of American Holidays*. Princeton: Princeton University Press.

Wakefield, Alan (2006). *Christmas in the Trenches*. Stroud: Sutton Publishing.

Wallace, James C. (2013) 'A Religious War? The Cold War and Religion', *Journal of Cold War Studies*, 15, no. 3, Summer: 162–80.

Weintraub, Stanley (2001). *Silent Night: The Story of the World War I Christmas Truce*. New York: The Free Press.

PART II
THEOLOGY

CHAPTER 6

THE OLD TESTAMENT

JOHN BARTON

A highlight of the annual Christmas celebrations in England, and for many throughout the English-speaking world, is the Festival of Nine Lessons and Carols held at King's College, Cambridge, on Christmas Eve, and much imitated in ordinary parish churches in many places. The service has been held every year since 1918, and is based on an earlier form that had been used at Truro Cathedral in Cornwall since 1880. The carols vary from year to year, but the lessons (readings) follow a fairly fixed pattern. The complete list is: Genesis 3:8–19; Genesis 22:15–18; Isaiah 9:2–7; Isaiah 11:1–9; Luke 1:26–38; Luke 2:1–7; Luke 2:8–16; Matthew 2:1–12; and John 1:1–14. (Sometimes Micah 5:2–5 is included, and two Lukan readings amalgamated.) The four (or five) Old Testament readings reveal much about the understanding of the Christmas message. All of them have been understood as bearing a messianic significance throughout the history of the Christian Church.

Genesis 3:8–19 records God's conversation with Adam after he and Eve had eaten from the tree of the knowledge of good and evil and have become aware of their nakedness. It contains God's curse on the man, destined to thankless toil, on the woman, who is to have pain in childbirth, and on the snake, condemned to live in the dust—the implication is that originally snakes walked on legs like other animals. One major reason for the inclusion of this passage is to be found in the words to the snake, 'I will put enmity between you and the woman, and between your offspring and hers; he will strike your head, and you will strike his heel.'

On the face of it, this simply means that humans and snakes will always be at war, humans stepping on the heads of snakes and snakes biting the feet of humans. It is a 'Just So' story or, to put it more technically, an aetiological legend, explaining an aspect of the world as we experience it by referring back to a primordial event. But throughout Christian history the words to the snake have been interpreted as a messianic oracle. Taking the snake to represent, or be, the devil, Christian writers saw in the mutual striking of snake and man an allegorical reference to Christ defeating Satan, as we find in the Latin Easter hymn *Chorus novae Ierusalem*:

> How Judah's lion bursts his chains,
> And crushed the serpent's head. (*English Hymnal* 1906: 125)

Jesus Christ is the one destined to fulfil this 'prophecy', as it was seen: the one who so many centuries after Adam and Eve would accomplish God's eventual subjugation of the devil. This is surely the chief reason why this passage was included as the first reading in the carol service, even though to many congregations today the reference is not apparent. It is signalled (somewhat obscurely) in the traditional introduction by the reader, 'God foretells that the seed of the woman shall bruise the serpent's head', but it may be doubtful if the reference is picked up by most who hear it.

Genesis 22 contains the words of the angel of the Lord to Abraham after his near-sacrifice of his son Isaac:

> By myself I have sworn, says the LORD: Because you have done this, and have not withheld your son, your only son, I will indeed bless you, and I will make your offspring as numerous as the stars of heaven and as the sand that is on the seashore. And your offspring shall possess the gate of their enemies, and by your offspring shall all the nations of the earth gain blessing for themselves, because you have obeyed my voice. (Genesis 22:16–18)

From a biblical–critical point of view this seems to be an addition to an already completed story, as can be seen from its reference to the angel speaking 'a second time' (verse 15). What it draws out is that God's blessing, in response to Abraham's obedience, will not be for Abraham only but for 'all nations'—another theme of Christian messianism. The Messiah is not to be only a Jewish Messiah, but a deliverer who will bring blessing to all. All nations will find a blessing for themselves, 'from the LORD, the God of Israel, under whose wings [they] have come for refuge' (Ruth 2:12). Originally, the meaning may have been that other nations will invoke the God of Abraham in wishing blessings on themselves—'May we be blessed as Israel was blessed by God'; but it has been understood to mean that the nations will come to *share* in the blessings afforded to Abraham. This is a major theme of Christian messianism as understood by St Paul. As he expounds the Christian conviction in Galatians and in Romans, God's favour has through Christ been extended to the Gentiles, who are now 'Abraham's offspring':

> And the Scripture, foreseeing that God would justify the Gentiles by faith, declared the gospel beforehand to Abraham, saying, 'All the Gentiles shall be blessed in you.' (Galatians 3:8)
>
> ...in order that the promise may rest on grace and be guaranteed to all his descendants, not only to the adherents of the law but also to those who share the faith of Abraham (for he is the father of us all, as it is written, 'I have made you the father of many nations'). (Romans 4:16–17)

The two passages from Isaiah were for early Christians obviously messianic in intention:

> The people who walked in darkness have seen a great light;
> those who lived in a land of deep darkness—on them light has shined.
> For the yoke of their burden,
> > and the bar across their shoulders,
> > the rod of their oppressor,
> > you have broken as on the day of Midian.
>
> For a child has been born for us,
> > a son given to us,
> authority rests upon his shoulders;
> > and he is named
> Wonderful Counsellor, Mighty God,
> > Everlasting Father, Prince of Peace.
> His authority shall grow continually,
> > and there shall be endless peace
> for the throne of David and his kingdom.
> > He will establish and uphold it
> with justice and with righteousness
> from this time onwards and for evermore. (Isaiah 9:2, 4, 6–7)
> A shoot shall come out from the stock of Jesse,
> > and a branch shall grow out of his roots.
> The spirit of the LORD shall rest upon him,
> > the spirit of wisdom and understanding,
> > the spirit of counsel and might,
> > the spirit of knowledge and the fear of the LORD.
> The wolf shall live with the lamb,
> > the leopard shall lie down with the kid,
> the calf and the lion and the fatling together,
> > and a little child shall lead them.
> The cow and the bear shall graze,
> > their young shall lie down together;
> > and the lion shall eat straw like the ox.
> The nursing child shall play over the hole of the asp,
> > and the weaned child shall put its hand on the adder's den.
> They will not hurt or destroy
> > on all my holy mountain.   (Isaiah 11:1–3, 6–9)

Both refer to the birth of a royal child, and many commentators think one or both were originally meant as dynastic oracles celebrating a son for one of the Judaean kings: if either is genuinely by Isaiah, then this will be a son of Ahaz or Hezekiah, kings of Judah in the eighth century BCE. Or they may be 'all purpose' oracles for use in some kind of royal ritual around the time of the birth of an heir to the throne, or even of a coronation, which was widely understood as the day of the new king's metaphorical 'birth' (Williamson 2018).

Isaiah 11:1–9 clearly implies that the royal 'child' comes from the stock of Jesse, that is, is a descendant of Jesse's son, David, whereas Isaiah 9:2–7, with its reference to 'the day of Midian', may be thinking more of a person like one of the judges (see Judges 6–7, for the conquest of the Midianites). But the royalty of the child is stressed through the attribution to him of a series of four 'throne names', possibly modelled on Egyptian titles of the pharaoh. Both oracles were interpreted messianically, however, by Christians, and were seen as fulfilled in Jesus Christ. The authority resting on his shoulder was his rule over all things as God and Lord, as a result of his literal, not metaphorical, birth at Christmas, when in him God became incarnate. Isaiah 11 provides the reading in the Roman-rite divine Office for the Office of Readings on Christmas Day, and had long stood in Matins in both Roman and monastic use. It is also commonly read in Anglican churches on Christmas Day.

The Micah passage (Micah 5:2–5) is occasionally included in the carol service because of its explicit reference to Bethlehem:

> But you, O Bethlehem of Ephrathah,
>   who are one of the little clans of Judah,
> from you shall come forth for me
>   one who is to rule in Israel,
> whose origin is from of old,
> from ancient days.
> Therefore he shall give them up until the time
> when she who is in labour has brought forth;
>   then the rest of his kindred shall return
>   to the people of Israel.
> And he shall stand and feed his flock
>   in the strength of the LORD,
> in the majesty of the name of the
> LORD his God.
>   And they shall live secure, for now he shall be great
>   to the ends of the earth;
>   and he shall be the one of peace.

This oracle is referred to by king Herod's advisers in Matthew 2:5–6 when he is visited by the wise men following the star, and wishes to know where the Messiah is to be born. Again the passage is susceptible of a non-messianic interpretation, implying simply that all Davidic kings come from Bethlehem (at least metaphorically), since that is where David was born. But it seems likelier that it really is foretelling a coming deliverer of David's line, that is, a Messiah in the strict sense, who will be 'the one of peace'. The reference to 'she who is in labour', a reference to the Messiah's mother, was of course seen by Christians as concerning the Virgin Mary. A sceptic might speculate that this passage generated some details of the Nativity stories, and especially their insistence that Jesus was indeed born in Bethlehem, the city of David, even though he was known as coming from Nazareth in Galilee. Whether this is the case or not, the oracle of Micah does correspond closely to the Gospel stories, and has long been read liturgically in Christian practice even though it is not always part of the King's College service.

All of these passages are thus an important part of the Christmas celebration because they predict, or have been thought to predict, the coming of the Messiah, and hence to have been fulfilled in the birth and life of Jesus. Taken in this way, however, they may seem occasional and rather random, scattered through the Old Testament like stamps stuck at odd places in an album. In fact there is much more unity and coherence to the Christian use of the Old Testament in giving an account of the Christmas events than this may seem to imply, because the oracles belong in a continuous story that Christians told themselves using the Old Testament Scriptures. That story is encapsulated in the Bidding at the beginning of the King's College service, where we are invited to 'read and mark in Holy Scripture the tale of the loving purposes of God from the first days of our disobedience unto the glorious Redemption brought us by this Holy Child'.

The story begins with Adam and Eve in the garden ('the first days of our disobedience'), not merely because they heard the prophecy of the woman's offspring striking the snake's head, but because through them the whole human race ('*our* disobedience') was corrupted and put, apparently, beyond help. The subsequent history of the world, which soon in Genesis narrows down to the history of Abraham and his descendants, is a continuing story of disobedience and disloyalty to God, as the prophets bear witness, though occasionally (as in the oracle of Micah) a gleam of hope appears. God does not leave himself without a witness to his longer-term favourable purposes, as the story of Abraham in particular shows, for he promises that through Abraham's offspring (understand: Jesus, compare Galatians 3:15–18) all nations (understand: the Gentiles) will eventually be blessed (understand: be gathered into the Church). This will come about through the miraculously born Saviour predicted by Isaiah as the one who will exercise authority over the whole of humanity. And this rescue mission for a lost human race is not a mere promise, but has already been inaugurated, since Jesus has come and been born among us.

Thus there is a coherence to the story the Bible tells: it is not inconsequential. The story moves from an opening catastrophe in the garden of Eden, through repeated failure but also hope, to an eventual salvation brought about by the coming of Christ. This is how Christians have read the Old Testament since the work of St Paul, and the addition of the Gospels to the Old Testament confirms this way of seeing the story, by fleshing out the form the salvation took. I have elsewhere described this Christian reading of the story the Bible tells as one of a disaster followed by a rescue mission (Barton 2019), and this is beautifully illustrated by the shape and form of the King's College service.

It hardly needs saying that this represents a thorough Christianizing of the Old Testament/Hebrew Bible. In Judaism no one reads the garden of Eden story as at all central, or thinks of the Hebrew Bible as describing a plight from which humanity needs rescuing. The Bible is seen far more as a guide for conduct—as *torah*—than as depicting a human catastrophe and its promised solution. As we have seen, the 'messianic' texts were in most cases probably not messianic at all in origin, and the idea of a human race crying out for a Saviour is alien to Judaism, at least in the forms that have come down to modern times. There were messianic hopes around the time of

Jesus and Christians adopted them from Judaism, but they were concerned with the rescue of Israel from foreign domination, not with any kind of worldwide, let alone cosmic, intervention. But, as used in the Church, the Old Testament has come to have a forward-looking aspect, with the books of the prophets playing a dominant role such as they never had in Judaism. Thus the Christian reading of 'the Old Testament story' is not a Jewish story with the addition of Jesus and the New Testament, but rather a wholly different way of construing the entire Hebrew Bible.

Once this construal has been accepted, it becomes possible to see yet more details in the Old Testament as pointing forward to people and events described in the Christmas story. From the early Church onwards a large number of passages in the Old Testament have been drawn on for this purpose. The most obvious is Isaiah 7:10–17, which is quoted in Matthew 1:22–3, the prophecy that 'the young woman is with child and will bear a son, and will name him Emmanuel'. 'Young woman', Hebrew *almah,* is in the Greek Bible rendered *parthenos*, which usually means 'virgin'. The original oracle is probably another dynastic promise like Isaiah 9, but Christians took it as a prediction of the birth of Jesus from a virgin. One often hears it said that 'the virgin birth idea results from a mistranslation of the Hebrew', but it is not as simple as that (Vermes 2012). This passage of Isaiah was not treated by Jews as a prediction of the birth of the Messiah anyway, and the very first Christians, who spoke Aramaic, and read Hebrew rather than Greek, would not have been aware of it as speaking about a virgin. Something must have made them *notice* the passage, once they started to read the Bible in Greek, and that can only have been the fact that it appeared to speak of a virgin bearing a child. But they cannot both have read the Virgin Birth out of the passage and at the same time have read it into the passage. It is thus probable that the belief that Jesus was born of a virgin predates the use of Isaiah 7 as a messianic oracle. People must have been predisposed to think that Jesus's mother was a virgin, for them to alight on this passage as important: it is not probable that the Greek translation of a non-messianic oracle actually generated the belief.

Be that as it may, Isaiah 7 is a central Christmas text and has been so since Matthew saw it as fulfilled in the birth of Jesus. Other texts too became central to understanding the birth stories, and this is specially clear where the events we refer to as the Epiphany are concerned: the wise men, the star, the massacre of the innocent children. Here it may well be that the Old Testament texts have in some cases generated the Gospel stories. The star that led the wise men to the house where Jesus was (rather than to the manger, according to Matthew 2:11—the manger is in Luke's version of the birth narrative) is surely the star prophesied by the seer Balaam in Numbers 24:17: 'a star shall come out of Jacob, and a sceptre shall rise out of Israel'. This oracle was certainly interpreted messianically in second-century Judaism, since it is the reason why Simon bar Kosiba (died 135 CE) was nicknamed 'Bar Kokhba', that is, 'son of a star', when he rebelled against the Romans. Christians are seldom aware of this oracle, however, and it is never read in churches at Christmas nowadays, though it appears in antiphons for the season:

> Germinavit radix Iesse, orta est stella ex Iacob, virgo peperit Salvatorem;
> te laudamus, Deus noster.
> The root of Jesse has budded, a star is risen out of Jacob, a virgin has borne
> the Saviour; we praise you, O our God.
> (Lauds antiphon for 1 January—*Liturgia* 1972: I: 303)

But the two major Epiphany texts from the Old Testament are Isaiah 60 and Psalm 72:

> Arise, shine; for your light has come,
> and the glory of the LORD has risen upon you.
> For darkness shall cover the earth,
> and thick darkness the peoples;
> but the LORD will arise upon you,
> and his glory will appear over you.
> Nations shall come to your light,
> and kings to the brightness of your dawn.
> Lift up your eyes and look around;
> they all gather together, they come to you;
> your sons shall come from far away,
> and your daughters shall be carried on your nurses' arms.
> Then you shall see and be radiant;
> your heart shall see and rejoice,
> because the abundance of the sea shall be brought to you,
> the wealth of the nations shall come to you.
> A multitude of camels shall cover you,
> the young camels of Midian and Ephah;
> all those from Sheba shall come.
> They shall bring gold and frankincense,
> and shall proclaim the praise of the LORD. (Isaiah 60:1–6)
> May he have dominion from sea to sea,
> and from the River to the ends of the earth.
> May his foes bow down before him,
> and his enemies lick the dust.
> May the kings of Tarshish and of the isles render him tribute,
> may the kings of Sheba and Seba bring gifts.
> May all kings fall down before him,
> all nations give him service.   (Psalm 72:8–11)

When Isaiah 60:3 predicts that 'nations shall come to your light, and kings to the brightness of your dawn', and speaks of people coming from Sheba bringing gold and frankincense, the original reference is to the rebuilding of Jerusalem after the exile of the sixth century (the situation envisaged in the books of Haggai and Zechariah); and 'you' is personified Jerusalem. But the suitability of the passage as a reading for Epiphany is obvious: Matthew adds the myrrh, but the gold and frankincense are already there in this prophecy. Add from Psalm 72:10–11 'may the kings of Tarshish and of the isles render him tribute, may the kings of Sheba and Seba bring gifts', and we have apparent predictions both of the scene in Matthew 2 and of the subsequent interpretation that the 'wise men' were actually kings. Again, one might think that the prophecies have generated the story, but against this is the addition of the myrrh and the fact that it does not make the identification with kings—which may suggest that there is some underlying narrative that was not simply produced by reflection on biblical texts, however much it has been elaborated by the evangelist. This does not mean that the story must be true, but only that it is not purely a product of 'midrashic' reflection on existing Scripture.

Thus the Christmas season is rich in references to the Old Testament, thought of as source of often quite detailed predictions of the events the New Testament describes. At times the old texts may have helped to generate the stories, but this is not invariably the case. Sometimes the fit between prophecy and fulfilment is loose, so that it is unlikely that the story deemed to fulfil the prophecy was spun wholly out of that prophecy. An example is the prophecy in Isaiah 7, where it is unlikely that the Greek *parthenos* is the actual source of the idea of the virginal conception of Jesus (who was after all not called 'Immanuel'); rather, a story and a prophecy were felt to have a basic congruence.

Once it was established that the events of Christmas fulfilled ancient prophecy, and were part of a continuous story of sin, suffering, and redemption, the way was open for seeing much broader patterns of correspondence between Old Testament and New. This results in what is normally called typology, where similarities between events or people in the two Testaments are deployed to indicate the consistency of God's action throughout history. Typological correspondences became a commonplace of Christian thought in the Middle Ages, exemplified above all in the phenomenon of the *bible moralisée*, in which pictures illustrate events in the two Testaments in parallel roundels down the page (de Hamel 2001). But typology goes back well into the patristic period. Consider for example this sermon by St John Chrysostom (died 40 CE):

> If you reflect upon the Scriptures and the story of our redemption, you will recall that a virgin, a tree and a death were the symbols of our defeat. The virgin's name was Eve: she knew not a man. The tree was the tree of the knowledge of good and evil. The death was Adam's penalty. But now those very symbols of our defeat—a virgin, a tree and a death—have become symbols of Christ's victory. In place of Eve there is Mary; in place of the tree of the knowledge of good and evil, there is the tree of the cross; and in place of the death of Adam, there is the death of Christ.
> (Chrysostom, *de coemeterio et de cruce*)[1]

Writers also play with the name Joshua, which in Greek is the same as Jesus (*iesous*), seeing 'our' Joshua as the one who leads his people into the promised land that is heaven; and with Bethlehem, which in Hebrew can be construed (by a false etymology) as the 'house of bread', so pointing to the Eucharist. Chrysostom's parallel between

---

[1] Migne, *Patrologia graeca* 49, col. 396.

Mary and Eve goes back at least to St Irenaeus (died 202 CE), and is celebrated in a medieval hymn to the Virgin, *Ave maris stella*:

> Sumens illud 'Ave'
> Gabrielis ore,
> Funda nos in pace,
> Mutans Evæ nomen.

Taking that 'Ave' ['hail'] from the mouth of Gabriel, set us up in peace, changing the name of Eva. (*Liturgia* 1972: I: 1034)

Typology is a powerful instrument for showing the unity of the Old and New Testaments, though also for pointing up contrasts between them. What it signals in either case is that the two Testaments are the same kind of thing, writings among which there is a certain intertextuality, as it would now be called. Events in the New Testament can be foreshadowed in the Old, as well as explicitly predicted there. Such would be the case with the massacre of the Innocents by Herod in Matthew 2:16–18:

> When Herod saw that he had been tricked by the wise men, he was infuriated, and he sent and killed all the children in and around Bethlehem who were two years old or under, according to the time that he had learned from the wise men.
> (Matthew 2:16)

This is not fore*told* in the Old Testament (though Matthew construes Jeremiah 31:15–17, 'Rachel weeping for her children', as referring to it), but is fore*shadowed* by Pharaoh's killing of the Hebrew boys in Exodus 1:15–22:

> The king of Egypt said to the Hebrew midwives...'When you act as midwives to the Hebrew women, and see them on the birthstool, if it is a boy, kill him.'...[After the midwives failed to comply, then] Pharaoh commanded all his people, 'Every boy that is born to the Hebrews you shall throw into the Nile.'
> (Exodus 1:15–16, 22)

Thus something similar happens in both the old and the new dispensations, and the correspondence brings out the divine providence behind the history told in both Testaments.

In a similar way, Abraham's willing giving up of his only son in Genesis 22 can be seen as a foreshadowing of God's giving up his only Son in the sacrifice of Jesus Christ, as is surely hinted at by St Paul in Romans:

> He who did not withhold his own Son, but gave him up for all of us, will he not with him also give us everything else? (Romans 8:32)

This accords with St Paul's idea that things which happened in time past (that is, things recorded in the Old Testament) were in general recorded for our benefit, so that we can see the consistency with which God acts in every age and especially in 'our' (Paul's) own:

> These things happened to them to serve as an example, and they were written down to instruct us, on whom the ends of the ages have come. (1 Corinthians 10:11)

Christmas and its associated festivals thus interweave texts from all over the Old Testament to create a new fabric that shows us Jesus Christ as the culmination of prophecies, but also of God's providential guidance of his people's history. The texts had never been stitched together in this way before the church got its hands on them: the pattern is not taken over from contemporary Jewish reading of the Old Testament Scriptures, but is a new and distinctively Christian creation. It is the Old Testament read with Christian hindsight.

REFERENCES AND FURTHER READING

Barton, John (2019). *A History of the Bible: The Book and its Faith.* London: Allen Lane.
de Hamel, Christopher (2001). *The Book: A History of the Bible.* London: Phaidon.
Lindars, Barnabas (1961). *New Testament Apologetic: The Doctrinal Significance of the Old Testament Quotations.* London: SCM Press.
Liturgia horarum iuxta ritum Romanum (1972). Vol. 1. Vatican City: Typis Polyglottis Vaticanis.
Migne, J. P., *Patrologia graeca.* vol. 49. Paris.
The English Hymnal (1906). London: Oxford University Press.
Vermes, Geza (2012). *Christian Beginnings: From Nazareth to Nicaea, AD 30–325.* London: Allen Lane.
Williamson, H. G. M. (2018). *Isaiah 6–12: A Critical and Exegetical Commentary* (vol. 2 of *A Critical and Exegetical Commentary on Isaiah 1–27*). International Critical Commentary. London: Bloomsbury T & T Clark.

CHAPTER 7

THE NEW TESTAMENT

MARKUS BOCKMUEHL
AND EVANGELINE KOZITZA

INTRODUCTION: CHRISTMAS IN THE NEW TESTAMENT?

An intercultural space tourist from the planet Alpha Centauri might be forgiven for wondering what the New Testament has to do with most of the themes that come to mind when discussing Christmas. Jesus of Nazareth was, it appears, a man of historical and religious consequence, so it stands to reason that his Nativity might prove to be of at least passing interest in the history of his cultural footprint. Hence, perhaps, the utility of studying the festival that celebrates his birth. And yet the slender ancient biblical accounts of that Nativity evoke virtually nothing of what Christmas has now meant to most people for well over a century. Scripture supplies no stable, donkey, three kings, or numerous other props of seasonal children's pageants—and certainly no hint of the implausibly hirsute and pot-bellied delivery driver and fluffy theme-park menagerie whose mythology services the insatiable appetite of a global consumer behemoth.

Perhaps there is little or nothing to be said about 'Christmas' and the New Testament? Quite apart from the contemporary connotations, our interstellar visitor might well conclude that even the Bible's own interest in the birth of Jesus looks remarkably constrained.

Virtually all New Testament writers foreground the death and Resurrection of Jesus, while the Gospels additionally focus on his public ministry of teaching and healing. But only two of them—Matthew and Luke—care to narrate his birth. More puzzlingly still, even these two do so in disparate ways that are not easily reconciled. They conjure up his genealogical descent through different sons of David; with or without a connection to the priestly family of John the Baptist; either Bethlehem or Nazareth as the home of Mary and Joseph; either Mary or Joseph as the recipient of angelic instruction; either shepherds in the fields or astrologers from the East as the first visitors to worship the divine child; either Jerusalem or Egypt as the Holy Family's first destination before eventually settling in Nazareth.

Even in these two Gospels the opening story of Jesus' birth seems almost entirely disconnected from the bulk of their account about his public life, death, and Resurrection: none of the events and protagonists around his birth and infancy plays any further part in the bulk of their narrative. In what sense, then, does Christmas really matter for the New Testament, and vice versa? This chapter aims to show that in fact it matters a great deal. We will find the narrative accounts of the Nativity to constitute just two of several important threads in a richly textured and colourful tapestry of reflection on the reality of 'Jesus becoming Jesus'—or in more traditional terms, of how in Jesus, God became man.

The New Testament in its canonical order begins with Matthew, and thus with the origin and birth of Jesus. But the reader soon realizes that what Matthew and Luke narrate, Mark either ignores or presumes, and John engages instead in the soaring mystical language of his Prologue. We will begin our discussion of the four Gospels with Mark and end with John, before going on to consider the New Testament's other non-narrative conceptions of Christmas. Our conclusion synthesizes these findings in relation to their reception among the earliest Christian readers.

Mark

This earliest of the four Gospels opens on a strikingly taciturn and mysterious note regarding the origins of Jesus, with no opening reflection of any kind on his birth or background. Identified as 'Messiah' without any human descent, he appears out of nowhere to be baptized by John (1:1, 9), who suddenly emerges 'in the wilderness' with a message of repentance fulfilling Old Testament prophecy (1:1–4, quoting Mal. 3:1; Isa. 40:3). There is no mention of either Bethlehem or Nazareth as the place of Jesus' birth, no genealogy of either parent, no virginal conception or Nativity, no childhood or youth. Mark's striking silence on our subject of Christmas explains his historic absence from seasonal readings, carols, or pop tunes, Handel's *Messiah*, or Bach's *Christmas Oratorio*.

Although Mark nowhere mentions Bethlehem, he does feature the open scepticism of Nazareth, whose villagers object to implausible claims about a Jesus they have known all his life: a mere carpenter, with four well-known brothers and several sisters still living in the same place (6:3). Their words intend to insult or perhaps to patronize and co-opt, but Mark implies no doubt about their factual truthfulness.

That said, one noteworthy feature of this encounter is that it identifies Jesus as the son not of Joseph but of *Mary*. Jesus has a *brother* called Joseph in this Gospel (6:3), but not a father—even if Jewish naming custom would leave the existence of a Joseph senior perfectly plausible (cf. Luke 1:59–61). Mark also envisages no continuing role for the mother of Jesus, who has by this point already been compared to his female disciples (3:31–5). Attempts to identify her with Mary the 'mother of James and Joseph' are implausible (15:40, 47; 16:1; cf. Marcus 2000; 2009: 1060).

Might 6:3 represent a jibe at Jesus' supposed bastard birth? That became a standard trope of subsequent anti-Christian polemic (e.g. in Origen, *Against Celsus* 1.32, 69) and is occasionally suspected already in the Gospel of John (8:41). But there is no evidence for such an accusation here, nor any attempt to address it.

One unexpected upshot of Mark's studied silence about any human father of Jesus is that it renders Mark's truncated account concordant with the other evangelists in two key respects. First, even Matthew and Luke feature Joseph only in passing at the beginning of the narrative before he completely disappears without further comment. Might this be, as early Christian tradition soon envisaged (e.g. in the *Protevangelium of James*), because he was a much older man, perhaps with children from a previous marriage, who died long before the public ministry of Jesus?

Secondly, even more clearly than Matthew and Luke, Mark nowhere pictures Jesus as the son of a man called Joseph; nor is there ever any human father figure on the scene. Indeed, this evangelist downplays even the significance of Davidic descent more than the other Gospels (12:35–7).

What accounts for this studied silence? True, it could in theory be a way of hush-hushing an illegitimate birth. But much more likely is the deliberate literary shrouding of human origins for a figure perceived throughout this Gospel as divine. Some ancient writers achieved this by narrating the circumstances of a divinely favoured birth. But certain Lives of Homer similarly capitalized on the poet's emergence from obscurity in order to assert his divine origins as the son, for example, of Apollo (cf. e.g. Ps.-Plutarch's *Life of Homer*; cf. also Collins 2007: 291).

What matters here is precisely the mystery surrounding the place from which, humanly speaking, Jesus 'has come' (1:14, 38; 2:17; 10:45; cf. controversially, Gathercole 2006). Thereby, Mark evokes a whole world of reflection on the heavenly origin—and unanticipated epiphany—of the one whose divine identity is revealed as empowered to forgive sin, Israel's bridegroom whom wind and waves obey and who is explicitly the Son of God (2:1–12, 18–22; 4:41; 14:61–2; cf. further Bauckham 2017b; Frey 2011; Geddert 2015).

MATTHEW

Readers familiar with the traditional Advent hymn, 'O come, o come, Emmanuel', have encountered already in the transliterated Hebrew of that carol's title one of the names that forms the central theological claim of Matthew's account of Jesus' birth: the infant's identity as 'God with us'. This extraordinary claim sits among Matthew's narration of scenes both commonplace (including details of biological descent and the vulnerability of a young family in the face of political stratagems) and unusual (including angelic visitations, supernatural dreams, and the appearance of a star that attracts foreign attention). Moreover, the claim is presented against a richly woven backdrop of citation and allusion to Jewish Scripture.

Matthew's Gospel introduces itself as a 'book of origin of Jesus the Messiah, son of David, son of Abraham' (1:1). This opening heading, 'book of origin'—echoing the only two other occurrences of the phrase in Scripture, at Gen. 2:4 (a narrative of creation) and Gen. 5:1 (an account of humanity descended from Adam)—positions Matthew's Gospel among these biblical antecedents as one that likewise records a cosmic narrative of origins, here that of Jesus the Messiah. Furthermore, it places Jesus himself within a specific Jewish lineage—he is 'son of David', key to establishing his Messianic identity, and more basically, 'son of Abraham', an ancestry he shares with the whole Jewish people. Matthew's genealogy in 1:2–17 fills in the details as he sees them, concluding with 'Joseph, the husband of Mary, by whom was begotten Jesus, who was called Christ'.

Portraying Jesus' genealogy through Joseph may seem an odd move for the evangelist to make—especially given Mark's previous disinterest in a human paternal figure, and Matthew's own clarity that Mary's conception is 'from the Holy Spirit' and not Joseph himself. However, Joseph plays an important—albeit silent—role in Matthew's infancy narrative as the recipient of divine revelation concerning the child's identity, and enactor of divine instructions to protect the child from harm (1:20–5; 2:13–14, 19–23).

Having located his protagonist within a specific genealogical framework, Matthew proceeds to relate the circumstances surrounding his 'origin' or 'birth' in several scenes: the revelation to Joseph concerning Mary's conception of Jesus through the Holy Spirit (1:18–25), the adoration of the Magi (2:1–12), and Herod's pursuit of the child, the Holy Family's flight to Egypt, and their eventual settlement in Nazareth (2:13–23). These scenes are punctuated by five 'fulfilment quotations'—a distinctive exegetical feature of Matthew's Gospel as a whole, but one that is especially concentrated in his infancy narrative (Soares Prabhu 1976). Through the invocation of prophetic texts from Jewish Scripture, Matthew makes sense of events in the life of the infant Jesus. Thus the angel, appearing to Joseph in a dream, famously cites Isaiah 7:14 to underscore Mary's virginal conception and to link the child's name, Jesus ('for he will save his people from their sins'), to the name Emmanuel ('God with us'). Similarly, Micah 5:1 and 2 Samuel 5:2 are invoked to prophesy the Messiah's birth in Bethlehem when the Magi arrive at Herod's court searching for the 'king of the Jews'; Hosea 11:1 is fulfilled in the infant Jesus' flight to Egypt, and subsequent journey out of it; Rachel's weeping in Jeremiah 31:15 is linked to the massacre of the Innocents; and an ambiguous quotation from 'the prophets' serves to underline the Holy Family's settling in Nazareth at the conclusion of the infancy narrative.

These explicit appeals to Jewish Scripture to elucidate specific scenes are combined with a more subtle feature of Matthew's text, in which the life of the infant Jesus parallels the life of Israel's great leader and lawgiver, Moses, as recorded in the Hebrew Bible and in later midrashic traditions (e.g. both children are saved from the cruelty of a powerful king; see further examples in Davies and Allison 1988: 192–3). Even beyond the parallels with Moses, the infant Jesus' flight to Egypt and return is depicted as repeating the experience of the nation of Israel more broadly—particularly through Matthew's use of Hosea 11:1, which in its original context unambiguously refers to Israel as God's son. For Matthew, the fate of Jesus is closely bound to the fate of his people.

At the same time, a key element of Matthew's narrative indicates that the infant's impact extends well beyond Israel's borders. The 'Magi from the east' have captivated readers from antiquity; depictions of the Magi and the star that guides them are among the first to appear in early Christian art (cf. Jensen 2001). Interestingly, while interpreters have theorized Persia, Arabia, or perhaps Babylon as the Magi's location of origin, and tradition has long presented them as a trio, Matthew's text reveals neither of these pieces of information. Instead, the details that matter to Matthew are those that relate to their pilgrimage to the newborn 'king'. The magi's story is one of vision ('we have seen his star at its rising') and devotion ('we have come to worship him'); juxtaposed with these elements are King Herod's inability to find the child and disinterest in paying him homage. Interpreters of this passage have often noticed its irony: while foreign astrologers display a keen recognition of the child's royal significance, others among Jesus' own people lack this insight.

What does Matthew's account offer to our picture of Christmas in the New Testament? On the literary level, it uniquely sketches details of Joseph's experience surrounding Jesus' birth, and provides the only New Testament account of the star, the Magi, and circumstances surrounding the flight to Egypt. Theologically, it constitutes the first scriptural attestation of a cornerstone of Christian faith—Mary's virginal conception of Jesus by the Holy Spirit—and in drawing attention to two names, Jesus and Emmanuel, provides key information about the child's mission and identity. As noted previously, the notion of 'God with us' encompasses much of what Matthew accomplishes theologically in his infancy narrative. In his opening combination of Davidic genealogy and revelation of divine conception, Matthew begins to illuminate the mystery of God entering the drama of human history at his birth. Through illustrating Nativity scenes against a wider panorama of scriptural citation and allusion, the infant is shown to be in a close solidarity with his people; at the same time, Matthew's account of the Magi hints that the child's identity as 'God with us' would hold far-reaching significance, even beyond Israel.

LUKE

Luke's infancy narrative furnishes such familiar Christmas motifs as the swaddled baby Jesus in a manger, the 'Gloria' of singing angels, and shepherds watching their flocks by night. Yet within the profound literary and theological artistry of Luke's composition it is difficult to isolate a single line or motif that encompasses the whole. Perhaps the words of the angel to the shepherds on that holy night provide a fitting point of entry: 'Behold I bring you good news, a great joy for all people: for to you is born this day in the city of David a Saviour, who is the Messiah, the Lord. And this will be a sign for you: you will find the baby wrapped in swaddling clothes and lying in a manger' (2:10–12). In a manner analogous to the angel's message, Luke's infancy narrative has spoken in a particularly compelling and intimate way to readers throughout history, inviting them into its evocative scenes to encounter the mystery of a child who is both Lord and lowly.

Luke accomplishes this in an account that in literary terms is remarkably different from Matthew's. He offers the perspective of Mary rather than Joseph; introduces characters who do not appear in Matthew (the angel Gabriel; John the Baptist and his parents, Zechariah and Elizabeth; shepherds; Simeon and Anna); and does not mention others whom Matthew does feature (the Magi; King Herod). Theologically, however, Luke provides resonance with Matthew's account in several important ways. He affirms the virginal conception of Jesus through the Holy Spirit, and illustrates the child's inextricable connection to his native Judaism while simultaneously asserting his significance for 'all people.'

Luke begins his Gospel not with Jesus' genealogy (which he provides later, in 3:23–38), but with a short preface (1:1–4). Here he references previously written accounts of Jesus' life, and emphasizes the orderly and reliable nature of his own account, based on eyewitness testimony. Interpreters often wonder how far this claim extends to the infancy narrative: Did Luke have access to any eyewitness sources for the birth and childhood scenes that he relates? One older, yet nonetheless intriguing suggestion is that Mary herself was a key source; this is based on Luke's ambiguous references to Mary 'storing up' and 'pondering' events surrounding her son's Nativity (2:19, 51), as well as his featuring of her personal experience. More recently, many have doubted Luke's access to any such source (notably Brown 1993); others have raised the possibility of Lukan contact with someone from Jesus' family, even if not Mary herself (e.g. Bauckham 2017a). However, we may construe the redaction history of the infancy narrative, on the purely literary level, at least: Luke's preface sets a tone for its reception as biographically trustworthy.

Following the preface, Luke begins to intertwine the story of Jesus' birth with that of his relative, John the Baptist. The respective annunciations and births of the Messiah's forerunner, and the Messiah himself, are recounted in parallel. Thus the angel Gabriel announces John's birth to Zechariah (1:5–25) before announcing Jesus' birth to Mary (1:26–38); there is a joining of the two families as Mary visits Elizabeth (1:39–56); and Luke completes the parallel in the corresponding nativity of John (1:57–80) and nativity of Jesus (2:1–7). Following the birth of Jesus in Bethlehem, several more scenes are narrated from his infancy and youth: the proclamation of angels and visit of shepherds (2:8–20); the circumcision and presentation of Jesus in the Jerusalem Temple, with Simeon and Anna as witnesses (2:21–40); and the finding of the 12-year-old Jesus in the Temple (2:41–52).

Luke's account of Jesus' origins connects the child deeply and intimately with his native Judaism. In agreement with Matthew, Luke repeatedly affirms that Jesus is of

Davidic lineage; furthermore, according to ancient interpretations of Luke 1:27, Jesus' connection to the 'house of David' is portrayed not only through Joseph, but even more substantially through his mother Mary (Bockmuehl 2011). The Temple in Jerusalem features in three of Luke's infancy scenes; details of its liturgical cult set the stage for the priest Zechariah's encounter with Gabriel before the altar of incense. Mary and Joseph are shown to be faithfully observant of Jewish laws and customs, including circumcising their son, performing acts of purification, sacrifice, and consecration after childbirth (see further Kozitza 2020), and making the pilgrimage to Jerusalem for the Passover feast.

While Luke does not employ Matthew's method of using 'fulfilment quotations', his infancy account similarly resounds with Jewish Scripture, and other Jewish modes of writing in the Second Temple period. This is perhaps most clearly exhibited in the four canticles interspersed throughout the infancy narrative: Mary's Magnificat (1:46–55), Zechariah's Benedictus (1:67–79), the angelic multitude's Gloria in Excelsis (2:14), and Simeon's Nunc Dimittis (2:29–32). These texts are strikingly evocative of the poetry we find in the Psalter, Isaiah, and elsewhere in the Hebrew Bible (Farris 1985), and even more contemporaneously with Luke, in some of the Dead Sea Scrolls (Brooke 2005: 272–81). In the Annunciation to Mary, we find further tantalizing resonance with Qumran; specifically, 4Q246, in its prophecy of a future royal figure, shares several parallels with Gabriel's announcement of Jesus' greatness, eternal kingdom, and divine sonship (Brooke 2005: 263–4). While claims about contact between the Lukan and Qumranic texts are likely taking things too far, the striking resemblances nevertheless invite the possibility that both texts arise out of a similar Jewish milieu of Messianic expectation.

Another important Christological aspect of the Annunciation echoes an assertion of Matthew's infancy narrative: Mary's conception of the child through the Holy Spirit. Luke elaborates on Matthew's somewhat sparser version, with Gabriel's answer to Mary's questioning: 'The Holy Spirit will come upon you, and the power of the Most High will overshadow you; and therefore the one born will be called holy, the son of God' (1:35). Other Christological details emerge in the responses of characters throughout the infancy narrative. Both Elizabeth and Zechariah refer to the son in Mary's womb as the 'Lord' (1:43, 76), terminology that overlaps with that of God himself (e.g. 1:68). The angel who appears to the shepherds adds two more titles: the child is 'a Saviour, who is the Messiah, the Lord' (2:11). Later, the Holy Family encounters Simeon in Jerusalem, a man waiting for 'the consolation of Israel' (2:25), as well as to behold 'the Lord's Messiah' (2:26). When Simeon takes the infant Jesus in his arms, he addresses God in his canticle, the Nunc Dimittis: 'My eyes have seen your salvation, which you have prepared before the face of all peoples, light for the revelation of the nations and the glory of your people Israel' (2:30-2). At the age of 12, Jesus astonishes Jerusalem rabbis with his religious understanding, and Mary and Joseph with his devotion to the affairs of 'my Father' (2:49). Each of these details lends a layer of colour to Luke's portrait of the child's identity and mission. The various titles present a complex mix of salvific, Messianic, and divine attributes.

Simeon's pronouncement on the significance of Jesus' birth strikes a balance between the child's importance within his native Judaism, and his impact on a more global scale. The final scene of Jesus' childhood gestures forward, toward his adult teaching ministry and his personal focus on a divinely appointed task understood by few.

Because of Luke's emphasis on Mary's role in the birth of Jesus, his narrative also contains seeds of Mariological reflection which continue to develop in later apocryphal narrative (especially the second century *Protevangelium of James*) and early doctrinal debates. Luke's portrait of Mary foregrounds her virginity (1:27, 34), and associates her with the 'grace' or 'favour' of the Lord (1:28, 30). The Annunciation is presented as a dialogue, in which Mary freely interrogates Gabriel's message before offering her consent: 'Behold, the handmaiden of the Lord; let it be for me according to your word' (1:38). During her pregnancy, Mary is hailed by Elizabeth as 'blessed among women' and 'the mother of my Lord' (1:42–3)—epithets that anticipate what Mary herself prophesies in her Magnificat: 'from now on all generations will call me blessed' (1:48).

Before concluding this section, it is perhaps worth noting that the book of Acts— another New Testament writing widely attributed to Luke, which recounts the early history of the apostles and Christian mission following the ascension of Jesus—is strikingly silent about how Christ came to be in the world. Mary 'the mother of Jesus' and his siblings are mentioned briefly in 1:14, and Peter and Paul allude to Jesus' Davidic lineage in their speeches to Jewish audiences in 2:30 and 13:23, respectively. For the most part, the narrative of Jesus' life in Acts (notably in the Petrine Gospel summary of 10:34–43) looks more like that of Mark than that of Luke: beginning with his baptism, not birth. Still: on the substantive conviction that Jesus of Nazareth was both Son of David and Son of God, Acts is at one with the Gospels.

This puzzle in Acts notwithstanding, Luke's overall contribution to the celebration of Christmas cannot be overestimated. Uniquely within the New Testament he offers the extended perspective of Jesus' mother, Mary, as well as miniature portraits of Zechariah and Elizabeth, the manger in Bethlehem, angels and shepherds, Simeon at the presentation of the infant in the Temple, and finally Jesus at 12 years old. Theologically, his complex portrayal holds the exalted identity of the newborn child ('Lord', 'Messiah', 'Son of God'; etc.) together with the modest circumstances of his birth in the city of David. His account vividly highlights the child's Jewish identity, while hinting at his broader significance 'for all people'.

Readers of both infancy narratives have long been curious about historical questions surrounding the events they contain, as well as the process of their respective stories' composition. For modern readers, such questions have become more persistent, and answers more sceptical. How much of what Matthew and Luke relate really happened? How can we reconcile the two accounts historically, when they differ so strikingly? There remains a spectrum of scholarly reflections on these issues. For some, only the barest of overlapping details qualify as historical fact—Jesus' name, perhaps the names of his parents, Mary and Joseph—and the rest is pure invention. There are also a range of approaches to the distinction between historical fact and theological truth. For some, various scenes might express a theological truth while remaining unhistorical in terms of factual events (see, e.g. this approach in Brown 1993). Still others defend the historical value of additional details (e.g. Kozitza 2020 on the Jewish customs cited in Luke's presentation scene), or even of the narratives more broadly (e.g. the more popular, though intellectually thoughtful treatment of Benedict XVI 2012). However one might be inclined to approach such questions, if the infancy narratives are understood in the way described here—as accounts that seek to paint in words the paradox of the divine entering history—then the narratives themselves resist facile answers to issues of history and theology. Rather, their purpose is to invite each reader to grapple with these questions for herself.

JOHN

John, like Mark, lacks a narrative of the birth and the early life of Jesus to match those of Matthew and Luke. But whereas the theme of 'Christmas'—Jesus becoming Jesus—remains evocatively quiescent in Mark, it is keenly explicit and extravagantly spread all over this fourth Gospel.

Twentieth-century scholarship often regarded this evangelist as less interested in history and historical narrative. But this is to misunderstand a writer with a keen eye for historical detail, particularly of the passion story in Jerusalem, and who characteristically rolls history and significance into one. Where the other three Gospels unfold a cumulative picture of Christ that turns out to be more than the sum of its parts, the fourth Gospel's Christology bursts onto the scene fully fledged from the start—and each part already radiates and presupposes the whole. Beginning with the opening lines, we are in no doubt that in Jesus the Eternal Word, the light of humanity, came into the world, 'becoming flesh' and taking up residence among us to overcome the darkness (1:4, 5, 9, 14), thereby 'exegeting' who God is for us (1:18). His birth, although never narrated, marks the point at which, as one 'sent into the world' by the Father 'from above', he 'came down from heaven' (3:17; 6:41, 51; cf. 8:23; 10:36; 12:46; 17:18; 18:37, etc.). This daring assertion understandably meets with just the kind of incredulity (6:42) that Mark reports in Nazareth.

At one level, this heavenly origin patently downplays the question of Jesus' birth, and gives his life and purpose a timelessness that sets him apart from others, famously including Abraham: 'Before Abraham was, I am' (8:58). And yet his birth is at the same time vital to his mission. Before Pilate he testifies about his own birth, 'I was *born* and *came into the world* to bear witness to the truth' (18:37).

What is more, that divine birth is vitally interwoven with the Gospel's affirmation that human salvation is quite concretely through union with Christ. This theme is fully developed in the discourse about the Bread of Life (6:35–58), the branches abiding in the vine (15:1–11), or in the so-called High-Priestly Prayer for the disciples (17:21, 23, 26). At the same time, his heavenly birth is instrumental to the notion that believers must be 'born from above', as followers of the Son of Man who descends and is born 'from above... from heaven' precisely for this purpose: to save the world through him (3:3, 5, 7, 13, 17, 31; cf. 8:23).

THE LETTERS AND REVELATION

Space precludes a fuller consideration of Christmas in the non-narrative writings of the New Testament. But as Mark and John demonstrate and the Fathers from Ignatius to Athanasius and the Creeds amply illustrate, early Christian writers were often strikingly eloquent about the importance of Christmas—Jesus becoming Jesus—without requiring a birth narrative of their own.

Despite his claim to be an eyewitness of the risen Lord (1 Cor. 9:1), St Paul was not an apostolic eyewitness and tradition-bearer of Jesus' life and teaching. He receives and transmits authoritative tradition about the Last Supper and about Jesus' death and Resurrection (1 Cor. 7:10; 9:14; 11:23–5; 15:3–8), and most scholars accept his additional familiarity with some gospel teachings about the Parousia (e.g. 1 Thess. 4:15–17; 5:1–7) or the moral instruction and example of Jesus (e.g. Rom. 12:14–21; 13:7–10; 14:14). But Paul's theological and 'quasi-narrative' interest in Jesus is overwhelmingly focused on his death and Resurrection rather than on his birth and youth. He appears to know nothing of either Bethlehem or even Nazareth, and the only concession to the family of Jesus is his naming of James as 'the Lord's brother' (Gal. 1:19; cf. 2:9, 12; 1 Cor. 15:7).

Nevertheless, what Paul does say about the Incarnation is both clear and in key essentials remarkably consistent with the wider early Christian witness. Being in the form of God, in being born human Jesus made himself nothing, taking on a slave's form in humble obedience all the way to the cross (Phil. 2:6–8). Being rich, he deliberately became a pauper to make his people rich (2 Cor. 8:9). Despite Paul's overwhelmingly Gentile readership, he insists on Jesus' birth to a Jewish mother and Messianic mission to Israel (e.g. Gal. 4:4–5; Rom. 9:5), and at vital points affirms the Messiah's Davidic descent in terms reminiscent of the Lucan Paul's exposition to the synagogue at Pisidian Antioch (Acts 13:23, cited earlier; cf. Rom. 1:3; 2 Tim. 2:8).

The later Pauline letters affirm that the fullness of God came to reside in Jesus, so that the 'Christmas event' of the Incarnation was the moment of his saving divine 'epiphany' when he was 'manifested in flesh' (Col. 1:19; 2 Tim. 1:10; Tit. 2:11; 3:4; 1 Tim. 3.16). A comparable reading of Christmas as theophany surfaces briefly in Hebrews (1:6; cf. 9:28), typically interpreted as Pauline from antiquity (including Origen: see Thomas 2019) to the King James Version.

This same conviction that Jesus was 'manifested' (1:20) at his Incarnation is undergirded in 1 Peter, as also in the famously anti-Docetic 1 John: being sent into the world as God's only Son, Jesus was the Word of Life 'made manifest' to take away our sins and to destroy the devil (4:9, 14; 1:2; 3:5, 8). That moment is his 'coming in the flesh' (1 John 4:2; 2 John 7).

The Book of Revelation's singular focus is on Jesus Christ's revelation of 'what must soon take place' (1:1) rather than on his first coming at Christmas (while retaining some awareness e.g. of his Davidic descent: 3:7; 5:5; 22:16). Yet the entire message of this book is bracketed by the 'Advent' affirmation of his 'coming' (1:7; 3:11, 20; 12:10; 16:15; 22:7, 12, 20) in judgment and redemption, which recapitulates and completes the New Testament's 'God with us' theme of Christmas: 'Look! God's dwelling place is now among the people, and he will dwell with them. They will be his people, and God himself will be with them and be their God. He will wipe every tear from their eyes' (21:3–4 NIV).

THE EARLIEST READERS

The earliest readers of the New Testament reflected on various aspects of its witness to the origins of Jesus. Much of this early interest is of an apologetic nature, as ancient Christians sought to tease out the theological implications of their texts and to clarify their beliefs in the face of opposition and debate. For example, the *First Apology* of Justin Martyr (100–165 CE), and his *Dialogue with Trypho* defend the divine and human descent of Christ, contrasting the virgin birth with Graeco-Roman myths and drawing extensively from prophetic Scripture. Irenaeus of Lyons' (c. 130–220 CE) *Against Heresies* is another key text in early theological reflection on the Incarnation. Origen of Alexandria (c. 185–254 CE) takes on early polemics surrounding the circumstances of Jesus' birth in *Against Celsus*.

Furthermore, multiple traditions that historically have been associated with the Christmas narrative arose through ancient interpretations of the New Testament. Key examples are found in the second-century apocryphal *Protevangelium of James*—including Mary's riding of a donkey into Bethlehem, the birth of Jesus in a cave, and a bright light appearing inside it (see Bockmuehl 2018 for more examples). This and other ancient infancy gospels attempted to fill gaps in the New Testament birth narratives: the *Protevangelium* fills in details of Mary's biography from her childhood up to and including the events recorded in Matthew and Luke, while the similarly early *Infancy Gospel of Thomas* sketches a somewhat disconcerting account of Jesus' early childhood as a precocious and tyrannical young miracle worker. Other more well-known motifs—such as the ox and ass at Jesus' manger, and the Magi as a trio—begin to appear in early Christian art.

Finally, the New Testament infancy narratives held a strong devotional and liturgical appeal to readers in antiquity. An early tradition (attested both in the *Protevangelium* and Justin Martyr) located the Lukan 'manger' in a particular cave in Bethlehem—a site which attracted the devotion of pilgrims at least from the third century (cf. Origen, *Against Celsus* 1.51; as well as the pilgrim Egeria's *Itinerarium* 42; and Jerome, *Epistles* 46.11; 58.3; 108.10), and over which the Constantinian Basilica of the Nativity was built in the fourth century. The four canticles of Luke's infancy narrative were variously incorporated into the prayer of the Church at least from the fourth century, and three important ancient feasts—Epiphany, Candlemas, and of course, Christmas—aided early Christians in liturgical reflection and participation in these events.

Conclusion: The New Testament in Christmas

This chapter has presented several distinct strands in the New Testament's tapestry of reflection on the nativity of Jesus—from the mystery surrounding his origins in Mark (and similarly in Acts), to the respective infancy narratives of Matthew and Luke, to the assertion of the Word's heavenly origin that permeates John, and non-narrative conceptions of Jesus' coming into the world in the letters and Revelation.

We have endeavoured to show that the New Testament texts are vitally central to the celebration of Christmas; in doing so, we have observed that they contribute to our conception of Christmas—the event of 'Jesus becoming Jesus'—in sometimes surprising ways. Familiar motifs such as the Christmas star and baby's manger, for example, originate in two very different accounts of Jesus' birth, which nonetheless agree on several essential points: the infant's Davidic and divine descent, his Messianic mission to Israel, and global significance. Even beyond the more recognizable infancy narratives, other layers in the New Testament's witness have been shown to have a significant bearing on our theme—as is partially illustrated by the fact that in ecclesial communities John's prologue is often read at Christmas alongside the infancy narratives, and that portions of Revelation are often read during the preceding season of Advent, which looks toward the coming of Christ. Even Mark's ambiguity surrounding human genealogy gestures meaningfully toward divine origins, and non-narrative statements in Paul and other letter writers contribute strokes in harmony with an overall picture that is complex, but strikingly consistent.

The New Testament may not appear to our opening paragraph's interstellar tourist to have much in common with contemporary connotations of Christmas. In fact, however, and as we have confirmed in its earliest reception, the New Testament bears strong and complex witness to an idea that has constituted the reason and the heart of this celebration for many throughout history: God came into the world as a man, born to a human mother, in solidarity with the human race and to save it.

References And Further Reading

Bauckham, Richard (2017a). 'Luke's Infancy Narrative as Oral History in Scriptural Form', in *The Christian World Around the New Testament: Collected Essays II*. Wissenschaftliche Untersuchungen zum Neuen Testament 386. Tübingen: Mohr Siebeck: 131–42.

Bauckham, Richard (2017b). 'Markan Christology According to Richard Hays: Some Addenda', *Journal of Theological Interpretation*, 11: 21–36.

Benedict XVI, Pope (2012). *Jesus of Nazareth: The Infancy Narratives*. London: Bloomsbury.

Bockmuehl, Markus (2011). 'The Son of David and His Mother', *Journal of Theological Studies*, 62: 476–93.

Bockmuehl, Markus (2018). 'Scriptural Completion in the Infancy Gospel of James', *Pro Ecclesia*, 27: 180–202.

Brooke, George J. (2005). *The Dead Sea Scrolls and the New Testament*. Minneapolis: Fortress.

Brown, Raymond E. (1993). *The Birth of the Messiah: A Commentary on the Infancy Narratives in the Gospels of Matthew and Luke*. 2nd edn. New York: Doubleday.

Collins, Adela Yarbro (2007). *Mark: A Commentary*. Hermeneia commentary series. Minneapolis: Fortress Press.

Davies, W. D. and Allison, Dale C. (1988). *A Critical and Exegetical Commentary on the Gospel According to Saint Matthew*. International Critical Commentary. Vol. 1. Edinburgh: T&T Clark.

Farris, Stephen (1985). *The Hymns of Luke's Infancy Narratives: Their Origin, Meaning and Significance*. JSNTSup 9. Sheffield: JSOT.

Frey, Jörg (2011). 'How Could Mark and John Do Without Infancy Stories? Jesus' Humanity and his Divine Origins in Mark and John', in C. Clivaz et al. (eds.), *Infancy Gospels: Stories and Identities*. Wissenschaftliche Untersuchungen zum Neuen Testament 281. Tübingen: Mohr Siebeck: 189–215.

Gathercole, Simon (2006). *The Preexistent Son: Recovering the Christologies of Matthew, Mark, and Luke*. Grand Rapids: Eerdmans.

Geddert, Timothy J. (2015). 'The Implied YHWH Christology of Mark's Gospel: Mark's Challenge to the Reader to "Connect the Dots"', *Bulletin for Biblical Research*, 25, 3: 325–40.

Jensen, Robin (2001). 'Witnessing the Divine: The Magi in Art and Literature', *Bible Review*, 17, no. 6: 24–32, 59.

Kozitza, Evangeline (forthcoming 2020). 'Legal Exegesis and Historical Narrative in Luke 2: 22–4,' *Journal of Theological Studies*.

Marcus, Joel (2000; 2009). *Mark: A New Translation with Introduction and Commentary*. The Anchor Yale Bible 27–27A. 2 vols. New Haven/London: Yale University Press.

Soares Prabhu, George M. (1976). *The Formula Quotations in the Infancy Narrative of Matthew: An Enquiry into the Tradition History of Mt 1–2*. Analecta biblica 63. Rome: Biblical Institute Press.

Thomas, Matthew J. (2019). 'Origen on Paul's Authorship of Hebrews', *New Testament Studies* 65: 598–609.

CHAPTER 8

JESUS CHRIST AND THE INCARNATION

KATHERINE SONDEREGGER

'Love came down at Christmas', Christina Rossetti wrote, 'love all lovely, love divine; love was born at Christmas: star and angels gave the sign.' Enthralled by love, this poem repeats in every form the cognates of love, composing a garland of love, graced with twelve instances of love in three short stanzas. Published at the end of the nineteenth century, this Rossetti poem was soon set to music; with the tune 'Gartan', this hymn has become a beloved Christmas carol in the English-speaking world. The tune infectious, the lyrics gentle and warm and tender, the poet much admired, it is little wonder that 'Love came down at Christmas' graces many Christmas liturgies. But we have another reason to turn to Rossetti's words: their distinctive and rich Christology. Many of the complex themes that attend the Christian festival of the Incarnation are sounded in this poem; and those that are not are distinctive by their absence.

We might begin with the central leitmotiv of the poem itself: Love as the identity and subject of the Incarnation. Here Rossetti gives us a name for Jesus Christ that links the Incarnation to the work of redemption, a linkage as old as the First Letter of John and a widespread thematic of the Patristic era. Christology, for the theologians of the early Church, was a doctrine about the saving purposes of God: it was a teaching about what the Greek Fathers called the 'Economy', the redeeming intervention of God into the creaturely realm. That purpose Rossetti sums up as 'love'. In the celebrated fourth chapter of 1 John—surely a golden text for Rossetti—the author sets out an economic account of love that joins the Father to the Son, and in the sending, or 'mission' of the Son, the enactment of love that is to rule the community of disciples:

> Beloved, let us love one another, because love [agape] is from God; everyone who loves is born of God and knows God. Whoever does not love does not know God, for God is love. God's love was revealed among us in this way: God sent his only Son into the world so that we might live through him. In this is love, not that we loved God but that he loved us and sent his Son to be the atoning sacrifice [hilasmon] for

our sins. Beloved, since God loved us so much, we also ought to love one another. No one has ever seen God; if we love one another, God lives in us, and his love is perfected in us. (1 John 4: 7–12)

Here the author of 1 John does not explicitly name the Son as Love, yet the purposes of God are caught up in the pattern of love: a sending, a self-offering or sacrifice, a revelation that is life giving, and an indwelling that is love's perfection in the believer. The divine Economy, praised in Patristic theologians as diverse as Athanasius, Irenaeus, Theodore, and Cyril, can be recognized in this pattern that links the Incarnation to redemption, and is characterized by agapic love, both divine and human, given and sent in the Son, born and increased in the disciples.

For Cyril, as for many in the Alexandrian tradition, Christology joins together this pattern of love to the cosmic movement of *descent*. Time and again, Cyril in his quarrels with Nestorius, ties the Person of Christ, narrated in the Economy, to the 'lowering' or 'self-emptying' of the Son as set out in Philippians 2. This Christological hymn, thought to be traditional already by the time of the Apostle Paul, characterizes the 'mind of Christ' as humble—ready to set aside the 'form of God' for the 'form of a slave', obedient to the terrible way of the cross, a descent to shameful death. Rossetti's 'coming down at Christmas', for Cyril, was the pattern of descent, exhibited first in the Word's leaving realms of light for the world of suffering, human flesh, then perfected and disclosed in the lowliness of a crucifixion that took our suffering and guilt for His own. The Economy, we might say, is a double descent: first in Bethlehem, in the 'likeness of human flesh', and then in Golgotha, in the 'form of a slave', humbled, crushed down, marred by the callous execution of an inconvenient troublemaker at the edge of empire (McGuckin 2004). The artistic tradition in the European world conformed to this downward pattern by developing an iconography of the birth of Jesus that incorporated, sometimes hidden, sometimes unmistakably, a cross or foreshadowing of the Passion, and its instruments of torture, within the Nativity itself. Parallel to this close tie between manger and cross is the frequent depiction of Christ's birthplace as surrounded by ruins—a once glorious realm now in decay, a visible sign of sin's dominion and empire's long and weary collapse.

As intimate as is this joinery in Scripture and the early Church, the portrait of Jesus Christ set out at Christmastide does not always or easily conform to this pattern. The Person of Jesus Christ—the explicit domain of Christology—can be set out in idiom that is sharply distinct from the Johannine narrative of atoning sacrifice. Rossetti's hymn might also serve, by way of silence, as exemplar of this modern practice. Strikingly in this carol—though not to be sure in other works by Rossetti—the work of sin-bearing, the Passion and sacrifice for sin, do not find explicit mention here. Rather, we are presented with Love who is with us at Christmas, all lovely, love divine: this is Christ who is Immanuel, God with us. Now, love most certainly can embrace the whole of the Economy of the Word, and it is reasonable to assume that Rossetti leaned upon the wide, atoning connotations of divine love in her poem. But the absence of the 'second descent' in the hymn points us to a distinctive development in modern Christologies at work in Christmas celebrations.

The charge that the Festival of the Incarnation is 'sentimental'—that it allows Christians to dwell upon a tiny, helpless, yet loveable baby, and to ward off the costly adulthood that awaits him, and the unrelieved pain that awaits all the world's sufferers—this charge trades on the notion that modern Christologies separate the Person of the Incarnate from his work. The Person of Jesus Christ, that is, can be studied, even adored, as the one who comes to us as an infant, present to us as God in the flesh, or in William Temple's arresting image, Spirit inhabiting and elevating matter. In this way, the Incarnation can be considered a 'principle': the central story, or Economy, of Jesus Christ is the presence of the divine within the creaturely realm of matter. As principle, Jesus Christ is the instance or, perhaps, exemplar of the transcendent embracing and assuming immanence: God is not contrary to the finite but rather indwells it. From such considerations spring the notion that Christ is to be ranged among the Christian sacraments: He is himself the holy present in, with, and under the visible species, the flesh and bones of human life. William Temple and John MacQuarrie called this notion the 'Sacramental Principle' (Temple 1953; Macquarrie 1997) and, in different form, we see an instance of this in the early Christology of Edward Schillebeeckx, Christ as primal sacrament (Schillebeeckx 1963).

It might serve as archetype of this whole development to consider the high-minded introduction to the 1890 translation of Friedrich Schleiermacher's *Christmas Eve: Dialogue on the Celebration of Christmas* by the English scholar and priest, W Hastie. In his warm recommendation of the Dialogue he writes this about Christmas:

> As a Christian observance Christmas was specially based upon the tenderest and loveliest page in the Gospel History, and on what is most touching and fascinating in human life. Its essential purity, its higher symbolism, and its universal significance, invested it with a charm, a freedom, and a simplicity all its own. It accordingly gave full scope for all that is brightest and most joyous in religious celebration; and it increasingly gathered around it the fairest and gayest forms of art....But it has been above all by the domestic hearth that the dear delightful festival has showed its subtlest power; and its crowning glory was reached not so truly in high altar service, or in gay representation, as in its consecration of the sweet sanctities of home...Christmas became above all things the children's festival, and it gave a new and diviner significance to the feeble pulsations of infant life.
> (Schleiermacher 1890: vii, viii–ix)

Hastie speaks for a time and an era; one that is not ours—perhaps to our loss. But in this lofty air of sentiment and spiritual elevation, this Victorian essayist captures something our shabbier and more deflationary era has called the 'Christmas spirit', a hope, often broadly secularized, that what is mean in us can be broken open, if only for a day, and child-like wonder returned to the stony hearts we prize in a caustic and angry world. Hastie, however, has not wholly secularized Christmas. Indeed his central conviction is that Frederich Schleiermacher has uncovered in the birth of the Christ

Child the key and source to the 'higher life' that is the mainspring of the Christian Gospel. Here is his commendation of Schleiermacher and the *Dialogue*:

> For the great theologian [Schleiermacher] has shown us in the Christ as the Divine ideal of humanity, that the glory of the Nativity is essentially involved in all human birth, and is consciously diffused by the higher Birth over all; and that all human life has thus become sacred and divine. Let his cheerful yet solemn voice, then, be heard, along with all besides, bidding us celebrate the mystery of this higher life joyfully and freely, yet without the profaning presence of an unhallowed thought, and recognise it in its harmony with all the wonders of love and science.
> (Schleiermacher 1890: xiv–xv)

Of course, we must let Schleiermacher speak for himself! But not without pausing a moment to assess this broad theme of spiritual elevation and renewal Hastie so endearingly evokes.

The emotion or sentiment of Christmas—the higher life Christ brings—has become attached in a particular way to Jesus *as infant*. Though we catch glimpses of the charm of the baby Jesus in medieval art forms (we might think of the 'beautiful Madonna' tradition of medieval Germany), the patristic era seemed unimpressed by the domestic touch of Jesus at his birth. Not for them the sense of playfulness or joy in a divine child! Rather childishness, ignorance, frailty, and danger were the hallmarks of childhood that the Word condescended to, in great humility, and took as his own. It may well be that the 'discovery of childhood', explored so deftly by Philippe Aries, had to await an era in which childhood was prized as a time of freedom, not labour; and one in which parents might reasonably expect children to grow before them into adulthood. From the late modern period forward, the image of Jesus Christ as an infant has come to symbolize and express the nostalgia and longing for a love undiluted and a dependency undefiled by disappointment and betrayal. The infant Christ, in these ways, becomes a symbol of love, certainly; but even more, of innocence. Unlike the royal child of much medieval sculpture, the late modern Child Jesus is fully infant-like, rounded and open-armed, soft, vulnerable. He has become something *universal*: a child in love and in need, the delight of His adoring Mother.

In his elevated tone, Hastie has captured an enduring element in all Christology: Jesus Christ as representative. To say that the name of Jesus is Love is to capture in different idiom this same representative or universalizing office of Christ. In the Holy Infant we do not look for the concrete or particular elements of this one Jewish life— how the earthly Jesus may have looked and acted in his swaddling clothes—but rather see in him all children, and discover in this one life what should captivate us in all young life, a holy gift of God. It is a small step from here to a Christology that is embedded or 'indigenized' to every human culture. The love that is born at Christmas may take the form and appearance of an Asian child, come to expression as a member of a Dinka family, or belong in an Inuit home; He is Everychild, and his universality can be measured by his hiddenness within the childhood of the whole human family.

As in all representative Christologies, a subtle inversion can threaten this welcome note of universality. Is it exactly that Jesus Christ is present as Holy Child within every human child? Or is it perhaps that every human child lives out what Jesus, too, assumes at birth? Or to use Rossetti's idiom for a moment: Is it quite that Jesus Christ is Love, who descends at Christmas; or is it Love that Jesus Christ also is? Thus is reversed the subject and the predicate, and the true universal in this schema appears to be the predicate—love, say; or infancy and need—and the subject a member of that larger class. Such reversals were a special neuralgia for the Reformed theologian, Karl Barth, who sought always to anchor Christ's representative life in His own particularity and uniqueness (Barth 1956). It may well be that Barth, prescient in so much, sensed early on the broad, secularizing impulse that lies hidden in such depictions of the human, Holy Child. It is a continuing task of present-day Christology to properly express and integrate the universality of Christ—his gracious assumption of human *flesh*, all flesh—with the singularity and sovereignty of his unique life, this very one.

In this, as in so much, Schleiermacher will serve as instructive example. We can see in this early dialogue, for example, the inversion that has come to be known as Relationalism, a hallmark of German academic liberal theology. Early in the *Dialogue*, Sophie, one of the guests at this Christmas party, sees in her mother, Ernestine, the very icon of Holy Mother and Child. Ernestine and Sophie, a Maternal Madonna and Child, embody the sanctity and purity of higher life with us. Even Sophie spies in her mother the very Mother of God: 'Suddenly Sophie was aware that her mother was standing just behind her, and without shifting she turned to her and exclaimed with deep feeling: 'Oh, Mother, you might just as well be the happy mother of the divine babe!' (Schleiermacher 1890: 9). And her mother soon returns the high praise: 'In a certain respect', Ernestine says, 'I truly feel that she did not say too much when she thought that I might well be the mother of the blessed child, because I can in all humility honor the pure revelation of the divine my daughter, as Mary did in her son, without in the least disturbing the regular relation of mother to child.' Shortly she expands upon this intuition: 'In this sense, every mother is another Mary. Every mother has a child divine and eternal, and every mother devoutly looks out for the stirrings of the higher spirit within that child.' Even her husband, Edward, echoes this universalizing strain:

> In Christ, then, we see the Spirit, according to the nature and means of our world, originatively forming itself to the point of self-consciousness in individual persons.... Devotion and love are Christ's very nature. Thus it is that every mother who, profoundly feeling what she has done in bearing a human being, knows, as it were by an annunciation from heaven, that the spirit of the church, the Holy Spirit, dwells within her.... Such a woman also sees Christ in her child—and this is that inexpressible feeling a mother has which compensates for all else. In like manner, however, each one of us beholds in the birth of Christ one's own higher birth whereby nothing lives in oneself but devotion and love, and the eternal Son of God appears in each of us too.   (Schleiermacher 1890: 72)

So too in his extended speech on Christology and Christmas, Edward finds his highest exemplar of Christ to be the 'Word made flesh' or as he puts it, in implicit Johannine idiom, the 'whole human being' or, perhaps, 'the Man'. He says:

> The Gospel according to John hasn't any Christmas even, recounted as an external event. Yet, in his heart prevails an everlasting, childlike Christmas joy. John gives us the higher, spiritual view of our festival.... This is how I prefer to regard the object of this festival: not a child of such and such an appearance, born of this or that parent, here or there, but the Word become flesh, which was God and was with God. The flesh, however, is, as we know, nothing other than our finite, limited, sensory nature, while the Word is thinking, coming to know; and the Word's becoming flesh is therefore the appearing of this original and divine Word in that form. Accordingly, what we celebrate is nothing other than ourselves as whole beings—that is, human nature, or whatever else you want to call it, viewed and known based on the divine principle.... One finds redemption in that the same union of eternal being and of the coming into being of the human spirit, such as it can be manifested on this planet, arises in each person, and thus each contemplates and learns to love all becoming, including oneself, only in eternal being.
> (Schleiermacher 2010: 117–18)

Here we see the powerful clash and integration of universal concepts—the eternal and temporal; the unbounded and the limited, the absolute and the individual—come to their fullness in the festival of Christmas, God with us. From such speculative inversions issue the conviction that Christology is a form of 'symbol' or 'mythos' which translates the idea of 'mediated transcendence' into the narrative and concreteness of an individual life. Students of the German philosophical tradition will recognize immediately the Hegelian tone of much of this speculation. Schleiermacher, to be sure, was no Hegelian; but we are on firmer ground to say that academic theology in the early, post-Kantian era drank from the same well, a form of speculative idealism that found in concepts and ideas the very constitution of the cosmos. For such idealists, the Scriptural narratives do not themselves ground or specify the New Testament Christology; rather, they *illustrate* or render visible and tactile the idea that is divine transcendence become immanence. In this way, the 'history-like' narratives (the phrase is Hans Frei's) become subtly displaced by a concept, such that the Incarnation is not directly *about* the birth 'taking place in this way' but is rather truly about the infinite in finite matter, the eternal in the midst of time. In the *Dialogue*, Edward represents such a view, especially in its Schleiermacherian key: it is Johannine, through and through. But this is not all that Schleiermacher says; not by a good measure!

In the *Dialogue*, as in the later *Christian Faith*, Schleiermacher develops two themes that will prove strongly generative in modern Christology—themes that echo a tradition more ancient than the high liberalism of progressive Germany. Ernst, in his closing speech to the Christmas gathering, highlights the axiom that Christ is the *Origin* of the higher life, the ground and commencement of human redemption. Here Schleiermacher is searching for a means by which the historical Christ can remain absolute and essential to Christian piety, even in the face of historical development and change. In the *Dialogue*, he begins to sketch out a concept of originality that will be brought to maturity only in his later, second edition of the *Glaubenslehre*. The problem he faces is one Søren Kierkegaard will enunciate clearly a generation later: Is Christ a teacher who could be surpassed and left behind, once the lesson is mastered? Or is he a teacher who can never be excluded from the lesson he conveys, for he is source but also sustenance, without whom no lesson can be mastered? It seemed that history taught that Christ must be only the first genre of teacher; the relentless transformation of human society swept the past into a receding horizon, always further away, further alien from the now that consumes the present. After all, once the higher life is born, the Child introduced, the higher life inaugurated, can we not now continue along in the same way, following this pattern, perhaps, but under our own banner?

Influenced by the early modern historians of culture, Schleiermacher understood the Church to be a community whose language, thought-form, and practice were bearers of such evolutionary history. The past saints and doctors of the faith would be remembered, of course; commemorated and honoured, but their influence belonged to that past age, and the engines that drove the future belonged to a new generation. Such a corrosive historicism seemed poised to undermine Christ Himself. He might be founder, yes—a title the nineteenth century was happy to confer on Jesus—but could he not also be subsumed now into the Church, its teachings and ways, and be found dependent upon the pious community to recall, honour, and make relevant his teachings for a new day?

Once again it seemed possible that the predicate could swallow up the subject, the Church in its evolution and steady re-fashioning, now the ground of the Christian faith, Jesus Christ the Church's gift to the world. From such speculations the contemporary anxieties about Christology are born: Could Jesus Christ be one among many religious adepts and founders? Could he be surpassed as source of wisdom, replaced as Redeemer of the lost? Could the Church in some future day combine Jesus Christ with other master teachers; or perhaps find in some future spiritual leader that 'something greater is here?' Famously, Ernst Troeltsch considered history itself—its unconstrained future, its unanticipated twists and turns, its radical pluralism—powerful enough to unseat Christ from his throne of absoluteness, and make him, as are we all, subject to the sands of time, a Christian Ozymandias, pitiful in lost grandeur (Troeltsch 2006). Not so far from such radical relativism are present-day worries that Christ and his example must be shown relevant to an utterly changed society. How can a first-century Jew, a man (as is thought) of his time, a prophet of the end-times who apparently could not imagine a world spinning on two millennia later, be the Saviour of an urban, technological, egalitarian, and war-soaked society such as we exhibit today?

Schleiermacher answered, Christ is unsurpassable. Jesus Christ as origin meant for him that every re-birth from sin, every freedom from God-forgetfulness, every recognition that God inhabits even sorrow and tragedy, was a birth of Christ in us, and wholly initiated by Christ. Every moment of the Christian life was the working of the supernatural becoming natural: the grace of the Redeemer blessing, conserving, elevating, and healing the divided and sin-sick soul. To confess this is to acknowledge Christ as Lord of the Church, the present giver of the Spirit, and continual source of joy. Christ is Kierkegaard's irreplaceable teacher, the one who is himself the lesson and the truth. In this sense, Christmas does not belong to the past; it is rather the festival of Christ's continuing birth into the world of sinners, the Risen One with healing in his wings. Schleiermacher echoes here a theme as old as Athanasius: the Christ who is worshipped in the Church is *alive*, not dead in the past, and remains sovereign and priest over the world He has redeemed.

The *Dialogue* echoes a second ancient theme, as well, though dressed out in modern idiom: Christmas is a vividly *gendered* festival. The Christology on display in this dialogue anchors the Christ Child firmly in a world framed by the intuitions and habits of men and women, of the masculine and feminine. A German feminist, Schleiermacher hoped to advance the spiritual and cultural aims of women through an acknowledgement of what we now call 'difference': the women of the Christmas Eve Dialogue are the bearers of a higher naturalism in religious life, and their musical harmony and inner peace manifest an integrity that men, in their public, controverted, and alienated lives, can only admire and find refuge in. Significant for our task is the Christological purchase of this gendered imagination. In the *Dialogue*, Jesus Christ is feminized: He is the origin of the inner peace and harmony and joyful self-presence just because he—like Mary, like the spiritual women gathered in this warm, pious home—never tasted inner conflict or suffered under a clouded God-consciousness. He is blessed; he is blessing. (The medievalist Caroline Bynum has explored with wonderful novelty the significance of Christ's Marian, female flesh in her now classic works, *Jesus as Mother* and *Holy Feast, Holy Fast*.) Historians of modern Protestant culture have long noted the feminization of Christ in nineteenth-century piety (Douglas 1998). Here is a man (as is thought) who expresses the tenderness, and spontaneity, reserved for women (some women) who make a private reserve into a home of warmth, creativity, and nurture. For Horace Bushnell and other Protestant liberals, men who follow Christ become more as he is, more compassionate and sensitive, more loving and forgiving, more feminine in their cultural idiom and sign. Once again, Schleiermacher echoes an ancient Christological theme: the place of Mary in the Christology of the early Church.

In the years leading up to the Ecumenical Council at Chalcedon, the Metropolitans of Alexandria and Constantinople poured out invective over the proper title for Mary, the Mother of Jesus. Cyril, Metropolitan of the ancient see of Alexandria, favoured the title God-bearer, *Theotokos*, as an ancient and popular recognition of Mary's unique place in the Economy of Salvation. Nestorius, the Metropolitan of the upstart Imperial capitol, Constantinople, insisted that Mary could be only the 'Man-bearer', or more precisely, the 'Christ-bearer', *Christokos*. Certainly, these were debates over Mary and her singular role as virginal Mother of Jesus Christ. But more centrally, these were debates over Christology, the proper interpretation of his Person as 'composite', containing and in some way, unifying both divine and human natures. Once again, Cyril took ancient practice as his guide: it was entirely proper, he thought, to take qualities and properties that belonged to one of Christ's natures and apply them to the other. So the faithful had long said, and Cyril would endorse their conviction: the divine Word suffered; the human flesh was God. Such expressions were given the title, the 'communication of idioms', and under its aegis, Christians were invited to see the wonder, even paradox, of the God who came down at Christmas. Nestorius considered such talk dangerously loose and undisciplined. The wonder of Jesus Christ, he said, was that the God–man bore both natures, divine and human, without mixing or confusing either: Christ was no pagan deity, turned into a golden shower, or a golden warrior, half god, half mortal, such as Perseus or Achilles. Jesus Christ, rather, is a unitary subject whose natures do not combine or properly modify one another, but rather in perfect harmony and goodwill, enter into the singular life of the Incarnate Word. Mary, a human mother, gives birth to a human child—who is the Christ of God, the Eternal Son sent as the world's Saviour.

In the end, it required an Ecumenical Council to settle this dispute (though not the Christology it aimed to define): Mary was the God-bearer; the Eternal Word of God was born of her, suffered under Pontius Pilate, and died, mocked and rejected, in the Place of the Skull. After AD 451, or perhaps, better, after the Second Council of Constantinople in AD 553, the Chalcedonian Creed or Definition became the bedrock of ancient and medieval Christology, and of bitter debate, both in Late Antiquity and beyond, and in theological schools, East and West. In the end, this Chalcedonian Christology will shape our final examination of the Love that came down at Christmas: it will tell us—under certain conditions and with strict limitations—who is this Love who descended from realms of light to become the world's Redeemer.

Axiomatic to the Chalcedonian definition is the confession that Christology is an expression of the doctrine of God: the Person and work of Jesus Christ has to do, principally and primarily, with the Eternal Word or Son of God. The full deity of Christ is not *argued for* in this ancient creed; it is rather assumed. The rhythmic phrase that pulses through the definition—one and the same Son—refers clearly and consistently to the Eternal Son, who in these last days takes human nature for his own. The crisis that attended the Chalcedonian Council did not concern whether this man was God; all sides of the debate recognized the divine subject who was enfleshed at Christmastide. Unlike our modern worries about the proper limitation and historical groundedness of Christ's human life, the ancients addressed themselves almost entirely to the manner in which deity could assume and be joined to the humanity. Their preoccupation, that is, turned on the form of union the divine Son could make with a human and rational body. To express this for a moment in Rossetti's vocabulary: Love was for the fifth-century Church the Eternal Word; his descent to the flesh was visible manifestation of his divine nature as love. To say it simply: Christmas is about God. It is no simple matter, however, to say just how God can be the agent or acting subject of the Incarnation. The theologians of the early Church were keenly aware that the Incarnation was not closed up in itself: it was rather the starting-point for the *via crucis*, the journey to the cross. Even Athanasius, who in his early treatise, *On the Incarnation*, could speak unguardedly about the Word wielding his body like an instrument, knew that this divine subject 'came to die': the body of the Word was not merely the teaching tool of the Eternal Son but was rather the source of salvation through its passion and death. The Gospel narratives, that is, constrained early Christologies such that a 'life of Jesus' could not be envisioned without Jerusalem and Golgotha. The early Church was not a 'theology of the cross' in Luther's style, but it did recognize in the crucifixion the goal and saving purpose of the Incarnation. Now, how was such a life to be predicated of God? That was the great dilemma of Patristic Christology.

On one hand, it seemed that the Gospel depiction of Jesus—his thirst at the well at noon-day; his grief over the death of his friend Lazarus; his steady obedience to his Father; and his signal suffering and mortality, from Gethsemane to Calvary—pointed to a deity who could undergo all these things. Might the incursion of God into the world require a divine being that could put on visibility, vulnerability, passibility? Might this be a *mixture* of some kind—a mediator who belonged in the liminal realm between the High God and the frail mutability of creatures? Such were the speculations of Arians, early and late. A natural Christology of the early Church—and not altogether missing from the modern—was to combine deity and humanity in such a way that the acting subject of the Incarnation was a deity fit for mortality, a lesser god. Of course the ancient world knew of mixed genres of this kind: most of the heroic sagas of Antiquity concerned mortals with a tincture of the Immortals in their veins. We need not say that Arianism is pagan, or paganizing; that is far stronger than the surviving literature could support. It is rather that the broader cultural world in which Arians moved allowed for degrees of divinity—and that seemed to fit the Gospel narratives like a glove. Jesus Christ could be angelic; or he could be the 'first-born of all creation', as Proverbs 8 would have it; or he could be the Begotten God, the Second who at his begetting was turned toward creation and creatures. He was human-scale, from the first, and was in this way, the Love that took creatures to his heart and to his very being. It was no puzzle that this Son of God died; it was rather a puzzle to know just how this one was God.

The Ecumenical Council at Nicaea (AD 325) determined that Arianism could not defend the axial confession that the acting subject of the Incarnation is God. The Nicene Creed which issued from the Council stipulated that the Eternal Son was indeed 'Begotten of the Father', but was 'not made'—not a creature at all—'true God from true God', 'of One Being, *homoousious*, with the Father, by whom (the Son) all things were made'. The compressed Gospel narrative that occupies the second paragraph of the Nicene Creed reintroduces the central problematic: How does the 'God become Man' suffer under Pontius Pilate and die? The controversies of late Antiquity can be gathered under this catch-all: How does the Eternal Word join to human nature in such a way that this saving narrative can be true of Jesus Christ, and be true of God?

The Incarnation, Chalcedon later decrees, teaches of a divine Son who, as fully and eternally God, comprises also a fully human nature—and these two natures, divine and human, cannot be understood to be 'divided or separated' nor can they be 'confused or mixed'. They exist in a full 'Personal or Hypostatic Union'. More striking still, the human nature, assumed by the Word, must be 'of one being, *homoousious*, with us', consisting in an ensouled body, both inwardly and outwardly human. The mystery of the Incarnation is only heightened by the conviction that a fully human life, manifested to us from Bethlehem to Golgotha, is also and at once, the divine life of the Eternal Son of God. This 'two-nature Christology' led Cyril to speak of the Eternal Word 'suffering impassibly', the *Logos* entering into the Passion through his own flesh, even as he entered into the human family through the womb of Mary, the Mother of God. The one acting subject of the Incarnation is God enfleshed, at once eternal and temporal, cosmic and individual, heavenly and altogether of the earth, earthy. The Christology proposed at Chalcedon does not remit but rather heightens the tensions of all other attempts to speak of the Person of Christ: this one Lord is holy, yet become sin for us; is immortal and eternal, yet born under Caesar Augustus; is omniscient and utterly intelligible, yet the hidden one, the Man of Sorrows, who is driven by the Spirit into the wilderness, to be tempted of God; the Living God, yet entombed in a garden grave, left among the dead. The mystery of Christmas, in this tradition, is the astonishing word that God is and has done all this, for us and for our sake, yet remains fully, truly, eternally God.

'Love came down at Christmas,' Christina Rossetti wrote, a 'lovely love' that aims to be 'born in us' as love of stranger and friend and of enemy. Christology is the study of the scriptural and Church debate to set out and investigate how such Love can be of God and be God, yet ours, fully, completely, sacrificially. Christians who approach the manger with this Christology in heart and mind, will never come to the end of this mystery, for it is God with us, Immanuel, Love Divine.

REFERENCES AND FURTHER READING

Barth, Karl (1956–1958). *Church Dogmatics*. Vol IV, Parts 1 and 2. Trans. G. Bromiley. Edinburgh: T & T Clark.
Bulgakov, Sergei (2008). *The Lamb of God*, trans. B. Jakim. Grand Rapids, Mich: Wm Eerdmans Press.
Douglas, Ann (1998). *The Feminization of American Culture*. New York: Farrar, Strauss, & Giroux.
Frei, Hans (1997). *The Identity of Jesus Christ*. Eugene, Oregon: Wipf and Stock Publishers.
Grillmeier, Aloys (1975). *Christ in Christian Tradition*, trans. J. Bowden. Atlanta: J Knox Press.
Macquarrie, John (1997). *A Guide to the Sacraments*. London: SCM Press.
McGuckin, John Anthony (2004). *Cyril of Alexandria and the Christological Controversy*. Crestwood, New York: St Vladimir's Press.
Schillebeeckx, Edward (1963). *Christ, the Sacrament of Encounter with God*. New York: Sheed and Ward.
Schleiermacher, Fredrich (1890). *Christmas Eve: A Dialogue on the Celebration of Christmas*, trans. W. Hastie. Edinburgh: T & T Clark Co.
Schleiermacher, Fredrich (2010). *Christmas Eve Celebration: A Dialogue*, trans. T. Tice. Eugene, Oregon: Cascade Books.
Schleiermacher, Fredrich (2016). *The Christian Faith*, trans. T. Tice, C. Kelsey, and E. Lawler, Louisville: Westminster/John Knox Press.

Tanner, Kathryn (2010). *Christ the Key*. Cambridge: Cambridge University Press.
Temple, William (1953). *Nature, Man, and God*. New York: Macmillan Press.
Troeltsch, Ernst (2006). *The Absoluteness of Christianity*, trans. D. Reid. Louisville: Westminster/John Knox Press.
White, Thomas Joseph (2017). *The Incarnate Lord: A Thomistic Study in Christology*. Washington, DC: Catholic University of America Press.

CHAPTER 9

THE BLESSED VIRGIN MARY AND THE VIRGIN BIRTH

KATHERINE G. SCHMIDT

IN 1897, American painter Henry Ossawa Tanner took on a familiar subject in Christian art: the Annunciation. For centuries, Christian artists have been intrigued by the visit of the Angel Gabriel to the Mother of Jesus. Mary is often depicted in her characteristic blue, and the Gabriel in the robes and trappings of the artists' imaginations for angelic beings. Tanner's Annunciation, however, is singular in its ability to draw from the story the truly human elements. Mary sits on an unmade bed in a modest room, glaring at a glowing figure in the left portion of the painting. On her face is a mix of scepticism, awe, and fear. The viewer is drawn into Mary's home, and the scene somehow appears more intimate than other artistic renderings. Here we have a young woman at the turning point of her life, which also happens to be the turning point for all of humanity.

BIBLICAL SOURCES FOR THE MOTHER OF JESUS

Given her enormous place in some Christian traditions, Mary appears relatively little in the record of the New Testament. Mark, the oldest of the four Gospels, only mentions her once, and the mention reflects the Gospel's overall ambivalence about her role in Jesus' mission. She remains unnamed for the writer of Mark, called simply 'your mother' by those around Jesus. A crowd says to Jesus, 'Your mother and brothers [and your sisters] are outside asking for you' (Mark 3:31). Jesus' response isn't the warmest, to say the least, and he insists, 'Who are my mother and [my] brothers? . . . Here are my mother and my brothers. [For] whoever does the will of God is my brother and mother' (Mark 3:33–5). Mark's Gospel does have many women in the account of the Passion and Resurrection, even ones named Mary, but his mother remains totally absent from the scene of her son's suffering and death.

The Gospel of Matthew begins with a genealogy of Jesus, broadly understood to underscore his Jewish heritage and the theological meaning therein. This genealogy, however, is patriarchal. Though it does end with Mary—named here in Matthew unlike in Mark—it does so as she relates to Joseph, 'husband of Mary'. Throughout the Matthean infancy narrative (the account of Jesus' birth), Mary is mentioned either as mother or wife. The focus for the writer of Matthew is the role Joseph plays in bringing Jesus into the world, and in protecting him from Herod's violence (Matthew 2:13–23).

Like Mark's Gospel, Matthew's Gospel has women at Jesus' death and Resurrection, and the Gospel writer follows the writer of Mark in leaving out Mary the mother of Jesus and naming the other Marys: 'Mary Magdalene and the other Mary came to see the tomb' (Matthew 28:1).

In John's Gospel, Mary features more prominently than in Mark and Matthew. Although she does not appear many times in the Gospel, she appears in important moments: at the beginning of Jesus' ministry and during his death on the cross. Throughout John's account, however, she remains unnamed. She is presented only as 'his mother'.

Her first appearance is for Jesus' first miracle, as John's Gospel contains no infancy narrative. We meet Mary (though unnamed), therefore, when Jesus is already an adult. In John 2, the mother of Jesus approaches her son in order to tell him, 'They have no wine.' Jesus' response echoes the interaction from Mark 3 in tone: 'Woman, how does your concern affect me? My hour has not yet come' (John 2:2–4). Apparently unmoved by her son's refusal, Jesus' mother tells the waiters, 'Do whatever he tells you.' (These words feature prominently in the founding documents and ethos of the Society of Mary, or Marianists, one of many Catholic religious orders centred on Mary.) Jesus goes on to change water into wine, thus saving the newlyweds the embarrassment, and beginning his ministry, or what the writer of John calls his 'signs'.

The second appearance of the mother of Jesus in the Gospel of John is at the foot of the cross. Even here, she remains unnamed, even though other women in the scene are named, including 'his mother's sister, Mary the wife of Clopas' (John 19:25). Here she appears next to another unnamed character in John's Gospel, the much-discussed 'disciple whom [Jesus] loved' (John 19:26). From the cross, Jesus draws the attention of these two characters towards one another, saying, 'Woman, behold, your son', to his mother, and 'Behold, your mother', to the disciple (John 19:26–7). The last we hear of Jesus' mother in this Gospel is that 'from that hour the disciple took her into his home' (John 19:27).

Of the four Gospels, the writer of Luke gives us the most detail about the mother of Jesus. The writer does so not only through the Gospel but also in the book of Acts, which most scholars understand as a continuation of the Gospel narrative. It is in Luke's Gospel that the Christian tradition finds the story of the Annunciation, within which we find many of the details of Mary that continue within the doctrine and practice of the Christian faith. The angel Gabriel finds Mary in a particular place, Galilee, and in a particular state of life, as 'a virgin betrothed to a man named Joseph' (Luke 1:26–7). Unlike the other Gospels, Luke's Gospel gives us Mary's words, songs, and even feelings. Mary is 'troubled . . . and pondered' what the angel was saying. She asks questions, and we even learn about her family, as Gabriel also announces that her relative will bear a son as well. By the end of her time with Gabriel, after her question has been answered and she has pondered her announcement, Mary even offers a prayer: 'May it be done to me according to your word' (Luke 1:38).

The Annunciation itself prefigures the theology of the Incarnation at the heart of Christianity. God breaks into the world through Gabriel and comes not to the rich or powerful but to a very young woman, herself in 'such mean estate' (Dix 1865). God chooses the lowliness of his son by choosing a lowly young woman, barely more than a girl by most speculations. Mary is not, however, a mere instrument in the plan for salvation. She is its handmaid and steward. Luke's Gospel includes Mary's canticle, her own theological account of God's covenant being kept through her. To her relative Elizabeth, Mary sings her canticle. The two women are rejoicing at the good work of God, and it is in their fellowship that we learn of the triumph of God in Jesus Christ.

But Mary's canticle is no meek tune. 'My soul proclaims the greatness of the Lord; [she sings] 'my spirit rejoices in God my savior.' Sometimes called the Magnificat (in Latin, the canticle begins 'magnificat'—that is, 'I magnify'), Mary's canticle is more than just a personal reflection on God's blessings. In just ten short verses, she interprets her present circumstance in light of salvation history as well as eschatological promise. Mary recounts the works of God in the promises to Abraham and the rest of Israel, among whose descendants is Mary and her unborn child. This is no disinterested God, Mary reminds us, as she recalls that God has 'dispersed the arrogant', 'thrown down rulers', and sent the rich away empty (Luke 1:51–3). Thus Mary recounts the deeds of the God of Israel in order to praise Him but also to recognize the ongoing and forthcoming work. If we are to take Mary's interpretation seriously, we will expect to find God in Jesus continuing such social reversals in terms of prestige, power, and money. Indeed, the Jesus of Luke's Gospel is truly his mother's son during the Sermon on the Plain, which (unlike the Gospel of Matthew) offers no qualifying 'in spirit' to 'blessed are the poor'. (Matthew's Gospel also reads, 'Blessed are those who hunger and thirst for righteousness', as opposed to Luke's: 'Blessed are the hungry.')

The Christian tradition, specifically Catholic, hold Mary to be 'Blessed' and 'Virgin'. Both are theologically important and biblically grounded. With regard to 'blessed', the writer of Luke is placing Mary in the line of blessed women from the Hebrew Bible. Judith, for example, is called 'blessed' by Uzziah after she saves the nation of Israel from ruin (Judith 13:18). In the book of Judges, Deborah sings of the triumph of Jael, calling her 'blessed among women' (Luke 1:42). Jael, like Judith, saved the Israelites by triumphing over a man who would bring them destruction. The honour is Elizabeth's in the Gospel of Luke to situate Mary in this company of women: 'Most blessed are you among women,' says Elizabeth to her relative (Luke 1:48). Like Judith and Jael, Mary will usher victory into the nation of Israel, and 'from now on all ages will call [her] blessed' (Luke 1:52).

The Gospel of Luke gives us the detail of Mary's virginity, for while we might surmise this in Matthew's infancy narrative given her historical context, the writer of Matthew does not specify it. The Gospel of Luke's larger project is to situate Jesus as the fulfilment of God's promises to Israel. His explicit description of Mary as virgin is in reference to Isaiah 7:14. The text reads: '[T]he virgin shall be with child, and bear a son, and shall name him Immanuel.' In Hebrew, the word is *almah*, which can be simply translated as an unmarried young woman. The Christian tradition has long maintained that this implies virginity, both by historical context and by an understanding of Mary's sinless (Catholic) or morally superior (Protestant) nature. In the Catholic tradition, Mary's virginity is perpetual, meaning that even after giving birth to Jesus, Mary remained a chaste spouse to her husband, Joseph. It is for this reason that she retains the title 'Virgin' within the Christian tradition, especially within Catholicism.

The writer of Luke continues his narrative with an account of the early Church in the book of Acts. We find Mary in the upper room with the disciples where they 'devoted themselves with one accord to prayer' (Acts 2:14). It is possible to say, then, that Mary is the only figure in the Gospels to be present at both the birth of Jesus and the birth of the Church. She is counted among the first disciples, but truly, she is the first disciple full stop. She is the first to hear the good news in the Annunciation, and she responds in song. She is, in a real sense, the first Christian, the first person to have her life transformed by the love of God in Christ.

The Council of Ephesus

Mary's precise role in the ministry of the early Church and the details of her death are unknown to us from the biblical record. In the fourth century, the Emperor Constantine converted to Christianity, and it became 'the favored religion of the Roman Empire' (Tanner 2001). This favoured status meant that church leaders could safely come together to discuss and decide church doctrine from around the Christian world. The first of the major councils, Nicaea, would address the relationship of the Second Person of the Trinity, arguing against Arius who suggested that Jesus was not divine in the same, full sense as the Father. The Council of Nicaea insisted upon the full divinity of Jesus, putting forth a 'baptismal creed adapted to provide a conciliar test of orthodoxy' (Tanner 2001). Bishops would return to the creed in 451 at the Council of Chalcedon, more fully insisting on the full divinity and full humanity of Jesus.

Between Nicaea and Chalcedon, however, Mary became a topic for great debate at the Council of Ephesus in 381. In a sense, the debate over Mary's title is really a debate about the nature(s) of Jesus. In Christian practice, Jesus had come to be identified as the New Adam, for just as Adam brought sin into the world, Jesus defeated it by his cross. Consequently, Mary was identified somewhat naturally with Eve, and she was understood to have been obedient to God in the way that Eve was not. But if Jesus was truly Saviour, then he was truly God. It was a given that Mary was the mother of the man Jesus; now arose the question of her maternity in relationship to his divinity.

As part of his argument against Arius from back in 324, Alexander of Alexandria gives Mary the title of *Theotokos*. His encyclical against Arianism is the first documented use of this title for Mary. Mary was *Theotokos*, the God-bearer, according to early Christian practice and later the Council of Ephesus. The Council's interlocutor, Nestorius, felt that the title could not be applied to Mary because as a mere human, she could not be said to bear divinity. He preferred the term *Christotokos*, or Christ-bearer, because while Mary could not bear God, she did bear the man Jesus Christ in whom divinity dwelt. For the council fathers, Nestorius' position drove a wedge between the humanity and divinity of Jesus, the danger of which would be downplaying or subordinating his divinity (Arianism). At the other extreme, Monophysitism would insist that Jesus' divinity 'swallowed up' his humanity, and the Council of Chalcedon would need to undertake a more careful formulation of the relationship between Jesus' natures.

Mary in the Medieval and Reformed Church

Theologians of the Middle Ages, including Thomas Aquinas, Bonaventure, Bernard of Clairvaux, and others, wrestled mightily with what to maintain about Mary's holiness given the doctrine of original sin. In the *Summa*, Thomas follows Augustine (as he often does) in confirming Mary's bodily Assumption into heaven, a doctrine which would not become dogma until the nineteenth century (see section entitled 'Mary in the Millenium'). Popular devotion to Mary continued throughout the Middle Ages, and she collected many titles in this period: 'Queen of Heaven', 'Queen of Mercies', and 'the woman clothed with the sun' from the Book of Revelation (Pelikan 1996).

Before the onset of the Protestant Reformation, Thomas à Kempis took to calling Mary 'mediatrix' during the fifteenth century, a title that would persist through the Reformation and beyond. In fact, she retains this title both in the Catechism of the Catholic Church and in the Dogmatic Constitution on the Church, *Lumen Gentium*, from the Second Vatican Council: 'the Blessed Virgin is invoked in the Church under the titles of Advocate, Helper, Benefactress, and Mediatrix' (*Lumen Gentium* 1964). Whenever the Catholic Church would insist on the primacy of the communion of saints in the life of faith after Luther, they would insist on Mary as the first among saints. She was compared to Jesus—in a way that would make and continues to make Protestants uncomfortable—insofar as Jesus mediates between God and humanity, and Mary mediates between humanity and Jesus.

In the midst of the Church's response to Luther, Mary once again became a topic for discussion of doctrine. Much like the Council of Ephesus, discussion of Mary served to facilitate and distil the debate over revelation itself. Many Protestants would come to assert that Mary's perpetual virginity, her bodily Assumption, and her Immaculate Conception (not yet dogma but widely taught) did not have biblical warrant. Protestant Reformers did affirm the Virgin Birth, given the testimony in the Gospel of Luke. They could not, however, give assent to the Assumption or Immaculate Conception. Martin Luther did confirm, however, the title of *Theotokos* for Mary as a matter of biblical faith.

Although it existed prior to the era of Reform in the early Modern period, the Rosary became a widely popular devotion across Europe in the wake of the Protestant Reformation. Praying a Rosary typically involves using beads to count several sets (decades) of Hail Marys, as well as intermittently the 'Glory Be' and 'Our Father' (the Lord's Prayer). One uses the Rosary to meditate on stories from Scripture known as 'mysteries', which are determined by the day of the week. As a personal devotion, it allows individual Catholics to practise a distinctly Catholic ritual without public liturgy, which may have proved contentious in some places. This also places the ritual outside of the lay/clergy relationship as a practice that does not require the sacramental office of the ordained. Nathan Mitchell summarizes the advantages of the Rosary as a devotional practice thus:

> It was portable, it appealed to both laypeople and clergy, its prayer could be easily memorized and recited in either Latin or the vernacular, and its mediations required not literacy but simply the exercise of one's imagination.
> (Mitchell 2009: 6)

Furthermore, since the prayers are offered in sets of ten, one may pray a Rosary using one's fingers if beads are not handy. While this represents a bodily element of prayer found in most religious traditions, the popularity of the Rosary following the Reformation could also be seen as an insistence on the outward, external, and even institutional elements of the Christian tradition against the Reformer's emphasis on the internal and personal elements.

Devotion and Dogma

Although devotion to Mary has existed through church history, Marian devotion in the Catholic Church hit a high point in the nineteenth century. During this period, popular devotion dovetailed with official church teaching in the promulgation of the dogma of the Immaculate Conception. The doctrine of the Immaculate Conception—the concept that Mary had been conceived without sin—had been widely taught in the Church for centuries. In 1854, however, Pope Pius IX released *Ineffabilis Deus*, defining the dogma once and for all. In 1858, the dogma's definition gained notoriety thanks to a young French girl named Bernadette.

In February of 1858, Bernadette Soubirous went out with a few other children to the outskirts of Lourdes. While gathering wood, Bernadette encountered the figure of a woman whom she called *Aquero*, or 'that one', in a grotto. The woman appeared to her a total of eighteen times, with different messages and instructions. On February 25, *Aquero* told Bernadette to drink from the spring and to eat the herb growing there. On March 25, the woman finally told Bernadette who she was, saying: 'I am the Immaculate Conception' (Laurentin 1999). The dogmatic confirmation of Mary's own sinless conception from four years earlier both reflected and exacerbated popular piety surrounding the Virgin Mary. Coupled with the new, seemingly miraculous spring waters, Lourdes quickly became a place of pilgrimage for Catholics.

Millions of pilgrims travel to Lourdes every year. Many of them suffer from physical ailments, and they travel to Lourdes in hope of physical and spiritual healing. Scholars are quick to point out that these pilgrimages have turned the tiny town of Lourdes into one of the most visited tourist destinations in the world, complete with the shops, hotels, and restaurants of other destinations. Many more people can go on pilgrimage to Lourdes now than in the nineteenth century. A system of importing and distributing water from Lourdes sprung up as a result of a growing American demand for a physical connection to Lourdes from across the Atlantic Ocean. This system was maintained predominantly by the Holy Cross community, whose aim was to cultivate 'a national Marian piety' among the various Catholic immigrant groups now living in America (McDannell 1999). It should come as no surprise that the Basilica of the National Shrine of the Immaculate Conception in Washington, DC was first conceived in the mid-nineteenth century, when 'the Bishops of America declared the Blessed Virgin Mary the patroness of the United States under her title of the Immaculate Conception' (National Shrine 2019).

In lieu of undertaking the dangerous and expensive trip to Lourdes itself, American Catholics wrote letters to Edward Sorin, the founder of Notre Dame in Indiana, in order to obtain water from Lourdes. They would also write letters after receiving the water, telling of the great miracles and healings caused by using it. The water itself formed a connection between the individual in America and the miraculous events of the grotto at Lourdes. Across the United States and Europe, replica Grottoes of Lourdes stand in churches, on church grounds, or campuses—and even in gardens and yards—as a connection to the nineteenth-century apparition.

But Our Lady of Lourdes shares her pride of place in the American context with an earlier apparition of Mary, Our Lady of Guadalupe (Mexico). In fact, there are two Marys who bear the name Guadalupe: Our Lady who appeared to Juan Digeo in Spain, and the original Spanish Guadalupe, who is sometimes referred to as the Black Madonna because of the tone of her skin. In all three cases—Lourdes, Guadalupe Mexico, and Guadalupe Spain—one can use Mary and Marian devotion as a cipher for the political and social dynamics of political contexts. In France, for example, Lourdes can only be understood in light of the reconfiguration of the religio-political dynamics of the French nation-state after the Revolution. One cannot understand Our Lady of Guadalupe, for example, outside of the history and consequences of Spanish colonialism. This is in no way to diminish the religious significance of the Marian apparitions; rather, it reinforces an incarnational theology celebrated at Christmas to say that God acts within history even as God transcends it.

Mary in the New Millennium

Though the nineteenth century reflects a climax in Marian devotion in the West, the importance of Mary did carry on into the twentieth century. In fact, the next dogma to be defined infallibly by the Church was also Marian: the dogma of the Assumption, defined in 1950. The dogma maintains that because of her sinlessness (her Immaculate Conception, as already discussed), Mary, the mother of Jesus, was assumed into heaven, body and soul. This has a connection to the tradition of holy saints in the Catholic Church remaining uncorrupted in body after death. Reading this dogma historically, it makes sense for the Church to affirm the goodness of the physical body in the wake of its desecration during the horrific human rights abuses of World War II.

As for the twenty-first century, we can divide the attention paid to Mary into two broad categories: the traditional devotional form similar to Lourdes and Guadalupe, and a critical form among second- and third-wave feminists and others, mostly but not exclusively from an academic perspective.

One Marian devotion that has bridged the twentieth and twenty-first centuries is the contested apparition of Mary in Medjugorje, Bosnia and Herzegovina. Because of the location, this devotion has also persisted through shifting geopolitical realities (the dismantling of Yugoslavia), as well as war and ethnic cleansing. Like Lourdes, Medjugorje has become a place of pilgrimage, especially for the sick. Unlike Lourdes, however, the people to whom Mary has appeared are still alive. They also claim that Mary is still appearing to them on a daily basis. Pilgrims flock to her here, as well as to Fatima, Portugal, and Knock, Ireland. Marian devotion, often taking its nineteenth century or even older form, is alive and well in the West and beyond.

Like the Council of Ephesus, academic theologians and other scholars continue to focus on Mary because she gathers up so many other topics. For modern scholars, Mary provides an occasion for addressing the issues of gender and race from a theological perspective. This is especially true when it comes to images for Mary and the way in which these images reinforce notions of both race and gender that are problematic for women and people of colour: 'Images of Mary matter for Christian women because of the degree to which she has been idealized and, often, contrasted to other women' (Zimmerman 2012: 183). In light of the realities of the world's women, they argue, the idealized image of a white Mary both reflects and perpetuates notions of idealized womanhood that oppress.

Two recent examples in the American context reflect this critical turn. Benjamin Wildflower's ink drawings of Mary reflect a dissatisfaction with the meek virgin of the 1950s, and instead recast Mary as a powerful revolutionary. Wildflower's most popular piece shows Mary cloaked in a somewhat traditional robe and crown of stars, but her fist is raised in defiance as the words of her Magnificat surround her. He also produced a piece that reimagines the Miraculous Medal, another devotion centred on the Immaculate Conception. Wildflower titles his piece 'Miraculous Metal', and shows Mary standing on a pile of symbols for white supremacy in the United States, including a Confederate flag, an assault rifle, and a Nazi flag.

In a similar vein, Our Lady of Ferguson is a modern icon of Mary as a black woman in America, protector of all victims of gun violence. The icon's style is somewhat traditional and bears resemblance to icons in the Orthodox tradition. It was written (painted) by Mark Dukes, at the request of Revd Dr Mark Francisco Bozzuti-Jones, pastor of Trinity Church Wall Street, an Anglican church in New York. Here we have a new devotion to Mary focused not on an apparition but on a social reality that the faithful believe needs her special attention. It is telling and quite remarkable that this particular devotion comes not from Catholics but from the Protestant tradition, who clearly vary in their focus on Jesus' mother depending on their liturgical and doctrinal particularities. Regardless of confessional differences, Mary, the mother of Jesus, persists as a subject for theological reflection and a focal point of spiritual practice. Her place in the story of the Nativity means that at least once a year, she takes centre stage with her son in the celebration of Christmas.

REFERENCES AND FURTHER READING

Dix, William C. (1865). 'What Child Is This?'

Laurentin, Rene (1999). *Bernadette Speaks: A Life of Saint Bernadette Soubirous in Her Own Words.* trans. John W. Lynch and Ronald DesRosiers. New York: Pauline Books and Media.

Lumen Gentium (1964). *Dogmatic Constitution on the Church.* Second Vatican Council.

McDannell, Colleen (1999). *Material Christianity: Religion and Popular Culture in America.* New Haven, CT: Yale University Press.

Mitchell, Nathan (2009). *The Mystery of the Rosary: Marian Devotion and the Reinvention of Catholicism.* New York: New York University Press.

National Shrine of the Immaculate Conception (2019). Available at www.nationalshrine.org/ (accessed 16 March 2020).

Pelikan, Jaroslav (1996). *Mary Through the Centuries: Her Place in the History of Culture.* New Haven: Yale University Press.

Tanner, Norman P. (2001). *The Councils of the Church: A Short History.* New York: Herder and Herder.

Zimmerman, Mary Ann (2012). 'Being Immaculate: Images of Oppression and Emancipation', in Laurie M. Cassidy, Maureen H. O'Connell, and Elizabeth A. Johnson (eds.), *She Who Imagines: Feminist Theological Aesthetics.* Collegeville, MN: Liturgical Press: 181–204.

PART III

WORSHIPPING COMMUNITIES

CHAPTER 10

ROMAN CATHOLICISM

ANNE McGOWAN

The etymology of Christmas, from the Old English 'Cristes maesse', underscores the centrality of participation in 'Christ's Mass' to the celebration of the holiday for generations of Roman Catholic worshippers. Crowds in churches swell with 'Christmas and Easter Catholics' who prioritize Mass attendance alongside the more routinely devout on the two central feasts of the Roman Catholic liturgical calendar (Cidade 2011). The continued popular appeal of Christmas as an event prompting people to worship certainly derives in part from its very *human* holiness. The Incarnation as Christmas's central theological claim becomes accessible through one of its premier manifestations—the birth of a baby—an event often swaddled in wonder and mystery even for secular souls. The official Christmas liturgies of the Roman rite, however, do not dwell extensively on the Christ Child born in Bethlehem but rather on the salvation of humanity ultimately made possible through the Incarnation. Therefore, the celebration of Christmas in Roman Catholic worshipping communities involves situating Christ's birth in the broader context of his death and Resurrection, negotiating the placement of paraliturgical and cultural customs that nourish the piety of the people, and preaching the Gospel to people who probably know the story of the Christmas crèche but may not have embraced its connections with the cross and the call to Christian discipleship.

THE CONTOURS OF THE CHRISTMAS SEASON AND THE *COMITES CHRISTI*

The Nativity of the Lord on 25 December follows the Paschal Triduum in importance on the Catholic liturgical calendar; like Easter Sunday, the celebration of Christmas extends for an octave and beyond, encompassing a festive, celebratory season. Christmas officially begins with First Vespers (Evening Prayer I) of the Nativity of the Lord on 24 December and extends through the Sunday after Epiphany or after 6 January (*Universal Norms* 1969: nos. 33, 37–8). Regional bishops' conferences may opt to transfer Epiphany's observance to the Sunday between 2 and 8 January in locales where 6 January is not already designated a holy day of obligation. The Feast of the Baptism of the Lord, a relative newcomer to the Catholic liturgical calendar introduced in 1960, closes the Christmas season on the Sunday after Epiphany (or Monday when Epiphany is kept on a Sunday numbered 7 or 8 January). Within the octave, the Church keeps Sunday (or 30 December) as the Feast of the Holy Family and the eighth day, 1 January, as the Solemnity of Mary, the Mother of God.

The three days immediately following Christmas commemorate key witnesses to Christ (Stephen the protomartyr, John as apostle and evangelist, and the Holy Innocents), seen by medieval commentators like Jacobus of Voragine as typifying three kinds of martyrdom: 'the first willed and endured, the second willed but not endured, the third endured without being willed' (1993: I:50) Although only Holy Innocents perhaps settled in late December because of an intrinsic connection to Christmas, the calendrical confluence of these paradigmatic *comites Christi* ('friends of Christ') yields opportunities for theological reflection on the saving significance of human death and (re)birth in Christ, as in the Roman Missal's Prayer after Communion for Stephen's feast: 'we give thanks to you, O Lord,/ who save us through the Nativity of your Son,/ and gladden us with the celebration of the blessed Martyr Stephen'(2011: Proper of Saints, 26 December).

In the Roman rite, the birth of Christ and the death of martyrs are closely connected historically. The oldest extant reference designating 25 December as Christ's birthday comes from Rome, in a civic–ecclesiastical compilation known as the Chronograph of 354 or the Philocalian Martyrology (Roll 1995: 83–6). A notation of the earthly birth of Christ in Bethlehem of Judea on the eighth of the Calends of January heads a list of martyrs venerated in Rome arranged according to their 'birthdays' to eternal life from December to November, thus situating the one to whom all the other martyrs gave witness in a place of prominence at the head of the calendar. The core of a complementary necrological listing of bishops of Rome can be dated quite precisely to 336, suggesting that Christ's birth formed a festal anchor to the Christian year at Rome by that time.

Even today, Roman euchological texts for Christmas largely bypass narrative details about Christ's birth, emphasizing instead 'the marvelous consequences of that event for the regeneration of a human race fallen but destined for glory' and doctrinal reflections on its significance (Regan 2012: 45). (The solemn blessing for the Nativity of the Lord in the Roman Missal is a rare exception that *does* mention shepherds and an angel.) The first psalm antiphon for Evening Prayer I of Christmas announces, 'He comes in splendour [*magnificátus est*], the King who is our peace; the whole world longs to see him' (Liturgy of the Hours 1975: I: 394), incorporating aspects of the entire paschal mystery and alluding especially to Christ's death portrayed in the Johannine tradition as his kingly exaltation on the cross (see John 12:23, 32; Parsch 1959: 200). A traditional chant from the Roman Martyrology announcing 'The Nativity of Our Lord Jesus Christ according to the flesh' may still be sung either during the celebration of the Liturgy of the Hours on 24 December or prior to the beginning of Christmas Mass during the night (Beitia 2004).

The Masses of Christmas

Whereas the more important solemnities on the Roman Catholic liturgical calendar might be celebrated with a Mass during the day and a vigil Mass, each with its own distinctive lectionary readings and proper prayer formularies, Christmas stands alone with *three* separate Masses prescribed for 25 December (Mass in the night, Mass at dawn, and Mass during the day), plus a vigil Mass that is less a true vigil in its historical origins than an anticipatory celebration. The three Masses for 25 December evolved from the cycle of papal stational liturgies in Rome connected to celebrations in particular churches. The original Roman Christmas Mass is the Mass during the day, associated with the mid-morning papal Mass and featuring the reading of the Prologue of John's Gospel (Ruth 1994). The full set of three is first attested in a homily of St Gregory the Great (d. 604) by way of an apology for preaching succinctly at the night Mass: 'Because [by the Lord's bounty] I am going to celebrate the eucharist three times today, I can comment only briefly on the Gospel lesson' (*Homilia 8 in Evangelia* 1, 1990: 50). This set of Masses spread throughout Europe during the early Middle Ages, although perhaps not as rapidly as had once been supposed (van Tongeren 2001). Charlemagne's promotion of Roman liturgical usages in his empire helped circulate this triad of Christmas Masses throughout the West, still linked to their designated times; celebrating the three Masses in immediate succession, which sometimes happened in the modern period prior to the Second Vatican Council, is a ritual aberration (Jounel 1985: 83–4).

'Holy exchange' between divinity and humanity in Christ incarnate that opens a way for human redemption accomplished historically, celebrated liturgically, and fully realized eschatologically is the pre-eminent theological motif of Roman Catholic Christmas liturgies, as exemplified in the third Christmas Preface for the Eucharistic Prayer:

> For through [Christ] the holy exchange that restores our life
> has shone forth today in splendour:
> when our frailty is assumed by your Word
> not only does human mortality receive unending honour
> but by this wondrous union we, too, are made eternal.
> (Roman Missal 2011: Order of Mass, no. 37)[1]

---

[1] Excerpts from the English translation of *The Roman Missal* © 2010, International Commission on English in the Liturgy Corporation, (ICEL); excerpts from the English translation of *The Liturgy of the Hours*, vol. 1 ©1974, ICEL; excerpts from the English translation of the *Directory for Masses with Children* © 1973, ICEL. All rights reserved.

Exchange themes dominate the daytime liturgy, complementing themes of light, life, and the glory of God revealed in Christ. The Gospel passage (John 1:1–18) expounds them, and the first two readings already raise them—Isaiah 52:7–10 on the revelation of God's salvation to 'all the ends of the earth' and Hebrews 1:16 on God's firstborn, 'the reflection of God's glory'. They are also threaded through the prescribed prayers of the Mass. The opening collect in the current Roman Missal, inspired by a prayer from the sixth-century Verona 'Sacramentary' (Pristas 2013: 76), stresses in euchological form the deep connections between creation and the possibility of human redemption in Christ opened up when God's word dwells among people:

> O God, who wonderfully created the dignity of human nature
> and still more wonderfully restored it,
> grant, we pray,
> that we may share in the divinity of Christ,
> who humbled himself to share in our humanity.
> (Roman Missal 2011: Proper of Time, Nativity of the Lord)

This incarnational theology impacts the celebration of every eucharistic liturgy, since a variant of this prayer has been recited for centuries by the priest at the mixing of water and wine at the preparation of the chalice, giving a theological interpretation to the liturgical action: 'By the mystery of this water and wine / may we come to share in the divinity of Christ . . .' (Roman Missal 2011: Order of Mass, no. 24; on the history of this practice, see Jungmann 2012: II:62–4; Pristas 2013: 76–7).

Some older vernacular translations notwithstanding, official Latin liturgical sources never refer to 'Midnight Mass' but rather to Mass during the night (*in nocte*). The midnight time of celebration became traditional for practical reasons, as the earliest possible time of celebration, as well as theological ones, such as a Christological reading of Wisdom 18:14–15 ('while . . . night in its swift course was now half gone, [God's] all-powerful word leapt from heaven, from the royal throne'). A night-time celebration also corresponded well with the Gospel pericope, Luke 2:1–14—the angels' 'annunciation' of Jesus' birth to shepherds watching over their flock by night. Relaxed restrictions on the timing of Mass in the twentieth century and permission to schedule anticipated Masses on Sundays and holy days for pastoral reasons now make it possible to begin Mass before midnight. In some places, this night Mass was historically celebrated toward cockcrow, around 3 a.m.; a vestige of this timing survives in references to the night Mass as the rooster's Mass (*Misa de Gallo*) in Spain and countries influenced by Spanish culture (Weiser 1952: 52). In historical and contemporary settings, the timing of Christmas feasting has been connected to this night Mass, with worshippers sometimes arriving devoid of spiritual *and* physiological sobriety after prior festivities (Miles 1976: 97–8) and/or departing from church to continue celebrating Christmas with their communities and families.

The Mass during the night may have originated with Pope Sixtus III (432–50), a staunch advocate of the Marian title of *Theotokos* legitimated by the Council of

Ephesus in 431. He supervised the rebuilding and rededication of a Roman basilica honouring the Mother of God, including a chapel modelled after the Bethlehem grotto and its manger (Irwin 1986: 174; Regan 2012: 46). Once a small-scale celebration, the night Mass grew in importance during the Middle Ages as 'popular spirituality sought to commemorate the events connected with the incarnation as exactly as possible' (Irwin 1986: 174). This pious impulse coincides with the deep sacramentality foundational for Catholic liturgical theology: humans can 'experience God through signs, and the signs are efficacious because of the incarnation of God, who thereby allowed himself to be seen and touched' (Nocent 2013: 201). The other Scripture readings for Mass during the night again serve to set the Gospel account of Jesus' birth in a larger context. The passage from Isaiah 9:1–6 [9:2–7] proclaims that the child 'born for us' is none other than a descendant of David and Son of God; Titus 2:11–14 interprets this manifestation of God's grace as a source of salvation for all people.

The Mass at dawn acquired a connection to Christmas that it had only circumstantially at first. In Constantinople December 25 was celebrated as the feast of the martyr St Anastasia, and Pope John III (561–74) likely inaugurated a custom of celebrating an early-morning eucharistic liturgy commemorating this saint with representatives of the Byzantine community, stopping at St Anastasia's basilica between the night Mass at St Mary Major and the daytime Mass then celebrated at St Peter's. It became a Christmas Mass with a supplemental commemoration of Anastasia in the eighth century, perhaps in the wake of declining Byzantine influence, and thus took its place among Rome's other two Masses for Christmas Day (Regan 2012: 46). This Mass developed for a specific community and never gained great prominence. Many priests, however, took advantage of permission to celebrate all three Masses at Christmas although the dawn Mass usually was celebrated privately (Parsch 1959: 205).

Even if they are now heard by the people only in churches with early morning Masses on their Christmas schedule, the texts for the Mass at dawn have a rich theology of their own, revelling in the growing light of day and inviting a response of faith in followers 'illuminated' by the incarnate Word. The Gospel (Luke 2:15–20) features the shepherds' response to the angels' good news; they embody the 'Holy People, the Redeemed of the Lord' mentioned in the first reading (Isaiah 62:11–12). The second reading (Titus 3:4–7) connects the incarnational appearance of God's love and kindness with human sharing in the mystery of divine life through faith and baptism.

The vigil Mass of Christmas evolved from a eucharistic celebration appended to the vigil office on the afternoon of 24 December, giving it the quality of a 'forefeast' rather than the full celebration *of* the feast (Irwin 1986: 173–4; Parsch 1959: 191–2). It functioned as the final Mass of Advent on the morning of 24 December after afternoon and evening Masses were officially forbidden in the sixteenth century—although its importance as a popular celebration waned much earlier after most laypeople stopped frequenting the church's hours of daily public prayer. The legacy of the vigil as an anticipatory celebration of Christmas is still reflected in the use of Scripture readings and texts that speak of waiting for redemption and looking forward to the Lord's coming, rendering this service a ritual bridge between the Advent and Christmas seasons even though it now officially belongs to the latter, restored to an early evening celebration with the Missal of Paul VI in 1970 (Regan 2012: 47). The first reading, Isaiah 62:1–5, would not be out of place at an Advent liturgy, and the Gospel reading from Matthew 1:1–25 concludes with a brief mention of Christ's birth. The contemporary multiplication in some parts of the world of 'vigil' and anticipated 'midnight' Masses in the late afternoon and early evening hours of 24 December meets a legitimate pastoral need for convenient worship times, echoes romantic notions of Christmas Eve in popular culture, and frees 25 December for family celebrations; however, it is a historical anomaly that blurs the theological distinctiveness of the four Christmas Masses (McConnell 2007: 12).

Unlike Ash Wednesday, Palm Sunday, and the Easter Vigil, the Masses of Christmas feature no unique symbols and rituals that distinguish their order from a Sunday Mass. The abundant symbolism of light and darkness in the liturgical texts, however, suggests opportunities to emphasize Christ as the preeminent light that dispels the world's darkness, especially by augmenting the use of candles at the entrance, Gospel, and offertory processions (Irwin 1986: 181). Two regular features of Masses on Sundays and solemnities, the Gloria and the Nicene Creed, have Christmas connections. When the Gloria, a festive hymn of praise whose opening words—'Glory to God in the highest,/ and on earth peace to people of good will'—are based on the angels' praise of God in Luke 2:14, was introduced to the Roman rite, it was naturally sung at Christmas—although only at Masses celebrated by bishops until the eleventh century (Jungmann 2012: 356–7). The Gloria is not sung on Sundays during Advent or Lent, so it returns at Christmas with a particular festive potency. As a 'credal' feast, Christmas was a logical occasion for the Creed's recitation when this became a regular feature of Roman-rite liturgy in the eleventh century (Jungmann 2012: I:469–70). In current practice, the collective recitation of the Nicene Creed on Sundays and solemnities is distinguished by a change in posture underscored further at Christmas; instead of a profound bow at the words 'and by the Holy Spirit was incarnate', all who are physically able kneel at these words on the solemnities of the Nativity and the Annunciation of the Lord.

Liturgical Accommodations

The publicly appropriated meaning of a liturgy may differ considerably from the official interpretations inscribed in ritual books and promoted by theologians since people come to the liturgy bearing their own expectations, devotions, and hopes. Crèches and children are especially prominent at many Christmas liturgies, leading to inevitable 'negotiation' between people's expectations of liturgy and the rubrics of rites. Other paraliturgical customs are particular to certain countries or regions; some examples are documented online by the Catholics & Cultures initiative (Landy 2019).

In Western tradition, a trajectory can be drawn from the cave and manger complex of the Bethlehem crèche venerated by pilgrims since the fourth century to the sixth-century manger at St Mary Major in Rome to medieval liturgical plays hosted by abbeys and cathedrals to Francis of Assisi's first outdoor Nativity scene in 1223 where Masses and the manger converged (Jounel 1985: 86; Kelly 2010: 54–65). As Nativity scenes set up in or near churches grew as focal points for popular devotion to the Christ Child, some of them began to vie visually with the altar as sites for communal prayer, at the risk of 'mak[ing] the liturgy appear as merely a reminiscence of Christ's birth instead of a commemoration of the incarnation by which Christ came to accomplish our redemption through the paschal mystery' (Irwin 1986: 177).

Official liturgical texts provide minimal guidance about seasonal decoration but do either implicitly or explicitly suggest that a Nativity or manger scene should not be located in the immediate vicinity of the altar (see Roman Missal 2011: *General Instruction of the Roman Missal*, no. 299; *Book of Blessings* 1989: no. 1544). Regional and local guidelines can be more specific. For example, *Built of Living Stones* from the United States bishops' conference specifies that the altar 'should remain clear and free-standing, not walled in by massive floral displays or the Christmas crib' (2000: no. 124). Although the crèche is an extra-liturgical addition, its great importance in the popular piety of many cultures requires some accommodation of its presence within Christmas Masses, both in terms of its physical placement and devotional activities directing attention towards it. Such practices might range from a simple procession depositing the figure of the Christ Child into the Nativity scene at a point overlapping the beginning or end of Mass to an elaborate enthronement of the newborn king during Mass accompanied by 'a shower of flowers, tolling church bells, and choir voices raised in song' (Fertig 1990: 38).

In parts of the world where the Christmas vigil Mass(es) overflow with families and young children, the composition of the assembly qualifies as a 'Mass with Children'. Those preparing Christmas liturgies may make accommodations to foster the active participation of young people using their pastoral judgement and suggestions in the *Directory for Masses with Children*, such as acknowledging the presence of children 'by speaking to them directly in the introductory comments . . . and at some point during the homily' (1974: no. 17). Lectionary readings are often adjusted, especially by swapping the prescribed Gospel dominated by Matthew's genealogy of Jesus (1:1–25) for the more familiar treatment of Jesus' birth from Luke 2:1–14. The Directory's recommendation 'to give some task to the children' (no. 18) could be implemented in ways that foster children's liturgical participation (e.g. decorating the worship space, singing during Mass, ringing a bell during the Gloria, assisting at the preparation of the gifts) but also in ways that detract from it, such as assuming a role in a Christmas pageant. While not exclusive to children, abbreviated versions of devotional Christmas pageant traditions connected to Christmas Eve (including *Las Posadas* and *La Pastorela* in Mexico and parts of central and South America, the *panunúluyan* in parts of the Philippines, and *hoat canh Giang Sinh* in Vietnamese cultures) may entertain and delight worshippers of all ages when they migrate into Mass itself. Such practices, however, counter ritual dynamics demanding a fresh proclamation of salvation during the Liturgy of the Word at Mass rather than a dramatic re-enactment of past events.

CULTURAL CONSIDERATIONS

Although the liturgy of the Roman rite is celebrated worldwide according to official prescribed texts, worshippers' experiences of Roman Catholic Christmas liturgies are shaped by culture and context. These considerations impact the verbal dimensions of the liturgy to some extent. Liturgical presiders and preachers can help local assemblies relate the salvific impact of the Incarnation and its consequences for redemption to the particular situations of their lives by leveraging opportunities to address the assembly informally in ways that contextualize Christmas for the people gathered in a very particular time and place.

Cultural considerations, however, will especially impact the nonverbal dimensions of the liturgical celebration such as music and singing (including the forms, melodies, and instruments that express and support it); gestures, postures, processions, and other forms of external embodied expression; and the arrangement and decoration of the worship space and everything used and displayed within it, including 'all the liturgical furnishings, vessels, vestments and colors' (*Varietates Legitimae* 1994: nos. 38–44). The principle of progressive solemnity makes Christmas an appropriate time to bring out the best and most festive elements the local community can produce or procure in terms of music, decoration, vestments, ceremonial, and quality in the exercise of preaching and other liturgical ministries. What this looks, feels, sounds, and even smells like will vary according to factors as diverse as the natural materials available in the local environment, the socio-economic status of the congregation, and cultural expectations and assumptions about what makes for a dignified yet joyous liturgical celebration. All these nonverbal dimensions interact with the prior experiences of Christmas worshippers as part of the context in which the Scriptures are proclaimed and expounded and prayers of praise, petition, and thanksgiving are made to God in the course of the liturgical celebration as the meaning of who Christ is for this community in light of the ongoing movements of the Spirit unfolds.

In some regions, priests and communities take pride in celebrating the liturgy of the Roman rite 'by the [ritual] book'; elsewhere worshippers are more open to liturgical adaptation and inculturation. Even a very 'traditional' Christmas Mass may incorporate cultural elements, such as fireworks during the Gloria in some regions of mainland China or extended periods of singing and dancing in Kenya during parts of the liturgy that already feature movement (e.g. the entrance, Gospel, offertory, communion, and recessional processions). Worshippers in many Asian and African cultures expect the priest to prepare and deliver a lengthy, well-polished homily replete with relevant theological and catechetical content. In parts of Africa, especially more rural areas, the Christmas Eve and/or Christmas Day liturgy may be the four- to five-hour centrepiece of a day of worship, feasting, and fellowship. As one Kenyan priest recounted, 'It *is* the holiday – to be at church'. (This information is drawn from personal interviews and e-mail correspondence collected during the 2018–2019 academic year by Scott Jakubowski, CM, who surveyed Vincentian priests and seminarians serving around the world about cultural nuances in the celebration of Christmas Masses.)

Another cultural consideration related to the celebration of Christmas involves the timing of the feast in relation to natural cycles of light and warmth. For those in the southern hemisphere, Christmas comes not in the bleak midwinter but rather in close conjunction with the summer solstice. The frequent references to light and darkness in the liturgical texts of Christmas are necessarily experienced and interpreted differently in these places, and theological reflections arising from such contexts can expand and enrich the meaning of Christmas for Catholics around the globe. For example, as an Australian liturgical consultant notes, 'Christ the sun bursts upon the earth not only to dispel the darkness but to sear and scorch the land with power and might' (Pilcher 2007: 515).

Preaching Christ, Child and Crucified

Worshippers who pay close attention to the Scriptures proclaimed and the proper texts of the Christmas liturgies might experience cognitive dissonance if they seek festivities focused on the infant Jesus but find all-encompassing theological claims about salvation through an adult Christ that challenge them towards conversion. Preachers help people navigate this tension by connecting the proclamation of salvation in the liturgy with an invitation to respond to Christ with faith in life. Catholic preachers have used diverse imagery, styles of expression, and practical applications to achieve this goal in light of the real or perceived needs of their auditors. Even when the paschal implications of the Incarnation are not emphasized by preachers, they are inevitably in view within or near discussions of salvation through Christ, light and darkness in the world, and the larger eucharistic context within which such preaching is usually embedded.

Many early preachers complemented the content of the Christmas liturgy by emphasizing doctrine to safeguard their flocks from the deception of heresy (Connell 2006: I:112). For example, Pope Leo I (d. 461) insists, 'Corporeal birth did not take anything away from the majesty of God's Son, nor add anything to it, for the unchangeable substance can neither be diminished nor increased' (Leo I, Sermon 27.2,1996: 111). Catholic preachers have returned to this theme throughout the centuries to promote understanding of the Incarnation as an impetus to love God. Francis de Sales (d. 1622) explores several extended analogies to help his hearers grasp the union of divine and human natures in Christ—the three 'tastes' of the Exodus manna, iron heated in fire, and a sea-saturated sponge (1987: 67–81). Bernard of

Clairvaux (d. 1153) reflects on God's wisdom, mercy, and love incarnate in the union of soul, flesh, and divine Word for the sake of salvation: 'what did not exist was created; what had perished was restored; what was above all things was made a little lower than the angels' (2007: 110). Óscar Romero's homily for Christmas Day in 1977 extends incarnational insights to the human and divine aspects of the Church as an ongoing revelation of Christ in the world, acknowledging the suffering of the people of El Salvador and the Church's capacity for growth even 'during the darkness of night' (2015: II:148–51).

Catholic preachers have also drawn on details of the biblical infancy narratives proclaimed in the Christmas liturgies, encouraging their hearers to encounter themselves and their world in the story such that Christ comes to spiritual 'birth' anew in them. In a 2017 homily, Pope Francis juxtaposed Mary and Joseph's journey with the experience of twenty-first-century migrant families searching for space and welcome (Francis 2017). Bernard of Clairvaux preaches on the lowliness of Bethlehem: 'If only we too may be found a Bethlehem of Judah, that he may deign to be born within us too . . . [that we might] see within us the Lord's majesty' (2007: 93). Preaching to fellow Cistercian monks in the twelfth century, Guerric of Igny proposes that Christ's birth calls all Christians to embrace a maternal vocation in accepting the gift of this newborn child: 'faith working in you through charity has been born of the Holy Spirit. Guard it, nurture it tenderly, as the Infant Christ, until the Child Who was born for you may be formed in you' (1959: 45). In a series of homilies likely intended as spiritual instruction for members of her religious community, Hildegard of Bingen (d. 1179) dwells extensively on the virtues Christ's birth might foster in the soul, such as the sign of a swaddled infant the shepherds should seek in a manger: 'Clearly, through revelation, you will find Obedience, hold it in your embrace, and "place it" in Humility' (2011: 54). Contemporary Catholic women preaching on Christmas (also in contexts outside of Mass) have emphasized the decision of accepting a child and the 'labour' of bringing God's love to birth in the world (see Vieyra Alvarez 2018; Schenk 2016). Pope Benedict XVI in 2007 reflected on Christmas as a 'feast of restored creation'; Christ's coming has the potential to restore not just humanity but the entire universe.

Catholic Christmas preaching can also focus attention on who Christians are and might yet become through their identification with the glorious light and life of Christ. In a paradigmatic example of Christmas preaching, still read annually on Christmas Day in the Roman Catholic Office of Readings, Pope Leo casts a wide narrative arc from Incarnation to final Judgement that sweeps up Christians from their 'rebirth' in the baptismal font:

> Christian, remember your dignity, and now that you share in God's own nature, do not return by sin to your former base condition. Bear in mind who is your head and of whose body you are a member. Do not forget that you have been rescued from the power of darkness and brought into the light of God's kingdom.
>
> (Sermon 21.3, in Liturgy of the Hours, I:405)

The Venerable Bede (d. 735) presents Christ as the New Adam who restores humanity to the Paradise they lost: 'He chose a time of utmost peace to be born in the world that he might lead the human race back to the gifts of heavenly peace' (Bede 1991, I: 52). Catholic belief in Christ's eucharistic presence makes it natural to reflect on Jesus' birth in a place called 'house of bread' and the child Jesus as 'the One who, under the sign of broken bread, would leave us the memorial of his Pasch' (John Paul II 2004). Giovanni Battista Cardinal Montini (the future Pope Paul VI) appealed to those drawn to the night Mass of Christmas for various reasons to draw close to Christ who has revealed himself:

> Jesus comes to us in the moving form of infancy to flood us with boundless confidence in his divine innocence and to awaken in us again the good and joyous child that we were and that, with him at our side, we can be once again.
> (Montini 1964: 61–8)

With the Incarnation, God's divine Word assumed a new mode of participation in the world's unfolding story, intensifying God's offer of salvation. Roman Catholic Christmas liturgies promote a 'unitive' liturgical piety that situates the Incarnation and birth of the Son of God within the context of the entire paschal mystery, albeit often in ways that emphasize doctrinal formulations and thus demonstrate how what was to be believed (*lex credendi*) influenced what came to be prayed (*lex orandi*). Narrative and symbolic dimensions of the Christmas liturgies, including day and darkness and the birth of Christ, can foster liturgical participation insofar as they might shape a 'rememorative' piety that helps worshippers experience God's invitation to salvation in the present. On the other hand, 'representational' piety at the periphery of the Christmas liturgies that dwells on tangible 'access' to details of the biblical infancy narratives can cast worshippers in the role of observers rather than participants in God's ongoing drama of salvation (on these three 'pieties', see Stevenson 1988: 9–12). Considered incorporation of paraliturgical and cultural customs into Christmas liturgies and kerygmatic preaching can help foster a fruitful amalgamation of the unitive and rememorative dimensions of the liturgy that leads worshippers to embrace the saving mystery encountered anew at Christmas, Easter, and every other time the Church gathers to pray. Devotional experience can still shape the piety of those who comprise the Church, such that baptized witnesses who initially imagine themselves as Christ's friends might truly become his companions, fellow sharers in God's own life through the Spirit, first in worship and then in life.

References and Further Reading

Bede the Venerable (1991). *Homilies on the Gospels, Book One*, trans. Lawrence Martin and David Hurst. Kalamazoo, MI: Cistercian Publications.

Beitia, Philippe (2004). 'L' annonce de la naissance du Christ dans le Martyrologe romain: histoire, évolution et sens théologique'. *Bulletin de Littérature Ecclésiastique*, 105, no. 4: 339–52.

Benedict XVI [Pope] (2007). 'Midnight Mass homily'. Available from https://w2.vatican.va/content/benedict-xvi/en/homilies/2007/documents/hf_ben-xvi_hom_20071224_christmas.html (accessed 16 March 2020).

Bernard of Clairvaux (2007). *Sermons for Advent and the Christmas Season,* trans. Irene Edmonds, Wendy Mary Beckett, and Conrad Greenia. Kalamazoo, MI: Cistercian Publications.

Book of Blessings (1989). For use in the dioceses of the United States of America. Collegeville, MN: Liturgical Press.

Built of Living Stones: Art, Architecture, and Worship (2000). Washington, DC: United States Catholic Conference.

Cidade, Melissa (2011). '"C and E" Catholics Decoded'. *Nineteen Sixty-Four: A Research Blog for the Center for Applied Research in the Apostolate.* Available at http://nineteensixty-four.blogspot.com/2011/12/c-and-e-catholics-decoded.html/(accessed 16 March 2020).

Connell, Martin (2006). *Eternity Today: On the Liturgical Year.* Volume 1. New York: Continuum.

Directory for Masses with Children (1974). Vatican City/Washington, DC: United States Catholic Conference.

Fertig, Theresa Kryst (1990). *Christmas in the Philippines.* Chicago: World Book.

Francis [Pope] (2017). 'Midnight Mass Homily'. Available at https://w2.vatican.va/content/francesco/en/homilies/2017/documents/papa-francesco_20171224_omelia-natale.html/ (accessed 16 March 2020).

Gregory I (1990). *Forty Gospel Homilies,* trans. David Hurst. Kalamazoo, MI: Cistercian Publications.

Guerric of Igny (1959). *The Christmas Sermons of Bl. Guerric of Igny,* trans. Sister Rose of Lima. Trappist, KY: Abbey of Gethsemani.

Hildegard of Bingen (2011). *Homilies on the Gospels,* trans. Beverly Mayne Kienzle. Collegeville, MN: Cistercian Publications/Liturgical Press.

Irwin, Kevin W (1986). *Advent Christmas: A Guide to the Eucharist and Hours.* New York: Pueblo Publishing Company.

Jacobus de Voragine (1993). *The Golden Legend: Readings on the Saints,* trans. William Granger Ryan. Princeton, NJ: Princeton University Press.

John Paul II [Pope] (2004). 'Midnight Mass Homily'. Available at http://w2.vatican.va/content/john-paul-ii/en/homilies/2004/documents/hf_jp-ii_hom_20041224_christmas-night.html/ (accessed 16 March 2020).

Jounel, Pierre (1985). 'The Christmas Season', in Aimé Georges Martimort et al. (eds.), *The Church at Prayer: An Introduction to the Liturgy,* New ed., Vol. 4. Liturgical Press: Collegeville, MN: 77–90.

Jungmann, Josef A. (2012). *The Mass of the Roman Rite: Its Origins and Development [Missarum Sollemnia],* trans. Francis A. Brunner. Notre Dame, IN: Christian Classics.

Kelly, Joseph F. (2010). *The Feast of Christmas.* Collegeville, MN: Liturgical Press.

Landy, Thomas M. (2019). 'Christmas, Advent & Epiphany'. *Catholics & Cultures.* Available at https://www.catholicsandcultures.org/feasts-holy-days/christmas-advent-epiphany/ (accessed 16 March 2020).

Leo I (1996). *Sermons,* trans. Jane Patricia Freeland and Agnes Josephine Conway. Washington, D.C.: The Catholic University of America Press.

Liturgy of the Hours (1975). 4 vols. New York: Catholic Book Publishing Corp.

McConnell, Christian (2007). 'Timing Midnight Mass', *Rite* 38, 5: 8–12.

Miles, Clement A. (1976). *Christmas Customs and Traditions: Their History and Significance*. New York: Dover Publications. [Reprint of 1912. *Christmas in Ritual and Tradition*. London: T. Fisher Unwin.]

Montini, Giovanni Battista (1964). *Homilies on Christmas and Epiphany*. Trans. Michael Campo. Baltimore/Dublin: Helicon.

Nocent, Adrien (2013). *The Liturgical Year, Vol. 1: Advent, Christmas, Epiphany*, trans. Matthew J. O'Connell, annotated by Paul Turner. Collegeville, MN: Liturgical Press.

Parsch, Pius (1959). *The Church's Year of Grace: Vol. I: Advent to Candlemas*, trans. William G. Heidt. Collegeville, MN: Liturgical Press.

Pilcher, Carmel (2007). 'Poinsettia: Christmas or Pentecost—Celebrating Liturgy in the Great South Land that is Australia', *Worship* 81, no. 6: 508–20.

Pristas, Lauren (2013). *Collects of the Roman Missals: A Comparative Study of the Sundays in Proper Seasons before and after the Second Vatican Council*. London: Bloomsbury T & T Clark.

Regan, Patrick (2012). *Advent to Pentecost: Comparing the Seasons in the Ordinary and Extraordinary Forms of the Roman Rite*. Collegeville, MN: Liturgical Press.

Roll, Susan K. (1995). *Toward the Origins of Christmas*. Kampen, The Netherlands: Kok Pharos Publishing House.

Roman Missal (2011). *Third Typical Edition, for Use in the Dioceses of the United States of America*. Collegeville: Liturgical Press.

Romero, Óscar A. (2015). *A Prophetic Bishop Speaks to His People: The Complete Homilies of Archbishop Oscar Arnulfo Romero*. Vol. 2. Trans. Joseph V. Owens. Miami: Convivium Press.

Ruth, Lester (1994). 'The Early Roman Christmas Gospel: Magi, Manger, or Verbum Factum?', *Studia liturgica*, 24, no. 2: 214–21.

de Sales, Francis (1987). *The Sermons of St. Francis de Sales for Advent and Christmas*, trans. Nuns of the Visitation. Rockford, IL: Tan Books.

Schenk, Christine (2016). 'Nativity of the Lord'. *Catholic Women Preach*. Available at http://catholicwomenpreach.org/preaching/12252016/ (accessed 16 March 2020).

Stevenson, Kenneth (1988). *Jerusalem Revisited: The Liturgical Meaning of Holy Week*. Washington, DC: The Pastoral Press.

Universal Norms on the Liturgical Year and the General Roman Calendar (1969). Available at www.vatican.va or in any current printed edition of the Roman Missal.

van Tongeren, Louis (2001). 'Transformations of the Calendar in the Early Middle Ages', in Paul Post, Gerard Rouwhorst, Louis van Tongeren, and Anton Scheer (eds.), *Christian Feast and Festival: The Dynamics of Western Liturgy and Culture*. Peeters: Leuven: 287–317.

Varietates Legitimae: Inculturation and the Roman Liturgy (1994). Vatican City/Washington, D.C.: United States Catholic Conference.

Vieyra Alvarez, Yadira (2018). 'Christmas'. *Catholic Women Preach*. Available at http://catholicwomenpreach.org/preaching/12252018/ (accessed 16 March 2020).

Weiser, Francis X. (1952). *The Christmas Book*. New York: Harcourt, Brace and Company.

CHAPTER 11

EASTERN ORTHODOXY

MARY B. CUNNINGHAM

CHRISTMAS in the Eastern Orthodox Churches is considered the second most important feast after Easter. It is primarily a religious, as opposed to commercial or secular, event. Families and communities do come together for feasting and merriment, following the rigorous offices and liturgies that take place in church, but gifts are more often exchanged either on the feast day of St Nicholas (6 December) or at the beginning of the New Year (1 January)—depending on particular ethnic or national traditions. The term 'Eastern Orthodoxy' is applied in this chapter to the various Christian Churches that accept the Fourth Ecumenical Council of Chalcedon (AD 451): these include the Churches of Greece, Eastern Europe (Albania, Bulgaria, Cyprus, Georgia, Romania, and Serbia), and Russia (Ware 1993: 6). Although these separate Churches may have different patriarchs or archbishops and thus be self-governing, they are for the most part in communion and share the same liturgical tradition. The latter, although spoken or sung in different languages including Greek and Old Church Slavonic, was established during the long period of the Byzantine Empire (c.AD 330–1453). It is based on a synthesis of the Jerusalem and Constantinopolitan liturgical rites that occurred between approximately the eighth and twelfth centuries (Taft 1992). It is also worth noting that the liturgical tradition that persists in modern Orthodox Churches is heavily influenced by monastic practice; it may thus appear long and repetitive to those who are unused to this form of worship.

Since liturgical worship represents such an important part of the Eastern Orthodox Christmas, it is worth examining its content in some detail. The first section of this chapter, after a brief discussion of the history of the feast, shows how the liturgical services that occur during the Christmas period both re-enact and expound the doctrine of Christ's Incarnation. Because doctrine is taught not only by means of texts, but also with the help of images, or holy icons, in the Orthodox tradition, a second section explains the iconography (or visual meaning) of an icon of the Nativity of Christ. The third and final section of the chapter deals with the celebration of Christmas in communities and homes, according to separate Orthodox traditions. Some customs, such as those of the Serbs, are distinctive, bearing no resemblance to the practices that are observed, for example, in Russian or Greek homes. As in the case of some traditions in the West, some of these rituals may have pagan origins; however, they are 'baptized' through association with the Christian understanding of this holy day.

Theology and Liturgy: The Celebration of Christ's Nativity in Church

'Christ is born, give praise! Christ comes from heaven, rise up to meet him! Christ is on the earth, be lifted up! Sing to the Lord, all the earth!' (Gregory Nazianzen 1990: 104).

This is the joyful opening of a famous sermon by the early Byzantine theologian and bishop, Gregory Nazianzen, which was preached in Constantinople towards the end of the fourth century (Daley 2006: 117; Mossey 1965: 9–10). It influenced later hymns including especially a canon, which is attributed to an early eighth-century hymnographer known as Kosmas the Melodist and is still sung in Matins on Christmas Day (*Festal Menaion* 1998: 269). The text sets the tone for the Orthodox celebration of the Nativity of Christ: his birth from the Virgin Mary represents a new beginning. After the creation of humanity in Genesis, followed by the Fall—along with all of its unfortunate consequences both for human beings and the rest of the natural world—God has taken on mortal flesh and thus renewed, or recapitulated, the original creation. Both Gregory and Kosmas exhort not only human beings, but also the whole of creation, to rejoice. Heaven and earth are reunited and death gives way to eternal life.

This positive theological message pervades the liturgical services that take place throughout the days that lead up to Christmas and for five subsequent ones. In fact, it continues through the feast of Theophany, which occurs twelve days later, on 6 January, and which celebrates another aspect of Christ's manifestation in creation at the time of his baptism. It is worth interjecting here that the date of Theophany should not be confused with celebrations of Christmas according to the Julian calendar, which take place in some jurisdictions (such as the Russian patriarchate of Moscow and most of the Oriental Churches), on 7 January. The offices for Christmas and Theophany emphasize the Incarnation of Jesus Christ, which is celebrated in both historical and cosmic terms. Such teaching is delivered in church with the help of biblical (both Old and New Testament) readings, hymns, and sermons (*Festal Menaion* 1998: 199–294). The extent to which congregations understand Orthodox liturgical services is open to question, since both prayers and hymns are composed in ancient languages. They also employ complex (but rarely explained) typology or symbolism and are usually chanted or sung. Nevertheless, the unchanging liturgical rites, which are carried out on an annual basis, have a cumulative effect on worshippers. Most Orthodox Christians, if questioned about the theological meaning of Christmas, will respond with correct doctrinal formulations, thanks to the teaching that they receive in church.

Above all, however, they will communicate the joy that is associated with all of the major Christological and Marian feasts. A festival such as this is celebrated not only in church, but also at home with family and friends.

The Nativity of Christ is one of twelve major feasts (both Dominical and Marian) in the Orthodox Church. Like several other important feasts, including Easter, Christmas is honoured with a period of preparation and an 'afterfeast' during which the festival continues to be observed (*Festal Menaion* 1998: 42–4). The preparation takes the form of a forty-day fast, which begins on 15 November. Orthodox Christians are expected to avoid meat, dairy products, wine and oil, just as they do during Great Lent; the purpose of such fasting is to both to purify and to assist the faithful in their prayers to God. The two Sundays that precede Christmas are dedicated, first, to the 'Forefathers' (or the ancestors of Christ) and second, more broadly, to all of the righteous men and women of the Old Testament, from Adam to Joseph who was betrothed to the Virgin Mary (52–3). Then, on 20 December, the celebration of the Christmas begins in earnest. Hymns and prayers for the liturgical offices for the next ten days are concerned with Christ's Nativity, with the most elaborate being reserved for Christmas Eve and Day. And on Christmas morning, the fast is broken with a feast of pork, lamb, milk, cheese, wine, and oil—in short, all of the products that were avoided during the period of preparation. As Juliet du Boulay points out, 'the feast is, then, an act of reverence as much as is the fast' (du Boulay 2009: 145); this rule also applies to other major feasts of the Orthodox Church.

The celebration of Christmas originally took place in Jerusalem on 6 January; this date later came to focus solely on the baptism of Jesus Christ. In its original form, the feast of 'Epiphany' celebrated the birth of Jesus Christ, with a vigil taking place at the 'place of the shepherds' near Bethlehem on 5 January, the eve of the feast (*Armenian Lectionary* 1971: 210–11). In the morning, a liturgy was celebrated in the Church of the Resurrection (Anastasis) in Jerusalem (*Armenian Lectionary* 1971: 214–15; Bradshaw and Johnson 2011: 146; Getcha 2012: 126). Other Eastern Churches, apart from Jerusalem, celebrated both the birth and the baptism of Christ on 6 January, calling both events 'the Epiphany'. However, by about the end of the fourth century, the Roman practice of assigning Christ's birth to 25 December—originally in order to supplant the pagan feast of Sol Invictus (the 'Invincible Sun') at the winter solstice—also began to be adopted in the East (Talley 1986: 79–162). Gregory Nazianzen may have preached the Christmas homily that was cited at the beginning of this section on 25 December, although some scholars believe that it was still intended for 6 January (Daley 2006: 117; McGuckin 2001: 336–7). Gregory also adapted the theme of 'light' that was associated with the winter solstice to the Christian message. Jesus Christ was thereafter described in both sermons and hymns as the 'Sun of Righteousness' who brought enlightenment and truth to the world, as we see in a festal troparion (or short hymn) that is sung to this day in Orthodox Churches:

> Your Nativity, O Christ our God, has shone the light of knowledge upon the universe; for by this means, those who adored stars were taught by a star to worship

you, the Sun of Righteousness, and to know you as the Dayspring from on high.
O Lord, glory to you.   (*Festal Menaion* 1998: 266 [with adjustments])

The services that are celebrated in Orthodox Churches today still use many of the readings, hymns, and prayers that were composed for the feast of Christ's Nativity from the fourth century onward. And, although they mostly no longer include processions from one holy site or church to another as they did in the Late Antique and Byzantine periods, these services continue to induce an emotional response in those who attend them. The texts of the hymns encourage listeners metaphorically to see, hear, and participate in the scene at the manger in Bethlehem—along with associated events such as the angelic message to shepherds in a field (Luke 2: 8–15) and the arrival of the Magi from Persia (Matt. 2: 1–12). The Gospel accounts of Matthew and Luke provide the basis for the narrative, but added to these is a second-century 'apocryphal' or extra-canonical text known as the Protevangelium of James (Elliott 1993: 48–67). The Gospel of Pseudo-Matthew, which was compiled several centuries later and replaced the Protevangelium in the West, did not circulate widely in the Christian East (Elliott 1993: 84–6). Certain details, including Christ's birth in a cave rather than in a stable and the attendance of a midwife named Salome, became current in both texts and images associated with the Nativity story.

The story begins much earlier, however, according to the Eastern Christian compilers of liturgical services associated with Christmas. The biblical readings that are used in the offices for this feast evoke God's creation of the universe, followed by the prophecies that foretell the coming of the Messiah. A passage from the first chapter of Genesis, which is read in Vespers on Christmas Eve, reminds congregations of the original goodness of creation before it was tarnished by humanity's fall from grace. Readings from the prophets, including Micah, Isaiah, and Daniel, then inform them of God's plan for redemption which would culminate in the sending of his Son, Jesus Christ, into this fallen world. Whereas the prophets could only foresee some kind of reconciliation between God and humanity occurring with the help of the Messiah, it was witnesses after this birth, including the Evangelists and apostles, who testified to the combined divinity and humanity of this Saviour. The readings that take place during various offices on Christmas Eve and on the day itself thus include Matthew 1–2, Luke 1, and some from the Epistles—especially that which is addressed to the Hebrews (Wybrew 2000: 47–8; *Festal Menaion* 1998: 199–289). The New Testament passages thus not only provide the narrative of Jesus's birth in Bethlehem, along with their separate accounts of shepherds, angelic hymns, and the arrival of the Magi, but also bear witness to the Christological mystery that was revealed at this event.

The hymnography that fills out the rest of these liturgical services builds on this biblical basis, weaving not only the narrative but also the prophecy and symbolism of Old and New Testament witnesses into its poetic celebration of the feast. Such hymns, which are sung either by individual cantors or by choirs according to the traditions of separate Orthodox jurisdictions, teach the theological meaning of the feast according to a hermeneutic tradition that was formulated by the early Christian Fathers (Breck 2001; Stylianopoulos 2006). The songs date from about the sixth to the twelfth century, after which they were organized into service books that are still used in Orthodox Churches today. Since it is impossible to examine all of these hymns in the context of this chapter, I will choose two that are representative of the rich poetic, theological, and symbolic quality of this hymnographic corpus.

The first and most famous hymn, called a kontakion, was composed in the sixth century by a Constantinopolitan hymnographer known as Romanos the Melodist (Kontakion on the Nativity). This is a long, narrative work, which includes twenty-five stanzas, including a prologue. The kontakion was originally sung, probably by one cantor, during an all-night vigil on Christmas Eve; it served, as a kind of sung homily, to teach the assembled congregation that God himself was born of a virgin and placed in a cave (according to the Protevangelium of James), where both shepherds and Magi came to worship him. A typological form of exegesis, which juxtaposes the cave in Bethlehem with the Garden of Eden, suggests the importance of this event in the history of God's dispensation for salvation:

> Bethlehem has opened Eden, come, let us see;
> we have found delight in secret, come, let us receive
> the joys of Paradise within the cave...
> There a virgin has borne a babe
> and has quenched at once Adam's and David's thirst.
> (Romanos the Melodist (1963), trans. Lash 1995: 3)

Romanos sees the arrival of Jesus Christ, the Son of God, into creation as counteracting the original Fall from grace; human beings—or at least those who accept this revelation—are invited to re-enter paradise since they are deified by Christ's participation in their nature. Rich poetic symbolism also pervades this text: the secrecy of the cave, which evokes the purity of Mary's womb, also suggests an erotic fecundity that is fulfilled in the birth of this divine and human infant (Arentzen 2017: 87–119). Above all, Romanos aims to draw his listeners into this mysterious scene, calling on them to see and understand the paradoxical message of Christmas.

Owing to changes in liturgical practice from about the thirteenth century onward, compilers of the service books (or Menaia) began to include only the prologue of Romanos the Melodist's kontakion. This short stanza nevertheless became famous, since it encapsulates the Christological message of the feast of the Nativity:

> Today the Virgin gives birth to him who is above all being,
> and the earth offers a cave to him whom no one can approach.
> Angels with shepherds give glory,
> and magi journey with a star,
> for to us there has been born a little Child, God before the ages.
> (Romanos the Melodist (1963), trans. Lash 1995: 3)

The prologue is sung during the various offices of Christmas Eve and Christmas, as well as in the Divine Liturgies that take place on both days (*Festal Menaion* 1998: 221–89).

The second hymn which I have chosen for discussion is attributed to an eighth-century Palestinian hymnographer called Kosmas the Melodist (or 'of Maïuma') (Emereau 1923: 20–2; Savas 1983: 103–4). It is sung in Matins for Christmas Day in conjunction with another, which is assigned to Kosmas's brother or friend, the theologian, preacher, and hymnographer, John of Damascus (*Festal Menaion*: 269–84). Both hymns belong to the hymnographic form known as the canon. This is structured as a set of responses to nine biblical canticles of the Old and New Testaments; each ode is set to a different melody, known as the heirmos, and refers both to the canticle on which it is based and to the subject matter of the canon as a whole (Wellesz 1961: 198–245; Krueger 2014: 138–43). Kosmas begins his canon by quoting the homily by Gregory of Nazianzen that was cited at the beginning of this section: he calls on his audience to celebrate the birth of Christ and to glorify him. Not only human beings but the whole of creation should sing praises in honour of this world-changing event. Although this ode is inspired by the first canticle, namely, the victory hymn of Moses after crossing the Red Sea (Ex 15: 1–19), it alludes to it only in tone; the emphasis is rather on the story of salvation from the Fall to Redemption in the Incarnation of Christ (*Festal Menaion*: 269).

An eighteenth-century commentator on the Festal Menaion, Nikodemos the Hagiorite, noted that Kosmas the Melodist wove Old and New Testament passages into his canon on the Nativity of Christ, thus creating an intertextual tapestry of biblical allusions (Heortodromion: 65–99). This method of exegesis, which was common in Patristic and Byzantine liturgical texts, underlines both the unity of Scripture (which was believed to be written by separate human authors with the inspiration of the Holy Spirit) and its prophetic or typological fulfilment in the Incarnation of Christ (Young 1997: 97–116, 140–60). The fourth ode of Kosmas's canon opens with a good example of such intertextuality, which in this case is used typologically:

> Rod of the root of Jesse, and flower that blossomed from his stem, O Christ, you have sprung from the Virgin. You came from the mountain overshadowed by the forest; you were made flesh from the one who was not married, O God who are not formed out of matter. Glory to your power, O Lord.
> (*Festal Menaion*: 273 [with adjustments])

This stanza begins with an allusion to Isa. 11: 1, associating the rod and the flower or blossom with Christ. The view that Mary, as well as Joseph, was descended from Jesse was generally accepted on the grounds that most Jews married within their own tribes (Eusebius, *History of the Church* I.7.14; Eusebius of Caesarea, trans. Williamson 1965: 56). Kosmas then alludes to the prophet Habbakuk, describing the Virgin Mary as a 'mountain overshadowed by the forest'. The full biblical reference says that 'God will come out of Thaiman, and the Holy One from a shady, densely wooded mountain'

(Hab. 3:3 Septuagint; trans. Piertsma and Wright 2007: 809). As Nikodemos explains, Mary is described as a mountain because the latter is not ploughed or planted by humans; it produces tall trees, bushes, and grasses without cultivation. In other words, Mary's virginity needed no human seed to produce Christ. She was 'overshadowed' by the 'power of the most High' when she accepted the archangel Gabriel's message, according to Luke 1:35. Habbakuk's shaded mountain is thus an Old Testament type that was fulfilled in the Virgin birth of the new covenant. Kosmas the Melodist's fourth ode uses typology to emphasize the humanity and the divinity of Christ, as revealed at the time of his Nativity. The intertextual nature of his hymn writing reinforces an understanding of God's redemptive plan throughout the history of the Old Testament. Prophecies or types that are hidden in Scripture became visible after his Son was conceived by a virgin and born in Bethlehem.

The hymns of Romanos and Kosmas the Melodists continue to be sung—either by solo singers or by choirs—in modern Orthodox churches at Christmas. It is worth repeating the question that was posed at the beginning of this section, that is, how much of this material did congregations actually understand? The fact that the hymns are sung in ancient languages (usually earlier forms of Greek and Slavonic) in many churches, compounded with problems of varying acoustics and diction, may mean that some Orthodox Christians absorb more holy atmosphere than verbal sense in church (du Boulay 2009: 9). However, many congregants carry service books and follow the services word for word; they may also be educated in the typological or poetic meaning of hymnography. In any case, the Church's decision not to change or abridge Byzantine service books must reflect a view that such complex expressions of incarnational theology remain meaningful to both ordained and lay Christians. The underlying message of joy and celebration shines through the Christmas services, causing experienced churchgoers to know and sing for themselves a few of the simpler hymns, such as the prologue to Romanos the Melodist's famous kontakion.

Iconography of the Feast of the Nativity

Icons, or painted images of Jesus Christ, the Virgin Mary, saints, or festal scenes such as the Nativity, provide another method for teaching Orthodox Christians the theological meaning of these holy subjects. Icons of the feast of the Nativity, which typically follow the iconographic form that appears in Figure 11.1, portray the narrative of this miraculous birth in a condensed form: the Christ Child lies in a manger within the cave of apocryphal tradition, flanked by an ox and an ass, while Mary reclines beside him. An angel delivers the joyous news to a shepherd at the top right of the icon, backed by more angels to the left of a highly stylized mountain that is intersected by rays of light from heaven. At the bottom right of the icon, midwives prepare a bath for

FIGURE 11.1. Icon of the Nativity of Christ by Onufri, 16th century, National Museum of Medieval Art, Korce, Albania © PRISMA ARCHIVO/ Alamy Stock Photo.

the newborn baby while at the left, a disconsolate Joseph is approached by a simply dressed male figure who is sometimes identified as the Devil (Ouspensky and Lossky 1983: 160). The lower right-hand scene reflects apocryphal narratives such as the Protevangelium of James, which record the presence of midwives at Christ's birth (Protevangelium of James 19–20, trans. Elliott 1993: 64–5); that on the left offers a visual representation of Joseph's initial doubt concerning Mary's conception of Jesus, as recorded in Matthew 1: 18–25.

The theological message of this icon consists in its portrayal of the simultaneous humanity and divinity of the incarnate Son of God, Jesus Christ. The cave in which he lies, which is depicted as a black hole in the middle of the mountain, symbolizes the fallen world or the darkness into which light now shines (cf. John 1: 5)—although it is sometimes also equated with the tomb in which he would later be interred. But above all, this vulnerable figure, which is wrapped in white swaddling bands, reveals the self-emptying (kenosis) of the Godhead when he chose to assume human nature (Ouspensky and Lossky 1983: 157). The ox and the ass represent not only the fulfilment of prophecy (Isa. 1:3), but also the recognition of Christ's divinity by animals as well as by human beings. The Virgin Mary lies beside the cave, often in an attitude of lassitude and dejection. This is understood to indicate her participation in a fully human (although also virginal) conception and birth, as well as her maternal premonition of future suffering for her son. Mary's eyes are sometimes directed not towards Christ, but rather at the unhappy figure of Joseph. This indicates her compassion not only for him, but also for all who are unable to understand or accept the mystery of the Incarnation (Baggley 2000: 38). The divinity of Christ is indicated by means of the rays of light from heaven (symbolizing the Trinity) that shine on the cave, the angelic host, and the haloes of the Christ child, his mother, and Joseph. The Magi, who approach on horseback from the left side of the icon with their gifts, show that Christ, the Messiah, was recognized not only by Jews but also by the 'nations' or the whole world. The economic use of narrative detail in this icon conveys the message of the Christmas story with concise focus to Orthodox believers.

The primary purpose of icons is not to teach, however; it is rather to offer an opportunity for spiritual encounter. Holy images such as this are understood to have a direct symbolic link with the figures or scenes that they portray. The 'theology of images', which developed during the Byzantine period of Iconoclasm (cAD 730–843), justifies the role of holy icons (whether miraculous or man-made) in religious worship (Barber 2002: 39–81; Pelikan 1990: 7–66). It is based on the belief that objects such as this in some way reflect divine prototypes. More specifically, it became possible in the new dispensation to portray Jesus Christ in paintings or other media because he took on human nature and, following the Resurrection, remained incarnate. The acceptability—or indeed necessity—of creating images of Christ applies by extension to his mother Mary, the saints, and biblical or festal scenes. Icons are believed to represent 'windows' into the divine world (Constas 2014: 15–33). This theology of images also helps to explain the abstract quality of icons, as well as the gold, rather than realistic, backgrounds that they are given: these are images of a deified world, reflecting its transformation following Christ's presence and ongoing example within it. The icon of the Nativity is placed in the centre of the nave in Orthodox churches at Christmas. On entering the church, the faithful approach and venerate the icon, bowing down before it and kissing the figure of Christ or his mother Mary. Candles are also lit and placed on brackets surrounding this central icon; these symbolize the light that entered creation with the birth of Jesus Christ.

CHRISTMAS CELEBRATIONS IN THE COMMUNITY

The celebration of Christmas in local communities varies widely, according to different ethnic or local traditions throughout the Eastern Orthodox world. Furthermore, recent studies of such customs already require revision, as their authors themselves admit (du Boulay 2009; Papachristophorou 2013): improved communication networks, globalism, commercialism, and secularization are all helping to erase the memory of traditional practices in Eastern Christian communities. What happens in the homes of many Orthodox families at the time of religious festivals such as Christmas nevertheless remains distinctive, even though their communities have changed dramatically in the last fifty years or so or have been dispersed around the world. Such customs often reinforce feelings of national and religious identity and are therefore encouraged. It is worth examining what we might call extra-liturgical, or non-ecclesial, Christmas beliefs and rituals in the final section of this chapter because these remain significant from both historical and ethnographic points of view.

As we saw earlier in this chapter, certain practices are shared among Orthodox countries and their diaspora populations with regard to the celebration of Christmas: although feasting occurs both on Christmas Eve and Day, gifts tend to be exchanged either on the feasts of St Nicholas (6 December) or St Basil (1 January). Apart from this, separate traditions have developed over the centuries in the Orthodox nations of Russia, Eastern Europe, and Greece. I have chosen for reasons of space to focus here on two distinctive examples: first, Serbia (French 1942); and second, a village called Ambeli in Evia (or Euboea), a Greek island just north of Athens (du Boulay 1994; du Boulay 2009). Although my source for the former example is somewhat dated (French 1942), I have witnessed the Serbian Christmas rites still being celebrated by a modern family that lives in the United Kingdom. As for the latter example, I can only claim that this represents one anthropologist's in-depth study of an isolated community in late twentieth-century Greece. Although it may not precisely reflect the wider beliefs and practices of this country, du Boulay's study is remarkable in its documentation and analysis of one local Greek community.

Serbian Orthodox Christians begin their celebrations on Christmas Eve by sending two young men of the household out to cut the trunk (or branch) of an oak tree (called the *badnyak*), which is then divided into three pieces. These are taken back to the house where the housewife breaks an unleavened cake over the longest of the three branches. The log is burned in the fireplace overnight, with one of the men keeping watch to make sure that it does not go out. An accompanying ceremony, which is carried out by the woman, involves scattering straw and corn throughout every corner of the house. She imitates the clucking of a hen while the children run behind her pretending to be chickens. After this, the family assembles in the kitchen. The father throws a few walnuts into the corners of the room, places a lighted wax candle into a bowl or box of wheat, censes each person, and offers up a prayer, asking for God's blessing on the household. The family then consumes a hearty meal of fish, bread, and vegetables before going to bed. In the morning, following a lengthy Divine Liturgy (or Mass) at church, the family feasts on roast pig and other rich foods. A special cake, known as the 'chesnitsa' and in which a coin is hidden, is served—although in some regions of former Yugoslavia this was saved for St Basil's day on 1 January (French 1942: 24–8). Aspects of the Serbian Christmas ritual, as in the Christian West, have links with pagan practices or beliefs. The log, which may be compared to the Western Yule log, reflects the need to affirm the survival of nature through the long, cold winter. Other references to fertility, the harvest, and the passage through death to new life appear in the words and actions of Serbian Christians at this time. Nevertheless, such Christmas celebrations frequently invoke the Christian God who was born on this holy night. The spreading of straw throughout the house serves to remind the family of his humble birth in a stable, while in some families the evening meal is taken while sitting on the floor, rather than at the table (French 1942: 26). Gender roles are well defined in the Serbian rituals surrounding Christmas, thus reinforcing a traditional understanding of household and society.

According to Juliet du Boulay, the small Greek mountain village of Ambeli possessed (at least until the early 1970s) a cosmology that was based on ancient ideas about God's relationship with the natural world. This world view in many ways resembled those of Late Antique and Byzantine Christianity (Brown 1971; Cunningham 2002: 141–58). The villagers believed that a stable earth was positioned at the centre of the universe, with planets and stars revolving around it. It was spherical and held up through its central axis by a great tree. Hobgoblins (*skalikantzoúria*), besides living in ravines around the village, spent their time hacking through the roots of this tree so as to 'bring the earth crashing down' (du Boulay 2009: 31). At Christmastime, however, they were allowed to come up and create mayhem among the villagers; they infested houses, streets, and especially mills—to which it was dangerous to go during this period (du Boulay 2009: 81). Finally, after the twelfth day of Christmas, or Theophany (6 January), the hobgoblins were banished again to the underworld. There they found the tree restored and their work of the previous year undone (du Boulay 2009: 31). The anthropologist suggests that the disturbances of the goblins during these twelve days may be related to the vulnerability of the Christ Child as he lies in the manger; after his baptism and the blessing of the church and houses with holy water at Theophany, full power over these evil forces is restored. She further argues that this mythology reflects the natural processes of the winter solstice: the period during which the sun is weakest is dangerous for humans and all other creatures. Stories of accidents, near misses, and other terrifying events that took place between Christmas and Theophany were common in village folklore (du Boulay 2009: 41–3). The idea that goblins, or evil spirits, stalk the streets and fields over the Christmas period appears to be widespread in Greece; however, this is also a period of feasting and merriment. After the Christmas meal for family and friends, at which roast pork is usually consumed, Greeks celebrate the new year and St Basil's day by baking a special cake known as the 'basilopitta' in which a coin is hidden. Although village beliefs and rituals may sometimes be abandoned, thanks to modern communication networks and education, many Greek Orthodox Christians continue to attend the night offices and liturgies that form part of their Christmas celebrations.

Russians, Bulgarians, and other Orthodox nations observe the same liturgical offices and liturgies as do the Serbs and Greeks; they also celebrate the feast with family meals on Christmas Eve and Christmas Day. However, the beliefs and practices of these Christians differ significantly from those that have just been described. National or local rituals, which vary throughout the Orthodox world, play an important part in the Christmas celebrations of all of these jurisdictions. Such diversity contrasts with the uniformity of the official liturgical celebrations of the Nativity of Christ.

Conclusion

We have surveyed three major aspects of Eastern Orthodox Christmas in this chapter: first, the liturgical celebration of the feast, along with its theological meaning; second, its visual expression in an icon of the Nativity of Christ; and third, the celebration (or perception) of Christmas in two quite different Orthodox settings. Whereas the first two topics reveal continuity across the jurisdictions of the Chalcedonian Churches of Russia, Eastern Europe, and Greece, the third shows considerable variation. It is possible that local beliefs and practices, which have not received much coverage in standard textbooks on Eastern Orthodoxy, belong more to the fields of anthropology, sociology, and ethnography than they do to theology or church history. However, this subject should be explored further since it uncovers rich and varied aspects of Christian tradition. We may label some customs, such as the burning of the Yule log or the idea of a world tree as 'pagan'; however, these have been completely integrated into Christian faith and ritual in both Serbia and Greece. Christmas, like its more important counterpart, Easter, reflects the way in which a system of faith, or doctrine, may be intertwined with popular mythology in human culture. Ritual actions help to embed both doctrine and less official 'mythologies' in the memories of the communities that belong to separate jurisdictions of the Eastern Orthodox Church.

References and Further Reading

Primary Sources

Armenian Lectionary (1971). Ed. and trans. A. Renoux. Le Codex Arménien Jérusalem 121, Patrologia Orientalis 36, fasc. 2, no. 168. Turnout: Brepols.
Eusebius of Caesarea (1965). *History of the Church*. Trans. G. A. Williamson. Harmondsworth: Penguin Books.
Festal Menaion (1998). Trans. Mother Mary and Archimandrite K. Ware (1969). London: Faber and Faber; repr. S. Canaan, PA: St Tikhon's Seminary Press.
Gregory Nazianzen (1990), *Oration 38, On the Theophany*. Ed. and trans. (Fr.), C. Moreschini, Grégoire de Nazianze, Discours 38–41, Sources Chrétiennes 358. Paris: Éditions du Cerf; trans. (Eng.) N. V. Harrison (2008), St Gregory of Nazianzus, *Festal Orations*. Crestwood, NY: St Vladimir's Seminary Press.
Nikodemos Hagiorites 'Heortodromion: etoi hermeneia eis tous hasmatikous kanonas ton Despotikon kai Theometerikon heorton' (repr. 1970) Athens, C.I. Spanou; trans. E. Theokritoff. Unpublished. (I am grateful to the translator for sharing her draft with me).
Protevangelium of James (1853). Ed. C. Tischendorf, *Evangelia Apocrypha*. Leipzig: Avenarius and Mendelssohn. 1–50; Ed. E. de Strycker (1961), *La forme la plus ancienne du Protévangile de Jacques*, Subsidia hagiographica 33, Brussels: Société des Bollandistes; Trans. Elliott, *The Apocryphal New Testament*, 57–67.
Romanos the Melodist (1963), *Kontakion on the Nativity*. Ed. P. Maas and C. A. Trypanis, *Sancti Romani Melodi Cantica: Cantica Genuina*. Oxford: Oxford University Press: 1–9; Trans. Archimandrite E. Lash (1995), St Romanos the Melodist, *Kontakia on the Life of Christ*. San Francisco: HarperCollins: 1–12.
Septuagint (LXX) (2007). Ed. and trans. A. Pietersma and B. G. Wright. Oxford: Oxford University Press.

Secondary Works

Alfeyev, Metr. H. (2016). *Orthodox Christianity, Vol. 4: The Worship and Liturgical Life of the Orthodox Church*. Crestwood, NY: St Vladimir's Seminary Press.
Arentzen, T. (2017). *The Virgin in Song: Mary and the Poetry of Romanos the Melodist*. Philadelphia: University of Pennsylvania Press.
Baggley, J. (1988). *Doors of Perception: Icons and Their Spiritual Significance*. Crestwood, NY: St Vladimir's Seminary Press.
Baggley, J. (2000). *Festival Icons for the Christian Year*. London: Mowbray.
Baldovin, J. F. (1987). *The Urban Character of Christian Worship: The Origins, Development, and Meaning of Stational Liturgy*, OCA 228. Rome: Pontifical Institute.
Barber, C. (2002). *Figure and Likeness: On the Limits of Representation in Byzantine Iconoclasm*. Princeton and Oxford: Princeton University Press.
Boulay, J. du (1994). *Portrait of a Greek Mountain Village*. Limni, Evia, Greece: Denise Harvey.
Boulay, J. du (2009). *Cosmos, Life and Liturgy in a Greek Orthodox Village*. Limni, Evia, Greece: Denise Harvey.
Bradshaw, P. F. and Johnson, M. E. (2011). *The Origins of Feasts, Fasts, and Seasons in Early Christianity*. London: SPCK; Collegeville, MN: Liturgical Press.

Breck, J. (2001). *Scripture in Tradition: The Bible and Its Interpretation in the Orthodox Church*. Crestwood, NY: St Vladimir's Seminary Press.

Brière, E. A. (1983). 'Scripture in Hymnography: A Study in Some Feasts of the Orthodox Church'. DPhil thesis, University of Oxford.

Brown, P. (1971). *The World of Late Antiquity: AD 150–750*. London: Thames and Hudson.

Casiday, A. (ed.) (2012). *The Orthodox Christian World*. London and New York: Routledge.

Constas, Fr Maximos (2014). *The Art of Seeing: Paradox and Perception in Orthodox Iconography*. Alhambra, CA: Sebastian Press.

Cunningham, M. B. (2002). *Faith in the Byzantine World*. Oxford: Lion Hudson.

Daley, B. E., SJ (2006). *Gregory of Nazianzus*. London and New York: Routledge.

Elliott, J. K. (ed.) (1993). *The Apocryphal New Testament: A Collection of Apocryphal Christian Literature in an English Translation Based on M.R. James*. Oxford: Clarendon Press.

Ellis, J. (1986). *The Russian Orthodox Church: A Contemporary History*. London and New York: Routledge.

Emereau, C. (1923). 'Hymnographi byzantini: Quorum nomina in litteras digessit notulisque adornavit (Cont.)', *Échos d'Orient* 22, no. 129, 11–25.

French, R. M. (1942). *Serbian Church Life*. London: SPCK.

Getcha, Archbishop J. (2012). *The Typikon Decoded: An Explanation of Byzantine Liturgical Practice*, trans. P. Meyendorff. Yonkers, NY: St Vladimir's Seminary Press.

Iswolsky, H. (1962). *Christ in Russia: The History, Tradition, and Life of the Russian Church*. Kingswood, Surrey: Worlds Work.

Krueger, D. (2014). *Liturgical Subjects. Christian Ritual, Biblical Narrative, and the Formation of the Self in Byzantium*. Philadelphia: University of Pennsylvania Press.

Louth, A. (2013). *Introducing Eastern Orthodox Theology*. Downers Grove, IL: Intervarsity Press.

McGuckin, J. A. (2001). *Saint Gregory of Nazianzus: An Intellectual Biography*. Crestwood, NY: St Vladimir's Seminary Press.

McGuckin, J. A. (2011). *The Encyclopaedia of Eastern Orthodox Christianity*. Chichester and Malden, MA: Wiley-Blackwell.

Mossey, J. (1965). *Les Fêtes de Noël et d'Épiphanie d'après les sources littéraires cappadociennes du IVe siècle*. Louvain: Peeters.

Ouspensky, L. and Lossky, V. (1983). *The Meaning of Icons*. Crestwood, NY: St Vladimir's Seminary Press.

Papachristophorou, M. (2013). *Myth, Representation and Identity: An Ethnography of Memory in Lipsi, Greece*. New York: Palgrave Macmillan.

Pelikan, J. (1990). *Imago Dei: The Byzantine Apologia for Icons*. New Haven and London: Yale University Press.

Savas, S. J. (1983). *Hymnology of the Eastern Orthodox Church*. Brookline, MA: Byzantine Melodies.

Stylianopoulos, T. G. (ed.) (2006). *Sacred Text and Interpretation: Perspectives in Orthodox Biblical Studies*. Brookline, MA: Holy Cross Orthodox Press.

Taft, R. F. (1992). *The Byzantine Rite: A Short History*. Collegeville, MN: Liturgical Press.

Theokritoff, E. (2005). 'Praying the Scriptures in Orthodox Worship', in S. T. Kimbrough, Jr (ed.), *Orthodox and Wesleyan Scriptural Understanding and Practice*. Crestwood, NY: St Vladimir's Seminary Press: 73–87.

Talley, T. J. (1986). *The Origins of the Liturgical Year*. Collegeville, MN: Pueblo.
Ware, T. (1993). *The Orthodox Church*. New Edition, London: Penguin Books.
Wellesz, E. (1949; rev. ed. 1963). *A History of Byzantine Music and Hymnography*. Oxford: Clarendon Press.
Wybrew, H. (1997). *Orthodox Feasts of Jesus Christ and the Virgin Mary: Liturgical Texts with Commentary*. Crestwood, NY: St Vladimir's Seminary Press.
Young, F. M. (1997). *Biblical Exegesis and the Formation of Christian Culture*. Cambridge: Cambridge University Press.

CHAPTER 12

LUTHERANISM

KIRSI STJERNA

Global and Ethnic Celebration of Light

For Lutheran worshipping communities, Christmas is loaded with meanings and traditions—religious and folk and cultural—with global and local ingredients. An amalgamation of medieval practices, pre-Christian ('pagan') customs, and idiosyncratic ethnic preferences, the Lutheran Christmas includes lights, the ubiquitous decorated Christmas trees and flowers, Advent wreaths, seasonal hymns and songs, particular foods—where the ethnic traditions can be tasted—and the liturgical services offered by the Church. Music, with roots in Martin Luther and Johann Sebastian Bach, features prominently in Lutheran Christmas, at church and in homes.

Theologically, for Lutheran Christians standing on the ecumenical, creedal faith, Christmas is the annual celebration of the birth of Jesus of Nazareth as the Saviour of humankind. At the heart of the varied traditions to mark the birth is the radical Christian belief that a young maiden called Mary of Nazareth gave birth to a child she named Jesus, a real child, who was also truly God. This Incarnation of God, as Jesus came to be understood in the early Church's doctrinal decisions, was to bring light and hope to the world, and freedom from death and life eternal. Christmas marks the beginning of this logic where humanity and divinity become united in one big story of salvation.

The church's liturgical calendar gives a rhythm to the days of the Christmas season, in which Lutherans follow the pre-Reformation Christian convention on the dating of Christmas on 25 December—while acknowledging the historical uncertainty regarding the actual birthday. As a festival of light, Christmas for Lutherans—from its timing to the forms of festivities—merges amicably its 'pagan' and Christian elements. Christmas is a theologically articulated religious holiday with a specific liturgical calendar and lectionary, while it is also a cultural event with often no explicit spiritual agendas but strong household traditions. Lutherans over the centuries have developed their local customs to celebrate, with the considerable influence of Northern European traditions.

The German reformer Martin Luther has set the tone for the Christmas proclamation in a particularly Lutheran faith grammar, leaving an abundancy of model sermons, translated into several languages, and he also has furnished Lutherans with many beloved hymns (Bainton 2017). The most far-reaching Lutheran influence could be argued to come from Johann Sebastian Bach's Christmas music (Pelikan 2003). Some of the most frequently performed works are his Christmas Oratorio from 1734, composed for the St Thomas and St Nicholas churches in 1734, and his Magnificat in E-flat Major (BWV 243a) from 1723 for St Thomas, originally written for another feast (the Visitation—in July) and that involves four Christmas hymns.

The roots of the Lutheran tradition being in the northern parts of Europe with long winters, Lutheran Christmas distinctly marks the importance of light. The desire to break free from the cold and dark in the deep mid-winter is manifest in the decorations, activities, and lyrics of the seasonal music. In worship, the birth of Christ as the light for the world is proclaimed in Word and celebrated in liturgy and music, and the worship space is typically decorated with an abundance of lights.

Many Lutheran congregations opt to have a Christmas tree in the sanctuary, with ceremonies around decorating it. While theologically speaking and in Christmas hymns and Scripture readings, the infant Jesus as the promised light to the world takes—or should take—precedence, the Christmas tree with lights is prominent and essential. In many of the Western countries different types of evergreen, pine, or spruce trees are decorated with stars and candles, and other precious ornaments with a more ethnic distinction, for example in India a mango or a palm tree gets to hold the lights. Unlike the legend suggests, Martin Luther or Lutherans did not invent the tradition with Christmas trees, but he may have contributed to the custom of decorating them with lights.

In addition to the ubiquitous Christmas tree, other anticipated aspects of Christmas for Lutherans are the festive meals and gift-giving, and going to the Christmas Mass. What is served at the Christmas dinner, when the gifts are exchanged—and how they appear, with or without the reindeer, secretly during the night or in the evening with the appearance of the Santa Claus—and when the Christmas service is, these are areas where inter-Lutheran differences reveal local and ethnic variations.

Sharing Christmas gifts has long roots, but the Reformation introduced a change to the timing of it. Typically this happens on Christmas Eve or on Christmas Day, per Luther's preference to focus on the Christ Child with the gifts, rather than adhering to the earlier tradition of giving gifts on St Nicholas Day on 5 or 6 December—which is still a custom in some European countries (e.g. Poland, Germany, and Netherlands). It appears that Luther himself practised gift-giving during Advent, shaping the tradition of Advent calendars that afford tiny gifts or messages for each day leading up to Christmas. In the climax of Advent, those celebrating Christ's birthday are invited to exchange gifts with one another, if not in goods, then in deeds; the gift of compassion and freedom being the greatest of them all, per Luther's emphasis.

Not all Lutherans feast on gingerbread cookies and Stollen and plum pudding (aka Figgy Pudding). Some Lutherans eat ham and goose, others nibble on turkey or goat, some crave for the infamous lutefisk or other fish dishes (abundant in Scandinavian Christmas), others sample festive curries or special tamales, yet others prepare casseroles—anything from liver or rutabaga casserole to Janson's Temptation—and refined pies, savoury and sweet, with particular Christmas recipes. Christmas tastes different in different corners of the world, involving traditional foods shared on Christmas Eve or Christmas Day, per local traditions.

Martin Luther's Christmas

Martin Luther, a religious reformer, loved Christmas. He preached hundreds of sermons, and left a strong theological and liturgical legacy that has shaped Lutheran proclamation and interpretation of the Christmas Gospel, Christmas singing, and many other customs that have been carried on in Lutheran homes and faith communities around the world.

In his Christmas and Advent sermons Luther was at his best as a proclaimer of the Christian Gospel and as a theologian whose primary concern was that human beings get to hear the liberating promise from God about their freedom and dignity, regardless of their status, gender, wealth, age, ability, or other factors. Mary, for Luther, connects ordinary human beings personally to the Christmas Gospel. Luther's Christmas sermons warmly contemplate the biblical texts and draw the listeners to think of their own lives, with ample references to the daily experiences of men and women, and with an effort to arouse feelings and inspiration that would have an impact in people's personal situations (Bainton 2017).

Luther wrote, at the very least, five carols that equip people of faith to both proclaim the Christmas Gospel and to respond to it in singing. In addition to the gold standard, 'From Heaven Above to Earth I Come', another has survived in his own handwriting: 'To Shepherds as They Watched by Night'. Also the following are attributed to Luther: 'We Praise You, Jesus, at Your Birth' (a fourteenth-century hymn adapted by Luther); 'Christ Jesus Lay in Death's Strong Bands'; 'Flung to the Heedless Winds'; 'O Lord, We Praise Thee'; and 'Saviour of the Nations, Come'.

Luther's fundamental theology and his passion for the Christ story—as well as his jubilation about Christmas—are featured poignantly in his now classic hymn, 'From Heaven Above to Earth I Came', from 1535. This hymn, based on Luke 2:1–18, was originally written for a Christmas pageant for children. In the words attributed to the angel and the verses given for children to sing, Luther gives a synopsis of his teaching on the revelation offered in Christ in flesh and in Word, and of the true Incarnation of God in the humanity in Christ, of his theology of the cross as a lens to see how God appears in human life, and of the proper responses human hearts should have for this gift. Much of Lutheran Christmas preaching underscores these points that congregants can together proclaim in their singing of this hymn, which happens in most Lutheran churches at least once in worship during Christmas time.

In the articulation of the hymn, first, the Christmas proclamation is about the revelation of the good news for humanity found in the infant Jesus in the arms of his human mother, Mary. In the words of the angel (translation from Evangelical Lutheran Worship Book #269):

> 1. From heaven above to earth I come
> to bear good news to ev'ry home!
> Glad tidings of great joy I bring
> to all the world, and gladly sing:
> 2. To you this night is born a child
> of Mary, chosen virgin mild; this new
> born child of lowly birth, shall be the joy of all the earth.

Second, even if his birth is humble and the setting lowly, the gift the baby Christ brings is the greatest: freedom for the human heart. The angel continues:

> 3. This is the Christ, God's Son most high,
> who hears your sad and bitter cry, who will himself your Savior be
> and from all sin will set you free.
> 4. The blessing that the Father planned
> the Son holds in his infant hand,
> that in his kingdom, bright and fair,
> you may with us his glory share.

Third, Christ's birth in its humbleness turns around the human expectations of glory and reminds us of the real presence of God in the midst of all human experience:

> 5. These are the signs that you will see
> to let you know that it is he:
> In manger-bed, in swaddling clothes
> the child who all the earth upholds.
> 6. Now let us all with joyful cheer
> go with the shepherds and draw near
> to see the precious gift of God,
> the blessed child to us bestowed.
> 7. Look, look, dear friends, look over there!
> What lies within that manger bare? Who is that lovely little one?
> The baby Jesus, God's dear Son.
> 8. Welcome to earth, O noble Guest,
> through whom the sinful world is blest! You turned not from our needs away;
> how can our thanks such love repay?

Fourth, in contrast to the theology of the glory, Luther's theology of the cross expects God to appear in the opposite of what human beings might imagine—in the midst of suffering, even death:

> 9. Oh Lord, you have created all!
> How did you come to be so small,
> to sweetly sleep in manger-bed
> where loving cattle lately fed?
> 10. Were earth a thousand times as fair,
> and set with gold and jewels rare,
> still such a cradle would not do
> to rock a prince so great as you.
> 11. For velvets soft and silken stuff
> you have but hay and straw so rough,
> on which as king so rich and great
> to be enthroned in humble state.

Fifth, the revelation of Christ is not theory but a transformative truth that needs to become personal and therewith shift people's orientation in life to that of compassion and joy, in which humans join the angels in their adoration of the one God:

> 12. Ah, dearest Jesus, holy child
> prepare a bed, soft, undefiled,
> a quiet chamber in my heart,
> that you and I may never part.
> 13. My heart for very joy now leaps;
> my voice no longer silence keeps;
> I too must sing with joyful tongue
> the sweetest ancient cradle-song:
> 14. Glory to God in highest heav'n,
> who unto us His Son have giv'n!
> While angels sing in pious mirth
> a glad new year to all the earth!

Martin Luther's Christmas Sermon

In addition to joining the singing of hymns, there is hardly a better way to understand Christmas for Lutherans, religiously speaking, than to take a few moments with Luther preaching on a pivotal Christmas text, 'Gospel for Christmas Day, Luke 2:1–14' (AE 75/1, 209–29; also found in WA 10/1.1:58–95, LW 52:7–31, from 1522).

Luther starts with the big picture, the cosmic, earth-shaking impact of Christ's birth:

> Haggai records God's words: 'I will shake heaven and earth when He whom all nations desire shall come' (Haggai 2:7). This is fulfilled today, for the heavens were shaken; that is, the angels in the heavens sang praises to God. And the earth [was shaken], that is, the people on the earth, so that everyone had to get up and make a journey, one to this city, another to that, throughout the whole land, as the Gospel tell us [Luke 2:1–3]. It was not a violent, bloody uprising, but rather a peaceful one awakened by God, who is the God of peace. (Luther 2013: 209.)

Luther proceeds to give historical background information to make a theological point about the nature of the rule of Christ: because 'the birth of Christ occurred in the time of Caesar Augustus' and at the time of the 'first taxing' of the Jews in the land of Syria, under the Roman governor, there is no doubt that 'His kingdom was not to be worldly, nor would He rule over worldly power in a worldly way, but that He and His parents were subject to it' (Luther 2013: 210).

The preacher proceeds to explain the Gospel text, point by point, with the premise that this 'Gospel is so clear that it requires very little explanation, but it should be well considered, regarded, and taken deeply into the heart. No one will receive more benefit from it than those who keep quiet, banish everything, and diligently look into it' (Luther 2013: 210). The reason to look at the Gospel closely is so that you can be transformed:

> Therefore, if you want to be enlightened and warmed, to see the divine grace and miracle, so that your heart is kindled, enlightened, devout and joyful, then go where you are quiet and take this picture deep into your heart, and you will find miracle upon miracle. (Luther 2013: 210)

Luther emphasizes the humility and the unexpected in the ways God communicates with the world: the most ordinary and the most miraculous come together in the birth of the world's Saviour who once upon a time was nursed in a crowded stable by his teenage mother:

> First, see how plainly and simply things happen on earth, and yet how high they are regarded in heaven. On earth it happens this way: Here is a poor young woman, Mary of Nazareth, regarded as nothing at all and thought of as one of the last citizens of the city. No one is aware of the great miracle she carries; she is silent, keeps her own counsel, and regards herself as the least in the city.
> (Luther 2013: 211)

Luther expresses considerable attention to the discomfort of the pregnant woman, who is at the heart of the story and gives a concrete starting point from which to understand the God of the cross from very much a woman's point of view. He continues to transport the listener to the scene and stir emotions:

> The evangelist shows how, when they arrived at Bethlehem, they were the most insignificant and despised... No one took pity on this young woman who was giving birth for the first time.... There she is, alone, without any preparation, without light, without fire, in the middle of the night, in the darkness. No one offered her any service as is customarily done for pregnant woman.

Luther invites the listener to get closer to the newborn and 'imagine what kind of cloths they were in which she wrapped the child' (Luther 2013: 212).

The question of the Virgin Birth did not bother Luther, or really Lutheran worshippers in general since; theologically, it has not been a major cause of concern or preoccupation. In his time, when discerning the disassociations with Catholic beliefs, Luther had to address it, and set the tone with his stress on the words 'natural' birth and 'true birth':

> Some debate about how this birth took place, whether she was delivered of the child in prayer, in great joy, before she was aware of it, without any pain. I do not reject that opinion, possibly invented for the sake of the simple. But we must abide by the Gospel, which says that she gave birth to Him, and by the apostles' Creed, which says, 'Born of the Virgin Mary.' There is no deception here, but, as the words read, a true birth. (Luther 2013: 212)

Just in case anyone would miss his point, Luther gets more specific, highlighting aspects of the divine birth as if he knew firsthand the specifics of making and birthing babies—knowledge he would gain some years later when married to Katharina von Bora at which time he would experience the birthing miracle with her:

> It is well-known what I meant by giving birth and how it happens. It happened to her just like other women, with good reason and the assistance of her body parts, as happens at birth, so that she is His natural mother and He is her natural son. Therefore, her body did not lose its natural function in giving birth, except that she gave birth without sin, without shame, without pain, and without injury, just as she had also conceived without sin. The curse of Eve did not come on her.
>
> And, tenderly he ponders how, 'Likewise, she also fed Him with milk from her breast in the natural way. (Luther 2013: 212–13)

Luther's attention to the natural and physical is remarkable, and was definitely a new kind of preaching in his context, that of a theologian of the cross who calls the thing what it is and corrects falsities (as he articulates in his 1518 Heidelberg Disputation). His reasons are theological and based on the scriptural evidence about God's intentions revealed through Christ's birth: God could have not found a better way to show divine goodness than by sinking Godself 'deep into the flesh and blood' in Christ's birth: 'From now on even that can be regarded as godly, honorable, and pure, which in all men is the most ungodly, shameful, and impure. These are the real miracles of God'

(Luther 2013: 213). The Christmas gospel reminds us of the pivotal event when God took away human shame and glorified the lowly.

Moving forward, Luther takes a look at 'the mysteries or secret things' the Christmas history holds. He involves the listener in the Christmas story with the reminder that the holy and innocent birth of Christ is a matter of believing 'that Christ is born *for you*, and that this birth is *yours* and occurred for *your* benefit [*emphasis added*]. The Gospel teaches that Christ was born because of us, and that He did and suffered everything because of us' (Luther 2013: 215). The impact of this is oneness with God in what Luther later would call a 'happy exchange', in which all that is Christ's becomes mine, and vice versa:

> See, in this way Christ takes our birth away from us and absorbs it into His birth, and give us His, that in it we might become pure and new, as if it were our own, so that every Christian may rejoice and glory in Christ's birth as if he also, like Christ, had been born bodily of Mary. (Luther 2013: 216)

The Christmas Gospel goes beyond a historical narrative for Luther: it is a personal invitation for the believer to find themselves on Mary's lap in an intimate communion with God:

> Therefore, see to it that you do not find pleasure in the Gospel only as a history, for that does not last long; also not only as an example for that does not stick without faith. *But see to it that you make this birth your own and trade places, so that you are freed from your birth and receive His. This happens when you believe. So sit in the lap of the Virgin Mary and be her dear child.* But you must exercise this faith and ask for it, because while you live you cannot establish it too firmly. This is our foundation and inheritance, on which good works must be built. [*emphasis added*]
> (Luther 2013: 216)

As Luther's preaching reveals, the virgin Mother Mary features prominently in Lutheran Christmas imagination, implicitly, even if her role in Lutheran spirituality has been minimal. Listening to Luther's sermonizing about Mary thus offers a healthy corrective. Luther's sermon also gives the theological rationale for the spirit of hospitality and compassion that is especially expected in the Christmas season. Because of the gifts given to all of humanity in Christ, human beings are called to love their neighbour; where this shows concretely is that invitations and opportunities for charitable giving are enhanced at Christmas time:

> Here you see that He loved us and did everything for us in order that we may do the same, not for Him—for He does not need it—but for our neighbor. This is His commandment, and this is our obedience. Therefore, faith makes Christ ours, and His loves makes us His. He loves, we believe, thus we are united into one cake. Again, our neighbor believes and expects our love, we are therefore to love him also and not let him want and expect it in vain. One is the same as the other: as Christ helps us, so we help our neighbor, and all have enough. (Luther 2013: 217)

The manger scene is the foundation for Luther's theology of the cross, which is a theologically founded orientation that looks for the empowerment of the weak and naming God's presence and work in the opposite of what misguided human beings might expect in their foolishness and hunger for vainglory. Luther reminds us regarding the manger scene with Mary and Joseph: 'No one noticed or recognized what God was doing in that stable.... Oh, what a dark night this was for Bethlehem, which was not conscious of that glorious light!' And further: 'See, this is the very first picture with which Christ puts the world to shame and shows us that all it does, knows, and is, is objectionable, that its greatest wisdom is foolishness, its best action is injustice, and its greatest good is misfortune' (Luther 2013: 211).

In the spirit of Luther, Lutheran proclamation at Christmas never moves far from the Holy Week's remembering of the crucifixion but rather maintains the tension between life and death as the place to reckon the miracle of Resurrection and eternal life, the promise of which became incarnate through Mary's womb. Lutheran theology being done in the truth-telling shadow of the cross, it makes sense even when deciphering the events of the first Christmas, that the human standards of glory and success do not measure up with those of God who has chosen to come to humanity in surprising ways, in the lowliest and loneliest of places, as a God who knows suffering and stays close to those who suffer and die, a God who is not known in pomp and tinsel, but in humility and meekness.

For Luther, Christmas is an invitation to humility and simple awe before the miracles of life. After the model of Mary, human sojourners are led to different humble mangers, to find God in unexpected places, to both host and be hosted by strangers, and both receive and offer the kind of warmth and compassion Mary gave to her child. Christmas texts and hymns reverberate feelings of compassion that God has shown to humanity, in and through the holy infant Jesus. The Lutheran theology of Christmas is anchored in the experience of Mary mothering the infant Christ in the stable.

To conclude, Luther's Christmas preaching focuses on Christ and aims to bring joy to the listeners' hearts, making the Christ-offering personal and life-changing:

> See here what the Gospel is, namely, a joyful preaching concerning Christ, our Savior. Whoever preaches Him rightly preaches the Gospel and pure joy. How can a heart hear a greater joy than that Christ is given to him as his own? He not only says that Christ is born, but he also makes His birth our own by saying 'your Savior'.
> (Luther 2013: 220)

LITURGICALLY

Fast-forwarding from the sixteenth-century Lutheran reforms to the experience of contemporary Lutheran faith communities: the liturgy for Christmas today follows the framework set up in Luther's time and it resembles in essential parts that of the Catholic Mass, even to keeping the name: it is common—while not ubiquitous—for Lutherans to speak of Christmas Mass. (The word Mass has been reclaimed since the Reformation era criticisms of Catholic practices that the Evangelicals considered extraneous if not harmful, and ones that arose, in their understanding, from a misunderstanding of what the Eucharist was for and what the prerogatives for the priestly office were.)

As a reformer, Luther kept much of the order of the medieval Catholic worship that had formed his own spirituality from his youth. He underscored the importance of the heard and proclaimed Word, elevating thus the role of the sermon (including at Christmas), which shows, for example, in the ornate preaching pulpits in German churches. Two sacraments, Baptism and Eucharist, were maintained, and with them an invitation was extended to all individuals to join in contemplation of the mysteries of the birth of God in human flesh as a gift and to decipher the ensuing responses and responsibilities for Christians whose journey starts and ends with the child in the manger, Jesus. Christmastime, thus, was an especially important time for Christians to gather around the Gospel message and set the tone for the rest of the Church year.

Lutheran churches around the world have their own liturgical handbooks and worship manuals. Generally speaking, Lutherans follow a Western calendar and are in their liturgical orientation and form, design, and content, closest to that of the Anglican or Episcopalian Church. Historically, the liturgical elements for Christmas arise from the Catholic format, with modest changes negotiated slowly from the Reformation onward. In terms of scheduling, Christmas is part of the organized 'temporal schedule', which is paired with the 'sanctoral cycle' that has a fixed schedule for important commemorations of saints and special holy days. The temporal year, with Christmas and Easter as the lifeline, begins with the first Sunday in Advent (Pfatteicher 1980).

In accordance with this calendar, Lutherans' Christmas season follows after four Sundays in Advent, and lasts twelve days, from 25 December until Epiphany on 6 January. Christmas, the Feast of the Nativity, is one of the main festivals. The others are Epiphany, Baptism of our Lord, Transfiguration, Annunciation, Palm Sunday, Good Friday, Easter, Ascension, Pentecost, Holy Trinity, All Saints, and Christ the King. Most of them are so-called moveable feasts, as their date changes annually, a sequence set by first determining the date of Easter, and each having their own prayers, including special Eucharistic prayers.

In liturgy, different readings and prayers are allocated in the lectionary and different colours are designated for different Sundays and feast days. There is some variation about the colours used: for instance, in the Evangelical Lutheran Church of America, the colour for Advent is typically blue—although purple has been used also—and for Christmas the colour is white, whereas in the Evangelical Lutheran Church of Finland, white is used for the First Advent and Christmas, with other colours in between.

Advent

The First Advent Sunday marks the beginning of the Church Year, liturgically. Four Advent Sundays give a festive and anticipatory rhythm for the life of worship, as well as the framework for specific traditions followed at homes. Just as the four Sundays in Advent typically include lighting of a candle in a Christmas wreath and hymns with words of anticipation and the promise given to Mary, and special Advent music; also at home candles and anticipation lift up the mood. In many Lutheran countries, children receive Advent calendars to ease—and enhance—the anticipation, with twenty-four windows to open with a token of a gift or a Christmas message inside. Similarly, Christmas markets (aka Christkindlsmarkt) are common during Advent, a Reformation era tradition that has spread from Germany to other countries.

A special Advent tradition is that of Santa Lucia, celebrated on 13 December, which not coincidentally is also at the same time of year as the winter solstice. The third-century martyr Lucia is remembered with a celebration of light, with procession and candles, in Italy and in Scandinavia in particular. In Sweden and other Scandinavian homes, the day can involve parades, girls wearing lighted advent wreaths and serving special saffron breads; sometimes St. Lucia's celebration is incorporated into a Lutheran church's Advent offerings.

In Advent, candles decorate not only churches and houses, but also graveyards: for instance, in Finland and Iceland, it is common to light candles at graves and for families to visit the graveyard before or after attending the Christmas Mass.

Christmas Eve and Christmas Day

Advent leads to the Feast of the Nativity, celebrated on December 25th. It is preceded by Christmas Eve on December 24th, one of the days most pregnant with meaning and customs among Lutherans. Christmas Mass is offered typically on either Christmas Eve or Christmas Day, and sometimes both, with the liturgical colour of white, with or without the Eucharist.

With a great variety in detail from culture to culture, Lutheran churches typically offer different types of festival worship on Christmas Eve, anything from family afternoon service to later night worship to Midnight Mass. Christmas morning worship time varies from early morning to later morning time and is in some contexts less attended than the Christmas Eve service, if even offered at all. Whereas in some countries, like Finland and Germany, early-morning Christmas worship has been the standard, elsewhere Christmas Eve worship may mark the beginning of festivities in homes and towns. Ethnic and cultural and local differences are many and liturgical variances are allowed. (Just looking at the different schedules in North American Lutheran churches would illustrate this.) This is an area where the amalgamation of cultural and religious factors is tangible: in contexts where the home traditions with gifts and festive meals focus on Christmas Day, the worship time on Christmas Eve may be preferred; in other contexts the opposite is the case. In short, the main divide between Christmas Eve and Christmas Day service offerings is in the local (culturally rooted) traditions regarding which day is the main coming together, feasting, and gifts exchange, and what works the best for the local community.

The Christmas services typically feature high liturgy and rich music and familiar Christmas hymns—although new ones have been composed as well. If in the past the Eucharist was not always part of Christmas worship per se, recently it has become more common to include the sacrament in the Christmas Mass. The order includes the regular elements of Lutheran worship, with readings from the Bible, prayers, hymns, confession of faith, confession of sins, and proclamation. The Bible readings are set in the lectionary, with rotating options.

The days post-Christmas Day each bear their own historic meaning and often include specific customs. Worship is offered when these days fall on Sundays, and always for New Year's Day and Epiphany. The so-called second Christmas Day, St Stephen's Day, on 26 December, remembers the first Christian martyr (Acts 8:1), and the colour is red. In Finland, this was traditionally the day one was (finally, after Christmas Peace) allowed to visit others' houses, and go to sauna! Following this, St. John the Apostle is remembered before the fourth day of Christmas, the Day of the Innocents, remembering the killing of the baby boys (under 2) in Bethlehem by the order of King Herod; neither of those days have specifically Lutheran rituals. New Year's Day recognizes the circumcision of Jesus, and worship is offered with the colour white. Epiphany notes Jesus' baptism, and the visitation of the Magi, still with the liturgical colour white. Somewhere during the Christmas season, typically a worship with 'lessons and carols' or some other musically oriented service is offered. For Finnish Lutherans, a cherished tradition, at home and abroad, is 'Kauneimmat Joululaulut', the chance to sing the 'most beautiful Christmas songs'. For many, the Christmas hymns from childhood are the highlight and the most powerful invitation to still the mind, to contemplate the gift of the Christ Child, and let one's heart be warmed with compassion—the kind Luther preached about as the power that can shake heaven and earth.

References and Further Reading

Anttila, Miikka E. (2017). *Luther's Theology of Music: Spiritual Beauty and Pleasure*. Berlin/Boston: De Gruyter.

Bainton, Roland H. (2017). *Martin Luther's Christmas Book*. Minneapolis, MN: Fortress Press.

Evangelical Lutheran Book of Worship: Manual on the Liturgy. Minneapolis: Augsburg Fortress Press, 2006.

Luther, Martin. (2013). *Luther's Works*, Church Postil I, Volume 75, eds. Benjamin T. G. Mayes and James L. Langebartels. Missouri: Concordia Publishing house.

Pelikan, Jaroslav (2003). *Bach: Among the Theologians*. Eugene Oregon: Wipf and Stock.

Pfatteicher, Philip H. (1980). *Festivals and Commemorations: Handbook to the Calendar in Lutheran Book of Worship*. Minneapolis: Augsburg Fortress Press.

Pless, John T. (1998). 'Learning to Preach from Luther in Advent and Christmas', *Concordia Theological Quarterly*, 62, no. 4, October: 269–86.

CHAPTER 13

ANGLICANISM

MARTYN PERCY

ARGUABLY, the originality of Anglicanism lies in the very its lack of originality. It claims no creeds of its own. It has no distinctive doctrines. It is a broad church, encompassing a wide range of practices and beliefs. It is something of an 'ecclesial magpie', borrowing from other traditions to build its own nesting habitats. The genius of Anglicanism, wherever it is encountered across the world, lies in its blendedness and breadth. It is a faith marked by hybridity: high, low, middle; Catholic and Reformed; liberal and conservative; modern and traditional—and more besides. It as an ecclesial compound—an alloy of theologies, cultures, and traditions.

As a global denomination, Anglicanism is creative, to be sure; yet also plagiaristic, often pirating the traditions and practices of other denominations. Some of its liturgical jewels such as Evensong and Matins come from other ecclesial ecologies. Anglican polity has 'homed' these liturgies—just as it also speaks at Christmas, effortlessly, of 'Midnight Mass', even though its own doctrines and congregations seldom speak of the Eucharist in such terms. Indeed, 'Midnight Mass' is primarily a Roman Catholic service, so is a curious term for Anglicans to bestow upon their traditional late-night Christmas Eve Eucharist, given the history of the Reformation. However, the term is also used by Lutherans and Methodists who observe the same ritual. Eastern Orthodoxy observes an all-night vigil ending with Matins on Christmas Eve. In the same way, an adapted and modern service such as Christingle—and which enjoys enormous popularity in the Church of England, with around 6,000 celebrations a year—often marks the start of Advent, with many services functioning as a liturgical prelude to Christmastide, or in some cases at Epiphany. Perhaps typically for Anglicanism, the prominence of the service into the informal–pastoral–liturgical calendar of most clergy and congregations in the Church of England was not something foreseen at the outset. (The service was introduced by one John Pensom in 1968, merely as a vehicle for raising funds for the Church of England's Children's Society.)

Nowadays, Christingle services are enormously popular within British Anglicanism, and for many herald the commencement of the Christmas season. 'Christingle' is a word of Germanic origin, meaning 'Christ Child', and the service is usually geared towards children. The liturgy is celebrated at the darkest time of the year in the northern hemisphere, and was originally popularized amongst the Scandinavian churches. The roots of Christingle services lie with the German Moravian Church, and involve the custom of holding a 'Christingle'—a symbol—comprising an orange (representing the world), a candle pushed into the centre of the orange, then lit (representing Jesus as Light of the World), a red ribbon is then wrapped around the orange to represent the blood of Christ, and then some dried fruit sweets skewered into the orange, to represent the fruits of the earth and the four seasons.

The relative resilience of Christmas as a religious festival has meant that Christian faith continues to enjoy particular prominence in the public sphere, in a way that can no longer be said of festivals such as Whitsun. However, it is probably an axiomatic truth that most Anglican clergy will have an ambivalent relationship with Christmas.

The Christmas season—for 'season' is what it is—inspires an almost natural turn towards the sacred (Deacy 2016). Whether it is Carols by Candlelight, Christingle, traditional nativity plays and festive liturgies—all combine to produce an intense and widely shared public expression of religious sentiment and spiritual sentience. On the other hand, Christmas is a season with remarkably secular currents, and can seem to some to be the very antithesis of any religious celebration, mired in conspicuous consumerism and consumption. Indeed, the Christmas season was ushered in by some with a nodding reference to the Collect for the Sunday next before Advent (sometimes known as 'Stir Up Sunday'), where the *Book of Common Prayer* Collect begins 'Stir up, we beseech thee, O Lord, the wills of thy faithful people...', prompting many households to literally stir the mixture in the bowl of fruit, alcohol, and flour for the Christmas pudding that was to be served a month hence. Then again, the nostalgia that Christmas evokes can lead to a reconnection with that sustained chain of memory which is religion (Hervieu-Leger 2000). Alternatively, the season can just be viewed as one long prolonged holiday.

'Ambivalence' is a relatively modern word, and generally refers to simultaneous conflicting feelings. The term was first coined in 1910 by Swiss psychologist Eugen Bleuler, but it did not take long for the word to migrate into wider use. However one might view Christmas, it continues to provide enchantment within the modern world; people know there is more to life than the explainable and visible. Christmas is one thread or link in the chain of social memory that enables society to cohere. Whether or not churches are well attended at Christmas—and they generally are—the popularity of nativity plays at school and carol singing remains significant and pervasive (Graham 2000).

The particularity of the Church of England can lead to some quite bold forays into public life, including attempts to reclaim Christmas as primarily Christian. A number of English Anglican Evangelical proponents of such views have lobbied hard to identify Christmas as Jesus' birthday, mainly in order to remind society of its indebtedness to Christian faith, and to use the occasion as an opportunity for evangelism. Many Conservative Evangelical Anglican churches (and their associated campaigning organizations) have sometimes appeared to suggest that Christmas can only be truly celebrated and understood in a Christian context (e.g. at the millennium: '2000 – ©

Christianity'). Such views were reminiscent of the claims—often seen on wayside pulpits and signboards—that 'It isn't a genuine Christmas without the church', or that 'Christmas without Christ is *Xmas*'.

Although such claims have some merit, they generally lack subtlety. Time and seasons, and the way in which they are marked and measured, are not owned outright by any one group—religious or otherwise. In attempting to christen Christmas in such an exclusivist way, or monopolize its meaning, some Christian organizations have misunderstood the contemporary ambivalence of the feast; not understood that this ambivalence has a long-standing pedigree; and not perceived how pervasive and subtle the implicitness of Christmas continues to carry significant and meaningful spiritual meaning that still enjoys widespread public value.

To be sure, some Christians have bewailed the perceived loss of Christian feasts to 'bank holidays', holy days to holidays, the passing of the once widespread observance of Good Friday and Whit Monday, and more besides. For some Christians, Christmas and Easter are perceived as being lost to the forces of consumerism, and overtaken by secular interpretations, replete with myths involving rabbits, reindeer, and Father Christmas.

However, this sense of 'Christian time' somehow being stolen—the sacred being subsumed by the secular—may in fact be a kind of misplaced nostalgia. Many of the central Christian seasons, particularly Christmas and Easter, were originally and deliberately located within complementary or competitive calendar systems and celebrations that were pagan. The location of Christ's birthday is linked to winter and darkness, and the coming of the light. It is a solar feast that does not move. Easter, in contrast was a Christian 'baptism' of several pagan festivities, and is linked to the lunar calendar. Moreover, its deepest roots lie in another religion, namely the Passover of Judaism.

This might suggest that the task for the churches in (re-)claiming time and seasons such as Christmas is daunting, and has become even more complex in a secular and consumer-led world. Yet the scale of the problem probably depends on the extent to which one is willing to accept a general secularization thesis. Jib Fowles notes that Christmas has had a curiously brief social history (Fowles 1996). He also discusses how ambivalent this 'sacred season' had been for centuries throughout the northern hemisphere (see also, Horsley and Tracy 2001; Marling 2000). At a time when the daylight was weakest, pagan festivals included excessive drinking and eating, the exchange of gifts, normal rules and prohibitions being suspended, and even roles reversed (women and men cross-dressing, masters waiting on servants, and so on). The fifth century saw the festival Christianized, but with the old customs maintained, even if they were then reinterpreted (Nissenbaum 1996; Horsley 1993; Roll 1995).

For Anglicans in England in the sixteenth century, the censorious attentions of Protestant reformers led to the heavy policing of religious festivals that we might now regard as liturgically and socially exuberant. Similarly, in the colonies of New England in the seventeenth century, and in Great Britain under Oliver Cromwell's and Richard Cromwell's rule (i.e. the brief republican phase from 1649 until 1660), the celebration of Christmas was largely prohibited. However, this merely paved the way for the reinvention of the season in the nineteenth century. It is from this capitalist and industrial base that the extent of Christmas has widened. The season itself lasts much longer.

Fowles suggests that in the United States it runs from Thanksgiving in late November to Super Bowl Sunday (which is now usually held in early February). In this season, families are more in focus, gifts are exchanged, and our connectedness and interdependence are celebrated. So, contrary to what one might perceive, 'soft-sacred' ideology is usually given a particular voice during this notably secular of seasons, and the materialism and consumerism should probably be seen as an extension of an inborn human and religious instinct. The way we tell time is invariably a weaving together of secular and sacred symbols and seasons that point to the innately spiritual nature of our society (Deacy 2016: 125–46).

This in itself is thought provoking for Anglicanism and the (virtually) worldwide celebration of Christmas. Anglican polity, after its troubled birth in the sixteenth century, and the revolutions of the seventeenth century, has 'settled'. The word is used advisedly here, for the so-called Elizabethan Settlement is an attempt (and still 'work in progress', arguably) to establish a normative state of affairs in which unresolved tensions (e.g. between Catholic and Protestant expressions of Christianity and a national church) can live together in a kind of tense peace, which seeks to model a capacious hybridity. This finds expression, as we shall see, in liturgies.

The Anglican spirit that embraces hybridity—inculcating it into its 'ecclesial DNA', effectively—does so knowing that there will be a degree of ambivalence in the polity and the performative (i.e. pastoral and liturgical). But it is precisely this ambivalence that has enabled festivals such as Christmas to evolve so easily within it, and then be exported wholesale during the expansion of missionary endeavour and the burgeoning British Empire in the nineteenth century, which laid the foundations for what we now know as the Anglican Communion. (The Anglican Communion numbers approximately 85 million people, spread across 165 countries (Percy 2017a: 4–9)).

In Anglican polity and identity, wherever it is encountered in the world, there is a disposition towards comprehensiveness, breadth, and inclusion. The Anglican vision of the church is first and foremost, a blueprint for the ordering of society; a kind of 'social skin'. Anglican polity is therefore, first and foremost, a social vision that has ecclesial consequences. It is not (merely) an ecclesiastical polity with accidental social consequences (Avis 2016).

The ambivalent hybridity is arguably mirrored in the distinctive theological emphasis that Anglicanism is probably best known for—namely for its focus on the Incarnation. Although this is somewhat of a speculative remark, there is a case to be made for Anglican theology being particularly drawn to this doctrine. One can sense socio-ecclesial reasons for this that emerge in paradigms of practice. The emphasis can be detected in the poetry of T. S. Eliot (who borrowed freely from Launcelot Andrewes 'Sermon on the Nativity', preached before King James I on Christmas Day—a Wednesday, 1622, at Whitehall) and U. A. Fanthorpe, and in the prose of writers such as Dorothy L. Sayers and Charles Dickens. It emerges in performance too, with the Service of Nine Lessons and Carols broadcast from King's College Cambridge being, arguably, the voice and face of Anglicanism that is most seen and heard around the world (TV, radio, and Internet). First broadcast in 1928 by the BBC,[1] Nine Lessons and Carols has been copied and adapted by many other denominations.

The service of Nine Lessons and Carols was introduced by Eric Milner-White, the Dean of King's College, whose own experience as an Anglican army chaplain in the First World War had led him to champion more accessible forms of worship for the Church of England, and to some extent also to honour and memorialize those who had lost their lives in the conflict. Indeed, casualty rates from the university, city, and county of Cambridge were exceptionally high, and this may have partly moved Milner-White to inaugurate the new service.

Other very early exponents of the festival have included Brown University (Providence, Rhode Island) from 1916, Groton School (Massachusetts) from 1928, and Magdalen College School (Brackley, Northamptonshire, England) since 1899. Beginning in 1928, and with the exception of 1930, the service from King's College has been broadcast every year. It gained global influence when the BBC began broadcasting the service on its overseas programmes from the 1930s. Indeed, even during the Second World War, despite the stained glass being removed from the chapel and the lack of heating, the broadcasts continued.

The origins of the service of Nine Lessons and Carols originated from Truro Cathedral in Cornwall, with Bishop Edward Benson formalizing the service with Nine Lessons for use on Christmas Eve 1880. The service that is typically referred to as 'The Festival of Nine Lessons and Carols', tells through Scripture readings, carols, and anthems, the story of the Fall of humanity, the promise of the Messiah, and the birth of Jesus in nine short Bible lessons from Genesis, the prophetic books, culminating with one of the birth narratives from the Gospels (Matthew or Luke), and concluding with the reading of the opening of John's Gospel, proclaiming that 'the word became flesh and dwelt amongst us' (John 1:14). The service is interspersed with the singing of carols, hymns, and choir anthems, and there are often other embellishments, such as poetry and prose to complement the Scripture readings.

The popularity of 'Nine Lessons and Carols' may well lie in Milner-White's original and highly cultivated Anglican pastoral instincts, namely to provide a form of worship at a liminal time of year that was more geared to a non-churchgoing public, and was accessible and succinct. There are few occasions in the liturgical calendar when the Christian story can be told more or less in its entirety, but Milner-White's perceptive adaption of Bishop (later Archbishop) Edward Benson's 1880 template clearly struck a chord. The hybridity of the liturgy, coupled to the pastoral ambivalence the Church of England attempted to address in the aftermath of the First World War (Wilkinson 1978), probably played an important part in the sustained popularity of the festival.

---

[1] However, the current broadcast comprises seven readings, not all from Scripture, and tends to major on carols and anthems. The programme is recorded earlier in December and then broadcast on Christmas Eve, and is currently listed in the programme schedule as *Carols from King's*.

Anglican Ambivalence and Christmas Past

However, and as we noted earlier, Christmas has not always enjoyed uncritical reception and appreciation within Anglicanism. The Reformations of the sixteenth and seventeenth centuries saw a sustained socio-religious interrogation of the pervasive influence of Christmas celebrations, as Anglicanism buffered against the growing strength of Puritanism and the theology of Calvinism. Lawrence Stone has shown how the social and religious revolution of the 1640s began with reformation and counter reformations in the previous century (Stone 2017). What precipitated the revolution is complex: a lack of external threat to the nation at the time; unresolved internal tensions, and emergent inter-generational fissures; instability, including economic disequilibrium; social change, including new ideas and values; and accelerants, or actors, who are precipitants.

That Christmas came under Puritan scrutiny is not so surprising. Feast days in the Catholic liturgical calendar could be viewed as occasions of conspicuous consumption, and free occurrences of unlicensed revelry. Even under the Laudian-Royalist tradition, which might have inculcated the festivity of Christmas into a socialization that gave ventilation to a kind of implicit religion, Christmas would have flourished as a richly participative civil occasion. The Laudian presumption of faith was that monarch, bishops, clergy, and church somehow constituted the social skin of the world. Correspondingly, whatever it affirmed, or did not oppose, gained significant social licence. There were parallel issues in early New England (Nissenbaum 1996).

The Puritans saw things differently, however, and liminal mediations between congregation and society were under much greater scrutiny. Dancing, gaming, carnival, and festivity were all vested with negative value, and the potential for sin and public disorder duly flagged. Correspondingly, when the Puritans settled in America, they 'made a point of abolishing the Calendar of Christian feasts and saints' days ... [and] the celebration of Christmas was forbidden on pain of a five shilling fine' (Fischer 1992: 163). It was illegal to celebrate Christmas in Massachusetts from 1659–81. It took until the middle of the nineteenth century for Christmas to become a public holiday in New England. Up until that point, it was a normal working day, and there were no religious services in the most churches (in the early period none at all) unless Christmas fell on a Sunday.

Yet whilst life in Puritan Massachusetts might have been experienced as plain and simple, the contrast with the later colony of Virginia could hardly have been greater. David Hackett Fischer points out the differences in diet. For Puritans, simple fare of peas or beans (hence Boston beans) formed a staple (Fischer 1992: 351–2). In Virginia, which was largely settled by Royalists who fled after losing the English Civil War in 1649, the fare was rich and spiced, with dishes including veal fricassee and fried chicken—often with additional accompanying meats. For Virginians, Christmas was a twelve-day festival, a 'happy season of parties, dances, visits, gifts and celebration' (Fischer 1992: 370). The raucousness of these celebrations should not be understated, involving as they did firecrackers, bonfires, letting off guns, and games that could be quite violent in character—all with ample quantities of food and drink.

Our ancestors lived under a social *and* theological construction of reality. Moreover, these constructions of reality were far more localized, not necessarily intra-regionally putative, let alone national. So, for Virginians, the Anglican notion of 'killing time' was partly achieved through licensed festivity such as Christmas. For Puritans, 'improving time' was the order of the day, and this led to certain kinds of socio-religious prohibition, including the banning of Christmas. For the later Quaker arrivals in North America, 'redeeming the time', though different from their Puritan neighbours, still placed them at odds with the Anglican ethos of Virginia.

To understand the ferment of the Reformation era around the celebration of Christmas in early Anglicanism, and how this was, to some extent, transported to the New World, one needs to trace the origins of ambivalence rooted in the religious syncretism that was tolerated and fostered in England from earliest times. A letter sent by Pope Gregory to Abbot Mellitus on his departure for Britain in AD 601, stated that:

> ... we have been giving careful thought to the affairs of the English, and have come to the conclusion that the temples of the idols among that people should on no account be destroyed. The idols are to be destroyed, but the temples themselves are to be aspersed with holy water, altars set up in them, and relics deposited there... In this way we hope that the people, seeing their temples are not destroyed, may abandon their error and, flocking more readily to their accustomed resorts, may come to know and adore the true God. And since they have a custom of sacrificing many oxen to demons, let some other solemnity be substituted in its place such as a day of Dedication or the Festivals of holy martyrs whose relics are enshrined there... If the people are allowed some worldly pleasures in this way, they will more readily come to desire the joys of the spirit. (Bede 1955: 86-7)

'Worldly pleasures' may indeed be one pathway to ensure that others 'readily come to desire the joys of the spirit', and it may be this that provides the nascent foundation for the Anglican ambivalence towards Christmas. As Rodney Stark has pointed out, 'by thinly overlaying pagan festivals and sacred places with Christian interpretations, the seventh-century missionaries made it easier to become Christian—so easy that actual conversion seldom occurred' (Stark 2001: 114). Perhaps this partly accounts for the relaxed attitude displayed in James Woodforde's *Diary of a Country Parson*—that invaluable window into the life of the clergy and the state of English Christianity in the eighteenth century. He clearly thinks it is reasonably good to have 'two rails' (about 30 communicants) at Christmas or Easter, from approximately 360 parishioners. As Woodforde notes, his church is only ever usually full when either there is a war on or a member of the royal family is gravely ill.

Anglicanism, Christmas, and Cultural Adaptation

To some extent, the contemporary Christmas that many will now experience across the English-speaking world is in no small part a strongly Anglican (or Episcopalian) creation. Stephen Nissenbaum's work identifies the popular stories of Washington Irving, and the influence of the (so-called) Knickerbocker Set, who were Episcopalian, High Church, and conservative.[2] Irving's *Knickerbocker's History* is a significant book, as it describes things that become prompts for many of the modern Christmas traditions in the United States. Irving wrote his satirical history in 1809, under the pseudonym Diedrich Knickerbocker, and in his book-length parody of colonial America, Irving satirizes the early Dutch settlers of New York and their traditions, including their patron saint, Nicholas, whom they referred to as Sancte Claus. Indeed, Saint Nicholas is mentioned more than two dozen times in the book.

Oloffe, one of the characters created by Irving, dreams one night that St Nicholas comes riding over the tops of the trees in a wagon in which he brings his yearly presents to children. Irving's Saint Nicholas is:

> an amusing caricature of the old-time Dutch gentry who inhabited Irving's imaginary New Amsterdam: a genial yet obviously patrician saint, dressed in a broad hat and invariably smoking a long pipe. (Nissenbaum 1996: 177–8)

After that, Clement Moore, another prominent Episcopalian, wrote 'A Visit from Saint Nicholas' in 1822 in which Santa Claus is no longer appearing with a wagon and horses, but is now in a sleigh with a reindeer. The Dutch 'Sinterklass' was, in other words, transmogrified by an Episcopalian into a benevolent minister of gifts and charitableness.

For Christopher Deacy, the emergence of Santa Claus is a kind of 'quasi-religious epiphany' (Deacy 2016: 50), and was essentially a form of social and cultural re-enchantment. It is perhaps no accident that the sentimentalizing of Christmas gains significant traction following the emergence of social dislocation as a result of the Industrial Revolution and the burgeoning growth of towns and cities. Anglicanism cannot claim any monopoly on this in relation to Christmas, but in a range of cultural forms, it can justifiably assert some pre-eminence. It would be quite something to stake a claim that Santa Claus is the creation of a small group of Episcopalians. However, it is not unreasonable to suggest that in the evolution of the character, and the development of Christmas as a globally celebrated festival, Anglicanism has played a significant part.

We can see the echoes of this in Charles Dickens' *A Christmas Carol*, with strong sentiments of ethics and spirituality woven through the drama. There is also, arguably, some eliding with the character of Scrooge, in his misanthropy, representing a kind of

---

[2] Nissenbaum, 1996, pp. 177–8.

censorious Puritanical world view in driving away the carol singers. However, the character of Scrooge as Puritan-like would have reached back into Victorian folk memory. One should not forget that in medieval and early modern England, the carol singers would be 'wassailing'. This would be groups of peasants going from house to house, and in 'a seasonal mood of social inversion, entering unbidden into the homes of their socioeconomic superiors with demands for favours and treats' (Horsley and Tracy 2001: 3). A wealthy homeowner would have understood the threat of 'give us some figgy pudding; we won't go until we get some', since the failure to supply food and drink might mean the visit of the unwelcome guests who had effectively invaded the house might develop into a sourer occasion.

Because Christmas never had an immaculate conception—it is inherently a hybrid in origin, purpose, and practice—its cultural form has evolved from 'a peasant celebration marked by excess, carnality, and a significantly, at least momentary, social inversion' (Horsley and Tracy 2001: 2–3). We should not gloss over just how ambivalent its reception was, as its very celebration was socially divisive. As Nissenbaum notes, Christmas festivity was an occasion that platformed the mockery of established authority and aggressive begging (with menacing threats directed towards the allegedly uncharitable). Social hierarchy was symbolically turned upside down, with designated roles of gender, age, and class all subverted (Nissenbaum 1996: 7–9). Elders and betters were often sardonically mocked. A boy might dress as a bishop, and a peasant might be designated as the 'Lord of Misrule', as an ersatz representation of the actual lord of the manor or the landed gentry. Men dressed as women; and women as men. Servants dressed as masters. (This cross-dressing and wearing of disguises was known as 'mumming' or 'mummering', and is still practised in parts of Great Britain, Ireland, Canada, and the United States.) There was considerable social pressure for masters to wait on servants. And 'chambering' (a euphemism for fornication) was commonplace. In the emerging towns and cities of the early nineteenth century, the Christmas celebrations had evolved into more anti-social behaviour, with a movement from carnival rowdiness to Christmas season riots and, in some places, even developed into urban gang violence (Nissenbaum 1996: x–xi).

The antecedents for this behaviour were, in part, what the Puritans had reacted against. Whereas the tendency of Anglican polity had been largely permissive towards Christmas, the Puritans mainly saw social nuisance and widespread vice. The Reverend Increase Mather of Boston complained in 1687 about Christmas being a season of debauchery, drunkenness, gaming, and mad mirth (Nissenbaum 1996: 6–7). His son, the Reverend Cotton Mather observed that the celebration of Christ's Nativity was marked by displays of lewdness and licentiousness, with heavy drinking, excessive eating, and revelry. In England, similarly, the Reverend Henry Bourne of Newcastle, in 1725, complained of Christmas as an excuse for drunkenness, rioting and wantonness, with the season stretching up to Candlemas (February 2) (Nissenbaum 1996: 7).

Perhaps recognizing that Christmas was always a difficult holiday or season to Christianize, and that there were only a handful of citizens for whom it was a time of pious devotion, Anglican polity had largely left Christmas to its own devices for the three centuries following the Reformation. However, this changed in the nineteenth century, and to a large extent, the missiological pulse of Anglicanism that focused on re-enchantment has shaped the worshipping practice and wider social celebration of Christmas. Anglicanism's vocational response to the socio-economic and cultural challenges of the nineteenth century found their fullest expression in vigorous forms of Evangelicalism and Anglo-Catholicism. The former stressed piety and probity, and the latter aesthetics and enchantment. Both expressions had some investment in a degree of nostalgia, and a significant impact on the evolution of Christmas as a festival, and here we can make three observations.

First, and partly through groups such as the Knickerbockers, Christmas began to be transferred from un-licensed public merrymaking into a more domestic domain, which in turn found expression in local churchgoing. The class-based demand of gifts from elites—hitherto reciprocated only by the promise of 'goodwill' from a recipient underclass—shifted to an ecology that was more family-based, with children receiving gifts from parents. Christmas became, through Santa Claus, domesticated, and more focused on the home. Second, the old ways of celebrating Christmas—public rowdiness, threats, and extensive drunkenness—were now seen as anti-social, or even as crimes. These were replaced by the notion of the 'real' or 'traditional' Christmas, an affective re-enchantment of the festival that now stressed charity and reciprocity. Third, the celebration of Christmas emerged as a new form of social control, in much the same way as harvest festival had tamed and domesticated the earlier and rather rowdier celebrations of Lammas.[3] Now, at Christmas, Santa Claus became that 'mythical mediator for the exchange of gifts [which] also served to ease the guilt about indulgence and the ambivalence towards mass-produced goods felt by middle-class parents in the early nineteenth century' (Horsley and Tracy 2001: 4). Put another way, Christmas became a fusion of capitalism and Christianity—and so the perfect blend of festive-feasting for developed societies in the modern era.

Conclusion

The relatively recent cultural history of Christmas is rooted in a diverse range of sources, of which religion constitutes one portion. For example, Mark Connelly suggests that

---

[3] Modern British traditions of celebrating harvest festival largely owe their origins to the inventive Revd Robert Hawker, who in 1843, invited parishioners to a special thanksgiving service at his church at Morwenstow in Cornwall. Hawker's Service of Harvest Festival captured the churchgoing imagination, and the fashion for such services quickly spread. Victorian hymns such as *We plough the fields and scatter*, *Come, ye thankful people, come* and *All things bright and beautiful*, along with translated Dutch and German harvest hymns, also helped to popularize the mid-Victorian celebrations of harvest festival, which included the annual custom of bedecking churches with local produce.

the material produced by the BBC and American and British cinema about, and for, Christmas tended to emphasize family values, the antiquity of Victorian Christmas...[it is] a moment of spiritual communion for the English-speaking communities across the globe. (Connelly 2012: xiii)

The notion of Christmas as a vehicle of 'spiritual communion' is suggestive. The festival may be a kind of 'Implicit Religion' (Bailey 1997; Bailey 1998), albeit one especially shaped by an Anglican ethos. The concept of Implicit Religion can act as a counterbalance towards the tendency automatically to equate 'religion' with specialized institutions, articulated beliefs, and specific religious behaviour. Above all, the lens of Implicit Religion allows us to read aspects of contemporary society for elements of religiosity within what, to the more casual observer, might conventionally be seen as a 'normative' secular sphere. Christmas celebrations within Anglicanism arguable fall into this category.

Implicit Religion is an approach that is neither 'civil' nor 'folk' in broad outlook. It is, rather, an intentional focus on ordinary everyday activity that may appear, at first sight, to have no element of spirituality or religion to it at all. Moreover, the participants may have no explicit idea that what they are doing can be read and understood as 'religious'. So, their participation is often unconscious. For example, John Hardy, drawing on the work of Edward Bailey, discusses how ordinary weather-related talk is a form of sublimated spirituality, and hints at the almost reassuring liturgical-like chant of the shipping forecast on *BBC Radio 4*, every midnight. (Hardy 2017). In a similar way, the resonant themes of 'Christmas culture', even when seemingly detached from religion, produce evocative resonances of the sacred and divine (Brown 1999: 102–4). The gift-exchange ecology of the festive season, reflected and amplified in Anglican worship, meets this religious impulse (Bailey 1990).

So, we should not be surprised at the continuing rise in the number of attendees or worshippers in Anglican churches at Christmas. But as with much statistical analysis, there is a deeper story behind these numbers that tells us how to interpret the bare arithmetic. To understand the growth of Anglican worshippers at Christmastide, one needs to have some grasp of the nuanced ecology of English churchgoing. Social exchange theory can help with such interpretations. Arguably, for the population as a whole, classic Christmas church attendance is a 'low-threshold' pursuit—that is to say, anyone can come, without any need or pressure to join a rota, group, class, or other supplementary activity. However, this kind of 'low threshold' at Christmastide—be it Nine Lessons and Carols, Christingle, or Midnight Mass—is most likely complemented by some 'high reward' for attendees and worshippers. From an English Anglican perspective, and as David Brown comments, 'far from being embarrassed by the greater popularity of Christmas, the Church might take note of the fact that the infant provides a more easily accessible symbol of new life than the resurrection of Easter Sunday' (Brown 1999 102).

The ambivalent hybridity of Christmas is apparent wherever you scratch the surface of seemingly traditional customs. Christmas carols have invariably consisted of a secular–sacred 'musical-mash'. Old folk tunes have acquired spiritual verse, such that we can no longer tell the secular apart from the sacred. Much of our Christmas food, movement, and traditions have been rechristened with sacred meanings. Christianity has always taken the pagan, or the secular, and used it as a vehicle for the religious. Indeed, Brown argues that some of the cultural customs of Christmas—mistletoe, holly, Yule logs, and Christmas trees—which to some are just pagan, are actually pregnant with spiritual meaning, drawing on ancient religious roots:

> even the custom of kissing under the mistletoe, surprising as it may seem, was once associated with explicit Christian symbolism. In fourteenth-century England it was the custom to embrace anyone visiting one's home at Christmas under the Holy Bough, a nativity scene placed in the shape of a bough hanging inside the front door and surrounded by mistletoe. (Brown 1999: 104; Morris 1992: 67–8)

As Brown reminds us, the power of the Christmas story is not lost or undermined if 'external material from the surrounding culture is used to illuminate or even to rewrite its story' (Brown 1999: 104). It is this assimilation, leading to an ambivalent hybridity, that the Anglican tradition does naturally so well, and so authentically at Christmas. So, at Christmastide, and despite familiar clergy ambivalence, Anglicanism is arguably at its best and most authentic. It is likely that the festive music will invariably be of finer quality. The preaching will be of a high calibre. (For modern examples of Christmas sermons, see Ladd 1942: 29–33; Farrer 1991; Perham 2018: 12–23; Percy 2017c: 48–56; Percy 2007). And the liturgy will be both accessible and elegant. Indeed, extensive efforts to produce evocative and engaging liturgy for Christmas—liturgy that connects with the wider public—continues to be part of the Anglican repertoire of worship (see, for instance, Stancliffe 1991). This is in contrast to the standard modus operandi for the Church of England, which has in recent years drifted into something more akin to a denomination of 'high threshold and high reward' for 'members-only'. True, a 'high-threshold' church may offer members a rich menu and a variety of groups and activities, which visitors might want to join. But there is a sense in which the spirit of Christmas—a church that offers a 'low-threshold-high-reward' experience—expresses the *true* essence of English Anglicanism. That is to say, the services will embody a quality and commitment in pastoral and liturgical endeavour for *all* those attending, quite independent of any reciprocation on their part (Percy 2017b). In that sense, the ecclesiology expresses the theology: the Christ Child is for all, and not just the committed. This is meaning of the incarnation, after all, and a modern Collect used by many Anglican churches at Christmas reflects this spiritual sentiment:

> Blessed are you O Christmas Christ,
> that your cradle was so low that shepherds,
> poorest and simplest of earthly folk,
> could kneel beside it and look level-eyed
> into the face of God. (Morley 1992: 45)

At Christmastide, Anglicanism rediscovers and renews itself as a form of ecclesiology that expresses the particularity and theology of the Incarnation, dwelling in the midst of the communities the churches serve. In gift, festivity, and exuberance, new life and hope is celebrated in the darkest of seasons. Charity to all is affirmed, and the church once again resumes its vocation as the social skin of the world. The Word made flesh dwells amongst us once again, full of grace and truth; and a symbol of enduring light amidst the darkness.

REFERENCES AND FURTHER READING

Andrewes, Launcelot (2005).'Sermon preached before the King on Christmas Day, 1609', in Peter McCullough (ed), *Launcelot Andrewes: Selected Sermons and Lectures*, Oxford English Texts. Oxford, Oxford University Press: 162–77.

Avis, Paul (2016). 'Polity and Polemics: The Function of Ecclesiastical Polity in Theology and Practice', *Ecclesiastical Law Journal*, 18: 2–13.

Bailey, Edward (1990). 'The Implicit Religion of Contemporary Society: Some Studies and Reflections', *Social Compass*, 37: 483–97.

Bailey, Edward (1997). *Implicit Religion in Contemporary Society*. Kampen, Netherlands: Kok Pharos.

Bailey, Edward (1998). *Implicit Religion: An Introduction*. London: Middlesex University Press.

Barnett, James (1954). *The American Christmas: A Study in National Culture*. New York: Macmillan.

Bede (1955). 'A Copy of the Letter Sent by Pope Gregory to Mellitus on his Departure for Britain, AD 601', in *Bede: A History of the English Church and People*, translated by Leo Sherley-Price, London: Penguin: 86–7.

Brown, David (1999). *Tradition and Imagination*. Oxford: Oxford University Press.

Connelly, Mark (2012). *Christmas: A History*, London: I. B. Tauris.

Deacy, Christopher (2016). *Christmas as Religion*. Oxford: Oxford University Press.

Eliot, T. S. (1974). 'Journey of the Magi', in T. S. Eliot, *T. S. Eliot: Collected Poems 1909–1962*. London: Faber and Faber: 99.

Austin Farrer, Austin (1991). *Austin Farrer: The Essential Sermons*. ed. Leslie Houlden. London: SPCK.

Fischer, David Hackett (1992). *Albion's Seed: Four British Folkways in America*. New York: Oxford University Press.

Fowles, Jib (1996). *Advertising and Popular Culture*. Thousand Oaks, Calif.: Sage Publications.

Graham, Elaine (2000). '"The Story" and "our stories": Narrative Theology, Vernacular Religion and the Birth of Jesus', in George Brooke (ed.), *The Birth of Jesus: Biblical and Theological Reflections*. Edinburgh: T & T Clark: 89–100.

Hardy, John (2017). 'Overheard in Passing: Talking (of) Weather, Funerals and Implicit Religion', *Theology*, 120, no. 2 (July/August): 271–8.

Hervieu-Leger, Danielle (2000). *Religion as a Chain of Memory*. Cambridge: Polity Press.

Horsley, Richard (1993). *The Liberation of Christmas*. London: Continuum.

Horsley, Richard and Tracy, James (eds.) (2001). *Christmas Unwrapped: Consumerism, Christ and Culture*. Harrisburg PA: Trinity Press International.
Ladd, William Palmer (1942). *Prayer Book Interleaves*. Oxford: Oxford University Press.
Marling, Karal Ann (2000). *Merry Christmas!* Cambridge, MA: Harvard University Press.
Morley, Janet (1992). *Bread of Tomorrow*. Maryknoll, NY: Orbis, 1992.
Morris, Desmond (1992). *Christmas Watching*. London: Jonathan Cape.
Nissenbaum, Stephen (1996). *The Battle for Christmas*. New York: Alfred A. Knopf.
Percy, Martyn (2017a). *The Future Shapes of Anglicanism: Currents, Contours, Charts*. London: Routledge.
Percy, Martyn (2017b). 'The Household of Faith', in Paul Avis and Benjamin Guyer (eds.), *The Lambeth Conference: Theology, History, Polity and Purpose*. London: Bloomsbury: 316–40.
Percy, Martyn (ed.) (2017c). *Untamed Gospel*. London: Canterbury Press.
Percy, Martyn et al. (eds.) (2007). *Darkness Yielding*. 4th ed. London: Canterbury Press.
Perham, Michael (2018). *One Unfolding Story*. London: Canterbury Press.
Roll, Susan (1995). *Towards the Origins of Christmas*. Kampen: Kok Pharos Press.
Stancliffe, David (ed.) (1991). *The Promise of His Glory*. London: Liturgical Press/Continuum.
Stark, Rodney (2001). 'Efforts to Christianize Europe, 400–2000', *Journal of Contemporary Religion*, 16, no. 1: 105–23.
Stone, Lawrence (2017). *The Causes of the English Revolution 1529–1642*, rev. ed. London: Routledge.
Wilkinson, Alan (1978). *The Church of England During the First World War*. London: SPCK.

CHAPTER 14

REFORMED AND DISSENTING PROTESTANTS

ANDREW R. HOLMES

THE meaning and observance of Christmas has always been contested, and perhaps those most associated with opposition are to be found amongst Reformed and Dissenting Protestants. In the aftermath of the Reformation, Puritans, Scottish Presbyterians, and their heirs in both the Old and New Worlds most vociferously opposed and effectively proscribed the religious and secular observance of Christmas. Yet taking a longer perspective demonstrates that they too wavered between protest and participation and had to adapt their principles to changing circumstances. Was Christmas a holy day, a holiday, or neither? How could church leaders and theologians transform popular opinion and practice? Complexity of attitudes and often-pragmatic accommodation were inescapable as marking the passage of time involved a range of knotty issues—'biblicism, primitivism, Sabbatarianism, anti-Catholicism, the re-evaluation of the uses and role of tradition, Christian liberty, issues of adiaphora, and the reform of popular calendrical customs and the folk mores reflected in them' (Schmidt 1994: 94). Their attitudes were further complicated by Church–State relations and denominational differences in which the celebration of Christmas became a sign of difference. Most of the groups belonging to these traditions dissented from Episcopalian state churches and objected to liturgies that followed the Christian year; even in Scotland, where Presbyterians became the state church, the religious non-observance of Christmas became a symbol of Scottish identity against their larger English neighbour. Opposition to Christmas was also tempered over time by the involvement of Reformed and Dissenting Protestants in the broader evangelical movement and the commercial and industrial revolutions of the period. Groups belonging to this tradition were both the cause and the victim of the secularization and commercialization of the season.

Opposition to Christmas in the Old and New Worlds, c.1560–1690

Reformed Protestants throughout Europe rejected the yearly cycle of holy days that marked the late medieval church in favour of a view of sacred time that was focused upon weekly Sunday worship. At the same time, most continental Reformed churches, apart from Geneva, did approve of the religious observance of the main events in the life of Christ, including his Nativity, though this was rejected by Puritans and Presbyterians in Britain and Ireland (Benedict 2002: 495–6). The observance or non-observance of holy days in general was significant because the ritual year was central to the life-cycle of early-modern communities. As a consequence, the assault on the religious and secular observance of Christmas in Britain and Ireland was part of a broader campaign to transform popular culture by the application of biblical principles. Those opposed to Christmas objected to any religious observance that was not explicitly commanded in the Bible (the so-called regulative principle) and which was seen as a vestige of popery. Puritans in England were reacting against what they believed was a half-Reformed Elizabethan Church of England, which, in Conrad Russell's memorable phrase, 'looked Catholic, and sounded protestant' (Russell 1996: 280). As the debates between mainstream churchmen and Puritans gained momentum by the early seventeenth century, different approaches to marking sacred time became 'vivid symbols' of their differences. On the one hand, there was the yearly Christological cycle of Anglicans and Roman Catholics, while, on the other, there was 'the iconoclastic reductionism of the Puritan calendar' that replaced the Christian year with weekly Sabbath observance (Davies 1975: 216). The religious observance of Christmas came to represent the growing tensions between the Crown and Parliament that would eventually issue in the wars of the three kingdoms of England, Scotland, and Ireland after 1638. For the Stuart monarchy which wanted to unite the kingdoms through state churches that observed the authority of bishops and followed the same liturgy, the observance of the Christian year reinforced the bond between rulers and the ruled. For their Puritan opponents, such a course ran counter to biblical teaching, encouraged popery and superstition, and perverted the moral life of the nation. This clash of world views explains in part the brutal treatment of William Prynne during the reign of Charles I. In *Histriomastix* (1633), Prynne produced an exhaustive—and exhausting—denunciation of the evils of the period in which Christmas became the embodiment of excess and popish saturnalia:

> When our Saviour was borne into the world at first, we heare of no feasting, drinking, healthing, roaring, carding, dicing, Stage-plays, Mummeries, Masques or heathenish Christmas pastimes; alas these precise puritanicall Angels, Saints and shepherds (as some I fear account them) knew no such pompous pagan Christmas Courtships or solemnities, which the Divell and his accursed instruments have since appropriated to his most blessed Nativity. (Prynne 1633: 768)

Histriomastix was one of a number of criticisms published by Prynne against the rule of Charles I and his reforms of the Church of England, and for his efforts, Prynne was fined £5,000, imprisoned, had his ears clipped, and was branded on the cheeks for seditious libel (Lamont 2011). For the Royalists who responded to the charges of Prynne and others, Christmas was linked 'with the good old days and the cause of King and Church' (Pimlott 1960: 834).

It was the influence of a different religious culture in another of the Stuart realms that brought to a head tensions between the Crown and Puritans. The Reformation in Scotland was a popular Calvinist movement in defiance of the Catholic monarchy of Mary, Queen of Scots. The First Book of Discipline (1560) abolished the Christian year and its holy days because they were not commanded in the Bible. This was confirmed when the Kirk welcomed the Second Helvetic Confession in 1566 but excluded those clauses that allowed for the religious observance of events connected with the life of Christ (McMillan 1931: 300–1). An active campaign of suppression on the part of the Kirk was carried out from the 1570s. In 1573, Aberdeen Kirk session put on trial fourteen women for 'playing, dancing and singing of filthy carols on Yule Day at even'; from 1583, Glasgow session 'ordered that those who kept Yule were to be excommunicated and also punished by the secular magistrates' (Hutton 1996: 26). The General Assembly of the Scottish church in 1575 asked the Regent to abolish 'Yule Day, Saints' Days and such others', and to impose penalties upon those who marked those days with festivities (McMillan 1931: 302). Yet, there was widespread resistance, including in the royal court of James VI of Scotland, later James I of England, Scotland, and Ireland. The resolutions against Christmas and other holy days in the 1570s testified to the slow pace of reform, and it was only in 1592 that the Scottish Parliament abolished previous acts requiring the religious observance of Easter and Christmas (Todd 2002: 184–5). Though the pronouncements of the Kirk were not always enacted upon, many clergy and church courts were serious in their opposition. As a consequence, when James I imposed the Articles of Perth on Scotland in 1618, Presbyterian resolve was intensified. The fifth of the five articles stated that, 'Christ's Nativity, Passion, Resurrection, and Ascension, and of Pentecost should be devoutly observed' (McMillan 1931: 312). The General Assembly compiled a lengthy protest, the ninth clause of which offered a wholehearted critique of holy days: 'They sett loose the filthie minds and mouths of fleshlie livers, to triumph against the most sound and best reformed professors, and to rejoice in their rotten opinions, and restored opportunities of sensuall observation, of guysing, gluttonie, carells, &c' (Calderwood 1844: 329). James was unmoved by such protests and matters deteriorated further under his son and heir, Charles I. In 1638 the General Assembly formally abolished the Five Articles, forbade any future discussion of them, and required some ministers to condemn their previous practice and preach 'penitential sermons' (McMillan 1931: 326).

The opposition of Scottish Presbyterians to the policies of Charles I led to the Bishop's Wars of 1639 and 1640 that began the descent into war in all three of the Stuart kingdoms. In 1643, Scots Presbyterians and English Puritans entered a formal alliance—the Solemn League and Covenant—that bound the signatories to 'the extirpation of Popery, prelacy... superstition, heresy, schism, profaneness' (Anon. 1894: 277). This was a significant moment as it brought together the two groups most opposed to the observance of Christmas and created the opportunity for shaping public opinion against the religious and secular misuse of the 25 December. Their reasons for doing so were a mixture of the theological, moral, and practical—they objected to Christmas because no date was given for Christ's birth in the Bible, the celebrations were associated with paganism and carnival, and it was a time of misrule that involved inverting and mocking social norms. As Stephen Nissenbaum observes, part of the explanation for the Puritan attitude was a recognition that the religious observance of Christmas was a compromise made with popular culture a thousand years previously. 'It may not be going too far to say that Christmas has always been an extremely difficult holiday to *Christianize*. Little wonder that the Puritans were willing to save themselves the trouble' (Nissenbaum 1997: 8).

The first flashpoint occurred in 1644 when 25 December fell upon a religious fast day appointed by the English Parliament. Dutifully, many parliamentarians attended sermons, including one delivered before the House of Lords by Edmund Calamy. This day, according to Calamy, had been 'much abused to superstition and prophanenesse', and it was difficult 'to reckon whether the superstition hath beene greater, or the prophanenesse'. The only way to deal with these evils was root and branch reform. 'This yeare God by a Providence hath buried this Feast in a Fast, and I hope it will never rise again. You have set out... a strict Order for the keeping of it, and you are here this day to observe your own Order, and I hope you will do it strictly' (Calamy 1644: 41). The following year, Parliament issued a number of documents aimed at the reform and reorganization of the national church, including 'The Directory of the Public Worship of God'. An appendix to the Directory stated, 'There is no Day commanded in Scripture to be kept holy under the Gospel, but the Lord's Day, which is the Christian Sabbath. Festival Days, vulgarly called Holy-Days, having no Warrant in the Word of God, are not to be continued' (Anon. 1894: 300). In June 1647, Parliament abolished the observance of Christmas and the other feast days of the Christian year. Later that year, a concerted effort was made in some areas to enforce the non-observance of 25 December. This was met with 'passive and active' resistance in London, Norwich, Ipswich, Ealing, and Canterbury. Shops that remained opened were attacked, there were skirmishes between rival groups, and there were fatalities in Ipswich (Pimlott 1960: 835–6). A pamphlet war between supporters and opponents of Christmas was undertaken. One anonymous author rehearsed the usual Puritan critique and claimed that, 'It is no wonder... that so many popish, ignorant, idle, deboyst, superstitious, Atheistical, loose, and profane people, are unwilling to part with Christmas, it being a time so suitable to their corrupt humours, and base lusts' (Anon. 1651: 4).

Puritanism, of course, crossed to the New World. In New England it was illegal to celebrate Christmas in Massachusetts between 1659 and 1681, while the authorities in Connecticut proscribed Christmas and mince pies (Nissenbaum 1997: 3; Bowler 2000: 186). Once more, Christmas became a convenient means of lamenting the ills of society. Increase Mather in 1687 included Christmas as an example of declining moral standards alongside stage plays, dancing, and maypoles. Most of the 'Christmas-keepers' paid no attention to the religious significance of Christ's birth but instead were 'consumed in Compotations, in Interludes, in playing at Cards, in Revellings, in excess of Wine, in mad Mirth; Will Christ the holy Son of God be pleased with such Services?' Such behaviour was bad anywhere, but was especially so in New England—'Immanuels Land'—and they could expect God's displeasure to be revealed unless they repented of their sinful ways (Mather 1687: 26, 31). It seems that popular attitudes, even in Puritan New England, remained difficult to change, and Cotton Mather repeated his father's charges in 1712:

> Can you in your conscience think, that our Holy Saviour is honoured, by mad mirth, by long eating, by hard drinking, by lewd gaming, by rude revelling; by a Mass fit for none but a Saturn, or a Bacchus, of the night of a Mahometan Ramadan?   (Mather 1712: 20)

The testimony of the Mathers is suggestive. Generally speaking, the Puritan and Presbyterian assault on Christmas was more successful in outlawing religious observance than eradicating popular pastimes. This 'offers a striking example of the law of unintended consequences: condemned by puritans as profane, Christmas had become even more secular once its religious dimensions had been supressed' (Capp 2012: 24). Christmas was revived in England after the Restoration of the monarchy in 1660, though popular festivity was less obvious than previously, and Scottish Presbyterians continued to oppose Christmas as they chafed under episcopal dominance. The so-called Glorious Revolution of 1688–9 uncoupled Christmas in England and Scotland and allowed Presbyterian Scots to abolish Christmas as a religious festival, but with ambiguous implications. The New-Year celebration of Hogmanay became the principal midwinter festival. It had none of the Christian connotations of Christmas and has continued ever since to offer an alternative to the domesticity and safety of the Victorian Christmas. Into this atmosphere, it 'blew like a raw northern wind, smelling of alcohol. Its "natural" community was that of friendship, not family, and its deity was not Father Christmas but the more menacing one of Father Time' (Hutton 1996: 122).

The persistence of popular observance may be interpreted as a sign of failure, yet it also testified to the pragmatism—the canny sense of priorities—of the reformers. They wanted to create a new, Bible-based religious culture of self-discipline and simplicity. As Margot Todd reminds us, elders in local Kirk sessions, 'were no fools; they chose their battles carefully, and with the priorities of the larger church and community in mind'. They 'tempered voluble disapproval with relative tolerance, until they had developed viable alternatives that would in the end redefine the festal culture of early modern Scotland'. The records of church courts are full of discipline cases against improper behaviour at Christmas and efforts to change popular perceptions, including a minister in Elgin who searched kitchens on Christmas Day for the 'superstitious goose, telling them that the feathers of them would rise up against them one day'.

Yet, unless 'festivity degenerated into serious disorder, destruction of property or violence', kirk sessions stuck to denunciation (Todd 2002: 185–6, 217, 224).

ENLIGHTENMENT, COMMERCE, AND EVANGELICALISM, C.1690–1800

In the eighteenth century, objections to the religious observance of Christmas endured while opposition to the excesses of the holiday season were reinforced by social and economic developments. The commercial and industrial revolutions prioritized time-management and economic efficiency, and contributed to the cult of respectability that dominated Victorian mores. Leigh Eric Schmidt has argued that by 1800, the 'confluence of Protestant Sabbatarianism, Enlightenment rationalism, industrial work discipline, and commercial capitalism had forged a consensus: Popular forms of celebration, plebeian patterns of leisure, and the bountiful round of holy days were bad for business' (Schmidt 1997: 29–30). This was expressed in 1840 in the sixth report of the Select Committee of the House of Commons for the Regulation of Mills and Factories. One witness noted that, 'Mill-owners who belong to the Church of England will very often become Dissenters, so far as denying the sacredness of Christmas-day and Good Friday, if the law does not absolutely prohibit working on those days' (Anon. 1840: 156).

In England, the religious non-observance of Christmas helped define Protestant Dissenters against the Church of England. Comprising between 5 and 10 per cent of the population, Dissenters were in no position to enforce their views. They sought instead a toleration for their distinctive position, a task that was given added urgency as they divided into Trinitarian and non-Trinitarian groups. In December 1706, Benjamin Robinson, the Trinitarian minister of Little St Helen's Presbyterian congregation in Bishopsgate, London, preached a sermon on relations between Church and Dissent. As both groups agreed upon the principal facts of the Gospel, Robinson urged forbearance on minor matters. Though the evidence clearly supported the view that 25 December was not the birthday of Jesus, 'I think it better to leave this still, a doubtful thing' (Robinson 1707: 13). James Peirce, another Presbyterian minister, though anti-Trinitarian, came to a similar conclusion about the observance of holy days in a sermon preached on 25 December 1716. Christians 'ought...to bear with one another's differing sentiments and practices, without envying, or grievously censuring, the liberty which is used on both sides' (Peirce 1728: 286). In a sermon preached in 1770, Joshua Toulmin, the Unitarian minister of Mary Street General Baptist Chapel in Taunton, dutifully listed the usual reasons for opposing the observance of special days. What is significant about Toulmin's analysis is the clarity with which he reflected the values of the new commercial and industrial age:

> A Disinclination to Industry is contracted: and Habits of Idleness and Debauchery are formed. Every such Day is an Incentive to personal Vice, and a Loss to the civil

Community; for it is deprived of the Fruits and Advantages, which would otherwise be derived from the Diligence and Labours of its most numerous and useful Members; so that if the Time lost to the Employments of Trade and Manufacture, was spent in Sobriety and innocent Mirth, yet the Publick would receive no inconsiderable Detriment.   (Toulmin 1771: 15)

Though the rational biblicism of eighteenth-century Unitarianism was replaced in the nineteenth century by James Martineau's emphasis on individual spirituality and conscience, many of the heirs of rational Dissent continued not to observe Christmas well into the Victorian age (Reed 2009/10).

Opposition to Christmas was connected by some to the Enlightenment-inspired call to public virtue, reasonable religion, and radical politics. David Williams, a former Presbyterian minister in England and friend of Benjamin Franklin, argued that the only acceptable response to the Incarnation was to practise disinterested virtue and charity towards the poor (Williams 1774: 76–91). Protestant Dissenters throughout Britain and Ireland were supporters of political reform and sympathetic to both the American and French Revolutions (Bradley 2001). An example of this interplay was William Steel Dickson, a theologically liberal Presbyterian minister in Ulster and at one time Adjutant General of the Society of United Irishmen who organized an ill-fated rebellion against British rule in Ireland in 1798. On 25 December 1792, Dickson preached a sermon to his congregation in Portaferry, County Down, on the angelic anthem recorded in Luke 2. Dickson stated that there was no biblical authority for observing Christ's birth, yet, as the day was still observed, '[I]t is better to apply it to religious services, than spend it in dissipation, drunkenness, and blasphemy—a practice equally injurious to religion, inconsistent with the purpose of a Saviour's coming, and dishonorable to men.' Dickson then focused on the angel's call for 'Peace on Earth', and how religious disputes since Constantine had been caused by 'the religion of the state, and not the religion of Jesus'. Yet in the wake of the French Revolution, a new age was at hand that would result in the removal of political disabilities against those who dissented from the religion of the state:

> That national 'justice may roll down as waters, and righteousness as a mighty stream'—that civil pains and penalties, on account of religion, may be abolished for ever—and that equal liberty—equal privilege, and equal protection, may henceforth, be the portion of all the people; unite them in the bonds of inviolable brotherhood; and perpetuate their attachment to their king and constitution, by a community of interest in the peace and prosperity of their country!
> (Dickson 1812, Appendix 37, 53, 56)

In his sermon, Dickson also noted that the Church–State connection had held back the global extension of Christianity. From a Protestant perspective, this became a priority as Evangelicalism expanded rapidly in the second half of the eighteenth century. One of the most obvious expressions of this was the gradual emergence of Methodism out of the Church of England and its spectacular transatlantic growth during the Age of Revolutions. Reflecting their Anglican roots, Methodists embraced Christmas as an opportunity to remind individuals about the state of their souls and to encourage communal piety (Schmidt 1994: 101). This was reflected in the Advent hymns of Charles Wesley, most famously, 'Hark! The Herald Angels Sing' (Baker 2007). The evangelical call to personal conversion and missionary activism helped reduce denominational tensions and gradually brought Protestants together. This even had an effect on attitudes to holy days. Joseph Hart, an Independent minister who was converted in 1757, reflected this attitude in one of his hymns, 'Holy Days':

> Some Christians to the Lord regard a Day;
>   And others to the Lord regard it not.
> Now though these seem to choose a different Way;
>   Yet both, at last, to one same point are brought...
>
> Let not the observer, therefore, entertain
>   Against his brother any secret grudge:
> Nor let the non-observer call him vain;
>   But use his freedom and forbear to judge.
>
> Thus both may bring their motives to the test;
>   Our condescending Lord will both approve.
> Let each pursue the way that likes him best;
>   He cannot walk amiss, that walks in love (Hart 1759: 49–50).

The contribution of Old Dissenters and Evangelicals to Christmas hymnody is significant, though often under-appreciated. For instance, Isaac Watts, the most important composer of sacred song amongst Old Dissent, composed 'Joy to the World', while James Montgomery, a Moravian from Ulster, penned 'Angels from the realms of glory' (Bowler 2000, 124–5, 8). Hymns proved to be very important in weakening the opposition of Protestant Dissenters to the observance of Christmas in New England. In concert with Anglicans, Evangelical Dissenters helped undermine hostility to Christmas by choosing hymns that prioritized 'lyrical and emotional effectiveness', a process that was underpinned by singing schools and choirs that attracted young people (Nissenbaum 1996: 150).

Acceptance and Continued Opposition to the Present Day

How did Reformed and Dissenting Protestants respond to the emergence of the modern Western Christmas in the second quarter of the nineteenth century? In many respects, the story is one of capitulation to the relentless logic of commercialization, Victorian respectability, and the elevation of childhood innocence. For many scholars, religious considerations did not play a significant role in this process. When religious developments are mentioned, the focus is on the revival of Anglican ritualism and theological moderation that concentrated on the Incarnation rather than Christ's atoning death on the cross. Yet such developments deeply worried many Reformed and Dissenting Protestants. For instance, the *Baptist Magazine* in 1868 linked the resurgence of popular interest in Christmas directly to the so-called Catholic turn within the Church of England. Given these developments, 'it behoves every one who prizes the name of Protestant to set his face like a flint against all practices which savour of the superstitions which Popery has bequeathed to us' (Anon. 1868a: 772). It is clear that the religious observance of Christmas continued to be opposed for theological and moral reasons by many of the leaders of Reformed and Dissenting Protestantism in the nineteenth century. In an introduction to Presbyterian principle and practice published in 1836, Samuel Miller, one of the founders of Princeton Theological Seminary and its first professor of Ecclesiastical History and Church Government, succinctly summarized the continued opposition of American Presbyterians in a section entitled, 'Presbyterians do not observe holy-days' (Miller 1836: 73–8). Samuel Cozens, a Strict and Particular Baptist in London, described Christmas in 1862 as 'the second edition of the Heathen Saturnalia, revised and corrected by a nominal Christian public. Feasts and jests, gluttony and drunkenness, revelry and riot, singing profane songs, and dancing the passions into unbridled lust, are more befitting Heathendom than Christianity' (Cozens 1862: viii). New forms of Protestant Dissent were equally censorious. Edmund Gosse's *Father and Son* (1907) is a remarkably unflattering description of his Plymouth Brethren upbringing in the 1850s under his father, Philip Henry Gosse. Festivity in general was frowned upon:

> but the keeping of Christmas appeared to him by far the most hateful, and nothing less than an act of idolatry. 'The very word is Popish,' he used to exclaim, 'Christ's Mass!' pursing up his lips with the gesture of one who tastes asafoetida by accident. Then he would adduce the antiquity of the so-called feast, adapted from horrible heathen rites, and itself a soiled relic of the abominable Yule-Tide. He would denounce the horrors of Christmas until it almost made me blush to look at a holly-berry. (Gosse 1907: 132)

Secularism, ritualism, and theological moderation are important to the emergence of the modern Christmas, yet the contribution of conservative forms of Protestantism should not be ignored or reduced to futile opposition. In particular, evangelicalism was central to shaping the Victorian values of philanthropy and domestic ideology that did so much to inform the new Christmas (Armstrong 2011: 748; Schmidt 1997: ch. 3). The infrastructure of Evangelicalism and its ability to energize ordinary churchgoers proved to be crucial. Katherine Lambert Richards demonstrated in *How Christmas Came to the Sunday Schools* (1934) that, 'Christmas returned to Protestant church life because the rank and file of the membership wanted it.' In particular, the early appropriation of elements of the Christmas story by Sunday schools made the holy day more acceptable amongst Protestant churches that had until then rejected religious observance. The pattern of adoption was obvious in one of the last churches to embrace Christmas, the Presbyterian Church in the United States, which was located primarily in the southern states:

> The process followed the familiar lines of official disapproval and ignoring of the day, of an increasing number of local celebrations, many of which were of the holiday, Santa Claus, party type, and finally of official recognition and attempts to change the character of the local observance. (Richards 1934: 220, 186)

The religious observance of Christmas was also supported within Reformed churches by those who were beginning to re-examine their forbears' rejection of the Christian year. Robert Lee, Professor of Biblical Criticism at the University of Edinburgh, chaplain to Queen Victoria, and minister of Old Greyfriars Kirk, was a champion of the renewal of public worship in the Church of Scotland. He freely admitted that none of these festivals and their accompanying rituals were sanctioned in the New Testament, but that no church was able to adhere solely to biblical principle. This was evident amongst Presbyterians in the elaborate non-scriptural rituals that grew-up around the Scottish communion season. As a consequence, to reject Christmas, Good Friday, or Pentecost, 'through fear of superstition, is nothing else than to indulge one superstition through fear of another, and a less'. Lee found the traditional opposition difficult to sustain as the European Reformed churches from which the Kirk had derived its theology and church government continued to observe these festivals. The non-observance of Christmas was, 'in every respect unnatural, and a blunder', and pleading ignorance about the actual date of Christ's birth was 'a paltry and ridiculous objection'. It was unedifying that Scottish Presbyterians kept 25 December as 'a day of domestic festivity' while ignoring the religious reason for its observance. Furthermore, he did not feel that it was necessary in the modern age 'to perpetuate for ever the results or symbols of ecclesiastical and civil feuds'. Significantly, Lee distanced himself from Catholic practice and sought instead to 'return to some practices of the universal Church' as approved by 'our earliest and wisest Reformers' and welcomed by 'the more enlightened portion of the Scottish people' (Lee 1864: 173, 192, 195).

Both Richards and Lee recognized that embracing Christmas as a holiday was an essential step prior to its adoption as a holy day. In that regard, the Victorian emphasis on charity and domesticity aided this process, though this was often at odds with the materialism of the season. In particular, setting aside Christmas as a special day was a means of providing a day of rest for hard-pressed and exploited workers. One of the greatest preachers of the age, Charles Haddon Spurgeon, reflected this imperative in a sermon on the birth of Christ preached in December 1855. Spurgeon could not see 'how consistent Protestants' could observe the Christmas holy day, yet he wished 'there were ten or a dozen Christmas-days in the year; for there is work enough in the world, and a little more rest would not hurt labouring people'. In addition, the holiday 'enables us to assemble round the family hearth and meet our friends once more'. Although Baptists did 'not fall exactly in the track of other people, I see no harm in thinking of the incarnation and birth of the Lord Jesus' (Spurgeon 1857: 25). For Dwight L. Moody, the most successful revivalist of the Victorian era, Christmas was a time of family and for deciding to follow Christ. In one Christmas Day sermon, he recalled how that morning he had thanked God for the advent of Christ:

> How it has lit up my little home. How my children are filled with joy that Christ came. And the best thing you can do to-day is to receive Christ and then thank God for sending Him; and then there will be light, peace, and joy; all of these blessings will come right into your heart.   (Moody 1880: 783)

The mixture of charity and religious activism can be seen in the pages of the *Banner of Ulster*, the mouthpiece of Presbyterian Evangelicals in Ulster. In December 1843, the usual objections to the religious observance of Christmas were listed along with a recognition that it was also a period 'of social intercourse and hilarity'. The editor placed the unknown individual who invented this mid-winter festival with Sir Richard Arkwright, James Watt, 'or any other modern mechanician', for the benefit he had conferred to humanity by setting aside a long-anticipated period of rest and conviviality. Of course, 'riot and dissipation' were not uncommon, but these were not caused by the old holidays but 'the dangerous practices of society' that they as Christians must struggle against throughout the year. Besides, Christmas and other holidays had their use. 'They check the utilitarian spirit of the age—a bad spirit, that deals with men as with machines—that is sustained by Mammon worshippers, and would banish from earth all considerations excepting those of gain' (Anon 1842). Twenty-five years later, the joyous celebrations in England were still not replicated in Presbyterian Ireland and Scotland, yet the *Banner of Ulster* was sure that, 'notwithstanding all the frost within, or without, our round faced, merry King [Christmas] is slowly making his way to the hearts of all'. The message of peace and goodwill was worth remembering, and so was the imperative to look out for those less fortunate. Christians ought to use this God-given opportunity to rest and prepare for the perennial battle against the 'dead weight of woe and misery' that remained 'in the Bethnal Green of London, in the Smithfield of Belfast, in the Liberties of Dublin, and elsewhere' (Anon. 1868b).

The concern with social action was expressed in the formation of the Salvation Army in London in the 1860s. The Army soon spread to the United States and became a symbol of the values of Christianity at Christmas time; indeed, a stereotypical American Christmas usually includes Salvation Army brass bands and charity collections. The first such kettle collection was devised by Joseph McKee in San Francisco in 1891 and soon, 'Santa Claus, kettles, and free food became the nucleus of the Army's Christmas fundraising scheme.' These expressed the values of domesticity and non-sectarianism while also raising the brand profile of the Salvation Army. In December 1899, 20,000 people were fed at a sit-down Christmas dinner in Madison Square Garden. Beforehand, 3,200 baskets had been distributed throughout the city; during the dinner the staff band played festive tunes and there was a screening of the Oberammergau Passion Play. According to Diane Winston, the 'positioning of the Army as a Christmas charity was a strategic coup'; it was both an attempt to reinstate religion within Christmas but also to profit from the 'acquisitive spirit' of the season (Winston 1999: 131, 132, 134).

The 'acquisitive spirit' of the season was no better demonstrated than in the department stores of John Wanamaker. While a leader of a Sunday school in Bethany Presbyterian Church, Philadelphia, Wanamaker 'developed children's Christmas programs into extravaganzas' (Cashdollar 2000: 68). Wanamaker's love of the Christmas season had a significant influence on his retail empire. Schmidt has described how his Philadelphia stores became 'Christmas Cathedrals' in which Evangelical Christianity was combined with hard-headed commercial considerations. Christmas had 'long stood out as a revelatory mix of religion, community, and commerce', and Wanamaker's stores 'were simply his loftiest temples'. The Grand Court of his Philadelphia store was transformed into a church with the world's largest pipe organ. Crowds of around 14,000 sang carols from specially-produced Christmas hymnals and toured the elaborate decorations with their detailed guidebook. 'During the holidays people did not just shop at Wanamaker's; they received devotional reminders and religious encouragement.' For many, this 'spectacle of spirituality' was awe inspiring and helped negotiate the tension between commerce and Christian values. According to one female correspondent:

> You have taken a big step in dispelling the fear that so many of us have these days— that of a completely commercialized Christmas. You have shone [sic] that it is possible to combine merchandising with a religious background. I feel sure that your Christmas Sales will not suffer because of your effort to bring a feeling (if not a reality) of Peace into the hearts of those who gaze upwards from your Grand court.
> (Schmidt 1997: 159, 161–2, 162, 163, 166–7)

By the turn of the twentieth century, Christmas had been embraced by Reformed and Dissenting Protestants because of popular demand. According to an anonymous English writer in 1898:

> Christmas amongst modern Nonconformists is a bright and joyous time in most of our places of worship, as well as in our home circles. We are getting rid of the idea that it is a superstitious festival, and therefore a hurtful custom to observe it; nor do we—as did our stern Puritan forefathers of old—regard the decoration of our homes with holly and mistletoe as a device or snare of the Evil One. Christmas services abound in our midst, and in many places are made the occasion of felicitous reunions and of common gatherings of different denominations for united praise and prayer. (Anon. 1898: 143)

Yet the acceptance of Christmas was not a foregone conclusion, and criticism remained; only in 1958 did 25 December become a public holiday in Scotland. In many respects, this was a legacy of the war waged on Christmas by early-modern Protestant Dissenters and it is interesting to note that some of the contemporary criticism of Christmas comes from those who trace their heritage back to the period before 1800. For some modern Unitarians, Christmas is an opportunity to assert their reasonableness and to mock the naivety of the orthodox:

> God rest ye, Unitarians, let nothing you dismay;
> Remember there's no evidence there was a Christmas Day;
> When Christ was born is just not known, no matter what they say,
> O, Tidings of reason and fact, reason and fact,
> Glad tidings of reason and fact.   (Bowler 2017: 110)

On the other hand, there is the unmistakable echo of the Puritan critique of the mid-seventeenth century in the following words that are to be sung to the tune of 'Joy to the World':

> Enslave the world with Godless lies
> And help the pope to reign
> Let every Protestant prepare to celebrate:
> *Chorus*
> And keep that popish mass
>   and keep that popish mass
>   and keep, and keep, that popish mass.
> He'll rule the world in tyranny
> And make the nations bow
> Before his triple crown
> the Protestants he'll make to crouch.   (Dobson 1995)

Perhaps more reflective of mainstream opinion is R. C. Sproul who in 2014 responded to his fellow Calvinists who rejected the observance of Christmas on the basis of its commercialism, appropriation of Santa Claus, and lack of historical and biblical warrant. For Sproul, all 'this carping is but a modern dose of Scroogeism, our own sanctimonious profanation of the holy'. He proceeded to justify the commercial character of the season because the desire to give gifts to others was simply an expression of 'the supreme gift God has given the world' (Sproul 2014). Even Puritans, it seems, have always found Christmas impossible to ignore and even harder to manage.

References and Further Reading

Anon. (1651). *Mercurius Religiosus: Faithfully Communicating to the Whole Nation, the Vanity of Christmas*. London.
Anon. (1840). *Sixth Report from the Select Committee on the Act for the Regulation of Mills and Factories; Together with the Minutes of Evidence Taken Before Them, and Appendix, and Index*. London.
Anon. (1842). 'Christmas Day', *Banner of Ulster* (23 December).
Anon. (1868a). 'Christmas', *Baptist Magazine*, 60: 769–72.

Anon. (1868b), 'A Merry Christmas!' *Banner of Ulster* (25 December).

Anon. (1894), *The Confession of Faith: The Larger and Shorter Catechisms, with the Scripture-Proofs at Large; Together with The Sum of Saving Knowledge (contained in the Holy Scriptures, and held forth in the said Confessions and Catechisms,) and Practical Use Thereof. Covenants, National and Solemn league. Acknowledgement of Sins, and Engagement to Duties. Directories for Publick and Family Worship. Form of Church-Government, &c., of Publick Authority in the Church of Scotland. With Acts of Assembly and Parliament, Relative to, and Approbative of, the Same.* Edinburgh: Johnstone, Hunter, and Co.

Anon. (1898). 'From Our Nonconformist Correspondent', *The Organist and Choirmaster: A Mid-Monthly Musical Journal*, 5 (January): 143.

Armstrong, Neil (2011). 'The Christmas Season and the Protestant Churches in England, c. 1870-1914', *Journal of Ecclesiastical History*, 62: 744-62.

Baker, Frank (2007). 'The Metamorphosis of Charles Wesley's Christmas hymns, 1739-88', in K. C. G. Newport and Ted A. Campbell (eds.), *Charles Wesley: Life, Literature, and Legacy*. Epworth: Epworth Press: 378-93.

Benedict, Philip (2002). *Christ's Churches Purely Reformed: A Social History of Calvinism*. New Haven & London: Yale University Press.

Bowler, Gerry (2000). *The World Encyclopaedia of Christmas*. Toronto: McClelland & Stewart.

Bowler, Gerry (2017). *Christmas in the Crosshairs: Two Thousand Years of Denouncing and Defending the World's Most Celebrated Holiday*. New York: Oxford University Press.

Bradley, J. E. (2001). 'The Religious Origins of Radical Politics in England, Scotland, and Ireland, 1662-1800', in J. E. Bradley and D. K. van Kley (eds), *Religion and Politics in Enlightenment Europe*. Notre Dame: University of Notre Dame Press 2001: 187-253.

Calamy, Edmund (1644). *An Indictment Against England Because of her Self-Murdering Divisions: Together with an Exhortation to an England-Preserving Unity and Concord. Presented in A Sermon Preached Before the Right Honourable House of Lords in the Abby Church at Westminster; At the Late Solemn Fast, December 25. 1644*. London.

Calderwood, David (1844). *The History of the Kirk of Scotland*...vol. 7, (ed.) Thomas Thomson. Edinburgh: The Wodrow Society.

Capp, Bernard (2012). *England's Culture Wars: Puritan Reformation and its Enemies in the Interregnum, 1649-1660*. Oxford: Oxford University Press.

Cashdollar, C.D. (2000). *A Spiritual Home: Life in British and American Reformed Congregations, 1830-1915*. University Park, PA: The Pennsylvania State University Press.

Coldwell, Chris and Webb, A. J. (2015). 'American Presbyterianism and the Religious Observance of Christmas', *The Confessional Presbyterian*, 11: 142-87.

Cozens, Samuel (1862). *A Christmas Box, Or the Great Festival; by S. Cozens, Minister of the Rehoboth Chapel, Victoria Street, Shadwell, London; To Which is Added the Author's Faith, Call to the Ministry, and Eventful Life up to the Present Time*. London: T. Matthews.

Davies, Horton (1975). *Worship and Theology in England, Volume II: From Andrewes to Baxter and Fox, 1603-1690*. Princeton: Princeton University Press.

Dickson, W. S. (1812). *A Narrative of the Confinement and Exile of William Steel Dickson, D. D.*, 2nd edition. Dublin: J. Stockdale.

Dobson, James (1995). 'Enslave the World (1995)'. Available at http://www.swrb.com/newslett/actualNLs/HoHoSong.htm (accessed 17 June 2019).

Durston, Chris (1985). 'Lords of Misrule: The Puritan War on Christmas 1642-60', *History Today*, 35, no. 12 (December): 7-14.

Gosse, Edmund (1907). *Father and Son: A Study in Two Temperaments*. London: William Heinemann.

Hart, Joseph (1759). *Hymns, &c. Composed on Various Subjects. With a Preface, Containing a Brief and Summary Account of the Author's Experience, and the Great Things That God Hath Done for His Soul*. London.

Hutton, Ronald (1994). *The Rise and Fall of Merry England: The Ritual Year 1400–1700*. Oxford: Oxford University Press.

Hutton, Ronald (1996). *The Stations of the Sun: A History of the Ritual Year in Britain*. Oxford: Oxford University Press.

Lee, Robert (1864). *The Reform of the Church of Scotland in Worship, Government, and Doctrine. Part I—Worship*. Edinburgh: Edmonston and Douglas.

Lamont, William (2011). 'Prynne, William (1600–1669), Pamphleteer and Lawyer'. Available in *Oxford Dictionary of National Biography*. Available at www. Oxforddnb.com/ (accessed 19 March 2020).

Mather, Cotton (1712*). Grace Defended. A Censure on the Ungodliness, by which the Glorious Grace of God, is Too Commonly Abused. A Sermon Preached on the Twenty Fifth Day of December, 1712*. Boston.

Mather, Increase (1687). *A Testimony Against Several Prophane and Superstitious Customs, Now Practised by Some in New-England, the Evil Whereof is Evinced from the Holy Scriptures, and from the Writings Both of Ancient and Modern Divines*. London.

McMillan, William (1931). *The Worship of the Scottish Reformed Church, 1550–1638*. London: James Clarke & Co.

Miller, Samuel (1836). *Presbyterianism the Truly Primitive and Apostolical Constitution of the Church of Christ*. Philadelphia: Presbyterian Tract and Sunday School Society.

Moody, D. L. (1880). *The New Sermons of Dwight Lyman Moody*. New York: Henry S. Goodspeed.

Nissenbaum, S. W. (1996). 'Christmas in Early New England, 1620–1820: Puritanism, Popular Culture, and the Printed Word', *Proceedings of the American Antiquarian Society*, 106: 79–164.

Nissenbaum, S. W. (1997) *The Battle for Christmas: A Cultural History of America's Most Cherished Holiday*. New York: Vantage Books.

Peirce, James (1728). *Fifteen Sermons on Several Occasions, Eight of which were never before printed. To which is added a Scripture Catechism: or, the Principles of the Christian Religion Laid Down in the Words of the Bible*. London.

Pimlott, J. A. R. (1960). 'Christmas under the Puritans', *History Today*, 10, no. 12, December: 832–9.

Pimlott, J. A. R. (1978). *The Englishman's Christmas: A Social History*. Hassocks.

Prynne, William (1633). *Histrio-mastix. The Players Scourge, or, Actors Tragaedie, Divided Into Two Parts...* London.

Reed, Clifford (2009/10). '"Sparrows Sang of Christmas Pies": Beatrix Potter and Unitarian Attitudes to Christmas in the 19th and Early 20th Centuries' *Faith and Freedom* 62: 91–102; 63: 3–21.

Richards, K. L. (1934). *How Christmas Came to the Sunday-Schools: The Observance of Christmas in the Protestant Church Schools of the United States, an Historical Study*. New York: Dodd, Mead & Company.

Robinson, Benjamin (1707). *The Practical Improvement of Christmas Day. A Sermon Preached at the Reverend Mr Shower's, in Old Jewry, December the xxvth, 1706*. London.

Russell, Conrad (1996). 'The Reformation and the Creation of the Church of England, 1500-1640', in John Morrill (ed.), *The Oxford Illustrated History of Tudor and Stuart Britain*. Oxford: Oxford University Press: 258–92.

Schmidt, L. E. (1994). 'Time, Celebration, and the Christian Year in Eighteenth-Century Evangelicalism', in M. A. Noll, D. W. Bebbington, and G. A. Rawlyk (eds.), *Evangelicalism: Comparative Studies in Popular Protestantism in North America, the British Isles, and Beyond 1700–1900*. Oxford: Oxford University Press: 90–109.

Schmidt, L. E. (1997). *Consumer Rites: The Buying and Selling of American Holidays*. Princeton: Princeton University Press.

Sproul, R. C. (2014). 'Don't Be a Scrooge This Christmas' (24 December). Available at https://www.ligonier.org/blog/dont-be-scrooge-christmas/ (accessed 17 June 2019).

Spurgeon, C. H. (1857). *New Park Street Pulpit, Containing Sermons Preached and Revised by the Rev. C.H. Spurgeon, Minister of the Chapel, During the Year 1856*, Vol. 2. London: Passmore & Alabaster.

Todd, Margo (2002). *The Culture of Protestantism in Early Modern Scotland*. New Haven: Yale University Press.

Toulmin, Joshua (1771). *The Observation of Festivals and Holy-Days, Considered, in A Sermon Preached at Taunton, on Christmas Day, 1770*. Bristol.

Williams, David (1774). *Sermons, Chiefly Upon Religious Hypocrisy, by the Author of the Essays on Public Worship, &c. In two volumes*, vol. 1. London.

Winston, Diane (1999). *Red-Hot and Righteous: The Urban Religion of the Salvation Army*. Cambridge, Mass.: Harvard University Press.

PART IV
THE NATIVITY STORY

CHAPTER 15

THE HOLY FAMILY

HOLLY TAYLOR COOLMAN

In the year 2006, *The Nativity Story*—a feature-length film chronicling the events surrounding Christ's birth—appeared in theatres. An elegant and understated film, it featured a strong sense of historical realism in the landscapes, costumes, and the actors cast to play the key roles. In one key element, though, the makers of the film had to exercise creative imagination: the relationship between Mary and Joseph, the mother of Christ and the man whom she marries. As is almost certainly historically accurate, the two had relatively little personal contact until after their marriage. In the course of the film, their journey to Bethlehem, however, chronicles a relationship of growing mutual respect and tenderness. Joseph is vigilant and protective. In one scene, as they cross a river, he fends off a snake and holds Mary close. In another, he falls into a deep sleep, exhausted from the long journey. In a foreshadowing of Jesus' own actions, Mary takes his dirty, bloodied feet and gently washes them. When, towards the end of the film, the expected baby is born, Joseph delivers Jesus himself. It is a scene of awe and joy, but also profound tenderness and connection. The viewer sees clearly that this child is born into a circle of love and care.

BIBLICAL WITNESS

Narratives of the Nativity story were not always so explicit in this regard. The figures of Mary and Joseph do, of course, appear in the earliest accounts, including the written Gospels themselves. The Gospel of Matthew begins with Joseph's genealogy, while the Gospel of Luke give Mary's. Each is introduced in detail, and particularly Mary's story of becoming Jesus' mother is emphasized. In an event that Christians will memorialize as the Annunciation, she is told by an angel that she is to be the mother of 'the Son of the Most High'. In a meeting that will be remembered as the Visitation, she travels to see her cousin Elizabeth, who is also expecting a baby. (There, we see the first recognition that the baby Mary carries is very special, when Elizabeth's unborn child senses the presence of that baby—though he, too, is not yet born—and 'leaps for joy'.) Mary responds with her own hymn of praise to God. It is clear that her role as the mother of Jesus makes her very important to those who follow him. After Jesus' childhood, however, her prominence in the scriptural narrative fades, with the exceptions of her involvement in the first miracle ascribed to Jesus, at the Wedding of Cana, and of a brief but striking scene in which, at the foot of the cross, Jesus himself commends his mother to the care of the beloved disciple, John. Joseph receives less attention, but he is described as a man who keeps the Law, as a woodworker, and, in the Gospel of Matthew as the one who bestows the name 'Jesus'.

Mary's and Joseph's connection to one another is also treated. In Matthew 1:20, an angel is described as appearing to Joseph specifically in order to overcome his understandably negative response to the unexpected pregnancy of his betrothed: rather than ending their plan to marry, the angel instructs Joseph to take Mary as his wife, knowing that her pregnancy does not result from infidelity. The focus of this episode, we should note, is precisely to ensure the creation of a secure family unit consisting of Joseph, Mary, and Mary's unborn child.

In two other places, these three figures are specifically pictured by Scripture as a family unit: at the birth of Christ, and at the flight into Egypt. The first, as we shall see later, does not become an an iconic image until the medieval period. The second, the flight into Egypt, is a clearer case of this little family on its own, and, as we shall see further on in this chapter, certain Christmas customs firmly establish this image in the Christian imagination.

In a larger sense, though, the account of these three as what we would now call a 'nuclear family', is decidedly not the focus of the earliest accounts. Affirmations of a virgin birth, for example, imply precisely that Joseph is not the biological father of Jesus, and the years of Jesus' childhood, in which we would likely find the accounts of this familial unit are mostly absent from the canonical gospels. (Non-canonical sources such as the Infancy Gospel of Thomas offer more in this regard.)

Within the Christian canon, in fact, the only story of the years Jesus spends with his family seems to emphasize the way in which he does not belong to his family in the way that other children do. Having made a Passover pilgrimage to Jerusalem, Mary and Joseph are on the return trip home when they realize that Jesus is not with the caravan with which they are travelling. After three long days' search, they find him in the Temple, and Mary admonishes him: 'Child, why have you treated us like this? Look, your father and I have been searching for you in great anxiety.' But Jesus' reply calls into question precisely the expected familial obligations: 'Why were you searching for me? Did you not know that I must be in my Father's house?' (Luke 2:42–9). The Holy Family, then, is presented in Scripture not as something standing on its own, nor emerging as ultimately important, but rather as a reality carefully and deeply woven into a larger narrative, the narrative of God-becoming-human.

HISTORICAL–CRITICAL

This story of Jesus remaining in the Temple also reminds readers to consider further the historical contexts in which these accounts of the Holy Family were recorded. The 'nuclear family', especially, was not the phenomenon in the first century that it is for many—especially those in post-industrialized cultures—today. Traditionally, it is not the nuclear family, per se, but rather the extended family, the household, and even the tribe or village, that formed the context for children's lives, and this was so for first-century Jews, as well. It would be unusual, in fact, for a mother and father and their children to be separated from extended family and from that larger community (Adams 2014). (The 'flight to Egypt', would appear to be such an anomaly.)

This observation, in turn, opens the door to other forms of historical investigation, and another perspective on the Holy Family. Both Joseph and Mary belonged to the peasant class, a community for whom life was generally hard. They owed three different forms of taxes: to Rome, to Herod the Great, and to the Temple (to which, traditionally, they owed 10 per cent of the harvest). Both would have spent long days at work, with Mary attending more to domestic chores. In Judea at that time, women were generally married at about 13 years of age, so we can assume that Mary was fairly young. She was most likely illiterate, but she lived in a highly oral culture, and she very likely would have been quite able to sing hymns from memory, as Luke 1:46–55 records her doing. About Joseph, we also have only modest historical data. He probably was of the lineage of David, as the New Testament records. He was a woodworker, and he spoke a dialect of Aramaic. Artisans like Joseph, who made up about 5 per cent of the population, had an even lower median income than those who worked the land full time. Consequently, in order to have a steady supply of food, they usually combined their craft with farming. In his role as father, Joseph would have attended to Jesus' religious education, but by the time Jesus moves into public ministry, Joseph receives no further mention. It seems that, by this point, he may have already died.

This leads to another question, that of Joseph's age. Historical norms predict that Joseph would have been older than Mary, but most early traditions imagine him as much older, and even elderly. Eastern Christian tradition relies heavily on the extra-canonical Protoevangelion of St James, in which Joseph, upon being selected as husband for Mary, protests because he is already an old man, with children. Farkasfalvy notes also that this 'old Joseph' may have been a projected archetype of the priestly guardians of the consecrated virgins, upon whose lives the traditional depictions of Mary's childhood are modelled (Farkasfalvy 2014). Early portraits do exist of a younger Joseph, though, and Jerome describes him in this way, insisting he died a virgin and not a widower. This 'young Joseph' later gains favour, as discussed in the last section of the chapter.

So, what is the path that leads from these individuals to the tender portrayal of *The Nativity Story*? The focus on the threesome of Jesus, Mary, and Joseph as a family unit seems to come even later, in a way likely connected to a number of historical and intellectual turns.

Coptic Tradition

First, though, one phenomenon should be noted as relatively exceptional. Coptic Christians in Egypt have long tended to remember the Holy Family, in specific connection to 'the flight to Egypt', recorded in the second chapter of Matthew. Warned by an angel of King Herod's intention to harm the infant Jesus—whom he saw as a rival after wise men from afar reported that they were looking for a newborn king—Joseph gathers Mary and the baby and travels to Egypt for safety. In this event, the three members of the Holy Family are in fact described as together, and apart from their larger community. To this day, the Church of St Sergius in Cairo stands where the Holy Family is believed to have rested while on their journey.

A secondary point to be noted here is the dynamic—apparent in virtually all cases going forward—in which remembrance and veneration of Joseph is closely tied to the remembrance of the Holy Family. The Copts, for example, also produced and treasured a text called *The History of Joseph the Carpenter*, written in the fourth or fifth century. This text did much to establish the tradition of an 'elderly Joseph', and includes a tender scene of Jesus with him at his deathbed. By the year 1,000, Coptic Christians included St Joseph in their annual calendar.

Medieval Beginnings

Beyond this devotional habit of Coptic Christians, though, there is remarkably little attention paid to the Holy Family as a threesome. Mary and Jesus are remembered and revered, of course, both separately and together. But Joseph is noticeably absent, in comparison with modern practice.

At the midpoint of the medieval period, though, small stirrings began to change that. In twelfth-century Bologna, Bernard of Clairvaux, gave a series of sermons emphasizing Joseph's importance in the Holy Family. In the thirteenth-century, in his *Life of St. Francis of Assisi*, Bonaventure offers a detailed account of Francis organizing the first 'living Nativity'. In a scene now familiar to many in miniature sets displayed at Christmas time, a tableau representing the moments after Jesus' birth were depicted by actors, with the three members of the Holy Family at the centre.

LATE MEDIEVAL FLOWERING

In the late medieval and early modern period, both Joseph and the Holy Family are claimed in new and powerful ways. The upheavals and scandals of the era may play a role here. The Hundred Years' War, peasant revolts, and religious scandals like the Babylonian Captivity of the papacy left both clergy and the laity reeling. In the midst of this, St Joseph, dignified and faithful, and the Holy Family, a well-ordered unit, emerge as a new spiritual ideal.

Jean Gerson, an influential French scholar and reformer, joined forces with Bernardine of Siena, and the two together accomplished much in this regard. Gerson penned a broadly published poem, the *Josephina*, that praised St Joseph's loyalty and selfless responsibility. St Bernardine preached about St Joseph in a similar way to his urban audiences. Further, the two scholars argued that St Joseph had been bodily assumed into heaven after death, as had Mary. Thus, they said, the Holy Family was reunited in heaven in a way that maintained the exact form of charity they had experienced on earth.

As the movement of Catholic reform grew, Joseph found a growing place of honour there, too, as did the Holy Family: Catholic families were encouraged to imitate the well-ordered Holy Family, headed by Joseph (Koschorke 2003). In 1570, a leader of Catholic Reform, Johannes Molanus, launched an energetic effort to rehabilitate and re-present St Joseph, with the Holy Family under his care, to the faithful. Molanus rejected the 'elderly Joseph' described in apocryphal accounts in favour of a husband closer to his wife's age and more like the families whom he hoped would be inspired. Charlene Villaseñor Black notes that St Joseph was not only the most frequently represented saint in Spanish Golden Age and Mexican colonial art, but also the most important (Black 2006).

Ignatius's *Spiritual Exercises*, written in the early sixteenth century and still widely used, drew participants, through imaginative prayer, into the presence of the Holy Family. Indeed, in Ignatius's own private chapel, an image of the Holy Family hung over the altar. In the seventeenth century, St Teresa of Avila was known for her devotion to the Holy Family. And Francis de Sales influenced by both the *Exercises* and by Teresa, likewise elevates and praises the Holy Family, and describes it as an ideal for human relationships. Overall, regional and sporadic devotion, both to St Joseph and to the Holy Family, gradually grew into powerful and widespread devotion by the sixteenth century.

THE NEW WORLD

As colonization of, and subsequent migrations to the New World took hold, the Holy Family gained new importance. Francois Laval, a Catholic priest and missionary, arrived in Quebec in 1659 and ultimately became the first Catholic bishop of that city. Laval encouraged devotion to the Holy Family in a number of ways, including establishing a feast and a Mass in honour of the Holy Family on the third Sunday of

Easter. Devotion to the Holy Family flourished among Canadian Catholics, as well as among Canadian–American communities of immigrants to the United States.

Further south, in Mexico, a new tradition appeared. Believed to have been celebrated first by Augustinian friars near Mexico City, at the end of the sixteenth century, 'Las Posadas' became a beloved Christmas devotion centred on the Holy Family—celebrated not only in Mexico, but throughout Latin America. Spanish for 'lodging', or 'accommodation', Las Posadas is a celebration lasting for a nine-day interval (called the novena) during the Christmas season, during which Mary and Joseph's quest for a place to rest in Bethlehem is re-enacted. A procession accompanies the holy couple as they travel to various locations designated as 'inns' and seek welcome there. Once the 'innkeepers' let them in, there is opportunity for prayers and celebration.

The Modern World

In the modern world, with challenges to the family, a new turn to the Holy Family appears. In the nineteenth century, the Holy Family is increasingly pictured as a contrast to, and cure for, the family unit embattled and undermined by industrialization and urbanization. Joseph is increasingly described as a quiet hero in his work (Koschorke 2003: 135). Joseph the pious worker, furthermore, is offered as an alternative of the worker as envisioned by the Communist movement.

A particularly striking example of attention to the Holy Family appears in mid-nineteenth-century Barcelona, where many were deeply concerned about the way in which industrialization was stripping away older traditions. In the 1870s, a small group of wealthy citizens came and formed a plan for a new church, a project that they hoped would restore religious devotion, civic pride, and the dignity of the people. That church, now designated a basilica even while it is still under construction, they named La Sagrada Familia, the Holy Family. In 1921, Pope Benedict XV proclaimed that the Feast of the Holy Family was extended to the liturgical calendar of the worldwide Catholic Church.

New attention to St Joseph is also obvious. In 1870, Pope Pius IX declared St Joseph to be the patron saint of the Catholic Church. The shift is seen in sacred spaces, as well: in the nineteenth century, St Joseph becomes increasingly common as the focus of the second side altar in Catholic Churches (the first always going to Mary) (Bouyer 1955). By now, he is virtually always depicted as younger, a contemporary of Mary.

Present Day

In recent years, the Catholic world has looked to the Holy Family in more substantive and theological ways. *Casti Connubi,* a 1930 papal encyclical on marriage from Pope

Pius XI, and *Familiaris Consortio*, a 1981 encyclical on the family from Pope John Paul II, both include prominent invocations of the Holy Family. *Redemptoris Custos* (Guardian of the Redeemer), a 1989 apostolic exhortation from Pope John Paul II sees St Joseph at the centre of efforts to renew family, society, and the Church. Pope Francis concludes his 2016 apostolic exhortation, *Amoris Laetitia* (The Joy of Love), on the pastoral care of families with an extended prayer to the Holy Family.

And, of course, in both the Catholic and Protestant worlds, the Holy Family has become the most central symbol of Christmas. The 'Christmas pageant', or 'Nativity play', a re-enactment of the Christmas story most often performed by children, is a beloved tradition in many parts of the world, in Catholic, Protestant, and Orthodox communities. In an increasingly secularized context in the West, a miniature Nativity scene, or crèche, has become synonymous with the attempt to maintain or recover the religious dimensions of Christmas. In one of the most important precedents affecting religious freedom in the United States, in fact, the Supreme Court decided in Allegheny v. ACLU (1989) that a Nativity scene in a county courthouse accompanied by a banner that read 'Gloria in Excelsis Deo' ('Glory to God in the Highest'), was unconstitutional because it was 'indisputably religious', rather than secular, in nature.

New inflections of meaning continue to appear. In an age of culture wars, the Holy Family has become an emblem for those championing 'traditional marriage'. Or, it is sometimes argued, the Holy Family stands as an emblem of vulnerable immigrants and refugees. And in the setting of the developed world, where families often feel harried and anxious, they are reminded that the Holy Family, sojourning in an animal dwelling, or fleeing through the night to Egypt, themselves suffered indignity and trial. Two thousand years after the birth of Christ, all that the Holy Family may yet mean remains to be seen.

REFERENCES AND FURTHER READING

Adams, Samuel L. (2014). *Social and Economic Life in Second Temple Judea*. Louisville, Kentucky: Westminster John Knox.

Black, Charlene Villaseñor (2006). *Creating the Cult of St. Joseph: Art and Gender in the Spanish Empire*. Princeton: Princeton University Press.

Bouyer, Louis (1995). *Liturgical Piety*. Notre Dame, Indiana: University of Notre Dame Press.

Chorpenning, Joseph F. and von Barghahn, Barbara (1996). *The Holy Family as Prototype of the Civilization of Love: Images from the Viceregal Americas*. Philadelphia: St. Joseph's University Press.

Chorpenning, Joseph F. and von Barghahn, Barbara (1998). *The Holy Family in Art and Devotion*. Philadelphia: Saint Joseph's University Press.

Farkasfalvy, Denis M. (2014). *The Marian Mystery: The Outline of a Mariology*. Staten Island, New York: St Paul's.

Johnson, Elizabeth (2003). *Truly Our Sister: A Theology of Mary in the Communion of the Saints*. Notre Dame, Indiana: University of Notre Dame Press.

Koschorke, Albrecht (2003). *The Holy Family and its Legacy: Religious Imagination from the Gospels to Star Wars*. New York: Columbia University Press.

CHAPTER 16

GABRIEL AND THE ANGELS

DAVID LYLE JEFFREY

WHEN angels now appear in Christmas greetings or as tree ornaments their appearance is more charming than is warranted by the texts of either the Old or New Testament. This modern characterization badly misrepresents the nature of angels in the Bible, and it misconceives the role of Gabriel in the Christmas story. The purpose of this chapter is succinctly to contextualize the character and narrative role of angels both in the canonical Scriptures and the most illustrious texts of Second Temple Judaism in such a way as to reveal the substantial consistency of their representation in these texts, and then to show how the particular role of Gabriel, especially in Luke's Gospel, is at once an extension and a development of the representation of angels in the Bible generally. Actual biblical angels, as it happens, are neither feminine nor cute; rather, they have a male appearance and are stern rather than sweet. Except for the cherubim over the altar (Exod. 25:18–20), the seraphim in Isaiah's vision (Isa. 6:1–3) and the 'four living creatures' in Ezekiel's *merkabah* vision of the *shekinah kavod* (Ezek. 1:5–6), they are not normally depicted as winged; in the Bible itself it seems that angels of the Divine Presence are distinctive in this respect, while extension in visual iconography of wings for Gabriel, Michael, and the angels in Revelation may draw upon Talmudic associations of Gabriel and Michael with the Divine Presence. What is universally of importance is angels' role as divine couriers who declare a specific calling or vocation to their hearers.

ANGEL VOICES

From the angels which appear to Abraham (Gen. 18: 1–22), to Lot (Gen. 19:1–22), and to Hagar and Ishmael (Gen. 21:17–19) right through to the Revelation to John, angels (sometimes described simultaneously as 'men') appear at critical points in salvation history to chosen persons. They speak nothing on their own behalf, but only as messengers of God, and so their words are of utmost consequence for their hearers. The Greek word *angelos* and its Latin equivalent, *angelus*, both mean 'messenger'; the Hebrew word *mal'ak* warrants this translation in the LXX and Luke's Gospel, but it contains an additional etymological resonance with *melech*, 'king', thus conveying delegation and a specific chain of command. Gabriel's appearance to Zacharias (Luke 1:11–25) and Mary (Luke 1:26–38) are in this respect entirely typical of angelic appearances throughout the Old Testament. Recent contentions that angels emerge in the Jewish Scriptures largely after the Babylonian captivity, suggesting a Persian mythological syncretism (e.g. Jenkins 2017:150), may thus mislead; actually, angels appear in thirty-four books of the canonical Christian Bible, a total of 305 times. Half of those books and 121 of the references are in the Old Testament (Lockear 1995: 28; 94).

As messengers of God, biblical angels can convey divine intent through actions or deeds (*daverim*) as well as words (*davarim*). Both the Apostle Paul and the writer of Hebrews clearly believed that Torah itself was transmitted by angels (Gal. 3:19; Heb. 2:2), and Paul reflects the normative angelology of his time in noting that they are not eternal spirits, but specifically created beings (Col. 1:16–17). One way they serve God is by acting as guardians and protectors, as for Hananiah, Azariah, and Mishael in the fiery furnace (Dan. 3:25) or Daniel in the lions' den (Dan. 6:22). They are guides through the wilderness (Exod. 14:19; 23:20), leaders of the forces of Israel into battle (Josh. 5:13–15), and at important junctures act as interpreters of visions and events (Dan. 10:11–12; Luke 24:5–8; Acts 1:10–11; Rev. 17:7–18). Biblical poetry offers assurances that God 'will give his angels charge over thee, to keep thee in all thy ways' (Ps. 91:11; 34:7; cf. Matt. 4:6; Luke 4:10–11), and the idea of personal guardian angels further develops from a saying of Jesus about little children, whose 'angels do always behold the face of my Father which is heaven' (Matt. 18:10). While it remains doubtful if human beings of any age can look on God directly, we are told that angels can and do (Matt. 18:10).

Perhaps most significantly in the context of the Christmas story, angels announce the birth of special characters already in Old Testament narrative, such as Samson (Judg. 13:2–8), Ishmael (Gen. 16:11–12) and, according to traditional Jewish exegesis, Isaac (Gen. 17:19). All three of these announcements of impending birth are to barren parents, just as will be the case in Gabriel's announcement of the birth of John the Baptist to Zacharias and Elizabeth; in the narrative about Ishmael the announcement entails the Bible's first account of God making a covenant with a woman (Gen. 21:17–18), an event not to be paralleled until Gabriel's annunciation to Mary. This portion of Jewish Scripture concerning Ishmael is shared with Muslims, where Gabriel is said to dictate the *Q'ran* to Muhammed.

Angelic appearances throughout the Bible, especially when a message is to be delivered, typically involves a single angel. Among memorable exceptions in Torah is Joseph's dream at Bethel ('house of God') of the ladder reaching from earth to heaven with angels ascending and descending on it (Gen. 28:11–12); Moses also spoke of the Lord coming from Sinai 'with myriads of holy ones' (Deut. 33:2). But there are other important Old Testament precedents for the 'heavenly host' which appears to the Shepherds in Luke's Gospel. These include the 'host of heaven' seen by the prophet Micaiah in his vision of God's judgment on Ahab (1 K. 22:19), as well as the 'sons of God' (Job 1:16) who, in the gloriously poetic divine rebuff to Job are referred to as having been present after the Creation, like a choir 'singing for joy' because of it (Job 38:7). Jewish worshippers in the time of the Nativity would have been familiar with references to the 'heavenly hosts' in the Psalms (e.g. Ps. 193:21; 148:2), and the apocalyptic vision of Daniel speaks of the Ancient of Days with 'thousands and thousands' of celestial beings attending him (Dan. 7:9–10). Nehemiah confesses before God, 'You give life to everything, and the multitudes of heaven worship you' (Neh. 9:6). Later on, Jesus will tell his disciples that angels rejoice over each sinner who repents (Luke 15:10). In Revelation, there similarly appear groups of angels, such as the four who stand at the corners of the Earth (Rev. 7:1), the seven who blow trumpets (Rev. 8–9) and pour out the bowls of wrath (Rev. 16), and the writer of the Letter to the Hebrews speaks of the celestial Jerusalem as echoing with the sound of 'thousands upon thousands of angels in joyful assembly' (Heb. 12:22). Here too the heavenly hosts join in singing the praises of God.

The content of what angels throughout the Bible communicate is never extraneous to the grand narrative: theirs are words of direct revelation, though often received with anxiety as well as joy. By the time we get to the New Testament, the appearance of angelic beings typically occasions genuine fright, as we see in Luke's Gospel, where their first words to their apprehensive hearers is 'Fear not!' (Luke 1:13; 20; 2:10; cf. Matt. 28:3–4; Judg. 6:22; Job 4:15; Dan. 10:12). For first and second-century Jewish readers, including early Jewish converts to Christianity, this element of angelic appearance to chosen persons would have seemed a striking contrast to the angelic appearances in Genesis, where angels seem to have produced awe in some of their hearers (e.g. Lot in Gen. 19:1), but often something more like simple recognition and polite respect (Gen. 18:1–3). The wrestling Jacob story (Gen. 32:24–32) is distinctive in its foregrounding of fierce resistance on the part of Jacob, acceptance of the angel's message coming only after many hours of struggle.

Naming the Angels

When Jenkins draws attention to the development of angelology as a distinct branch of Jewish religious study appearing in force after the Babylonian captivity, he is certainly correct (Jenkins 2017:152–64). For one thing, before that late time in the composition of biblical texts angelic beings are consistently anonymous, their words and actions being simply an expression of the divine regal will to the degree that the writers sometimes seem to assume that God himself is the speaker. When asked, the angels in Judges 13:18 and Genesis 32:30 decline to give their names. So also with actions; even so crucially important an angel as the one that stays the hand of Abraham at the almost sacrifice of Isaac (Gen. 22:10-12) is referred to only as the 'Angel of the Lord' in the biblical text itself; later Jewish association of this angel with Michael comes via various Talmudic commentaries dated c.AD 200 (Ginzberg 1983:5. 251, n. 242). In the deutero-canonical and apocryphal texts written during the Second Temple period this original anonymity of the angels had changed, if not yet so dramatically as during the Talmudic era, possibly through the influence of elaborate Persian angelology. Most of that expansive lore is not pertinent in our context, but the Persian belief in 'watchers,' guardian angels appointed to nations (Aramaic *irin*—etymologically residual in nation names such as Iran and Iraq) may have influenced the writer of the second part of Daniel, in which an angelic being mentions to Daniel the role of an archangel, 'Michael, your prince' (Dan. 10:13; 12:1). It is this apocalyptic text which first introduces us to Gabriel, who interprets to Daniel the meaning of his eschatological vision (Dan. 8:16-27), a passage which helps give rise in Talmudic teaching to the notion of Gabriel as one of the angels whose mission is interpretation (Collins 2000: 311; Melvin 2013: 156-7; Beyerle 2007). In response to Daniel's intercessory prayer of repentance for the disobedience and apostasy of his nation, Gabriel appears to him again, 'at the time of the evening offering' (Dan. 9:21) to continue his interpretation of the vision portending salvation for Israel. All these are clearly important precursors to Gabriel's appearance in the first chapter of Luke's Gospel.

GABRIEL IN THE CHRISTMAS STORY

The angel Gabriel, whose name means 'power of God' or 'emissary of God', appears four times in the canonical Scriptures, each time with a Messianic message. For a Jewish audience, it would probably have been of interest that he had appeared frequently also in inter-testamental literature precedent to Luke's Gospel (2 Enoch 24:1; 1 Enoch 20:40; 40:3) and in the Qumran scrolls (1 QM 9:15-16); he is there regarded as one of the 'glorious ones' who survey all humankind (1 Enoch 40:3), one of four angels who lift up the prayers of the martyrs (1 Enoch 9:1-11), and he is even said to sit at God's right hand (2 Enoch 24:1). If we assume that oral tradition of some duration lies behind at least portions of Talmud, it may well be a relevant rabbinical tradition that, as in the Q'mran Book of Jubilees (Vanderkam 2000: 378-93), Gabriel is said to be the angel that stands directly before the throne of God, making him thus an angel of the Presence, implying wings, and that he is accorded special guardianship over Judah (Bamidbar Rabbah 2.10). Also associated with the 'man clothed in linen' in Ezekiel 10:2 (WR 26.8, Tan.B. 3.41; 84), he is credited in later Jewish commentary with being the figure who wrestled with Jacob and gave Israel its 'new name' (Bereshit Rabbah 78.3; Zohar 2.41b). Among the many details introduced in Talmud (cf. Iavoschi 2004), perhaps most pertinently, Gabriel's appearances were thought by Jewish teachers to indicate proximity of the *Shekinah kavod* itself, the glory of God's own presence (Sh R 2.5; 32.9; Bereshit Rabbah 97.3; also Trypho, in Justin's *Dialogue with Trypho* 20, 28). How much of this tradition Luke knew we can only guess, but the associations are largely consistent with the two canonical Old Testament references that he doubtless did know, both of which clearly identified Gabriel with God's direct agency in delivering Messianic assurances (Dan. 8:15 ff.). That Gabriel appears a second time in Daniel (9:20–1) to clarify the eschatological significance of Daniel's vision, precisely when Daniel is praying in repentance for the sins of the people 'about the time of the evening sacrifice' most obviously bears on the manner of his appearance to Zacharias in Luke's Gospel; the reiteration is unmistakable (Luke 1:11). That the angel is 'standing on the right side of the altar of incense' suggests that he stood nearest the entrance to the Holy of Holies, as if he had come directly from the Presence. These details would seem to be anticipated in the Book of Jubilees. One might expect Zacharias to have known at least the canonical references and perhaps more.

It is characteristic in all of biblical literature that an encounter with an angel is profoundly unsettling. The doubled verbs used here (*etaracthe* and *phobos*—'terrified with fear'), suggests something even stronger. As we have seen, it is equally characteristic that when bringing a message of consolation or promise the angel will say, 'Fear not!' (cf. Dan. 10:12, 19). This echoes the 'fear not' assurances of God speaking to Abram and Moses (Gen. 15:1; Num. 21:34), to the destitute Hagar (Gen. 21:17), and the insecure Isaac (Gen. 26:24). 'Fear not!' is often on the lips of prophets who announce to a distraught and suffering Israel that their salvation is coming (Isa. 41:10; 41:13; 43:5; 44:8, etc.). All these associations resonate in Gabriel's assurance to Zacharias, even as later in his address to Mary (Luke 1:30). (When the shepherds on the hills of Judea are frightened by an angel, even before a host of angels appear in the skies above them singing, the same assurance is given [Luke 2:10].) Such fear at the sight of an angelic being is hardly irrational; deeper than the element of surprise for most is an instantaneous apprehension of being confronted unexpectedly by a presence of the Holy. As John Chrysostom would later note, 'The most righteous of men cannot see an angel without feeling fear' (*De incomprehensibili Dei natura*); Calvin suggests of Zacharias that 'he was frightened to the point of collapse.' The assurance 'Fear not!' presupposes at an intuitive level a recognition that, as at the first Passover, angels can be emissaries of God's judgment, of death and destruction. Yet fear of an emissary of God is consistent with fear of the Lord himself. Assurance that there is no need to fear God's immanent judgment is then already a sign of grace, coming redemption, and future hope.

Gabriel's assurance continues with a word of comfort: both for the community and for the priest: the prayer of Zacharias has been heard and Elizabeth will bear a son—despite being, like her husband, well past the age for such an event to occur naturally (7). Augustine understood his priestly prayer of repentance for the sins of the people to be analogous to the prayer of Daniel (Dan. 9:20–1), and the word about a son to be an answer to the separate, private prayers of Zacharias and Elizabeth (Sermon 291, *For the Nativity of St. John the Baptist* [PL 38.133]). Here is a further analogy with the situation of Abraham and of Manoah and the birth of their respective sons, Isaac and Samson. Yet the longed-for birth of a son is not here envisioned merely as fulfilment for his parents' sake, since 'many will rejoice at his birth, for he will be great in the sight of the Lord' (14-15). That is, Gabriel here conveys one answer to two prayers, fusing private desire with representative desire for the common good of Israel. This answer is to be bodied forth in the person of a prophet and a preacher who will call the people to that very repentance for which intercessors have for centuries been praying at the time of the evening sacrifice.

Gabriel specifies the fashion in which John the Baptist is to be prepared for that purpose, notably his Nazarite vows, much as were dictated by the angel to the wife of Manoah in regard to Samson (Judg. 13:3-7). But he adds something else: John will be 'filled with the Holy Spirit, even from his mother's womb' (15). This is an arresting detail. It is possible that Zacharias would have remembered what the Lord said to Jeremiah at the time of his calling: 'Before I formed you in the womb, I knew you; before you were born I sanctified you; I ordained you a prophet to the nations' (Jer. 1:5). The Hebrew word *qodesh*, translated 'sanctified', means literally 'set apart'; the concept of vocation or calling is inscribed in it. Here in Luke the conception of a prenatal consecration is intensified: Zacharias is told that even in Elizabeth's womb the child will already be 'filled with the Holy Spirit' (Luke 1:15). Though the plain sense makes Calvin uncomfortable, Ambrose more representatively notes that later, when John leaps in his mother's womb when Mary comes to visit Elizabeth (1:44), it is a confirmation of the Spirit's indwelling John already.

Gabriel declares further that John 'will turn many of the children of Israel to the Lord their God', the very thing for which, in the evening sacrifice, Zacharias has been praying, namely national repentance (cf. Jer. 3:7; Dan. 9:13) precisely in the fashion called for in the prophecy in Malachi that before the Messiah will come, God will send Elijah the prophet to 'turn the hearts of the fathers to the children and the hearts of the children to their fathers' (Mal. 4:5-6). As Gabriel frames this prophecy concerning John, 'he [that is, the Messianic forerunner] will also go before him in the spirit and power of Elijah, "to turn the hearts of the fathers to the children" and the disobedient to the wisdom of the just, to make ready a people prepared for the Lord' (Luke 1:17; cf. Ps. 24). At this moment in Gabriel's proclamation, the Messianic portent is overwhelming, not least because it synthesizes so much that had gone before.

Yet it is at just this high point that Zacharias, faithful priest though he has been, stumbles. He is not, of course, the first to doubt such a promise of God, given that it runs against the probabilities of nature. Chrysostom, Bede, and other patristic commentators have seen Zacharias's demand for a sign as the reflex of an incipiently rebellious spirit (Gk. *tolma*; Lat. *audacia*), one contrary to faith. In the light of analogous biblical stories, this seems too strong. A difference between this story and its most famous parallel, the assurance to Abraham of a son and heir by Sarah, is that Abraham's laughter is muted and his articulation of fundamental doubt is 'in his heart' (Gen. 17:16-17). By contrast, Zacharias asks aloud, like Gideon (Judges 6:17), for a sign, and yet, in a way unprecedented in either that or the Abraham story, Gabriel is offended enough to admonish him severely, apparently for forgetting those earlier stories. Gabriel now identifies himself and his purpose as plainly as one might to one with no knowledge of Jewish history at all, telling him that he will be unable to say another word himself until the child is born, because, Gabriel says, 'you did not believe my words which will be fulfilled in their own time' (Luke 1:19–20). The silencing of Zacharias serves to conceal the revelation from everyone else—perhaps including even the apparently embarrassed Elizabeth—until the event takes place (Marshall 1978: 61). That this is one of the ironies of Providence which everywhere characterize the unfolding master design of biblical grand narrative is suggested by the words *pleroo*, 'fulfil' and *kairos*, 'appointed time'. Gabriel's stern judgment, as well as his good news, thus hangs over the whole of the narrative. Zacharias tries in vain to communicate with the waiting worshippers when he comes out from the inner court; shortly afterward, his service completed, he retreats home. The child is conceived. Elizabeth's pregnancy is hidden for more than five months. Suspense gathers concerning the outcome.

But the looked-for birth is not to be before suddenly Gabriel appears again, this time not in the Temple, nor even Jerusalem, but to an apparently unheralded young woman in a small village. Mary is described simply as a 'virgin betrothed to a man whose name was Joseph, of the house of David' (Luke 1:27). Thus, we should not be at all surprised that Mary was taken aback by the appearance of the angel Gabriel. Mary's has been a hidden life, even as her extraordinary choosing is to be itself hidden, by contrast with the annunciation to Zachariah which is immediately a subject of public knowledge. Here, we get a stark reversal of that expectation: the family of the forerunner or herald is much more auspicious in its circumstances than is the proleptic family of the Lord. Cultural embarrassment regarding this aspect of Luke's account may lie behind the representation of Mary as a child of affluent parents and raised in the Temple in the second-century *Protoevangelion,* in which, interestingly, Gabriel has become simply 'the Angel of the Lord' (9: 9–17).

In Luke's text the fact that Mary is a virgin is emphasized by repetition of the term (*parthenon*), heightening the sense of the extraordinary in the event of Gabriel's direct address to Mary (Miriam in Hebrew), since it was so unusual in Jewish culture for any man, let alone a strange man, to salute a woman, especially an unmarried woman, directly (Lightfoot 1979: 25). But Gabriel's words are still more extraordinary: 'Rejoice, highly favored one, the Lord is with you; blessed are you among women!' (Luke 1:28). The term *kecharitomene*, 'highly favored one', is precedented only in the Septuagint of Daniel (ch. 10) when Gabriel is likewise the speaker, and it establishes here a connection between Mary as singular 'chosen one' and her saintly Old Testament predecessor in relationship to the eschatological fulfilment of God's purpose to redeem his people. (Gabriel's form of address to her, his calling her *kechartomine,* suggests in historic Catholic exegesis her having found favour *before* the angel declares it; the parallel with Daniel supports that implication.)

The subversion of normative cultural expectation is intensified by the pairing of this annunciation with that to Zacharias: special births in Scripture had, with one exception, always been announced to the father-to-be; this time, as with the mother of Samson, it is the woman who hears first. When Gabriel says to Mary, 'The Lord is with you', it is not merely a greeting but, in this context, a strong affirmation of her chosenness. The following phrase, 'Blessed are you among women', is missing from some manuscripts, but anticipates the response of Elizabeth (Luke 1:42), hence its later conjunction liturgically.

That Mary is 'troubled at his saying' should hardly, given this context, be surprising to us. Instead, in Luke's phrase, she 'considered what manner of greeting this was' (Luke 1:29). When Gabriel then says, 'Fear not, for you have found favour with God' (KJV), his calm clarification not only assures her he means no harm but further elevates the regal gravity of his address; when he then tells her that she will conceive and bear a son whose name is to be called Jesus, one who will not only be called great but will be 'the Son of the Highest', and that this son will be given the throne of 'his father David' and will be the eternal ruler of Israel, she must have been astounded at the eschatological magnitude of what was being said to her. After all, the earthly throne of David had been supplanted by Babylonians, Greeks, and Herodians, and the Romans now occupied the land.

But when she asks, 'How can these things be?'—she is betrothed, but not married, espoused but still a virgin, thus 'knows not a man'—another gospel distinctive emerges. *Ginosko,* like its Hebrew counterpart, *yadah,* is the polite but practical euphemism of a modest culture for sexual relations. How could she be pregnant? The suggestion of some ancient commentators that she had previously made a vow of perpetual virginity has no support in Luke or any other first-century or canonical Scripture. *Ginosko* is present tense; in Luke's narrative Mary does not say she is already or will be a dedicated virgin. The suggestion of the apocryphal *Protevangelium* of James that Mary was 'devoted to the Lord from her infancy' (2:10), lived in the Temple (3:3), having daily 'conversation of angels' (5:2) and that she had formally pledged her virginity at the age of 14 (5:5–6) attempts to warrant Gabriel indicating here in Luke that Mary has 'found favour with the Lord', because she has already made virginity her choice of life (7:9, 16). That is, in the later (cAD 140) apocryphal text a relation of meritorious and formally religious life and divine election is putatively established and her previously consecrated role is made to be public knowledge. All of this retrospective material contradicts the central emphasis of Luke's presentation.

Another distinctive point is the frank biological realism that undergirds Mary's question in Luke (1:34). Gabriel does not, as in the case of Zacharias, regard her question as an expression of doubt in the authority of the divine word to her, but rather as a genuine desire for clarification concerning something that she would recognize as entirely without precedent, even in biblical history. Nonetheless, there is a hint of that history in Gabriel's response: 'The Holy Spirit shall come upon you, and the power of the Highest will overshadow you' (Luke 1:35). The clue is in the verb, *episkiasei,* 'will overshadow'. In the LXX Old Testament this verb refers either to the Shekinah cloud that rested on the tabernacle (Exod. 40:34–5; Num. 9:8; 10:34), or to God's presence in protecting his people (Ps. 91:4 [LXX 90:4]). Thus, the divine presence in the Holy of Holies is here made to 'overshadow' and inhabit, as tabernacle, the person and womb of the Virgin. Thus, 'that Holy One who is to be born will be called the Son of God.' There is a 'doubling' or reiteration in these paired events, anticipating perhaps a third in Luke 9:14: the cloud in the Transfiguration (Bock 1994: 1. 122).

Gabriel's revelation to Mary of her aged cousin Elizabeth's pregnancy serves to signify that 'with God nothing will be impossible' (Luke 1:37); this immediate analogy with another providential event in her family seems intuitively confirming for Mary. Her response is now immediate: '*ecce ancilla domine*' says Mary in the famous Vulgate Latin translation: 'behold the handmaiden of the Lord' (KJV). Mary's words echo those of Hannah (1 Sam. 1:11), guiding our appreciation that her consent is offered not to Gabriel himself but to the Lord: 'be it unto me according to thy word' (KJV). This is effectively captured in the *Ghent Altarpiece* of the Van Eyck brothers, where Mary's *ecce ancilla domine* appears over her head as she looks up, praying, but the words are upside down and reversed, so as to indicate that she speaks neither to us nor to the courtly Gabriel, but directly to God (Jeffrey 2017: 134–5).

Typically when Gabriel appears in Annunciation paintings (especially after Giotto) his courtly body language bespeaks the regal posture of a royal suitor; also typically he finds Mary reading a Psalter or the prophecy of Isaiah (7:14); her 'be it unto me according to thy Word' is often signified by her hand held, palm down, over the open page of Scripture (e.g. Roger Van de Weyden, *Three Kings Altarpiece*). In this context we are led both by Luke's narrative and such well-composed painterly commentaries to see Mary as a devout virgin being 'courted', and her willing obedience as an exemplar for all faithful persons in whom, in a real and analogous sense, the Word of the Lord seeks also a nuptial habitation (Jeffrey 2009: 3–21). This conception transforms Gabriel into a medieval or Renaissance courtier, acting as an ambassador for the king in bringing to Mary a proposal of most holy marriage, and it is this image that has most influenced Christmas representations of Gabriel subsequently.

It may be Bonaventure who most strongly emphasizes the conversation between Mary and Gabriel as reflecting the decorum of gracious medieval courtesy. Giotto picks up this emphasis in his Arena Chapel *Annunciation*, by showing Gabriel kneeling in the fashion of a medieval courtier, white lily in hand (to signify Mary's virginal purity). Bonaventure's primary theological contribution is his emphasis on Mary's free will—her agency. As he summarizes it, Mary's fruitfulness 'took place *through God's action, the angel's annunciation,* and *the virgin's consent,* so that the restoration might correspond to the fall' (*Commentary*, 1.1.40). Bonaventure is not original here—he acknowledges his debt to St Bernard of Clairvaux as well as to Bede—but he develops the point more fully. To the many virtues of Mary celebrated by the great Cistercian, Bonaventure adds an emphasis on Mary's active intelligence, so that the reader cannot fail to appreciate that when the Virgin says, 'Be it unto me according to thy word', it is as 'the perfect consent of love... a sign of desire, not an expression of doubt.' It is at the precise moment of the Virgin's consent, for Bonaventure, that 'the Son of God was conceived' (1.1.70).

For medieval and Renaissance readers also, aware as they were of myriad pagan stories of the gods (perhaps especially the numerous stories of rapes of mortal women by a disguised Jupiter or Zeus), Gabriel's courtesy in the Annunciation was a distinctive feature of Luke's narrative, one with large theological implications. In Gabriel's address, Mary's free agency is theologically foregrounded in a way that makes her *fiat* a contrary not only of Eve, but of faithless Israel, the would-be espoused of God who went off into harlotry, and then into the captivity experienced by Daniel. For early Jewish readers, Gabriel in Luke's Gospel is thus both an interpreter of God's faithfulness throughout some of the darkest hours of Israel's history, and a sign of God's perseverant goodness in bringing Israel's redemption to pass in 'the fulness of time'. In that respect, characteristic of angels generally in the Old Testament, Gabriel lends to the Christmas story a note of high courtliness and joyous eschatological expectation.

REFERENCES AND FURTHER READING

Augustine of Hippo (1997). *Newly Delivered Sermons*. Translated by Edmund Hill. Works of Augustine 3/11. New York: New City Press.

Begg, Christopher (2007). 'Angels in the Work of Flavius Josephus', in *Angels: The Concept of Celestial Beings—Origins, Development and Reception*. Deuterocanonical and Cognate Literature Yearbook. Edited by Friedrich V. Reiterer, Tobias Niklas, and Karin Schöpflin. Berlin: de Gruyter.

Bernstein, Moshe J. (2011). 'Angels at the Aqedah: A Study in the Development of a Midrashic Motif', *Dead Sea Discoveries*, 7, no. 3, Angels and Demons: 263–91.

Beyerle, Stefan (2007). 'Angelic Revelation in Jewish Apocalyptic Literature', in *Angels: The Concept of Celestial Beings—Origins, Development and Reception*. Deuterocanonical and Cognate Literature Yearbook 2007. Edited by Friedrich V. Reiterer, Tobias Niklas, and Karin Schöpflin. Berlin: de Gruyter: 205–23.

Bock, Darrell L. (1994–6). *Luke*. 2 vols. Grand Rapids: Baker.

Bonaventure (2001–2004). *Commentary on the Gospel of Luke*. 3 vols. Translated by Robert F. Karris. Collected Works of Bonaventure 8. St. Bonaventure, NY: Franciscan Institute.

Bonino, Serge-Thomas, OP (2016). 'Angels and Demons in the New Testament' and 'The Developments of Christian Angelology until St. Thomas Aquinas', in *Angels and Demons: A Catholic Introduction*. Translated by Michael J. Miller. Washington, DC: Catholic University of America Press.

Cline, Rangar H. (2005). 'Ancient Angels: Hellenic Angel Veneration and Christian Reaction (*c*200–450 CE)'. PhD diss., Pennsylvania State University.

Collins, John J. (2000). 'Powers in Heaven: God, Gods, and Angels in the Dead Sea Scrolls', in John J. Collins and Robert A. Kugler (eds.), *Religion in the Dead Sea Scrolls*. Studies in the Dead Sea Scrolls and Related Literature. Grand Rapids, MI: Eerdmans: 9–28.

Coogan, Michael D. (2010). *The New Oxford Annotated Apocrypha*, Revised Fourth Edition. New York: Oxford University Press.

Evans, Annette H. M. (2006). 'The Development of Jewish Ideas of Angels: Egyptian and Hellenistic Connections'. PhD diss., University of Stellenbosch.

Gabra, Gawdat (2002). 'The Monastery of the Archangel Gabriel in al-Faiyum', in Gabra (ed.), *Coptic Monasteries: Egypt's Monastic Art and Architecture*. New York, NY: The American University in Cairo Press: 47–54.

Ginzberg, Louis (1983). *Legends of the Jews*. Philadelphia: Jewish Publication Society.

Heiser, Michael (2018). *Angels: What the Bible Really Says about God's Heavenly Host*. Bellingham, WA: Lexham Press.

Henze, Matthias (ed.) (2011). *Hazon Gabriel: New Readings of the Gabriel Revelation*. Early Judaism and Its Literature 29. Atlanta: Society of Biblical Literature.

Iavoschi, Roxana-Ileana (2004). 'The Archangel Gabriel in History and Tradition: An Analysis of his Role and Function in Judaism, Christianity, and Islam'. PhD Diss., Concordia University (Canada).

Jeffrey, David Lyle (2009). 'Sacred Proposals and the Spiritual Sublime', in Faith Holly Nelson, Lynn Szabo, and Jens Zimmerman (eds.), *Through a Glass Darkly: Suffering, the Sacred and the Sublime in Literature and Theory*. Waterloo: Wilfrid Laurier University Press: 3–21.

Jeffrey, David Lyle (2012). *Luke: a Theological Commentary*. Grand Rapids: Baker Academic.

Jeffrey, David Lyle (2017). *In the Beauty of Holiness: Art and the Bible in Western Culture*. Grand Rapids: Eerdmans.

Jenkins, Philip (2017). *Crucible of Faith: the Ancient Revolution that made our Modern Religious World*. New York: Basic Books.

Landau, Brent and Tony Burke (2016) *New Testament Apocrypha: More Non-Canonical Scriptures*. Vol. 1. Grand Rapids: Eerdmans.

Lightfoot, Janes (1979). *A Commentary on the New Testament from the Talmud and Hebraica*. Oxford: Oxford University Press, 1859; reprinted Grand Rapids: Baker.

López, René A. 2010. 'Identifying the "Angel of the Lord" in the Book of Judges: A Model of Reconsidering the Referent in Other Old Testament Loci', *Bulletin for Biblical Research*, 20: 1–18.

Lockyer, Herbert (1995). *All the Angels in the Bible*. Peabody, MA: Hendrickson.

Marshall, I. Howard (1979). *Commentary on Luke*, New International Greek Commentary. Grand Rapids: Eerdmans, 1978.

Melvin, David P. (2013). *The Interpreting Angel Motif in Prophetic and Apocalyptic Literature*. Minneapolis, MN: Augsburg Fortress, Publishers.

Friedrich V. Reiterer, Tobias Niklas, and Karin Schöpflin (eds) (2007a) *Literature Yearbook 2007*. Berlin: de Gruyter: 525–36.

Reiterer, Friedrich V., Tobias Niklas, and Karin Schöpflin (eds.) (2007b). *Angels: The Concept of Celestial Beings—Origins, Development and Reception*. Deuterocanonical and Cognate Literature Yearbook. Berlin: de Gruyter.

Rofé, Alexander. (2012). *Angels in the Bible: Israelite Beliefs in Angels as Evidenced by Biblical Traditions*. 2nd ed. Jerusalem: Carmel.

Van der Kam, James (2000). 'The Angel of the Presence in the Book of Jubilees'. *Dead Sea Discoveries*. Leiden: Brill, 2000.

van Dijk, Ann. (1999). 'The Angelic Salutation in Early Byzantine and Medieval Annunciation Imagery', *The Art Bulletin*, 81, no. 3: 420–36.

CHAPTER 17

BETHLEHEM AND THE CENSUS

LEROY A. HUIZENGA

ALTHOUGH the events each Gospel presents are combined in Christmas pageants and other retellings of the Christmas story, the Gospel of Matthew and the Gospel of Luke present very different birth narratives. In the Gospel of Matthew, the narrator recounts an angel telling Joseph to keep Mary as his wife, since the child in her womb is from the Holy Spirit (Matthew 1:20), and the angel later instructs Joseph to take the Holy Family and flee to Egypt, since Herod (the father of the clan of Herods whom history has deemed 'the Great') is about to attempt to kill the child (Matthew 2:13). Eventually the Holy Family makes its way to Nazareth, in Galilee in the north, avoiding Judea since Herod's wicked, brutal, and stupid son Archelaus was ruling there after his father's death. In the Matthean version, then, neither Joseph nor Mary have any speaking parts; the narrator bears the burden of recounting the stories of Jesus's conception and birth, escape to Egypt, and return to Israel.

The version presented in the Gospel of Luke is quite different. While in the Matthean version there is the general atmosphere of darkness and threat, in the Lukan version there is an atmosphere of light and expectative receptivity. The birth narrative in the Gospel of Luke recounts no threat to the Christ Child, has Mary (though not Joseph) uttering a battery of highly significant words, and evinces a general atmosphere of warmth and welcome: the archangel Gabriel makes joyous, momentous announcements to Zechariah about the baby who will become John the Baptist (Luke 1:8–23) and to Mary about the baby who will be Jesus the Messiah (Luke 1:26–38). Angels praise God and direct shepherds to go to Bethlehem to see the child. The characters of Mary, Zechariah, Simeon, and Anna speak and sing stirring words of praise and prophecy.

Each evangelist has composed his birth narrative in accord with his literary–theological purposes, whatever sources were or were not to hand. Further, literary–theological analysis involves reading for the model or ideal author's intention as determined by the text itself, which has an indexical relationship with the empirical author (Huizenga 2012: 71-4). That is, narrative tools, as opposed to redaction-critical tools, give us more purchase on the theological dynamics of a Gospel since they take account of the entirety of the text the author actually produced, instead of basing estimations of an evangelist's theology on perceived edits, additions, and omissions of material in prior sources, as those changes comprise a tiny percentage of the words a Gospel itself comprises (Huizenga 2012: 2-9). Examining the story of Jesus's birth in Bethlehem, the events surrounding it, and the census that brings the Holy Family there (Luke 2:1-21) is first a matter of literary and theological analysis before it is a matter of historical analysis, for the poetic function must always precede the referential function; the first thing readers—or those specialized readers known as scholars— encounter is the text itself as the author has (consciously and unconsciously) shaped it (as determined of course by modern editors using the scientific art of textual criticism, which itself can only be performed adequately with recourse to narrative analysis; see Huizenga 2011).

The Gospel of Luke is a gospel of continuity, comity, and concord. Unlike the other three canonical Gospels, which in various ways and to various degrees emphasize conflict between Jesus and his disciples on one hand and their fellow Jews on the other (see, for instance, Jesus' seven woes against the scribes and the Pharisees in Matthew 23), the Lukan author usually downplays conflict among Jesus, his disciples, their fellow Jews, and the Romans, instead emphasizing Jesus' and the Church's continuity with Judaism and its Scriptures, and its harmony with the *Pax Romana* established by Octavian, who became Caesar Augustus. For instance, in the version in the Gospel of Luke, it is a Jewish expert in the law who delivers the teaching that the two greatest commandments are to love God and to love neighbour (Luke 10:25-8), and not Jesus himself, as is the case in the Gospel of Matthew (Matthew 22:34-40) and the Gospel of Mark (12:28-34). As regards relations with the Roman world, in the Gospel of Luke the centurion at Jesus' crucifixion declares Jesus 'innocent' or 'righteous' (Luke 23:47), and in the companion volume to the Gospel of Luke, the book of Acts, no Christian is ever convicted by a Roman, and Paul and other apostles are routinely let go without charge (see, for instance, Acts 16:35-40, 17:1-9, 18:12-17, 19:21-41, 22:22-9).

In Luke 1 in particular the reader encounters a picture of continuity with Judaism; with obvious allusions to the situation of Abraham and barren Sarah, the archangel Gabriel appears to the aged priest Zechariah and informs him that his barren wife, Elizabeth, will bear a son who will come 'in the spirit and power of Elijah' (Luke 1:17) to bring many sons of Israel back to the Lord their God (Luke 1:5-17). Then the reader encounters a story about a pious Jewish girl, Mary, a virgin, to whom the archangel Gabriel announces that she will bear a son who will receive 'the throne of his father David' and who 'will reign over the house of Jacob forever' (Luke 1:32b-33a). Both archangelic declarations are marked by traditional Jewish prophetic beliefs. Mary's Magnificat (Luke 1:46-55) is also marked by traditional Jewish concerns: 'He has helped his servant Israel, in remembrance of his mercy, as he spoke to our fathers, to Abraham and to his posterity for ever' (Luke 1:54-5). The Jewish character of this first chapter might be obvious to certain readers, but New Testament scholarship has had an unfortunate history of downplaying the essential Jewish identity of Jesus and the early Christian Church. Even those scholars who would declare their rejection of anti-Semitism outright have all too often let the ghost of Martin Luther colour their estimation of Judaism and reading of the New Testament, which has often led to insufficient appreciation of the fundamental Jewish character of Christianity. Indeed, the scholar most responsible for shaping twentieth-century understandings of the theology of the Gospel of Luke, the German Hans Conzelmann, held that the first two chapters of the Gospel were largely irrelevant for its interpretation, going so far as to entertain the idea that they were a later addition: 'the authenticity of these first two chapters is questionable' (Conzelmann 1961: 118). Leaving the first two chapters aside as unimportant for the interpretation of the Gospel of Luke probably stemmed from Germanic scholarship's reflexive disdain for anything perceived as too Jewish (and thus also too Catholic, given both religions' emphasis on ritual and law), though it must be said that Conzelmann himself was no anti-Semite. It also violated two principal rules of literary interpretation: first, that beginnings set the stage in decisive ways for the story that follows, and second, that the whole (being the widest literary context) determines the meaning of the parts.

In Luke 2, the scene shifts from the Jewish setting of the Temple in Jerusalem and the Jewish girl Mary in the Jewish town of Nazareth of Galilee to an imperial Roman horizon with the mere mention of Caesar Augustus, who according to the narrator issued a decree 'that all the world should be enrolled' (Luke 2:1) in some sort of census. The mention of Augustus brings to the reader's mind the enduring Roman Peace that was established by the ultimate victory of Gaius Octavius Thurinus ending the Roman civil wars of the first century BCE. Octavius is better known to history (in English) as Octavian, nephew and adopted son of Gaius Julius Caesar, who would become the Caesar Augustus mentioned in Luke 2:1. The period of Augustus' rule (27 BCE–14 CE) is regarded as a golden age in Roman history, an era of peace and prosperity after a near century of civil war and its attendant depredations and deprivations.

Augustus' decree causes Mary (who had returned from Judea to Nazareth where she was visiting Elizabeth and Zechariah, Luke 1:39–40, 56) to go with Joseph from Nazareth to Bethlehem, the city of David, where Joseph was to register 'because he was of the house and lineage of David' (Luke 2:4). On one hand, then, the reader sees the narrator concerned to tie Jesus' birth and lineage (here by adoption, as Joseph is not the biological father of Jesus) to King David by virtue of the Holy Family's return to Bethlehem for the census. David was the original anointed one (which Christ and Messiah mean, derived from the Greek and Hebrew for 'anointed one', respectively; see 1 Samuel 16:1–13, where David is anointed king by Samuel) and thus the primary prototype for later Jewish conceptions of the Christ/Messiah. The Lukan author likely wishes to suggest Jesus' Davidic connections by locating the Holy Family in Bethlehem so that Jesus will be born there (although the author, who otherwise seems to know the Greek Old Testament very well, does not mention the striking prophecy of Micah 5:2, which predicts that a ruler of Israel will rise from Bethlehem; compare

Matthew 2:5–6, where the prophecy of Micah 5:2 finds explicit quotation); the reader, it is to be surmised, is supposed to see here an allusive reference to Micah 5:2. (Further, the lack of explicit reference to Micah 5:2 suggests that the author did not invent the story of Jesus' birth in Bethlehem, but knows it from tradition, or, if one rejects the Q hypothesis, from the Gospel of Matthew; in any event, had the author simply invented the Bethlehem story, an explicit quotation of Micah 5:2 would in all likelihood have been included.) On the other hand, the reader also sees the subtle Lukan theme of divine providence working through the Roman Empire (as will become a common Christian understanding once Constantine makes Christianity licit and begins favouring it, thanks largely to his historian Eusebius, whose *Ecclesiastical History* presented Rome as the agent of God's providence in setting socio-cultural and technological conditions for the ready spread of the Gospel and the Church). Rome, in the Lukan presentation, serves God's providence. And, on a third hand, the Lukan author's presentation of Joseph and Mary's compliance with this taxation census fits the theme of Christian–Roman harmony found in Luke–Acts, in which no Christian after Jesus is ever convicted by a Roman, and in which even the very centurion responsible for Jesus' execution declares him 'innocent' (*dikaios*, Luke 23:47).

But that does not mean Rome is simply good, or benign, in the Lukan vision. For the very mention of a census evokes the parallel accounts of David's sinful census in 2 Samuel 24 and 1 Chronicles 21 (the latter passage making Satan the ultimate instigator); as Edwards (2015: 68) writes, 'Mention of the word "census" should alert readers to danger, for in the OT only God legitimately counts his people.' What is more, the very claims made about Jesus Christ in the Gospel of Luke and the book of Acts rival claims made by and about Roman rulers like Caesar Augustus. Augustus' full official titular name was *Imperator Caesar Divi filius Augustus* (Emperor [or Commander] Caesar Augustus, Son of God) and Augustus would later be deified (declared divine and in soul ascended to the heavens) upon his death in 14 CE. The famous Priene inscription eulogizes Augustus in language familiar to readers of the New Testament:

> Because providence that has ordered our life in a divine way [...] and since the Caesar through his appearance (*epiphaneis*) has exceeded the hopes of all former good messages (*euangelia*), surpassing not only the benefactors who came before him, but also leaving no hope that anyone in the future would surpass him, and since for the world the birthday of the god (*theos*) was the beginning of his good messages (*euangelion*) [...]
> (Dittenberger 1960: 2, 40–2, quoted Koester 1992: 12)

Providence, epiphany, the 'good messages' (or, as *euangelion* is routinely translated in the New Testament, 'gospel'), divinity—all these terms resonant in the Christian grammar surround also the advent of Caesar Augustus and the age of peace and glory he brings.

Many scholars, then, have begun to examine Roman imperial realized eschatology, in which Augustus is thought to have ushered in a decisive, ultimate age of peace

(Koester 1992: 10–13), as an important context for understanding Jesus and the earliest Christians and the documents they produced. Koester summarizes the characteristics of this Roman eschatology as follows:

> There are several characteristic features of this Roman imperial eschatology: (1) The new age is the fulfillment of prophecy, and it corresponds to the promises given in the primordial age. (2) The new age includes this earth as well as the world of the heavens: Apollo as Helios is the god of the new age; the zodiac sign of the month of Augustus's birth appears on the shields of the soldiers. (3) The new age is universal; it includes all nations: the new solar calendar is introduced by the vote of the people of the cities all over the empire. (4) There is an enactment of the new age through the official celebrations of the empire, like the secular festivities of the year 17 BCE, mirrored by the subsequent introduction of Caesarean games in many places. (5) The new age has a savior figure, the greatest benefactor of all times, the *divi filius*, usually translated into Greek as υἱὸς τοῦ θεοῦ [*huios tou theou*]—"Son of God"—the victorious Augustus. (Koester 1992: 12–13)

The Roman vision and the Christian vision, then, attempt to occupy the same conceptual and cultural space: that is, each claims ultimacy, and each claims there is one divine ruler of the world. Recognizing this, certain statements in the Gospel of Luke take on a new light. The archangel Gabriel informs Mary that the child to be born to her will be called 'the Son of God' (Luke 1:35b). Mary's Magnificat in response contains words speaking of how God scatters the proud and pulls down the mighty from their thrones (Luke 1:51–2). Zechariah's prophecy speaks of the Lord God now moving to deliver Israel from her enemies (Luke 1:71, 73) thanks to the advent of the Christ Child, who will usher in an age of peace (Luke 1:78–9). And, as too few have noticed, Satan himself suggests that Rome, being one of the empires of the world, is under his domination (Luke 4:6). The Gospel's claims about Jesus, then, present an incipient challenge to the imperial Roman order with its realized eschatology. And while the earliest Christians were not political revolutionaries as such, the book of Acts records that Paul and Silas are charged with turning the world upside down (Acts 17:6). Perhaps the mention of Caesar Augustus in Luke 2:1 does not in the end signal Christian comfort and compatibility with the Roman order, but rather a challenge to the powers that then were. Indeed, in terms of geography the action in Luke–Acts begins in Jerusalem in its Temple (Luke 1) and centres on Jerusalem (see Luke 24:47, 52 and Acts 1:4–8; 9:26–31; 15:1–29; 21:15–25) but makes it way eventually to Rome; Jesus himself sketches this missionary movement in Acts 1:8: '[Y]ou shall be my witnesses in Jerusalem and in all Judea and Samaria and to the end of the earth.' Thus the great city of the Jews, Jerusalem, and the great city of the Gentiles, Rome, function as the two geographical poles of the known world in Luke–Acts, suggesting the universality of the Gospel message, which, as St Paul reminds his readers, first comes to and from the Jews, and then proceeds to the Gentiles (Romans 1:16; see 2:9–10).

The empirical author of the Gospel of Luke is usually regarded as an ancient historian of the first rank, but modern historians also regard him as making a massive blunder in mentioning that Joseph and Mary were subject to a census under Quirinius, governor of Syria, just before Jesus was born, for Herod the Great died as early as 4 BCE (and perhaps as late as 1 BCE; see Steinmann 2009) and Quirinius did not begin his administration of Syria until 6 CE in the wake of the Roman removal and banishment of Herod Archelaus (Herod the Great's son, who had been governing Judea as 'ethnarch' after his father's death) in 6 CE.

The invocation of Caesar Augustus in Luke 2:1 evokes the Roman Empire, and thus the Roman rule of Israel that had begun in 63 BCE, when the Roman general Pompey, in the east contending with Parthians, intervened in the last Hasmoneans' rivalry, conquering Jerusalem and removing both claimants to the throne, Aristobulus II and Hyrcanus II, and reduced southern Israel to a Roman protectorate, Judea, ruled by a Roman prefect but under effective control of the legate in charge of Syria. Roman rule of Judea did not mean that there was a legion stationed near Jerusalem providing a legionary for every street corner to keep law and order: neither the province nor the city were under formal martial law. The nearest legion was in Syria, while there was a small garrison of troops in the Antonia fortress, part of the Temple complex. It would be inaccurate to describe the situation in Roman-ruled Judea as one of occupation. Nevertheless, Rome made her rule felt through violence when it was judged the situation called for it, and through taxation, and many Jews resented Roman rule, however miniscule the actual Roman footprint in Judea and the holy city of Jerusalem.

Now, Josephus records a census of Judea for purposes of taxation near the beginning of P. Sulpicius Quirinius' administration of Syria, which began in 6 CE (Josephus, *Ant.* 18.1–10, 26). This census led to an insurrection led by Judas the Galilean, which the Lukan author refers to in Acts 5:37, in the context of a speech delivered by Gamaliel, a Pharisee and member of the Sanhedrin. Judas' insurrection was no minor affair and loomed large in the memory of first-century Jews, as Josephus' account and Acts' mention of it suggest. The Lukan author, therefore, certainly knew the census and rebellion of 6 or 7 CE well, and presumably their timing. The question, then, is whether the Lukan author really made a blunder in placing the time of Jesus's birth both after Quirinius' census (Luke 2:2) but also within the lifetime of Herod the Great (Luke 1:5), which simply didn't overlap, however late Herod the Great actually died. Most scholars, even Evangelical ones, will simply accept that the Lukan author erred: Edwards (2015: 71) writes, 'Why Luke twice refers to the same event, the latter [Acts 5:37] in essential correspondence with external historical records and the former [Luke 2:1] at variance with them, remains a mystery.' Some attempts at solving the mystery in ways that preserve the Lukan author's integrity as a good historian here in Luke 2:1 have been made, however. As Smith (2000: 283) writes, 'The fact that Luke's account of Quirinius and his census is falsifiable as historical evidence and is so easy for him to verify and correct makes it most improbable that he made the error of which he is often accused.'

One solution relies heavily on conjectured emendations, but has the strength of Tertullian's ancient witness behind it. Rist (2005) suggests that instead of reading 'Quirinius' in Luke 2:2 we should read 'Quintilius,' namely P. Quintilius Varus, who began governing Syria in 7 or early 6 BCE, replacing C. Sentius Saturninus, who had been in charge from 10/9 BCE (Josephus, *Ant.* 16.9.1). Tertullian (*Adv. Marc.* 4.19.10) asserts that Jesus' birth occurred when Saturninus was yet ruling the province of Syria. Tertullian, it is thought, would not contradict Luke 2:2, a crucial part and parcel of the Church's Scripture, unless he had very good reason to: he must have had a source (oral or written) that he trusted implicitly. Rist (2005: 490) suggests that 'Luke or his source (or just possibly a very early copyist) may indeed have confused Quintilius (Varus) with Quirinius, after which every further copy would repeat the mistake.'

Smith (2000) suggests that interpreters have misunderstood the reference to 'Herod, King of Judea' in Luke 1:5. Instead of Herod the Great, Smith argues, we should understand Herod Archelaus. Smith (2000: 286) notes that if 'Herod' in Luke 1:5 is meant to refer to Herod the Great, it would be the only reference to him in the entirety of Luke–Acts. Further, Archelaus is called 'Herod' on his coinage, and Dio Cassius names him 'Herod of Palestine' (Smith 2000: 286). Smith (2000: 286) also observes that Josephus records that Herod the Great gave Archelaus the title 'King' in the former's last will and testament ('Salome and Alexas...read aloud the letter that Herod had written to the soldiers to thank them for their faithfulness and goodwill to him and to ask them to give the same support to his son Archelaus, whom he had appointed king') and that the title was accepted by royalty, soldiers, and citizens (*Ant.* 17.8.1–2). Josephus himself calls Archelaus 'king': 'Herod's successor as king, his son Archelaus' (*Ant.* 18.4.3; Smith 2000: 286). As regards the glaring conflict with the Matthean account, Smith (2000: 292) opts for midrash:

> I do not think that Matthew had any intention of offering a historical account of Jesus' birth...it is much more probable that Matthew adopted a different chronology to fit his theological and literary scheme (or that he ignored chronological considerations altogether) than that Luke, who, in my opinion, did intend to maintain a historical framework for his narrative, made an easily falsifiable chronological blunder, which would hurt his credibility as an author and which would contribute little if anything to his central theological or literary themes.

Smith (2000: 292) thus concludes, 'Jesus was probably born in Bethlehem in 6 CE'

Another possibility is to find Josephus in error instead of the Lukan author, as Rhoads (2011) contends in a detailed, lengthy article. He argues that 'the account which Josephus tells of the census conducted by Quirinius, and the corresponding revolt by Judas the Galilean, is actually a mistaken duplication, broadly speaking, of events which occurred much earlier...the census began before Herod the Great's death' (Rhoads 2011: 67). Rhoads (2011: 69–70) notes that there are three accounts of insurrections involving a Judas in Josephus' works, the first in *Ant.* 17.148–67, the second in *Ant.* 17.269–85, and the third in *Ant.* 18.4–23 and *J.W.* 2.117–18; it seems Josephus is engaging in 'mistaken duplication' (Rhoads 2011: 70). Rhoads concludes that the three accounts concern one single Judas who led a rebellion in the final years of Herod the Great (2011: 79–80) and believes that the Sabinus mentioned in *Ant.* 17.221 and *J.W.*

2.16 and Quirinius are the same person (2011: 82–4), with Josephus not understanding that 'Sabinus', 'the Sabine', was a Semitic nickname for Quirinius. This would put Quirinius/Sabinus in Judea in the final year or two of Herod the Great's reign, conducting a census for the purposes of taxation, and if we accept a date for Herod the Great's death in 1 BC (Steinmann 2009), then the timing of Jesus' birth just after a census as detailed by the Gospel of Luke would seem to work. It is also of interest that Eusebius, in his *Ecclesiastical History* 1.5, dates the Lukan census to 3/2 BCE on our calendar in claiming it happened in Augustus' forty-second year and twenty-eight years after the battle of Actium.

Rhoads' article is relatively recent, and so has not yet found sufficient consideration among Lukan commentators, and it also suffers the disadvantage of appearing in a publication mainline biblical scholars esteem too little. The argument presented in and of itself is detailed, well researched, well argued, and rooted in prior studies suggesting similar conclusions (Schwartz 1988; Zahn 1893; Lodder 1930; Spitta 1906; Weber 1909)—it is not idiosyncratic. As such, the article merits serious consideration among scholars and historians.

The ultimate, most promising solution may lie in grammar, though many (but not all) commentators reject it (see, for example, Edwards 2015: 70). In Luke 2.2, the census described is the *apographē prōtē*, either the 'first census' taken when Quirinius was governor of Syria, as in many translations, or some other census 'before' the famous census of Quirinius. The latter option saves the Lukan author as a historian by understanding him to be making a reference to another, less well-remembered census that occurred just before Jesus' birth under Herod the Great and well before Quirinius' administration of Syria. The author would have done so to avoid the very charge with which modern scholars often charge him. On this view, Luke 2:2, which in any event sits awkwardly between vv. 1 and 3, reads as an aside designed to inform readers that Quirinius' famous census was not in view, but an earlier census, precisely because Quirinius' census of 6 or 7 CE loomed so large in Jewish memory. The author does not want his readers to be confused and thus regard him as a poor historian, so he has to clarify that he is not speaking about the famous census that would most naturally come to his readers' minds. Wright (2014: 89) observes, 'But in the Greek of the time, as the standard major lexicons point out, the word *prōtos* came sometimes to be used to mean "before", when followed (as this is) by the genitive case.' Scholars like Wright who favour this grammatical solution point to similar usage of *prōtos* + genitive in John 1:15, 1:30, and 15:18 (see Liddell and Scott 1996: 1535, and Bauer et al. 2001: 888–9; this reading of Luke 2:2 was also put forward and defended by Lagrange 1921: 66–8, and Nolland 1989: 101–2). Acts 1:1 also employs *prōton* to mean 'prior', and is particularly important because it comes from the Lukan author himself: *Ton men prōton logon* refers to the volume prior to the Acts of the Apostles, namely the Lukan author's first volume, which we call the Gospel of Luke, and so reinforces the possibility of a similar usage in Luke 2:2.

Assuming the standard interpretation of Josephus and Roman history, Quirinius carried out a major census in 6/7 BCE, and assuming the grammatical solution above,

Luke would be referring to some other census before the death of Herod the Great in 4 or 1 BCE. Joseph and Mary would have gone to Bethlehem to register either because Joseph owned property there (so Eusebius, *Hist. Eccl.* 3.20), or because under Herod the Great such a census would have been conducted in accord with Jewish customs (Edwards 2015: 69). Modern historians concur that no empire-wide census was ever taken in Roman history. The Lukan author might here be engaging in hyperbole when he states that Augustus decreed that 'all the world should be enrolled' (Luke 2:1), for in Acts 11:28 the author recounts a prophecy that a great famine would strike 'all the world', and that it took place during the time of the Emperor Claudius. The famine was serious, but it did not in fact occur over 'all the world'. So, the Lukan author is likely referring to a census that happened sometime before Herod the Great's death and just before Jesus' birth that is otherwise lost to history. Yet absence of evidence is not evidence of absence, and in any case the Lukan account—so reliable on so many other matters—is itself evidence of the census it mentions. Wright (2014: 116) opines, 'We don't know, from other sources, of a census earlier than Quirinius'. But there are a great many things that we don't know in ancient history...My guess is that Luke knew a tradition in which Jesus was born during some sort of census, and that Luke knew as well as we do that it couldn't have been the one conducted under Quirinius, because by then Jesus was about 10 years old. That is why he wrote that the census was the one before that conducted by Quirinius. The Lukan account of Jesus' birth during a census, then, is historically plausible.

References and Further Reading

Bauer, Walter et al. (2001). *A Greek-English Lexicon of the New Testament and Other Early Christian Literature*. 3rd ed. Chicago: University of Chicago Press.

Brown, Raymond (1999). *The Birth of the Messiah: A Commentary on the Infancy Narratives in the Gospels of Matthew and Luke*. Anchor Yale Bible Reference Library. New Haven, Conn.: Yale University Press.

Conzelmann, Hans (1961). *The Theology of St. Luke*. New York: Harper.

Dittenberger, Wilhelm (1960). *Orientis Graeci inscriptiones selectae*. 2 vols. Hildesheim: Olms.

Edwards, James R. (2015). *The Gospel according to Luke*. Pillar New Testament Commentary. Grand Rapids, Mich.: Eerdmans.

Huizenga, Leroy (2011). 'The Confession of Jesus and the Curses of Peter: A Narrative-Christological Approach to the Text-Critical Problem of Mark 14:62', *Novum Testamentum* 53, no. 3: 244–66.

Huizenga, Leroy (2012). *The New Isaac: Tradition and Intertextuality in the Gospel of Matthew*. Supplements to Novum Testamentum 131. Reprint. Leiden: E. J. Brill.

Koester, Helmut (1992). 'Jesus the Victim', *Journal of Biblical Literature*, 111, no. 1, January: 3–15.

Lagrange, M.-J. (1921). *Evangile selon Saint Luc*. 2nd ed. Paris: Gabalda.

Liddell, H. G. and Scott, R. (1996). *Greek-English Lexicon: With a Revised Supplement*. 9th ed. Oxford: Clarendon Press.

Lodder, Willem (1930). *Die Schätzung des Quirinius bei Flavius Josephus. Eine Untersuchung: Hat Sich Flavius Josephus in der Datierung der Bekannten Schätzung (Luk.2,2) Geirrt?* Leipzig: Dörffling & Franke.

Nolland, John (1989). *Luke 1–9:20.* Dallas, Tex.: Word Books.

Rhoads, John H. (2011). 'Josephus Misdated the Census of Quirinius', *Journal of the Evangelical Theological Society,* 54, no. 1, March: 65–87.

Rist, John M. (2005). 'Luke 2:2: Making Sense of the Date of Jesus' Birth', *Journal of Theological Studies,* 56, no. 2, October: 489–91.

Schwartz, Daniel R. (1988). 'On Quirinius, John the Baptist, the Benedictus, Melchizedek, Qumran, and Ephesus', *Revue de Qumran,* 13: 635–46.

Smith, Mark D. (2000). 'Of Jesus and Quirinius', *Catholic Biblical Quarterly,* 62: 278–93.

Spitta, Friedrich (1906). 'Die Chronologische Notizen und die Hymnen in Lc 1 U. 2', *Zeitschrift für die neutestamentliche Wissenschaft und die Kunde der älteren Kirche,* 7: 281–317.

Steinmann, Andrew E. (2009). 'When Did Herod the Great Reign?' *Novum Testamentum,* 51: 1–29.

Weber, Wilhelm (1909). 'Der Census des Quirinius nach Josephus', *Zeitschrift für die neutestamentliche Wissenschaft und die Kunde der älteren Kirche,* 10 (1909): 307–19.

Wright, N. T. (2014). *Who Was Jesus?* Grand Rapids: Eerdmans.

Zahn, Theodor (1893). 'Die Syrische Statthalterschaft und die Schätzung des Quirinius', *Neue kirchliche Zeitschrift,* 4: 633–54.

CHAPTER 18

THE MAGI AND THE STAR

D. H. WILLIAMS

In the time of King Herod, after Jesus was born in Bethlehem of Judea, Magi from the East came to Jerusalem, [2]asking, 'Where is the child who has been born king of the Jews? For we observed his star in the east and have come to pay him homage.' [3]When King Herod heard this, he was frightened, and all Jerusalem with him; [4]and calling together all the chief priests and scribes of the people, he inquired of them where the Messiah was to be born. [5]They told him, 'In Bethlehem of Judea; for so it has been written by the prophet: [6]"And you, Bethlehem, in the land of Judah, are by no means least among the rulers of Judah; for from you shall come a ruler who is to shepherd my people Israel.' [7]Then Herod secretly called for the Magi and learned from them the exact time when the star had appeared. [8]Then he sent them to Bethlehem, saying, 'Go and search diligently for the child; and when you have found him, bring me word so that I may also go and pay him homage.' [9]When they had heard the king, they set out; and there, ahead of them, went the star that they had seen in the east until it stood over the place where the child was. [10]When they saw that the star, they were overwhelmed with joy. [11]On entering the house, they saw the child with Mary his mother; and having fallen down they worshipped him. Then, opening their treasure chests, they offered him gifts of gold, frankincense, and myrrh. [12]And having been warned in a dream not to return to Herod, they left for their own country by another road.

(Matt. 2:1–12)

IT would not be Christmas without a performance of 'Amahl and the Night Visitors' playing on the radio (Menotti 1951). Amahl was the first opera to be composed for television in the United States. Its production was inspired by Hieronymus Bosch's painting, 'Adoration of the Magi' (late fifteenth century), and with it we encounter the quintessential portrait of the three Magi that has coloured the celebration of Christmas and Epiphany. There are three splendidly dressed kings, one of whom is black, and another who is aged, each bearing respectively presents of gold, frankincense, and myrrh. We are told in the opera that the names of the kings are Kaspar, Balthasar, and Melchior and that they have come a long way in their journey and still have far to go as they follow the star.

Matthew's account of the Magi (magoi) is unique in the Bible and we have nothing else with which to compare it. This has naturally led to a great many questions about what such an account of Persian astrologers is doing in the Gospel, what was the identity of the Magi and whether they were of royal blood, and what about the 'star' that the New Testament says prompted their trip in the first place and led them to the Christ Child. We are faced with the situation that there are more questions about the identity of the Magi than there are answers.

The fact that Jesus is called a 'young child' (paidion) and not an infant tells of an elapse of time between the original birth announcements made by the angels with the resulting visit by the shepherds and this later event. Exactly how much time is unknown, though 'paidion' could apply to someone from eight days after birth up to 7 years of age. Partly for this reason, the story of the Magi is associated with the feast of Epiphany (January 6) rather than Christmas, as Peter Chrysologus (fifth century) notes, '[T]he feast was conceived on different occasions and bore three characteristic signs of divinity' by the three 'mystical' gifts presented (Serm 157). By the fourth century, the Magi's arrival was celebrated as the Feast of Epiphany on January 6 (which is twelve days after Jesus' birth on December 25). Eastern Christianity refers to the holy day as Theophany (Basil of Caesarea, PG 31:1472–3) and also commemorates the manifestation of Jesus' divinity at his baptism in the River Jordan. In some parts of the Christian world, January 6, rather than December 25, is a time for exchanging presents, in commemoration of the gifts of the Magi.

We must ask what image or images did Matthew assume the word 'Magi' would evoke for his readers? Astrologers? Pagan star worshippers? Officials of the Persian court? Use of the commonly printed 'wise men' in older versions of the English Bible (Geneva; KJV; RSV) is too vague to be of any descriptive help. Matthew's narrative itself offers no evaluative comments about the Magi in general except that they were observers of the stars and their meaning (Hegedus 2003: 83). They would have presumably dedicated themselves to gleaning from the heavens insights pertaining to human affairs. There is still much ambiguity here. Magi (or a magus) has been used in reference to those engaged in sorcery, augury, or magic of various kinds. Acts 8 alludes to Simon from Samaria as a magos in the sense of magician; one who 'practised magic' (mageuon) (8:9) and amazed the people with his 'magic' (magiais) (8:11). We are informed by the Greek historian Herodotus that the magi were originally one of the tribes of the Medes, who functioned as priests and diviners under the Persians (sixth–fourth century BC) (*Histories* I.101).

The picture of those magicians who divine the future from the stars in the Old Testament is decidedly negative (see Deut. 18:9–14; Isa. 47: 13; Jer. 10:1–2). In Daniel 2 when King Nebuchadnezzar summons his magi and orders them to interpret his dream, they are presented as ineffective. Their learning and their art do not enable them to know what needs to be known. Their role in the story is to serve as foils to Daniel who received true knowledge from God. Daniel is presented as the bearer of true wisdom; magi and other so-called wise men are exposed as fools (Powell 2000a: 8). In the story of Balaam (Num. 24:17), this Gentile prophet thwarts the plans of an evil king by announcing that God is with Israel and that a ruler ('star') will arise out of Jacob. Despite Balaam's divinely inspired rehabilitation, a midrash on Balaam presented by Philo in *Vita Moysis* 1 identifies him as a magus and he is said to be the 'most foolish of all men' (Powell 2000a: 7). Balaam and his company are also called 'magi' in the *Palestinian Targum*.

Catacombs and Magic

The earliest representations of the Magi (and often the star) are found in third- and fourth-century catacombs. In several depictions, the Magi are depicted quite similarly as three individuals with indistinct 'gifts' held out in offering, approaching the seated Mary and the Christ Child (Mignozzi 2010: 103). They usually are wearing Phrygian (or Persian) caps, typifying that they are from the east and represent foreign Gentile nations. One of the few catacomb artworks that retains its colour and is most graphic, though somewhat corrupt, is the image found in the Basilieus (Marcus and Marcellianus) catacomb. The Magi's clothing reflects another common catacomb, that of Daniel's three friends in the fiery furnace who are likewise wearing Phrygian dress, in this case, Babylonian, since they too are being trained as magi (Via Latina Catacomb).

It is natural to ask why the magi are represented at all in the catacombs, which raises similar questions about why Matthew's Gospel saw fit to include them. Several themes have prevailed when it comes to interpreting their presence.

Their coming could be regarded as the earliest recognition of Christ by the Gentiles. From the beginning of the Gospel, Matthew gives prominence to the salvific inclusion of the Gentiles: The four women at the forefront of the genealogy are incorporated into the life of Israel (1:3, 5–6); Jesus heals the servant of a Roman centurion and expresses amazement at his faith in contrast to those of Israel (8:5–13); a Canaanite woman's daughter is healed of demoniac torments and Jesus declares the greatness of her faith (15:21–8). So, the Magi are the first Gentile characters in the early story of Jesus who acknowledge his messianic role. Matthew presents this acknowledgement as a fulfilment of divine prophecy in 2:6 (Mic. 5:2; II Sam. 5:2).

A further and just as likely rationale is the worship of Christ as the rightful king of Israel. As opposed to Herod who is called 'king' but does not know the Scriptures and the messianic heritage of his people, the Magi show that Jesus the Messiah is worthy of worship, 'we have come to worship him' (proskunein, to worship or pay homage; Matthew 2:2; cf. 2:11). This is a theme expressed several times in Matthew (Bauckham 2009: 56–7), signalling that such worship is the correct response to Jesus (Brown and

Roberts 2018: 35). In the catacombs, the Magi never appear apart from their obeisance to the child Jesus and Mary.

On the darker side, an alternative interpretation is that the Magi's presence reveals the subservience of the powers of magic. The idea that magic was overthrown by the Advent of Christ is frequent in the Fathers, and this overthrow was commonly connected with the visit and worship of the Magi. Justin states quite clearly that the worship of Christ was a revolt on the part of the Magi who were then freed from demonic power (*Dialogue with Trypho* 78). The association of the Magi with pagan magic is also assumed by Tertullian. '*Magia*', he says, 'is the manifold plague of the human mind, the contriver of all error, the destroyer both of salvation and the soul' (*On the Soul* 57.2). In particular, the feats worked by *magi* are nothing more than phantoms, produced through trickery and the agency of demons (*Apol.* 23.1). So strongly did Tertullian contrapose the goal of the Gospel and that of magicians, that his interpretation of the Magi's role in Matthew 2 is exceedingly qualified, for magi of any kind are involved in idolatry and deception: 'We know the mutual alliance of magic and astrology.' The interpreters of the stars, nevertheless, were the first to announce Christ's birth, the first to present Him gifts (*On Idol.* 9.3).

By this act were they placing Christ under obligation to themselves? Surely the magical arts are not being condoned by the Gospel. For two reasons, we are told this is clearly not the case. First, Tertullian observes that the Magi's gifts—frankincense and myrrh and gold—are given to Christ because they are representative of the end of 'worldly (that is, pagan) sacrifice and glory, with which Christ was about to do away.' Secondly, the dream given to the Magi after they arrived at Bethlehem told them they should go home, but by another way, not that by which they came. The upshot of this was that they should not walk in their ancient path. Just so we ought to understand by it the right Way and Discipline (*On Idol.* 9.3).

Tertullian is not alone in his interpretation about the appearance of the Magi in the Gospel narrative. Origen likewise takes the arrival of the Magi in Matthew 2 quite literally and therefore as problematic: Magi are said to be in communion with demons and by their formulas invoke them for the ends which they desire. But on their way to Bethlehem, the Magi encountered the 'multitude of the heavenly host praising God and saying, *Glory to God in the highest, and on earth peace, goodwill among men*' (Lk 2:14). Its effect was to negate the demons' strength and, as a result, the Magi's sorcery, says Origen, was confuted and their power overthrown. They nonetheless presented their gifts with the realization that a greater, divine power was at work. Thus, the Lord 'rewarded the piety of the magi in worshipping Jesus by warning them not to go to Herod but to return to their own country by another route' (*Contra Celsum* I.60). A similar logic is taken by Leo of Rome when he states:

> when the wise men had adored the Lord and completed their whole devotion, according to a warning in a dream they do not return by the same way which they had come. It was proper that now believing in Christ they not walk through the paths of their old way of life, but enter upon a new path and abstain from the wanderings they left behind. (*Sermon* 34.3)

The Magi of the early Church are themselves seen as transformed and redeemed by the majesty of Christ's divinity.

Who Were They?

There's no early evidence to suggest that the Magi were also kings. This despite the connection between the Old Testament passages on Gentiles (nations) and kings that have been historically applied to the magi of Matthew.

> Nations shall come to your light
> And kings to the brightness of your dawn (Isa 60:6).
> May the kings of Tarshish and of the isles
> Render him tribute
> May all kings fall down before him,
> All nations give him service (Ps. 72:10–11).

Exactly when Christian writers first ascribed kingship to the Magi is unknown, but attribution of royalty to the Magi appears to have been established by the onset of the sixth century. It is clearly stated by the author of the sixth-century Syriac work *Cave of Treasures* who gives the names of the Magi as Hormizdah, king of Persia, Yazdegerd, king of Saba, and Perozadh, king of Sheba (Budge 1927: 208–9).

Pictorial elevation of the Magi to kings is asserted in illuminated manuscripts of the tenth century: the Benedictional of St. Æthelwold and the Fulda sacramentary. Thereafter, the three kings become commonplace in European art forms (Kehrer 1909: 81ff). The (tenth-century) mosaic constructed in the Basilica of the Hagia Sophia in Istanbul (the basilica itself was completed and then consecrated on 27 December 537) that portrays Constantine and Justinian—two of the most eminent emperors of the Roman Empire—making offerings to the Virgin Mary and the child Jesus is designed to imitate the kings adoring Jesus. Drawing on such connections, Western painters and sculptors were keen to represent their kings in such a way that they too 'needed to pay fealty to the higher authority of Christ' (Gilbert 1996: 14). The Wilson Diptych from the fourteenth century (commissioned by Richard II) is a prime example. Before the Virgin Mary holding Christ are three English kings, evident from their crowns: Richard II, St Edward the Confessor, and St Edmund (National Gallery, London, c.1395).

The best-known and most detailed medieval account of the legendary travels of the Three Kings was the *Historia trium regum*, written around 1370 by the Carmelite scholar John of Hildesheim. The work enjoyed great popularity in the late medieval period and was also translated into German, Dutch, French, English, and Danish. According to this account, the star was first sighted in the forty-second year of Augustus Caesar in the East by a group of pagan astrologers, who, mindful of the Old Testament prophecy of Balaam (Num. 24:17), had for many generations watched the heavens for a sign of the Messiah.

The identification of the Magi in Matthew 2 as kings remained unchallenged for centuries, until the time of the Protestant Reformation. Luther polemically dismissed the Magi's alleged royalty. Calvin labelled the tradition 'dubious', and Maldonado admitted that it was 'less than certain'. Up to the present day, scholars of Evangelical, Reformed, and Roman Catholic churches are generally united in their scepticism regarding identifying the Magi with royalty (Powell 2000a: 459).

Nevertheless, the Byzantine emperor Zeno claimed to discover the remains of these 'kings' in 490 somewhere in Persia and brought them to Constantinople. The relics eventually reached the West during the Crusades—first travelling to Milan and then subsequently to Cologne by Frederick Barbarossa in 1164. Today, they reside in Cologne, in a magnificent reliquary shrine built for them in the late twelfth century. There they are known to pilgrims and tourists as the 'Three Kings of Cologne' (Jensen 2001: 28).

Number, Names, and Place

A variety of traditions evolved in the East and West concerning the number of Magi, including their names, geographical origin, and age. Although it is generally assumed that the Magi were three in number (because Matthew mentions that they presented three gifts), three is not the only accounting. In the later Eastern sources, especially in Syria, the names of twelve magi are listed. The sixth-century Syriac work, *Cave of Treasures* (already noted) mentions three magi, as do other sources in Coptic, Georgian, Armenian, and Persian, using a variety of different names (Metzger 1970: 81–3). In Persia the names attributed to the Magi are Amad, Zud-Amad, and Drust-Amad. Then there are lists of twelve magi each with a name from Syriac texts and others. In such cases, the three gifts are attributed to groups of four.

In the West, the three names which prevailed were (different spellings of) Gaspar, Melchior, and Balthas(s)ar. The earliest literary reference to these names occurs in a Latin translation of a sixth-century Greek chronicle from Alexandria known as the *Excerpta Latina Barbari*: Bithisarea, Melchior, and Gathaspa (Yamauchi 1989: 16). Three Magi appear in the famous sixth-century mosaic of the basilica Sant'Apollinare (Nuovo) at Ravenna (c.565). Above their heads stand the names +SCS BALTHASSAR +SCS MELCHIOR+SCS+SCS GASPAR. Among artistic depictions of the Magi in manuscripts, the oldest example is a miniature in the Codex Egberti (c.977–993) which is preserved in the Civic Library in Trèves. Adjacent to each magus are the names Caspar, Melchias, and Pudizar (Metzger 1970: 81).

Along with the three names evolved the notion that each magus represented varying ages and nationalities. The Ravenna mosaic shows the three as young, middle-aged, and elderly. More details are supplied by a treatise called *Excerpta et Collectanea* that is now generally thought to reflect an Irish tradition:

The first is said to have been Melchior, an old man with white hair and a long beard... who offered gold to the Lord as to a king. The second, Gaspar by name, young and beardless and ruddy-complexioned... honored him as God by his gift of incense and oblation worthy of divinity. The third, black-skinned and heavily bearded, named Balthasar... by his gift of myrrh testified to the Son of Man who was to die. (Brown 1977: 199)

While a black magus does not appear in artwork until the end of the fourteenth and start of the fifteenth centuries, Europeans became familiar with the notion that one of the Magi was a black African (e.g. Bosch's painting, 'Adoration of the Magi'). The establishment of a black magus was first connected with the idea that each of the Magi had a separate country of origin. An excellent and early example comes from the *Historia trium regum* (already mentioned). He describes Melchior as from the lands of Nubia and Arabia, Balthasar from Godolia and Saba, and Jaspar from Tharsis 'and a black Ethiope without any doubt' (Freeman 1955: 24).

Earlier writers, as did Matthew (2:12), understood the Magi to come from a single region, but by the eighth century, the Anglo-Saxon historian, the Venerable Bede, recorded a contemporary tradition that the three Magi signified the three parts of the world—Africa, Asia, and Europe—and that these were linked with the sons of Noah, who fathered the three races of Earth (Genesis 10; Patrologia Latina 92.13A). This line of thinking that interrelated the three sons of Noah with the three Magi was widely propagated. The influential *Glossa Ordinaria* unambiguously refers to the three Kings/Magi as prefiguring the nations sprung from the three sons of Noah coming to the Gospel (Aquinas, *Catena*; Newman 1999: I.62). For Anslem, the Magi simply represented three parts of the world: Asia, Europe, and Africa, that is, the three sons engendered by Noah (*Enarrationes in Matthaeum*, PL 162.1257). Hard evidence is lacking (Kaplan 1985: chap. 2), but a conceptual link between the Magi and the sons of Noah may have encouraged the view that one of the Magi/Kings was a black African.

THE GIFTS

Their gifts are essential to the story in that they portray the ultimate purposes of the Christ Child. As Hilary says: '[T]hey offered of gifts which represented their understanding of the fullness of Christ's identity: the gold proclaims Him as King, the incense as God, the myrrh as man.' Each gift contains an aspect of the mystery of Christ's purpose. Gold is for his kingship, myrrh for his death as a man, incense for his resurrection as God. The gifts celebrate not only the newborn Christ but also a new humanity (*In Mattheaum* I.5).

Leo of Rome believed that the gifts were threefold, honouring his royal character with gold, his human character with myrrh, his divine character with incense (Sermon 34.3). Similarly, for Origen, the Magi offered gifts to him who was, so to speak, a combination of God and mortal man. These gifts were symbols, the gold being offered as to a king, the myrrh for one who would die, and the frankincense to God (*Contra Celsum* I.60).

> Hasten after the star, and offer gifts with the Magi,
> gold, incense and myrrh; offer them to Christ
> as king, the gold; as him who died for you, the myrrh.
> (Gregory of Nazianzus, Sermon 38.17–18)

As far as the earliest interpretations go, the Magi's gifts demonstrated a Christological recognition of the child as both human and divine, intimately present and cosmically meaningful, mortal and eternal (Jensen 2001: 32). For later writers, the gifts had to do with Christian principles of piety. Gregory the Great considered them wisdom, prayer, and mortification of the flesh; for Luther, they are faith, hope, and love—'every Christian can bring these gifts, the poor man no less than the rich man' (Luz 2007: 109). There have been no end of meanings attributed to the gifts.

THE STAR

Like the Magi, the 'star' of Matthew's account has perplexed many through the ages.

> A star shone forth in the heaven above all the stars; and its light was unutterable, and its strangeness caused amazement; and all the rest of the constellations with the sun and moon formed themselves into a chorus about the star; but the star itself far outshone them all; and there was perplexity to know whence came this strange appearance which was so unlike them. (Ignatius, *Ephesians* 19.2)

It has been often argued that the star of Matthew 2 derives from the widespread belief (found already in Plato, *Timaeus* 41D-E; cf. Pliny, *Natural History* II.6.28) that all people have a 'natal star' that appears at their birth and passes away with them. More generally, celestial phenomena are frequently associated with important terrestrial events in ancient literature. Josephus tells of a star that stood over Jerusalem and a comet which remained visible for a year at the time of the city's destruction by the Romans (*War of the Jews* VI.5.3). It seems plausible to read the Gospel text as yet another example of this literary topos (Hegedus 2003: 84). Certainly, Matthew's readers would not have found bizarre the claim that a star rose to herald the birth of the king of the Jews (Brown 1977: 170).

But if the star has more than a literary basis, exactly what was it? Many attempts over the centuries have been made to identify the star of Matthew with celestial phenomenon such as a planetary conjunction, a supernova, or a comet. The astronomer Johanes Kepler speculated in the early seventeenth century that the 'star' was in fact a thrice-repeated conjunction of Jupiter and Saturn in the 'sign' of Pisces that occurred in 7 BC. This perspective remains a common one. There is the additional argument that Matthew would have been familiar with Jewish astrological tradition linking the appearance of the Messiah, and other great events, with the conjunction of the planets Jupiter and Saturn (Rosenberg 1972: 105–9).

A nova or supernova, which is when a very distant star explodes, corresponds most literally to Matthew's 'star'. The light is apparent for a few months or years and in some cases can be brighter than the moon. A case for this view has been articulated by David H. Clark who attempts to challenge the problem that there is no known evidence for such a phenomenon around the time of Jesus' birth (Clark et al. 1977: 443–9).

More widespread is the opinion that the 'star' was actually a comet (Nicholl 2015; Phipps 1986–1987: 88–92). As early as Origen, it has been argued that the moving star should be classed with:

> those celestial bodies which appear at times, such as comets, or those meteors which resemble beams of wood, or beards, or wine jars, or any of those other names by which the Greeks are accustomed to describe their varying appearances.
> (*Contra Celsum* I.58)

That the star appeared suddenly and was visible for over a year (something that makes sense only if it were a comet) and that the star surprised the Magi with its impressive 'rising', points to it being a comet: of all the celestial bodies, only comets behave in this manner. ('Rising' refers to the period when a celestial body re-emerges on the horizon after being hidden by the Sun.)

Then one can take into account the star's movement, in the space of a couple of months, from the eastern morning sky to the southern evening sky, where the Magi see it when they are travelling from Jerusalem to Bethlehem. That kind of movement is only possible for an object in the inner solar system, once again indicating that the star had to be a comet.

Regardless of which theory one accepts as most feasible, the Magi considered the revelation of the star as sure guidance for making the trip to Judea and inquiring into the birthplace of the king of the Jews:

> Beholding a divine sign in the heaven, they desired to learn its significance... because they supposed that the man whose appearance had been foretold along with that of the star, had actually come into the world; and having predetermined that he was superior to all evil and worldly powers... they resolved to offer him homage. (*Contra Celsum* I.60)

As a result of their recognition and adoration of the Messiah, the *Infancy Gospel of James* (21.4) claims that an angel rewarded the piety of the Magi by making known to them (in a dream) that they were not to go back to Herod, but to return to their own homes by another way. Matthew makes no mention of an angel, but the Gospel narrative implies the same, having stipulated the angel's instrumentality in dreams (1:20; 2:13 and 2:19).

References and Further Reading

Anselm (1854). *Enarrationes in Matthaeum. Patrologia Latina* 162. Ed. J. P. Migne.
Aquinas. J. H. Newman, trans. (1999). *Catena Aurea: Commentary on the Four Gospels Collected out of the Works of the Fathers*. London: Saint Austin Press.
Basil of Caesarea (1857). *Homilia in sanctam Christi generationem. Patrologia Graeca* 31. Ed. J. P. Migne.
Bauckham, Richard (2009). *Jesus and the God Israel: God Crucified and Other Studies on the New Testament's Christology of Divine Identity*. Grand Rapids: Eerdmans Publishing Company.
Bede (1862). *In Matthaei Evangelium Expositio. Patrologia Latina* 92. Ed. J. P. Migne.
Brown, Jeannine K. and Kyle Roberts (2018). *Matthew*. Grand Rapids: Eerdmans Publishing Company.
Brown, Raymond (1977). *The Birth of the Messiah*. Garden City, NY: Doubleday and Co.
Budge, E. A. (1927). *The Book of the Cave of Treasures*. Trans. Wallis Budge. London: The Religious Tract Society.
Clark, David H. et al. (1977). 'An Astronomical Re-Appraisal of the Star of Bethlehem—A Nova in 5 BC', *Quarterly Journal of the Royal Astronomical Society*, 18: 443–9.
Freeman, Margaret B. (1955). *The Story of the Three Kings: Melchior, Balthasar and Jaspar which originally was written by John of Hildesheim and is now retold by Margaret B. Freeman*. New York: The Metropolitan Museum of Art.
Gilbert, Adrian G. (1996). *Magi: The Quest for a Secret Tradition*. London: Bloomsbury.
Hegedus, Tim (2003). 'The Magi and the Star in the Gospel of Matthew and Early Christian Tradition', *Laval théologique et philosophique*, 59, no. 1: 81–95.
Jensen, Robin (2001). 'Witnessing the Divine', *Bible Review*, 17, no. 6: 24–30, 32.
Kaplan, Paul H. D. (1985). *The Rise of the Black Magus in Western Art*. Ann Arbor: UMI Research Press.
Kehrer, Hugo (1909). *Die Heiligen Drei Könige in Literatur und Kunst*, 2 vol. Leipzig: E.A. Seemann.
Luz, Ulrich (2007). *Matthew 1–7: A Commentary*. Trans. J. E. Crouch. Minneapolis: Fortress Press.
Menotti, Gian Carlo (1951), *Amahl and the Night Visitors*. First performed by the NBC Opera Theatre on 24 December 1951.
Metzger, Bruce M. (1970). 'Names for the Nameless in the New Testament', in P. Granfield and J. Jungmann (eds.), *Kyriakon: Festschften J. Quasten*. Münster: Aschendorf: 79–99.
Mignozzi, Marcello (2010). 'Dal Profeta ai Magi: storia di una migratio iconografica in età paleocristiana', *Vetera Christianorum*, 47: 99–116.
Nicholl, Colin R. (2015). *The Great Christ Comet: Revealing the True Star of Bethlehem*. Wheaton, IL: Crossway.
Phipps, William E. (1986–1987). 'The Magi and Halley's Comet', *Theology Today*, 43: 88–92.
Powell, Mark A. (2000a). 'The Magi as Kings: An Adventure in Reader-Response Criticism', *Catholic Biblical Quarterly*, 62: 459–80.

Powell, Mark A (2000b). 'The Magi as Wise Men: Re-examining a Basic Supposition', *New Testament Studies*, 46: 1–20.

Rosenberg, R. A. (1972). 'The Star of the Messiah Reconsidered', *Biblica*, 53: 105–9.

Yamauchi, Edwin (1989). 'The Episode of the Magi', in J. Vardaman and E. Yamauchi (eds.), *Chronos, Kairos, Christos: Nativity and Chronological Studies Presented to Jack Finegan*. Winona Lake: Eisenbrauns.

CHAPTER 19

THE INN, THE MANGER, THE SWADDLING CLOTHS, THE SHEPHERDS, AND THE ANIMALS

JODY VACCARO LEWIS

WHETHER we consider early Christian sarcophagi, the live Nativity originated by St Francis, the *Mystical Nativity* painting by Botticelli, or the onstage monologue by Linus in *A Charlie Brown Christmas*, we are indebted to Luke. Given the centrality of the Christian doctrine of the Incarnation, two of the Synoptic evangelists recount the circumstances of Jesus' birth in their opening chapters. While these accounts differ substantially from one another, addressing different audiences and stressing different themes, they nevertheless serve as complements. Matthew contextualizes the birth in relation to King Herod and Judea, while Luke begins with Caesar Augustus and the Roman Empire. Matthew explicitly notes the fulfilment of scriptural prophecies, but Luke subtly alludes to various biblical precedents. Matthew portrays the discovery of the star of Bethlehem by the Magi, who offer their treasures to the infant and return to their country, and Luke relates the angel's annunciation to the shepherds, who make known the messianic identity of the babe. The infant Jesus is indeed a universal saviour.

When it comes to a depiction of the scene of the Holy Family itself, however, only Luke provides any details. Representations of the Nativity in written form, fine art, folk culture, and our imaginations sometimes include the star and three Magi with their gifts from Matthew's Gospel, but the focus naturally rests on Joseph, Mary, and the baby. Typically, they are in a shelter of some sort, with the infant lying in a manger, in or on a swaddling cloth, all owing to Luke's description. While Luke's shepherds are not uncommon figures, the ox and ass are ever-present, added by the earliest tradition into Luke's portrait even though surprisingly neither biblical account mentions them.

This chapter concerns the inn, manger, swaddling cloths, and shepherds in the infancy narrative of Luke 2:1–20, as well as the animals who have come to accompany them. These verses reflect the literary skill of the evangelist, whose artful writing is cast into the genre of Greco-Roman historiography but also mimics the Semitic style of the Old Testament. In this way Luke fittingly introduces the Jewish Messiah who brings salvation to the whole world. The account of Jesus' birth is relatively spare by modern biographical and historiographical conventions and, combined with Luke's allusive style, demands attention to each element, both in its historical and literary context. Many aspects of the inn, manger, swaddling cloths, and shepherds would intuitively resonate with the Greco-Roman and Jewish audiences of the first century for whom these were common, familiar objects and figures of everyday life, but not so for most twenty-first century readers. The discussion of each element will therefore begin with the semantic range of the word and the attendant historical connotations.

Luke, of course, is not writing a work of mere history but salvation history. Through his mention of the inn, manger, swaddling cloths, and shepherds, Luke invokes a host of Old Testament texts, events, and personages, all of which further imbue his narrative with theological significance. Biblical literature often relies on textual connections to establish meaning. The inn, manger, swaddling cloths, shepherds, and eventually the animals are polyvalent in this way, conveying multi-layered meaning. The patristic and medieval exegetes recognized this polyvalence, which led them to interpret these Lukan verses within the entirety of Scripture, especially the Jewish messianic prophecies. Thus, the possible allusions to Old Testament texts will also be treated.

It is this symbolic richness that illuminates Christian art of the Lukan Nativity through the centuries. Artistic depictions of the inn, manger, swaddling cloths, shepherds, and animals is the final subject of this chapter, though given its extent, this treatment will be very selective. The goal is a brief survey that reflects the interpretation of the biblical text in visual form. While the main elements remain more or less constant, there are intriguing variations in the way they are rendered.

The Inn

In Luke 2:7, the evangelist comments that Mary swaddled and laid the newborn baby in a manger 'because there was no place for them at the inn' (RSV). With this explanatory remark, Luke suggests that, in lieu of other accommodations, the manger sufficed to cradle the infant. Since Luke says nothing more about the environs of Jesus' birth, exegetes have scrutinized this 'inn' in search of a more precise understanding of the locale. Moreover, since Luke mentions the inn, one may presume there is some significance to it beyond the literal lack of room there.

In classical Greek usage, the term *kataluma* generally means lodging or quarters, which may include an inn. From the verb *kataluo*, usually to destroy or put down but transitively to unloose, it connotes taking up lodging by loosing one's garments and travel gear, as used by Thucydides and Plato, for example. Accordingly, *kataluma* is used in the Septuagint, the Greek Old Testament, for several different words, variously meaning dwelling, lodging place, or resting place. (Here we will prescind from a discussion of Luke's exact use of the Septuagint and simply note that he appeared to have direct access to the Greek text at least in part and from other sources (Fitzmyer 1981: 113–6)). Moreover, while the common English translation of *kataluma* in Luke 2:7 is 'inn', in 10:34, in the parable of the Good Samaritan, Luke uses the Greek *pandocheion*, which appears only once in the New Testament and has the more particular sense of inn or hotel. Such inns, lacking modern luxuries, were quite simply one large room where all travellers slept together with their animals, known as a caravansary. Therefore, despite the oft-quoted King James' 'no room for them in the inn', the generic 'lodging place' or 'lodgings' seems to be a better translation in line with Greek usage and one that suits the intended distinction of Luke's terms (preferred by Brown 1977: 393; Fitzmyer 1981: 408; Johnson 1991: 50). In support of this reading, the only other instance of *kataluma* in the New Testament is Mark 14:14, with a parallel in Luke 22:11. This verse concerns Jesus' directive to the disciples to secure the upper room of a house for the Passover dinner, the Last Supper. The explicit context of the house thereby produces the translation 'guest room'. We might thus conclude with Brown that Luke intended *kataluma* in 2:7 to be an ambiguous lodging place (Brown 1977: 400). It has been occasionally suggested that *kataluma* be understood as the guest room in a private home (e.g. Bailey 1979). This reading is based on certain cultural presumptions, including at-home births and ancient hospitality norms, and the potential inclusio with 22:11.

Luke's mention of the 'inn' is evocative in two other ways. First, given his theological-narrative goal to demonstrate that Jesus is the fulfilment of Jewish messianic promises, Luke may be subtly alluding to certain Old Testament passages. As mentioned, *kataluma* occurs frequently in the Septuagint, but three passages seem especially relevant. In the Septuagint 1 Samuel 1:18, Elkanah and Hannah stay at a *kataluma* near the sanctuary of Shiloh after Eli tells the childless Hannah that God will grant her prayers for a son, who will be Samuel, the consecrated Nazirite, judge, and prophet. In the Septuagint 2 Samuel 7:6, after King David expresses the desire to build a permanent structure to house the Ark of the Covenant, the dwelling place of the Lord, the Lord tells the prophet Nathan to inform David that he will not build Him a house. Since He brought His people out of Egypt, says the Lord, 'I was moving about in a temporary abode (*kataluma*) and in a tent' (NETS). Lastly, in Jeremiah 14:8, in a time of drought, the suffering people of Jerusalem plead with the Lord, asking why He is like an alien in that land or like a traveller who stays in lodgings (*kataluma*).

Luke likely makes a connection to at least one of these passages, but taken together, within the unity of Scripture, they supply a rich hermeneutical basis for interpreting *kataluma* in Luke 2:7. For instance, Luke may recall the miraculous birth of Samuel to prepare his readers for the even more miraculous birth of Jesus to parents who, unlike Samuel's, cannot even stay in a *kataluma*. While it is Solomon who will build the Temple, in 2 Samuel 7 the Lord promises David that He will establish an everlasting kingdom from David's seed (2 Sam. 7:12–16), which constitutes one of the main messianic prophecies. The link to Jesus, whom Luke has already identified four times as being of the house of David, is patent: here at last is the promised Davidic Messiah. Finally, in Jeremiah, the language touches upon the household imagery in which God is present with His people. Their sinfulness is a rejection of the Lord so that He is more like a traveller than a resident. When the people 'remind' the Lord that He is among them, He responds that it is they who are the wanderers deserving of punishment for their sins. With the newborn babe, God dwells among His people.

Second, if Jesus was *not* born in the 'inn', it raises the question, where *was* He born? Early Christian tradition identified the site as a cave. While birth in a cave might seem crude to our modern sensibilities, many Palestinian homes, given the terrain, were built fully or partially in caves. Justin Martyr, *c*.160, comments that Joseph and Mary lodged in a cave near Bethlehem (*Dialogue with Trypho* 78.5), subsequently attested to by Origen in the third century (*Against Celsus* 1.51). Justin further notes that the birth in a cave fulfils the Septuagint version of Isaiah 33:16 that the righteous one 'will live in the high cave of a strong rock' (NETS). In the second century apocryphal work the *Protevangelium of James* (18), which embellishes the biblical account, Joseph leads Mary into a cave, then he leaves, after which the baby is born. Based on the strength of the tradition of this holy site, the Emperor Constantine commissioned the building of the Basilica of the Nativity over the designated cave in Bethlehem, which was completed in the 330s and remains a popular pilgrimage site today. Indeed, many paintings depict the birth of Jesus in a cave, especially in Eastern traditions, but others portray a stable or other form of shelter, all interpretations in response to the lack of perspicuity of the biblical textual evidence.

THE MANGER

Related to the discussion of the 'inn' is the significance of the newborn's makeshift cradle. Like *kataluma*, Luke's use of the Greek term *phatnē* admits of some ambiguity, which has been variously resolved. A relatively uncommon word in classical Greek, *phatnē* denotes primarily a manger, or a feeding trough or crib, for animals, often horses and oxen, and secondarily a stall for animals, though not a stable, barn, or other such building. The manger may be located outside or inside, and it may be carved from rock or wood.

In the New Testament, interestingly *phatnē* is only used by Luke, which he does in 2:7, 12, and 16, and also in 13:15. In the infancy narrative, when Mary sets the baby in the manger, Luke neither specifies whether it is found indoors or not, nor of what material it is made. The subsequent two mentions shed no further light. Many commentators, discontented with this imprecision, draw some logical conclusions. Derrett, for example, argues that the manger must have been cut out of rock, since there was not much wood in the region (Derrett 1971: 568), which is compatible with the cave scenario. Nevertheless, artwork often portrays the manger as made of wood or sticks, housed in a stable or other shelter, sometimes elaborate, sometimes meagre or even in decay, although some renderings feature the manger in a cave or just outside. Again, we might ask whether Luke intends the ambiguity to be purposeful and what that purpose may be. After all, the singular usage by Luke among New Testament writers suggests its importance beyond the merely descriptive.

The fact that Luke repeats 'manger' three times in the space of ten verses is intriguing. The manger is clearly an improvised cradle, which many construe as an indication of the poverty of Mary and Joseph, but this is not the main point. In addition to Mary laying the swaddled baby in the manger, the angel's proclamation to the shepherds includes the assurance, 'And this will be a sign for you: you will find a babe wrapped in swaddling cloths and lying in a manger' (2:12 RSV), which is realized in verse 16 when the shepherds find the baby lying in the manger. This last verse further highlights only the manger, not the swaddling cloths, which prompts more intrigue.

The angel tells the shepherds that the swaddling cloths and manger will be a *sign* to them when they find the baby. All babies were swaddled, though not all lay in a manger, so the sign cannot be a manner of identifying the baby. The shepherds also trust what the angel tells them because they go right away to see the 'thing that has happened' (2:15 RSV), so the sign is not a guarantee of the truth of the angel's proclamation. Instead, the sign of the swaddling cloths and manger must be a way of explaining the significance of the baby (Baily 1964: 3, Giblin 1967: 92). Giblin stresses that 'a sign to you' is used in a formulaic way in the Old Testament partly to explain the meaning of a divine action. Baily, perhaps in an overly literal reading, concludes that the nomadic shepherds often had to improvise on dwellings, caring for their families as best they could. The sight in Bethlehem of the swaddled baby in the manger indicates to them that He is one of them, poor, but He is also the Davidic Messiah, the promised shepherd of Israel (Baily 1964: 16). Derrett notes the likely inclusio, a rhetorical bracketing device, of Mary placing Jesus in (what he concludes is) the rock-hewn manger, and the Marys near the end of the Gospel watching where the body of Jesus was laid in the rock-hewn tomb (Derrett 1971: 570), so that Jesus passes into the rock and out again.

Once again, Luke's possible allusions to mangers in the Old Testament seem likely. Only three passages refer to a manger, all of which use *phatnē* in the Septuagint. In Job 39:9, when God conveys His sovereignty over all of creation through a series of rhetorical questions put to Job, He asks if the wild ox would serve Job and stay the night at his crib (*phatnē*). Proverbs 14:4 offers the adage, 'where there are no oxen, the cribs (*phatnē*) are clean; but where there is much produce, the strength of an ox is apparent' (NETS). Isaiah 1:3 proclaims, 'The ox knows its owner, and the donkey its master's crib (*phatnē*), but Israel has not known me, and the people have not understood me' (NETS). Of particular relevance is Isaiah 1:3, which both Origen and Jerome cited in relation to Luke 2. The link is further strengthened by the term *kurios* for master, the Greek word for Lord. The shepherds' witness to the baby Jesus in the *phatnē* thus suggests that Israel is at last coming to know the Lord (Brown 1977: 419).

Does Luke's use of manger in 13:15 relate to its meaning in 2:7? Here Jesus heals a woman who has been doubled over for eighteen years, but he thereby incurs the indignation of the synagogue ruler for breaking the Sabbath, the day of rest. In response, Jesus accuses him of hypocrisy, since some work was permissible on the Sabbath, asking, 'Does not each of you on the sabbath untie his ox or his ass from the manger (*phatnē*), and lead it away to water it?' (RSV). Jesus specifies the ox and ass, and while they were commonplace livestock, they may also signify Jesus' own allusion to Isaiah 1:3. Jesus, born and laid in a manger, is the Lord of His flock, who need to recognize Him.

Lastly, there is the symbolism of the manger in relation to its being, literally, a trough that holds food, one that now holds the baby Jesus. The Messiah, after all, is born in Bethlehem, 'the house of bread'. The thrice-repeated manger may also be Luke's way of stressing 'the sign of God's being the sustenance of his people' (Giblin 1967: 100). Isaiah 1:3 and Jesus' question in Luke 13:15 both portray the lord or master leading his ox and ass *away* from the manger, but in the Nativity, Jesus, the Lord, Himself lies *in* the manger. The early Christian authors perceived this imagery in relation to the Eucharist. Jesus in the manger liturgically symbolizes receiving the bread of life at the altar (e.g. Cyril of Alexandria, *Commentary on Luke* 1; Ambrose, *Exposition on the Gospel of Luke* 2.43).

THE SWADDLING CLOTHS

Following the birth of Jesus, Luke tells us in 2:7 that Mary 'wrapped him in swaddling cloths' (RSV) before laying Him in the manger. The verb *sparganoō*, to swathe or wrap in swaddling cloths, derives from the noun *sparganon*, which denotes the cloth bands or strips used to swaddle newborns. The familiar translation of the verb *sparganoō*, 'wrapped...in swaddling cloths' (RSV) is redundant, and the KJV includes the archaic 'clothes' for 'cloths' (Brown 1977: 399; Fitzmyer 1981: 408; Johnson 1991: 50). To resolve these and modernize the language, the NRSV has 'wrapped...in bands of cloth', while the NIV simply has 'wrapped...in cloths'.

Swaddling a baby was a common ancient custom, practised by the Greeks (though not Spartans!), Romans, and Jews, dating back to at least 4000 BC. Swaddling, then as now, involved wrapping an infant in woven strips of cloth in order to restrain the limbs. A series of actions, shared by these cultures and imbued with varied ritualistic significance, was followed in an orderly way by the midwife and other attendants. When the baby was delivered, his umbilical cord was cut, and then he was bathed with water and rubbed with salt (and sometimes wine) as antiseptics for cleansing. Then the baby was soothingly massaged with olive oil (sometimes mixed with salt) and, finally, swaddled (Soranus, *Gynecology* 2.13; Dasen 2011: 300–1). The ritual aspects associated with these acts broadly speaking concern the cleansing of impurities with water and anointing with oil (Grey 2001: 66–8).

Swaddling served various purposes. Emotionally, swaddling replicated the nurturing environment of the womb, securing and comforting the baby. Medically, the ancients believed that swaddling the limbs, thought to be malleable like wax, corrected any bending during delivery that might impede strong and straight growth (cf. Plato, *Laws* 7.789e; Galen, *On Temperaments* 2.2). Socially, for some ancients swaddling signified the uniqueness of humans among other animals, as straight limbs allow for walking upright (Dasen 2011: 302). Binding methods differed, though the second-century Greek physician Soranus provides a remarkably thorough discussion of precise techniques (*Gynecology* 2.14–15).

That Mary swaddles her newborn baby, then, is to be expected. It is not a sign, as some readers see it, that the Holy Family is poor. All babies were swaddled, rich and poor alike, dictated by maternal care and cultural custom. Though Luke does not specify it, Mary must have cleaned the baby, perhaps with Joseph's help, with some combination of water, salt, and oil. Many later renditions, both textual and visual, also include the presence of a midwife. This convention may be traced to the *Protevangelium of James*, when Joseph seeks a midwife, who goes into the cave to assist Mary after the baby is born, seemingly a later insertion into the Nativity story based on common experience. The point here is that of all of these typical practices, Luke mentions only the swaddling, and he does so twice in verses 7 and 12. Why is this detail so germane to his account?

One of Luke's goals is to convey the reality of the Incarnation. Mary's swaddling of the infant Jesus stresses his true humanity—and in a way familiar to Luke's audience. That is, Jesus was born into the world and cared for like all babies. He was fully and truly human. The medieval Benedictine monk Bede notes that Jesus took on our mortality but did not come like a king, for he was not wrapped in the purple cloth of royalty but in simple cloth (*Exposition of the Gospel of Luke* 1). Many commentators also see yet another inclusio between the Lukan Nativity and Passion symbolized by the swaddling cloths. As the infant Jesus is wrapped in cloth strips by Mary, so Jesus' body is wrapped in linen cloths for burial (e.g. Johnson 1991: 53). The fourth century Cappadocian theologian Gregory of Nazianzus likewise comments that as Jesus was wrapped in swaddling bands at his birth, so he released the swaddling bands of death at his Resurrection (*Oration* 29.19). Further drawing out the soteriology, the fourth-century Latin bishop of Milan Ambrose writes that Jesus was wrapped in swaddling cloths to free us from the bonds of death (*Exposition of the Gospel of Luke* 2.41).

That Luke is alluding to one or more scriptural texts seems highly probable. While a commonplace practice, swaddling is mentioned in the Old Testament only three times, despite the fact that there are many birth stories and birth imagery. The poetic, symbolic use of swaddling in these three passages invokes several prominent theological themes. In Job 38:8–11, in that same discourse when the manger is mentioned, God describes His creation of the world, dramatically depicting the birth of the sea, 'when it burst forth from the womb, when I made clouds its garment, and thick darkness its swaddling band' (38:8–9 RSV). God's swaddling of the sea with bands of darkness conveys His providential care for all of creation. In Ezekiel 16:1–4, the prophet recounts the covenantal origins of the people of Israel, who were as of foreign birth and neglected, for 'on the day you were born your navel string was not cut, nor were you washed with water to cleanse you, nor rubbed with salt, nor swathed with bands' (16:4 RSV) but left to die. The Lord, however, rescues the baby and lovingly nurtures her, entering into a covenant that becomes a type of rebirth (Grey 2001: 76). The last example comes from the Book of Wisdom, written in Greek in the first century BC and found in the Septuagint. In a speech under the persona of King Solomon, the author stresses the common mortality of mankind, including kings, who were traditionally thought to be godly in the ancient world. 'Solomon' outlines the stages of human life from conception onward and states that after his birth, 'I was nursed with care in swaddling cloths' (7:4 RSV). Even kings are swaddled. Thus, by specifying that Mary swaddles the newborn Jesus, Luke may be artfully suggesting Mary and Joseph's recognition of the sovereignty and providence of God, the fulfilment of God's covenantal promises, and the kingship of Jesus, the messianic son of David who is fully God and fully man. This is one part of the angel's sign to the shepherds.

Some scholars discern a resemblance to birth stories in Greco-Roman mythology. Most pertinent, in the myth of Ion, borne of the god Apollo's attack on Creusa, the baby is swaddled and then, when left to die, taken in his swaddling cloths by Hermes to the temple of Apollo. Years later the cloth strips allow the mother to identify the now grown baby (Derrett 2012: 260–1; Phillips 2011: 32–5). The myth is preserved in Euripides' play *Ion*, which was widely read in antiquity. The Homeric hymn to Hermes also features swaddling cloths, which function for the protagonist to prove his innocence (Phillips 2011: 35–7). The ancient Greek poet Hesiod further recounts how the god Kronos, who ate his children to preserve his power, was fooled by the shrewd Gaia, who gives him a swaddled stone to preserve the life of her son Zeus. Since these myths feature the motif of the birth of sons to gods and use swaddling cloths as a plot device, they are perceived as a direct influence on the Lukan Nativity. Such influence, though not demonstrable, would resonate with Luke's audience, who may have encountered this motif through its cultural appropriation. If so, Luke offers a challenge to his audience to accept the true Son of God, who became man and was swaddled by his mother.

THE SHEPHERDS

In Luke 2:8, the evangelist paints a bucolic scene of shepherds overseeing their flocks during the night watch, suddenly enlightened by the glory of the Lord and the proclamation of an angel. The angel brings the good news of the Saviour's birth and the sign of the swaddled baby in the manger, followed by an angelic chorus of praise to God. When the angels depart, the shepherds immediately resolve to go to Bethlehem to 'see this thing that has happened' (Luke 2:15 RSV). They do not doubt. They do not hesitate. Instead, they readily accept the truth of the proclamation and, upon seeing the infant Saviour, they themselves proclaim the good news to the wonder of all. Socially, the shepherds, who strikingly occupy a considerable portion of the narrative, present a humble counterpart to the learned Magi of Matthew's infancy narrative, but they evoke a wealth of themes.

The Greek term for shepherd is *poimēn*, whose literal meaning of keeper of the flock also connotes a manager or overseer. As ancient peoples tended to be largely nomadic, shepherding was an early, widespread occupation, with sheep the most common livestock due to their usefulness (meat, milk, and fur). The shepherd could be the owner of the flock, one of his children, or a hired hand, guaranteeing that the animals had enough food and water and were kept safe from predators and thieves. While pastoral work is often evocative of romantic notions, it was a lonely and demanding job, and it was considered among the lowest class of labourers because it was unskilled. A misconception prevails that shepherds in biblical times were disdained as sinners and thieves, to some extent due to their asocial trade. This view also anachronistically derives from later rabbinic texts (e.g. Babylonian Talmud Sanhedrin 25b and Mishnah Kiddushin 4:14). Upon closer scrutiny, the context indicates that the criticism of shepherds concerns those who pasture their flocks on others' land, as well as the inferiority of shepherding as a profession to the study of Torah—along with all other professions (Harris 2012: 19–20)! The first-century Jewish author Philo rather depicts shepherds as having dignity (*On Agriculture* 12.50).

The connotations of leading and protecting a flock transferred to the shepherd imagery that developed in ancient Israel and other cultures for gods, kings, and military and political leaders. Greek literature and mythology reflect the imagery, and Plato philosophically typifies the image of a shepherd for the just ruler (*Republic* 1.343b-345d). The shepherd is one of the main motifs of the Old Testament. Many great leaders in Israel's history tended sheep, including Abraham, Moses, and David. The image of God as Shepherd, moreover, runs from the Book of Genesis through the prophets and writings to express God's covenantal relationship with Israel. Ezekiel 34 elevates the image further as God indicts the rulers of Israel as bad shepherds and promises to rescue His flock with justice, hinting at the Messiah to come. This passage also serves as a prophetic precursor to Jesus' 'I am the Good Shepherd' discourse in John 10, where He claims it is intrinsic to the good shepherd to lay down his life for his sheep (John 10:11).

The role of the shepherds in Luke 2:8–20 presents a juxtaposition between the reality of the hardworking, lowly shepherds and the idealized image of the strong, just leader. Many interpreters merely regard the shepherds as the lowly or sinners whom Jesus comes to save, but this is to ignore the prevalent Old Testament shepherd motif. Among the many shepherd passages previously suggested, one more stands out here. Micah 4–5 prophesies the restoration of Zion, Jerusalem, and the ruler who will come forth from Bethlehem (5:2, a verse that Matthew quotes in his own infancy narrative in 2:6), who, like a shepherd, 'will stand and feed his flock in the strength of the Lord' (5:4 RSV). In Luke 2:11, the angels locate the birth of the Saviour in the city of David, which the shepherds properly construe as Bethlehem. Micah 4:8 also mentions Migdal Eder, which was near Bethlehem and means 'tower of the flock' (Cf. Brown 1977: 421–2, Fitzmyer 1981: 396). Altogether, the Micah prophecy forms a subtext to Luke 2 so that the shepherds, watching their flocks near Bethlehem, go to see the one who fulfils the messianic promise to David the shepherd boy-king (Harris 2012: 29–30).

THE ANIMALS

Finally, animals frequently appear in Nativity scenes, usually an ox and an ass, yet Luke never speaks of a single animal. Animals were omnipresent in ancient society, working in fields, carrying travellers, and kept inside homes at night. It would logically seem that a manger suggests animals, but why these two in particular? As the section on the manger indicates, Job 39:9, Proverbs 14:4, and Isaiah 1:3 all include a manger and an ox, with the last passage also specifying the ass. Quoted by early Christian authors, Isaiah 1:3 appears to be the major source for the animals that come to figure so prominently in the tradition (e.g. Ambrose, *Exposition of the Gospel of Luke* 2.42). The verse may also explain why the ox and ass usually stand close to the manger, aside from the obvious source of food. In Isaiah, the ox and ass know their owner, the Lord, and in the Nativity, the Lord lies in the manger. Some sources also cite the Septuagint version of Habakkuk 3:2, which states that the Lord shall be known between two living creatures (*Gospel of Pseudo-Matthew* 14). The convergence of the Jewish and Christian Scriptures have rendered the ox and ass a permanent fixture of the Lukan nativity.

THE MANGER, SWADDLING CLOTHS, SHEPHERDS, AND ANIMALS IN ART

Some final, brief comments on the Lukan Nativity concern the treatment of the manger, swaddling cloths, shepherds, and animals in Christian art. In the absence of descriptive detail in the text, artists have imaginatively added several features. As text and art merge, many of these features have coloured popular understandings of the biblical account.

Mangers vary in style, determined by cultural custom. They are made of stone, wood, sticks, or a basket of reeds, the latter evocative of both the feeding miracles and the Eucharist. Sometimes the ox and ass are eating from the manger while Mary holds the baby. Some painters of the Italian Renaissance make the manger resemble an altar to give the scene a more liturgical look (e.g. Duccio di Buon Insegna).

Luke's emphasis on the manger, and the consequent animals, apparently explains why there is almost always a stable of some kind in Nativities. The architecture of the stable is also culturally dependent. Eastern, Byzantine traditions often situate the scene in or just outside the mouth of a cave, clearly derived from the Bethlehem cave, whereas Western, Latin art prefers a simple roofed structure made of wood. In the Renaissance, the stable becomes grander like a palazzo but parts of it may be in ruin, meant to convey the triumph of Christianity over pagan culture.

Early Christian art tends to show the baby Jesus fully swaddled with only his face visible. This continues through the medieval period and into the fourteenth century, during which, for example, Giotto portrays the completely wrapped infant. Later in the century, however, the baby Jesus often has very little or no clothing, but he is encircled by a bright light. This shift is attributed to the vision of the Nativity by the medieval Birgitta of Sweden (1303–73), who writes in her *Revelations* that she saw the newborn baby naked and glowing with an ineffable light (7.21). Even though Birgitta next observes Mary swaddling her son, paintings in the fifteenth and sixteenth centuries portray the infant Jesus lying naked on top of the swaddling cloth and shining forth a bright light (e.g. Fra Bartolommeo, Rogier van der Weyden, El Greco).

The shepherds are predictably portrayed in simple dress, but sometimes this is accentuated so they represent the poor or to contrast them with the Magi. The number of shepherds varies, from one to three. They are sometimes depicted as young, middle-aged, and old to convey the stages of life. The shepherd's staff is often in hand, on which he occasionally leans. Some shepherds raise their hand in acclaim over the baby, while others kneel in homage or stand or sit off to the side, sometimes playing a horn.

Animals are integrated into the Lukan Nativity scene very early (e.g. the fourth-century Roman sarcophagus of Marcus Claudianus), integrated from the interpretive link to Isaiah 1:3. The ox and ass are typically close to and behind Jesus, often open-mouthed, sometimes eating from the manger and sometimes even touching him with their mouths. They stand at his feet in other depictions, seemingly nibbling on his toes. A fifteenth-century French sculpture has the ox biting on Jesus' fingers. The Eucharistic imagery is unambiguous. St Francis initiated the live Nativity in 1223, complete with manger, ox, and ass, and set in a cave. Additional animals sometimes are added in paintings (Jan Brueghel the Elder has many, including lizards and a stork!), but the ox and ass remain by Jesus' side. Even eighteenth-century County Louth headstones have engravings of the Nativity and emphasize the ox and ass (Mytum 2015: 27).

The convergence of Luke 2:1–20 and the artistic imagination highlight Luke's stress on the manger, swaddling cloths, and shepherds, yet also appropriates these elements to inculturate them to become more familiar to observers. In the end, this actuates one of Luke's main themes of the Nativity and the Gospel: the universal Saviour.

References and Further Reading

Bailey, Kenneth E. (1979). 'The Manger and the Inn: The Cultural Background of Luke 2.7', *Theological Review*, 2: 33–44.

Baily, Michael (1964). 'The Shepherds and the Sign of a Manger', *Irish Theological Quarterly*, 31: 1–23.

Brown, Raymond E. (1977). *The Birth of the Messiah: A Commentary on the Infancy Narratives in the Gospels of Matthew and Luke*. New York: Doubleday.

Carlson, Stephen C. (2010). 'The Accommodations of Joseph and Mary in Bethlehem: Κατάλυμα in Luke 2.7', *New Testament Studies*, 56: 326–42.

Dasen, Véronique (2011). 'Childbirth and Infancy in Greek and Roman Antiquity', in Beryl Rawson (ed.), *A Companion to Families in the Greek and Roman Worlds*. Hoboken, NJ: Wiley-Blackwell: 291–314.

De Orellana, Margarita, et al. (2006). 'The Traditional Art of the Nativity Scene', *Artes de México*, 81: 81–96.

Derrett, J. Duncan M. (1971). 'The Manger: Ritual Law and Soteriology', *Theology*, 74: 566–71.

Derrett, J. Duncan M. (1973). 'The Manger at Bethlehem: Light on St. Luke's Technique from Contemporary Jewish Law', in L. A. Livingstone (ed.), *Studia Evangelica VI*. Berlin: Akademia-Verlag: 39–47.

Derrett, J. Duncan M. (2012). 'Oracles, Myth, and Luke's Nativity Story', *Novum Testamentum*, 54: 258–68.

Feinberg, Larry J. (2006). 'Fra Bartolommeo's Nativity: A Rediscovered High Renaissance Masterpiece', *Art Institute of Chicago Museum Studies*, 32: 32–43, 91.

Fitzmyer, Joseph A. (1981). *The Gospel According to Luke I–IX*. Anchor Bible 28. Garden City, New York: Doubleday.

Giblin, Charles H. (1967). 'Reflections on the Sign of the Manger', *Catholic Biblical Quarterly*, 29: 87–101.

Grey, Matthew J. (2001). 'Becoming as a Little Child: Elements of Ritual Rebirth in Ancient Judaism and Early Christianity', *Studia Antiqua*, 1: 63–85.

Harris, Sarah (2012). 'Why Are There Shepherds in the Lukan Birth Narrative?' *Colloquium*, 44: 17–30.

Johnson, Luke Timothy (1991). *The Gospel of Luke*, ed. Daniel J. Harrington, SJ. Sacra Pagina 3. Collegeville: Michael Glazier.

Mytum, Harold (2015). 'Christmas in the Graveyard? Nativity Scenes on County Louth Headstones', *Archaeology Ireland*, 29: 26–9.

Phillips, Thomas E. (2011). 'Why Did Mary Wrap the Newborn Jesus in "Swaddling Clothes"? Luke 2:7 and 2:12 in the Context of Luke-Acts and First-Century Literature', in Steve Walton et al. (eds.), *Reading Acts Today*. New York: T&T Clark: 29–42.

Sarnecka, Zuzanna (2019). '"And the Word Dwelt amongst Us": Experiencing the Nativity in the Italian Renaissance Home', in Maya Corry et al. (eds.), *Domestic Devotions in Early Modern Italy*. Leiden: Brill:

Stracke, Richard. 'The Birth of Jesus: The Iconography'. Available at https://www.christianiconography.info/nativity.html/ (accessed 19 March 2020).

PART V
TRADITIONS

CHAPTER 20

THE WINTER SOLSTICE AND OTHER CELEBRATIONS OF THE SEASON

DANIEL GIFFORD

Search 'Winter Solstice Stonehenge' on YouTube.com and the plethora of results suggests a modern ritual in the making. The collection of uploaded videos spans most years of the twenty-first century, all depicting large crowds gathered for winter solstice at the famous British site. Watch enough of these videos and familiar faces appear, along with annual costumes and customs. There are drums and robes, songs and Green Man masks. But more importantly, the vast crowds swaddled in coats, hats, and scarves all hold their cellphones and smartphones aloft to capture both the scenes around them and one particular moment—sunrise.

Each year more of these videos are made and shared. Winter Solstice at Stonehenge has become a spectacle of display to be recorded and disseminated through social media; a mixture of history, memory, myth, and performance; a marriage of ancient traditions and the digital age. That these newly-born traditions of digitally capturing and sharing images have become their own festive rituals in a modern era should not be a surprise. Winter Solstice has been a wellspring of inspiration for festivals, rituals, and traditions that reflect both longstanding beliefs as well as contemporary contexts, with Christmas itself being widely considered the most prominent and successful among them. But Christmas hardly stands alone, and over the centuries there has been an ongoing process of competition, appropriation, and recontextualization between Christmas and these other winter festivals. Just as a new ritual has been born in which hardy tourists brave a cold dawn to capture digitally a particular sunrise at a particular place, so too have other annual traditions emerged from recognizing the shortest days' worth of sunlight all year.

It is the tilt of the Earth, and its elliptical orbit around the Sun, that conspire to bring about the annual occurrence of winter solstice. Such a combination requires that at some point each year, the North Pole will experience its furthest tilt from the Sun, resulting in both the shortest amount of sunlight in a day and the Sun's lowest arc across the horizon between sunrise and sunset. Cultures throughout the northern hemisphere have for millennia noted that this day transpires in what we now call December and assigned ritualized significance to the occurrence. A series of festivals and festivities were born.

Although the aforementioned Stonehenge has gained the lion's share of attention in recent times, numerous ancient sites were built to maximize their visual impact, specifically during the winter solstice. The Neolithic passage graves of Newgrange in Ireland, for example, contain a 'roof box' that would have channelled a single, thin beam of winter solstice 'first light' into a chamber, bisecting it and indirectly illuminating a three-leafed spiral figure on the wall. Newgrange predates Stonehenge by approximately 1,000 years (Ray 1989: 343–5) Solstitial orientation was a common feature in Egyptian temple construction—so much so that some have argued that temples were re-erected several times until a perfect orientation to solstitial light was achieved. Both the temple of Karnak and the temple of Amun at Medinet Habu are representative examples of this ancient architectural focus (Belmonte 2010: 65–93). Eight thousand miles to the east, similar orientations can be found in the ruins of Alta Vista near the modern town of Chalchihuites, Zacatecas, in north-west Mexico (Aveni et al. 1982: 316–35). In fact, the northern hemisphere is filled with examples of ancient architecture gathering, harnessing, and directing winter solstitial light. While the specific rituals surrounding this moment of radiant appropriation have often been lost, the fact that buildings themselves were designed to address specifically the winter solstice's solar patterns is itself illuminative, if one will pardon the pun. Light *mattered*.

Thus, it is no accident that festivals roughly corresponding to Christmas on worldwide calendars are themselves heavily focused on light: bonfires, candles, tapers, and lamps are all associated with winter festivals throughout the world. Christmas itself borrows heavily from this genre of iconography and symbolism, from the bright shining star in the Nativity story to the liberal use of candles, fires, and eventually electrified lights in festive decorations. The tradition of a Yule log is also heavily connected with the interplay of light and dark. Writes one chronicler of winter solstice traditions: 'The Yule Log itself is above all a reminder of the importance of fire in the depth of cold and darkness of Midwinter' (Matthews 1998: 98).

Perhaps no other winter holiday captures this quite as completely as Hanukkah, often called the Festival of Lights. Hanukkah was a relatively minor Jewish festival that had largely 'fallen off the radar' within Reform traditions of Judaism. It was, however, still celebrated among many of the European Jews who joined the massive wave of immigrants to the United States in the late nineteenth and early twentieth centuries. In the context of both rising Jewish identity and the establishment of an American identity, the ancient, pre-Christian ritual of Hanukkah enjoyed something of a rebirth in American popular culture as 'the Jewish Christmas' (Stein 2012: 40). Central to making this connection was light.

Serving as a remembrance of the rededication of the second Temple in Jerusalem, Hanukkah occurs over eight nights in late November or early December, during which a candle is lit each evening in a menorah or candelabra, using a ninth central candle or shammash. 'The most obvious similarity between Christmas and Hanukkah outside the calendar is the use of lights', writes Blair Stein, 'either on the Christmas tree or menorah. [American] Newspapers, whether informed by a local rabbi, reporter, or the JHPNB [Jewish Holidays Press Notice Bureau], were quick to point out these parallels' (Stein 2012: 43). Although such newspaper accounts emphasized the parallels to Christmas specifically, others might have also noted similarities to the rituals of Advent—the liturgical lead-up to Christmas in Catholic and some Protestant denominations—in which specifically arranged and selected candles are lit at set increments. Instead of Hanukkah's nine, Advent typically employs four candles, one lit each Sunday before Christmas. Practices of light pervade both sets of religious tradition.

However, symbols of light and luminescence were not the only overlap people saw between Christmas and Hanukkah. Particularly within the American milieu of a rising mass media, exploding consumer culture, the growth of department stores, and civic celebrations such as holiday parades, there was a newfound parallel between the holidays when it came to gift-giving, and presents for children especially. Writes Stein: 'Beginning around the turn of the century, giving gifts became just as important to the Hanukkah spirit as lighting candles, both of which took place almost exclusively in the home' (Stein 2012: 45). Still, although certainly amped up by the context of American consumerism, gift-giving—like symbols of illumination—has deep roots in winter festivals across a range of cultures.

Traditional, pre-Christian/pre-conversion Inuit winter festivals involved gift-giving, for example, as did rituals among Finns and Laplanders, some of which featured a central gift-giving figure with striking parallels to a modern Santa Claus (Laugrand et al. 2002: 203–25; Matthews 1998: 117). In the Kalash cultures of Pakistan, winter solstice rituals include the baking of small animal figures from dough which are eventually given to children (Cacopardo and Cacopardo 1989). Indeed, the ancient Roman festival of Saturnalia—often identified as one of the major precursors to Christmas and its placement on the calendar in December—made gift-giving so central that an entire day was devoted to it. *Sigillaria*, the culminating day of the Saturnalia festival, shared its name with the small terracotta and wax figures that were given as gifts among friends and family. It was Ovid who suggested in *Ars Amatoria* that the practice was getting more lavish and potentially out of hand with each passing year, a lament surely recognizable to today's holiday shoppers (Tóth 2014: 17; Hollis 1989: 106).

In addition to a heavy reliance on light symbolism and a strong bent toward gift-giving, Christmas inherited a third batch of customs from winter solstice and other ancient, seasonally adjacent festivals and traditions—the use of evergreen. 'Just as the Midwinter fires celebrated the longed for return of the sun,' writes John Matthews, 'so did the evergreen tree signify the continuing presence of burgeoning life in the midst of Winter's sleep of death' (Matthews 1998: 78). The list of plants is an impressive one—cedars and firs, holly, ivy, hawthorn, myrtle, bay, and mistletoe to name a few. All of these had relevance in pre-Christian winter traditions that carried forward into the wreaths, garlands, adornments, and decorations of modern Christmases. In their exploration of the ethnobiology of Christmas, Christian Rätsch and Claudia Müller-Ebelin likewise remind us that many of the flavours and smells of Christmas originated in pagan times. Smudging in wintertime to ward off evil spirits often involved many of the very plants we combine into holiday potpourri today: juniper, thistle, fir, crabapple, thyme, and fennel (Rätsch 2003: 15).

From this thick stew of pagan and pre-Christian festivals—winter solstice, Saturnalia, and Hanukkah among them—we can see the seeds of what would eventually flower into several Christmas traditions recognizable today. With light symbols, gift-giving, and the use of evergreens (and other plants) there was a clear process of borrowing and reappropriation at work, a process that provided a sort of cultural feedback loop to earlier traditions as Christmas customs fell into place. However, this was really just the beginning of the process. The entire holiday calendar did not freeze into place like hardened amber with the arrival of a winter-time celebration called Christmas. Instead, new holidays continued to emerge and take shape, finding their own place on the calendar in the weeks and months surrounding Christmas. In other words, the process of collaboration and competition between winter season holidays—including those very same ones that had predated and inspired Christmas traditions—would continue for hundreds more years right up to the present day.

Certainly, one of the most prominent of these additional holidays is Epiphany, observed on January 6. Derived from the Greek work for 'revelation', Epiphany suggests that moment when Christ was revealed to a larger world, although different Christian denominations offer different explanations of what that moment actually was—either the arrival of the Magi or the baptism of Christ in the River Jordan (Frodsham 2008: 99–100). The split over meaning is also indicative of the split over Epiphany itself, with the holiday gaining traction first in the Eastern church as early as the second century, while its adoption in the West—and connection to the Magi story—occurred later into the fourth century, by which time Christmas itself was largely finding its footing as a holy day on December 25.

Epiphany thus also developed into a sort of opposite bookend to Christmas, setting up the '12 Days of Christmas'. Because the two have thus been bound together for centuries, it is perhaps unsurprising that traditions have migrated between them. For example, in several cultures, Spain and Latin America included, gift-giving occurs on Epiphany rather than (or sometimes in addition to) Christmas. Baked goods specific to Epiphany have also emerged from a larger seasonal palate of spices, fruits, nuts, and chocolate. Parades and processions are also common throughout the world, often with a focus on children.

Still, perhaps one reason Epiphany lacks the worldwide appeal of Christmas (one author suggests that it is 'the Rodney Dangerfield of liturgical feasts'—that is, the one that does not get much respect) is its signifier as the end of revelry (Brancatelli 1997: 51). Many families and churches take down their Christmas decorations at Epiphany, and the day puts a definitive endnote to the holiday season. There are no carols to the thirteenth or fourteenth days of Christmas. And while the longest night of the year has already passed with winter solstice, the coldest night of the year is most certainly still to come. Epiphany closes the chapter on festivities for another year, with little to look forward to until spring. Except for where it doesn't close...

In New Orleans, Brazil, the Caribbean, and other warm climes with both a strong Catholic heritage and the ability to gather in the streets during peak winter months, Epiphany marks the beginning of Carnival season. King cakes have become a signature of this kick-off in New Orleans, where they are decorated with green and purple icing and feature a hidden bean, prize, or token to be found by a reveller who is then named king (or queen) for the day. Like so many other traditions, this too has great cross-cultural elasticity. Similar Twelfth Night cakes proved popular throughout medieval Europe and Tudor England, before being 'rediscovered' in the eighteenth and nineteenth centuries. But it is in New Orleans specifically that the bridges between cake, Epiphany, and Carnival all come together, as Marcia Gaudet writes:

> While the present form of the cake is not genuinely traditional with the southwest Louisiana Cajuns, the celebration of Mardi Gras and the Carnival season is. Thus, it is a symbolic link with a tradition of long standing. It is a regional, cultural, festive food custom that originated as a religious folk way (Epiphany) and became a festival cake associated with Mardi Gras. (Gaudet 2003: 56)

If the specific link of king's cake to Carnival's launch on Epiphany is unique to Louisiana, the larger assumption that the Carnival season begins at Epiphany is much more widespread. Throughout the Caribbean, a welter of conditions gave rise to Carnival rituals that begin on January 6, including a 'privilege' provided to African slaves that allowed them to organize their own street parades and dances on certain Sundays between Epiphany and Ash Wednesday. Slaves in Cuba, Martinique, Brazil, and other colonies capitalized on the opportunity to draw from their African heritage, music, dances, and food for these festivities, combining them with colourful costumes, lanterns, and masks. These traditions became even more meaningful and resonant after emancipation. As Lizbeth Paravisini-Gebert writes, 'Despite its many similarities to the European carnival, the Caribbean carnival is not a European-inspired nature festival, but rather a celebration rooted in the experience of slavery and the commemoration of emancipation' (Paravisini-Gebert 1997: 216–17). The affiliations with European-born Epiphany traditions thus take a backseat to the much more significant, unique, and personal experiences of slaves—Caribbean and South American Carnival was born from the miseries of human trafficking.

Still, the Carnival season between Epiphany and Ash Wednesday does share certain other DNA markers with European winter holiday festivities, as Paravisni-Gerbert also writes: 'Carnival's appeal to the Caribbean masses rests on its temporary inversion of accepted norms of behavior, on the subversion of the "natural" social order it promotes' (Paravisini-Gebert 1997: 216). Such inversions were a hallmark of Christmas and Christmas-adjacent festivities, often to the chagrin of church leaders, political rulers, and social elites. The phenomenon has any number of terms—carnivalesque, misrule, reversals—and any number of manifestations including mumming and wassailing. As noted earlier, Twelfth Night was especially prone to these sorts of inversions, with cake-based customs pointing the way to a 'Lord of Misrule' who would oversee the all-night party. Such traditions migrated to the New World as evidenced by the emergence in the 1870s of the 'Twelfth Night Revellers' of New Orleans who launch the Carnival season.

Inversions and licence for misrule also seeped deep into Christmas itself, leading to its brief (and often mocked) outlawed status by Puritans in the 1600s. Yet Christmas, Twelfth Night, and Carnival were not the only winter holidays that trafficked in notions of the carnivalesque. Particularly as the popularity of Christmas was channelled towards domestic, interior-based, child-centric traditions and rituals, a sense of winter misrule was redirected towards other holidays, New Year's Eve perhaps most of all.

Of course, cultures around the world had celebrated the beginning of a 'new year' for over 4,000, years, with some of the earliest celebrations occurring in Babylonia. But the problem of a 'new year' celebration is the assumption of when one year ends and another begins—a day that could be based on any number of factors and resulting in new years beginning in practically every month and season, depending on history, culture, and location. In 45 BCE the Julian calendar confirmed the Western new year as January 1; however, little did anyone know that a new religion would be ascendant within a few short generations of setting that milestone. Thus, situated between the increasingly important Christian holidays of Christmas and Twelfth Night/Epiphany, New Year's Eve (and indeed New Year's Day as well) ended up on the largely overlooked list of winter holidays.

This began to change with the industrial and urban revolutions that occurred throughout Europe, North America, and colonial outposts in the nineteenth century. Hannah Forsyth writes of Sydney's transformation into a world-class New Year's Eve destination: 'Time at New Year's Eve is an industrialized paganism, for it represents our technological ability as a society to know the exact stroke of midnight, with no natural phenomenon to assist us—the triumph of Father Time over Mother Nature' (Forsyth 2011: 71). Additionally, New Year's Eve pushed the carnivalesque and misrule tendencies of the season towards cities where large, often inebriated crowds could gather, frolic, and make merry along wide streets and in spacious squares. Holiday postcards from the early twentieth century reveal the dichotomy between the rural ideal of a peaceful Christmas tableau of snowy fields and quiet villages, and the city-based revelries of an urban New Year's Eve (Gifford 2013: 111–13). Scotland has produced both an exception and an exception that proves the rule to the suggestion that New Year's Eve primarily became a product of the industrial/urban transformations. Called Hogmanay among the Scottish, this New Year's Eve holiday had, for centuries, been connected to more bucolic and familial roots among the Scots. Writes David Hayes, 'Well into the 1950s, 25 December was a normal working day in Scotland; the important festival was Hogmanay, 31 December. The Scots tradition was to reflect quietly on the dying year, to nurture an inner space which after midnight would fill with warm companionship.' This would seem to reflect the more idealized vision of Christmas seen elsewhere with its snow-covered hills and crackling fires of home and hearth. But Hayes too is forced to admit this tradition has migrated away from the rural ideal and into the cities, Edinburgh especially. He writes:

> Six years ago, the ritual new year gathering at the Tron kirk on the Royal Mile was expanded into a range of events—concerts, funfairs, a torchlight procession—stretching over a week. The centrepiece was a late-night Hogmanay party against the city's incomparable skyline, with a firework display and live bands on several stages. (Hayes 1999: 15)

Even Scotland's Hogmanay had largely conceded the rural space to Christmas and turned the midnight stroke of the clock over to an urban marketing machine.

As Christmas and Epiphany established themselves as the nearly two-week juggernauts of the winter calendar, other holidays jockeyed for position and relevance within their orbit. If New Year's Eve found its place as the urban venue for seasonal misrule, then feast days dedicated to St Nicholas and St Lucy took the largely opposite approach of focusing on children and domesticity in the lead-up to Christmas's big day. The Feast of St Nicholas is not Christmas Day as some might assume; rather it is December 6 on the Western liturgical calendar and December 19 on the Eastern calendar. It is also another child-centric day focused on giving small gifts to children, often by filling empty shoes left by the fireplace overnight—a tradition that had transmuted in America to stockings 'hung by the chimney with care' in Clement Clark Moore's famous 1820s poem, 'A Visit from St Nicholas'. Of course, socks were not the only or even the most important transmutation, with the feast of St Nicholas providing the larger framework, central figure, understood iconography, and ritualized behaviour of Christmas's own Santa Claus or Father Christmas. St Nicholas, writes Stephen Nissenbaum, could so readily be adapted into Santa Claus, precisely because the ancient bishop and saint was 'a figure of great authority as well as great charity'[1] (Nissenbaum 1996: 72).

The Feast of St Lucy or Santa Lucia likewise operated as a two-way street between a relatively minor saint's day and larger Christmas traditions. Celebrated on December 13th, this particular day was an opportunity to further emphasize the importance of both light and baked goods as part of the winter holiday season. Candles, torches, and bonfires were used to mark the occasion, as were wreaths of evergreen. Later in the eighteenth century, similar combinations of evergreen wreaths and candles would surface in Germany as Advent iconography. Likewise, specific holiday loaves and buns associated with Santa Lucia would find broader appropriation as part of a seasonal flow of sweets, breads, and pastries special to the holidays.

---

[1] In some Germanic cultures, St Nicholas Eve is a time for Krampus—a goat-headed, black furred, demon-like creature—to visit and potentially kidnap naughty children.

As the recognizable traditions, iconography, and consumerist patterns of modern Christmas largely settled into place over the ninetieth and twentieth centuries, emerging holidays had to account for Christmas's pre-eminence. Thanksgiving in the United States provides a particularly good example. Championed by Sarah Josephina Hale, editor of the wildly popular magazine, *Godey's Lady's Book*, Thanksgiving emerged in the second half of the 1800s as a family affair in which loved ones gathered around a communal table for a proscribed feast (for which the ladies' magazine provided all the instruction, recipes, and decorating tips). Hale linked the festival to a historical event that took place in 1621 in Plymouth, Massachusetts. This 'first Thanksgiving' between Pilgrims and Native Americans was almost completely a mythology created in the 1800s through the lens of white Manifest Destiny and racial superiority, with just enough basis in fact to keep historians busy for the next two centuries.

However, in addition to the necessity of her holiday having an 'origin story', Hale recognized the need to differentiate her holiday from the more dominant Christmas. 'Christmas is a day set apart by Christendom to commemorate the nativity of our blessed Lord,' Hale wrote in 1837. By contrast, Thanksgiving would have 'a national character' in which those gathering would cherish 'the best affections of the heart—the social and domestic ties' (Hale 1837). Even as Christmas itself had been moving by this time to a similar emphasis on domestic ties, Hale understood the need to differentiate between a largely religious holiday and the civic/nationalist one she was proposing. And she was enormously successful. By the turn of the twentieth century, not only was Thanksgiving firmly entrenched on the American calendar, its iconography was rife with flags, Uncles Sams, and bald eagles at levels Christmas never could have sustained (Gifford 2013: 144–170). Hale had found a niche that Christmas had yet to fulfil. The ideas behind Thanksgiving proved so successful that Canada adopted a similar holiday by the late nineteenth century, but eventually moved it up on the calendar to early October, tying it more closely to autumn harvests rather than winter celebrations.

In the twentieth century this process of holiday invention and reinvention continued. For some this meant revisiting the traditions of the past. A growing consciousness of humans' impact on the planet, wildlife populations, and natural resources such as clean air and water led to waves of conservationism and environmentalism. Particularly the latter movement—which gained widespread popularity and awareness starting in the late 1960s and 1970s—offered an opportunity to consider the natural rhythms of life from a pre-modern age, including humans' attunement to events like the winter solstice. In his call for rectifying humans' disconnection with the natural world, Anthony Weston's 1994 *Back to Earth: Tomorrow's Environmentalism* encouraged a re-engagement with such festivals and their nature-based roots: 'Suppose that we take it upon ourselves to re-root our festivals explicitly in the natural and pagan soil from which they sprang' (Weston 1994: 139).

The link between environmentalism and nature-centric religious movements like Neopaganism also encouraged exploration of ancient winter festivals and practices in a modern context. Layered upon this too was the feminist movement (or, more accurately, movements) that sought to eschew traditions and rituals that reinforced sexist hierarchies and other forms of exclusion such as racism and homophobia. Many saw these hierarchical structures and mechanisms for oppression encapsulated in the religious holidays of organized Christianity, Christmas included. Wicca practitioners developed an alternative festival calendar or 'Wheel of the Year' that reimagined the annual rhythms of practice and celebration including those of winter:

> A midwinter ceremony or Yule ritual might celebrate the return of the sun during the longest night and the rebirth of the sun god. Wiccan festivals are intended to remind participants of the cycle of life, of human death and rebirth, and the changes evident around them in the natural world. (Pearson and Pike 2005: 1740)

But not all re-examinations of pagan folklore, ancient traditions, and winter customs were benign. 'One of the most striking features of the Nazification of Christmas', writes historian Joe Perry, 'was its redefinition as a neo-pagan, "Nordic" celebration that drew on winter solstice rituals allegedly practiced by ancient German tribes.' Perry reveals how 'return to light' festivals capitalized on past patterns and traditions (some authentic, some invented) to craft new metaphors for the Nazi movement in which darkness would be conquered and light would usher in 'the new German ascension' (Perry 2005: 575, 578). Fascist Italy likewise developed new holiday rites and rituals in the 1930s—such as the *Giornata della Madre e del Fanciullo* [Day of the Mother and Child on December 24]—that converted Christmas Eve into a 'celebration of fascist female duty: Patriotic procreation and the nurturing of healthy young fascist Italians' (Ferris 2012: 101). In Cold War-era Romania, officials repurposed centuries-old Christmas carols to fit with new ideological goals. Popular songs that emphasized the star iconography from the Nativity story were converted so that Christ as the 'light of the world' instead became the light of Socialism shining from the East (i.e. the Soviet Union) (Pieslak 2004: 7–30).

In the early 2000s interest in pagan and pre-Christian rituals connected to the winter solstice took a decidedly different turn. An assortment of books, articles, and websites began to gain popular traction by variously suggesting that the ancient Mayan Long Count calendar had indicated 2012's winter solstice would mark apocalyptic change for the planet. Although the theory never received scientific support—and was in fact debunked in a variety of ways—the linkage of a mysterious ancient culture, the winter solstice, and various tendrils of New Age mysticism and millennial enthusiasm for 'the End of Days' proved irresistible. Popular culture especially capitalized on the 2012 movement, most notably Roland Emmerich's disaster movie *2012* which earned $770 million worldwide.[2] Still, the episode was another example of appropriation of past winter seasons for modern purposes. In an article published in 2006, Robert Sitler argued,

---

[2] '2012' Box Office Mojo. Available at https://www.boxofficemojo.com/movies/?id=2012.htm/ (accessed 20 March 2020).

> Many of the self-proclaimed leaders of the 2012 movement have successfully appropriated this date from an ancient Mayan calendar by explicitly linking themselves to the living Mayan world.... In doing so, 2012 proponents have transformed belief in the global significance of the December 21 date into a snowballing phenomenon that no amount of evidence can constrain. (Sitler 2006: 34)

Repurposing the past to create new holiday rituals and customs continued in other ways throughout the twentieth and into the twenty-first century. In the aftermath of the Watts riots of 1965, African-American leaders looked for ways to reaffirm African and African-American identity, pride, and culture. One result was Kwanzaa. Invented in Baltimore, Maryland, by black activist and scholar Maulana Karenga and first celebrated over the 1966/67 season (Kwanzaa begins on December 26 and ends January 1), the festival draws on an amalgam of African harvest festivals and pan-African traditions including tributes to ancestors and a communal feast or *karamu*. Reconstructing Kwanzaa's paths to mainstream awareness and acceptance, Anna Day Wilde notes the rapid dissemination of information about the festival that occurred through newspapers, churches, museums, and schools, along with more commercial avenues such as expos, product lines, and corporate sponsorships (Wilde 2004: 120–30).

In addition to the importance of a large family meal, Kwanzaa has other elements that are at least superficially similar to Christmas, although all are given an Afrocentric purpose, meaning, and name to underscore their importance in creating a connection to African culture. The lighting of candles is one example, as well as the giving of gifts—often books, musical instruments, or other educational items—to children. The timing of the festival is likewise conspicuous in its overlap with Christmas. However, Karenga has always maintained that Kwanzaa is not an alternative to Christmas; rather, it is a cultural celebration that can take place alongside religious celebrations such as Christmas or Hanukkah. 'They have a religious purpose,' he offered in a 2013 interview, 'but Kwanzaa has cultural purposes: reaffirming our rootedness in African culture, reaffirming the bonds between us ... and reaffirming the importance of communal values, those that stress and strengthen family, community and culture' (Kaltenbach 2013).

The fact that the path of Kwanzaa's mainstream acceptance passed through the commercial realms of consumer product lines, largescale expos, and purchased goods is indicative of how much holiday culture in the modern era has become mediated and understood as an outgrowth of consumption. Black Friday has become its own holiday tradition, one based around the ritual of shopping for holiday presents. In fact, the ritualized behaviours of Black Friday are themselves extensions of recognized Christmas and winter season rituals—spending time with family members (trips to the mall often involve multiple relatives), making wish lists of desired goods, getting presents wrapped, visiting Santa, and of course, ultimately giving gifts (Boyd and Peters 2011: 522–37). The term 'Black Friday' is thought to have been coined sometime in the 1960s; however, recognition of a definitive and distinct 'shopping season', including a kick-off day, existed well before then. President Franklin Roosevelt famously moved Thanksgiving up a week in 1939, explicitly to expand the number of shopping days between Thanksgiving and Christmas. His controversial 'Franksgivings' lasted until 1941, when

Congress passed a joint resolution officially declaring Thanksgiving as the fourth Thursday in November. The entire episode reveals that shopping itself was a specific holiday tradition by the first half of the twentieth century, with its own set of dates set aside specifically for the consumerist rituals.

Whether because of its explicit emphasis on consumption or its association with Christian religious traditions, Christmas was clearly not for everyone. Counter- or anti-Christmas rituals began to crop up particularly in the final years of the 1990s and into the new millennium. Advanced by a swath of comedians, parodists, social commentators, atheists, and others disenfranchised by Christmas's ubiquity, Festivus became a protest holiday 'for the rest of us'. Given its most popular introduction to Americans through a 1997 episode of the hit TV show *Seinfeld*, Festivus was presented as a made-up holiday with its own set of traditions, rules, and customs devised by Frank Costanza. The holiday took on life beyond the single episode, with Festivus becoming a canvas upon which participants could create their own quirky rituals based on those laid out in the original Seinfeld script such as 'The Airing of Grievances' and 'Feats of Strength'.

Festivus thus became part of a popular conversation that in many ways pulled back the curtain on Christmas rituals: Why is one ritual any more 'real' than another? Are not all holiday traditions ultimately made up by someone? This great levelling of the sacred and the silly is a hallmark of the postmodern era, as noted by Ilona Mikkonen and Domen Bajde: 'We can therefore connect Festivus with broader tendencies of contemporary consumer culture; skepticism, even disrespect of metanarratives (or grand narratives) is a trait that is often attributed to postmodern consumers' (Mikkonen and Baide 2013: 322).

By the 2010s it was clear that 'celebrations of the season' could mean just about anything: Christmas dinner at a Chinese restaurant; travel to the remotest regions; going to the movies; taking a 'polar bear' swim in icy waters; surfing with Santa, or posting on any number of anti-Christmas social media sites. The gathered crowds at Stonehenge every winter solstice—clutching their cellphone cameras tight in their gloved hands—are but a tiny piece in the mosaic of what falls under the heading 'holiday traditions' today. Even the modern semantic debate of 'Happy Holidays' versus 'Merry Christmas' is indicative of the fact that the calendar has grown quite crowded with festivals, holidays, rituals, and days of tradition and meaning. More importantly, none of these holidays exist in a vacuum, removed and isolated from the others. Instead, they are part of an ever-expanding constellation *and* conversation across time that links histories, cultures, and people through a basic understanding of winter as a special and unique time of year.

REFERENCES AND FURTHER READING

Aveni, Anthony F., Hartung, Horst, and Kelley, J. Charles (1982). 'Alta Vista (Chalchihuites): Astronomical Implications of a Mesoamerican Ceremonial Outpost at the Tropic of Cancer'. *American Antiquity*, 47, no. 2: 316–35.

Belmonte, Juan Antonio et al. (2010). 'On the Orientation of Ancient Egyptian Temples: (5) Testing the Theory in Middle Egypt and Sudan', *Journal for the History of Astronomy*, 41, no. 1: 65–93.

Boyd Thomas, J., and Peters, Cara (2011). 'An Exploratory Investigation of Black Friday Consumption Rituals', *International Journal of Retail & Distribution Management*, 39, no. 7: 522–37.

Brancatelli, Robert (1997). 'Three Gifts, Three Kings and Three Ways to Celebrate Epiphany', *Journal of the Liturgical Conference*, 14, no. 2: 51–5.

Cacopardo, Alberto, and Cacopardo, Augusto (1989). 'The Kalasha (Pakistan) Winter Solstice Festival', *Ethnology*, 28, no. 4: 317–29.

Dennis, Matthew (2002). *Red, White, and Blue Letter Days: An American Calendar*. Ithaca: Cornell University Press.

Ferris, Kate (2012). *Everyday Life in Fascist Venice, 1929–40*. London: Palgrave Macmillan.

Forsyth, Hannah (2011). '"Making Night Hideous With their Noise": New Year's Eve in 1897', *History Australia*, 8, no. 2: 66–86.

Frodsham, Paul (2008). *From Stonehenge to Santa Claus: The Evolution of Christmas*. Stroud, UK: The History Press.

Gaudet, Marcia (2003). 'The New Orleans King Cake in Southwest Louisiana', in Marcia G. Gaudet and James C. McDonald (eds.), *Mardi Gras, Gumbo, and Zydeco: Readings in Louisiana Culture*. Jackson, MS: University Press of Mississippi: 48–58.

Gifford, Daniel (2013). *American Holiday Postcards, 1905–1915: Imagery and Context*. Jefferson, NC: McFarland Press.

Hale, Sarah (1837) in *The Thanksgiving Editorials of Sarah Josepha Hale from the Pages of Godey's Lady's Book*. Pilgrim Hall Museum, Plymouth, MA. Available at https://pilgrimhall.org/pdf/SJH_Editorials.pdf Last retrieved May 24, 2019.

Hayes, David (1999). 'Just Another Marketing Opportunity', *New Statesman*, 128, no. 4417: 15.

Hollis, Adrian S. (1989). *Ovid: Ars amatoria, Book 1*. Oxford: Clarendon Press.

Kalapos, Gabriella (2006). *Fertility Goddesses, Groundhog Bellies & the Coca-Cola Company: The Origins of Modern Holidays*. Toronto: Insomniac Press.

Kaltenbach, Chris (2013, December 20). 'Kwanzaa Creator Maulana Karenga Will Speak at Lewis Museum', *The Baltimore Sun*. Retrieved from https://www.baltimoresun.com/features/bs-ae-kwanzaa-20131220-story.html (Unavilable in Europe at time of writing).

Laugrand, Frédéric and Oosten, Jarich (2002). 'Quviasukvik. The Celebration of an Inuit Winter Feast in the Central Arctic', *Journal de la Société des Américanistes*, 88, no. 88: 203–25.

Matthews, John (1998). *The Sacred Traditions of Christmas*. Wheaton, IL: Quest Books.

Mikkonen, Ilona and Baide, Domen (2013). 'Happy Festivus! Parody as Playful Consumer Resistance', *Consumption Markets & Culture*, 16, no. 4: 311–37.

Nissenbaum, Stephen (1996). *The Battle for Christmas*. New York: Vintage.

Paravisini-Gebert, Lizbeth (1997). 'Writers Playin' Mas': Carnival and the Grotesque in the Contemporary Caribbean Novel', in A. James Arnold (ed.), *A History of Literature in the Caribbean: Volume 3*. Amsterdam: John Benjamins Publishing Company: 215–38.

Pearson, Joanne and Pike, Sarah M. (2005). 'Wicca', in Bron Taylor (ed.), *Encyclopedia of Religion and Nature*. London: Continuum: 1739–1742.

Perry, Joe (2005). 'Nazifying Christmas: Popular Culture and Popular Celebration in the Third Reich', *Central European History*, 38, no. 4: 572–605.

Pieslak, Sabina Pauta (2004). '"Lenin in Swaddling Clothes": A Critique of the Ideological Conflict between Socialist State Policy and Christian Music in Cold War Romania', *Current Musicology*, 78: 7–30.

Rätsch, Christian and Müller-Ebelin, Claudia (2003). *Pagan Christmas: The Plants, Spirits, and Rituals at the Origins of Yuletide*. Rochester, VT: Inner Traditions.

Ray, T. P. (1989). 'The Winter Solstice Phenomenon at Newgrange, Ireland: Accident of Design?' *Nature*, 337, no. 6205: 343.

Restad, Penne L. (1995). *Christmas in America: A History*. New York: Oxford University Press.

Stein, Blair (2012). '"The Charnukah Being Observed Now": Understanding Hanukkah through American Newspapers, 1880–1915', *Journal of Religion and Culture*, 23: 39–61.

Sitler, Robert K. (2006). 'The 2012 Phenomenon New Age Appropriation of an Ancient Mayan Calendar', *Nova Religio: The Journal of Alternative and Emergent Religions* 9, no. 3: 24–38.

Tóth, Orsolya (2014). 'The Roman Saturnalia and the Survival of its Traditions Among Christians', *Történeti Tanulmányok—Acta Universitatis Debreceniensis Series Historica*, XXII: 10–20.

Weston, Anthony (1994). *Back to Earth: Tomorrow's Environmentalism*. Philadelphia: Temple University Press.

Wilde, Anna Day (2004). 'Mainstreaming Kwanzaa', in Amitai Etzioni (ed.), *We Are What We Celebrate*. New York: New York University Press: 120–130.

CHAPTER 21

ST NICHOLAS TO SANTA CLAUS

ADAM C. ENGLISH

NICHOLAS OF MYRA

ST NICHOLAS, whose life can be dated uncertainly between 260 and 343, originally hailed from Patara, a Lycian port-town on the coast of the Mediterranean about 85 km from Myra. Linguistically, the name 'Nicholas' represents a combination of the Greek words for 'victory' and 'people', meaning something like 'victory of the people' or 'people's champion'.

Some sources list Nicholas's parents as Epiphanius and Nonna, but that is a mistake. Epiphanius and Nonna parented a different individual, a certain Nicholas of Sion, named after Nicholas of Myra. This second Nicholas lived from 480 to 564, two hundred years after the first (*Bios* 1984). In the tenth century, the hagiographer Symeon Metaphrastes combined the lives of the two Nicholai, either by accident or on purpose, and created an enduring error (Cioffari 1987: 101–10). Even today, stories from the two Nicholai continue to be repeated and interlaced into a single biography.

In Patara's necropolis, located outside the arched gate to the city, the remains of a church known as the 'Spring Church' can be found. The ruins themselves date to the fourth century, but Christians certainly gathered long before then in the cemetery around the tomb of an unknown saint for worship and community. This is most likely where Nicholas first learned the faith.

Three Dowries

Patara not only marks the place of his birth, but also provides the stage for the most celebrated scene of his life, one that directly connects him to Christmas and Santa Claus. The earliest written account comes from Michael the Archimandrite's *Life of*

Saint Nicholas, the first full-length biography of Nicholas (Michael n.d.; Anrich 1913; Falconi 1751). Composed in the eighth or ninth century, the Greek text consists of twelve episodes in fifty-two paragraphs, ten of which are devoted to the story in question, known simply as 'the three daughters' or 'the three dowries'. According to Michael, Nicholas lost his parents while still in his youth. Although they left him a sizable financial inheritance, the money proved more of a spiritual burden than a material blessing. As he considered what he should do, he learned of a neighbour who had recently lost his fortunes.

> Michael the Archimandrite describes the dilemma as follows:
>
> He [the neighbour] had gone from being well-off to extreme indigence. He had three daughters who were both shapely and very attractive to the eye, and he was willing to station them in a brothel so that he might thereby acquire the necessities of life for himself and his household. For no man among the lordly or powerful deigned to marry them lawfully, and even among the lower-classes and those who owned the least bit of something there was no one well-minded enough to do this.
> (Michael n.d.: section 10)

The man's resolution to prostitute his daughters not only demonstrates the family's desperation but also reminds modern-day readers of the precarious and often tragic nature of life in Late Antiquity. Emperors Augustus and Constantine are among those who prohibited parents from selling their children into slavery or prostitution, an indication itself that the practice was common.

Nicholas chose to intervene. He slipped by the man's house at night and tossed a bag of gold through the window. In the morning the father found the gold coins and decided to use them as dowry so that one of the girls might marry out of her plight. When Nicholas observed how the money had been handled, he returned by night with a second gift. Again, the gold became dowry for the second daughter.

When Nicholas returned yet a third time under cover of darkness, the father was prepared to discover the identity of his secret benefactor. When the bag of gold hit the floor the father sprang up and chased down the anonymous gift-giver. 'When he recognized who he was, he threw himself face-first at his feet with cries, and gave thanks to him over and over' (Michael n.d.: section 17).

From Antiquity, chapel frescoes and painted wood-panels reproduced the signature scene: Nicholas tossing his gift through the open window. In popular usage, St Nicholas came to be represented by three bags of gold, or more symbolically, by three gold discs or spheres.

In later retellings of the tale, minstrels and sermonizers embellished the plot by imagining that, upon arriving at the house, Nicholas found the windows barred shut. He was compelled to drop the gold down the chimney where it landed in the girls' stockings hung by the fireplace to dry. Eventually, French nuns in the twelfth century began to re-enact the story by setting out gifts for poor children and signing them from St Nicholas (Bowler 2005:18). Dutch and German parents followed the nun's lead and left little presents—an orange, a handful of nuts, a candy cane—for their children. Children dutifully set out their shoes or stockings on the eve of St Nicholas for the purpose, along with a carrot for Nicholas's horse, Amerigo.

Praxis de stratelatis

In his own day and time, people remembered and venerated Nicholas for attributes other than his generosity. In point of fact, the earliest story to gain popularity was not the three dowries but the *praxis de stratelatis*, the story of the military officers (Anrich 1913: 67–91). By the early 500s, the *praxis de stratelatis* circulated widely in Greek and Latin territories. Clues within the story date its events to the year 331 (English 2012: 137). If this date is correct, two important pieces of historical context should be highlighted. First, the date indicates that the episode occurred late in Nicholas's life, after a long and distinguished record of service to his community and church. Second, it occurred during the eventful reign of Constantine, the emperor who ended persecution against Christians and consolidated the Roman Empire with policies advantageous to Christians. In the lands under Constantine's rule, public funds built new churches while at the same time traditional shrines and temples were emptied and dismantled, even in Myra.

The *praxis de stratelatis* opens with Nicholas going down to Andriake, the port of Myra, to quell a riot between local residents and a recently docked Roman military convoy. Nicholas negotiates with three military officers, Nepotianus, Ursus, and Eupoleonis and is able to resolve the matter peaceably. He then returns to the city centre to halt a beheading ordered by a judge who had accepted bribes in exchange for a conviction. In the background stand the three military officers watching Nicholas at work. They do not forget what they see.

The three military officers and their Roman convoy depart from Myra, complete their expedition, and in the end return to Constantinople. Upon arrival they are immediately arrested on the accusation of treason and conspiracy to assassinate the emperor. From their prison cells, they pray to the God of Nicholas for help. A vision of Nicholas appears to Emperor Constantine and his prefect, Ablabius. In the morning Constantine summons the officers and accuses them of sorcery, but when the men relate what they had witnessed in Myra, Constantine orders them released.

The *praxis de stratelatis* was for many generations the most widespread and popular story about Nicholas, as can be demonstrated by the vast number of historical church frescoes, sculpture work, and stained glass depicting scenes from the story: Nicholas grabbing the sword of the executioner and visiting the dreams of the emperor while three imprisoned men pray.

In the Middle Ages, these churchly images gave rise to other more imaginative and gruesome tales. In one such tale regularly reproduced by troops of actors on stage, three boys are lured inside by an evil butcher (or innkeeper, depending on the version of the story) where they are hacked and stuffed into pickling barrels (Jones 1978: 128–40). Nicholas arrives on the scene to play the role of detective, 'taking the lid off' the foul crime and restoring the boys to life.

The Council of Nicaea

Nicholas of Myra attended the celebrated Council of Nicaea in the year 325. This historic gathering of bishops met at the behest of Emperor Constantine and produced the most widely recognized creed of Christianity, the Nicene Creed. Scholars have questioned Nicholas's presence at the council, and with good reason. The earliest and most reliable lists of attendees do not include his name. In the late twentieth century, the Dominican scholar Gerardo Cioffari performed an exhaustive study of the matter. He investigated sixteen extant lists of attendees and found that Nicholas does not appear in ten lists, all of which record less than 300 bishops in attendance at Nicaea. His name does appear in the six lists that name over 300, an attendance figure closer to the probable number (Cioffari 1987: 23–9).

Nicholas's presence at the council gave rise to one of the most memorable legends about him: that he punched a heretic while at the council. In the most well-known version of the story, the heretic Arius stands before the council of bishops and the Emperor Constantine and spouts false teachings about Christ. Nicholas listens until he can contain himself no longer. He steps forward and strikes Arius in the jaw. For his rash act in the presence of dignitaries and the emperor, the bishops deprive Nicholas of his episcopal robes and mitre. They then temporarily imprison him and guards burn off his beard. But that night, Mother Mary and Jesus appear to Nicholas and commend his zeal for the truth. They restore his beard and his garments. His fellow bishops take it as proof of his righteousness and discernment.

The story persists today by way of online memes featuring the stern looking Byzantine saint with the tagline: 'I came to hand out presents and punch heretics, and I just ran out of presents' or 'I saw Santa punching Arius'. Unfortunately, the tale has no basis in history. No record of the incident can be found prior to the fourteenth century, more than a thousand years after Nicholas's death. In the late 1300s, the Venetian chronologist Petrus de Natalibus recorded perhaps the earliest version (Anrich 1913: 459). The tale quickly caught hold and became part of the standard Nicholas lore.

Spreading Popularity

Sources agree that Nicholas of Myra died on 6 December of natural causes in old age. The medieval hagiographer Jacobus de Voragine assigned this event to the year 343 (de Voragine 1969: 21, Cioffari 1987: 206–7). Nicholas's feast day, 6 December, quickly became a grand opportunity for parades, dramatic impersonations, gift-exchanges, and family meals. It served as the first major holiday in a season filled with feasting, from the Greek Lenaea to the Roman Saturnalia, the Germanic Yuletide, the Irish Wren Day, the Latin Christian feast of the Nativity of Jesus, 25 December, and New Year's Day, 1 January.

Soon Nicholas's popularity extended far beyond the reach of a regional saint. By the mid-500s, a church was dedicated to him in the harbour of Constantinople and Latin authors in Rome were collecting and reproducing tales of his deeds. His notoriety spread to the remote corners of Britain and Spain and as far east as Russia, where he became especially beloved by the people and in the life of the Orthodox Church. Parents named their children Nikolai, Nicole, Colette, Colin, Nick, and Klaus. Churches, boats, businesses, and cities took their names from Nicholas and were dedicated to him. His patronage extended to a wide range of professions and stations in life, including apothecaries, bakers, barrel-makers, boatmen, brides, butchers, captives, dock workers, fire-fighters, the falsely accused, judges, law-clerks, longshoremen, merchants, murderers, newlyweds, old maids, orphans, pawnbrokers, perfumers, pilgrims, sailors, and travellers.

New legends sprang up to celebrate his quick action, sound judgement, and tender mercy: Nicholas rescued sailors caught on the stormy sea, restored stolen merchandise, guided poor souls lost at sea or in mountain passes, miraculously returned the boy Basileos to his parents from Arab captivity, discovered coins hidden in a hollow staff, supplied a pauper with a gold coin on St Nicholas Day, punished a man who broke a golden-cup vow, and restored an accidentally boiled infant to life.

Three reasons might explain the quick swell of devotion to Nicholas beginning in the early Middle Ages. First, Myra was on route to the Holy Land. Pilgrims voyaging by boat to the sacred biblical sites frequently stopped over at Myra. Second, pilgrims who came to Myra were awed and blessed by the manna, myrrh, or ointment (as it was variously known) collected from the tomb of Nicholas. Pilgrims bottled and used it as holy water. Thirdly and most significantly, sailors, boatmen, dock-workers, and those who operated in sea travel fervently devoted themselves to Nicholas as their patron saint. The devotion of this particular segment of the population had significant results. As seamen travelled from port to port, they shared tales of maritime miracles, wore Nicholas medallions, kept small wooden icons on their ships, threw 'Nicholas bread' on the water at the start of a voyage, prayed to the saint for protection, and thanked him with votive offerings upon return. They named their ships for him as well as islands and harbours they discovered. In Greenland the first cathedral erected by Vikings was dedicated to him; Christopher Columbus named a port in Haiti after him; Spanish settlers bequeathed his name to a township in Florida.

By the end of the Middle Ages, his image appeared inside thousands of churches around the world, on Russian and Greek icons, in stained-glass representations in France and Britain, and on mosaics, frescoes, canvases, and medallions in Germany, Switzerland, and Italy. Nicholas became the second most popular name for a church dedication after Mother Mary. At the time of writing, his name currently appears on fifty-two churches in Australia, five in Tanzania, seventeen in China, eighteen in Argentina, eighty-three in Canada, nearly 400 in the US, and over 500 in Russian territories (Myers n.d.).

The Fate of Myra

But, what became of the tomb and the church in Myra? From 2009 to the present, Professor Sema Doğan of Hacettepe University has led a major effort to excavate, study, and preserve the Church of St Nicholas, known locally as the Aziz Nikolaos Müzesi. Meanwhile, Professor Nevzat Çevik of Akdeniz University has focused on Myra and its port Andriake, culminating in 2016 with the opening of new museum facilities and new finds at Andriake (Cevik 2017; Akyürek 2016). While the oldest wall of the St Nicholas Church in Myra dates to the sixth century (the time when Nicholas's popularity began to soar), much of the construction seen today came in the tenth to twelfth century. Tragically, two major misfortunes befell the church around the same time.

First, in 1087, sailors from Bari, Italy, arrived in port at Myra and entered the church under the guise of pilgrims. Once inside however, they drew out axes and hammers, smashed open the tomb, lifted the bones, and transferred them to Bari. The event, piously referred to as the 'translation of the relics', is commemorated in Italy every 9 May as the Festa di Bari, where Nicholas is known as St Nicholas of Bari (Jones 1978: 172–209; English 2012: 180–4). A dozen years later, in 1099, Venetian sailors also paid a visit to Myra and took the remaining bone fragments left behind by the Barians (Martino 1994). These are now interned at San Nicolò al Lido in Venice.

A second misfortune to visit the Church of St. Nicholas in Myra came less than two hundred years later, in the latter half of the thirteenth century, when the Myros River changed course (Cevik 2017; Akyürek 2016). In a short span of time, the rerouted river buried the ancient city and the Church of St Nicholas under six to nine metres worth of deposited silt. Nevertheless, by that time Nicholas's fame and legend had already spread well beyond Myra and the province of Lycia to all corners of the Christian world.

Here Comes Santa Claus

On 6 December 1810, John Pintard (1759–1844) distributed a pamphlet to the New-York Historical Society meeting featuring a woodcut image of St Nicholas in bishop's attire, complete with a halo and the emblem of the cross stitched on his cassock. Pintard, a classic promoter for social causes, solicited the image of Nicholas in order to redirect holiday attention from carousing and boozing toward thoughts of good deeds, rewards and punishments, and the upbringing of children. In the woodcut, Nicholas holds a money purse in one hand and a birch rod in the other. He is flanked by a beehive on his right and a dog on his left, symbols of industry and fidelity, respectively. Pintard chose this saint as the city's patron for an additional reason: he hoped to reinvigorate New York's Dutch heritage marked by St Nicholas Day celebrations of family meals and gifts for children (Nissenbaum 1997: 49, 56, 70).

In America, St Nicholas quickly shed his traditional European ecclesial garb for a new look. Washington Irving (1783–1859), also a member of the New-York Historical Society, published a humorous *History of New-York*, in which Nicholas appeared with 'a low, broad-brimmed hat, a huge pair of Flemish trunk hose and a pipe' (Irving 1881: 96). James K. Paulding (1778–1860) extended Irving's comic vision in 1836 with his own fictional stories and exaggerated the odd Dutch appearance of the saint even more (Paulding 1836). In 1821, a New York publisher produced *The Children's Friend: A New Year's Present, to Little Ones from Five to Twelve*, the first lithographed book published in America and the first to picture Santa Claus, here called 'Santeclaus'. The lithograph plates showed the saint wearing a coat and a tall fur cap and driving a sleigh of toys 'O'er chimney tops, and tracks of snow, To bring his yearly gifts to you' (Bowler 2005: 35–7).

The definitive depiction of this new and Americanized St Nicholas came in 1823 when *The Sentinel* of Troy, New York, published an anonymous poem. It began with these memorable lines:

> 'Twas the night before Christmas, when all thro' the house,
> Not a creature was stirring, not even a mouse;
>   (Foster 2000: 222–3; Nissenbaum 1997: 76–7)

Initially, the poem was given the title, 'An Account of a Visit from Saint Nicholas', but it soon came to be known by its celebrated opening phrase. Historian Gerry Bowler has observed that the poem's 'impact on the development of Santa Claus and Christmas itself cannot be overstated' (Bowler 2005: 42). At just the time when Christmas festivities were shifting from the streets and pubs to hearth and home, 'The Night Before Christmas' set the holiday scene by the family fireplace.

The issue of the poem's authorship has received scrutiny in recent years. Vassar College professor Don Foster has presented significant evidence to demonstrate that Clement Clarke Moore (1779–1863) did not in fact pen 'The Night Before Christmas' (Foster 2000: 221–75). According to Foster and other scholars who have studied the matter, the more likely author was an eccentric Dutch American named Henry Livingston (1748–1828). Livingston regularly submitted quirky poems, engravings, and satires to newspapers and magazines under whimsical pseudonyms like 'Henry Hotspur' and 'Peter Pumpkineater' or anonymously, as in the case of 'The Night Before Christmas'.

As the poem gained in popularity over the next ten years, someone finally ventured a guess as to the author of this beloved poem: Clement Clarke Moore, perhaps because Moore was a well-known public figure who occasionally dabbled in poetry. Historian Stephen Nissenbaum describes Moore as 'an old-style country gentleman, a patrician man of leisure' who owed his financial security to his large, lucrative, and inherited Manhattan estate, Chelsea (Nissenbaum 1997 : 67). Moore did not respond to the attribution one way or the other and the true author, Livingston, could not contest it because he had died in 1828. Livingston's children protested on his behalf to no avail.

The issue might have been easily resolved by producing the original autograph of the poem in the penmanship of either Livingston or Moore, but unfortunately, no such proof exists. Suspiciously, Moore wrote to Norman Tuttle, the former owner of the *Troy Sentinel*, in 1844 to ask where, how, and from whom the newspaper had obtained a copy of the poem. But the poem had come by way of a third party, and Tuttle never knew the identity of the author. Only at this point did Moore accept responsibility for the poem. If Foster's argument is correct, Moore ultimately claimed authorship because it became too awkward and personally embarrassing for a prominent gentleman like Moore, thrust suddenly into the limelight, to disown the poem.

The case for Henry Livingston and against Clement Clarke Moore must be constructed from a close analysis of the style, rhythm, and word-choice within the poem itself and a comparison of the poem with the other written works of the two men. Two findings from Foster's analysis bear repeating. In the initial printing, the list of reindeer names included Dunder and Blixem, two Dutch expressions that would have made sense to Livingston but not to Moore, who knew German but not Dutch. Later printings changed the names to Donder and Blitzen (Foster 2000: 265–6). Secondly, in the poem's original ending, St Nick calls out 'Happy Christmas to all', not 'Merry Christmas to all', as it often appears in later editions. Editors changed the wording from 'Happy' to 'Merry' most likely because 'Merry Christmas' was a much more common greeting than 'Happy Christmas' and because it sounded better lyrically. Why, then, would the original author have used the expression, 'Happy Christmas'? As it happens, 'Happy Christmas' was a peculiar expression of Henry Livingston, as can be demonstrated from his personal correspondence. Clement Clarke Moore, by contrast, never greeted anyone, in personal letters or public writings, with either expression (Foster 2000: 261; also see Jones 1954: 357–83; Jones 1978: 348).[1]

The issue of authorship aside, perhaps the most surprising and innovative aspect of 'The Night Before Christmas' is the physical appearance of Nicholas himself. The poem's description of Nicholas's clothing, 'dress'd all in fur' and 'tarnish'd with ashes and soot' brings to mind a rather frightening Germanic predecessor, variously called Aschen Klaus (Ash Claus) or Pelznichol (Furry Claus), Ru-klaus (Rough Claus), Pelze-Nicol, Belsnickel, Belschnickle, or Bellsschniggle (Miles [1912] 1975: 230–2; Restad 1995: 50; Siefker [1997] 2006). Twigs and leaves stuck out from his hair and beard and soot smudged his face. Dressed in fur-skins and patched rags, it was the custom of this creature of the woods to go from house to house. Jingling bells sewn onto his costume announced his approach. He carried a whip to frighten naughty children and a bag of nuts to toss to the well behaved. The overall effect ranged from terrifying through

---

[1] The authorship question is by no means settled. The majority position still favours Clement Clarke Moore as the true author, an opinion shared by other authors in this volume.

strange and exciting to amusing. In 'The Night Before Christmas', St Nick has some of the physical characteristics of the traditional Pennsylvanian Germanic Pelznichol/ Belsnickel, but, importantly, none of the fearsome aspects. The eyes that twinkle and dimples that stay merry assure us we have 'nothing to dread' (Foster 2000: 222; Nissenbaum 1996: 77; Siefker [1997] 2006: 165–190).

'The Night Before Christmas' does not show Nicholas as a stern bishop, a mischievous Dutchman, or a Germanic wild-man of the woods, but as 'a right jolly old elf'. He drives a reindeer-pulled sleigh to the rooftops where he then drops down chimneys and into homes. He has not come to judge character or spook children, but 'like a peddler just opening his pack' he has dropped in to fill stockings with goodies (Foster 2000: 222; Nissenbaum 1996: 77).

Domestication and Commerce

As historians Penne Restad and Judith Flanders have separately demonstrated, the forces of domestication and commerce emphasized Nicholas's role as a magical bearer of gifts to children (Restad 1995: 123–42; Flanders 2017). Diaries, letters, fictional accounts, and artwork from the time confirm the tradition: late on Christmas Eve, St Nick would visit each home, riding on his sleigh. He would slip magically down the chimney and place gifts in stockings and under the Christmas tree. He might pause for cookies and milk, but would quickly move on to the next house without being seen. According to Restad and Flanders, this is Christmas domesticated: the central event in the Christmas season was now located in the home, not the church or the public square or the pub. This is also Christmas commercialized: the routine by which parents bought toys and candies and books from department stores for their children was elevated, disguised, and ultimately separated from their commercial origins by the Christmas ritual of wrapping, hiding, and finding presents on Christmas morning. In Santa's hands, mass-produced commodities for parental purchase became specially prepared gifts for children (Restad 1995: 129–30, 150).

Throughout the nineteenth century Santa's look and costuming took a number of forms, especially in the imaginative drawings of Thomas Nast (1840–1902), the German-born illustrator for *Harper's Weekly* (Nast 1890). Nicholas's name began to morph along with his appearance. Alternate spellings ranged from Kris Kringle (from the German Protestant Christkind) to various spellings of Sinterklaas, Saint Claas, Sancte Claus, Sandy Claus, Klaas, Sinti Klass, and Santaclaw. The name had been evolving at least since 1773, when a New York paper, *Rivington's Gazeteer*, noted the anniversary of St Nicholas, 'otherwise called St. a Claus' (Jones 1978: 330).

The needs of commerce standardized the identity of Santa Claus more than any other social or creative force during this era. By the early 1900s, advertisements, playing cards, toys, and magazines displayed the red suit uniform, black belt and boots, portly belly, and large white beard. The first Christmas card printed in the United States was a department store advertisement that illustrated Santa Claus with a family opening gifts. The holiday message read: *Pease's Great Varety [sic] Store in the Temple of Fancy*. Perhaps no one harnessed the marketing power of Santa Claus more effectively than Haddon Sundblom (1899–1976). Hired in 1931 by the Coca-Cola Co., Sundblom painted warm scenes of Santa with Coke in hand over the next thirty years and in so doing concretized the image of the American Santa Claus in iconic fashion (Bowler 2005: 121–4).

By the late 1800s, Santa Claus lookalikes could be seen ringing bells on sidewalks, waving at crowds from parades, greeting families in department stores, and taking gift requests from children. A cottage industry was born. The seasonal demand for Santa impersonators created a need for training in the craft. Charles W. Howard (1896–1966), who appeared in the Macy's Thanksgiving Day parade for nearly twenty years, opened a Santa Claus School in Albion, New York in 1937. Hundreds of Santa-would-be's earned BSC. degrees (Bachelor of Santa Claus). Soon other training centres and professional associations opened and organized. Today, seasonal Santas participate in conferences, workshops, associations, and meetings in New York City, Lavonia, Michigan, Gatlinburg, Tennessee, and Branson, Missouri, where, for example, more than 500 converge annually for the 'Discover Santa' gathering (Meehan 2016).

By the 1870s, children began mailing letters to Santa Claus. These letters often went unopened and unanswered until the first decade of the 1900s when various volunteer groups such as the Santa Claus Association of Elizabeth A. Phillips in Philadelphia, John D. Gluck's organization in New York, and the Silver Belt Santa Claus Association in Arizona tackled the ever-growing pile (Palmer 2016: 33–6). Citizens in the town of Santa Claus, Indiana (established 1855) devoted thousands of volunteer hours composing handwritten responses to letters delivered to the town post office.

Eight-year-old Virginia O'Hanlon bypassed the North Pole and directed her own correspondence to the newspaper: 'Some of my friends say there is no Santa Claus. Papa says, "If you see it in THE SUN it's so."' The printed reply, 'Yes, Virginia, there is a Santa Claus', has become the most reprinted editorial of all time, inspiring a musical cantata and an Emmy-awarded TV special. The author of *The Sun*'s editorial, Francis P. Church, explained to Ms Virginia that Santa Claus 'exists as certainly as love and generosity and devotion exist' (Church 1897). The tension between doubt and belief conveyed in this famous newspaper exchange has been played out on screen in countless Santa Claus movies: for example, Edmund Gwenn's *Miracle on 34th Street* (1947), Tim Allen's *The Santa Clause* (1994), and Will Ferrell's *Elf* (2003).

As the personality and character of Santa/Nicholas expanded and evolved in the twentieth century, new companions introduced themselves: Mrs Claus, elves, and talking snowmen. In the United States, Rudolf the Red Nosed Reindeer is perhaps the most popular and beloved new character to the Santa Claus story. Created by Robert L. May in 1939 for a Montgomery Ward department store promotional, Johnny Marks adapted the story into a song recorded by Gene Autry in 1949. The song sold 25 million copies and spurred the creation of a much-beloved stop-motion animated television special in 1964.

Across the Globe

Internationally, St Nicholas-related customs abound. In many Christian and formerly Christian regions, St Nicholas still strides about in bishop's robes, stole, and mitre, giving him a stately and religious presence. He is often accompanied by mischievous or clownish sidekicks such as the chain-rattling Krampus in Austria, Père Fouettard in parts of France, and the unwashed Schmutzli in Switzerland. In Slovak and Czech towns, children peek out from behind their parents to see the spectacle of a devil enter their homes, restrained by an angel or by the goodly St Nicholas himself.

Other European areas have created their own, unique gift-giver in place of St Nicholas or Santa Claus. In most of France, a tall and slim Père Noël wearing a white fur-trimmed hooded robe travels with his donkey to deliver presents, while in the British Isles, Father Christmas personifies the merriment of the season as he has since the fifteenth century. During the long winter of Russia's experiment with Communism, the Communists replaced St Nicholas with Dyed Moroz (Grandfather Frost). Since the collapse of the Soviet Union, St Nicholas has returned but Dyed Moroz has not disappeared. He has instead been repurposed and popularized through commercial use, becoming the Russian equivalent of Santa Claus.

As for the American Santa Claus, he has been embraced outside the United States with the same love–hate as any other American export. Families around the world enjoy Santa Claus movies and television shows, and many incorporate Santa Claus gift-giving into their own traditions. Nevertheless, certain sectors have resisted Santa for religious or cultural reasons. Gerry Bowler has documented the clashes in his recent *Christmas in the Crosshairs*. In one example, he notes banners hung in the central city of Xi'an, China, in 2014, that read: 'Strive to be outstanding sons and daughters of China, oppose kitsch Western holidays' (Bowler 2016: 152).

In recent years, a different kind of controversy has bedeviled the Dutch Netherlands. The Dutch cherish their own elaborate traditions of Sinterklaas, who dresses not as Santa Claus but as a bishop in full ecclesial regalia. He arrives by boat in early November from Spain and rides his horse through the streets handing out Spanish oranges. On 5 December, 'Sinterklaasavond', the eve of St Nicholas, families celebrate with a big meal and presents—for this reason it is also called 'Pakjesavond' (Presents Eve). The cause for dispute lies with Sinterklaas's travelling companion, Zwarte Piet, 'Black Pete'.

Zwarte Piet first appeared in an 1850 book as a Moorish servant travelling with Sinterklaas from Spain. Today, Zwarte Pieten characters parade in garish courtly attire or harlequin costumes, large feathered hats, and, controversially, blackened faces. Although the Zwarte Pieten remain popular with most Dutch, internal and external pressures to change the tradition have steadily intensified since about 2013. Municipalities such as Amsterdam, Rotterdam, and The Hague, and regions (including the entire country of Belgium), have prohibited certain racist and offensive features of the Pieten: no more exaggerated lips, Afro black wigs, or gold earrings. In many places, the blackface has been reduced to a few chimney smudges or eliminated altogether. Zwarte Piet has become Schoorsteen Piet (Chimney Pete), or just Piet (Myers n.d.).

History suggests that the traditions and customs of St Nicholas will not stop evolving with the times. Nevertheless, in some form and fashion, he will no doubt continue to visit homes and gladden hearts.

References and Further Reading

Anrich, Gustav (1913, 1917). *Hagios Nikolaos: Der heilige Nikolaus in der griechischen Kirche*. Leipzig: B. G. Teubner.
Akyürek, T. Engin (2016). 'Andriake: The Port of Myra in Late Antiquity'. *Trade in Byzantium: Papers from the Third International Sevgi Gonul Byzantine Studies Symposium*: 465–87.
Bios tou hagiou Nikolaou, The Life of Saint Nicholas of Sion (1984). Translated by Ihor Ševčenko and Nancy Patterson Ševčenko. Brookline: Hellenic College Press.
Bowler, Gerry (2005). *Santa Claus: A Biography*. Toronto: McClelland & Stewart.
Bowler, Gerry (2016). *Christmas in the Crosshairs: Two Thousand Years of Denouncing and Defending the World's Most Celebrated Holiday*. New York: Oxford University Press.
Cevik, Nevzat (2017). 'Myra: The Hidden Metropolis of Lycia', *Actual Archaeology Magazine*, 19: 39–51.
Church, Francis (1897). 'Yes, Virginia, there is a Santa Claus', *The Sun*, September 21. Available at http://www.newseum.org/exhibits/online/yes-virginia/ (accessed 20 March 2020).
Cioffari, Gerardo (1987). *San Nicola nella Critica Storica*. Bari: Centro Studi Nicolaiani.
English, Adam C. (2012). *The Saint Who Would Be Santa Claus*. Waco: Baylor University Press.
Falconi, Niccolò Carminio (ed.) (1751). *Sancti Confessoris Pontificis et Celeberrimi Thaumaturgi Nicolai Acta Primigenia*. Naples.
Flanders, Judith (2017). *Christmas: A Biography*. New York: St. Martin's Press.
Foster, Don (2000). *Author Unknown*. New York: Henry Holt.
Irving, Washington (1881). *The Works of Washington Irving, Volume 7: Knickerbocker's History of New York*. New York: Putnam's Sons.
Jones, Charles W. (1954). 'Knickerbocker Santa Claus', *The New-York Historical Society Quarterly*, XXXVIII, no. 4: 357–83.
Jones, Charles W. (1978). *Saint Nicholas of Myra, Bari, and Manhattan*. Chicago: University of Chicago Press.
Martino, Luigi (1994). 'San Nicola: La Grande Avventura.' Available at http://web.tiscali.it/luigimartino/ (accessed 20 March 2020).
Meehan, Mary (2016). 'Christmas in July—Inside a Santa Summer Camp', *National Geographic*. Available at https://news.nationalgeographic.com/2016/07/santa-claus-convention-branson-missouri-christmas-photos/ (accessed 2 April 2020). https://news.nationalgeographic.com/2016/07/santa-claus-convention-branson-missouri-christmas-photos/ (accessed 20 March 2020).
Meisen, Karl (1931, 1981). *Nikolauskult und Nikolausbrauch im Abendlande*. Mainz: Pädagogischer Verlag Schwann Düsseldorf.

Michael the Archimandrite (n.d.). *Bios tou Nikolaou.* Translated by John Quinn and Roger Pearse. Available at http://www.stnicholascenter.org/pages/michael-the-archimandrite/ (accessed 20 March 2020).

Miles, Clement (1912, 1975). *Christmas Customs and Traditions.* New York: Dover.

Myers, Carol (n.d.). The St Nicholas Center. Available at http://www.stnicholascenter.org/ http://www.stnicholascenter.org/ (accessed 20 March 2020).

Nast, Thomas (1890). *Christmas Drawings for the Human Race.* New York.

Nissenbaum, Stephen (1997). *The Battle for Christmas: A Cultural History of America's Most Cherished Holiday.* New York: Vintage.

Palmer, Alex (2016). *The Santa Claus Man.* Guilford: Rowman & Littlefield.

Paulding James K. (1836). *The Book of Saint Nicholas.* New York: Harper and Brothers.

Restad, Penne (1995). *Christmas in America.* New York: Oxford University Press.

Siefker, Phyllis (1997, 2006). *Santa Claus, Last of the Wild Men.* Jefferson: McFarland.

de Voragine, Jacobus (1969). *Golden Legend.* Translated by Granger Ryan and Helmut Ripperger. New York: Arno.

CHAPTER 22

TREES AND DECORATIONS

DAVID BERTAINA

The Christmas tree has become an indispensable part of winter seasonal imagery. Its presence in the home epitomizes an authentic Christmas. And yet, a decorated tree in a home seems anachronistic in the context of commemorating a historical feast dedicated to the birth of Jesus Christ. How did trees become a necessary display at Christmas? This chapter explains how the Christmas tree and its decorations became the main characteristic of Christmas celebrations thanks to medieval liturgies and guilds, the early modern accumulation of wealth, domestic values, child-rearing attitudes, private life, and the modern advances of industrialization, marketing, and global commerce. These shifts over time explain how the celebration of the Nativity feast is expressed through the display of a tree which symbolizes a festal identity.

THE ROOTS OF THE CHRISTMAS TREE

The origins of the practice of bringing a tree into the home has long stumped scholars. Some have mistakenly claimed that the tree can be traced to Late Antique pagan tradition. In 1858 the Protestant thinker Johannes Marbach asserted without solid evidence that the tree was a pre-Christian German folk custom. In 1861, Paulus Cassel echoed the idea of its ancient origins and its nationalist implications. In both cases their goal was to demonstrate that the tree's alleged Teutonic pagan roots made it a shared symbol common to all Germans. The tree would represent a unified German identity and could serve as a point of domestic piety for both Catholics and Protestants (Perry 2010: 16). The myth was an imaginary link constructed and reinforced by nationalists to promote the German Fatherland. These sources were used by Alexander Tille in his 1893 book *Die Geschichte der Deutschen Weihnacht.* In the English language, Clement Miles (*Christmas in Ritual and Tradition, Christian and Pagan,* 1912) cited Tille's claims that the tree was derived from pre-Christian Teutonic folk custom. Readers have accepted these 'historicist fantasies' (Perry 2010: 55) for their accounts of the Christmas tree, and the myth continues to be repeated by contemporary media today.

Other writers have connected the origins of the Christmas tree with medieval Catholic tradition. According to a legend about Saint Boniface, he went to a sacred site with an oak tree dedicated to Thor and cut down the tree to use the timber for a chapel (Robinson 1916: 62–4). However, the original source does not mention the time of year, the existence of an evergreen fir tree, or any words of Boniface connected to the Nativity feast. Others have tried to connect the Protestant reformer Martin Luther with the tree's roots, reporting that during a walk he was astounded at the shining stars twinkling through evergreens, which motivated him to bring home a fir tree and light it with candles at Christmas. But this legend only appears in the nineteenth century.

The Christmas tree tradition most likely developed from a combination of medieval liturgical traditions and guild patronage to local communities, which over time were transformed into a private practice beginning in the sixteenth century. In the medieval period, many people could not read and write, so plays were a way to communicate biblical stories. In that time, a Paradise Tree was set up for plays to represent the Tree of the Knowledge mentioned in Genesis 2:9. The actor playing Adam would later parade through the streets of the town with the tree. The tree symbolized humanity's downfall but also represented the tree of the cross, which would become the salvation of all people. Medieval tradition even claimed that Adam had taken a branch from the Tree of Knowledge and Jesus' cross was made from that tree. The trees were decorated with apples, representing the Fall of humankind, while round pastry wafers on the tree symbolized the Eucharistic host as the path to salvation. The plays were performed on 24 December, which was the feast day for Adam and Eve. The display of the Paradise Tree was meant to symbolize the Garden of Eden where they lived. The liturgical calendar placed their feast day here to remind Christians that Jesus' birth was a conduit of salvation allowing humanity to return to its perfect state in the Garden.

Medieval guilds sought to sponsor these mystery plays in order to build their prestige in the community. These groups connected the Church to the public, and guilds made a somewhat solemn occasion into one with more exuberance. This may have led to the Paradise Tree becoming not just a prop in a play but a guild-sponsored exhibition. As early as 1419, a baker's guild in Freiburg references a tree in the local Hospital of the Holy Spirit decorated with apples, wafers, gingerbread, and tinsel (Brunner 2012: 3). A tree was set up outside the town hall of Tallinn, Estonia in 1441. In 1444 in London, a standard was set up in a square with holly and ivy at Christmas (Bowler 2000: 227). There are references to trees decorated with apples, thread, and straw in Riga, Latvia in 1510 and in Reval, Estonia in 1514, also created by merchants' guilds. In 1570 in Bremen, a guild installed a tree in their hall, filled with apples, nuts, pretzels, and paper flowers (Brunner 2012: 5). Thus, guilds from the fifteenth and sixteenth centuries played an important role in introducing the tree to the public. However, none of these trees were dedicated to Christmas in the home.

The most certain historical knowledge we have of the tree used in home decoration during Christmas comes from the sixteenth-century German-speaking lands of the

Alsace region. There is a reference in 1531 to evergreens being sold in the markets there and then brought home (Snyder 1976: 11). The Strasbourg cathedral also displayed a tree ('Tannenbaum') in 1539. Other evidence suggests trees were popular, such as when Freiburg prohibited citizens from cutting down trees in 1554. A decree in 1561 in the Alsatian region permitted people to cut trees as long as they were no greater than eight shoe lengths (about 4 feet in height), which indicates smaller trees were popular for personal home use (Brunner 2012: 6). In 1605 in Strasbourg, a source notes that locals put fir trees in their homes, and they decorated them with paper roses, apples, flat wafers, gilded candies, and sugar figurines (Snyder 1976: 13). In Turckheim in Alsace, another ban was the first to refer to the tree as a 'Christmas tree' (*Weihnachtsbaum*) in 1611. In Germany, there were a variety of names for the tree besides *Weihnachtsbaum* (Christmas tree), including *Tannenbaum* (fir tree), *Christbaum* (Christ tree), *Lichterbaum* (light tree), and *Lebensbaum* (Tree of Life). The influence of the tree is clear from its earliest published critic, the Strasbourg theologian Johann Konrad Dannhauer who wrote in the 1640s:

> Among other trifles which are set up during Christmas time instead of God's word is the Christmas tree or fir tree which is put up at home and decorated with dolls and sugar... Whence comes the custom, I know not; it is child's play... Far better were it to point the children to the spiritual cedar-tree, Jesus Christ.
>
> (Snyder 1976: 14; Miles 1976: 265)

DEVELOPMENT OF AN IMAGE IN EUROPE

'O Tannenbaum' (which translates as 'fir tree' not 'Christmas tree') was a German folk song originally unrelated to Christmas. While the first verse was written from an anonymous author, the melody for the carol was first published in 1799, and the lyrics were first linked with the melody in 1820 thanks to folk song collector August Zarnack. Second and third stanzas were added in 1824 by the poet Ernst Anschütz and it was connected with the Christmas feast. Within two decades, the carol was well known across Germany and abroad (Collins 2006: 42–6). Such a carol could only appear after the popularization of the Christmas tree.

The display of the Christmas tree was propagated by wealthier urban families of German society. More affluent families during this period constructed homes with sitting/parlour rooms that provided space for tree displays. The tree was a nostalgic reminder of the realm of nature and agricultural folk life. During the seventeenth century, older homes with ceiling boards might hold decorated treetops hung upside down. In a description by Lisolette von der Pfalz, she recalled that boxwood trees would be placed in planters and decorated in her childhood home during the mid-seventeenth century.

Literature from this period played an instrumental role in disseminating tree rituals. Famed German writer Johann Wolfgang von Goethe wrote *The Sorrows of Young*

Werther (1774) in which he described the way that a Christmas tree would be decorated (Brunner 2012: 19). The Christmas tree was promoted as an authentic national folk tradition, making it easier to adopt across religious and national lines. Samuel Taylor Coleridge described a Christmas visit to Ratzeburg in 1798 in which he wrote that on Christmas Eve the children set up a Christmas yew bough on a table to unveil to the family (Brunner 2012: 50). Coleridge's account was influential because his story was published multiple times. In 1816, E. T. A. Hoffmann described a Christmas tree in his story about *The Nutcracker and the Mouse-King* (Hoffmann 1930: 13). The tree was meant to evoke feelings of surprise and enchantment for the children. By this point, the setting included all the essential components: an exotic and magical tree, a family parlour, an unveiling of the tree to the delight of the family, a childhood-centered experience, and a tree as the source of joy and spiritual renewal.

What is clear from these examples is that by the turn of the nineteenth century, the Christmas tree had become a ritualized object that bound families and peoples together. The common rituals included the decoration of the tree together, the unveiling of the tree on Christmas Eve, the emphasis on its display with candlelight, the distribution of presents in its branches, the production of seasonal foods and edible decorations, and scenery placed around the tree. Further, the tree was a top-down development. By class, trees were more common among royals and aristocrats along with middle-class people. By location, trees were more common in cities than in rural areas. By religion, the trees tended to be displayed among Protestants rather than Catholics. By geography, the tree began in central Europe and branched out to northern Europe first, then later to southern Europe.

The first Christmas tree in England of which we have record belonged to the Hanoverian Queen Charlotte, the wife of George III, who set up a yew tree with decorations and presents at Windsor Castle in December 1800. According to a witness, the tree was filled with 'sweetmeats, almonds and raisins in papers, fruits, and toys, most tastefully arranged, and the whole illuminated by small wax candles...after the company had walked round and admired the tree, each child obtained a portion of the sweets it bore, together with a toy, and then all returned home quite delighted' (Snyder 1976: 19). One of the most well-known images of the Christmas tree was published by the *Illustrated London News* in 1848 of Queen Victoria with her German husband Prince Albert alongside a table-top tree, adorned with ornaments and toys, with their joyful children looking on in delight. Earlier, in 1840, Prince Albert introduced a series of Christmas rituals tied to the tree at Windsor Castle. The crown also sponsored trees for military barracks, schools, and hospitals around the country. Later historians have argued that 'When the Christmas tree was introduced to England, it promoted the idea that the Germans were home-loving people, very capable of expressing simple and authentic emotions' (Armstrong 2008: 503). This idea of the tree as a common Anglo-Saxon tradition was also promoted in several publications. In 1840, *A Present from Germany: or, The Christmas Tree* was an English translation of a German story along with an account of the origins of the Christmas tree (Perry 1840). An anonymous 1844 children's book on *The Christmas Tree: A Present from Germany* recounts the story of a daughter and her father describing the German Christmas tree and how it should be displayed by her cousins in North America (Armstrong 2008: 493). Charles Dickens composed *A Christmas Tree* in 1850 describing the tree and its decorations as a 'pretty German toy' (Dickens 1907: 4), which 'made a lively realisation of the fancies of childhood' (Dickens 1907: 6).

Over the course of the first half of the nineteenth century, the Christmas tree established itself as a tradition beyond Germany to include Scandinavia, England, and America. The Christmas tree made a late appearance in France, with a reference in 1837 to its display by the German-born Helen of Mecklenburg (Bowler 2000: 226). The tradition spread into northern European cultures among the upper classes and was disseminated via media to other classes as trees became more accessible and affordable via markets created for the specific purpose of selling trees. By 1881 it was popular enough that Franz Liszt composed his piano arrangement known as 'Weihnachtsbaum' (Christmas Tree Suite). In predominantly Catholic countries the manger scene remained the most important symbol in the home until the twentieth century: 'Already in 1823 Archduke Johann of Austria complained that a tree decorated "with candles and an entire room full of toys of all kinds" threatened the sanctity of the traditional Nativity scene and disturbed the quiet moments of Christmas Eve prayer mandated by Catholic tradition' (Perry 2010: 37). In Spanish-speaking Catholic cultures, the tree was rare until the later twentieth century. Instead, the tree is displayed publicly by the local government, while the Nativity manger scene has been more common in homes.

The 'German Tree' in America

How did a country with religious misgivings about Christmas due to its Puritan heritage become a proponent of the tree? There is no Christmas tree in Clement Moore's 'A Visit from Saint Nicholas'. Most likely, German immigrants in the late eighteenth century brought the practice to Pennsylvania. Moravian settlers were known to use wooden pyramid trees adorned with evergreen boughs in Bethlehem, Pennsylvania in 1747. But the appearance of a Christmas tree in the home is first known only in the early nineteenth century. John Lewis Krimmel was a Philadelphia artist who made sketches around 1820 of a family gathered around a table-top holly tree, decorated with cookies, fruits, and figures and a village scene below with a fence around it, while delighted children looked on with joy. In 1821 Matthew Zahn also noted in his journal that a family member had gone out for Christmas trees in Lancaster County, Pennsylvania. In nearby York County, a bachelors' society set up a *Krischtkintle* (Christ-child) tree in 1823 for charity (Brunner 2012: 53). In Philadelphia, the *Saturday Evening Post* remarked in 1825 that Christmas trees with ornaments could be seen in windows (Snyder 1976: 28). These sources confirm that as German communities in Pennsylvania integrated with American society, their practice of displaying decorated Christmas trees was adopted by other Americans in the early 1800s.

Harriet Martineau has been credited with popularizing the Christmas tree in New England, in her 1832 retelling of the story of Charles (Karl) Follen and his family's Christmas tree. In her account, the Harvard College lecturer Follen opened his parlour on Christmas Eve to the delight of his children. The key point is not that the Follen family's tree was unique, but that Martineau's story appeared in the American Sunday School Union, introducing a national readership to the practice. The Christmas tree spectacle represented 'a private space, radically cut off from the pressures of the world outside and centered around the happiness of children' (Nissenbaum 1997: 187). The Christmas tree became the dispenser of gifts and a way for parents to direct children's behaviour. The tree was a shared familial endeavour whose sole purpose was for wonder and enjoyment. Family history, traditions, and values were embodied in the evergreen.

American literature also contributed to the popularization of the Christmas tree. Catherine Sedgwick published a story in 1836 that described a German maid decorating a Christmas tree (Snyder 1976: 31). Margaret Fuller in a *New York Tribune* editorial in 1844 already recognized the connection between the tree and children: 'The evergreen tree is often reared for the children on Christmas evening, and its branches cluster with little tokens that may at least, give them a sense that the world is rich, and that there are some in it who care to bless them' (Nissenbaum 1997: 216). These kinds of publications in America and Europe helped to contrast the ideal home with the artifice of public life. The Christmas tree in the home came to signify everything that was authentic in human relationships. It was the focus of domestic interaction, child-centered activities, handmade gifts, and moral instruction. Thus, the tree entered into American tradition as a pre-commercial German cultural tradition, but it was spread via the economic exchange of goods.

Charity has been connected to the Christmas tree since the nineteenth century. Displaying a decorated tree was an expensive endeavour. The Dorcas Society of York displayed an ornamented tree to raise funds for widows and orphans in 1830. Other entrepreneurs charged entry fees for people to view the Christmas tree.

Immigration was a major factor in the practice of displaying trees. As German immigration continued, it was common to hear of Christmas trees across the United States by the 1840s. By 1862 in San Francisco it was common for Christmas trees to be displayed there (Snyder 1976: 32). American tourism in Germany was also a factor in the diffusion of the tree. Tourists to Europe would bring back ornaments or other items for their homes. This exchange of people and goods led to a cultural transfer of German tree traditions abroad.

The nineteenth-century Romantic Movement provided the right factors to popularize the Christmas tree, including its predilection for nature as a symbol of purity, its emphasis on good morals, and promotion of sentimentality. In England, the Oxford Movement and Tractarians endorsed the Christmas tree as an ornate tradition. The tree had a religious connotation as it was adopted by Protestant Christians and later Catholics in America. Sermons, children's books, and other sources confirm the integration of the tree into the moral life of America. But by the end of the nineteenth century, the religious symbolism of the Christmas tree had been subsumed by its role in economic and civil life. In large parts of America and northern Europe, evergreens were accessible to meet the emerging demand for a tree. As Armstrong has argued:

> When contemporaries saw the Christmas tree, or the impact it had on children, they might express their joy, which was a word that could carry religious connotations in this period. Subsequently, however, the potential for religious meaning became largely obscured by convention and consumer desire.
> (Armstrong 2008: 496)

Mass-media marketing was one major reason for the increased popularity of trees and ornaments. The *New York Tribune* carried advertisements selling Christmas trees in 1843. In *Godey's Lady's Book*, their 1850 Christmas edition included an illustration taken from the 1848 image of Queen Victoria and Prince Albert with their royal tree, although the image was transformed to depict a well-to-do American family. Sara Josepha Hale, the editor of *Godey's*, published this image to influence how women were to ornament their homes for Christmas. For instance, in the 1860 *Godey's* Christmas edition, the magazine introduced the floor to ceiling tree, in contrast to a smaller tabletop tree (Snyder 1976: 33–4). Presents were to be moved beneath the tree, which allowed the tree to accommodate more ornaments. The *Golden Christmas Book*, for instance advised families about what specific items to display on their tree's branches.

Infrastructure development was also responsible for the wide availability of trees. Until the twentieth century, the Christmas tree was considered a status symbol, a sign of wealth and security. A tree in the home was already considered an old-fashioned tradition by the turn of the twentieth century, when perhaps 20 per cent of all families in the United States had Christmas trees. But due to railroads which transported trees, industrialization which created markets for trees and ornaments, mass marketing and commercialization of Christmas, increased purchasing power, Christmas tree farms, and electric lights, more than half of all Americans had Christmas trees in their homes by 1920.

In the 1957 story *How the Grinch Stole Christmas*, the Grinch steals Christmas trees from each family's home to take away the feast. Dr Suess' critique of materialism personified in the tree and its gifts was an acknowledgement that the tree had become an anchor for family life which consisted of material exchanges of goods. But at the same time, 'Today's Christmas tree is one of the few purely aesthetic objects created by families and individuals' (Marling 2000: 175). T. S. Eliot emphasized its novelty in 'The Cultivation of Christmas Trees', remarking: 'The child wonders at the Christmas Tree: let him continue in the spirit of wonder at the Feast as an event not accepted as a pretext' (Eliot 1956: 1).

The tree caused tremendous change to the setting of Christmas in the home. The tree was part of a standardization process, in which moral and domestic concerns, in contrast to public rowdiness, became the dominant trend in the Christmas celebration. A novel addition in the eighteenth century, trees are now considered normative to the

Christmas celebration. The centre of the celebration has been transferred from the Nativity crèche to the Christmas tree. Trees have become entertainment pieces as well. 'Rockin' around the Christmas Tree' (1958) by Brenda Lee indicates how the tree has become a homegrown American tradition. The tree augmented—for some, even replaced—liturgical ritual and domestic piety with a private family event that is more sentimental and child focused.

Decorations and Traditions

In the film *Elf* (2003), Buddy the Elf spruces up a tree, along with the entire room, to extravagant excess and to the delight of everyone at Gimbel's department store. The scene reminds us that tree decorating serves a therapeutic purpose. Decorating addresses a key need for human connection with surrounding family and friends and community. Most early decorations were made in the home, and many were edible. One of the oldest references to decorations on a tree comes from 1605 in Strasbourg. The tree was trimmed with paper roses to represent the Virgin Mary, apples to represent the Paradise Tree of Life, pastry wafers to represent the Eucharist, different types of fruits, and dried and pastry-style candied ornaments (Bowler 2000: 227). The treats would be eaten off the tree between Christmas and 6 January (The Feast of the Three Kings). The tradition was meant to evoke a reminder of the Magi's visit to Bethlehem with their gifts, which is still commemorated in some places in Europe and elsewhere.

Several types of German cookies were placed upon branches. Matzebaum, marzipan, and springerle were made into Christmas-themed designs as well as shortbread, gingerbread, spice, and sugar cookies. Apples and nuts, most often gilded, were displayed on trees to catch the eye. Popcorn became common in the 1860s, and later cranberries were added. Oranges were also added to trees, perhaps in connection with their distribution on 6 December for the feast of Saint Nicholas. Sugar confections and candies, such as pears and apricots, were popular because they could remain on trees for an extended time. Perhaps the most successful sweet introduced was the candy cane (Snyder 1976: 45–52).

The global transport of mass-produced ornaments, bought in stores, and gifted everywhere, altered the image of the Christmas tree. Industrialization provided a dizzying variety of options for sprucing up a tree. Tin and lead were used to make stars, crosses, and flowers. Wax moulds were made of the child Jesus and various figures. Tinsel was cut into designs using silver and lead foil. Three-dimensional embossed cardboard images known as 'Dresden' ornaments were popular. Glass ornaments from Germany became one of the most popular items across Europe and America by the 1860s. They were made in the shape of red glass balls to represent apples, or gold balls in the likeness of stars, or shaped into beads, icicles, pinecones, and candies. Tree toppers have varied over time, but ornaments of the angel Gabriel or the Star of Bethlehem are most common (Snyder 1976: 55–69).

Candles made from beeswax or tallow have been a regular feature on Christmas trees. As early as 1765, Goethe mentions a tree with candles in Leipzig (Brunner 2012: 41). Candles were lit upon the tree in the morning or at night, but never for too long due to the fire hazard. Some candle holders were made with counterweights while spring-clip holders were developed in 1879. The first electric lights appeared on a tree in 1882, and lights became affordable to middle-class buyers during the 1920s. In the aftermath of the Second World War, bubble lights were introduced. At the start of the twenty-first century, the advent of LED lights has changed the glow of Christmas trees, and light aesthetics continue to change over time.

Different trees have been used for decoration according to time and place, including the yew, boxwood, Scotch pine, Nordmann fir, silver fir, Norway spruce, Douglas fir, Fraser fir, white spruce, balsam fir, Eastern white pine, Colorado blue spruce and several other types. Live trees were placed in planters or wooden pieces were nailed to the bottom of the tree, or a tree was inserted into a stool with a hole in the middle. The Christmas tree stand spread rapidly after its introduction. By 1880, screws were introduced to the stand so that the tree would be firmer, and by 1899 stands were made to hold water. Tree skirts also became common during the latter half of the nineteenth century.

Christmas Trees in Public

In the 1965 *Peanuts* Christmas special, Charlie Brown introduces his audience at a play to a miserable spruce branch, adorned with a single red ball ornament. Despite mockery from others, the *Peanuts* gang reminds us that at that moment the tree transforms from a pathetic branch into a sacred symbol at the centre of public attention. In addition to the home, Christmas trees are displayed in churches, schools, markets, community centres, and civil locations.

In 1856, Franklin Pierce became the first American President to set up a Christmas tree at the White House. By 1895, the White House Christmas tree was decorated with electric lights. In 1923, Calvin Coolidge started the tradition of displaying a National Christmas Tree which is selected each year. In addition to sacred and civil sites, sometimes war zones have been homes to trees. During the First World War in 1914, the Germans and Allies unofficially instituted a Christmas Truce that involved the display of Christmas trees on the German front. During the Cold War in the 1950s, the West Germans put up illuminated 'Christ trees' on the Berlin Wall as a critique of the religious repression carried out by communist East Germany (Perry 2010: 246–7).

The appearance or disappearance of trees in public has also been tied to politics. The Soviet Union banned the Christmas tree from 1928 to 1935, only to allow its return as the New Year tree. Cuba banned the display of Christmas trees as a sign of American values. Revolutionaries from places in Latin America and southern Europe have burned publicly displayed Christmas trees as capitalist symbols of greed (Bowler 2017: 86, 141, 161–2).

For religious celebrants at Christmas, the public display of the tree is an image of the cross; Jesus' birth points toward his death upon a tree, evoking the image of the Tree of Life in Paradise. Referring to the Vatican Christmas tree in Saint Peter's Square, Pope John Paul II noted in his 2003 Christmas message:

> Beside the crib the Christmas tree, with its twinkling lights, reminds us that with the birth of Jesus the tree of life has blossomed anew in the desert of humanity. The crib and the tree: precious symbols, which hand down in time the true meaning of Christmas! (John Paul II 2003).

The public display of giving trees tied to charitable activities at Christmastime is found at sites such as schools, shopping centres, and civil offices. They unite local communities in a public effort to help a special cause. The trees are for the help of the needy, link social classes, encourage charity, and represent civic virtues.

In contrast to a Nativity scene, the display of a Christmas tree in a public space is widely considered acceptable in the United States. However, political debate over public religious expression has led to some controversies. In the 1984 US Supreme Court case of Lynch v. Donnelly in Pawtucket, Rhode Island, the plaintiff objected to a Nativity scene set up alongside other items including a Christmas tree. The court permitted the display because of its historical value, as well as what they considered the secularizing image of the tree and other images next to the Nativity scene. In 1989, in another Supreme Court case, Justice John Paul Stevens opined that the Christmas tree should not be allowed on public property, even though it was not even part of the case. Christmas trees have sometimes been banned from public schools and offices for fear of litigation. Universities have also restricted the manner in which Christmas trees may be displayed. In some cases, the use of a Christmas tree for charity has been discouraged or threatened with legal action, such as a giving tree in 2009 at the Orange County, California Superior Court. People with an axe to grind have produced alternative names including the Holiday Tree, Care Tree, Multicultural Tree, Tree of Lights, Community Tree, Winter Solstice Tree, Grand Tree, Family Tree, Annual Tree, Festive Bush, Unity Tree, Culture Tree, Season Conifer, Giving Tree, and Tree of Celebration (Bowler 2017: 234). These language games represent part of a wider culture war over the role of religion in public life. And yet, the public display of Christmas trees will remain common so long as it transcends its sacred features to evoke a host of common principles, including community, family, home, and moral values. The malleable nature of the tree's meaning makes it conducive to assimilation in the public mindset more easily than other ideological symbols of Christmas.

The Dynamism of the Contemporary Christmas Tree

In the closing scene of *It's A Wonderful Life* (1946), George Bailey holds his daughter Zuzu next to a Christmas tree when a bell ornament on the tree rings. The ringing signifies that the angel Clarence has earned his wings. The tree fuses religious faith, domestic tranquility, child-like joy, and communal unity—all of which continue today. The Christmas tree is a ritualized tradition, developed through institutional and devotional Christian life, popular culture, and societal ideals. This ritual is repeated annually, with families taking old things from storage, remembering past Christmases, decorating together with others, and enjoying the spectacle of a completed tree. The Christmas tree embodies those familial connections and shared values. At the same time, the tree's ability to embody a diversity of meanings allows it to set down roots in most global locations. A Christmas tree might be filled with origami in Japan or it might be a colourful palm tree in Australia. These traditions show how humans shape trees to envision them in an idealized form that inspires enjoyment.

The tree has remained a popular symbol for Christmas because it can signify a variety of religious, moral, familial, and national identities. Brunner calls the tree 'the product of centuries of custom, myth, vivid imagination, craftsmanship, and iconography' (Brunner 2012: 90). The tree has impacted the historical, social, cultural, and economic framework of the Christmas celebration. Trees have helped make Christmas the chief global holiday by connecting the public and private realms and promoting social civility with domestic joy. The Christmas tree is a malleable icon which can unite diverse groups.

The Christmas tree will continue to play an important role in the celebration of the Nativity feast. It remains the repository for gifts and charity. The tree represents a sacred gathering place, whether for a family or for a community. The tree reorients its surroundings to accommodate people and objects to itself. During the Christmas season, the home is organized around the tree's location. Whether one is at Rockefeller Place in New York or at Saint Peter's Square in the Vatican, the multiple layers of meaning in the display of a Christmas tree inspire wonder and joy at Christmas.

References and Further Reading

Albers, Henry, and Davis, Ann Kirk (1997). *The Wonderful World of Christmas Trees*. Parkersburg, Iowa: Mid-Prairie Books.

Archer, Sarah (2016). *Midcentury Christmas: Holiday Fads, Fancies, and Fun from 1945 to 1970*. New York: The Countryman Press.

Armstrong, Neil (2008). 'England and German Christmas Festlichkeit, c.1800–1914', *German History*, 26, no. 4: 486–503.

Bowler, Gerry (ed.) (2000). *The World Encyclopedia of Christmas.* McClelland & Stewart.
Bowler, Gerry (2017). *Christmas in the Crosshairs: Two Thousand Years of Denouncing and Defending the World's Most Celebrated Holiday.* Oxford: Oxford University Press.
Brunner, Bernd (2012). *Inventing the Christmas Tree.* New Haven: Yale University Press.
Collins, Ace (2006). *More Stories Behind the Best-Loved Songs of Christmas.* Grand Rapids: Zondervan.
Crump, William (2013). *The Christmas Encyclopedia.* Third Edition. Jefferson, NC: McFarland & Company.
Cullmann, Oscar (1990). *Die Entstehung des Weihnachtsfestes und die Herkunft des Weihnachtsbaumes.* Stuttgart: Quell.
Dickens, Charles (1907). *A Christmas Tree.* London: Foulis [Reprint from 1850].
Eliot, T. S. (1956). *The Cultivation of Christmas Trees.* New York: Farrar Straus Giroux.
Heinz, Donald (2010). *Christmas: Festival of Incarnation.* Minneapolis: Fortress Press.
Hoffmann, E. T. A. (1930). *The Nutcracker and the Mouse-King.* Trans. Louise F. Encking, Chicago: Albert Whitman.
John Paul II, Pope. (2003). *Urbi et Orbi Message, Christmas 2003.* Available at http://w2.vatican.va/content/john-paul-ii/en/messages/urbi/documents/hf_jp-ii_mes_20031225_urbi.html/ (accessed 20 March 2020).
Marling, Karal Ann (2000). *Merry Christmas! Celebrating America's Greatest Holiday.* Cambridge, MA: Harvard University Press.
Miles, Clement (1976). *Christmas in Ritual and Tradition, Christian and Pagan*, T. Fisher Unwin, 1912. Reprint by New York: Dover Publications.
National Christmas Tree Association. (2020). Available at http://www.realchristmastrees.org/ (accessed 3 April 2020).
Nissenbaum, Stephen (1997). *The Battle for Christmas: A Cultural History of America's Most Cherished Holiday.* New York: Vintage.
Perry, Emily, trans. (1840). *A Present from Germany: or, The Christmas Tree*, London: Charles Fox.
Perry, Joe (2010). *Christmas in Germany: A Cultural History.* Chapel Hill: University of North Carolina Press.
Restad, Penne (1995). *Christmas in America: A History.* Oxford: Oxford University Press.
Robinson, George (trans.) (1916). *The Life of Saint Boniface by Willibald.* Cambridge, MA: Harvard University Press.
Saunders, William (2018). *Celebrating a Merry Catholic Christmas: A Guide to the Customs and Feast Days of Advent and Christmas.* Charlotte, NC: Tan Books.
Snyder, Phillip (1976). *The Christmas Tree Book: The History of the Christmas Tree and Antique Christmas Tree Ornaments.* New York: Viking Press.
Tille, Alexander (1893). *Die Geschichte der Deutschen Weihnacht.* Leipzig: E. Kiel.

CHAPTER 23

GIFTS AND CHARITY

ELLEN M. LITWICKI

CHARLES Dickens, short of funds in 1843, published his novella, *A Christmas Carol*, in time for the holiday (Restad 1995: 136). During the summer of that same year, the philosopher Ralph Waldo Emerson published a brief essay on 'Gifts' in the *Dial*. These two works provide insights into the transformation of Christmas gifts and charity then under way. The period between the late eighteenth and the early twentieth century saw the domestication of Christmas, and this chapter considers its impact on Christmas giving. It focuses primarily on the United States in this period, with some consideration of British and German developments, to argue that domestication redefined Christmas giving, enmeshing it in both the family and the marketplace, and rationalized charity towards institutionalized forms.

To Christian believers, the first Christmas gift was Jesus himself: 'For God so loved the world, that he gave His only begotten Son' (John 3:16 KJV). The first recorded gifts for Christmas were the gold, frankincense, and myrrh the Magi brought to Jesus (Matthew 2:11). The gift customs typical in modern industrial societies where Christianity is prevalent, however, have a surprisingly short history. There is little historical record of Christmas gifts until the Early Modern era, when northern Europeans adopted St Nicholas (melding Christian and folkloric traditions) as a bringer of gifts (or punishment), and German towns introduced Christmas markets to sell food and crafts for the holiday season. Martin Luther apparently introduced the *Christkind*, who brought gifts on Christmas Eve (Perry 2010: 15, 23–5; Nissenbaum 1996: 64), as an alternative to Nicholas.

Early gifting traditions were predominantly communal, as this agricultural slack season allowed leisure, merriment, and feasting. From the processions of St Nicholas and his satanic/grotesque assistants to the Christmas plays and wassail traditions of England, peasants and apprentices demanded drinks and other treats (or gifts) from landowners, in exchange for raucous performances, while servants went home with Christmas boxes (Restad 1995: 6–8). Variants of these traditions crossed the Atlantic and were enacted annually in farming communities and cities. On American plantations during the Christmas season, enslaved individuals were 'treated' to varying levels of leisure, food, drink, and 'gifts' (Bigham and May 1998). By the turn of the nineteenth century, however, the streets of urban centres such as London and New York had become increasingly uproarious, as artisans and clerks paraded noisily and demanded drinks from reluctant elites (Nissenbaum 1996: 90–107; Restad 1995: 36–41). Dublin's *Hibernian Magazine* (1777) noted that 'the lower class... are rejoiced, from levying the taxes... of Christmas boxes', complaining that while the wealthy happily rewarded 'the industrious', the boxes were now 'almost demanded as a right, by our journeymen, and other servants'.

Such complaints led to the transformation of Christmas gifting in this period. Chief among the forces shaping this change was industrialization and its capacity to produce quantities of consumer goods, as well as the urbanization it hastened and the class system it created (Nissenbaum 1996; Restad 1995). Just as important were the cultural changes wrought by the new bourgeoisie, which defined itself around the (nuclear) family, the increasingly precious child, and the home as haven from the commercial city (Gillis 1996; Hamlin 2003). To reinforce its values the middle class created 'sentimental occasions' (Pleck 2000: 1), many of these commemorated with gifts that symbolized the ties of affection binding family and reaffirmed domestic values (Hamlin 2003: 861). Foremost among the new sentimental occasions was the domesticated Christmas, which replaced the carnivalesque public celebration with a private family holiday. Its main ritual was no longer 'treats' to the working poor but gifts to children, and a new distinction emerged between 'presents' to family and 'charity' to the needy (Nissenbaum 1996: 227). With regional variations, the emerging middle class in the United States and Europe created Christmas gifting traditions centred on family, domesticity, and the duty of charity to the worthy poor.

Although at first seasonal giving often occurred on New Year's Day, and some families gave presents on both occasions, there was a gradual but decisive shift towards Christmas. Nissenbaum (1996: 49–89) outlines the transformation by the 1820s of the Dutch Sinter Klass into Santa Claus, the deliverer of gifts to children on Christmas Eve, by Washington Irving, Clement C. Moore, and other New York patricians. Although Santa obscured the commercial origins of many gifts, the marketplace was clearly implicated in domestic giving even in this early period. The German Romantic writer E. T. A. Hoffmann published 'The Nutcracker and the Mouse King', which fancifully depicted a little girl's gifts come to life, while Caroline von Humboldt described Christmas gifts to her son of soldiers and a theatre (Perry 2010: 13–14, 18). Didactic books were popular gifts to German children (Perry 2010: 40), and lavish gift books produced annually for the holiday market sold briskly (Nissenbaum 1996: 140–150; Dickinson 1996). Wachelder (2013) and Schmidt (1995: 113–17, 122–7) demonstrate that newspapers advertised toys and books for Christmas presents in London and American cities in the early nineteenth century, while Hamlin (2003) illustrates the close connections between the toy market, Christmas, and domesticity in nineteenth-century Germany.

By the time Dickens and Emerson wrote, the transformation of Christmas into a gift-centred domestic holiday was thus in full swing. Despite a *New York Times* assertion

(16 December 1869) that its lesson was that 'a good man...will give away a large quantity of presents', *A Christmas Carol*'s most compelling message, according to Marling (2000: 139), was a secular sermon of Christmas benevolence. Dickens is silent on domestic gifts, although he did package his book as a Christmas present, complete with red binding and a stamped holly wreath (Marling 2000: 121). Ebenezer Scrooge's conversion to the Christmas spirit provokes instead a charitable impulse, leading him to have the large 'prize Turkey' sent (as an anonymous gift) to the Cratchits and to pledge a generous sum to a gentleman soliciting for the destitute, whom he had earlier rebuffed. Dickens signalled the change from communal Christmas 'treats' to a blend of institutionalized charity and direct gifts to those needy known to be worthy (Nissenbaum 1996: 228–9). Scrooge sends the turkey directly to the family of his employee, whose loyalty and work ethic, along with the innocent pathos of his son, Tiny Tim, had proven the family worthy of this gift (Restad 1995: 139–40). Rather than give directly to other poor Londoners, he donates through a charitable institution.

These two types of charity became characteristic of the domestic Christmas. Waits (1993: 169) notes both featured two types of gifts: practical items such as holiday meals and clothing and pleasure-inducing gifts such as toys. Stories of middle-class families and children providing gifts and food to their needy neighbours featured regularly in children's literature during the holiday season (Nissenbaum 242–4; Perry 48–53). In *Little Women* (Alcott 1868–69: 7, 27–8), the March sisters, after complaining, in Jo's words, that 'Christmas won't be Christmas without any presents', give up their Christmas breakfast to a poverty-stricken German immigrant family, at their mother's behest. An African Methodist Episcopal newspaper printed a French children's tale (DeWitte 1866) that taught Philadelphia children to remember the postbellum poor at Christmas. Young Lucie begs her uncle to give her an expensive doll for Christmas. On the way to the shop, they visit the Charity School, where she hears heart-rending stories from children who lacked coats, shoes, and sufficient food, much less toys. Newly educated about her privilege, Lucie asks her uncle to spend the doll money on food and toys for the poor children. Such stories educated young middle-class readers to their responsibility to curb their own desires and assist less fortunate children at the holidays.

While men such as Scrooge and Lucie's uncle often provided the means, bourgeois women provided most of the unpaid labour of the new Christmas charity; such work was safely within their 'sphere'. Madison, Wisconsin women raised funds for dinner and toys to brighten the Christmas of Civil War orphans, for instance (Bennett 1966). Sarah Hale, editor of *Godey's Lady's Book*, asserted that 'the season of charity' belonged 'properly' to women, since 'their presence everywhere...makes home'. She delineated those 'worthy' of such gifts: 'unhappy persons who, in hospitals, asylums, poor-houses, and prisons, are deprived of those associations of home' (1871). Nissenbaum (238–44) and contemporary accounts reveal these, along with orphanages, as the primary focus of Christmas charity. In New York in 1901, for example, charitable organizations provided food and toys for disabled children, as well as those at the Newsboys' Lodging House and the House of Industry (Anon. 1901). As this suggests, impoverished and suffering children were the most compelling targets of holiday charity (Waits 1993:

166–7). Louisa May Alcott (Cheney 1889: 352) wrote her siblings in 1875 about her trek to New York's Randall Island to give Christmas dolls to residents of the children's hospital and the asylum for the mentally disabled.

In her study of Christmas in British workhouses, Foster (2017) argues that these unreciprocated gifts to the needy reinforced the social hierarchy and the domestic ideal, disciplining the poor while assuaging bourgeois guilt about poverty. Foster describes the concomitant 'workhouse Christmas tourism' (556) by donors, who watched benevolently as needy individuals received presents and ate their gifted meals. Marling (2000: 142–8) and Nissenbaum (1996: 251–3) similarly discuss the voyeuristic aspects of the charitable Christmas for American spectators, whether viewed in person or through the lens of media reports and illustrations.

Institutional Christmas charity continued to evolve in the twentieth century. Thompson (1996) documents the expansion of giving in Sioux Falls, South Dakota, from religious organizations and the Salvation Army to the Kiwanis, American Legion, Elks, and Boy and Girl Scouts. A letter to the *New York Times* (13 December 1912) warned of the danger of 'promiscuous giving to applicants without investigation of their worthiness', and commended the more 'scientific' methods of charitable bureaus, which conducted research to find 'individual cases worthy of assistance'. That year, readers could give to the '100 Neediest Cases' thus identified and published in the *Times* (15 December 1912), with heart-tugging stories aimed at bourgeois readers such as 'Tuberculosis in Entire Family', 'Crippled Girl's Pluck', and 'Father and Mother Insane'. Variants of these pleas still appear in newspapers across the United States every holiday season. Despite warnings against personal charity, it too continued; for instance, Romanian Jewish immigrant Sam Stone anonymously sent $5 checks to destitute Canton, Ohio residents who wrote him personal accounts of their need at Christmas in the depths of the Great Depression (Gup 2010).

Stone's gifts would no doubt have pleased Ralph Waldo Emerson (1843), who famously postulated that the 'only gift is a portion of thyself' in an essay that illuminated contradictions at the heart of giving in an industrial capitalist society. Carrier (1990) notes the necessity of distinguishing gifts from commodities and argues that Emerson's 'ideology of the perfect gift' attempted to do so. Noting 'the difficulty experienced at Christmas and New Year,... in bestowing gifts', Emerson disparaged purchased presents, asserting that '[r]ings and other jewels are not gifts, but apologies for gifts'. He suggested that gifts should be occasional and not grounded in reciprocity. But the gifts of the domestic Christmas were by definition recurring and reciprocal, as well as primarily purchased rather than handmade, as illustrated in his own daughter's letters.

A series of letters in 1853 from Ellen Tucker Emerson (1982) to her mother (Lidian) provide rich insights into domestic gift-giving's extension from the family outward to friends, its gendered nature, its burden of reciprocity, and its links to the consumer market. The adolescent Ellen recorded her Christmas obligations at school, describing them as (in an echo of her father) 'a puzzling and expensive affair' (I: 42). The letters illustrate the complexity of selecting appropriate gifts and Ellen's fears of failing at this task. She explained that the girls gave each other gifts, conveyed her gift ideas (perfume, a thimble case, and 'a box of sealing wax' [I: 44]), and asked Lidian to provide further suggestions. By mid-December the pressure was mounting. Ellen fretted that 'Ida will give me a handsomer present than I have got for her', and worried that the thimble case was 'too mean a present'. She had discovered that the students spent 'about a dollar a piece for their presents' (I: 45); the rules of reciprocity suggested she must do the same. Therefore, Ellen requested that her mother send by December 21st a box with 'pretty little ornaments and trifles of that kind that are fashionable here' (I: 46), and Lidian responded with a vase, a bust, a 'tortoise-shell pen holder', and brushes. Ellen commented that she did 'not fancy the little books nor the penholder for presents so I will keep them' (I: 47), and asked that her mother choose two additional gifts. On Christmas Ellen thanked Lidian for her assistance, assuring her: 'Every one says that all the presents I gave were perfectly lovely' (I: 49).

Each of the gifts Ellen gave were purchased, not homemade. Illustrating the gendered nature of gifting, Ellen conferred exclusively with her mother about the presents and drew on Lidian's expertise to select most of those items. Middle-class women were responsible for maintaining the family's emotional bonds, and gift exchange played an important role in this effort; even today women select, give, and receive the majority of presents (Cheal 1988: 175–83; Komter 2005: 76–97; Rappoport 2012: 4–5; Sinardet and Mortelmans 2009). Although she initially shared her father's perplexity and anxiety about gift giving, Ellen soon settled into this duty herself. Five years later, she was advising her sister Edie about school gifts, suggesting '[p]uzzle your brain incessantly by day', but warning her not to think of them at bedtime: 'Presents are bad things to think about in bed [as] they...prevent one's going to sleep' (I: 161).

Ralph Waldo Emerson, like many men, was a much more tangential participant in this ritual, although he presumably paid for many of the Emerson household gifts. During the same months she was corresponding with her mother about Christmas gifts, Ellen wrote twice to her father (I:43–5), describing her coursework, thanking him for sending money, and pleading with him vainly to come to the school's Christmas party. Emerson apparently did follow his own suggestion of an ideal gift, 'the poet brings his poem' (1843), and Ellen reminded him in 1867 that poems were expected for each grandchild. She also informed him of what he would be giving 'to each of your dear family' (I: 455). On another occasion, Ellen recounted to Edie how their 'overjoyed' father reached for a set of knives Lidian called 'Father's present', utterly forgetting this was his own gift to his wife. Ellen commented wryly, 'It is real comedy the way we give presents for him' (I: 609). Although Emerson apparently came to appreciate presents to himself, he clearly remained baffled by and removed from the labour involved in giving them.

As the Emerson gifts suggest, most presents exchanged in middle-class households were purchased ones, as evidenced by the expansion of the market in Christmas gifts in the nineteenth century (Schmidt 1995). The *New York Times* (24 December 1879) hailed the throngs of shoppers in the city's shops on Christmas Eve as a sign of returning prosperity; one salesclerk claimed they were selling mostly 'very expensive toys' for children's gifts. At Christmas as at other times, bourgeois culture and the market economy were inextricably linked and mutually beneficial, as Nelson (2004) has argued, but purchased gifts contained the potential danger of commodifying sentiment. A variety of commentators followed Emerson in decrying the intrusion of the marketplace into the intimate province of the domestic gift. In *Godey's* Caroline Kirkland (1845) lamented the transformation of the gift into something 'whose worth can be reckoned in dollars', concluding that presents had 'become a meaner sort of merchandize' rather than 'owing all value to sentiment'. The (Methodist) *Ladies' Repository* warned readers that 'the *commercial* aspect of gift-making' threatened the nation's most precious population. Proclaiming that Christmas 'is so drowned in the patter of bonbons, and the jingle of gilded trinkets, that its higher meaning is almost unintelligible to our modern ears', the article cautioned that parents who made 'the *moneyed value* of gifts,... their chief expression' would create in their children 'a sharp, sordid, bargaining spirit!' (Anon. 1871).

Although magazines offered suggestions and instructions for handmade Christmas gifts, criticisms of purchased presents did little to stem their growth. Instead, individuals, aided by prescriptive literature, developed methods of transforming these commodities into gifts. Santa Claus and his nineteenth-century German counterpart, *Weihnachtsman* (Christmas Man) (Perry 2010: 34), constituted one such method for mystifying the commercial origins of children's presents (Nissenbaum 1996: 169–75), even as advertising and store Santas promoted their purchase. For adults, *The Nation* (Anon. 1865) suggested thoughtful shopping and the giver's intervention could transform merchandise. The giver could 'have a book bound after a design of his own;... he can buy cheap brown or buff earthen candlesticks and paint them with his own hands till they are more beautiful than the costliest porcelain.' Givers with less time could 'keep a memorandum-book for the purpose of recording wishes' and seek out the item most desired by the recipient. Carrier (1993) argues that such 'Christmas shopping is an annual ritual through which we convert commodities into gifts', and Perry (2010: 176) notes that advertisements taught German women that finding the right gifts was hard, if rewarding, work.

Perhaps the most important way to decontaminate commercial goods was to wrap them. Introduced in the second half of the nineteenth century, wrapping quickly became essential to Christmas gift presentation; in his study of Christmas in Middletown, Caplow (1984: 1310–11) found that the 'wrapping rule' was one of the most widely followed customs. Marling (2000: 1–42) provides the fullest historical discussion of boxes, ribbons, and wrapping paper. She suggests that the mid-nineteenth century Christmas stockings and the dramatic unveiling of the tree in the parlour were precursors that similarly 'covered' gifts. Although she acknowledges that wrapping disguises the commodity nature of a gift, Marling argues (19–20) that its main purpose was to mystify, surprise, and ultimately delight the recipients.

Prescriptive writers, magazines and newspapers, merchants, and advertisers all collaborated in the promotion of Christmas gifts, which constituted a significant portion of annual retail sales by the end of the nineteenth century. The gift customs created by the urban bourgeoisie spread to rural areas as well, helped by developments such as mail-order catalogues. Grace Snyder (1986: 441), a rural Nebraska woman, wrote in her memoir of ordering her children's Christmas presents from Montgomery Ward's in 1914. These customs also extended to working-class Americans, who mixed cheaper versions of popular gifts with homemade presents.

Christmas-giving grew well beyond the family circle, abetted by the proliferation of cheap novelties or gimcracks manufactured for holiday giving (Waits 1993:50–2, 70–2). Ellen Emerson (1982) commented in 1884 on the multiplying number of family gifts, noting that her sister's home was 'one vast store-room of Christmas presents...from each of her family of 9' to 'innumerable people' (II: 537). Advice literature abetted this expansion. At the turn of the century *Ladies' Home Journal* (December 1898: 28) offered suggestions for Christmas presents for household servants, the mailman, the laundress, invalids, and poor families. A few years later (December 1903: 47) this list had expanded to the family doctor and minister, uncles, aunts, nieces, nephews, and 'friends and acquaintances'.

Not only did the number of recipients expand, but the cost of gifts, particularly to intimates, mushroomed. By the mid-nineteenth century shops in New York were advertising items such as pianos and furs, and turn of the century critics condemned the growing number and expense of Christmas gifts. Rather ironically, Edward Bok, editor of the *Ladies' Home Journal* (December 1894: 16) called Christmas presents 'a burden' on women and demanded a modification of 'this senseless habit of excessive gift-making'. C. B. Wheeler (1904) complained: 'Every nursery is glutted with a perfect shopful of toys', producing jaded children who demanded 'give, give'. Wheeler suggested it was time for an 'Anti-gift League'.

Progressive reformers focused on the hardships Christmas gift customs worked on those who made and sold presents. Boxmaking was a 'sweated trade' (Marling 2000: 14) and workers in German toy factories were poisoned by the lead in toy soldiers (Perry 2010: 155). The seasonal rush in factories and stores led to overwork followed by post-holiday lay-offs; department stores required clerks to work up to six hours a day of unpaid overtime during the season. One worker testified that 'after demonstrating dolls' all day she 'cried from fatigue' (Anon. 1913). After a brief undercover stint in a department store, journalist Rheta Childe Dorr (1907: 1343–4) wrote that Christmas looked 'terribly different...from behind a counter'. The fifteen-hour workdays and customers crowding the counters until 10 p.m. led her to vow to 'never give or receive another Christmas present as long as I live'. A coalition of female reformers and workers in New York even launched the short-lived Society for the Prevention of Useless Giving, or SPUG, in 1912 (Litwicki 2011: 485–7; Collins 2012). It aimed to eradicate customs coercing retail and factory workers to contribute part of their meagre wages to Christmas gifts for their supervisors, but it also condemned the 'growing custom of exchanging gifts at Christmas without sentiment' throughout society (*New York Times*, 3 November 1913). Wheeler was presumably a fan.

Despite reformers' pleas, the proliferation and expense of gifts continued, with slowdowns during the World Wars and the Depression, when money and/or consumer goods were short. Americans pushed war bonds as appropriate Christmas gifts in 1917, for example, and Immanuel Schöch (2007) recalled Christmas celebrations with handcrafted gifts among Bessarabian Germans in the 1930s. Gift-giving has evolved since the nineteenth century, certainly. Gifts have reflected new technologies over the years (for example, radios and vacuum cleaners in the 1920s; computers and cell phones in the early 2000s), as well as shifts in gift philosophy. Waits (1993: 70–9) suggests that Christmas cards began to replace gifts for those outside the family circle in the early twentieth century. That period also saw a reaction against decorative presents, with advisers and merchants, some touting the SPUG idea, pushing such practical gifts as Hoosier cabinets, electrical appliances, and thermos bottles (Litwicki 2011: 498–503). Gifts have at times reflected political ideologies. Perry (2010: 211–15) notes that the Nazis 'redefined the Christmas gift to express a distinctly fascist mode of consumption' (211), promoting gifts crafted by German artisans.

Regional and ethnic variations have also marked Christmas giving. Alarmed by their children's desire for Christmas presents in the late nineteenth century, German and American Jews transformed Chanukah into a Jewish gift holiday (Perry 2010: 70–5; Joselit 1994: 230–43). Kwanzaa, a holiday originating in a Black Power critique of the commercialism of white Christmas, features handmade and Afro-centric presents for children (Mayes 2009: 43). In Spain and a number of Latin American countries, children receive gifts on Three Kings Day (Epiphany). On the night before, Mexican parents crowd *zócalos* (squares), searching for toys at vendors' stalls. In Puerto Rico children leave hay for the kings' camels in boxes under their beds and wake up to gifts of toys, candy, and nuts (Rodriguez 2016). The *Christkind* brings children gifts on Christmas Eve in parts of Europe. *Weinachstman* delivers them in places in Germany, England has Father Christmas, France *Pere Noel*, and Russia, Grandfather Frost (Marian). Secular Christmas giving has even spread to China and Japan. According to Kimura and Belk (2005), Japan's celebration is a hybrid whose central ritual is the exchange of expensive gifts by young lovers.

Recent trends continue to shape Christmas giving, both charitable and personal. Although local Christmas charity drives remain popular, national and international organizations have extended their search for Christmas donors with bulk mail and the Internet, as well as by mailing dubious 'presents' of calendars and cards meant to induce guilty gifts. A newer twist is the charity gift card offered by Charity Navigator, which enables recipients to choose the charity to receive the gifted 'donation' (Waldfogel 2009: 155–6).

As for personal presents, despite ongoing debates over the propriety of monetary gifts (Zelizer 1997: 71–118; Waldfogel 2009: 60–7), these have grown apace, along with creative variants such as gift certificates, which emerged at the dawn of the twentieth century (Litwicki 2011: 496–7), and the gift card, which was introduced in 1995 and soon became the top-selling gift item (Offenberg 2007). Gift registries expanded to include Christmas in the late twentieth century, becoming another means of enabling individuals to select their own gifts. Nostalgia for hand-crafted presents persists along with these trends and drives the recent upsurge in Christmas markets, which have also become tourist attractions. Eldridge and Pappalepore (2019: 191) note there were more than 150 Christmas markets in Europe in 2014, and many American cities have introduced Christmas markets in recent years.

Although critics such as economist Joel Waldfogel (2009: 18) oppose most individual Christmas presents as an economic waste, the custom is unlikely to even decline, much less die out, anytime soon. The forms of charitable and personal giving created by the bourgeoisie in the industrial age seem to have staying power, as shown by their continuing ability to deflect criticism and adapt to changing times, as well as their resonance with each new generation's conceptions of family and home.

REFERENCES AND FURTHER READING

Alcott, Louisa May (1868–69). *Little Women*. Boston: Roberts Bros.
Anon. (1777). 'Fugitive Thoughts on the Celebration of the Christmas Holidays', *Hibernian Magazine*, January: 47–8.
Anon. (1865). 'Presents', *The Nation* (21 December): 783–4.
Anon. (1871). 'Festivals and Presents', *The Ladies' Repository*, January: 43–5.
Anon. (1901). 'New York's Holiday Season of Charity', *Frank Leslie's Weekly* (26 December).
Anon. (1913). 'Christmas and the Shoppers', *The Outlook* (13 December).
Bennett, Katrina (1966). 'Orphans' Celebration—Top Christmas Charity', *Wisconsin Then and Now*. 13, no. 5: 4–5.
Bigham, Shauna and May, Robert E. (1998). 'The Time O' All Times? Masters, Slaves, and Christmas in the Old South', *Journal of the Early Republic*, 18 (Summer): 263–88.
Caplow, Theodore (1984). 'Rule Enforcement Without Visible Means: Christmas Gift Giving in Middletown.' *American Journal of Sociology*. 89 (May): 1306–23. Available at https://www.jstor.org/stable/2779184 (accessed 23 June 2019).
Carrier, James (1990). 'Gifts in a World of Commodities: The Ideology of the Perfect Gift in American Society', *Social Analysis*, 29: 19–37.
Carrier, James (1993). 'The Rituals of Christmas Giving', in Daniel Miller (ed.), *Unwrapping Christmas*. Oxford: Oxford University Press: 57–74.
Cheal, David J. (1988). *The Gift Economy*. London: Routledge.
Cheney, Ednah D. (ed.) (1889). *Louisa May Alcott: Her Life, Letters, and Journals*. Boston: Roberts Bros.
Collins, Paul (2012). 'The Original War on Christmas', *Slate* (13 December). Available at https://slate.com/human-interest/2012/12/the-war-on-christmas-it-started-100-years-ago-with-the-spugs.html/" https://slate.com/human-interest/2012/12/the-war-on-christmas-it-started-100-years-ago-with-the-spugs.html/ (accessed 21 March 2020).
De Witt, [Henriette] (1866). 'Christmas at the Charity School', *Christian Recorder* (13 January).
Dickens, Charles. (1843) *A Christmas Carol*. London: Chapman and Hall. Available at https://en.wikisource.org/wiki/A_Christmas_Carol_(Dickens,_1843)/ (accessed 21 March 2020).
Dickinson, Cindy (1996). 'Creating a World of Books, Friends, and Flowers: Gift Books and Inscriptions, 1825–60', *Winterthur Portfolio* 31: 53–66.
Dorr, Rheta Childe (1907). 'Christmas From Behind the Counter', *The Independent* 63 (5 December): 1340–7.

Eldridge, Adam, and Pappalepore, Ilaria (2019). 'Festive Space and Dream Worlds: Christmas in London', in Andrew Smith and Anne Graham (Eds.), *Destination London: The Expansion of the Visitor Economy*. London: University of Westminster Press: 183–204. Available at http://www.jstor.org/stable/j.ctvhrdot9.12/ (accessed 21 March 2020).

Emerson, Ellen Tucker (1982). *The Letters of Ellen Tucker Emerson*. Ed. Edith E. W. Gregg. Vols. 1 and 2. Kent, Ohio: Kent State University Press.

Emerson, Ralph Waldo (1843). 'Gifts', *Dial* (1 July): 93–5.

Foster, Laura (2017). 'Christmas in the Workhouse: Staging Philanthropy in the Nineteenth-Century Periodical', *Journal of Victorian Culture*, 22: 553–78. Available at https://doi.org/10.1080/13555502.2017.1295641/ (accessed 21 March 2020).

Gillis, John R. (1996). *A World of Their Own Making: Myth, Ritual, and the Quest for Family Values*. New York: Basic Books.

Gup, Ted (2010). 'A Yuletide Gift of Kindness', *Smithsonian Magazine* (December). Available at https://www.smithsonianmag.com/arts-culture/a-yuletide-gift-of-kindness-70852670/ (accessed 21 March 2020).

[Hale, Sara Josepha] (1871). 'The Season of Charity', *Godey's Lady's Book* (December).

Hamlin, David (2003). 'The Structures of Toy Consumption: Bourgeois Domesticity and Demand for Toys in Nineteenth-Century Germany', *Journal of Social History*, Summer: 857–69.

Joselit, Jenna Weissman (1994). *The Wonders of America: Reinventing Jewish Culture, 1880–1950*. New York: Hill and Wang.

Kimura, Junko and Belk, Russell W. (2005). 'Christmas in Japan: Globalization Versus Localization', *Consumption, Markets and Culture*, 8, September: 325–38.

[Kirkland, Caroline] (1845). 'Hints for an Essay on Presents', *Godey's Lady's Book*, January: 27–9.

Komter, Aafke E. (2005). *Social Solidarity and the Gift*. Cambridge: Cambridge University Press.

Litwicki, Ellen (2011). 'From the "Ornamental and Evanescent" to "Good, Useful Things": Redesigning the Gift in Progressive America', *Journal of the Gilded Age and Progressive Era* 10 (October): 467–505. doi: 10.1017/S1537781411000326.

Marian, Jakub (2019). 'Christmas Gift-Bringers of Europe', *Jakub Marian's Language Learning, Science, and Art*. Available at https://jakubmarian.com/christmas-gift-bringers-of-europe/ https://jakubmarian.com/christmas-gift-bringers-of-europe/ (accessed 21 March 2020).

Marling, Karal Ann (2000). *Merry Christmas! Celebrating America's Greatest Holiday*. Cambridge, Mass.: Harvard University Press.

Mayes, Keith A. (2009). *Kwanzaa: Black Power and the Making of the African-American Holiday Tradition*. New York: Routledge.

Nelson, Elizabeth White (2004). *Market Sentiments: Middle-Class Market Culture in 19th-Century America*. Washington, DC: Smithsonian.

Nissenbaum, Stephen (1996). *The Battle for Christmas: A Cultural History of America's Most Cherished Holiday*. New York: Alfred A. Knopf.

Offenberg, Jennifer Pate (2007). 'Markets: Gift Cards', *Journal of Economic Perspectives*, 21 Spring: 227–38.

Perry, Joe (2010). *Christmas in Germany: A Cultural History*. Chapel Hill: University of North Carolina Press.

Pleck, Elizabeth (2000). *Celebrating the Family: Ethnicity, Consumer Culture, and Family Rituals.* Cambridge: Harvard University Press.

Rappoport, Jill (2012). *Giving Women: Alliance and Exchange in Victorian Culture.* New York: Oxford University Press.

Restad, Penne (1995). *Christmas in America: A History.* New York: Oxford University Press, 1995.

Rodriguez, Ashley (2016). 'Discovering the Magic of Three Kings Day, from Puerto Rico to the US', *Quartz* (6 December): Available at https://qz.com/823973/ (accessed 21 March 2020).

Schmidt, Leigh Eric (1995). *Consumer Rites: The Buying and Selling of American Holidays.* Princeton: Princeton University Press.

Schöch, Immanuel (2007). 'Customs and Practices at Advent and Christmas Time, on New Year's Eve and New Year in the Old Homeland', trans. Victor Knell. *Heritage Review*, 37: 2–7.

Sinardet, Dave and Mortelmans, Dimitri (2009). 'The Feminine Side to Santa Claus: Women's Work of Kinship in Contemporary Gift-Giving Relations', *Social Science Journal*, 46: 124–42. Available at www.sciencedirect.com/ (accessed 21 March 2020).

Snyder, Grace and Yost, Nellie Snyder (1986 [1963]). *No Time on My Hands.* Lincoln, Neb.: Bison Books.

Thompson, Tommy (1996). 'Angels and Dollars: One Hundred Years of Christmas in Sioux Falls', *South Dakota History*, 26: 195–226.

Wachelder, Joseph (2013). 'Toys, Christmas Gifts and Consumption Culture in London's "Morning Chronicle", 1800–1827', *Icon*, 19: 13–32. Available at https://www.jstor.org/stable/23788118 (accessed 7 May 2019).

Waits, William B. (1993). *The Modern Christmas in America.* New York: New York University Press.

Waldfogel, Joel (2009). *Scroogenomics: Why You Shouldn't Buy Presents for the Holidays.* Princeton: Princeton University Press.

Wheeler, C. B. (1904). 'Gifts', *Living Age* 242 (24 September): 794–9.

Zelizer, Viviana A. (1997). *The Social Meaning of Money: Pin Money, Paychecks, Poor Relief, and Other Currencies.* Princeton, NJ: Princeton University Press.

CHAPTER 24

CHILDREN AND CHILDHOOD

MARCIA J. BUNGE

CHILDREN make up one third of humanity. They are members of homes, faith communities, and nations. Furthermore, every person on the planet once was or currently is a child. It is a role that all human beings share, and childhood experiences and memories shape human beings across centuries and cultures.

The birth of a child as well as children and childhood memories all play central roles in diverse Christmas traditions worldwide. Christmas celebrates the story of Jesus' birth and the mystery of the Incarnation. It highlights the glory and compassion of God as well as the vulnerability and tender care of a baby. In the history of Christianity, the wonder and joy surrounding the celebration of Jesus' birth is often coupled with a sense of wonder and joy for the children in our midst and a renewed obligation to protect and care for them. Memories of childhood experiences at Christmas also spill over into stories, songs, paintings, films, and other cultural and artistic expressions of Christmas.

Thus, no matter what period or context one examines, childhood and Christmas are interwoven. Christmas traditions in homes and faith communities have not only focused on the birth and childhood of Jesus but also been created for, carried out by, or inspired by children. Special attention is also paid at Christmas to the needs of children. Furthermore, childhood memories have sparked the creation of new traditions both inside and outside the Church.

Reflecting on interconnections between Christmas traditions and children is a highly fruitful yet also challenging task. Christianity is an ancient and highly diverse religious tradition that is being lived out in many parts of the world. Christianity is currently the world's largest religious group, making up about a third of the human population; Christian communities are growing around the world, particularly in sub-Saharan Africa and the Asia-Pacific region;[1] and there are over 30,000 Christian denominations

---

[1] These and other statistics can be found on the website of the Pew Research Center (pewresearch.org), including a report with the statistics cited here: https://www.pewforum.org/2011/12/19/global-christianity-exec/ (accessed 21 March 2020).

worldwide (Barrett 2001). With such an ancient, vast, and varied religious tradition, where does one begin to explore relations between children and Christmas traditions? Furthermore, although Childhood Studies is rapidly growing in all academic disciplines, it is still in its infancy (Bunge 2006). Thus, much like during the beginning stages of Women's Studies, Black Studies, or Disability Studies, scholarly attention is just beginning to be given to the vulnerabilities and strengths of one more often marginalized and exploited group of human beings on the planet: children. Many books and articles on Christianity past and present or even about Christmas might mention children marginally but, if so, often sentimentalize or minimize their role and active participation in Christian communities, rituals, and traditions. The terms 'child', 'children', or 'childhood' are often not even listed in the indexes of major studies about Christian faith and practice past and present, even though children have been members of Christian communities since the birth of Christianity.

Although reflecting on the complex interconnections between Christmas traditions and children is challenging for these and other reasons, a fruitful way to begin is by taking three lines of inquiry. The first is to focus on children's active participation and, at times, central role in Christmas traditions. Children are, after all, thinking human beings and active social agents, and they experience and contribute to familial and communal life. The second is to explore traditions in which both children and adults seek to address the needs of children locally and around the world. The Bible and Christian traditions emphasize obligations to help and seek justice for the most marginalized, including children, and attending to the needs of children has played a role in Christmas activities and the Christmas spirit. Finally, no form of Christianity lives in a vacuum, and a perennial concern in the history of Christianity and today is the spiritual and moral formation of children and how easily this task can be neglected by parents or undermined by wider cultural forces and trends, including at Christmas. Today, this concern is especially pronounced in consumer-oriented and technological cultures, yet even in the past, theologians and church leaders warned adults of the problems of focusing so much attention on other concerns that they lose sight of the meaning of Christmas. Although this chapter highlights only a few examples of the many intersections between Christmas traditions, children, and childhood, by exploring these three lines of inquiry, it demonstrates the central yet often neglected role of children in Christmas traditions as well as the need for further scholarly attention to children's participation in religious traditions and to the history of Christian obligations to the spiritual formation of children and the task of seeking justice for all children.

As is well known from histories of childhood, the definition of a 'child' changes across centuries and cultures. Today the *United Nations Convention on the Rights of the Child* and legal codes around the world generally define 'children' as persons 18 years of age and under. This chapter refers to 'child' and 'children' in this broad sense. Furthermore, even though children are central to many secular celebrations and cultural traditions associated with Christmas (not least those connected with Santa Claus), this chapter focuses primarily on the celebration of Christmas as part of the religious practices of Christian families and communities.

Children's Participation and Agency

In many parts of the world, one of the primary Christmas traditions in which children participate with families and their faith community is worship. All around the world, children attend various worship services during Advent and Christmas. With only a few exceptions, across almost all branches of Christianity and periods of history, one finds that attending services before and on Christmas Eve and Christmas Day are important traditions for children and families. In their faith communities, children might also participate in special Christmas programmes or Nativity plays designed for children and families.

In one of the most ancient Christian traditions, Ethiopian Orthodox, for example, families attend a special Christmas Day service and three-day festival. Like other Orthodox traditions, Ethiopian Orthodox Christians follow the ancient Julian calendar. Thus, they celebrate Christmas Day, called *Ganna*, on 7 January in the Georgian calendar currently used in the West. Ethiopian Orthodox Christians fast the day before *Ganna* and then wake early the next morning to participate in an early morning Christmas Mass. Everyone wears white robes or white clothing along with a cotton toga-like shawl called a *shamma*. Twelve days after *Ganna*, Ethiopian Orthodox Christians participate in a three-day and highly festive celebration called *Timkat* (the Amharic word for 'baptism'), which celebrates the baptism of Jesus in the Jordan River (Jenkins 2011). The three-day celebration includes entire church communities, including children. Together they spend the days feasting, singing, dancing, and participating in ancient and colourful pilgrimages and processions. In the processions, priests wear red and white ceremonial robes, wave incense, and carry embroidered umbrellas and replicas of the Ark of the Covenant called *tabot*. Women and men dress in white, and children wear colourful clothing and crowns, often representing the colours of their church's youth group. During a special candle-lit, early morning ceremony on the second day of *Timkat*, hundreds of believers, young and old, plunge fully clothed into consecrated pools to renew their baptismal vows.

Music plays a central role in Christmas services and traditions around the world past and present, and children have often participated by singing or playing instruments. Children along with adults sing Advent and Christmas hymns and carols in their homes, congregations, and communities. Children also sing in special Christmas pageants and programmes. Musicians have composed Christmas hymns and carols for children to sing. A host of other hymns and carols for the whole congregation directly refer to the baby Jesus and to children who come to worship him or who find comfort and joy in his presence. The Protestant Reformer and musician, Martin Luther (1483–1546), for example, encouraged congregational singing and composed a number of hymns, including several for Christmas. One of his most famous and child-focused, 'From Heaven Above', was composed in 1535 for his own children and designed for a children's pageant in the church (Bainton 1948: 6). Faith communities and their related institutions also host a range of special concerts and community sing-alongs. Church-related schools, colleges, and universities, for example, often hold annual Christmas concerts and programmes for the entire community.

From ancient times, children have also sung in choirs and helped lead services at Christmas and other times during the year. In the early Church, for example, the singing of psalms was often led by a young man, sometimes even a boy, 'who intoned the text as a solo or led the congregation in a responsive format', and 'from the later fourth century, church choirs became more common' (Dowley 2011: 44). Many choirs in the Middle Ages and Reformation period in Europe were made up of boys, and a host of well-known church musicians, hymnwriters, and composers in the West started their musical careers in boys' choirs. [See, for example, the biographies of Martin Luther (1483–1546), Giovanni Pierluigi da Palestrina (c.1525–1594), or Heinrich Schütz (1585–1672)]. Several famous boys' choirs today whose Christmas services and concerts are aired on television around the world have long histories, such as Leipzig's *Thomanerchor* (founded 1212) and the Vienna Boys' Choir (founded 1498). Children's choirs composed of both boys and girls are highly popular in Christian churches around the world today.

In addition to participating in special worship services and musical traditions, children are invited and encouraged to participate in a host of additional Advent and Christmas activities in their homes and faith communities. If one examines just a few common, Christmas traditions carried out in some North American homes and congregations today, for example, then one finds several activities that focus on children and encourage their participation. Children help light candles on the Advent wreath, open Advent calendars, set up manger scenes, help decorate Christmas trees, sing carols in the neighbourhood, and open presents. Children might help decorate or prepare special foods, such as Christmas breads or cookies, and wrap presents for others. In Ethiopia, men and boys play a game called *Ganna* (again, which means 'Christmas'). The game is similar to hockey and played on an open field with a curved stick and ball. At the start of the game, participants touch the ball, asking God to provide for them and help them live through one more rainy season (Alamayahu 1959).

Another Christmas activity enjoyed by children and their families in parts of the world is visiting or participating in live Nativity scenes. According to tradition, one of the first to create a crèche with living animals or figures was the thirteen-century friar, Saint Francis of Assisi. The tradition began in 1223 in the area around Greccio, Italy, when, according to the writer of his earliest biography, Francis asked a friend, John Velita,

> to portray the Child born in Bethlehem and to see somehow with my bodily eyes the hardship he underwent because he lacked all a newborn's needs, the way he was placed in a manger and how he lay on the hay between the ox and the ass.
> (Thomas of Celano 1997: 81)

The friend prepared a manger scene with an ox, ass, and manger in the nearby hills with honeycombed caves. On Christmas Eve, Franciscan brothers from the region as well as a crowd of nearby villagers brought candles and torches to the simple crèche in the hills, celebrating, participating in a Mass, and singing hymns of joy. Franciscan preachers promoted the tradition during the fourteenth and fifteenth centuries, and eventually many towns in Europe had their own crèche. Moreover, 'Carol singing accompanied the use of the crèche and grew in popularity during the same period' (Senn 2006: 152). The tradition of live Nativity scenes continues to be enjoyed by Christian communities around the world today.

In some Christmas traditions, children play such a central role that these traditions could not be properly practised without the active participation of children. In the popular Swedish tradition of Saint Lucia, for example, a girl or female teenager and other children play central roles. This tradition celebrates the life of St. Lucia, a young Sicilian virgin who was martyred in 304 CE.[2] According to legend, she was killed by the Romans for vowing to remain a virgin and secretly bringing food to Christians in Rome who were hiding from persecution in catacombs. The tradition of celebrating Saint Lucia's Day in Sweden probably began as early as 1000 CE, when communities incorporated southern European Christian practices into Norse celebrations of the winter solstice. The celebration, which takes place on Saint Lucia's Day, 13 December, grew in popularity during the seventeenth century, and it is still practised today in homes, congregations, and even schools and communities in Sweden, Swedish-speaking Finland, and areas of the world with Swedish immigrants. A girl is chosen to represent St Lucia. She dresses in white with a red sash around her waist and a crown of lingonberry branches with candles on her head. In homes, the oldest daughter is often chosen to represent St Lucia. She enters the room while the family sings a traditional St Lucia song, and she often carries a tray with coffee and special saffron buns (*lussekatter*). In larger settings, St Lucia is often accompanied in a procession by little 'star boys' (*stjärngossar*) who carry lanterns and by little girls who dress in white. The celebration emphasizes faith, service to others, and bringing light into the world.

Caring for Children in Need

Another important perspective on interconnections between children and Christmas in the past and today is studying the many traditions and special initiatives during Advent and at Christmas devoted to caring for children in need. Attending to the needs of children is a task undertaken by Christian families, congregations, and a host of national and international faith-based organizations, agencies, hospitals, clinics, orphanages, and child advocacy and lobbying ministries. For example, Christian congregations in North America today often sponsor projects that provide meals for families in need and Christmas presents for poor children. National church offices across

---

[2] https://www.britannica.com/topic/St-Lucias-Day/ (accessed 21 March 2020).

denominations launch special Christmas initiatives that focus on children in need locally and internationally. Faith-based organizations that work with children at risk also sponsor special appeals and fund-raising campaigns. These special Christmas campaigns help support children year-round.

Children themselves also often participate in these traditions or special appeals. They participate in several ways, such as by donating money, helping to prepare meals for needy families, working in soup kitchens, picking out toys for children in poverty, or singing carols in paediatric units of local hospitals. Many children's books, poems, choir anthems, musicals, videos, films, and songs tell stories of children who generously gave to others during Christmas. Some tell how children brought gifts to the baby Jesus or a child in need. In North American churches (and culture more generally), for example, one popular song at Christmas is 'The Little Drummer Boy', which conveys the story of a poor boy who visits the baby Jesus and, having no gift fit for a king to bring, plays his drum for him (Davis 1941). Children are also taught carols that emphasize giving, such as 'In the Bleak Midwinter', based on the poem, 'A Christmas Carol', by Christina Rossetti (1830–1894), which closes with these lines: 'What can I give Him, Poor as I am? / If I were a shepherd I would bring a lamb, / If I were a Wise Man I would do my part,— / Yet what I can I give Him, Give my heart.'

Such Christmas traditions are in line with biblical commands to help the vulnerable, Jesus' own example, and Christianity's long-standing commitment to children in need. The Bible states that all human beings are made in the image of God (Genesis 1:27), and numerous biblical passages explicitly command one to love and to seek justice for the most vulnerable—widows, orphans, and strangers. Deuteronomy 10:18, for example, states that God 'executes justice for the orphan and the widow, and...loves the strangers, providing them food and clothing'. The prophet Isaiah exhorts: 'Learn to do good; seek justice, rescue the oppressed, defend the orphan, plead for the widow' (Isaiah 1:17). Christian obligations to children are also grounded in Jesus' command to 'love the Lord your God with all your heart' and to 'love your neighbour as yourself'. In the Gospels, Jesus shows compassion directly to children. Each Synoptic Gospel gives an account of Jesus welcoming and blessing little children (see, for example, Mark 10:13–16; Luke 18:15–17; Matthew 19:13–15; also, Matthew 18:2–5; Mark 9:33–7; Luke 9:46–48), and several biblical passages tell stories of Jesus healing and including children.

Thus, since the early Church and still today, Christians have attended to children in need. For example, Roman law considered children to be property, and a father could legally allow unwanted infants to die. Early Christians, like Jews, consistently rejected infanticide, took in orphans, and affirmed the full humanity of infants and children. The early Christian bishop, Cyprian, for example, wrote that people, even infants, are 'alike and equal since they have been made once by God'. All share a 'divine and spiritual equality' (Cyprian 1964: 217–18). (Although Cyprian is making strong claims for the spiritual and divine equality of children, he does not draw implications for their social equality.) There are many powerful stories in the past and today of Christians who looked outside their doorways, saw children in need, and responded. In many cases, they started with nothing, but their efforts blossomed into thriving institutions. In the history of Christianity, one certainly finds examples of Christians who have harmed children yet also many others who have shown them compassion (Bunge 2001). In the Lutheran tradition, for example, we find many (sometimes neglected) stories of those who fully supported public education for all or showed compassion to children in need, such as Philipp Melanchthon (1497–1560); A. H. Franke (1663–1727); and N. F. S. Grundtvig (1783–1872).

Although Christians and people of other faiths and world views certainly attend to the needs of children throughout the year, it is interesting to note the number of specific appeals directed primarily for children in need during Christmas both inside and outside the church. Special appeals to children in need during the Advent and Christmas season are cited in histories of Christian charities, sponsored by secular and faith-based organizations, and woven into popular Christmas stories, plays, and films. One of the most popular Christmas tales of generosity to poor children is *The Christmas Carol* by Charles Dickens. Not as well known is the story behind the writing of this book, sparked by the author's serious concern for children. According to several accounts and biographies, Dickens was deeply disturbed by the plight of poor, uneducated, or exploited children, especially those forced to work in factories. He himself had been forced to work in a factory when 12 years old (DeVito 2014: 14–37). In 1843, he gave a speech on the education of the poor in response to a parliamentary report on Britain's harsh child labour practices. After the speech he planned to write a pamphlet titled 'An Appeal to the People of England, on Behalf of the Poor Man's Child'. However, when he realized that a pamphlet or more speeches might not be powerful or persuasive enough to turn the population's attention to the dire situation of children, he decided to write a story that might strike 'a sledgehammer blow' on behalf of poor children. The result was *A Christmas Carol* (Hawksley 2017).

Spiritual Formation and Recapturing the Meaning of Christmas

Another fruitful perspective on Christmas traditions and childhood is exploring the ways families and congregations past and present seek to help children remember the meaning of Christmas and strengthen children's moral and spiritual development amidst a variety of distractions. Christian parents and Church leaders recognize, for example, how easily the spiritual meaning of Christmas can be undermined by wider cultural forces and trends. Today this concern is especially pronounced in consumer-oriented and technological cultures, in which children are daily bombarded with messages trying to define for them who they are and whose they are. Through television, social media, and unrelenting marketing strategies directed at children, meaningful Christmas traditions are easily overshadowed by a focus on presents, possessions, and shopping. Even in the past, Church leaders warned of cultural trends and forces that can erode the spiritual message of Christmas, such as by focusing too much attention on food, feasting, and finery.

Church leaders and Christian parents past and present also acknowledge how easily they themselves can lose sight of the religious meaning of Christmas and the importance of children's faith formation generally. Even when they seek to pass on the Christmas story and the life-giving power of a life centred on love of God and neighbour, they recognize they face a number of obstacles. In many contexts around the world parents work long hours and struggle to make ends meet. Whether rich or poor, parents also admit that they themselves can lose sight of the significance of spiritual formation at Christmas and throughout the year by focusing too much attention on other concerns, such as their career, money, possessions, reputation, appearance, or their children's future financial success.

In the face of these and other obstacles, Church leaders and Christian parents past and present have sought ways to pass on the Christmas message and the Christian faith more intentionally. They have done so primarily by participating in the many kinds of Christmas and Advent rituals and traditions described earlier. Pastors have also preached sermons about the duties of parents and caregivers to focus on the message of Christmas. Theologians have written devotions for Advent to be used in the home. Some of these Advent books include activities for the family, such as songs to sing, biblical passages to read and discuss, or Christmas stories or poems to read aloud. One Advent book to be used in the home published in the 1950s in Germany, for example, is over two hundred pages and includes stories, poems, biblical verses, pictures, carols, and suggestions for various family activities (Gottschick 1954).

Conclusion

As we see in this short chapter, we can discover much about intimate connections between Christmas and children by re-examining various Christmas traditions with special attention to children's participation and agency, adults passing on the message of Christmas to their children, and Christian commitments to caring for all children in need.

Nevertheless, there is still so much we do not know about the role of children in inspiring, creating, or participating in these traditions. How closely were children involved? What traditions were created particularly with children in mind? What did these traditions mean to them? When did children's devotion to the Christ Child become a subject of stories, songs, and art? When did Christmas appeals to help children in need precisely begin? How have the many Advent books or devotions written for families over the centuries been used? Were they used? As Christianity continued to grow in diverse parts of the world, what child-focused cultural practices were incorporated into new expressions of Christmas traditions? What commitments to children in diverse cultural contexts were incorporated into or rejected by newly formed Christian communities in those contexts? What religious practices, songs, or forms of artistic expression do Christians around the world find most meaningful as they seek to strengthen the spiritual lives of children and youth in their midst and focus on the message of Christmas? What other questions and sources will help us uncover more about the active roles and experiences of children in Christmas traditions beyond simply assuming they were silent, passive, or insignificant players in 'communities', 'congregations', 'crowds', or 'villages'?

Greater attention to these and other questions would help us better appreciate the role of children in Christian communities and better understand the origin, power, and meaning of Christmas traditions. Further research into the intimate connections between children and many other religious traditions would also honour children's agency and their place as full members of faith communities and indeed the human population.

REFERENCES AND FURTHER READING

Alamayahu, Samuel (1959). 'The Game of Ganna', *Addis Ababa University College: Ethnological Society Bulletin*, 9, July–December: 9–27.

Bainton, Roland H. (1948). 'Introduction', in Martin Luther, *Martin Luther's Christmas Book*. Edited by Roland H. Bainton. Minneapolis, MN: Augsburg.

Barrett, David, B., Kurian, George, T., and Johnson, Todd, M. (2001). *The World Christian Encyclopedia: A Comparative Survey of Churches and Religions in the Modern World*, 2nd edition. Oxford: Oxford University Press.

Bunge, Marcia J. (2006). 'The Child, Religion, and the Academy: Developing Robust Theological and Religious Understandings of Children and Childhood', *Journal of Religion* 86, no. 4, October: 549–78.

Bunge, Marcia J. (ed) (2001). *The Child in Christian Thought*. Grand Rapids, MI: Eerdmans.

Cyprian (1964). *Letters*, trans. Sister Rose Bernard Donna. Washington, DC: Catholic University of America Press

Davis, Katherine K. (1941). 'The Little Drummer Boy.'

DeVito, Carlo (2014). *Inventing Scrooge: The Incredible True Story Behind Charles Dickens' Legendary 'A Christmas Carol'*. Kennebuport, ME: Cider Mill Press.

Dowley, Tim (2011). *Christian Music: A Global History*. Minneapolis, MN: Fortress Press.

Englebert, Omer (1965). *St. Francis of Assisi: A Biography*. Chicago: Franciscan Herald Press.

Gottschick, Anna Martina (ed.) (1954). *Weihnachtliches Hausbuch*. Kassel: Johannes Stauda Verlag.

Hawksley, Lucinda (2017). *Dickens and Christmas*. South Yorkshire: Pen and Sword.

Jenkins, Philip (2011). 'The Three Days of Timkat', *Christian Century* (27 December): 45.

Senn, Frank C. (2006). *The People's Work: A Social History of the Liturgy*. Minneapolis, MN: Augsburg Fortress.

Thomas of Celano (1997). *The Life of St. Francis of Assisi and The Treatise of Miracles*, trans. Catherine Bolton, Assisi: Editrice Minierva.

CHAPTER 25

FOOD AND DRINK

PAUL FREEDMAN

As this book makes clear, most countries, regardless of the degree of actual Christian religious affiliation, observe certain festive rituals associated with Christmas. This is true for food and drink as well and, in accord with other objects, icons, and ceremonies, Britain and Germany are paramount in originating influence, with the United States in a more recent but important international role. Rather than just surveying celebratory meals in different lands, which would provide a somewhat anodyne 'we're all the same even if we're different' message, this chapter emphasizes simultaneously archaic as well as recently invented food traditions.

Archaism, in the sense of fixed customs that resist change, would seem antithetical to the development of new practices, but in fact Christmas dining customs are seldom as old as they seem, and antiquity and innovation are two sides of the same proverbial coin. Eggnog and Christmas (plum) pudding are associated with Christmas in the United States and Britain respectively, appearing as 'ye olde' dishes revived from oblivion only for this occasion. They are indeed old in comparison with, say, kale salad or tandoori-flavoured crisps, and in their combination of spices (eggnog is usually served with grated nutmeg) and sweetness they even reflect a vaguely medieval aesthetic, but they are invented traditions, dating from the late-eighteenth and early-nineteenth century (Winn 2018: 138–41, 144). The Feast of the Seven Fishes, a supposedly venerable Italian Christmas Eve feast, is an innovation of Italian-Americans that started no earlier than 1900 (DiGiovine 2010: 181–208).

The archaic-seeming novelties evoke the Middle Ages, not only in their ceremonial aspects but in the plethora of spices and other exotic ingredients regarded with particular favour by the medieval upper classes. The medieval aura of Christmas fare is due to a number of factors. Many European public festivals, such as the *palio* races organized by Siena's neighbourhoods, or the Holy Week processions in Seville do actually go back to the Middle Ages. Beginning about two hundred years ago, it was discovered that borrowing from the medieval period provides a Christian religious patina that is considerably jollier than the austere solemnity of, for example, Lent and

Easter. The objects and symbols of contemporary Christmas were developed at the height of Romanticism, in the early- and mid-nineteenth century. While it is wrong to say that Christmas rituals are merely a Victorian invention, that period had a particular fondness for the medieval aesthetic, visible in everything from railroad stations to the houses of Parliament, not to say the endless number of Gothic revival churches. Whether revived or invented, Christmas foods made popular in the nineteenth century had to be appropriate to an overall medieval setting even if inaccurate, for example, turkey, the mainstay of the English Christmas dinner, is originally a New World bird, hence from the European perspective post-medieval.

The medieval aesthetic is particularly noticeable with regard to sweets. Gingerbread, the spiced and sugar-dusted German cookies known from the German as *Pfeffernüsse* ('pepper nuts'), Tuscan *panforte*, American fruitcake, Swedish saffron buns (*lussekatter*) involve spices such as cinnamon and cloves that were de rigueur in medieval dining, as well as sugar and dried or glazed fruit, all of which were in the Middle Ages expensive, prestigious, and credited with medically favourable effects. (Freedman 2008: 19–75) Marzipan is another medieval combination of sugar, honey, and ground almonds made or bought during Christmas. Spanish nougat (*turrón*) is available all year round, though particularly consumed during Christmas. There are two primary varieties, the hard *turrón de Alicante* which resembles Italian nougat, and the soft, crumbly, almost paste-textured *turrón de Jijona*. Both reflect Islamic confectionery traditions from Spain's inconsistently acknowledged multicultural heritage. At Christmas, a *turrón* variety made with eggs and another with marzipan are particularly popular.

In some cases dishes whose medieval antecedents would have been served at banquets all year round became identified with Christmas. The boar's head, for example, might be a featured item at any medieval feast that came on a day when meat was permitted, while by the eighteenth century it became more exclusively associated with Christmas and subsequently has fallen into desuetude (Shanahan 2019: 52–5). Boar's head glazed with two different brightly coloured sauces was featured in the cookbook of Master Chiquart, chef to the duke of Savoy in the early fifteenth century (Flandrin and Lambert 1998: 120). The Boar's Head dinner at Queen's College Oxford, supposedly commemorates the miraculous deliverance of a late-medieval undergraduate attacked by a wild boar while walking and reading. Somehow (miraculously indeed), he managed to kill the boar with his copy of Aristotle. The feast dates from the fourteenth century and is celebrated at Christmastime, although not precisely on Christmas Day or Eve itself (Aylmer 1995: 148).

The imprecision as to the date of the Queen's College feast, as well as that of *turrón*'s season in relation to Spanish Christmas brings us to the important but confusing aspect of Christmas food and drink: that celebrating Christmas is not limited to 25 December. Unlike Easter, there is no single day or meal set aside for the feast. In some countries Twelfth Night (the eve of Epiphany) is (or was until recently) more important than Christmas Day or Christmas Eve. Even with the compression of the holiday to December 24–26, there are distinctions not only among nations but within them. While in Britain it is generally agreed that Christmas dinner is on December 25 and takes place in the afternoon or evening, in the United States Christmas Eve might be more important, particularly among immigrants or descendants of immigrants from Catholic countries, or a kind of breakfast after opening presents on Christmas morning may involve the greatest ceremony or consumption of traditional foods.

For many, the sweet pastries, candies, and drinks that accompany the holiday, the days leading up to Christmas are more important than the day itself. During Advent, mulled wine, Christmas cookies, and gingerbread are repeatedly brought out at parties or family gatherings, before whatever the Christmas meal actually amounts to. *Lussekatter* are prepared in Sweden for St Lucia's Day, 13 December, but are regarded as a Christmas tradition.

In the English-speaking world, Twelfth Night lost its importance long ago and the Christmas holidays basically end with New Year's Day. In countries such as Spain, the influence of American commercialization has weakened the gift-giving of the *dia de los reyes* in favour of Santa Claus and Christmas Day, but Epiphany hasn't completely disappeared everywhere.

When Twelfth Night ruled, the Christmas season led up to a time of rowdy, carnivalesque festivity. Eating and drinking were deliberately excessive in keeping with the suppositious historical precedent of the Roman Saturnalia. The English and New World Puritans disapproved of all but the most perfunctory Christmas observance and objected particularly to this mob celebration, regarded as typically pagan and Catholic in their materiality, idolatry, and excess. If the laws of the Puritan Commonwealth and the New England colonies against Christmas revels were by-and-large impossible permanently to enforce, the Calvinists did succeed in quelling Twelfth Night. Henceforth (after the 1660 Restoration), feasting would centre, more-or-less, around the Nativity even if, as late as the nineteenth century, Britain retained elaborate 'Twelfth Cakes'. These were accompanied by comical, almost carnivalesque representations of Christmas kings, queens, and other more amusing characters such as Falstaff, 'Lady Warbler', or 'Jerry the Jester'. This centuries-long tradition was finished, however, by the last decades of the century (Henisch 1984).

More or less, again depending on the country, unlike American Thanksgiving or Russian Easter, there isn't in most places a single meal that defines the Christmas season's culinary repertoire. Some of this is due to the number of days between the beginning of Advent and the end of the 'Twelve Days of Christmas' with Epiphany, and some is the result of changing the holiday from a boisterous, adult occasion of feasting into a domestic, child-centred event. This is remarked upon elsewhere in this book in terms of the figure of Santa Claus. The climax of the holiday is usually not a celebratory meal but rather Christmas morning when the presents under the tree are opened at a time of day unsuitable for raucous or excessive dining.

The anticipation built into Advent thus focuses on the Christmas pay-off in terms of gifts, but initiates the culinary events with various sweet biscuits, cakes, and candies. The child-oriented Christmas also means overall less drinking. Unlike most secular feasts, Christmas Dinner is not an appropriate occasion for pleasant inebriation, at least not conventionally. The seasonal drinks such as Swedish *glögg*, American eggnog, or mulled wine are not pathways to Rabelaisian or even more moderate Breughelian excess.

With this context of a de-centralized Christmas food and drink repertoire, we can look at some specialties and specific practices. Generally speaking, the appearance of long-standing tradition and codification is strongest in northern Europe, while eccentricity and recent changes are characteristic of the southern hemisphere. There at this time of year it is too hot for plum pudding, but innovations encompass northern-hemisphere countries like Japan that have gone in for Christmas in a big way without having a substantial Christian background of real or invented culinary customs. The dish most commonly associated with Christmas in Japan is Kentucky Fried Chicken, followed by a sponge or layer cake resembling strawberry shortcake. The Japanese KFC custom dates from the 1970s and is an example of enjoying something readily available at any time of year rather than being, like plum pudding or roast goose, a one-off. The chicken and cake are also free of any medieval or pseudo-medieval evocation (Smith 2012).

BRITAIN

An online list gives no less than thirty Christmas dishes for the UK, ranging from Scottish Dundee cake to things found at other times of the year such as trifle, beef Wellington, or the classic savoury devils on horseback ('List of Christmas Dishes' 2019). Such diversity notwithstanding, Britain is exceptional because here there really is substantial agreement as to when the celebratory meal takes place and what its constituents must be. Christmas dinner, served in the afternoon or early evening, features roast turkey or goose, roast potatoes, Brussels sprouts, Christmas pudding and mince pies, and maybe a few sausages wrapped in bacon. As with so many aspects of Christmas, Charles Dickens can be credited or blamed for what are now regarded as age-old Christmas foods and ceremonies. *A Christmas Carol* (1843) actually mentions two meals, one the meagre but nevertheless joyous Christmas Eve feast that Bob Cratchit and his family manage to put together with their own resources, and then the immense turkey furnished by Ebenezer Scrooge's new-found largesse (Dickens 1843).

On his own, Bob Cratchit is able to serve a goose that is admirable simultaneously for its tenderness, flavour, size, and cheapness. The expense nevertheless means that its only accompaniments are apple sauce and mashed potatoes. Mrs Cratchit concludes the meal with a Christmas pudding, 'like a speckled cannon ball' soaked in brandy and set alight, with a holly sprig stuck on top. The repentant Scrooge happily buys the largest of the prize turkeys in the window of the poulterer's (open on Christmas Day). We don't learn how the gift turkey was served *chez* Cratchit, but the next day the clerk, amazed at his employer's sudden change of character, shares with Scrooge a bowl of smoking bishop, a type of mulled wine.

Turkey did have a long history of at least possible presence at the English Christmas table considerably before Dickens. In his *Five Hundred Pointes of Good Husbandry* (1573), a book about farming and the household, Thomas Tusser includes turkey ('well drest') along with various meats, brawn, pudding, souse, and minced pies as typical of Christmas. By 1727, turkey was so frequently a feature of Christmas that the well-known poet and dramatist John Gay could observe that:

> From low peasant to the lord,
> The Turkey Smokes on every board.

Nevertheless, goose and chicken remained less expensive than turkey and it was only in the aftermath of *A Christmas Carol* that turkey, otherwise not much eaten, became almost required. Currently, in the UK today between 76 per cent and 87 per cent of families eat roast turkey on Christmas Day, an index of conformity few if any other nations can rival (Shanahan 2019: 40–5). Dickens also receives credit, if that is the word, for the almost equally widespread service of Christmas pudding, certainly the holly sprig and flaming aspects. Christmas pudding is an essentially nineteenth-century creation, although based on precedents such as a more liquid 'plum pottage' or 'plum porridge'. Plums were not a necessary ingredient—any kind of dried fruit would do. Like mince pie, which it very much resembles in more concentrated form, plum pudding originally consisted of chopped meat, dried fruit (usually raisins and currants), and what are now considered sweet spices such as cinnamon and cloves. Dishes of this sort combine exotic Arab-Persian ingredients (the spices and dried fruit) with a European tradition of meat pies or thick soups or stews.

In 1728, a French traveller, noted that in Britain everyone 'from the King to the artisan' eats Christmas porridge and Christmas pies. César de Saussure describes the former ('a dish few foreigners find to their taste') as dried raisins and plums stewed in broth, spices, and wine. It is to be found within a few days of Christmas, before or after, but on no other occasions, though he does not know why this is. In the eighteenth century, it could be served as a first rather than last course (Shanahan 2019: 68–9).

Boiled plum pudding became the standard finish to the Christmas feast by the mid-nineteenth century, advanced if not completely created by Dickens. Plum pudding had been a common accompaniment to roast beef, the normal celebratory meat. It evolved by reducing and eventually losing meat and suet altogether, thus becoming more sweet, and identified definitively as a final course. Plum pudding also became identified commonly as 'Christmas pudding', a token not only of its place in the list of holiday dishes but a sign of its exile from every other sort of meal. Modern plum pudding has attracted a considerable amount of ritual: prepared the Sunday before Advent, stirred clockwise by each family member who makes a New Year's wish, and fortified with brandy or whisky periodically until the final unveiling on Christmas Day (Winn 2018: 139–42).

It is in the nature of the long and variegated Christmas season that even in Britain, the most conformist in terms of timing and menu of the Christmas meal, other occasions supplement if they do not supplant Christmas dinner. A modernized adaptation of *Mrs Beeton's Christmas Book* from 1900 (the original itself being a reworking of Mrs Beeton's *Book of Household Management* from 1861) includes what might be considered the 'authorized' Christmas dinner, but also describes a meal on Christmas

Eve, a Boxing Day buffet, and general suggestions for holiday dinners, lunches, drinks, and children's parties (Westland 1989). Nevertheless, Christmas, the one day of the year when everyone in Britain eats pretty much the same things, exalts bland abundance and predictability. Noting this, the English professor and crime writer Ian Sansom summarizes the meal in its English form as 'pathetic, good enough, resistant to change: Christmas on a plate' (Sansom 2018: 7). This seems a little harsh.

UNITED STATES

The American Christmas took off from the British developments. Here too, Dickens's *A Christmas Carol* transformed and, in effect, foregrounded the holiday. As stated earlier, the Puritans in New England had repressed attempts to take time off work or mark the occasion with feasting or dissipation. While this complete disapproval was not accepted by the other colonies, usually New Year's Eve and Day constituted the main seasonal holiday and Christmas was an almost routine day when stores, offices, and government agencies were likely to be open for business.

Before Dickens' influence was felt, it was only in the South that Christmas was a major festive occasion and by the 1830s it began to be recognized as a legal holiday in the slave-owning states. Christmas was an occasion for symbolic acts of patriarchal generosity on the part of plantation owners who might hold feasts of barbecued meat, offer their slaves once-a-year treats of whisky or eggnog, and give out small gifts such as pipes or articles of clothing. This ceremonial largesse fit the slave-owners' efforts to portray themselves as beneficent patriarchal figures, rebuking by counter-example the dour austerity of the North. Although carefully staged and controlled, these Christmas festivities evoked a medieval and Elizabethan tradition of exception, even a degree of social inversion and misrule, in keeping with the older Christmas as bacchanal (Bigham and May 1998: 263–88). Southern elites claimed the Royalist cavaliers as their ancestors and opposed their culture of honour and gaiety with the harsh materialism of the Puritan North.

In 1874, the celebrated Massachusetts divine Henry Ward Beecher recalled that when he was young, Christmas had seemed alien, something observed by papists and their close cousins, the Episcopalians. By this time, however, most of the country, under the influence not only of Dickens but of the 'Olde' English atmosphere evoked by Washington Irving's Squire Bracebridge stories, regarded Christmas as an occasion for lavish dining, gift-giving and, particularly, a family and children's holiday (Kaufman 2004: 147–57).

Distinct from Britain, no set menu or time was established for the American Christmas meal. Ham might be preferred to turkey (although there is a problem of repetition with Easter). Plum pudding might be served by Anglophiles, but it was as likely that the sweet course would consist of pumpkin pie, or chocolate *bûche de Noël* borrowed from France, or fruitcake, or some improvised confection. As a result of a combination of immigrant traditions, the length of the Christmas holidays, and the concentration on gratifying children, the United States has a lavish but indistinct repertoire of Christmas culinary possibilities regarding timing and particular dishes.

Insofar as there was to be a large, familial dinner on Christmas day, it would centre around turkey, given the influence of *A Christmas Carol*. The problem was that turkey was already the centrepiece for Thanksgiving, as firmly ensconced as was Christmas pudding in Britain. Thanksgiving arrives a month before Christmas, so in theory nothing imperatively prevents one from having turkey again, but to do so compromises its uniqueness. There is something odd about two similarly mildly religious but essentially secular, cold-weather holidays with the same main course. In Canada, outside of Québec, British traditions are stronger than in the United States and because Canadian Thanksgiving is celebrated in early October, there is not the same uncomfortable propinquity of timing. But many of the same factors as in the United States vitiate the maintenance of British conformity.

The undisputed reign of Christmas turkey in America from the 1840s ended around 1900. Already in the 1890s, American magazines suggested substituting saddle of venison, steak, crown roast of pork, or even veal curry. As part of the triumph of appearance over taste that marks much of the early-twentieth century American scene, magazines offered stylish ways to incorporate red and green colours or to create lighter innovations such as a Christmas pear salad, further obscuring whatever the traditional meal was supposed to be (Kaufman 2004b: 249).

Although not confined to the United States, the element of mockery for some of those durable, even 'iconic', food traditions is a notable feature of recent decades. The archaic appeal of eggnog and its banishment from all non-Christmas meals or parties moves it potentially and, eventually actually, from cherished seasonal symbol to ludicrous ritual, on the order of the now hopelessly comic and eye-rolling mistletoe. In the United States, fruitcake comes in for more amused contempt than any other food associated with Christmas. There is the widely diffused joke that there really is only one Christmas fruitcake, but it keeps on being re-gifted because no one actually wants to eat it. The fact that dense sweet confections of glazed fruits, nuts, raisins and other ingredients, highly prized during the Middle Ages, are not only old-fashioned but inedible provides the basis for newspaper and food magazine columns every holiday season on the order of 'actually fruitcake doesn't have to be unpleasant' or 'here is a recipe for *real* fruitcake'.

There is some anticipation of the dismissal of this superannuated treat in the Irish music hall reviews of the 1940s and 1950s that produced the memorable song, 'Mrs. Fogarty's Christmas Cake' with the chorus:

> And there were plums and prunes and cherries
> There were citrons and raisins and cinnamon too
> There was nutmeg, cloves and berries
> And a crust that was nailed on with glue
> There were caraway seeds in abundance

> You could work up a fine stomach ache,
> Sure you'd have to think twice
> Before eating a slice
> Of Mrs. Fogarty's Christmas cake.

Another quasi-Christmas dessert is the King Cake of southern Louisiana, especially New Orleans. As with all culinary matters, regional variation has diminished in the United States since the nineteenth century when modern technology and industrial food processing created a single food style impervious to seasons and environment (Freedman 2019: 3–49) Louisiana has the best preserved regional cuisine in the United States, a result of both its French traditions and the peculiar creation of New Orleans as a gastronomic destination as far back as the 1880s. Christmas in Louisiana is celebrated with the same flexibility as everywhere else in the United States. A recently developed Louisiana specialty, Turducken—a chicken stuffed inside a duck stuffed inside a turkey—has seized the imagination of much of the rest of the country (Roahen 2008: 119–34). The Lousiana King Cake, generally *not* imitated elsewhere (unlike the turducken) is an adaptation of the French *gateau des rois*. Many other Catholic countries have a similar ring-shaped pastry for Twelfth Night celebrations, the aforementioned English Twelfth Cake, or the Spanish *roscón de reyes*, for example. The New Orleans version is something like an oversize oval Danish (despite its name, a well-known American pastry type), with frosted sugar that is sometimes coloured green, purple, and gold. It can be filled with cheese or custard and is sometimes braided. Buried somewhere in the cake is a small figurine, called a *fève*, French for 'bean'. The original French *cake* had a hard bean hidden inside. Getting the slice with the *fève* makes you the king or the queen of the Twelfth Night festivities (Williams 2013: 167–9).

In an instance of American confusion or casualness about holiday celebrations, the cake, as its name implies, was originally a Twelfth Night treat in commemoration of the visit of the three kings to the Christ Child. Now, however, it begins the season of Mardi Gras, which comes at least a month later but is a big event in New Orleans, attracting thousands of tourists. The garish colours of the sugar are most certainly not French but rather reflect the colours of local Carnival parade societies ('krews'). But this is a different holiday and, as our concern is with Christmas, we can leave it.

The result in the United States has been a pick-and-choose repertoire of possibilities for Christmas regarding timing and particular dishes. The most durable food traditions are those such as candy canes, or eggnog, small items disassociated from serious meals. As Cathy Kaufman notes: 'Unlike our colonial ancestors, contemporary Americans think Christmasdinner very important: we simply cannot predict the menu' (Kaufman 2004c: 24).

Thanksgiving functions as a form of civic unification much as does the British Christmas, but Christmas in the United States can express a variety of class and ethnic identities as well as quirky, personal decisions. The most important culinary commemoration might be on Christmas Eve or Christmas Day. My in-laws used to prepare Christmas-day breakfast that featured German Stollen (a flat, dense rectangular cake covered with powdered sugar) and Canadian bacon. This was their only unchanging Christmas-season meal.

GERMANY

Germany is the home or point of origin of Christmas in many respects, from the tree to the plethora of spiced and sweet foods served during the holiday. In some instances it shares traditions with a considerable part of northern and eastern Europe so that it is impossible to say that the Christmas goose is of German origins. In other cases, as with Stollen, Germany is not only the source, but unlike many so-called Christmas foods, it actually can be traced back quite far, to 1329. Of course, as with all traditional preparations, it has changed. It was originally part of Advent, a period of fasting, and so only with papal indulgences in the late-fifteenth century and the Reformation's abolition of fasting regulations could it be made with butter. In original form, it seems to have been an oatcake made with water and rape-seed oil, shaped to resemble the infant Jesus in swaddling clothes. Although they were luxuries, spices, dried fruit, and sugar were permitted in fasting times so that the early forms of Stollen could be ostentatious but at the same time compliant.

German history has been affected by confessional division, and so Catholic and Protestant regions developed different Christmas culinary practices on the basis of not only local geography and environment, but on the nature of rules. The fancy Stollen that is familiar today is most closely identified with Protestant Saxony, Dresden in particular, but the entire panoply of Advent treats, notably gingerbread and Christmas cookies (*Plätzchen*), come from both sectors: Protestant Nürnberg is famous for gingerbread, while Catholic Ulm is noted for its star-shaped marzipan-filled Ulmer Weinachtssterne (Heinzelmann 2014: 111–12; Metzger 2008: 269–71).

FRANCE

The French have a standard meal, the Christmas-Eve réveillon, in keeping with the tradition of Catholic countries that celebrate an elaborate repast that conforms to Advent fasting rules. In modern times meat dishes such as pâté or even turkey are common, but still oysters and other shellfish are necessary, if not sufficient. What France is internationally famous for, however, is two kinds of dessert traditions, the *bûche de Noël* (a chocolate-covered cake made to look like a Yule-log) and an assortment of thirteen desserts, supposedly a Provençal tradition. *Bûche de Noël* originally referred to the actual Yule log burned during the long nights of the winter solstice and, perhaps, descended from some pre-Christian Nordic festive symbol of light in a dark season. The sponge cake roulade shaped like a log and covered with chocolate is an appropriate substitute in an era of central heating and dwellings with inconvenient or non-existent fireplaces. The cake dates back only to the post-Second World War period.

Another venerable-seeming practice is the thirteen Christmas desserts of Provence that form the conclusion to a *réveillon* dinner in that region. The meal might begin with typical regional items such as *bagna cauda* (a form of vegetable fondue with anchovy sauce), cardoons, something made with salt-cod, fish stew, and cheese. The thirteen desserts represent Christ and the Twelve Apostles. They come in three services or divisions: dried fruits, fresh fruit, and then various nougats, candied biscuits, and cakes. Dense spiced cake, marzipan, and fruit confections are part of a European-wide shared tradition. A *bûche de Noël* might even make an appearance amidst this display. Beloved though it may be, this Provençal custom is not much older than the cake version of *bûche de Noël*. There is no evidence for its existence before 1920. (http://www.saisons-vives.com/Origine-des-13-desserts-de-Noel,543.html). Unlike the thirteen desserts, the *bûche de Noël* has been adopted all over the world.

OTHER COUNTRIES

Christmas meals offer a kind of comfort food that is, paradoxically, not ordinary but usually unique to the occasion. The comfort can be in national identification, the repetition of family rituals, or the evocation of home for those who are in exile or merely travelling. Some of these are clearly traceable to an influential European tradition. Thus, in Argentina, a kind of Italian panettone reflects the large Italian immigration of the late-nineteenth and early-twentieth century while turrón evokes its Spanish colonial as well as immigrant past. The Piedmontese delicacy *vitello tonnato*, cold, thinly-sliced veal with a creamy tuna fish sauce, has become a 'typical' Argentine Christmas treat, locally referred to as *vitel toné*. This is another example of a dish that used to be ubiquitous and served throughout the year, but has become old fashioned and identified with fond memories of deceased grandmothers or festivities of the 1950s. It flourishes in the manner of plum pudding in Britain as a uniquely Christmas item.

Other southern hemisphere countries have moved away from their former colonial culture to conform more closely with the prevailing hot weather. Like Canada, Australia for a long time celebrated a traditional English Christmas, more faithfully the higher the social class and the closer the familiar identification with Britain. As part of Australia's movement away from cultural dependence on Britain, it has sought out its own general European borrowings, such as the pavlova cake, and dispensed with the wintry turkey and Christmas pudding tradition to embrace outdoor cooking, especially barbecued prawns.

In other lands, such as the Scandinavian nations, the pattern we have seen of consuming something only on Christmas that used to be eaten all the time is repeated.

Lutefisk is dried whitefish, usually now cod, whose reconstitution is by means of successive baths of lye and water over a period of at least a week. The lye is necessary because unlike salt cod, the dried product (known as stockfish) cannot return to its original texture by means of water alone. As with American fruitcake, this Christmas tradition is considered amusing, even repellant, but is all the more a sentimental favourite because of that. The use of lye, which actually has many processed food applications, as well as the strong not to say unpleasant smell of the fish while undergoing its painful resurrection, have given it a dubious reputation and *lutefisk* has become the mark of genuine affiliation with Scandinavian ancestry. *Lutefisk* is now considerably more popular with the descendants of Norwegian and Swedish immigrants in the United States, particularly in the northern Midwest, than in Scandinavia where is has been largely abandoned as an unpleasantly archaic reminder of an impoverished past (Janik 2011). Here once more, the attachment to a vivid if imagined past centres Christmas dining around a sense of place and identity by means of food, well known as among the most effective evocations of nostalgia and the individual and collective past.

References and Further Reading

Aylmer, Ursula (1995). *Oxford Food: An Anthology*. Oxford: Ashmolean Museum and Bodleian Library.

Bigham, Shauna and May, Robert E. (1998). 'The Time O' All Times? Masters, Slaves and Christmas in the Old South', *Journal of the Early American Republic*, 18: 263–288.

Dickens, Charles (1843). *A Christmas Carol in Prose: Being a Ghost Story of Christmas*. London: Chapman and Hall.

DiGiovine, Michael A. (2010). 'La Vigilia Italo-Americana: Revitalizing the Italian-American Family Through the Christmas Eve 'Feast of the Seven Fishes', *Food and Foodways*, 18, no. 4, October: 181–208.

Flandrin, Jean Louis and Lambert, Carole (1998). *Fêtes gourmands au moyen âge*. Paris: Imprimerie Nationale.

Freedman, Paul (2008). *Out of the East: Spices and the Medieval Imagination*. New Haven: Yale University Press.

Freedman, Paul (2019). *American Cuisine and How It Got This Way*. New York: Liveright.

Heinzelmann, Ursula (2014). *Beyond Bratwurst: A History of Food in Germany*. London: Reaktion.

Henisch, Bridget Ann (1984). *Cakes and Characters: An English Christmas Tradition*. Prospect Books.

Janik, Erica (2011). 'Scandinavians' Strange Holiday Lutefisk Tradition'. *Smithsonian Online*, 18 December. Available at https://www.smithsonianmag.com/travel/scandinavians-strange-holiday-lutefisk-tradition-2218218/ (accessed 21 March 2020).

Kaufman, Cathy (2004a). 'Nurturing a Holiday: Christmas Food in Eighteenth and Nineteenth Century America', in Richard Hosking (ed.), *Proceedings of the Oxford Symposium on Food and Cookery 2003*. Totnes, Devon: Prospect Books: 146–56.

Kaufman, Cathy (2004b). 'Christmas', in Andrew F. Smith (ed.), *The Oxford Encyclopedia of Food and Drink in America*, 1: 249.

Kaufman, Cathy (2004c). 'The Ideal Christmas Dinner', *Gastronomica*, 4, no. 4 (October): 17–24.

'List of Christmas Dishes' (2019). Available at https://en/wikiipedia.org/wiki/List_of_Christmas_dishes/ (accessed 21 March 2020).

Metzger, Christine (ed.) (2008). *Culinaria Germany*. Königswinter: H. F. Ullmann.

Roahen, Sara (2008). *Gumbo Tales: Finding My Place at the New Orleans Table*. New York: W. W. Norton.

Sansom, Ian (2018). 'Jubilant Devastation: Coded Messages in the Traditional Christmas Dinner', *Times Literary Supplement* (21 and 28 December): 7.

Shanahan, Madeline (2019). *Christmas Food and Feasting: A History*. Lanham, MD: Rowman and Littlefield.

Smith, K. Annabelle (2012). 'Why Japan is Obsessed With Kentucky Fried Chicken on Christmas', *Smithsonian* (online), 14 December. Available at https://www.smithsonianmag.com/arts-culture/why-japan-is-obsessed-with-kentucky-fried-chicken-on-christmas-1-161666960/ (accessed 20 March 2020).

Westland, Pamela (1989). *Mrs Beeton's Christmas Book: Practical Ideas for Creating the Traditional Christmas*. London: Ward and Lock.

Williams, Elizabeth M. (2013). *New Orleans: A Food Biography*. Lanham, MD: Rowman and Littlefield.

Winn, Christopher (2018). *The Book of Christmas: The Hidden Stories Behind our Festive Tradition*. London: Hardie Grant.

PART VI

THE ARTS

CHAPTER 26

CAROLS AND MUSIC TO 1900

TOVA LEIGH-CHOATE

> From the time when the angels inaugurated the custom, hovering over the stall-cradle of the infant Jesus, carols and songs have ever been the favorite music at the festal season of Christmas, and antiquarians with all their researches have not been able to fix a date at which the popular idea of celebrating the Nativity was not carried out by singing and merry-making.
>
> 'Christmas and Its Carols', *McCook Tribune* (December 24, 1885: 14)

ON Christmas Eve, 1885, the residents of McCook, Nebraska, received in their newspaper a special Christmas supplement called *Christmas Bells*. Along with stories, poems, and artwork, the supplement included a two-column spotlight on 'Christmas and Its Carols', which told a short, colourful history of the English carol tradition—only one part of the body of music associated with 'the festal season of Christmas' but one which had, over the previous half-century, received a lot of attention from English 'antiquarians with all their researches'. Indeed, the specific traditions mentioned in the article, from the singing at Oxford of 'The Boar's Head Carol' to the publication in Derbyshire of carols with woodcut images on ballad paper, would have seemed far removed from life in the frontier town of McCook, and from the other towns in which the same column appeared that year: several in Kansas, including Eagle, Ashland, and Caney; Danville, Kentucky; and Pine Grove, Pennsylvania. Only one of these, the *Kentucky Advocate* (25 December 1885) identified the column's author as Frank I. Jervis, an attribution matched in the *Chicago Current*, where it seems Jervis first published his piece on 20 December 1884.

United States census records and newspapers reveal that Frank Jervis was a 'Britisher' who settled first in Davenport, Iowa, then in Chicago, Illinois, where he worked as a newspaper editor, author, lecturer, and artist. A review of one of his lectures printed in the *Quad-City Times* (Davenport, 19 May 1870) called Jervis 'an encyclopœdia of history, biography, facts, fancy, humor, and things', a description supported by his foray into the history of carols. His interest reflected the broad development of antiquarian and popular engagement with traditional English carols over the course of the century, as well as the growing interest in reading about and celebrating an 'old-fashioned Christmas'. In his *Ancient Mysteries Described* (1823), the antiquarian William Hone included a list of eighty-nine English Christmas carols 'annually printed' in broadsheet form, which he expected would 'at no distant period become obsolete', unless collectors turned their attention to this 'class of popular poetry' (Hone 1823: 97–9, 106). What he did not realize was that, as he wrote, Gilbert Davies was in the midst of publishing his *Ancient Christmas Carols, with the Tunes to Which They Were Formerly Sung in the West of England* (1822), followed by a second, expanded edition in 1823. Davies's collection—a veritable 'cultural mustard seed'— spurred several others, including William Sandys's *Christmas Carols, Ancient and Modern* (1833), with its long introduction on past Christmas customs (Studwell and Jones 1998: 10). It has been argued that these early efforts may have inspired Charles Dickens to name his classic tale of the redemption of Ebenezer Scrooge, so influential in the urban revitalization of Christmas traditions, *A Christmas Carol*; to call its chapters *staves*; and to include within it the singing of carols. Jervis, who lectured on Dickens in Davenport in 1870, may also have drawn from a carol collection for his brief history of the English carol, in which he blamed 'cheap literature and national schools' for the custom's demise.

But the English carol tradition is just one part of the vast human project that is Christmas music. As Jervis highlighted, the presence of music was read into the original Gospel story and has been an important part of its commemoration ever since. The angel's announcement of Jesus's birth to the startled shepherds—the 'good tidings of great joy'—was reportedly followed by a 'multitude of the heavenly host praising God, and saying, Glory to God in the highest, and on earth peace, good will toward men' (Luke 2:10–14). Christians have typically read the angels' 'praising' and 'saying' as 'singing', and they have longed to join the Angels' Hymn. So, too, have they yearned to sing with the Old Testament prophets who foretold Christ's birth; witness with the shepherds who hurried to the manger; coo lullabies with Mother Mary; wonder alongside Joseph and the friendly beasts in whose presence baby Jesus lay; and join the gift-bearing Magi with gifts of song for the Christ Child. From the outset, composing and performing music for the Christmas season was a way to re-tell and participate in the drama of the biblical story, to increase the season's festivity through songs of joy and mirth, and to reflect on the feast's personal significance and interpret its theological meanings—in short, to 'gloss Christmas' (Lagueux 2004).

'Christmas' has always meant more than 24–25 December, and in this chapter, it includes the season of preparation leading up to Christmas Day (in religious terms, 'Advent'), the twelve-day period it begins, and the feast of the Epiphany, or appearance of the Magi, on 6 January. It also includes the prominent saints of the season—Nicholas (6 December), Lucy (13 December), Thomas (21 December), Stephen (26 December), and John (27 December)—as well as the Feast of the Holy Innocents (28 December), the Feast of the Circumcision (New Year's Day), and Twelfth Night (5 January). Indeed, the Christmas season has always been tangled up with the legends of the seasonal saints (especially Nicholas), and with the raucous festivities of the turning of the year. Christmas, then, must be viewed as a series of holy days and holidays, as in the challenged, yet apt, greeting, 'Happy Holidays!' (Studwell 1995: 5, 127).

In its music, as in other aspects of its celebration, Christmases of centuries past were, as now, both sacred and secular. Sandys's characterization of the fifteenth-century carol applies to Christmas music through 1900, namely, that it was

> divided into two sorts: one of a more scriptural or serious nature, sung in churches, and through the streets, and from house to house, ushering in the Christmas morning, and sung afterwards, morning and evening, until Twelfth-day; the other, of a more convivial nature, and adapted to the season of feasting and carousing. (Sandy 1860: cxxi)

Over the centuries, this 'carousing' has included revelry of all kinds: eating and drinking, wassail-bowl traditions, dancing and processions, carolling, gambling and other games, mumming (disguising) and pageantry, Lords of Misrule and other socially upside-down role-playing, mistletoe and Yule logs, decorating, hunting, and gift-giving. To fit all of these traditions, the music of Christmas has included liturgical song in a variety of genres, popular religious and secular songs, 'carols' proper, hymns, ballads, oratorios, cantatas, organ settings, spirituals, lullabies, and children's songs, as well as purely instrumental dance tunes, incidental music, and concert music.

In many ways, the history of Christmas music mirrors the wider histories of religion, culture, and even politics in the societies in which the birth of Christ has been celebrated. Unfortunately, much Christmas music has been lost to improvisation, faded oral traditions, and history's tumults. This chapter traces only some of the holiday's vast musical customs, focusing in particular on the foundational liturgical inheritance of the medieval West, Reformation-era traditions, and developments in the nineteenth century.

EARLY CHRISTIAN AND MEDIEVAL FOUNDATIONS

Even before the introduction of the formal feast of Christmas, Christians sang the Angels' Hymn (*Gloria in excelsis Deo*), and hymns and lyrics in honour of Christ's birth appear with regularity beginning in the fourth century. The earliest known Latin hymn for the season is credited to Bishop Ambrose of Milan: *Veni redemptor gentium* ('Come, Redeemer of the Nations'). The fourth-century poet Prudentius penned several lyrics taken up as hymns in the Latin liturgy, including *Corde natus ex Parentis* ('Of the Father's Love Begotten'), *Quid est, quod arctum circulum* ('Why Doth the Sun Re-Orient Take?'), and *Quicumque Christum quaeritis* ('Lift Up Your Eyes, Who'er Ye Be'). In the fifth century, Caelius Sedulius wrote the memorable lyrics *A solis ortus cardine* ('From Lands that See the Sun Arise') and *Hostis Herodes impie* ('How Vain the Cruel Herod's Fear'), both of which, like all of these early Latin hymns, would be used not only in the medieval Church but, in translation, in varied Christian denominations up to the present day.

As the Roman-rite cycle of feasts and seasons settled, so too did the musical foundations that would give it character and expression. By the eighth century, on the seven days leading up to Christmas Eve, most liturgical communities in the West adorned the chanting of Mary's canticle at Vespers, the 'Magnificat', with one of seven or more special antiphons known as the great 'O' antiphons. Each opened with an apostrophic invocation of the still distant Jesus by one of his titles or characteristics drawn from Old Testament prophecy: O Wisdom (*O sapientia*), O Lord and Leader (*O adonay*), O Root of Jesse (*O radix Iesse*), O Key of David (*O clavis David*), O Radiant Dawn (*O oriens splendor*), O King of All Nations (*O rex gentium*), and O Emmanuel (*O Emmanuel rex*). After the invocation and a short elucidation of its image, each 'O' antiphon ended with a longing petition for Jesus to 'come'—to teach, rescue, shine, or save mankind. All seven antiphons were sung to the same unique, six-phrase melody; they were often accompanied by the church's largest bell; and they were typically sung by the most prominent members of the liturgical community (Hiley 1995: 98–9). This festivity heightened the sense of anticipation on the final days of Advent and started a liturgical crescendo that would peak with the special festivities of Christmastide. Their performance instructions illustrate that it was not just *what* was sung but *how* it was sung—the manner of its performance—that made the Christmas season stand apart in the music of the medieval Church. This *how* comprised many different factors (including *who*, *when*, and *where*) that varied according to a feast's or season's festive rank and nature.

The Christmas Day liturgy of the Royal Abbey of St-Denis outside Paris, resting place of most of the French monarchs of the Middle Ages, illustrates many of the ways that even unison chant performance could be heightened to reflect the solemnity of Christmas. The abbey's first surviving ordinal, or instruction book, indicates that its thirteenth-century monks celebrated Christmas with a level of musical festivity in some ways even greater than at Easter, the 'feast of feasts' (Foley 1990: 306–9). In the special night Mass that followed the night Office of Matins on Christmas Day, for example, all the abbey's bells sounded from the beginning of the *Gloria in excelsis* to its end. This emphasis on the Angel's Hymn—withheld from the Mass throughout the penitential season of Advent—highlighted its joyous return on the actual anniversary of the blessed night 'when the angels inaugurated the custom' (to quote Jervis again). The abbot himself was to sing or intone some of the day's important chants: the eighth responsory and the reading of the Genealogy of Christ at Matins, and the special antiphon for the Benedictus canticle at Lauds. During some of the chants of the Hours, the community was to kneel for mercy. Two priests censed not only the altars but the entire community throughout the singing of Matins. All monks were to be 'festively dressed' in their finest vestments. Some chants of the main Mass were to be sung from precious ivories, likely ivory diptychs that could hold a sheet of parchment, and other precious relics, vessels, and objects were carried in the day's music-filled processions (Foley 2012: 356). Some chants, too, were to be sung in especially sacred places: the abbey's former and current *sancta sanctorum*, both associated with the abbey's patron saints and royal benefactors and reserved only for special moments on the highest-ranking feasts. Before the cantors intoned the Christmas Introit *Puer natus est* ('A Child is Born') to start the main Mass, for example, certain 'prepared monks' sang the three introductory verses (tropes) beginning *Hodie cantandus est* from the abbey's current Holy of Holies in the raised, twelfth-century chevet. In this same space, 'someone singing well' was chosen by the cantor to chant a rare antiphon before the Gospel. These colourful instructions show that then, as now, Christmas services required the best singers and careful preparation. In many medieval centres, as at Notre-Dame in Paris, strong soloists might introduce polyphony, or multi-voice music, at the highest moments of solemnity.

The Christmas liturgy of St-Denis provides an example of a trope: new material—text, music, or both—added to a pre-existing chant in order to make it more festive and appropriate to the day. Easter and Christmas received the lion's share of medieval tropes, which could be added at the beginning, middle (in one location or throughout), or end of many chants in the Mass and Office. Some tropes verged on the dramatic, such as the *Quem Quaeritis* ('Whom do you seek?') dialogue tropes for Easter, and the derivative Christmas dialogues representing the crib-side visit of three shepherds (*Ordo pastorum*) or the three Magi (*Ordo stellae*). In the shortest versions of these, an Angel announced Christ's birth and the witnessing shepherds or kings passed on the news to the congregation. These dramatic dialogues were sometimes integrated into the surrounding liturgy, as at Rouen, where the shepherds also lead the choir at the Christmas Mass and sang solos both at Mass and at Lauds. Also at Rouen, the stational play of the Magi took the place of the usual pre-Mass procession on the feast of the Epiphany and included the use of processional antiphons drawn from the liturgy, after which the Magi led the choir at Mass and sang the solo verses (Hiley 1995: 264–5). The Feast of the Holy Innocents on 28 December, too, sometimes included a version of Rachel's Lament (referenced in Matt. 2:17–18), or even a full Innocents' play. Fewer communities enacted a Prophets' Play (*Ordo Prophetarum*), including a Song of the Sybyl, as a culmination of the Advent season.

Robert Lagueux (2004, 2009) describes the special character of the musical 'glossing' that took place during the Christmas season at the cathedral of Laon by the end of the twelfth century. In the Prophets' Play, between each of the thirteen Jewish and pagan prophets who foretell the birth of Jesus, two Summoners lead the whole assembly in a poetic refrain-chorus that repetitively taunts the Jews for their errors, reminiscent of the Advent sermons read the preceding four weeks. In the *Ordo Stellae* performed on the Feast of the Innocents, as the children are slaughtered, they sing portions of a

Matins responsory; Rachel sings her lament; and the Consolatrix tries to console Rachel with verses from a sequence for the feast—all texts combining to highlight the tension between joy and sorrow in the feast. On the Feast of the Circumcision at Laon, the Apostles' Creed was farsed, or 'stuffed', with nineteen verses from other chants for Christmas or other feasts; after its traditional opening, 'Credo in Deum patrem omnipotentem' ('I believe in God, the Father almighty'), the clerics sang two lines of the hymn-like Christmas Sequence *Nato canunt omnia*, before returning to the next line of the creed, then another snippet of borrowed chant, and so forth (Hiley 1995: 234).

During the Christmas season, and often in the festive days following Christmas Day, many liturgical communities enacted special rituals of role reversal and frivolity. These both reflected and attempted to contain secular traditions involving misrule and excess, and they typically involved the singing of special songs. Such festivities could include the installation of a Boy Bishop or Boy Abbot: a choirboy who took on the senior ecclesiastical role (and vestments!) for a day. They could also involve a Feast of Fools or Feast of the Ass—often but not always on New Year's Day, the Feast of the Circumcision—at which more permissive kinds of music might be heard in the church and in or en route to nearby buildings including the refectory. Such festal music might include polyphonic processional songs called *conductus*, such as the catchy *Orientis Partibus*, or Song of the Ass; farced (troped) chants, creeds, and readings, including the Epistle at Mass and the refectory reading; or the addition of a sung drama like the *Ludus Danielis* ('Play of Daniel') at Beauvais (Fassler 1992). Circumcision/New Year's liturgies might also include clerical dance to Latin refrain songs, as suggested by lyrics and rubrics in the festal Circumcision liturgies at Le Puy (Caldwell 2013: 226).

Indeed, Latin refrain songs and, more broadly, the repertory of *nova cantica* ('New Songs')—rhymed, religious songs for one or more voices—figured prominently in the Christmas celebrations of the medieval Church, whether in or out of the sanctuary. Caldwell notes that Latin refrain songs, some with vernacular elements, formed the core of the Christmas repertory until the development of vernacular songs and carols, particularly in the thirteenth century, and that fully one third of the refrain-song repertory was written for the Christmas season (Caldwell 2013: 527ff.). Using many examples of Christmas-themed songs, Llewellyn (2018) highlights the frequent word play and expressions of excess found in the 'new song' repertory, as well as its common use of exclamations like 'eia', all of which tie the repertory to the festal traditions of troping. The joyful 'eia' features in some vernacular carols as well. In Germany, vernacular refrains known as *Leisen* sometimes punctuated the Latin liturgy on festive occasions, and the earliest known German Christmas song, 'Sei uns willkommen, Herre Christ', seems to have originated as a *Leise*.

Not everything sacred happened at church, of course. From peasants to princes, laypeople of all ages enjoyed music and singing, drama and dancing, and they celebrated the festivities of the Christmas season with vernacular song, some of it to religious texts, some not. It is in this music that we find the beginnings of the so-called Christmas carol, as a strophic, festive song of rejoicing, often with a refrain called a burden. Unfortunately, much of the festive music of the Middle Ages has been lost, having been created extemporaneously by popular minstrels or simply not recorded. With the music of the troubadours of southern France and the trouvères of northern France—notated, studied, and even parodied—strophic vernacular song blossomed, its influence quickly spreading to surrounding countries. A rondeau by the thirteenth-century French trouvère Adam de la Halle reflects a medieval Christmas tradition that continued for centuries: musicians performing at the homes of the wealthy in search of reward. The first stanza declares, 'Our Lord Noël / Sends us to his friends— / That is, to lovers, / And to the courtly and well-bred— / To collect some coppers as/A Christmas offering', while the refrain suggests that, for those who oblige, 'God [will] be in this house / And wealth and joy in abundance' (Keyte and Parrot 1992: 15). The personification of Lord Noel reflects the popular use of the word 'noel' as a festive cry particularly associated with Christmas; from the twelfth century on it appears in the liturgy in Latin refrain songs, and French carols would eventually be known by the term 'noel'.

In Italy, mendicant friars taught the people through dynamic preaching and song. St Francis himself reportedly bid his followers to be 'minstrels of the Lord', always following their preaching to the people with the singing of praises to God (Sorrell 2009: 107). Within this environment, the popular vernacular spiritual songs known as *laude* ('praises') developed in the Italian city-states, their influence spreading abroad with the spread of the Franciscan and Dominican orders. To Italy, too, is due the custom of publicly staging the manger scene, often accompanied by songs and music. Popularized by St Francis, if not invented by him as once thought, the *presepio*, *crèche*, *Krippe*, *Nacimiento*, *jeslicky*, crib, or living Nativity spread throughout Europe and remains a beloved tradition in many places today.

German Christmas plays and representations of the Nativity from the later Middle Ages included songs, sometimes known from beyond the plays. Such representations often included a *Kindelwiegen*, a scene in which baby Jesus was rocked to special songs and dances, like 'In dulci jubilo' and 'Joseph, lieber' (Heintzelmann 2001: 175). Mendicant influence may be found in 'In dulci jubilo', attributed to the fourteenth-century Dominican mystic Heinrich Seuse, who reportedly learned the song from angels who appeared to him and coaxed him into a dance of joy around the infant Jesus. Its macaronic text in German and liturgically inspired Latin bids all to rejoice and be glad because 'our heart's joy lies in the manger', the 'Alpha and O[mega]'—the O reminiscent of the frequent -O endings in liturgical refrain songs as well as the great O antiphons. One of the best-loved medieval carols, 'In dulci jubilo' has enjoyed a succession of settings by composers from Michael Praetorius to J. S. Bach to Franz Liszt. The beloved Polish carol 'W żłobie leży' ('Infant Holy, Infant Holy'), believed to date to the sixteenth century, may also have been composed for performance at a manger scene.

Medieval English drama, too, included songs, some pre-existing, some not, some vernacular, some not. One of the best-known English Christmas carols comes from the Nativity-focused *Pageant of the Shearmen and Tailors* in Coventry, one of ten or so plays in the city's summer *Corpus Christi* cycle, attested from the fourteenth century.

Surviving first in a sixteenth-century setting, the so-called Coventry Carol is a haunting lullaby sung by three 'mothers' of Bethlehem (originally played by men, of course), mourning the impending slaughter of their children by King Herod: 'Lully, lulla, thow littell tine child, / By by, lully, lullay'.

All of these festal songs could be called 'carols', a word appearing with increasing frequency in European literature and records over the course of the Middle Ages (as in Chaucer's reference to singing 'carole-wise'), even if they were known by another name. Beginning in the early fifteenth century, however, there appears in English manuscripts a specific form of art song called 'carol'. Its basic presentation is as an English or Latin (or macaronic) song with a refrain unit called a burden that both begins the song and returns after each of its uniform stanzas (Stevens 2018). Most of these surviving carols are polyphonic, that is, for multiple voice parts—usually two, with three often on the burden—but music for about ten monophonic carols has been found in manuscripts, and these may represent a larger, lost tradition. Even the carols for multiple voices were set mostly syllabically, with dancelike rhythms, and with light, open textures, often in the easy harmonies of thirds and sixths typical of English style. The usual poetic form consists of roughly equal four-line stanzas, rhyming aaab, and a burden that rhymes with the final line of the stanza, but this is not universal. There are also carols with two burdens and other variations. Although carols could touch on any subject, including politics (like the early and well-known Agincourt Carol [*circa* 1415]), they most often celebrated Mary, the Incarnation, or the saints of Christmas, and Christmas was the season when many carols, even those not about Christmas, were likely sung (Fallows 2018).

The development of this English 'art carol' remains complex and obscure. Its origins have been variously linked to the liturgical and vernacular song traditions and cultural currents mentioned above, as well as to the growing nationalist culture and propaganda in the reign of King Henry V. David Fallows (2018) highlights this last factor, arguing that the early manuscripts of the polyphonic carol can now be dated more consistently to the reign of Henry V, and that this very distinct and very *English* genre—more widely influential than previously thought—can be linked definitively to Henry V's court culture and to his political ambitions at home and abroad. Nevertheless, as Smaill reasonably argued (2003), the total picture of the carol's development must lie at the intersection of many cultural routes.

From Reformation to Enlightenment

The first printing of 'Christmasse carolles' took place in England in 1521, at the hands of Wynken de Worde, a German-born apprentice to the pioneering printer William Caxton. Unfortunately, only one leaf survives (Bodleian Library, Rawlinson 4to. 598[10]), with the end title and texts of two carols: the famous macaronic Boar's Head Carol sung at Queen's College, Oxford, and 'A carol of huntynge'. Worde's collection led a wave of sixteenth-century printings in England, some influenced by Reformation ideals. John Tysdale, for instance, reportedly received a licence to print a collection of *Certayne goodly carowles to be songe to the glory of God* in 1562 (Sandys 1833: cxxix). The tempering effect of the Reformation can also be seen in *Piæ Cantiones*, a collection of carols with tunes published in Sweden in 1582. Credit for the venture goes to Theodoric Petri, a Finnish Catholic studying in Sweden, and to the Lutheran pastor, editor, and printer Jaakko Finne. Thanks to Finne's heavy editing, Petri's collection reflected not only the theological leanings of Lutheranism—with sometimes awkward textual revisions, as for less emphasis on Mary—but also its democratizing spirit and international reach. Petri's collection included over seventy notated hymns and carols from all over Europe, and successive editions in both Sweden and Germany suggest that it was well known in northern Europe for a century or more (Studwell and Jones 1998: 4). Like the others, the twenty-four songs for Christmas are set for one to four voices. Among them is a Latin and Swedish version of 'In dulci jubilo' and the tune to which John Mason Neale would set 'Good King Wenceslas' nearly three centuries later.

Music played an important role in Lutheran worship from the beginning. In his own efforts to get sacred music to the people, Martin Luther adapted and translated into German some of the old Catholic hymns and chants, creating a new kind of congregational song called a 'chorale'—a theologically sound text paired with a simple melody sung by the entire congregation in unison, or featured in a multi-voice setting for choir or congregation. Chorale melodies could be drawn from the plainchant of the Catholic Church, from non-liturgical sacred song, or from vernacular folk songs. Two of Luther's earliest and best-known Christmas chorales were the Advent hymn 'Nun komm, der Heiden Heiland' ('Savior of the Nations, Come'), a rhymed adaptation of the venerable Ambrosian hymn *Veni redemptor Gentium*, and 'Christum wir sollen loben schon' ('We Should Praise Christ Beautifully'), based on the fifth-century Christmas hymn by Sedulius, *A solis ortus cardine*. Like many chorales, both of these went on to have an illustrious life in settings for various vocal and instrumental groups, by composers from Luther's friend Thomas Walter to J. S. Bach and beyond.

Beyond his many four-part chorales, organ preludes, and multi-movement Christmas cantatas, Bach's most important contribution to Christmas music is his *Weihnachts-Oratorium*, or Christmas Oratorio (BWV 248), a massive work written for performance in church across six days of the Christmas season of 1734: Part I, for Christmas Day, on the birth of Jesus; Part II, for 26 December, on the angels' message to the shepherds; Part III, for 27 December, on the adoration of the shepherds; Part IV, for New Year's Day, on the circumcision and naming of Jesus; Part 5, for the first Sunday after the New Year, on the journey of the Magi; and Part 6, for Epiphany (6 January), on the adoration of the Magi. Markus Rathey (2016: 8–9) has shown how this arrangement offered churchgoers in Leipzig an almost two-week reflection on the dramatic events of the biblical narrative, modelling and encouraging the 'internalization of religiosity' emphasized by Lutheran officials who opposed the exterior celebrations, including masked plays and door-to-door pageantry, that had marked German Christmastides past. Indeed, covering the same narratives as many of the special chants, tropes, and dramas performed over these same days in the medieval Church, Bach's oratorio, like his cantatas, emphasized not only the standard teachings regarding the first and second comings of Christ but, more particularly, the mandate to welcome Christ into one's own heart in the here and now, a concept common both to medieval mysticism and seventeenth- and eighteenth-century piety. (Isaac Watts's memorable line, 'Let ev'ry heart prepare him room', from 'Joy to the World' [1719] comes to mind.) In the closing hymn-chorale of Part I, *Ach mein herzliebes Jesulein* (from the thirteenth stanza of Luther's Christmas chorale *Vom Himmel hoch*), the believer invites baby Jesus to make his cradle in the believer's heart. The alto aria near the end of Part III, *Schließe, mein Herze*—the only newly composed aria in the whole work—encourages the believer's heart to hold this blessed wonder (of Jesus's Incarnation) fast within its faith. This emphasis on the interior emotions, not only of joy, but of wonder, trust, comfort, gratitude, deep love, and desire, and on the heart as the place for Christmas celebration, would endure through the eighteenth and nineteenth centuries.

If Lutherans promoted Christmas music as a means of evangelical teaching, and encouraged widespread participation in music-making, Protestants in England and Scotland placed Christmas increasingly under attack. In 1582, the Scottish Parliament outlawed the singing of 'caralles', whether in or out of the church, as 'superstitious and papist'. In England, William Slayter's publication in 1642 of a collection of *Psalmes, or Songs of Sion*, 'Intended for Christmas Carols' and set to solemn but familiar (i.e. popular) tunes may be seen as an effort to restore the psalter and temper the musical excesses of the season. This effort came to a head during the Civil War of 1642–51 and the subsequent establishment of the Puritan Commonwealth under Oliver Cromwell and his son Richard. Parliament outlawed seasonal plays in 1642; declared Christmas a day of penance in 1644; and outlawed any observance of the holiday at all in 1652, though observance of these laws was spotty at best. While the Puritan heyday certainly weakened carol-singing in urban centres, and ended composition of the polyphonic art carol, musical festivities and folk carols fared better in rural communities. In his *Vindication of the Solemnity of the Nativity of Christ* (1648), Thomas Warmstry defended the carol, within limits: 'Christmasse Kariles[,] if they be such as are fit for the time, and of holy and sober composures, and used with Christian sobriety and piety, they are not unlawfull, and may be profitable, if they be sung with grace in the heart' (p. 24). His message sounds much like Bach's.

If carols were officially discouraged in England, they were officially embraced in Bohemia. After the Catholic victory over the Protestant Hussites in the Thirty Years' War, the Jesuit writer and missionary Fridrich Bridelius published a collection of old and new Nativity songs, *Jesličky. Staré nové písničky* (Prague, 1658), as part of an effort to Catholicize the country.

In England, the Restoration in 1660 paved the way for a gradual softening of the hardline stance against Christmas music beyond the psalter. The first hymn to appear in an official publication was Nahum Tate's 'While Shepherds Watched Their Flocks' in the *Supplement to the New Version of the Psalms* in 1700 (Keyte and Parrot 1992: xviii). Over the course of the eighteenth century, in both England and America, poorly sung metrical tunes gave way to harmonic hymns and anthems, and congregational singing yielded some of its dominance to the emerging church choir. Inspired in part by the music-friendly Wesleyan reform movement, singing schools, singing treatises, and songbooks popped up everywhere, and huge new repertoires of sacred music—including some Christmas music—were produced by composers of varying abilities, often in shape-note settings. New Haven (Connecticut) composer Daniel Read's setting of Tate's 'While Shepherds Watched' was among the most popular of the American shape-note repertory; first published in 1785, his 'Sherburne' tune was reprinted over seventy times before 1810 (Crawford 1984).

Traditional carol texts continued to be circulated in broadsheets and chapbooks, and the traditional carol survived the eighteenth century in some of the more remote parts of England such as Cornwall. Increasingly, however, new carols, closer in style to hymns, replaced the old (Keyte and Parrot 1992: xix). In France, the philosopher and composer Jean-Jacques Rousseau distinguished between the popular *noël* (carol) and the *cantique* (hymn) in his *Dictionnaire de musique* (Paris, 1768). Rousseau's was the first music dictionary ever written, an expansion of his entry on music in the *Encyclopédie*. For Rousseau, a hymn is what 'one sings in honor of Divinity... what we sing in our Temples, excepting the Psalms which have preserved their own name'. Noëls, on the other hand, are 'types of musical airs destined for certain songs which the people sing in the festivals of Christmas... [they] must have a rustic and pastoral character matching the simplicity of the words, and of the Shepherds who one supposes sang them in worshipping the Child Jesus in the cradle' (my translation). Rousseau emphasized the rural, popular nature of *noëls*, while true *cantiques* had texts and music fit for worshipping God Almighty in the church.

In Italy, the prominent Neapolitan priest and philosopher Alphonsus Liguori composed the music and words (originally in *napolitano*) for the most beloved of all Italian carols, 'Tu Scendi dalle Stelle' ('From Starry Skies Descending') in 1732. The tune is set in *pastorale*-style, reminiscent of the *zampogna*, or Italian bagpipe, known to Italian cities by the annual Christmas-time return of piping shepherds from the countryside. The German creator of ethnography, Johann Gottfried Herder, preserved and published folk songs as an example of the unique character of every nation or *Volk*. To exalt their character, he invented the word *Volkslied*, or 'folk song'. In 1773, Herder published *Stimmen der Völker in ihren Liedern* [Voices of the Peoples in Their Songs], including the Sicilian mariners' melody that would later provide the tune for the famous German carol text 'O du fröhliche'. Herder's Enlightened sympathy for diverse national cultures provided a philosophical basis for collecting the oral cultures of peasant communities, a project taken up in different lands over the course of the nineteenth century.

THE NINETEENTH CENTURY

With the rise of nationalism following the French Revolution and Napoleonic era, carols became important to the ethnic identity of smaller nations close to larger neighbours. Along the geographical divide between Catholicism and Orthodoxy, carols (*kolęda*, *colinde*, etc.) became central to Finnish, Estonian, Latvian, Polish, Czech, Croatian, Romanian, and western Ukrainian popular identities. Their creation and retention united generations in singing, combining vernacular popular participation with the festive celebration of core religious beliefs. For example, isolated German-speaking communities in eastern and south-eastern Europe sang German *Weihnachtslieder* such as 'Silent Night', composed by Franz Gruber in 1818.

In general, Christmas music in the nineteenth century developed along several interconnecting paths: first, the widespread revival and restoration of the carol in England and elsewhere in Europe; second, the translation, adaptation, and spread of carols among diverse national and religious traditions; third, the explosion in hymn composition facilitated by the rapprochement of Reformed and Dissenting Protestant congregations with the Christmas feast and the acceptance of hymnody in the Church of England (due itself to pressures from the pro-hymn Evangelical churches and the push for a return to ancient hymnody characteristic of the Oxford Movement); fourth, the advent of cheap octavo music publishing, including hymn and carol collections, as well as concert music like Handel's *Messiah*, increasingly associated with Christmas; and fifth, separate from the others, the composition and early spread of music for the new, or revised, Christmas character of St Nick/Santa Claus. Encouraging these were related developments in the cultural meanings and expressions of Christmas, including the growing importance of the theology of the Incarnation and the increased domestication of the holiday, as it moved from a festival celebrated with outdoor games and pageants into an 'old-fashioned' celebration for church and, especially, home and family. Musical forces pushing the development of Christmas music included the growth of choral societies and festivals and the increasing prominence of church choirs, greater musical education and awareness among the general public, scholarly and antiquarian interest in folk customs and folk music, and, broadly, the appeal of the Christmas story, with all of its emotional and dramatic resonances, to the Romantic spirit.

As this chapter began with a newspaper column from the 1880s, so will it conclude by illustrating these themes in nineteenth-century newspapers—a source of cultural transmission that became affordable and widely disseminated at this time. The first piece under consideration is an advertisement for R[ichard] R[obert] Chope's collection of *Carols for Use in Church During Christmas and Epiphany*, printed in *The Guardian* (London) on 20 September 1893 ([p. 18], col. 1464). Published in 1875 (with earlier versions, differently titled, dating to the 1860s), Chope's carol collection was the century's largest, containing 112 carols with tunes edited by Herbert Stephen Irons. It followed his equally ambitious *Congregational Hymn and Tune Book* of 1857 (138 hymns) and 1862 (300 hymns), the first widely distributed source of the pairing of Charles Wesley's 'Hark! The Herald Angels Sing' with Mendelssohn's tune of 1840. As the advertisement makes clear, *Carols for Use in Church* could be purchased in eight variably priced formats, from the most expensive ('Cloth gilt, FULL SCORE, expression marks, &c.', costing 4 schillings) to the least expensive ('Words only, ONE PENNY'.) In between were two variations with the melody notated, a special cloth-gilt edition of the texts illustrated with woodcuts, and a cheap edition of the full score.

In terms of size, Chope's collection dwarfed the work of his predecessors, as outlined by Studwell and Jones (1998). Gilbert, mentioned at the start of the chapter, had published only eighteen carol texts, with eight tunes, in the two editions of his *Some Ancient Christmas Carols* (1822–3). These included the texts of 'While Shepherds Watched Their Flocks', 'The First Nowell', and 'A Virgin Most Pure', but no tunes known well today. Sandys's *Christmas Carols, Ancient and Modern* (1833) included thirty-four recovered 'ancient' English carols, forty still in use in western England, and six 'French Provincial' carols—a total of eighty carols—with eighteen tunes. His later *Christmastide: Its History, Festivities, and Carols* (1852) included a smaller sample of forty-two texts and twelve tunes but reached a wide audience. In 1853, the clergymen Thomas Helmore and John Mason Neale, musician and lyricist, respectively, published their *Carols for Christmas-tide*, with twelve carols adapted from those in Petri's *Piae Cantiones* of 1582, a rare copy of which they had been sent by the queen's envoy in Sweden. Neale translated the foreign lyrics (including 'Christ Was Born on Christmas Day' [from *Resonet in laudibus*], 'In the Ending of the Year' [from *In hoc anni circulo*], and 'Good Christian Men, Rejoice' [from *In dulci jubilo*]), or wrote his own (in the case of 'Good King Wenceslas'), and Helmore edited the old tunes preserved by Petri. Though not devoted to English carols, Helmore and Neale's work, published by J. A. Novello in London and marketed affordably to churches, did much to 'recover prestige for the carol' and 'rebuild the broken bridge between poets and people', more broadly (Dearmer et al. 1929: xvi). To their partnership as adapter-compilers, both sympathetic to the Oxford Movement, we also owe a *Hymnal Noted*, with Latin plainchant translations including 'Of the Father Sole Begotten', 'From Lands That See the Sun Arise', and the O-Antiphons; and the beloved Advent hymn 'O Come, O Come Emmanuel', whose eighteenth-century Latin text draws on the 'O' Antiphons (Studwell and Jones 1998: 18–19).

Other collections preceding Chope's drew on late medieval manuscripts in the British libraries (Thomas Wright's several publications) and on the song content of broadsides and almanacs (William Henry Husk's *Songs of the Nativity* [1868], which included many texts, divided into 'religious carols' and 'festive carols and songs', but only twelve tunes). In his introduction, Husk noted the changing tastes of the people, who gravitated more towards hymns than to 'the genuine Christmas carol'. Edmund Sedding published nine English and foreign carols in his *Ancient Christmas Carols* (1860), adding seven more in 1863. Most important for the widespread revival of the carol in England was the collection by the Reverend H. R. Bramley and music editor Dr John Stainer, *Christmas Carols New and Old* (1871). To their original forty-two carols with tunes were added twenty-eight more in a second edition of 1878, and these seventy carols were repeatedly printed through 1950, complete with illustrations, an index, and a well-written preface. Bramley and Stainer's collection was a public success and profoundly influenced church music in England and America. In Austria, collections of German-language Christmas songs appeared around this same time, including Karl Weinhold's *Weihnacht-Spiele und Lieder aus Süddeutschland und Schlesien* (Graz, 1853) and Wilhelm Pailler's *Weihnachtlieder und Krippenspiele aus Oberösterreich und*

Tirol (Innsbruck, 1881–3). French interest in preserving *noëls* likewise picked up in the second half of the century, with collections like Dom G. Legay's *Noëls anciens* (1875–6).

If not the first or best English compiler, Chope's reach was unmatched, as the nearly two hundred testimonials published in the *Guardian* advertisement suggest. Moreover, if we view Chope's anthology as just one manifestation of the Christmas music phenomenon in the latter half of the nineteenth century, the advertisement reveals the broader place of that phenomenon within the cultural and religious contexts of the time (see chapter 4 in this volume). The first testimonial, for instance, notes that Chope's work was 'a great help in teaching the fundamental doctrine of the Incarnation', a doctrine increasingly stealing priority from that of the Atonement, which held sway earlier in the century. With their focus on the coming to earth, in bodily form, of the Virgin-born Jesus, Christmas hymns and carols both reflected and promoted this shift. Similarly, another testimonial notes, 'Our Presbyterian neighbors come to church in crowds about Christmas time, simply because they are so fond of the carols. Our own people love the Carols very much, and would miss them if they were withdrawn'. The quotation demonstrates how the widespread use of festive Christmas music in Anglican/Episcopalian Christmas services, though technically proscribed through the nineteenth century, as well as in Catholic and Lutheran celebrations, did much to soften the anti-Christmas stance of the Presbyterian and other Reformed and Dissenting churches, whose members simply went elsewhere to enjoy the season's musical offerings. In addition to showing the carols' general popularity with congregations, as tuneful songs 'which breathe the purest and sweetest spirit of Christian joy', the testimonials show that Chope's carols were in frequent use by church choirs and in the religious education and entertainment of children, who otherwise 'seem to think that [the holiday's] chief feature is roast beef and plum pudding, while church has no attraction for them'. The testimonials also witness the rise of special carol services in and around Christmas.

Our second example comes from across the Atlantic in the *Boston Daily Globe* (24 December 1894: 5), and reflects the widespread tradition of reporting on past or upcoming Christmas programmes in area churches. Here the paper describes the special services held the Sunday before Christmas in dozens of churches in and around Boston. Though untitled, the reporting features numerous music-related headlines, including: 'Decorations and Music of Big Protestant Churches', '"Hallelujah Chorus" Favorite with the Choirs', 'Joyous Christmas Carols in Bay State Churches', 'Elaborate Musical Programs at Both Morning and Evening Services', and 'Chancels Decked in Green, Choirs Augmented, Classic Music Sung'. The reports, generally a paragraph long, almost universally report on the quality and quantity of the music in addition to the topic of the sermon and, often, the nature and extent of the decoration. That such elaborate services were held, both in church and in special afternoon or evening concerts, itself reflects the increasing domestication of Christmas in the nineteenth century, with even those Protestant churches who had once adopted the tradition of holding a Christmas Day service instead moving the pomp and ceremony to the Sunday just before Christmas. Two days later, the *Globe* showcased the Christmas services held on Christmas Day itself, primarily in Catholic, Episcopalian, and some Methodist churches, with children's festivals held by some Baptist congregations.

The *Globe* accounts highlight the Victorian-era craze for ever more elaborate decorations in tandem with ever more elaborate music: 'The flowers, the ropes of green, the carols, cantatas and oratorio strains all told of the Christmas time'. Indeed, the reports are filled with descriptions of the hymns and carols, anthems, processional pieces, cantatas, oratorios (or parts thereof), and organ or symphonic music performed by a variety of musical forces, from vocal and instrumental soloists and (double) quartets, to choirs of children or adults, to bands and orchestras. The spread of English hymn and carol arrangements abroad is evident throughout, as in the report that two Stainer arrangements (the Offertory anthem 'Hosanna in the Highest' and 'Sanctus') were performed at St Paul's in Boston. Among the local works performed was 'O Holy Night', an English translation by the Boston-area Unitarian minister John Sullivan Dwight of Adolphe Adam and Placide Cappeau's mid-century *Cantique de Noël*. Not only do the reports show the widespread singing of carols in the church, or in special carol services or evening concerts, they also reflect the growing musical education and participation of the public, with frequent mention of augmented choirs and individual naming of choir members and soloists. The emphasis on 'classic music', typical for the nineteenth century, shows not only in the heading, 'Classic Music Sung', but in the many reports of music by Haydn, Mozart, and especially Handel. Such emphasis is not surprising, as Boston was home to the Handel and Haydn Society, a choral society founded in 1815 with the purpose of improving the quality of singing and musical taste in the area. That the Hallelujah Chorus was a 'favorite with the choirs' reflects not only local interest in the work—the Handel and Haydn Society performed the American premiere in 1818—but also the growing trend of *Messiah* performances at Christmas time. Indeed, the *Globe* reports that several other movements of Handel's masterpiece, including the 'Pastoral Symphony', were performed that same day in area churches.

The final newspaper feature for discussion, 'Glad Little Folks, and Their Christmas Merrymaking', *Lancaster New Era* (23 December 1887: 1), reports on school Christmas programmes (so-called 'Closing Exercises') held in the public schools of Lancaster, Pennsylvania, in 1887, reflecting what seems to have been a country-wide tradition by this time. Here, too, decorations are noted, as are the elaborate programmes of songs, recitations, instrumental solos, and even plays. The songs, drawn almost entirely from J. P. McCaskey's *Franklin Square Song Collections* (New York: Harper, 8 volumes, 1881–92), span the spectrum of Christmas themes. McCaskey, a prolific educator, education reformer, editor, and songbook compiler, at the time served as the principal of the high school boys performing in the programme (Parsil 2016). Together with the high school girls, these boys performed the songs 'Christ is Born in Bethlehem', 'The Holly Wreath', 'The Little Children's Day', 'Jolly Old St Nicholas', 'Christmas is Coming', 'Deck the Halls', 'The Mahogany Tree', and 'Silent Night', attributed, as in the first *Franklin Square* songbook (1881), to [Michael] Haydn rather than Franz Gruber. The city's other schools performed some of the same, and numerous other, songs, likewise drawn primarily from McCaskey's collections.

These songs, the newspaper report, and McCaskey's song collections illustrate interlocking trends in Christmas music, music education, and, more broadly, the celebration of Christmas in the final decades of the nineteenth century. The song 'The Little Children's Day' illustrates the transformation of Christmas into a children's holiday: a dear 'festal day' welcomed by 'childish rapture' and 'the song, shout, and laughter' of children 'over hill and valley, / In cottage and in hall, / In schoolroom and on playground'. This is not just any noisy holiday, however, but one best centred in the family: 'But merriest is the music / Of childhood's voice at home'. McCaskey's *Franklin Square* songbooks were themselves 'Devoted to School and Home Enjoyment' (as indicated on the cover), and included 'Favorite Songs and Hymns for Schools and Homes, Nursery and Fireside'. In his *Songs of the Nativity*, Husk, too, had noted the increasing domesticity of Christmas: 'Perhaps the greatest characteristic of Christmas Day at present is the very general custom of regarding it as a domestic and family festival', and he expressed a hope that his carol collection might find a place within that home-centred holiday. Reflecting the desire for an 'old-fashioned' family Christmas, the beloved song 'Away in a Manger'—likely written by an unknown American—was widely disseminated as 'Luther's Cradle Song' in the final decades of the century, with the further explanation that Luther had sung it at home with his children.

The song 'The Little Children's Day' not only reflects the domestication of Christmas but the priority given to Santa Claus in its celebration. Like 'Jolly Old St Nicholas', 'The Little Children's Day' celebrates Santa Claus/St Nick with his 'pack and reindeer sleigh'. Henry Phillips's 'Christmas is Coming', too, highlights Santa Claus as the dependable deliverer of gifts to children everywhere. These images drew on the nineteenth-century transformation of the St Nicholas of 6 December into Santa Claus of 24/25 December, effected primarily by Washington Irving and Clement C. Moore. Drawing on Irving's vision of the saint as a pipe-smoking, wagon-flying gift-giver (1809), Moore's poem, 'A Visit from St. Nicholas', first published anonymously in the *New York Sentinel* on 23 December 1823, established the image by which Santa Claus would be celebrated ever after: as a jolly, chubby old man, landing on rooftops in a reindeer-driven sleigh, then sliding down chimneys with a bundle of toys on his back to deliver to the stockings of sleeping children. The first known Christmas song devoted to this American-made Santa seems to have been 'Up on the Housetop', written in the 1850s or 60s by Benjamin R. Hanby. 'Jolly Old St Nicholas', believed (wrongly) by some Lancastrians to have been composed by McCaskey himself, shares with 'Up on the Housetop' not only its characterization of a gift-giving St Nick but also its inclusion of specific children's names, including Nellie/Nell (Parsil 2016: 171).

That Santa Claus should receive his own Christmas music is not at all surprising. Even before his calendrical transfer and character transformation, St Nicholas—his feast on 6 December—had already received an inordinate amount of musical attention. Medieval monks and clerics across Europe composed a variety of special music in his honour: tropes and sequences, rhymed offices for the Hours, refrain songs, polyphony, and even several liturgical dramas—more than half of those in the *Fleury Playbook*, for example (Caldwell 2013: 410). Moreover, Santa Claus of the nineteenth century was still akin to St Nicholas, a saint in the religious sense, promoted by American churches as the ideal Christian gift-giver (see chapter 4). Performances of music in his honour at church services and concerts were not uncommon, as in a 'very pretty Christmas cantata, "Saint Nicholas"', performed in costume by the Sunday School of the Kountze Memorial Church in Omaha, Nebraska, in December 1889 (*Omaha Daily Bee*, 27 December 1889: 5).

Broadly speaking, Christmas music before 1900 was rooted in medieval traditions both sacred and secular. It has enabled two thousand years of Christians to join the Christmas story, whether through the official music of the church, centred on the biblical voices of the angels and prophets; or through the music of liturgical drama, Nativity representations, country carols, and spirituals, reflecting the sometimes imagined voices of the shepherds, the people of Bethlehem, the Magi, and Mary and Joseph themselves. Songs of Christmas have also always accompanied the season's secular merriments and pageantry, bringing light and warmth to a time otherwise dark and cold. While its diverse pasts illustrate the divisions among the various religious and national traditions, Christmas music has also been—through its dissemination, adaptation, and compilation across space and time—a means of uniting people of differing beliefs and backgrounds.

References and Further Reading

Bradley, Ian (ed.) (1999). *The Penguin Book of Carols*. London: Penguin.
Caldwell, Mary Channen (2013). 'Singing, Dancing, and Rejoicing in the Round: Latin Sacred Songs with Refrains, circa 1000–1582'. PhD dissertation. University of Chicago.
Crawford, Richard (ed.). *The Core Repertory of Early American Psalmody*. Madison, Wisconsin: A-R Editions.
Dearmer, Percy, Vaughan Williams, R., and Shaw, Martin (1929). *The Oxford Book of Carols*. Oxford: Oxford University Press.
Fallows, David (2018). *Henry V and the Earliest English Carols: 1413–1440*. Abingdon, Oxon.; New York: Routledge.
Fassler, Margot (1992). 'The Feast of Fools and *Danielis ludus*: Popular Tradition in a Medieval Cathedral Play', in Thomas Forrest Kelly (ed.), *Plainsong in the Age of Polyphony*. Cambridge: Cambridge University Press: 65–99.
Foley, Edward (1990). *The First Ordinary of The Royal Abbey of St.-Denis in France (Paris, Bibliothèque Mazarine, 526)*. Fribourg, Switzerland: University Press.
Foley, Edward (2012). 'A Tale of Two Sanctuaries: Late Medieval Eucharist and the Analogous', in Ian Christopher Levy, Gary Macy, and Kristen Van Ausdall (eds.), *A Companion to the Eucharist in the Middle Ages*. Leiden and Boston: Brill: 327–64.
Gilbert, Davies (1823). *Some Ancient Christmas Carols, with the Tunes to Which They Were Formerly Sung in the West of England. Together with Two Ancient Ballads, a Dialogue, &c.* London: J. Nichols and Son.
Greene, Richard Leighton (1935; rev. and exp. 1977). *The Early English Carols*. Oxford: Clarendon Press.

Heintzelmann, Matthew Z. (2001). 'Drama, Christmas Plays', in John M. Jeep (ed.), *Medieval Germany: An Encyclopedia*. New York: Garland.

Hiley, David (1995). *Western Plainchant: A Handbook*. Oxford: Clarendon Press.

Hone, William (1823) *Ancient Mysteries Described*. London: William Hone.

Husk, William Henry (1868). *Songs of the Nativity; Being Christmas Carols, Ancient and Modern*. London: John Camden Hotten.

Hymns and Carols of Christmas. Available at http://www.hymnsandcarolsofchristmas.com/ (accessed 21 March 2020).

Irving, Washington (1809). *A History of New-York*. New York: Inskeep and Bradford.

Keyte, Hugh, and Andrew Parrot ed. (1992). *The New Oxford Book of Carols*. Oxford: Oxford University Press.

Lagueux, Robert Charles (2004). 'Glossing Christmas: Liturgy, Music, Exegesis, and Drama in High Medieval Laon'. Ph.D. dissertation, Yale University.

Lagueux, Robert C. (2009). 'Sermons, Exegesis, and Performance: The Laon *Ordo Prophetarum* and the Meaning of Advent', *Comparative Drama*, 43: 197–220.

Llewellyn, Jeremy (2018). 'Nova Cantica', in Mark Everest and Thomas Forrest Kelly (eds.), *The Cambridge History of Medieval Music*, Vol. 1. Cambridge: Cambridge University Press: 147–75.

McCaskey, J. P. (ed.) (1887). *The Franklin Square Song Collection*, No. 4 (1887). New York: Harper and Brothers.

Nettle, Reginald (1960). *Christmas and Its Carols*. London: Faith Press.

Nissenbaum, Stephen (2013). 'How Handel's *Messiah* Became a Christmas Tradition', *Händel-Jahrbuch*, 59: 291–302.

Parsil, Dolores (2016). *Lancaster's Good Man: John Piersol McCaskey*. Morgantown, Pennsylvania: Masthof Press.

Rathey, Markus (2016). *Johann Sebastian Bach's Christmas Oratorio: Music, Theology, Culture*. New York: Oxford University Press.

Rousseau, Jean-Jacques (1768). *Dictionnaire de musique*. Paris: Chez la veuve Duchesne.

Routley, Erik (1958). *The English Carol*. New York: Oxford University Press.

Sandys, William (1833). *Christmas Carols, Ancient and Modern: Including the Most Popular in the West of England, and the Airs to Which They Are Sung. Also Specimens of French Provincial Carols*. London: Richard Beckley.

Sandys, William (1852). *Christmastide: Its History, Festivities, and Carols*. London: J. R. Smith.

Smaill, Adele Margaret (2003). 'Medieval Carols: Origins, Forms, and Performance Contexts'. Ph.D. dissertation. University of Michigan.

Sorrell, Roger D. (2009). *St Francis of Assisi and Nature: Tradition and Innovation in Western Christian Attitudes toward the Environment*. New York: Oxford University Press.

Stevens, John (ed.) (2018). *Mediæval Carols*. Third ed. by David Fallows. *Musica Britannica*, IV. London: Stainer and Bell.

Strohm, Reinhard (1993). *The Rise of European Music, 1380–1500*. Cambridge: Cambridge University Press.

Studwell, William (1995). *The Christmas Carol Reader*. New York: Haworth Press.

Studwell, William E., and Dorothy E. Jones (1998). *Publishing Glad Tidings: Essays on Christmas Music*. New York and London: Haworth Press.

Piæ Cantiones: Ecclesiasticae Et Scholasticae Veterum Episcoporum (1582, facsimile 1967). Helsinki-Helsingfors: Edition Fazer.

CHAPTER 27

CAROLS AND MUSIC SINCE 1900

TODD DECKER

When is it acceptable to play Christmas music? Only at sundown on Christmas Eve and during the twelve days to follow would be the answer of the stricter church organists and choir directors who follow the Christian liturgical calendar. Carols and songs of Christmas may resound in worship only from the celebration of the birth of Christ on Christmas Eve through Epiphany in early January (or, in some contexts, Candlemas at the start of February). The four weeks before Christmas Eve comprise the season of Advent, a penitential period with its own, rather small, musical repertoire centred in Protestant churches on the carol 'O Come, O Come Emmanuel'.

In contrast to the church calendar, Christmas music in mass media begins some five to eight weeks before Christmas Eve, then falls silent shortly after Christmas Day. Music Choice, a music content provider to digital cable companies across the United States, switches to Christmas music on its 'Sounds of the Season' channel on November 1, the same day the satellite radio provider SiriusXM adds fifteen Christmas channels to its line-up. Music Choice ends Christmas music on January 6; SiriusXM cuts it off (except for one year-round channel) on December 28 (Music Choice 2019; SiriusXM 2019). Most major radio markets in the US have at least one station that flips to all-Christmas programming just after Thanksgiving Day (celebrated the fourth Thursday in November) on Black Friday, the start of the Christmas shopping season. Such 'stunt' programming, according to Jon Miller, VP of Audience Insights for the media ratings-company Nielsen, 'creates a dynamic in the radio listening marketplace that doesn't exist during the rest of the year and it changes the way people use radio' ('Nielsen' 2017). The mass media Christmas season also changes the way people use music, and this seasonal use of music relies on a body of musical works enjoyed by most people only during the secular Christmas season of the four or so weeks before Christmas Day. Indeed, the music streaming service Spotify carefully marks Christmas tracks by way of algorithms and flags, which prevent holiday songs from appearing in a user's feed unless such music is specifically requested (Hickey 2015). These musical works—a group of Christmas carols and songs with overlapping media histories, lyrical tropes, and sonic signifiers—simultaneously mark and make the contemporary Christmas season as celebrated outside religious contexts.

This chapter on carols and music since 1900 centres on the repertoire of recorded Christmas music circulating at present in the popular music marketplace in the United States. Following musicologist Richard Crawford's concept (Crawford and Magee, 1992) of a core repertory (the most frequently printed or recorded works in a given genre), Table 27.1 lists seventy-five Christmas songs that have circulated widely in recorded form since about 1942, when the signal Christmas hit 'White Christmas' established the genre of the secular, popular Christmas song. The core repertory offered here is at once historical (including hits that made their strongest impact in the past) and cumulative (reflecting the enduring presence of songs and recordings from across the decades into the contemporary moment).

Sources informing the core repertory include sales charts from the trade publication Billboard and user data and playlists from the streaming service Spotify. Joel Whitburn's Christmas in the Charts: 1920–2004 provides several lists that account for the varying methodologies Billboard has used over the decades to quantify the sales of recorded Christmas music. Lists from Whitburn drawn on here include:

- Song titles with the most versions that charted as singles. 'White Christmas', 'Jingle Bells', and 'The Little Drummer Boy' top this list (Whitburn 2004: 76)
- Song titles appearing most frequently on charting albums. 'Silent Night', 'White Christmas', and 'The Christmas Song' hold the three top positions (Whitburn 2004: 269)
- Specific recordings that charted over consecutive years. Bing Crosby's original 1942 'White Christmas' holds the record, charting every year but one (1952) between 1942 and 1970. The Harry Simeone Chorale's 'The Little Drummer Boy' charted consecutively from 1958 to 1970, and Bobby Helms' 'Jingle Bell Rock' from 1960 to 1970 (Whitburn 2004: 76)
- Whitburn's most expansive list chronologically enumerates song titles that charted on at least six occasions and specific records that were either Top 10 hits on the Hot 100 chart or number 1 hits on the Country, R&B, Adult Contemporary, or Christmas charts. This list begins in 1934 with the songs 'Winter Wonderland' and 'Santa Claus is Coming to Town' (Whitburn 2004: 74–5)

Spotify provides three lists that capture the shape of Christmas music listening in the streaming era and confirm the rootedness of the twenty-first-century Christmas pop repertory in a past reaching back to the mid-twentieth century:

- Top 20 Christmas songs streamed globally (2017)
- Top 10 streamed in the US (2017)
- The Spotify-curated Christmas Classics playlist—the service's holiday playlist with the most followers (1.6 million in 2019)

Table 27.1 A Christmas Core Repertory

Title	Year Pub.	Music / Lyrics	Significant Recordings
God Rest Ye, Merry Gentlemen	c1760	Traditional (English)	Annie Lennox (2010)
Silent Night	1818	Franz Xaver Gruber / Joseph Mohr	Mahalia Jackson (1962), Barbra Streisand (1967)
The First Noel	1823	Traditional (English, Cornish)	Frank Sinatra (1957)
Joy to the World	1848	Isaac Watts (1719) / hymn tune 'Antioch' (1848)	Aretha Franklin (1995)
Jingle Bells	1857	James Lord Pierpont	Benny Goodman and his Orchestra (1935), Ella Fitzgerald (1960), The Singing Dogs (1971), Spongebob Squarepants (2005)
Santa Claus is Comin' to Town	1934	John Frederick Coots / Haven Gillespie	George Hall and his Orchestra (1935), Bing Crosby and the Andrews Sisters (1947), The 4 Seasons (1962), The Supremes (1965), The Jackson 5 (1970), Bruce Springsteen (1975)
Winter Wonderland	1934	Felix Bernard / Richard B. Smith	Guy Lombardo and his Royal Canadians (1934), Tony Bennett (1968), The Eurythmics (1987)
We Wish You a Merry Christmas	1935	Traditional (English, West Country)	John Denver and the Muppets (1979)
The Little Drummer Boy	1941	Katherine Kennicott Davis	Trapp Family Singers (1951, titled 'Carol of the Drum'), Harry Simeone Chorale (1958)
White Christmas	1942	Irving Berlin	Bing Crosby (1942), The Drifters (1956), Elvis Presley (1957), Louis Armstrong (1964), Taylor Swift (2007)
I'll Be Home for Christmas	1943	Walter Kent / Kim Gannon	Bing Crosby (1943), Michael Bublé (2011)
Have Yourself a Merry Little Christmas	1944	Hugh Martin / Ralph Blane	Judy Garland (1944), Sam Smith (2014)
Let It Snow! Let It Snow! Let It Snow!	1945	Jule Styne / Sammy Cahn	Frank Sinatra and the B. Swanson Quartet (1950)
The Christmas Song	1946	Robert Wells / Mel Tormé	Nat King Cole (recorded versions with his trio and strings in 1946 [2], 1953, and 1961)
Sleigh Ride	1948	Leroy Anderson (1948) / Mitchel Parish (1950)	Leroy Anderson (1950), The Ronettes (1963)

(Continued)

Table 27.1 Continued

Title	Year Pub.	Music / Lyrics	Significant Recordings
Blue Christmas	1949	Billy Hayes / Jay W. Johnson	Elvis Presley (1957)
Rudolph, the Red-Nosed Reindeer	1949	Johnny Marks	Gene Autry (1949)
It's Beginning to Look A Lot Like Christmas	1951	Meredith Willson	Perry Como and the Fontane Sisters (1951), Michael Bublé (2011)
Silver Bells	1951	Jay Livingston / Ray Evans	Dean Martin (1966), Stevie Wonder (1967)
Jingle Bell Rock	1957	Joseph Carleton Beal / James Ross Boothe	Bobby Helms (1957)
Rockin' Around the Christmas Tree	1958	Johnny Marks	Brenda Lee (1958)
It's the Most Wonderful Time of the Year	1963	Edward Pola / George Wyle	Andy Williams (1963)
A Holly Jolly Christmas	1964	Johnny Marks	Burl Ives (1964), Michael Bublé (2011)
Last Christmas	1984	Wham!	Wham! (1984)
All I Want for Christmas is You	1993	Mariah Carey / Walter Afanasieff	Mariah Carey (1993)

OUTER CORE
(Song title and composition date; listed in chronological order; carol dates reflect when tune and lyrics were first published together.)
O Come All Ye Faithful (1740); O Christmas Tree (1824 [German lyrics]); O Holy Night (1847); It Came Upon the Midnight Clear (1850); Hark, the Herald Angels Sing (1856); Deck the Halls (1862 [English lyrics]); What Child is This? (1865); O Little Town of Bethlehem (1868); Away in a Manger (1887); The Twelve Days of Christmas (1909); Carol of the Bells (1919); Christmas Island (1946); Here Comes Santa Claus (Right Down Santa Claus Lane) (1947); Merry Christmas Baby (1947); All I Want for Christmas is My Two Front Teeth (1948); You're All I Want for Christmas (two versions: 1948 and 1963); Baby, It's Cold Outside (1949); Frosty the Snowman (1950); Lonesome Christmas (Pts. 1 and 2) (1950); Mele Kalikimaka (1950); (Everybody's Waitin' for) The Man with the Bag (1950); I Saw Mommy Kissing Santa Claus (1952); Santa Baby (1953); (There's No Place Like) Home for the Holidays (1954); The Christmas Waltz (1954); Nuttin' for Christmas (1955); Mary's Boy Child (1956); The Chipmunk Song (Christmas Don't Be Late) (1958); Please Come Home for Christmas (1960); Do You Hear What I Hear? (1962); Pretty Paper (1963); Little Saint Nick (1963); Santa Looked a Lot Like Daddy (1965); Christmas Time is Here (1965); You're A Mean One Mr. Grinch (1966); Merry Christmas Darling (1970); Feliz Navidad (1970); Happy Christmas (War is Over) (1971); This Christmas (1971); Step Into Christmas (1973); If We Make It Through December (1973); Wonderful Christmastime (1980); Christmas in Dixie (1982); Grandma Got Run Over By a Reindeer (1982); Do They Know It's Christmas? (1984); Driving Home for Christmas (1986); Fairytale of New York (1987); I Only Want You for Christmas (1991); Mistletoe (2011); Santa Tell Me (2013).

Mariah Carey's 1993 track 'All I Want for Christmas is You' tops the first two lists. However, Crosby's 'White Christmas' appears ninth on the global Top 20 and eight tracks on the US Top 10 were originally released before 1965. The presence of old recordings on these lists indicate the sedimented nature of the core repertory: old songs, recordings, and artists endure for decades in the Christmas corner of popular music. The Christmas Classics playlist is dominated by mid-twentieth-century records and artists but points towards post-1970 releases that have attained 'classic' status (at least in this context) beyond Carey's 'All I Want for Christmas is You', such as Wham!'s 'Last Christmas' (1984) (Vacher and Van Buskirk 2017; Spotify 2019a).

An eighth and final list, also drawing on Spotify, rounds out the sources informing the core repertory. In 2015, Walt Hickey analysed Spotify's entire catalogue of 1.3 million holiday tracks (categorized as such by Spotify) for the statistics-oriented website fivethirtyeight.com (Hickey 2015). Hickey's list of the twenty-five most-covered Christmas songs on Spotify usefully highlights the oldest songs in the repertory: traditional carols in the public domain.

Table 27.1 sorts the core repertory into two prioritized groups. The twenty-five song titles in the inner core each appear on three or more of the eight lists described above. An outer core of fifty titles—some making only one of the lists—adds generic breadth and historical range. The distinction between song titles and recordings requires some flexibility here: some song titles have been frequently recorded and exist in many versions (Whitburn lists 337 album tracks of 'Jingle Bells'; Hickey counts 26,496 versions of 'Silent Night' on Spotify); some song titles endure chiefly by way of a singular, iconic recording (Brenda Lee's 'Rockin' Around the Christmas Tree'); and some combine both of these modes of transmission (Crosby's original 'White Christmas' is just one of eighteen versions of the song that have charted as singles). And so, while the core repertory enumerates song titles, in many cases one or two early recordings have had a lasting presence or influence on how a given song is arranged and sung. Michael Bublé's many twenty-first-century recordings of mid-twentieth-century holiday songs owe an audible debt to earlier singers. A Spotify playlist of the entire core repertory in alphabetical order, including all the songs and recordings discussed further on in the chapter, can be found at username ChristmasCoreRepertory (Spotify 2019b).

Carols, Songs, and Popular Music History

The core repertory has proven relatively stable since about 1970. Indeed, the survival of this body of relatively old songs in the ever-unfolding popular music present attests to the distinction of popular Christmas music within the larger context of popular music history, which favours continuous change in repertory. Dividing the core repertory into two content-based groups—carols and songs—helps clarify this aspect of Christmas music since 1900.

Thirteen titles in the core repertory fall into the category of carols. Carols express core aspects of the Christian Christmas story, are likely to appear in most Christian hymnals, and are strophic in form (a lyric made of several stanzas, each sung to the same, relatively short tune of about four phrases). Even performers who do not identify as Christian record carols: Barbra Streisand's 'Sleep in Heavenly Peace (Silent Night)' topped the Billboard Christmas chart in 1966. All of the carols in the core repertory were published before or during the nineteenth century; several draw on traditional tunes and texts reaching back centuries. They are, for many pop artists, by far the oldest works of music they perform.

Most of the titles in the core repertory are best understood as standard-issue popular songs on a Christmas or wintertime theme. Henceforth, use of the word song in this chapter indicates this narrowly defined group. Songs refer to, and in some cases originate, secular Christmas content (the Santa Claus narrative and the convivial winter festival nature of the so-called holiday season) and are under copyright (and thus require licensing for their use). Most follow the common form of the 'classical' popular song between the 1910s and the 1950s (a thirty-two-bar chorus with one set of lyrics that include the song's title, sometimes with an introductory and optional verse). Songs of this type—the vast majority written between 1940 and 1965—have been instrumental in defining Christmas as a decidedly secular holiday lacking any explicitly Christian content.

One notable inner core title falls between the carol/song dichotomy. 'The Little Drummer Boy'— composed in 1941, first recorded by the Trapp Family Singers in 1951—found enduring pop success in an evocative recording by the Harry Simeone Chorale released in 1958. The song's lyrics communicate explicitly Christian content. Like several secular Christmas hits of the 1950s discussed later in the chapter, 'The Little Drummer Boy' introduces a new character—the titular boy—to the tangle of narratives that make up Christmas. The boy even interacts with Mary—who nods at him—and the baby Jesus—who smiles at him. The boy's response to Jesus's smile receives extraordinary musical emphasis on the Simeone Chorale's recording, with a dramatic pause in the rhythm and a breathless absolute silence. The boy's heart-stopping encounter with Jesus captures a shared quality of most all the carols and songs in the core repertory: fruitful interaction between a given lyric and the narrative nature of Christmas as simultaneously an event, a period of time, and an annual recurrence. 'The Little Drummer Boy' (like traditional carols and two outer core titles with Christian content: 'Mary's Boy Child' [1956] and 'Do You Hear What I Hear?' [1962]) inserts the listener into the Christian story of Christmas. Secular Christmas songs similarly put the listener into various secular narratives of the season: some more general (going to parties or out shopping, sending seasonal greetings, just dreaming) but many centred on another Christmas Eve arrival: the annual return of Santa Claus with presents for all. The similar power of Christmas carols and songs to locate the listener within broadly shared cultural or religious narratives powerfully marks this repertory—and perhaps explains why Christmas carols and songs are unwelcome out of season. Virtually all Christmas music in the core repertory traffics in seasonal narratives. But while carols typically build on events and characters found in the New Testament and amplified in Christian tradition, popular songs have been a vibrant constructive site where secular Christmas narratives are not only amplified but also invented. In such cases, the space of a song literally contains the substance of the season.

While carols survive in popular music as remnants of a specifically Christian heritage, the core repertory songs boldly define an innovative, secular, distinctly American Christmas holiday and season. The next three sections sort the songs of the core repertory into three categories—'white', 'green', and 'blue'—based primarily on an analysis of lyrics. Implied holiday narratives—seasonal experiences of the weather, Santa's arrival, romance in wintertime—inform each category. The varied temporal identity of Christmas as event, season, and cyclical recurrence shapes the experience of these songs which, when listened to or sung, have the power to intensify or activate common holiday practices of reflection, expectation, and fulfilment. After considering the origins and content of these three song categories, a final section traces sonic continuities across the entire core repertory by lending an ear to the glistening timbres (or sound colours) that signal the season as expressed on recordings.

'White Christmas' and Other Songs of Experience

Songwriter Irving Berlin's 'White Christmas' originated the secular, popular Christmas song hit. Berlin's commercial savvy, historical happenstance, and dissemination by overlapping mass media forms launched 'White Christmas', and the song's huge success, in turn, initiated a commercially vibrant genre: songs—ballads, mostly—that construct the Christmas holiday around memories of Christmases past and the direct expression of warm greetings for Christmas present. In these songs, Christmas is an extended experience—a season, not an event—to recall and dream about and to share in sociable groups, often including children. Berlin firmly locates this re-imagined holiday 'in the snow'.

Berlin composed 'White Christmas' in 1940 as part of a film vehicle for singer Bing Crosby titled Holiday Inn. The success of Berlin's song 'Easter Parade', introduced in the 1932 Broadway musical As Thousands Cheer and included in Holiday Inn, inspired the always market-minded songwriter to compose a comprehensive catalogue of seasonal tunes. The plot of Holiday Inn strings together songs for Christmas, New Year's Eve, Lincoln's Birthday, Valentine's Day, Easter, the Fourth of July, and Thanksgiving. Only the Christmas and New Year's Eve tunes from the film have endured as seasonal standards. (Elsewhere I have detailed how Berlin's lyric for 'White Christmas' shaped the plot of Holiday Inn [Decker 2011: 468–75]).

Crosby first sang 'White Christmas' on the radio on Christmas Day 1941. Holiday Inn was in production at the time. Entrance of the United States into World War II in response to the attack on Pearl Harbor on 7 December surely influenced the decision to introduce 'White Christmas' several months before Holiday Inn's premiere: the content of the lyric spoke movingly, if coincidentally, to the new and unsure situation facing a nation mobilizing for war. 'White Christmas' was released on record and in the film in August 1942. The song became an immediate and surprising summer hit and, as Berlin had hoped, a reliable annual favourite. Indeed, Berlin's song and Crosby's recording are frequently cited as the best-selling popular music items in history.

The song's title unambiguously locates Christmas in places where it snows in December: Berlin's emphasis on snow locates a truly satisfying Christmas in the North, likely the American north-east and Midwest. Indeed, the seldom-sung verse to 'White Christmas' situates the singer in 'Beverly Hills, LA', where the sun shines on green grass and swaying orange and palm trees even on Christmas Eve. By implication, Christmas without snow—without 'white'—is less than complete. The chorus lyric proceeds to mention children listening for sleigh bells and the writing of Christmas cards. Both suggest social interactions outside of any romantic context: a key departure from most popular songs. And so, Berlin's lyric re-constructs a religious holiday out of a regional climate, multi-generational sociability, and the act of offering a formal Christmas greeting. Christmas, in this influential song, is an essentially social experience, even if the lyric, with its repeated 'I' sentences, hints at a solitary individual musing to himself or herself. Fragments of narrative haunt 'White Christmas': dreaming, listening, and writing messages to friends are all common acts that acquire special resonance during the holiday season. And simply listening to 'White Christmas' inserts the listener into a holiday narrative: humming or singing along goes a step further. In such ways, popular Christmas music, enjoyed in its season, enacts a repetition of words, melodies, and ideas that together constitute a wholly secular, informal, widely distributed ritual practice of a re-imagined Christmastime.

Many core repertory songs repeat the tropes and suggested narratives first set down by Berlin in 'White Christmas'. 'I'll Be Home for Christmas' (1943) lists 'snow' among its key Christmas signifiers—adding 'mistletoe' and 'presents'—and makes this sort of Christmas a place accessible in one's dreams: the song itself opens a sonic space where the dream can be achieved. 'Have Yourself a Merry Little Christmas' (1944) begins with a greeting, puts sustained friendships at the centre of the season, and returns obsessively to the title's rather modest wish. Both these songs appeared shortly after 'White Christmas' and during World War II, when military men and women were separated from their homes 'for the duration' of the conflict. 'White Christmas' speaks as well to themes of separation, longing, and dreaming (see, for example, Crosby singing to soldiers near the front lines in the Pacific Theatre in the 1946 film *Blue Skies* and the European Theatre in the 1954 film *White Christmas*). The melancholy of actual separation during the war, felt across the broad swath of American listeners when these songs first appeared, resounds in the many subsequent recorded versions of these songs as a more generalized nostalgia and longing for Christmases past.

Christmas songs experienced a boost in popularity after World War II (see next section) and the snow-children-greetings progression of 'White Christmas' remained a sturdy template open to less melancholy expression. 'The Christmas Song' (1946) follows the model closely: initial references to 'Jack Frost' and 'folks' in winter clothing are followed by children waiting for Santa's arrival; an explicit greeting closes the song. (The famous opening line about 'chestnuts roasting' carried a different resonance when the song first appeared. Adult Americans in the mid-1940s would likely remember the annual abundance of chestnuts—a gift of the land, relied on for centuries by the less fortunate—that had recently disappeared with the complete destruction by blight of North America's native chestnut forests [Vandermast 2008: 345]). Upbeat songs such as 'The Christmas Waltz' (1954), 'It's the Most Wonderful Time of the Year' (1963), and 'A Holly Jolly Christmas' (1964) also touch on snow, Santa, and sociability with friends, and leave off any longing for the past: these tunes insist that Christmas is 'the best' or 'most wonderful' time of year and that 'every' song seems to be offering holiday greetings. In a further reduction of the model, 'Feliz Navidad' (1970) offers only a greeting: first in Spanish, then in English. In a contrasting reflexive vein, 'Christmas Time is Here', introduced in the 1965 television special A Charlie Brown Christmas, recycles the tropes of 'White Christmas' then wishes, at the close, that 'such spirit' could be seen throughout the year.

In their evocation of a 'white' Christmas, several of these songs implicitly reference the song 'Jingle Bells' (1857), the lyric for which, without mentioning Christmas, celebrates snowy weather as experienced by apparently middle-class folks with access to a 'one-horse open sleigh'—a leisure vehicle used for courtship in the humorous narrative verses. The sound of jingle bells became synonymous with sleigh bells (referenced by Berlin in 'White Christmas') as early as 1934 in the lyric to 'Winter Wonderland' (also lacking the word Christmas) and the experience of moving delightedly through 'frosty' and 'lovely' weather in an old-fashioned conveyance recurs in songs like 'Sleigh Ride' (1948) and 'Jingle Bell Rock' (1957).

The 'white' Christmas song of seasonal experience as synonymous with winter weather in the north-eastern and Midwestern United States is gently challenged in songs like 'Christmas Island' (1946, where Santa arrives in a canoe), 'Mele Kalikimaka' (1950, the title offers a Hawaiian Christmas greeting), and 'Christmas in Dixie' (1982, where at least there's snow 'in the pines'). Such songs register by contrast the normative cold climate of most popular, secular Christmas songs on Berlin's original model and the enduring example of 'Jingle Bells', the oldest song (again, as opposed to a carol) in the core repertory.

"Green Chritma": Songs of Santa and Gifts

Berlin never specifies the origin of the 'sleigh bells' heard in 'White Christmas': it could be a passing 'one-horse open sleigh' or it could be Santa. Santa Claus in his American guise as a jolly bringer of presents on Christmas Eve looms large in a second group within the core repertory: songs that frame Christmas as an occasion for gift-giving and receiving. Songs for children prove central to this category, which grew rapidly, with the post-World War II expansion of the US economy, into a song type to rival the Christmas-as-experience songs modelled on 'White Christmas'. These are songs of Christmas as a transactional, unabashedly commercial holiday celebrating gifts, shopping, and Santa.

The two earliest, popular songs to mention Santa date to the mid-nineteenth century: 'Jolly Old Saint Nicholas' and 'Up on the Housetop' have seldom been included on Christmas albums and no single of either has ever charted (neither make the core repertory). Santa's real entrée into popular music occurred in 1934 with the song 'Santa Claus is Coming to Town'. A modest hit for George Hall and his Orchestra upon release and for Crosby and the Andrews Sisters in 1947, rock-era performers such as the 4 Seasons (1962), The Supremes (1965), and the Jackson 5 (1970) recorded it with success and rock icon Bruce Springsteen made it a signature inclusion at his holiday season concerts from early in his career. 'Santa Claus is Coming to Town' distils the Santa narrative to a reiterated warning: Santa's arrival is imminent so be good or no presents. The resonance of the lyric precisely matches the secular season: after Santa's Christmas Eve visitation, Christmas—and the need for the song— is over. (Brad Paisley's '364 Days to Go' [2006] captures the moment just after the gifts have been opened, when the next round of presents reappears in the most distant future imaginable in this cyclical system of exchange.)

But, of course, Santa is physically present everywhere in the weeks leading up to Christmas. Singer and movie star Gene Autry's experience leading the Hollywood Christmas Parade—an annual event in the Southern California sun that ended with Santa's arrival—inspired the 1947 children's hit 'Here Comes Santa Claus (Right Down Santa Claus Lane)', a song that gently sacralizes the Santa narrative. Autry's lyric dwells more on the promise of peace than on toys, and persistent references to 'the light', 'prayers', and 'the Lord above' hint at a non-specific sacred dimension accessible to all: no mention of good or bad here; all will be rewarded if they only 'jump in bed' when Santa makes his visit. Again, the lyric takes the listener to the brink of Christmas morning, after which the song's meaning lapses for another year.

Autry's next Christmas record was a number 1 pop hit and a historic contribution to American secular Christmas music: 'Rudolph, the Red-Nosed Reindeer' (1949). Rudolph is an original Christmas character—a copyrighted and licensed property (unlike Santa and his eight named reindeer from the poem 'A Visit from St. Nicholas', first published in 1823 and commonly known by its first line, "Twas the Night Before Christmas'). Robert L. May created and introduced Rudolph in colouring books—red crayon required—distributed free by the department store Montgomery Ward beginning in 1939. May's brother-in-law, Johnny Marks, penned a song about the character in 1949. Autry and others recorded 'Rudolph' to great commercial success, solidifying the children's record, in the still-new, 7-inch, 45 rpm single format, as an important element in the popular music market. Rudolph enjoys a delightfully tangential relationship to the Santa narrative: should Christmas night prove dangerously foggy, his glowing nose will lead the way and save the day. Autry's copyrighted holiday characters did not end with Rudolph. He also introduced Frosty the Snowman, a cold-weather Christmas tangent who bears no gifts but the joy he spreads marching around town. (And in a Berlin-esque move, in 1950 Autry expanded to other holidays and recorded the most successful version of 'Here Comes Peter Cottontail', a branded version of the Easter Bunny who, like Santa, delivers gifts.)

These Christmas songs for children (excluding 'Here Comes Santa Claus') found transmedia success and expanded narrative treatment as half-hour animated or stop-motion television specials in the 1960s. Annual not-to-be-missed broadcast events into the 1980s, with the advent of the home video market (VHS tapes, then DVDs), songs about the Santa-Rudolph-Frosty constellation were perpetuated across generations and reified as gifts, treasured holiday possessions, and points of reference for each song's many covers. Streaming video services keep these artefacts of earlier popular Christmas culture alive into the twenty-first century.

The Santa narrative reduces Christmas to a transactional holiday with gifts at the centre: Kay Starr's '(Everybody's Waiting for) The Man with the Bag' (1950) succinctly expresses this notion in its title. As noted, some Christmas-as-experience songs on the 'White Christmas' model also foreground presents. Almost every sign of Christmas enumerated in 'It's Beginning to Look a Lot Like Christmas' (1951) is specifically commercial, with toys in 'every store' and specific items for boys and girls in the song's patter trio. A carol sung in one's heart at the close of the chorus tries in vain to signal something besides things as the reason for the season. 'Silver Bells' (introduced in the 1951 film The Lemon Drop Kid, which involves a Christmastime con exploiting donation-collecting Santas) similarly paints the holiday city as given over entirely to 'Santa' and shoppers rushing around. The closing words of the chorus, 'soon it will be Christmas day', warn the listener—perhaps a parent doing Santa's work—of the impending end of a season defined by the act of shopping.

The Santa narrative and Christmas as all about gifts opens the way for comic and novelty songs about individuals with unique challenges or expectations as to the presents they will receive. Here, again, popular songs added new characters and situations to the narratives of the secular season. Many such songs appeared in the late 1940s and 1950s, often to substantial commercial success, suggesting a persistent place in popular music for inventive skewering of the retail pieties of the season. Spike Jones & his City Slickers took 'All I Want for Christmas is My Two Front Teeth' to the top of the pop charts in 1947, as did 13-year-old Jimmy Boyd with 'I Saw Mommy Kissing Santa Claus' in 1952. The latter, somewhat creepily, remains in the eyes of a child while also mining the erotic potential of the Santa narrative for adults. Eartha Kitt's number 4 pop hit 'Santa Baby' (1953) works similarly but with less discomfort (and no evident tots) by casting Santa as the sugar daddy to Kitt's gold digger recitation of a long and expensive list. 'Nuttin' for Christmas' (a number 6 hit in 1955) gifts its naughty child lyrical 'I' with an indulgent cameo. 'The Chipmunk Song' (a number 1 hit in 1958) rises to its height when the rascally Alvin belts out his consuming desire for a hula hoop: in such moments the secular Christmas song gives musical power to the simple desire for stuff.

All the songs discussed in this section thus far entered the core repertory between 1947 and 1960. The expansion of the American economy in these years, benefitting white Americans in particular, resounds across this category. And so, as with 'White Christmas' and its progeny, songs of Santa and presents speak to a comfortable middle class able to shape the Christmas season around abundant leisure and discretionary spending. This linking of Christmas to consumption and commercialism came in for skewering at the time in Stan Freberg's 1958 comedy record and cult favourite, 'Green Chritma'. Presented as a demented advertising meeting, the sketch lampoons how recognizable and imagined American corporations link their products to the season. As one executive says, 'Christmas has two 's's in it and they're both dollar signs.' Manic musical fragments, none coalescing into a recognizable tune, tie specific products, such as branded chestnuts, to the meaning of the season. Actual Christmas songs centered on Santa, children's hopes, and the buying of presents function similarly as more generalized advertisements and rationales for consumption. This would seem to be the default mode for a large swath of Christmas songs.

Critique of consumption or Christmas as transaction has never gained serious traction in the core repertory and only minor Christmas hits, such as Roy Orbison's 'Pretty Paper' (1963) and Band Aid's 'Do They Know It's Christmas?', have broached the topic with any success.

'Blue Christmas' and Other Songs of Romance

Romantic love occupies the narrative heart of popular music. A third category of Christmas songs explores familiar romance narratives in a Christmas or wintertime setting. Christmas as a set of tropes or string of seasonal nouns can, at times, seem merely decorative in these songs. Nonetheless, the link between the holiday and persistent romantic hopes and desires is strong.

A sizeable group of songs present failed romance during the holidays, when feelings of sadness are intensified by the good cheer all around. Elvis Presley's 'Blue Christmas' (1957) contrasts the singer's blue 'memories' with his absent lover's 'Christmas of white'. The specifics of the narrative are unclear but separation—Christmas 'without you'—proves a recurring theme, heard again in 'Merry Christmas Darling' (1970), which reworks the tropes of 'White Christmas' and sends the not especially seasonal wish, 'I want to be with you', to just one person—the beloved. In such moments, 'blue' Christmas songs narrow the holiday to the romantic couple: the sociability of the season, as well as the ubiquitous children underfoot, disappear.

Singing a Christmas-themed blues has been a common practice, especially for African-American performers. The blues singer and pianist Charles Brown set the pattern with his enduring 1947 hit 'Merry Christmas Baby', a twelve-bar blues record that was still regularly reaching the top ten of Billboard's Christmas chart into the 1970s. Brown extolls his lover's gifts to him, including a diamond ring, and declares his desire to kiss her underneath the ubiquitous mistletoe (an object and site of much pop music veneration; see Justin Bieber's 2011 'Mistletoe', among the newest additions to the core repertory). Other Christmas blues, such as Lowell Fulson's two-part 'Lonesome Christmas' (1950) and Brown's 'Please Come Home for Christmas' (1960), rehearse familiar territory (presents, children, snow, Santa, mistletoe) but, as their titles suggest, feature discontented personas meditating on separation from the beloved, framed in romantic and sexual, rather than nostalgic, terms.

Songs of Christmas and romance frequently declare themselves in their titles, and the combination of several direct words—Christmas, want, all, I, you—have been arranged to serve more than one song. The earliest example is 'You're All I Want for Christmas', which makes the claim that 'each day' with the beloved is like Christmas. Here, the once-a-year holiday is reconfigured as a metaphor for desire realized outside the cycle of the year: Christmas as a code word for wishes granted. The lyric ends with the odd desire to awake on Christmas morning to find 'my stocking filled with you'. While Frankie Laine had a hit with 'You're All I Want for Christmas' in 1948, Bing Crosby also recorded the song, demonstrating Crosby's capacity to deliver all the major types of Christmas song. An entirely different song with the title 'You're All I Want for Christmas' was released by the black singer Brook Benton in 1963. Over a sensual groove, Benton asks for his lover's 'arms' and 'kisses' instead of the season's 'tinsel and show' and ends with a repeated plea, 'please want me too'. Typical of 'blue' songs, this one lists Christmas tropes only to reject them in favour of nothing but the beloved.

The same five words rearranged as 'All I Want for Christmas is You' have served three different songs, each ringing changes on the identical theme. (Song titles cannot be copyrighted.) The earliest, introduced by Carla Thomas in 1963, places the desire for one person's love in a social context (the gist being, let everyone else have their toys and stuff, I just want you) and refers to Santa without naming him. The second, by Vince Vance and the Valiants from 1989, runs a long list of Christmas tropes (holly, mistletoe, silver bells, tinsel, the beloved described as 'the angel atop my tree') before arriving at the same declaration. The record's bluesy, old-time rock and roll sound—complete with backing vocals and a honking saxophone solo—signals a romantic slow dance. The third song titled 'All I Want for Christmas is You', featuring Mariah Carey and released in 1993, remains the single most popular Christmas record of the twenty-first century, an enduring global hit that takes the tropes of the 'blue' Christmas song in a joyous direction. After an extended and emotive opening that lets Carey display her gospel-style vocal prowess, a shuffle beat with triplets in the piano drops in, setting a tone of exultant and nostalgic rock and roll fun that does not sound old fashioned. Carey's record sounds of its moment but also feels rooted in 1960s pop. The desire for recorded Christmas music at once new and nostalgically old—similar to Bublé's faithful covers of mid-century hits, but using an original and romantic song—is met here with great panache. Carey's relatively recent record has remained potent even as it recycles and musically remakes lyrical tropes reaching back to the 1940s.

Truly original takes on Christmas romance are rare in the core repertory. In an unusual twist, the British pop group Wham!'s 'Last Christmas' pre-emptively addresses a lover to whom the singer gave their heart in the past: 'this year' will be different, the singer declares. Throughout, the word 'Christmas' carries a stripped-down seasonal meaning: with no descriptive or narrative embellishment, the singer pledges not to repeat a mistake made last year; he is, however, still singing to the lover who rejected him 'last' year. In an expressive contrast to the lyric, the sound of the record communicates bouncy and jangly good cheer. Perhaps the repeated word 'Christmas'—or the iconic status of the singer, George Michael—alone keeps this record in the core repertory.

Winter romance without mention of Christmas recurs throughout the core repertory. 'Winter Wonderland' established this trope in 1934 and added a snowman named 'Parson Brown' to the dramatis personae of the season's narratives. 'Let It Snow! Let It Snow! Let It Snow!' (1945) describes the pleasures of a twosome camped out by a cosy fireside. In both tunes the sensuous pleasures of cold weather—albeit for those with coats and hearths—provides the lyrical keynote. The much less often recorded 'I've Got My Love to Keep Me Warm' (1937) meditates on a storm and the 'worst December', but casts the experience in a negative light. For winter songs to stick as Christmas songs, enjoyment of the weather is key. Or—perhaps—bad winter weather might be put to romantic use, as in the duet 'Baby, It's Cold Outside'. In this much-sung song set in a private space (another core repertory fireside), the 'Wolf' repeats the title phrase and assorted endearments to the 'Mouse', who lists the reasons why she (or he) needs to leave. (As introduced in the film 1949 film Neptune's Daughter, 'Wolf' and 'Mouse' are unassigned as to gender. The 2010 Christmas episode of the TV series Glee featured a male–male version.) 'Baby, It's Cold Outside' has come in for critique in the age of #MeToo: the lyric suggests sexual harassment to some (Fortin 2018). Whether the song survives or not, it has for decades marked the erotic edge of the Christmas core repertory.

Beyond that edge lies a corpus of sexually explicit Christmas songs: naughty novelties for adults only. The possible fleshly contents of a Christmas present often provide a narrative conceit in these songs, with cult hits such as Kay Martin and Her Body Guards' 1958 'I Know What You Want for Christmas' (its lyric, like risqué songs by 1920s' blues queens, riffs on teasing descriptions of the female body before claiming the intended gift is a puppy) and the Saturday Night Live 2006 musical short 'Dick in a Box' (which similarly extends the explicit, sexually boastful language of 1990s' rappers).

The Unifying Sound of Christmas 'Glisten'

The lyrics of Christmas carols and songs alike situate the listener within the narratives of the season, whether the Christian story of Jesus' birth or secular stories of seasonal experience, gifts, and romance. In this way, the core repertory of popular Christmas music contains a measure of variety. However, in the sonic domain of musical timbre, recordings across the corpus of Christmas music share a common element: instruments and sounds that glisten. Here, again, Berlin's 'White Christmas' provides essential orientation.

Berlin uses the word glisten to describe the treetops in the snow-covered scene of his Christmas dreams. (The word recurs in 'It's Beginning to Look a Lot Like Christmas', where the 'five and ten' [a store full of affordable gifts] glistens 'once again'.) In the next line of 'White Christmas', Berlin imagines children listening for sleigh bells. As staged and arranged early on in Holiday Inn, the lyric about glistening treetops and sleigh bells is followed by the sound of bright, ringing bells, represented on screen as bell-shaped ornaments on a Christmas tree, struck by Crosby with the mouthpiece of his pipe (never mind that five bells struck in succession yield six pitches in a euphonious seven-note descending pattern). One characteristic timbre (or sonic colour) of commercial Christmas music finds a point of origin in this movie moment featuring brightly ringing bells.

Shiny, diminutive, chime-like, metallic, glistening bell sounds resound across the corpus of commercial Christmas music. Glockenspiels, celestas (as heard in 'The Dance of the Sugar Plum Fairy' from the ballet The Nutcracker, an American holiday staple since the later 1950s), triangles, finger cymbals, and—of course—actual sleigh bells are central members of the instrumentarium of recorded Christmas music. Examples from famous records include:

- Rolled celesta chords at the start and a phrase of the melody played on glockenspiel during the instrumental chorus of Autry's 'Rudolph the Red-Nosed Reindeer'
- Finger cymbals throughout the Harry Simeone Chorale's 'The Little Drummer Boy'—the only sounds on the record not made by the voices of the singers
- Four seconds of nothing but sleigh bells answering the electric guitar lick that opens Bobby Helm's 'Jingle Bell Rock'
- Two seconds of jingle bells joined by acoustic guitar at the start of Bieber's 'Mistletoe'
- The music box-like opening of Carey's 'All I Want for Christmas is You'
- Glockenspiel and piano creating a sense of 'cold down along the beach' at the start of Springsteen's live recording of 'Santa Claus is Coming to Town' (1975)
- Struck (not shaken) sleigh bells alone marking the backbeats for much of John Lennon and Yoko Ono's 'Happy Christmas (War is Over)' (1971)
- Strategic chimes throughout Crosby's 'Do You Hear What I Hear?'(1962) and The Beach Boys' 'Little Saint Nick' (1963)
- The Big Ben chimes made tiny and shiny at the start of Arianna Grande's 'Santa Tell Me' (2013), which also features a toy piano doubling the vocal on the chorus
- Just about any version from any era of 'Silver Bells'

Actual bell-like instruments are not always necessary. Vince Guaraldi's piano playing in 'Christmas Time is Here' evokes a chime-like effect throughout. With the introduction of synthesizers in the early 1980s, pop Christmas records indulged in simulated, digitally generated bells and chimes. Paul McCartney's 'Wonderful Christmas Time' (1980) contains a study in synthetic glisten, mixed throughout with jingle bells, bell-like vocals (the children in the song sing 'ding-dong-ding-dong'), and other short and resonant sounds often in complex rhythmic alignment.

The sound of bells is, of course, also part of Christian traditions around the celebration of Christmas. The four Sundays of Advent, prior to Christmas Eve, are a penitential season: sometimes bells are set aside entirely during this period (as they are during the weeks of Lent before Easter). Then, on Christmas Eve and Day, bells ring out loudly and repeatedly to announce the birth of Christ—as described in the carol 'I Heard the Bells on Christmas Day' (lyrics 1863). Here, again, American popular music follows exactly the reverse practice: ringing, bell-like timbres as heard in generations of pop recordings resound across the Christmas core repertory during the holiday shopping season in the weeks before Christmas Eve, only to fall silent for another year shortly after Christmas Day. The glistening timbres of these recordings signal—with no words necessary—the 'merry and bright' nature of the Christmas season as celebrated, made, and replayed each year in popular music since World War II.

REFERENCES AND FURTHER READING

ASCAP (2016). '"Santa Claus is Coming to Town" Is Most-played Holiday Song of the Last 50 Years'. Available at https://www.ascap.com/press/2016/11-21-top-holiday-songs (accessed 22 March 2020).

Crawford, Richard and Magee, Jeffrey (1992). Jazz Standards on Record, 1900–1942: A Core Repertory. Chicago: Center for Black Music Research.

Decker, Todd (2011). 'On the Scenic Route to Irving Berlin's Holiday Inn (1942)', Journal of Musicology, 28, no. 4: 464–97.

Fortin, Jacey (2018). 'How "Baby, It's Cold Outside" Went from Parlor Act to Problematic', New York Times, 13 December.

Hickey, Walt (2015). 'The Most-Covered Christmas Songs Ever'. Available at https://fivethirtyeight.com/features/the-most-covered-christmas-songs-ever/ (accessed 22 March 2020).

Music Choice (2019). 'Sounds of the Seasons Schedule'. Available at https://musicchoice.com/wp-content/uploads/2019/01/2019-Sounds-Of-The-Seasons-Schedule.pdf/ (accessed 22 March 2020).

'Nielsen' (2017). 'Nielsen: 72% Ratings Spike for All-Christmas Radio Leaders', INSIDERADIO. Available at http://www.insideradio.com/free/nielsen-ratings-spike-for-all-christmas-radio-leaders/article_e5b5f450-e6e5-11e7-9342-43a49939fb73.html/ (accessed 22 March 2020).

SiriusXM (2019). Available at https://www.siriusxm.com/holiday-music/ (accessed 22 March 2020).

Spotify (2019a). Christmas Classics by Spotify (playlist). Available at https://open.spotify.com/playlist/37i9dQZF1DX6R7QUWePReA?si=Ni77otaaQJaSML6Zg-ZDOw (accessed 22 March 2020).

Spotify (2019b). ChristmasCoreRepertory (playlist). Available at https://open.spotify.com/playlist/oN4Mt6k3ttlgC7ylPisvGO (accessed 22 March 2020).

Vacher, Martin and Van Buskirk, Eliot (2017). 'The Most Christmassy Songs & Countries on Spotify'. Available at https://insights.spotify.com/us/2017/12/18/christmas-listening-data/.

Vandermast, David (2008). 'Blighted Hopes', American Scientist, 96, no. 4: 345–46.

Whitburn, Joel (2004). Christmas in the Charts: 1920–2004. Menomonee Falls, Wisconsin: Record Research, Inc.

CHAPTER 28

PAINTINGS

BARBARA VON BARGHAHN

THE ANNUNCIATION

THIS chapter will explore twelve days of the Christmas story in Renaissance and Baroque paintings, which depict the Gospel infancy narratives of Christ. Just as every journey has a starting point, every tale has a beginning, and so, the story of Christmas in art which largely concerns events associated with travel, appropriately opens with the theme of the 'Word made Flesh', the Incarnation of Christ, the Messiah sent to earth by God to redeem mankind. Fra Filippo Lippi's *Annunciation* centres on the Virgin Mary's *fiat* [agreement] at Nazareth to be the mother of the prophesied Messiah (see Figure 28.1). Parameter walls encasing an inner sanctuary and cloister garden with closed portal stresses the privacy of the moment (Holmes 1999: 219–40).

These features typify a convent and constitute a spatial metaphor to extol the virginity of Christ's mother. The *Proto-Evangelium* of St James the Less (11:1–3) describes two visits by archangels, both of whom appear in the *Annunciation* bearing lily fronds. The messenger who approached Mary by an outdoor well stands beneath an arched portal leading to a garden. Archangel Gabriel takes compositional centre stage as the harbinger of grace who follows Mary after she retreats into her house. Encased by low walls, Lippi's cloistered *hortus conclusis* (enclosed garden) is visible through arches of an impressive classical screen. Bisecting the pedimented gate of the higher garden walls, and rising from the well, is the trunk of a lofty cypress. The tree's verdant bowers extend to the space above the entablature, where God appears on the left with angels. The celestial group forms the upper coordinate of a diagonal trajectory—a golden ray that intersects with the dove of the Holy Spirit and the heart of Mary. Wearing an azure blue *maphorion*, a hooded mantle, the Virgin Mary has just responded in the mystical conversation with Gabriel, who kneels with translucent peacock wings denoting immortality and a corona of pink and white roses. The same floral hues resurface in the Archangel's almost diaphanous raiment with its delicate folds of cloth. The striated marble bench of the lower wall functions to separate the Virgin Mary's inner

FIGURE 28.1 FRA FILIPPO LIPPI, The Murate Annunciation Altarpiece (tempera on poplar), 1443–45 (203×186 cm: 79.9×73"), Munich Alte Pinakothek 1072. © PRISMA ARCHIVO/ Alamy Stock Photo.

sanctum—a 'domestic' Temple sanctuary of God's House. The titles *Santa Maria Ara Coeli* (Mary as Altar of Heaven) and *Maria Ecclesia* (Mary as Church) affirm the divine selection of the Virgin to be a physical tabernacle for Christ's body. An open book of prophecies rests upon a wooden prie-dieu in the intimate space of Mary's private *camara*. Beside it, the crystal vase of roses confirms her role as a pure vessel for Jesus, an eternal wellspring of 'living water' (John 4:1–22). Mary's husband Joseph only speaks with angels, one of whom assured the just carpenter of her virginity (Matt. 1:18–23).

The Visitation

Luke relates that the Annunciate Virgin Mary travelled from Galilee to Judea to see her elderly cousin Elizabeth (Elisheba), who was then expecting a child, as announced by Gabriel to her husband Zacharias. In a biblical context, the 'visitation' concerns a theophany, a divine manifestation to humanity. Arriving at Hebron, Mary embraced Elizabeth, and with this sensory connection, the yet unborn John the Baptist leapt in his mother's womb. Mary's joyful *Magnificat* follows (Luke 1:46–56), as well as Zacharias prophetic *Benedictus* following John's birth (Luke 1:56–64). The trip to Judea was 82 miles, and Mary would not have ventured alone but with Joseph and plausibly her half-sisters, Mary Salome or Mary Cleophas. All would have served as familial witnesses when Zacharias named his son.

The Visitation theme concentrates upon paired figures. Frequently, Mary and Elizabeth embrace before a landscape and the home of Zacharias. Such was not the case with an exceptional 'Intercession Altarpiece' created by the German artist Konrad Witz and his Swiss workshop about 1445/7 for a convent in Basel (Brinkmann, Georgi, Kemperdick 2011: 170–90) (see Figure 28.2). The symbolism of the fifteenth-century ensemble is complex. When closed during the liturgical seasons of Advent and Lent, the exterior panels of 'Intercession Altarpiece' were a visual statement of the Redemption from the earthly birth of a Messiah to the triumph prognosticated in Revelation. The wing panel of the *Trinity with the Visitation* shows Mary and Elizabeth against a gold-patterned cloth of honour and an unusual trope—the infants Jesus and John displayed within their respective mother's wombs. Enthroned against a green and red lined cloth, the Trinity appears with an open book of blank pages that intimates not only the written testament of the future, but also the Incarnation of the Apocalyptic 'Word'. Beneath the sacred text is the sacrificial Lamb of God, a fulfilment of Isaiah's prophecy (53:7), and the emblem of John the Baptist, intercessor for sinners at the Last Judgment.

The Census in Bethlehem

The Flemish master Pieter Brueghel the Elder portrays Bethlehem not as a biblical town of Judea, but as a sixteenth-century Flemish village in winter (see Figure 28.3). A bit to the right of the foreground centre where barrels of ale rest on snow-laden, large-wheeled carts, Joseph walks as Mary, 'great with child', sits on a donkey beside a large ox. The tired group approaches a throng of figures paying their taxes. Census officials are behind a large open window, the bars of which form a cross. The crowd clusters about a popular inn, a structure identified by its hanging wreath and ale pitcher suspended on the wall. A glimpse of a warm interior is visible through the portal and

FIGURE 28.2 KONRAD WITZ, The Counsel of Salvation and the Visitation, left wing of a dispersed Redemption Altarpiece (tempera on fir), ca. 1445, (135.3×164 cm: 53.3×64.6"), Berlin, Gemäldegalerie, Staatliche Museen Preußischer Kulturbesitz, Basel, Alte Pinakothek. (Photo: Jörg P. Anders, No. 1673, 1910 donated by F. Kleinberger, Paris). © Peter Horree/Alamy Stock Photo.

FIGURE 28.3 PIETER BRUEGHEL THE ELDER, The Census at Bethlehem, S&D 1566, oil on panel (116×164.5 cm: 45.7×64.8"), Brussels, Musées Royaux des Beaux-Arts 3637. © Art Collection 2/Alamy Stock Photo.

the preparation of food for everyday travellers occurs outside. A cook leads a pig to slaughter while sturdy peasants make pancakes over a fire. Hens and a rooster peck at seed. Stacks of wheat reference the Hebrew meaning of Bethlehem as 'House of Bread'. A man opening the shutters in the attic area of the inn establishes there is no room left for boarders. Brueghel painted his panel in Antwerp, the primary port city of the southern Netherlands. Spanish Archdukes then governed Belgium and they collected taxes as administrative agents in Brussels for the Hapsburg Crown. The placard high on the wall above the tax-collection table bears the Hapsburg royal escutcheon, a double-headed eagle.

Due to religious conflict with the Protestants of Holland, the northern Netherlands, there were shifts in population. Ruins in the distant architecture of Brueghel's landscape are the result of societal turbulence; they are the walls of Amsterdam, a Dutch trading centre Brueghel visited in 1562 (Stechow 1990: 100). The composition also shows contemporary structures and quotidian activities of rural folk. A wealthy citizen's home dominates the upper centre, and it is across from an inn for poor travellers—a hollow tree with a signboard. Several village houses are solidly constructed; they have brick walls and stable roofs. However, one decrepit timber edifice stands close to an icy pond; the weight of snow has caused its roof to cave inwards. This ramshackle hovel appears deserted, and because of the cross over its gable, perhaps Brueghel intended the shaky dwelling to be the venue for Christ's birth. Playful children skate and play *kalf* on the frozen pond near the derelict hut. Their activities are a juxtaposition to the strenuous efforts of peasants with heavy sacks on their backs who cross the ice of a river in the upper left portion of the snowy composition. A blood red sun rises in this same sector of the panel and it dramatically contrasts with the stark silhouettes of branches that extend from the inn's solitary tall tree. The most distant of the village structures on the horizon line of the leaden grey sky is a parish church.

THE NATIVITY OF CHRIST

The *Nativity* by Robert Campin provides a theatrical setting reminiscent of a liturgical mystery play. A realistic and dilapidated thatch-roofed stable is the compositional anchor of the stage. Set at an angle, it is supported by weather-beaten dowelled beams which clearly were repurposed from an earlier structure. Attached to the brick foundation, the paper funnel of a wasp nest, an indicator of evil, is the type of Vespidae insect colony that habitually dies in winter. Campin's painting depends upon the *Revelationes Coelestes* of Brigid of Sweden, who in 1373 had an ineffable vision of the Nativity. She beheld the Virgin Mary in white kneeling by a stable column and the infant Christ lying on the earth naked and glowing brightly as angels sang. This 'glorious shining' contrasts with Joseph's candle, an artificial human product. Renaissance masters often sublimated the elderly Joseph, portraying him as mere staffage.

FIGURE 28.4 ROBERT CAMPIN, The Nativity of Christ, oil on panel (84.1×69.9: 33.1×27.5"), ca. 1425–30, Dijon, Musée des Beaux-Arts 150. © classicpaintings/Alamy Stock Photo.

Patinir accords Mary's husband the high status of protector in the painting; his hand shields a candle from extinguishment by wind.

Triadic arrangements abound in Campin's *Nativity* (Thürlemann 2002: 37–49). A celestial choir on the roof chants, 'Glory to God in the Highest . . .'. Three adoring shepherds in woollen apparel apposite for cold weather gaze into the sacred precinct. A wall's inner framework is open to reveal an ox and ass. Another triple ensemble originates from the story of midwives (Pseudo-Matt. 13–14) sought by Joseph—Salome

(Zelomi) and Azel (Zebel). Campin portrays both women in sumptuous attire, with woven robes either bordered in gold or articulated with jewelled borders. Like the shepherds, the women in their boldly colourful dresses seem to be inhabitants of Campin's world. These contemporary stage performers provide a moral lesson. Their heavy white linen headdresses unite them with an angel in white, who should form a quartet with the celestial group hovering over the thatched roof. The angel holds a phylactery, 'Touch the boy and be healed'. Salome faces the viewer and displays her open right palm, which withered because she doubted the Virgin Birth. Her scroll unfurls, 'I believe if only when I have proved it.' Azel is shown *de dos* and her raised right hand is a visual juxtaposition to Salome's palm healed by the newborn Christ. In the sacred language of gestures, Azel points towards the healer while simultaneously clasping a banderole, 'A Virgin shall bear a Son' (Isa. 7:14). Mary's pristine robe billows in angular folds, and its golden embroidery quotes the *Salve Regina*, an antiphon sung at evening prayers during the Christmas liturgical season.

The *Nativity*'s landscape iterates the notion of the travel, but the view shows the walled citadel of Huy and Meuse River valley in Liège. Contemporary travellers and a woman with a basket of eggs atop her head walk to market beside a stream flowing with icy slabs. A winding road leads ultimately to an intersecting pathway with men on horseback at a rural inn, a tavern, and town gate. The sun rises over the picturesque boats of the lake. With rays emanating from his tiny body, Jesus is the *Sol Invictus* and advent of a new age.

THE ADORATION OF THE SHEPHERDS

George de la Tour's *Adoration of the Shepherds* (1644) has a heightened spirituality due to its compositional simplicity, transcendent figures, and dramatic interplay between natural and divine light (Conisbee 1997: 119–23) (see Figure 28.5). His rural folk foregather intimately within the warmth of the Christ's parents. Joseph's taper resonates the same significance as in the *Nativity*. Golden wheat provides a soft bed for the swaddled infant—a symbolic monstrance containing the Eucharist; and a docile lamb, nibbles at a spring of wheat before the altar-manger summoning biblical prophecy (Isa. 53:7).

Enthralled by the child and illuminated against the dark stable walls, the triadic group of peasants—one of whom obsequiously lifts his hat—are gift-bearers. As such, they are pastoral counterparts to the august royal trinity of the magi-kings who travel to Bethlehem. Rather than gold, frankincense (perfume), and myrrh (anointing oil), they present modest offerings—a shepherd's crook, a flute, and a covered terracotta bowl of milk. La Tour's peasants likely have their source in the vernacular *chansons* carolled during Advent (Dunphy Wind 1998: 38–40). The French word for these popular songs—*noëls*—is synonymous with Christmas. Such melodic secular verses

FIGURE 28.5 GEORGES DE LA TOUR, The Adoration of the Shepherds, ca. 1644, oil on canvas (107×137 cm: 42×54"), Paris, Louvre Museum R.F. 2555. © Peter Horree/Alamy Stock Photo.

spring from seasonal plays performed in France and Belgium in which townspeople in regional dress play the parts of diverse characters in Christmas narrative.

La Tour's three *bèrgeres* wear warm clothes in neutral colours. The attire of their female companion, Mary, and Joseph, is tinctured the same brilliant hue of red. This selection of colour is unusual considering sumptuary laws in France separated factions of society and regulate ownership of luxurious garments. Prohibited from purchasing costly lace, brocades, velvets, damask, silk and furs, lower classes also were unable to wear woollen cloth tinted by expensive dyes such as red, purple, and green. Peasant clothing was restricted to colours of brown, grey, woad, and beige. For all its thespian qualities rooted in the French *noel* tradition, La Tour's *Adoration of the Shepherds* has a very limited palette save for his colouristic refrain of vermillion, which pervades his work with an unassailable sense of warmth. An iconographical *topos* for the fiery reds in La Tour's painting might be the feast of Pentecost, which was associated in France with the chivalric order of the Holy Spirit founded in 1578. His work assuredly shows the joy of pastoral folk, who are the first to hear the 'good tidings' and be infused with the Holy Spirit. The Eucharist wheat, sacrificial lamb, and body of an infant wrapped in white cloth are interrelated elements; they presage the events of the Passion and the lamentation of his devoted mother, the subsequent matriarch of the Pentecostal Church.

THE CIRCUMCISION OF CHRIST

When the Christ Child was 8 days old, he was circumcised as set forth in God's covenant with Abraham (Gen. 17:9–14) and according to Mosaic law (Exod. 4:24–6; Lev. 12: 30). After the rite (Luke 2:21), the name Jesus was formally given to him. Christ's *bris milah* (covenant of circumcision) marked the first shedding of his blood, and the rite prognosticated his Passion. A *mohel* (circumciser) could perform the Hebrew rite of *bris milah* in a domestic house. Christian artists traditionally illustrate the venue as a temple with an officiating priest of Bethlehem. A gilded chair—the 'Throne of Elijah' (*Kisey Eliyehu*)—is showcased in the ceremonial appointments of the *bris milah* to signify the Prophet of the Covenant.

Jacob Cornelisz van Oostsanen maintained an active workshop in Amsterdam (Middlekoop 2014; J. L. Carroll 1987). He inserted contemporary likenesses into his *Circumcision* (1517), a genre called *portraits-histoirés* (see Figure 28.6). Probably members of his family, these 'portraits' are presented within the context of the ceremony codified into Rabbinic Judaism before the sixteenth century. Having the highest honour at the *bris milah* is the primary *sandek* who grasps the baby during the physical act of circumcision and a second *sandek* who holds the baby as participants recite blessings during the bestowing of a name. Wearing an amethyst tunic with white fur collar, Van Oostsanen's primary *sandek* supports the infant Christ with both hands. Opposite him another figure genuflects, the *kvatter* [godfather]. Garbed in light blue and vibrant red stockings, he is a compositional and symbolic counterpart to the seated

FIGURE 28.6 JACOB CORNELISZ VAN OOSTSANEN, The Circumcision of Christ, 1517, oil and fabric on panel (109.2×60.5: 43×23.8), monogram and date bottom centre, Gift of the Samuel H. Kress Foundation, Portland Art Museum, Oregon 61.59.

temple priest as he lifts the lid of a golden offering vessel destined to contain Christ's foreskin.

Within the group surrounding the pedestal altar, a woman in brown dress with scarlet sleeves and gold-articulated headdress assumes the identity of the *kvatterin* (godmother), who has the high honour of carrying an infant to the *bris milah* space. The young Virgin Mary stands behind her in a coral dress with billowing white sleeves and gilded black headdress. Behind the godmother, a *sandek* wearing a black and crimson turban holds a recording book of names. Joseph, shown as an elderly man with a white turban and blue robe, touches this book. His purse denotes his position as family provider and his responsibility to pay the temple priest or *mohel*. Opposite Joseph is a stately man dressed entirely in black with a matching toque who perhaps is the artist. Behind the seated temple priest, another officiator holds a golden vessel, a perfumed incense offering (*qetoret*), and gestures with a brush towards the countryside. A landscape vignette conflates time between the public occasion of the infant Christ's circumcision and Jesus's solitude at Gethsemane (Luke 22:41–4). Paintings of the circumcision rarely show Christ's agony in the Garden—when he sweated blood in his anguish. Van Oostasanen's chalice-bearing angel gains importance in Amsterdam, where the municipal *Stille Omgang,* an annual devotional 'Silent Walk', commemorates the 'Miracle of the Host' (1345).

The Presentation in the Temple

Eastern pictorial representations of Christ's Presentation centre upon the *Hypapante* (*Obviatio*: Meeting) outside the Temple altar (*mizbēah*) between Jesus and Simeon, a righteous and devout man. Luke (2: 25–34) records Simeon's praise of Christ as a 'light unto the Gentiles' and the prophet's blessing of his parents. Gerbrand van den Eeckhout's *Simeon in the Temple* (1672) is close in spirit to Luke's account (see Figure 28.7). Not only does the work illustrate humble parents offering their first-born son to God, it centres upon the solemnity of the occasion in which Simeon holds Christ, the Messianic 'dayspring on high' (Luke 1:78). A disciple of Rembrandt in Amsterdam, Van den Eeckhout created variations of his *Simeon in the Temple* (Yeager-Crasselt 2018: 228–9; 248; Shorr 1946: 17–32). Frieze-like tenebristic groupings with foreground public and more private background sanctuary space are common to each.

Van den Eeckhout worked with a refined palette. He carefully applied colours to define participating figures in a scene. Treasures of the Temple of Jerusalem (*beit a'mikdash:*'Santified House') are shown in his painting, but the tabernacle (*vrishkan*) area is not visible. An exultant Simeon holds the swaddled infant Christ while reciting a canticle of praise (*Nunc Dimittis*). Three men stand behind Simeon, and a small boy in vermillion and silver holding a staff. This child is too old to be John the Baptist, but he could be a later 'apostle'. Five scribes sit to the right at a table covered in red velvet and laden with books. Missing from the setting is the *Cohen Gadol,* Jerusalem's High Priest,

FIGURE 28.7 GERBRAND VAN DEN EECKHOUT, Simeon in the Temple (The Presentation of Christ in the Temple), S&D 1672, oil on canvas (84.5×105.1 cm: 33.3×41.4"), Collection Thomas S. Kaplan and Daphne Recanati Kaplan, (cur.) Arthur Wheelock. The Leiden Collection GE-100.

who traced his patrilineal lineage to the biblical Aaron. Typically, the *Cohen Gadol* wears a *mitznefes* (turban) and breastplate (*efod*) adorned with twelve precious stones to signify each of Israel's Tribes.

Joseph and Mary kneel on the left side of the *Simeon in the Temple*. The Virgin Mary wears a roughened type of cloth that is tinctured red and brown. Next to her, Joseph holds two turtledoves by their wings and before him is a basket of carpenter's tools. Behind Joseph and looming over a crowd of visitors is an elderly woman with clasped hands, the widow Anna (Luke 2:36–8). The tabernacle lamp above her figure suggests her enlightened nature. With its figures attired in elaborate turbans and historical costume, Van den Eeckhout's composition has traits of a theatrical performance. Perhaps of inspiration was the inaugural play at Amsterdam's first public theatre (1638)—*Gijsbrecht van Amstel*—by the Mennonite Joost van den Vondel. Loosely based on Virgil's epic *The Aeneas*, the tragedy celebrates the founding in 1304 of a new Dutch Republic in Prussia by a hero forced by war to leave his homeland. He departs with a prediction of a new Golden Age in Holland. Because the story of *Gijsbrecht van Amstel* unfolded during the Christmas season, sacred tableaux with overtones of Messianic expectation such as 'Simeon in the Temple' were subsidiary episodes in the dramatic performance.

THE ADORATION OF THE MAGI

The paintings of Peter Paul Rubens defines the monumental Baroque style of the southern Netherlands. An artist who spent his professional career in Belgium, he was patronized by several European courts; his style is branded by grandiose compositions, a penchant for epical figures, bold colours, and painterly brushstrokes. Moreover, Rubens's technical expertise is equipoised by a demonstrated familiarity with humanist, historical, and sacred literature. He created several versions of the *Adoration of the Magi* theme. However, the one that likely resonated the most with the artist was his 1624 painting for the High Altar of the Antwerp Norbertine Abbey of St Michael (Haeger 1997: 45–71) (see Figure 28.8), the site of interment for members of his immediate family.

The most dynamic figure in Rubens's *Adoration of the Magi* stands on the left, the scarlet-robed, white-bearded Caspar, a personification of Europe. Gazing sternly towards the viewer, this formidable 'Pillar of Fire' pulsates with energy. Offering a finely tooled golden *tazza* having the look of an ecclesiastical monstrance, Caspar stands as a spiritual counterpart to the white-robed Melchior kneeling before him. Melchior swings a thurible, and this container with its wafting incense functions to identify him as a priest-king and personification of Asia. The swinging of the thurible typically occurs in groups of three in the service of the Mass. As incense burns, worshippers recite the *Tersanctus*. This Eucharistic prayer magnifies the priest's consecration of the bread and wine with a seminal chant of praise: 'Holy, Holy, Holy; Lord

FIGURE 28.8 PETER PAUL RUBENS, The Adoration of the Magi, 1624, oil on panel (447×336 cm: 14'81/8×11'43/10"), Antwerp, Koninklijk Museum voor Schone Kunsten, 194612. © ICP/incamerastock/Alamy Stock Photo.

God of Hosts . . .' Isaiah (6:1–8) describes six-winged angels flying around the throne of God. These Seraphim (Hebrew: 'burning') perpetually sing the *Tersanctus*. Supported by his mother, the infant Jesus in Rubens's *Adoration* leans forward from his swaddling cloth and looks towards Melchior. His diminutive nude body near an ox—Rome's customary sacrificial beast—hints at a future death at Calvary and entombment. The wheat of the stone manger references the Eucharistic Christ. Baltasar, the third magus, stands above Melchior. With his arms akimbo, he holds a gold container of myrrh. Costumed in a malachite hued outer cloak edged in marten fur, and front-buttoned tunic of dark peridot green, his white silk turban with red and gold stripes matches a silk belt with gold fringe. North Africa is his place of origin; camels are in his retinue (Trexler 1997; Kaplan 1985).

A fluted Corinthian column looms over the stable and combines with 'portraits' of men in armour to allude to the Augustan age into which Christ was born, and the supplanting of pagan worship with Christianity. A spider web hangs in the triangle of a stable rafter, a subtle footnote to Ovid's story (*Metamphoses*: 6) of Arachne and a mortal's hubris in challenging a god. The contrast to Athena is the Virgin Mary revered as a *Sedes Sapientiae* (Seat of Wisdom). Mounted on a walnut brown steed near the column the centurion Martin of Tours divides his cloak to share with a beggar, and thereafter, refused to wield his sword in Gaul on behalf of Rome. Opposite Martin on the right, the protector Joseph in shadows assumes the position of a fourth wise man. After the 'kings' leave Bethlehem, he journeys with his family to a distant land with undeniable courage, guided not by any atlas, but only by the night stars.

Joseph's Dream

The celebratory aspect of Luke's Gospel resounds in its songs: Mary's *Magnificat* (1:46–55); Zachariah's *Benedictus* (1:68–79); and Simeon's *Nunc Dimittis* (2:29–32). Even the angelic announcement to shepherds (2:10–11), the 'tidings of great joy', has all the hallmarks of a choir in exultation. By contrast, the angelic host is absent in Matthew's narrative; there are no hymns chanted by elated personae who portend the arrival of a Messiah. Rather, the events following the Magi's visit have a sober and chilling quality. Leaving Bethlehem in haste 'while it was still night' (Matt. 2:14), Joseph protected the child from certain death, and he obeyed without question the divine messages communicated to him.

Joseph's Dream about the Flight into Egypt (1620–30) by the Lombard Daniele Crespi is a painting extraordinary in its naturalism and sense of incipient movement (Ward Neilson 1996; Spiriti 2006) (see Figure 28.9). Matthew (2:11) intimates Joseph had property in Bethlehem when the Magi offered their treasures. Crespi portrays Joseph dominating the foreground workspace of a small dwelling. He rests his head against his hand, having apparently fallen asleep while working late into the evening. A small hand plane, chisel, and saw rest atop a solid and well-worn wooden table. Other tools of the carpenter's trade—axe, chisels, and clamps—are within a basket in front of the table.

FIGURE 28.9 DANIELE CRESPI, Joseph's Dream, 1620–1630, oil on canvas (297×203 cm: 116.9×79.9"), Vienna, Kunsthistorisches Museum GG 271. © Dipper Historic/Alamy Stock Photo.

Joseph's left foot is upon a larger smoothing plane and wood shavings are scattered about the room. Crespi, who trained in Milan and travelled to Genoa about 1622, admired Baroque Roman classical style and Venetian colourism. He likely entered the orbit of Cardinal Federico Borromeo and the Jesuits in Milan. Ignatius Loyola, founder of the Society of Jesus, elevated St Joseph as the patron of the order's humanist schools. Crespi in his *Joseph's Dream* contrasts the exhausted figure of a hard-working carpenter with the energetic archangel in an imposing white robe and flowing vermillion wrap patterned with shimmering gold. Caught in the immediate act of touching the slumbering Joseph, the celestial messenger at once gestures towards a dark bedchamber where the Virgin Mary watches her sleeping son. The hand placement in Crespi's composition unites not only spaces of the small house, but also connects Joseph and the infant Jesus, thus giving the impression they share the same dream.

Following the conclusion of the Council of Trent (1563), theologians instructed Catholic artists to support doctrinal points attacked by Protestants, such as the veneration of guardian angels. The Church recommended portraying Joseph as a much younger and *vir* caretaker of his family, reasoning he had to be physically strong to undertake so many journeys. The Wars of Religion witnessed considerable shifts in population as people sought safety from conflicting factions. In Protestant and Catholic centres alike, Joseph was extolled as the ideal protector for travellers and sentinel for displaced families.

REST ON THE FLIGHT INTO EGYPT

Joachim Patinir created his painting of the *Rest during the Flight into Egypt* (1518–20) in Antwerp when navigation was changing the global complexion of medieval Europe (see Figure 28.10). His broad panoramic vista with high horizon line and aerial perspective exemplifies the genre of art called 'world picture' (Koch 1968). Patinir's topography of low river valleys on the right stretches in bands of deep cerulean and pastel blue to encompass the land of Judea. To the left are rugged mountains—the terrain of Egypt. In the foreground of these geographical parentheses, Patinir tells the story of the Holy Family's journey in episodes drawn primarily from Apocryphal literature. The Massacre of the Innocents is on the landscape's upper right side, and the Flemish hamlet beneath a tranquil sky is a contradiction to the pandemonium of slaughter. Separated by a copse of trees, is a farm. A man sows seed in his fields while his helper guides a plough-horse. This rustic vignette recollects the Flemish proverb, 'no plow stands still when a person dies'. Additional maxims are suggested by: the sow with her five piglets ('The pigs run loose in the corn'); a peasant emerges from a forest with wood in his apron and a branch in his mouth ('The man biting into the wooden pillar is a hypocrite'); and a man defecating on ground by a barn ('to have disdain for the world'). The Sevillian scholar, Juan de Mal Lara (*Philosophia vulgar*, 1568) interpreted such ancient and vernacular expressions as vestiges of wisdom gleaned in Eden by Adam and Eve. The farm specifically recollects the 'Miracle of the Wheat' (*Infancy Gospel of*

FIGURE 28.10 JOACHIM PATINER, Rest during the Flight into Egypt, 1518–1520, oil on panel (121×177 cm: 47.6×69.6"), Madrid, Museo del Prado P001611. © Javier Larrea, agefotostock/Alamy Stock Photo.

Thomas 1:1), in which seed Jesus threw into a field instantaneously grew to a height for harvesting and tricked Herod's soldiers in close pursuit. Interrogated labourers commented they were seeding crops when the Nazarian family passed their farm.

The Virgin Mary in midnight blue robe and pale blue mantle sits on a hillock nursing her son (Mundy 1981–82; Silva 2007: 182–93). Joseph's donkey grazes in a meadow, and his posterior faces the round pedestal of a fallen idol on an outcrop. Joseph's water gourd, basket for gathering fruit, and a staff with saddlebags of clothes and objects bundled in haste are still life beneath a paradisiacal Tree of Knowledge laden with apples. Grape vines and ivy entwine about the trunk to signify the Eucharistic wine. Prickly plants foretell a Redeemer's bloody crown of thorns. Roses and purple irises of the rock grotto below Mary respectively symbolize her purity and sorrow. This spiritual garden gives her the twofold aspect of both a *Madonna Lactans* and *Mater Dolorosa*. Three forest trees on background hillocks affirm a symbolical association with Golgotha.

Patinir's landscape places Joseph walking on a winding route from town and carrying a bowl of porridge for Mary. Northern artists traditionally pictured him beating tree branches to obtain nuts. A chestnut tree stands alongside Joseph's path, its meaty fruit symbolic of chastity. An Egyptian temple dominates the town where Joseph obtained sustenance. Worshippers offer sacrifices at the complex to a rat god, which was sacred to Ra in Egypt. Two gilded images of pagan deities have toppled from a higher tower belonging to a classical rotunda. Homer (*Illiad* 1:39) identified Helios as a harbinger of light and dispeller of plagues. Strabo (*Geographica*: 13) mentions the 'Sminthian' Apollo—lord of mice—as the eponymous origin of several Mediterranean places (Lang 1884: 104–14). Patinir's golden statues suggest the fulfilment of Messianic prophecy regarding a 'sun of righteousness' with 'healing in its rays' (Mal. 4:2).

Ludolph of Saxony's *Vita Christi* (1374) describes the journey of the Holy Family as characterized by 'very long routes and deserted places' and passage through 'dark and uninhabited forests' (Ainsworth 1998: 308–11; Falkenburg 1988). Sacred landscapes by Patinir and his northern contemporaries have been associated with Ludolph's prayer book for meditation. Devout Catholics were encouraged to use the five senses of the body as a stimulant for introspective prayer. By using the imagination, therefore, a person could spiritually participate in the Gospel narratives—and in the case of the Flight into Egypt, could follow along with the Holy Family on an intrepid journey.

THE RETURN OF THE HOLY FAMILY TO ISRAEL

Nicolas Poussin, an expatriate French artist who settled in Rome for most of his professional career, painted arresting landscapes of the *Return from Egypt* (Oberhuber 1988). In the city by the Tiber River, he created incomparable interpretations of sacred

FIGURE 28.11 NICOLAS POUSSIN, The Return of the Holy Family from Egypt, ca. 1627, oil on canvas (134×99 cm: 52 3/4×39"), Cleveland Museum of Art, Gift of the Hanna Fund 1953.156. © ICP/incamerastock/Alamy Stock Photo.

themes, overlaying them with a classical aesthetic that paralleled Virgil's Messianic vision of a new Golden Age in the Eighth Eclogue of the *Aeneid*. Inspired by the glazes and colours of Titian, the smooth *factura* or polished surfaces of Raphael, and the poetic-idyll settings of panoramas by Domenichino and Carracci, Poussin's formal style seems to situate the Holy Family truly in the age of Caesar Augustus. He painted his *Return from Egypt* a mere three years after his first trip to Rome in 1624 (Francis 1953: 211–13).

He shows the Holy Family embarking in a boat (see Figure 28.11). Their donkey accompanies them; the beast's head is visible near the foot of the Virgin Mary. Using his pole to push away from the riverbank, the ferryman in a vermillion garment is reminiscent of the mythical Charon transporting souls to Hades. Encased by her voluminous sapphire blue robe, the Virgin Mary is as a symbolical counterpart as a mediator for sinners at the Last Judgment. A virile Joseph in burnt yellow tunic edged in blue, occupies a centre foreground position, as he steadies Jesus, who enthusiastically raises his arms to the sky. There in a flurry of clouds, and at the apex of the triangle of figures anchored by the barge, are five angels holding aloft a cross and they are the numerical equivalent of the five wounds of the adult Christ. Radiant vermillion and yellow colours in this heavenly zone compel the viewer to look directionally upwards as Christ-imitators. Disposed like sculpted images of a classical frieze, the Holy Family appears in the foreground against the setting of an ideal landscape.

Poussin captures water reflections of the river as adroitly as the luminosity of the sky he represents at dawn with its shifting clouds of rose-salmon wafting across an azure sky. Leafy bowers of trees to the sides of the riverbank further enhance a feathery effect. Triple saplings framing the distant *capricci* of Roman ruins also remind the devout of the wooden 'masts' of Calvary. In such a landscape—replete with architectural vestiges of antiquity—three arcadian shepherds on the opposite riverbank presage Christ's later exhortation to St Peter on the shores of the Sea of Galilee (Lake Tiberius), 'Feed my sheep' (John 21:15–17).

The principal actors of Poussin's painting present a vivid narrative of the return from Egypt, and yet the work has all the indicators of a pictorial elegy. Poussin causes the viewer to reflect upon a sober reality; once home, further dangers await Jesus. When he ultimately embraces the cross on the ascent to Calvary, and utters the words, 'it is finished' (John 19:30) in the presence of his distraught mother, he will have completed the end of his Redemption journey.

The Return of the Holy Family to Nazareth

Commonly depicted in art relating to the return of the Holy Family from Egypt is the outdoor representation of the infant John the Baptist greeting and embracing Jesus, often in the company of his mother, Elizabeth. Pseudo-Bonaventure (*Meditations* 13) states they met John in the wilderness where he was living in penitence. The *Protoevanglium of James* (22) informs that during the Massacre of the Innocents, Elizabeth had escaped with her son to the mountains, which split asunder to hide them and they beheld a 'light shining through the mountain' and an angel, their guardian. Perhaps the mountain range that hid Elizabeth and her son was—*Har Ha-karme* or Mount Carmel, a site in north-western Israel linked with Elijah, a prophet to whom John was compared

(Ma. 4:4–5; Matt. 11:10). John's father, Zacharias, remained in Judea. Herod's henchmen killed the priest in Jerusalem at daybreak in the Temple sanctuary because he refused to divulge the location of his son John (Matthew 23:35; *Protoevanglium*: 23–4).

Painted by Bartolomé Estéban Murillo about 1660 in Seville, *The Holy Family with the Infant St. John the Baptist* (see Figure 28.12) is a singular work with which to

FIGURE 28.12 BARTOLOMÉ ESTÉBAN MURILLO, The Holy Family with the Infant St. John the Baptist, 1655–1660, oil on canvas (156×126 cm: 61.4×49.6), Budapest, Szépművészeti Múzeum, 779. © Mariano Garcia/Alamy Stock Photo.

conclude the infancy narrative of Christ (Angulo 1980: II, 179, No. 196). Murillo completed many religious altarpieces for churches in Seville, Spain's port city to the Americas. His painting lacks the intense colours and dramatic flair of the sacred players in Poussin's *Return from Egypt*, as well as the ethereal Roman ruins of sweeping landscape. However, the realistic portrayal of adults at work and the naturalistic rendition of children engaged in play, combine to define the consummate perfection of biblical history's most renowned family. Mary's clothes, a coarse rust-red gown and chestnut-brown veil, accent her humility. She sews white cloth upon a yellow pillow. Murillo leaves the purpose of her textrix labours to the imagination. In a prophetic sense, she could be sewing either the 'seamless robe' worn by Jesus before his Crucifixion (John: 19:23–4), or the shroud of her son's entombment. Supporting this interpretation of the fabric are the objects riveting the attention of the two boys at play—a cross and banner inscribed *Agnus Dei* (Lamb of God).

Garbed in dark grey serviceable attire, Joseph attentively measures wood on a table. The nature of his project is difficult to discern, although the tools and the workbenches of his project are adjacent to a large stone building. While the structure historically should be the town's *beit k'nesset* (synagogue), it also summons a Christian church. Murillo's ambiguity of architecture in an outdoor setting confirms God's dwelling place is open to the world and always remains a home and destination for the traveller.

REFERENCES AND FURTHER READING

Ainsworth, Maryan W. (1998). 'Gerard David, "The Rest on the Flight into Egypt"' (No. 82), in Maryan W. Ainsworth and Keith Christiansen (eds.), *From Van Eyck to Brueghel. Early Netherlandish Painting in The Metropolitan Museum of Art*. New York: Harry N. Abrams: 308–11.

Angulo Iñiguez, Diego (1980). *Murillo*. 3 vols. Madrid: Espasa-Calpe.

Brinkmann, Bodo, Georgi, Katharina, and Kemperdick, Stephan (2011). *Konrad Witz*, Exh. Cat., Basel: Kunstmuseum: 170–90.

Carroll, J. L. (1987). *The Paintings of Jacob Cornelisz van Oostsanen (1472?–1533)*, Ph.D. Diss., UNC. Ann Arbor: UMI Research Press.

Conisbee, Philip (1997). *Georges de La Tour and His World*, Exh. Cat., National Gallery of Art, Washington. New Haven-London: Yale University Press: 119–123.

Dunphy Wind, Geraldine (1998). 'A Note on La Tour's "Adoration of the Shepherds"', *Source. Notes in the History of Art*, 7, no. 2, Winter: 38–40.

Falkenburg, Reindert (1988). *Joachim Patinir: Landscape as an Image of the Pilgrimage of Life*. Amsterdam-Philadelphia: John Benjamins Publishing Company.

Francis, Henry S. (1953). 'The "Flight into Egypt" by Nicolas Poussin', *The Bulletin of the Cleveland Museum of Art*, 40, no. 10, December: 211–13.

Haeger, Barbara (1997). 'Rubens's "Adoration of the Magi" and the Program for the High Altar of St. Michael's Abbey in Antwerp', *Simiolus: Netherlandish Quarterly for the History of Art*, 25, no. 1: 45–71.

Holmes, Megan (1999). *Fra Filippo Lippi, The Carmelite Painter*. New Haven: Yale University Press.

Kaplan, Paul H. D. (1985). *The Rise of the Black Magus in Western Art*, Ph.D. Diss., BU. Ann Arbor: UMI Research Press.

Koch, Robert A. (1968). *Joachim Patinir*. Princeton: Princeton University Press.

Lang, Andrew (1884). *Custom and Myth*. London: Longmans, Green and Company.

Middelkoop, Norbert (2014). *Jacob Cornelisz van Oostsanen (ca. 1475-1533). De Renaissance in Amsterdam en Alkmaar*, Daantje Meuwissen (ed)., Exh. Cat., The Amsterdam Museum-Akmaar Stedelijk Museum. Zwolle: Waanders.

Mundy, E. James (1981-82). 'Gerard David's "Rest on the Flight into Egypt", Further Additions to Grape Symbolism', *Simbiolus: Netherlandish Quarterly for the History of Art*, 12, no. 4 (1981-82): 211-22.

Oberhuber, Konrad (1988). *Poussin. The Early Years in Rome. The Origins of French Classicism*, Exh. Cat., Kimbell Art Museum, Dallas. New York: Hudson Hills.

Shorr, Dorothy C. (1946). 'The Iconographical Development of the Presentation in the Temple', *The Art Bulletin*, 28, no. 1, March: 17-32.

Silva, Pilar (2007). 'Rest on the Flight into Egypt', in Alejandro Vergara (ed.), *Patinir*. Exh, Cat. Madrid: Museo del Prado: 182-93.

Spiriti, Andrea (2006). *Daniele Crespi: Un grande pittore del Seicento Lombardo*. Milan: Silvana Editoriale.

Stechow, Wolfgang (1990). *Pieter Brueghel the Elder*. New York: Harry N. Abrams.

Thürlemann, Felix (2002). *Robert Campin. A Monographic Study with Critical Catalogue*. Munich-Berlin-London-New York: Prestel: 37-49.

Trexler, Richard C. (1997). *The Journey of the Magi: Meanings in History of a Christian Story*. Princeton: Princeton University Press.

Ward Neilson, Nancy (1996). *Daniele Crespi*. Soncino: Edizioni dei Soncino.

Yeager-Crasselt, Lara (2018). 'Simeon in the Temple', in Polina Lyubimova (ed.), *Age of Rembrandt and Vermeer: Masterpieces of The Leiden Collection,* trans. Daria Babich and Daris Kuzina, Exh. Cat. St. Petersburg-Moscow: Pushkin State Museum of Fine Arts-State Hermitage Museum: 228-9, 248 (no. 81).

CHAPTER 29

PLAYS

FRANCES CLEMSON

In an article published in the *Radio Times* on 23 December 1938, the novelist, playwright, and theologian Dorothy L. Sayers lamented the 'twaddling triviality' of many dramatic treatments of the birth of Christ:

> It is fatally easy for them to slip into Christmas-card prettiness, adorned with baby songs, bells, quaint shepherds, kneeling animals, and white-robed angels...all framed in holly and ivy and topped off with a tinsel star...It has all the charm of complete unreality; it could not disturb a fly; it arouses no urgent questions in the mind of anybody. (1938: 13)

What was wrong with such plays in Sayers' view? Why should a Nativity play be disturbing? Sayers' answers to these questions were rooted in her convictions about drama's capacity to explore and enact an Incarnational theology. In another *Radio Times* article some years later, Sayers argued that at the heart of Christianity is 'the personal irruption of God into human history' (1945: 3). Christmas marked the birth of Jesus Christ, one person, fully human and fully God, who comes for the sake of the salvation of the world. Sayers' complaint was that this divine dramatic action—God stepping onto the world stage—had become so 'barnacled about with sentimental accretions' that audiences could lose sight of *both* the humanity and the divinity of the Christ Child. Her experience was that Nativities too often encouraged her contemporaries to forget that God the Son was born into a 'confused and passionate world' not unlike their own (1938: 13). Whether we view this claim as 'revelation' or 'rubbish', Sayers insisted, we can hardly call it safe, saccharine, or 'dull' (1947: 5). A representation on stage of the Incarnation of God should startle us.

As an artistic form characterized by its attention to the fleshly and to human life in time, drama was able to present powerfully the *reality* of the Incarnation in Sayers' view. Earlier Christian thinkers tended to view dramatic performance suspiciously because of its connections to pretence and deceit (Dox 2004: 12–29; Castelli 2004: 114). Sayers was by no means unaware of this heritage. Nonetheless, she argued that drama does not deal only with appearances and illusions but with the real and the truthful. In her view, particular dramatic works were certainly capable of drawing audiences into a practice of paying attention to the embodied world as a place where God is present.

Beginning with the theme of Incarnation, as opened up by Sayers' comments, this chapter offers a thematic exploration of performative enactments that re-present Christmas and the birth of Christ for their audiences. Whilst it is impossible to give a comprehensive account of all such enactments, we will cover some distance chronologically and geographically as we see Christmas played on stages and streets, in churches and communities. Over the centuries, the Christmas season has created space for many kinds of festivity, playing, and playfulness. After considering drama's incarnational properties, the chapter's second theme will be the joyous and sometimes subversive exuberance of Christmas playing. Christmas is a time when roles can be reversed and when celebration can take ostentatious dramatic form.

The final theme is that of time. Putting on a performance and celebrating Christmas both involve non-identical repetitions over time (Pickstock 2013: 11–12). Each theatrical performance, like each Christmas we mark, is a distinctive event. Yet it is also shaped and informed by past performances and provides an occasion to look ahead to future enactments. A number of plays show their audiences multiple Christmases. Christmas in these plays is a 'gathering time' in more than one sense. In a series of non-identical repetitions, the past, present, and future are drawn together, allowing both characters and audiences to engage in performances of mourning, celebration, and expectation.

The Word Made Flesh: Performing the Nativity

In Richard Curtis' 2003 film *Love Actually* the following exchange takes place between Karen (Emma Thompson) and her young daughter Daisy (Lulu Popplewell):

DAISY: We've been given our parts in the nativity play. And I'm the lobster.
KAREN: The lobster?
DAISY: Yeah!
KAREN: In the nativity play?
DAISY: Yeah, *first* lobster.
KAREN: There was more than one lobster present at the birth of Jesus?
DAISY: Duh!

The film reprises this joke visually later on when the characters played by Hugh Grant and Martine McCutcheon find themselves travelling to the Nativity play with a small boy dressed as an octopus sitting between them. The humour here originates from two sets of expectations that the film's audience are likely to have about Nativity plays. The first is that the Nativity is an expansive, adaptable story, performed repeatedly with many cultural and contextual variations. The second set of expectations, situated in an often-unspoken tension with the first, is that we *know* what a Nativity play *should* be and our vision of the 'traditional' Nativity scene limits the levels of variation that we find permissible or plausible. Returning to the quotation from Sayers, if we have a 'Christmas-card' picture in mind we may anticipate some expansion of the familiar characters, but we are not prepared for the arrival of a lobster or an octopus.

Looking back to medieval Nativity plays, we find some familiar but also some potentially strange elements from the point of view of modern audiences. The earliest Nativity enactments were sung liturgical performances, such as the 'Office of the Shepherds' that developed at Rouen between the twelfth and fourteenth centuries. In the later forms of this enactment, the Choir, as angels, announced the good news to clerics acting as shepherds who then went to seek the Christ Child. Following this 'two priests of higher rank' acted as the 'midwives who were in the stable' and sang '*Quem queritis* [Whom do you seek]' before revealing an image of the Virgin and child to the searching 'shepherds'. The performance culminated with the adoration of the image 'on bended knee' (Young 1933: 14–16; Gibson 1981–2).

A more dramatically developed medieval depiction of the Nativity and the shepherds' role can be found in the *Second Shepherds' Play* from the (possibly) fifteenth-century Towneley plays. This play is intriguing both because of the insights it gives into the social and political concerns of its original context and because of an extensive comedic episode that precedes the actual Nativity scenes. The shepherds complain about their working conditions and the practices of landowners. They are interrupted by the arrival of a character named Mak who later steals a lamb from them. When the shepherds go to Mak's home looking for the lamb, Mak and his wife disguise the animal as a newborn infant in a comical paralleling of the Nativity. Whilst it is possible to view this episode as a purely parodic, and ultimately subversive, contrast to the solemnity of the Nativity scene, some scholars have suggested that the comedy here is fitting in a play that culminates in the joyful news of Christ's arrival (Gamboa 2018: 63). We might note particularly that the shepherds do not carry out the violent punishments they first consider for Mak when they discover his deceit, instead agreeing merely to the ludicrous penalty of tossing him about on a stretch of cloth. This can be understood to prefigure the 'charity' and 'forgiveness' embodied in Christ (Goodrich 2010: 543).

One less familiar element of the scriptural narrative that featured significantly in seasonal performances in the medieval era was the massacre of the Innocents. This event is found in Matthew's Gospel after the Wise Men are told in a dream not to disclose to Herod where the Christ Child has been born: 'When Herod saw that he had been tricked by the wise men, he was infuriated, and he sent and killed all the children in and around Bethlehem who were two years old or under' (Matt. 2:16). The script of the fifteenth-century N-Town Plays includes Herod's murderous plotting, the screams, laments, and protests of the mothers as they witness the death of their children, and culminates with Death personified and the devil carrying off Herod and his men. As Goodland observes, these massacre plays give direct voice to the victims, where the scriptural narrative does so only indirectly, quoting Jeremiah 31:15. The mothers' lamentation becomes a performative protest against evil, binding their experience to that of Mary (who will also one day witness the death of her son) and calling down divine justice on those who abuse worldly power (Goodland 2005: 56, 60–6).

Power and physicality return as themes in Nativity plays of the twentieth and twenty-first centuries. In Britain up until the 1968 Theatres Act, representations of Christ on stage were much restricted. These restrictions began as far back as the mid-sixteenth century and were codified in an Act to Restrain Abuses of Players in 1606. Over centuries a case-law approach to theatrical censorship established the precedent that the physical representation of the person of God in a dramatic performance was never permissible. By the 1930s, this policy was generating extraordinary lines of reasoning from the staff in the office of the Lord Chamberlain, who were responsible for operating the censorship system. In practice, many amateur or church-sponsored Nativity plays were already being performed without being brought to the notice of the Lord Chamberlain, but where permission *was* requested it seemed it would have to be denied. In 1937, faced with having to ban a perfectly innocuous Nativity play for children simply because the Christ Child was to appear on stage, the Lord Chamberlain's Reader of Plays suggested that Christ might be considered 'more an abstraction of an idea than a historical character' (Nicholson 2005: 142). It was the fleshly personhood of Christ on stage that was thought to threaten reverence and propriety. Drama's dangerous potential to make Christ appear as more than a concept had to be contained.

Two notable examples in this period of playwrights putting this potential to the test were John Masefield's *The Coming of Christ*, a Nativity play first performed in early summer at the Canterbury Cathedral festival of 1928, and Dorothy L. Sayers' *He That Should Come*, broadcast by the BBC on Christmas Eve 1938. Both were enacted in spaces deemed to be outside the control of the censors: a cathedral and a radio studio. Masefield attempted a new approach to the traditional Nativity, but was nonetheless wary of too direct or too embodied a depiction of Jesus. In the play's opening scene, Christ speaks as a 'male Spirit', given the title 'Anima Christi' (Soul of Christ) (Masefield 1928: 1). The dialogue with other 'spirits' makes clear that this is *not* Christ in Incarnate form, distancing the audience from the figure portrayed. At the play's conclusion, Mary and the infant Christ are shown but neither speak nor move; they are instead carried about the church in procession in a litter, in an action reminiscent of the liturgical origins of Nativity dramas. Despite the cautiousness of Masefield's production, the very act of staging the play was enough to generate controversy. One local newspaper placed the performance amongst the most shocking occurrences ever to have taken place in the cathedral, comparing it to the murder of Thomas Beckett (Pickering 2001: 121).

Masefield's decision to expand the characters of the Shepherds also sparked comment. Another contemporary newspaper announced with incredulity that 'revolutionary sentences are being put into the mouths' of scriptural characters (*The Dover Express*, 25 May 1928). Two of the three shepherds, 'Sandy' and 'Earthy' are disgruntled with the ways in which the 'workers' are made to bear the burdens imposed on them by the 'rich': 'It's time the workers should have the wealth they make.... In the next war the workers will not go' (Masefield 1928: 30). Ultimately, however, these complaints are quashed when they are reprimanded by the third shepherd, 'Rocky', who tells them to be 'thankful' (34). In response to Rocky's testimony that he trusts in God, Sandy scoffs, asserting: 'There never was a God and there never will be' (37). It is at this moment that the heavenly host appears. The overturning of Sandy's expectations undercuts the impact of his earlier protests. It is clear that it is the faithful words of Rocky, not the grumblings of his companions, that the audience should heed.

In *He That Should Come*, although Sayers was using the ostensibly disembodied medium of radio, she endeavoured to create a highly physical portrayal of the Nativity story. The main body of the action takes place inside the inn where there is no room for the Holy Family. The play seeks to convey the crowded atmosphere with multiple voices shouting and interrupting one another. Joseph and Mary are on the fringes of the action, making only a brief appearance before being sent out to the stable. Listeners eavesdrop on the conversations of the residents who are discussing religion, politics, taxation, and the joys and frustrations of everyday life. For those in the inn, the cry of a baby signals a birth like any other. Only when the shepherds clamour at the inn door do those within have a sense that something out of the ordinary may have happened. Even then, the scene closes with the same commotion over quotidian matters with which it opened. Sayers' aim was to underline the sheer ordinariness of Jesus' birth. Jesus was not born amongst '"sacred personages" standing about in symbolic attitudes... self-consciously awaiting the fulfilment of prophecies' (Sayers 1943: 22).

The Christian conviction that Christ was born on the margins of society has figured as a central motif in many modern Nativities. Langston Hughes' 1961 play, *Black Nativity*, was a ground-breaking expression of the connection between the marginalized Christ Child and the African-American experience of enslavement, poverty, and exclusion. The play gives voice to what theologian James Cone describes as Christ's inhabitation of the '*otherness* in the black experience' (Cone 1997: 114). Hughes 'deliberately allowed black music and religion to overwhelm the traditional play form' (Rampersad 1988: 345). The play uses carols and scriptural texts, alongside a wealth of Gospel songs and spirituals, weaving together acclamation and lamentation as God in Christ is born into poverty. Jesus is the 'LITTLE STRANGER / BABY WHO NEVER HAD NO CRADLE', the cast sing; 'THE WORLD TREATS YOU MEAN, LORD, TREATS ME MEAN TOO' (Hughes 2004: 362, 370). The narrator tells the audience that Jesus was born on the outside of 'a door closed to the poor... on an earthen floor / In a stable with no lock... At an address no one knows' and yet this is the child who shall make 'kingdoms tremble' (366). In the play's second act, the focus shifts to the contemporary world where the Church is 'but an extension of His manger' (371). Multiple voices testify in word and song to God's steadfast love, embodied in this infant. The impassioned performances were met with huge enthusiasm from audiences (Rampersad 1988: 347).

In 1979, the Philippine Educational Theater Association (PETA) created a version of the *panunuluyan*, a traditional street performance of Mary and Joseph's search for somewhere to stay immediately before Jesus' birth, with its origins in the period of Spanish colonial rule. PETA's version has since been performed many times in locations across the Philippines. The performance underscores the connection between Mary and Joseph's marginalization and the oppression of poor urban and rural communities. The Holy Family are shown being rejected by the rich and welcomed by the poor. They hear from the poor how their suffering is imposed upon them by the mendaciousness and corruption of landlords, managers, and foreign companies (Tiongson 1998: 149; Van Erven 1992: 40–1).

In December 2017, the anonymous British artist who goes by the name Banksy collaborated with directors Riham Isaac and Danny Boyle to stage a Nativity performance in the car park of Banksy's hotel in Bethlehem. 'The Walled Off Hotel' is situated next to the border wall constructed by Israel in the West Bank in the early 2000s. The performance, entitled 'The Alternativity', drew together local children, to perform a recognizably traditional Nativity with some striking variations drawn from the contemporary socio-political context. Joseph has to pass through a metal detector at a checkpoint every day on his way to and from work; three 'wise women' sing of their hopes for freedom. At one point, a narrator draws attention to the implausibility of certain elements of the familiar Nativity scene: 'It's always snowing in Bethlehem… The reality is no way!' Moments later fake snow falls onto the audience simultaneously enacting and ironizing the 'traditional' Christmas scene, as the unreal snowstorm suggests the dissonance between the imagined and the actual Bethlehem. Scholars have studied the border wall as a canvas for the art of resistance (Larkin 2014). In Isaac and Boyle's production, the wall becomes part of a theatre set. The searchlights of a nearby watchtower are refigured as perverse parallels of the lighting rig and particularly of the illuminated star suspended above the set. We might think of the way in which the walls of the *Globe*, one of the world's most famous theatres, have been understood as creating a temporary world-within-a-world for audiences. Here, a wall that encloses and shapes the audience's real world every day is made part of a performance space—a space where new imaginings are possible.

Festivity, Fooling, and Playing

The Christmas season provides an occasion for forms of play, celebration, and performance that break up (at least temporarily) the usual routines and structures of life. One early example is the 'Feast of Fools', when clergy of the lower ranks were raised to prominence and led celebrations. In his influential 1903 work, *The Mediaeval Stage*, E. K. Chambers characterized these feasts as a liberation for the clerics, an opportunity to 'burlesque the sacred and tedious ceremonies with which they were only too painfully familiar' (Chambers 1903: 325). This view of festivity and fooling as antithetical to the principles of the medieval Christian life has been challenged more recently by Max Harris. Harris argues that the feasts were in fact rooted in a particular Christian conception of 'foolishness'. In this understanding, the Fool is one who is of 'lowly status' by the world's standards. It is these 'foolish' individuals whom God has chosen, as Paul writes in his first letter to the Corinthians (1 Cor. 1:18–31, 4:10), for God in Christ acts in a way that appears 'foolish' in worldly terms, becoming 'weak' to the point of death on the cross. The 'Feast of Fools' was, Harris insists, firmly centred upon a liturgical celebration of this Christ-like foolishness, in which those in lower priestly orders were 'raised' to a central role, so as to foreground God's love for those of humble status (Harris 2011: 67–8). In certain places the Feast came to include dramatic performances of scriptural scenes, incorporating processional, liturgical, and possibly musical elements. The twelfth-century *Play of Daniel* at Beauvais is one example. Taking up the narrative of the faithful Daniel, who submits only to God and not to worldly powers, this was, Harris argues, an apt subject for the Feast (113–24). The Feast was genuinely playful, allowing for 'folly and discord' but doing so *within*, rather than *against*, ecclesial structures and culture (115).

Although it is unlikely that it received its first performance on Twelfth Night itself, the title of Shakespeare's 1602 play nonetheless conjures the festive period. Many of the themes of the play—illusion, disguise, disorder, and indeed play itself—can be connected to the reversal of roles and blurring of boundaries that was possible during the Christmas season (Greif 1982; Warren and Wells 1994: 5). One less well-known work of the same period that gives us an insight into the relationship between festive playing, playfulness, and power is Ben Jonson's *Christmas, His Masque*. This was an entertainment prepared for the Christmas season of 1616/17 to be performed at the Court of James I. It features Christmas personified appearing with '*a long thin beard, a Truncheon, little Ruffes, white Shoes, his Scarffes, and Garters tyed crosse, and his Drum beaten before him*' (Jonson 1941: 437). Christmas brings with him his children: Misrule, Caroll, Minc'd-Pie, Post and Paire (a card game), New-Yeares-Gift, Mumming (a form of Christmas folk drama), Wassail, Offering, and Babie-Cake (possibly a cake served at Epiphany). As Leah Marcus notes, James I had given a speech in the Star Chamber in 1616 that urged 'all Gentlemen of qualitie' to 'maintaine Hospitalitie' in their homes 'specially at Festiuall times' such as Christmas (Marcus 1986: 77; James VI and I 1995). It was also in this year that James first proposed the Five Articles of Perth. These were measures aimed at unifying Scottish and English Church practices and included among them was that the Scottish Church must observe and celebrate Christmas. The insistence of the character of Christmas that the players will '*present with all the appurtenances / A right* Christmas, *as of old it was*' is thus a politically and religiously freighted declaration (Jonson 1941: 443). Here festive play enacts royal authority.

There are many other examples we could discuss here from the mummers' plays alluded to above, to the Victorian pantomime. One work that allows us to look deeper at the themes of festivity and play is Henrik Ibsen's *A Doll's House* (1879). The dramatic action takes place over three days, beginning on Christmas Eve, and the plot centres on the relationship of Nora and her husband, Torvald. Nora discloses to a friend in the play's first act that she has borrowed money in secret in order to help Torvald during a period of serious illness. Not only has she concealed her action, she also forged her father's signature in the process of obtaining the money. During the course of the play Krogstad, who works with Torvald at a bank and is facing dismissal, reveals that it was he who arranged the loan and seeks to blackmail Nora so that she will help him keep his position.

The Helmer's Christmas tree and the festive trappings of the season play an important symbolic role throughout. In the play's opening moments, a porter carries the Christmas tree on stage and Nora Helmer instructs her maid to conceal it: 'The children mustn't see it before I've decorated it this evening' (Ibsen 2009: 23). Shortly afterwards Torvald recalls the previous Christmas, reminding Nora that: 'For three whole weeks you shut yourself away every evening to make flowers for the Christmas tree' (28). The audience learns later, however, that Nora actually spent this time taking in work copying documents in order to earn some money to repay the loan. Nora uses the task of decorating this year's Christmas tree to distract herself from the threat of her secret being exposed: 'Now—candles here—and flowers here. That loathsome man! Nonsense, nonsense, there's nothing to be frightened about. The Christmas tree must be beautiful' (51). At the beginning of the second act, which takes place on Christmas Day, the tree is (as the stage directions state) '*stripped and dishevelled, its candles burned into their sockets*' (55). It is in this act that Nora's own festive outward manner comes under strain. Krogstad enacts his threat and writes a letter disclosing Nora's secret to her husband, with Krogstad now seeking to blackmail Torvald directly. Immediately after seeing Krogstad leave his letter for her husband, Nora practises a dance for a party the next evening. Ulla Kallenbach argues that this dance—the tarantella—was: 'in Scandinavian and European cultural life...the epitome of liveliness and festivity...Nora's tarantella, however, is anything but that... [it] is a dance of desperation' (Kallenbach 2018: 189).

In some productions of *A Doll's House*, the Christmas setting has been replaced with another festival with similar resonance in the cultural context of the performance. Thus, in a Nepalese production of 2003 a Hindu festival of 'light and prosperity' was substituted for Christmas (Nilu 2008: 116–17). Yet in other cases, productions in non-Western contexts have emphasized this aspect of the work. In an Arabic version directed by Gamal Yaqoot in Egypt in 2006 the set dressing featured colourful decorations and gifts, creating an effect of a 'fairytale about to unfold in a glittering Christmas pantomime'. This gaiety was housed, however, within a roofless structure with transparent walls, conveying 'a poignant feeling of fragility, of transience' and presaging the vulnerability of Nora and Torvald's marriage (Selaiha 2011: 120–1). The Japanese play *Double Nora* (premiered in 2005) integrated elements of Noh theatre into *A Doll's House*. The production included an abstract Christmas tree on which dolls were hung, in line with the Noh practice of nonliteral, multi-functional props (Nilu 2008: 126).

As the title suggests, a major theme of the play is the notion that Nora has been treated as a doll, a plaything, by both her father and her husband. In the play's final scene it is Nora's independent action in obtaining the loan that becomes the catalyst for her to detach herself from Torvald and from her role as his 'doll-wife' (Ibsen 2009: 98). On one level the play's festive setting offers a striking contrast to the deep seriousness of Nora's fears and the audience's own growing sense of dread. Yet, in another sense, the play discloses to us the darkness that can lie at the heart of the playful and the festive. As Brian Johnston points out, the Christmas tree—for all its merry appearance—has been 'cut off' from 'full growth' and placed, artificially, in a 'domestic environment' (Johnston 1989: 145; Törnqvist 1995: 36). This parallels the control exerted over Nora by the men in her life. Through Nora's use of the excuse of decorating the tree as 'cover' for her secret paid work, the play prompts us to consider the connection between decoration and deception. Ibsen's play uses its festive setting to press upon its audiences in a new way the questions about appearance and reality, truth and falsity, liveness and pretence, that are inherent to theatre as a form.

Gathering Time

Christmas offers the dramatist a setting in which the joys and tensions of gatherings— as well as themes of exclusion, absence, and loss—can be explored. Christmas as a gathering time encloses characters in an atmosphere that can be comforting or claustrophobic. Christmas as a non-identical repeating event, happening year on year but never the same, has the power to gather memories and prompt us to look to the future. Where were we last Christmas? Where will we be next year? The most influential work in this respect is, of course, Dickens' *A Christmas Carol*, with its the ghosts of Christmas past, present and future, and it is no surprise that Dickens' story has been adapted for the stage many times.

Pulitzer Prize-winning playwright Paula Vogel's *The Long Christmas Ride Home* (first performed in 2003), gathers its cast in the oppressive setting of a Christmas car journey. A man and a woman and their three children (Rebecca, Stephen, and Claire) are driving to see the woman's parents on Christmas day. The play integrates Western dramatic conventions with Bunraku—a form of Japanese puppet theatre. The children in the car are represented by puppets, whilst their adult selves, shown later in the drama, are played by actors. The use of puppets is one way in which the play 'defamiliarizes' its subject, prompting its audiences to consider afresh the conventions of relationships, marriage, sexuality, and of Christmas itself (Mansbridge 2012: 219).

The early moments of the play show us an almost suffocating closeness without intimacy. Initially characters seem to read one another's minds and can speak on each other's behalf. They are nonetheless isolated from one another. Carsickness and bickering amongst the children—scenes familiar to many families on long Christmas trips—form the backdrop to much more serious tensions. The father is having an affair; the mother knows this but does not want him to leave. Rebecca is struggling with her adolescence, Stephen with his sexual identity, Claire (the youngest) cannot understand the interactions in her family and later blames herself for whatever is going wrong. Their journey takes them to another claustrophobic space: 'the grandparents' apartment: plain red-bricked/boxes, cramped, identical and cheap' (32). The Christmas gifts they exchange in the apartment demonstrate the lack of understanding amongst the family since it is clear that no one gets the gift they longed for. Claire's gift from her father is an expensive charm bracelet (when she asked for 'blazing six-shooters to conquer the west'(18)). The bracelet gets broken and the gathering unravels as the family fight and get back in the car.

In the second half of the play each child in turn escapes the car and becomes their future selves. In the Christmases of the future both Rebecca and Claire experience moments where their lives hang in the balance. They are each saved by the ghost of their brother. Stephen, it transpires, has died of AIDs but returns as a presence in his sisters' lives on the 26th December each year, the Feast of Stephen, the first Christian martyr. In the play's final scene, the action shifts back to the car. As the father is about to strike the mother, the car spins on the ice and comes to rest 'at the brink of a steep precipice' (70). In this moment the children link arms. The movement is described by Stephen's ghost in lines that parallel those spoken at the breaking of the bracelet but this time 'the thin strands of flesh / did not break' (73). The car pulls away and the family continue their long ride into their futures.

Vogel writes that her play was partly inspired by Thornton Wilder's one-act play of 1932, *The Long Christmas Dinner* (Vogel 2004: 5). In Wilder's play too, Christmas gathers time. The play depicts in *'accelerated motion ninety Christmas dinners in the Bayard household'*. The stage set consists of folding doors upstage and two 'portals', one signifying birth, the other death (Wilder 1933: 5). On stage there is a dining table around which the characters are constantly eating their Christmas dinner. The ordinary rising and sitting, arriving and departing that happens when families are gathered are used to enact the comings and goings of generations. Years pass in a few lines as smoothly as the motion of food and drink shared around the table. The play explores time and repetition. The same lines return again and again. Lucia, who is a young woman when the play begins, observes at the first Christmas: 'Every least twig is wrapped around with ice. You almost never see that' (7). The line is repeated by her daughter, her daughter-in-law, and (with a slight variation) by a distant cousin. The image of organic growth frozen in ice captures the duality of constancy and change that the play depicts. The phrase 'you almost never see that' is, in one sense, dramatically ironic. For the characters these icy winters are separated by at least a year, often much more, but for the audience they are only moments apart. Yet, in another sense the audience are not in a position of superior knowledge for, as unspeaking guests at the family's table, we are reliant on the characters' descriptions of the world beyond.

The themes of change and fixity are re-enforced as the characters remark on the passing of time. Lucia does not 'want time to go any faster' as she thinks of her small children; Leonora in the next generation, likewise, wants her children to 'stay just as you are' (11 and 19). In the face of grief characters fall back on 'the passing of time' as a source of healing. Roderick (Leonora's son) eventually leaves the family home complaining that time does not move in the house and he must go 'where time passes' (23). The passage of time in the play and the changes it effects could be taken as a sign of the meaninglessness of the family's commonplace experiences and worries. Yet: 'What the play emphasizes...is that family dinners, factory work, war, and weather are not petty concerns, but rather the very stuff from which lives and histories are made' (Mansbridge 2012: 218).

Small mundane acts are of great importance too in Alexander Zeldin's *Love*, first performed at the National Theatre in London in 2016. The play's characters have all found themselves homeless and are being temporarily housed in a shabby Bed and Breakfast by their local council. Christmas is coming and Dean, Emma, and Dean's two children, Paige and Jason, arrive at the B&B. The whole family will share one room. Emma is expecting a baby and is desperate to find a house as soon as possible but conversations with Colin—another resident and a carer for his mother, Barbara—reveal he has been in this 'temporary' accommodation for more than a year. The set is the common area that the residents share. The audience overhears phone calls made by Tarwa, who has come from Sudan and is separated from her children. Adnan, another new arrival, is a refugee from Syria. The performance is designed to be 'hyperreal', with much of the action taken up with the most commonplace tasks and conversations, including making tea and going to the toilet (Brennan 2017).

Christmas appears in fragments across the play: from Paige practising the carol 'Away in a Manger' for the school Nativity, to mince pies picked up from a local charity, to a few decorations that Dean and Paige put up in the common area. In a context of injustice and hardship, these glimpses of festivity may be thought to have little significance. Yet they are one of the mechanisms by which the play explores the possibilities for connection and hope, whilst also highlighting the gap between the characters' experiences and the extravagant gatherings that many participate in at Christmas. The play's opening directions state that the audience should be '*sat around in such a way that the actors can move freely amongst them*' (Zeldin 2016: 3). In the original production, the house lights were kept on and the actors looked at, sat amongst and even occasionally made physical contact with members of the audience (Brennan 2017). The audience are invited into this most haphazard, unwished-for gathering of strangers in an unwelcoming common space. What will they find there? There is plenty in this Christmas play to make the audience angry or uncomfortable. In the words of Barbara in the play's final moments, there is also 'love', 'as much as the sea, as big as the sea' (52).

Drama can generate suspicion because of its associations with pretence and disguise. Yet the examples of plays and playing explored in this chapter demonstrate that performance can also allow us to look beneath the glitter of Christmas, beyond the 'Christmas-card prettiness'. Christmas plays can disrupt the social order, call for justice, give voice to the excluded, and gather us together to remember and to hope.

References and Further Reading

Anon. (1928). 'The Whitsuntide Play at Canterbury Cathedral', *The Dover Express*, 25 May: 9.

Brennan, Clare (2017). '*Love*—Review: Homelessness Brought Close to Home', *The New Review, The Observer*, 8 January: 29.

Castelli, Elizabeth A. (2004). *Martyrdom and Memory: Early Christian Culture Making*. New York: Columbia University Press.

Chambers, E. K. (1903). *The Mediaeval Stage*, Vol. 1. London: Oxford University Press.

Cone, James H. (1997). *God of the Oppressed*, rev. edn. Maryknoll, NY: Orbis.

Dox, Donnalee (2004). *The Idea of the Theater in Latin Christian Thought: Augustine to the Fourteenth Century*. Ann Arbor, MI: The University of Michigan Press.

Gamboa, Brett (2018). *Shakespeare's Double Plays: Dramatic Economy on the Early Modern Stage*. Cambridge: Cambridge University Press.

Gibson, James M. (1981–2) '"*Quem queritis in presepe*": Christmas Drama or Christmas Liturgy?' *Comparative Drama*, 15, no. 4, Winter: 343–65.

Goodland, Katharine (2005). *Female Mourning and Tragedy in Medieval and Renaissance English Drama: From the Raising of Lazarus to King Lear*. Aldershot, Hants: Ashgate.

Goodrich, Jean N. (2010). '"So I thought as I Stood, To Mirth Us Among": The Function of Laughter in *The Second Shepherds' Play*', in Albrecht Classen (ed.), *Laughter in the Middle Ages and Early Modern Times: Epistemology of a Fundamental Human Behavior, its Meaning, and Consequences*. Berlin: De Gruyter: 531–45.

Greif, Karen (1982). 'Plays and Playing in Twelfth Night', in Stanley Wells (ed.), *Shakespeare Survey*, 34. Cambridge: Cambridge University Press: 121–30.

Harris, Max (2011). *Sacred Folly: A New History of the Feast of Fools*. Ithaca, NY: Cornell University Press.

Hughes, Langston (2004). 'Black Nativity: A Gospel Song-Play for a Variable Cast', in Leslie Catherine Sanders (ed.), *The Collected Works of Langston Hughes*, Vol. 6: *Gospel Plays, Operas, and Later Dramatic Works*. Columbia, MI: University of Missouri Press: 356–78.

Ibsen, Henrick (2009). *A Doll's House*, trans. Michael Meyer. Ed. Nick Worrall and Non Worrall. London: Bloomsbury Methuen Drama.

James VI and I (1995). 'Speech in Star Chamber of 20 June 1616', in J. Sommerville (ed.), *King James VI and I: Political Writings*. Cambridge: Cambridge University Press: 204–28.

Johnston, Brian (1989). *Text and Supertext in Ibsen's Drama*. University Park, PA: Pennsylvania University Press.

Jonson, Ben (1941). *Christmas, His Masque*, in C. H. Herford, Percy Simpson, and Evelyn Simpson (eds), *Ben Jonson*, vol. 7: *The Sad Shepherd; The Fall of Mortimer; Masques and Entertainments*. Oxford: Oxford University Press, 1941: 431–48.

Kallenbach, Ulla (2018). *The Theatre of Imagining: A Cultural History of the Imagination in the Mind and on the Stage*. Basingstoke, Hants: Palgrave Macmillan.

Larkin, Craig (2014). 'Jerusalem's Separation Wall and Global Message Board: Graffiti, Murals and the Art of Sumud', *The Arab Studies Journal*, 22, no. 1, Spring: 134–69.

Love Actually (2003). Dir. Richard Curtis. UK: Universal Pictures.

Mansbridge, Joanna (2012). 'Memory's Dramas, Modernity's Ghosts: Thornton Wilder, Japanese Theater, and Paula Vogel's *The Long Christmas Ride Home*', *Comparative Drama*, 46, no. 2, Summer: 209–35.

Marcus, Leah S. (1986). *The Politics of Mirth: Jonson, Herrick, Milton, Marvell, and the Defense of Old Holiday Pastimes*. Chicago: University of Chicago Press, 1986.

Masefield, John (1928). *The Coming of Christ*. London: William Heinemann.
Nicholson, Steve (2005). *The Censorship of British Drama 1900–1968.* Vol. 2: *1933–1952*. Exeter: University of Exeter Press.
Nilu, Kamaluddin (2008). '*A Doll's House* in Asia: Juxtaposition of Tradition and Modernity', *Ibsen Studies*, 8, no. 2: 112–29.
Pickering, Kenneth (2001). *Drama in the Cathedral: A Twentieth Century Encounter of Church and Stage*, 2nd edn. Calwell, Worcs: J. Garnet Miller.
Pickstock, Catherine (2013). *Repetition and Identity*. Oxford: Oxford University Press.
Rampersad, Arnold (1988). *The Life of Langston Hughes*. Vol. II: *1941–1967: I Dream a World*. New York: Oxford University Press.
Selaiha, Nehad (2011). '*Peer Gynt* by the Pyramids of Giza', in Erika Fischer-Lichte, Barbara Gronau, and Christel Weiler (eds), *Global Ibsen: Performing Multiple Modernities*. New York: Routledge: 117–30.
Sayers, Dorothy L. (1938). 'Nativity Play', *Radio Times*, 23 December: 13.
Sayers, Dorothy L. (1939). *He That Should Come: A Nativity Play in One Act*. London: Victor Gollancz.
Sayers, Dorothy L. (1943). 'Introduction' in *The Man Born to Be King: A Play-Cycle on the Life of Our Lord and Saviour Jesus Christ*. London: Victor Gollancz: 17–40.
Sayers, Dorothy L. (1945). 'The Execution of God', *Radio Times*, 23 March: 3.
Sayers, Dorothy L. (1947) 'The Greatest Drama Ever Staged', in *Creed or Chaos? And Other Essays in Popular Theology*. London: Methuen: 1–6.
Tiongson, Nicanor G. (1998). 'Mexican-Philippine Relations in Traditional Folk Theater', Philippine Studies, 46, no. 2: 135–50.
Törnqvist, Egil (1995). *Ibsen—A Doll's House*. Cambridge: Cambridge University Press.
Van Ervan, Eugène (1992). *The Playful Revolution: Theatre and Liberation in Asia*. Bloomington, IN: Indiana University Press.
Vogel, Paula (2004). *The Long Christmas Ride Home*. New York: Theatre Communications Group.
Warren, Roger and Stanley Wells (1994). 'Introduction', in William Shakespeare, *Twelfth Night, or What You Will*, Oxford: Oxford University Press: 1–76.
Wilder, Thornton (1933). *The Long Christmas Dinner: A Play*. London: Samuel French.
Young, Karl (1933). *The Drama of the Medieval Church*. vol. 2. Oxford: Clarendon Press.
Zeldin, Alexander (2016). *Love*. London: Bloomsbury Methuen Drama.

CHAPTER 30

POETRY

EMMA MASON

CHRISTMAS is one of few occasions in the calendar when poetry is read widely. Its rhythms, measures, sounds, and affects give form to the joy and love symbolized in the birth of Jesus Christ for those with and without faith. From the simple greetings printed in Christmas cards to Clement Clarke Moore's 1823 'A Visit from St Nicholas' ("Twas the night before Christmas'), poems associated with the festival offer a way of becoming intimate with an emotional experience at once loving, mysterious, communal, and faithful. Poetry's accommodation of the obscure and mystical aspects of Christmas allows for the expression of grace, incarnation, spirit, and sacrament, and its comprehension through intuition and imagination. Its line breaks and interludes reward the patient and attentive reader to whom the poem never explains but rather assists in acts of discernment, memory, perception, and reverence. It is a participatory mode whose meaning works through the experience of the reader for whom its propositions invite interpretation and invention rather than creedal obedience. Poetry is at once kin to religion and its festivals even as it summons and engages an abundance of ways to celebrate and praise befitting so broadly feted a holiday as Christmas. As John Hollander and J. D. McClatchy argue, poetry has been associated with Christmas from the start—'from the song of the seraphim above the manger to the cherished carols around the punchbowl'—because of its ability to voice what they call 'the marvellous' (1999: 11). For Hollander and McClatchy, 'the marvellous' provides them with a secular term for the spirit-filled, visionary, and incantatory cadences of the poem, a wonder or magic that is at once spell-binding but indefinite. Poetry captures something that escapes narrative and prose, but can be accessed by readers content to inhabit and reflect on the feeling it gives.

A reliance on feeling often provokes anxiety: we are reassured by the fantasy that our neighbours, communities, and governments make decisions based on reason rather than emotion. While feeling invariably influences our actions and choices, a nervousness at its ostensible precarity and impermanence polices its expression in many cultures, not least those who celebrate Christmas. Yet Christmas is a time when we are finally encouraged to enjoy feeling. While the season has become as associated with loneliness, conflict, and worry as joy and love, its negative connotations arise from a secular overlay of family, expense, and presumed comfort many expect or demand. These material expectations are distinct from the spirit and grace of Christmas that seasonal poems work to incarnate if not decipher or expound. From greeting-card rhymes and newsletter carols to songs and verse, Christmas poems take seriously the joyful mysteries and message of peace and communion the festival promotes. For every satirical jingle that champions insobriety there are countless poems that embrace Christmas as hallowed and divine. Poetry traditionally joins the ghost story and winter tale as the most popular form of the season, as well as providing a 'scriptural touchstone' on which celebrants might reflect and deliberate (Moore 2009: 121).

Poetry helps readers to process feeling and thought in what is often a frantic time of year, because of the way its metre, cadences, and rhythms alter our experience of language and therefore of time. As Isobel Armstrong suggests, poetry accomplishes this by inviting the reader to accept the energies of its stress patterns: its pulses are 'felt somatically' but leave no trace, 'a ghostly paradigm without obvious content' (2011: 26). In her reading of Hegel, Armstrong suggests that rhyme and stress emerge with Christian culture precisely because both value the spirit of meaning as well as its embodiment in language. In other words, rhythm is what allows us to experience the poem affectively as we feel its pulse within our bodies before we contemplate its meaning: it compels us to consciously and physically feel the moment even as its regularity and patterns stabilize us for long enough to reflect on our experience (Helsinger 2015). As William Wordsworth argued, poetry originates in the emotions we remember when we are quiet and, in such quietude, reflect on (1802). What is conjured and spirited in these moments is enhanced and amplified when such emotional and physical feeling is associated with a season whose meaning is affective for all and divine for many. Christmas creates a space and time in which feelings of joy, love, loss, and mystery can be safely experienced along with everyone else. This shared feeling might be exuberant and charismatic, but it might equally be silent and gentle. Either way, Christmas poems allow for an intimacy with both spirit and matter, with those who are absent and present, invoking a 'proximity between' things—people, relatives, strangers, the divine (Yousef 2013: 3). The recognition, attention, and appreciation that derives from such proximity goes beyond ethical responsibility into shared relationships and sympathies.

The poems this chapter discusses harness the affective charge of the season, its mood, atmosphere, as well as its spirit, as a counter to the affective challenges of modernity: anxiety, stress, boredom, paranoia, shock. Many critics address how affect produces and mediates these challenges (recent examples include Armstrong 2000; Brennan 2004; and Berlant and Stewart 2019). This chapter similarly identifies Christmas feeling, articulated through poems that activate its affective and divine experience, as a radical resistance to bad feeling. It addresses how poetry connects to and dwells with the Annunciation, Advent, Christmas trees, Christmas Eve, Epiphany, and Christmas Day in poems by Maya Angelou, e. e. cummings, Toi Derricotte, T. S. Eliot, Martín Espada, Robert Frost, Gerard Manley Hopkins, Langston Hughes,

Elizabeth Jennings, Peter Larkin, W. S. Merwin, Christina Rossetti, Evie Shockley, Sufjan Stevens, and W. B. Yeats. Woven through the chapter is the suggestion that poetry fosters our relationship with uncertainty and faith by replacing our desire for empirical reason and reassurance with the joy and love embodied in the birth of the Saviour.

Christmas begins, not with the joy and love of Christmas Day, but with feelings of anticipation, wonder, and fear. Amidst countless forms of commercial 'magic' promoted by those intent on selling Christmas via a storm of sentimental advertisements survive poems in which we are reminded to prepare ourselves for the miracle and mystery of the main event. Two events in the Christian calendar define this preparatory time: Advent or Parousia, in which Christians await the Nativity of Jesus; and the return of Jesus at the Second Coming. Both require Christians to commit to developing their capacity for attention, quietude, and reserve. Without this emotional vigilance and care, wonder becomes mere sensation and is stripped of its meaning as astonishment, amazement, and deliberation. As David A. Redding writes, 'that first Christmas was not / Simply for the children' (1965: ll. 5–6), but

> For the old folks –
> Bent backs
> And tired eyes
> Need relief and light
> A little more.
> No wonder
> It was grown-ups
> Who were the first
> To notice
> Such a star.   (1965: ll. 17–26)

Redding intimates that the wonder of Christmas goes beyond an innocent excitement and delight 'the children' might feel on other occasions such as a birthday, a song, a dance, or a dog walk. Christmas wonder has to be noticed and prayed for because it provokes uncertainty as well as hope, this 'climate of fear and apprehension' into which 'Christmas enters' as Maya Angelou declares (2006, l. 12). W. S. Merwin too writes in his 'Carol of the Three Kings' that the men walked 'upon the darkness' towards 'the lord' like a 'shadow': 'Many nights moving, / Swaying many nights / Between yes and no' (2000: ll. 5–12). Such swaying determines the lead-up to Christmas, the festival's very proclamation, its 'Annunciation', a visitation from the angel Gabriel to Mary to announce the Incarnation. This too is a tenebrous, obscure moment, frightening even, as W. B. Yeats conveys in his poem, 'The Mother of God':

> Wings beating about the room;
> The terror of all terrors that I bore
> The Heavens in my womb   (1968: ll. 3–5)

Elizabeth Jennings personalizes Mary's specifically female experience further in 'The Annunciation', echoing Yeats' depiction of terror but articulating the particular and troubling charge of Gabriel's visitation:

> Nothing will ease the pain to come
> Though now she sits in ecstasy
> And lets it have its way with her.
> The angel's shadow in the room
> Is lightly lifted as if he
> Had never terrified her there.   (2012: ll. 1-6)

Jennings deftly nuances the wonder of this scene through her guarded portrayal of Mary's fear, an emotion joined with love and divinity but still deeply felt. For Mary's exposure to God's love through Gabriel 'burns' into her emotional experience of preparing to be both a believer and a new mother:

> Though in her heart new loving burns,
> Something she never gave to man
> Or God before, and this God grows
>
> Most like a man. She wonders how
> To pray at all, what thanks to give
> And whom to give them to.   (2012: ll. 10-15)

Where Yeats conceives of the unborn Christ as a 'fallen star' that Mary has 'purchased with my pains' (1968: ll. 11–12), Jennings witnesses Mary incarnate new life: 'It is a human child she loves / Though a God stirs beneath her breast / And great salvations grip her side' (2012: ll. 22–4). Or, as Gerard Manley Hopkins ventures in his extraordinary 'The Blessed Virgin compared to the Air we breathe', Mary's 'work' is not only to carry Christ, but also to renew grace itself:

> This air, which, by life's law,
> My lung must draw and draw
> Now but to breathe its praise,
> Minds me in many ways
> Of her who not only
> Gave God's infinity
> Dwindled to infancy
> Welcome in womb and breast,
> Birth, milk, and all the rest,
> But mothers each new grace
> That does now reach our race—   (2002: ll. 13-23)

Hopkins proposes that Mary's role goes beyond that of mother of God to the equally immense role as giver of grace. His brief description of the maternal—wombs, breasts, milk, 'and all the rest'—is nestled in a poem that is entirely and effusively about Mary's delivery of grace, that divine love by which all things are gathered into relationship with God as 'one body' (1 Corinthians: 12:12). As such grace's closest synonym is air and atmosphere, an energy by which all things are sustained and loved, and in which Mary 'plays' as 'her flesh' becomes spirit 'And makes, O marvellous! / New Nazareths in us' (ll. 49, 59–60).

Hopkins persistently summons the marvellous through his work in order to invoke spirit and mystery: for the Catholic poet, grace is given freely to all by the Holy Spirit through the sacraments and sacred mysteries. The Anglo-Catholic Christina Rossetti shared his focus on the sacramental, but understood grace also to be 'prevenient', that which comes before existence as that force or energy that brings all into being and then transitions life into the 'new heaven' and 'new earth' described in Revelation (21:1). Grace not only sustains life for Rossetti, but assists creation as it waits and prepares for the arrival of heaven on earth, a New Jerusalem that would replace a world she perceived to be dominated by a secular obsession with money, possessions, greed, wealth, power, and cruelty. Her ecological vision for a transfigured world in which all species peacefully live together as one body in grace reveals her longing for a Second Advent (Mason 2018). In the first, however, she found a place to practise contemplation, anticipation, and devotional waiting by preparing herself and her readers for the birth and arrival of Christ. Rossetti's numerous Advent poems are marked not only by a painful patience and slow waiting and watching, but also by a deferral to fellow created beings who stand by in a gentler state of expectation. Her poem 'Advent (Earth grown old)', for example, blurs the line between material and spirit to remind us that the human waits alongside a green Earth and those beings who remain unseen until Christ returns:

> Earth grown old, yet still so green,
>   Deep beneath her crust of cold
> Nurses fire unfelt, unseen:
>   Earth grown old.
> We who live are quickly told:
> Millions more lie hid between
>   Inner swathings of her fold.   (Rossetti 1986a: ll. 1–7)

In 'Advent ("Come," Thou dost say to Angels)', a restorative Lord invites angels, spirits, lambs, and all who read the poem to '"Come home"' (1990: l. 4); whereas 'Advent (The End of All Things)' locates the same creation 'in the balance trembling' between a hell that 'looms vast' and a heaven that 'flings wide its gates to great and small' (1990: ll. 2, 9–10). But Rossetti also registers that what is so longingly yearned for during Advent is impossible to imagine or utter even as it requires discernment and love. As she writes in 'Advent (This Advent moon shines cold and clear)', those 'Heart-sick with hope deferred' might know that '"No speaking signs are in the sky"', but believe that their emotional waiting (they weep, laugh, and sing) will be met with affection: 'Then He shall say, "Arise, My love, / My fair one, come away"' (1979: ll. 6–7, 47–8).

The draw of such hope is especially striking in Jupiter Hamman's eighteenth-century Christmas poem, 'An Evening Thought: Salvation by Christ with Penitential Cries', wherein repeated internal rhymes—salvation, redemption, preparation, nation—intertwine anticipatory hope with deliverance from slavery as well as from a world in which such brutality is possible:

> Dear Jesus, give thy Spirit now,
>   Thy Grace to every Nation,
> That han't the Lord to whom we bow,
>   The Author of Salvation.
> Dear Jesus, unto Thee we cry,
>   Give us the Preparation;
> Turn not away thy tender Eye;
>   We seek thy true Salvation.   (1977: ll. 13–20)

Hamman accents poetry's capacity to make room for new and hopeful ways of thinking. Part of this capacity is poetry's potential to embrace meanings that are not yet developed or revealed, and about which we are uncertain and apprehensive and so seek a form that allows us to pause within contradiction. Christmas poems are frequently defined by such pause, one that allows the reader to think in a non-dualist and non-oppositional manner receptive to Christian unity. As Rossetti writes in her poem 'Christmas Eve', the arrival of Christ puts apparent oppositions into relationship and so conceives a gathered creation in which the darkness of Christmas night blazes with a noon-day brightness and the earth, birds, and angels all 'strike up' their music in a shared harmony. Evie Shockley's less obviously religious poem, 'you must walk this lonesome', also evokes this harmony, but shapes colliding thoughts about and memories of Christmas into a different kind of euphony:

> say hello to moon leads you into trees as thick as folk on easter pews dark but venture through amazing was blind but now fireflies glittering dangling from evergreens like Christmas oracles soon you meet the riverbank down by the riverside water bapteases your feet moon bursts back in low yellow swing low sweet chariot of cheese shines on in the river cup hands and sip what never saw inside a peace be still mix in your tears moon distils distress like yours so nobody knows the trouble it causes pull up a log and sit until your empty is full your straight is wool your death is yule moonshine will do that barter with you what you got for what you need draw from the river like it is well with my soul o moon you croon and home you go   (2009: 42)

Shockley gestures towards Christian rituals—Easter and baptism as well as Christmas—by interspersing abbreviated references to spirituals and hymns into a loco-descriptive poem about a walk in moonlit woods. References to 'Amazing Grace', 'Down to the River to Pray', 'Swing Low, Sweet Chariot', 'Peace Be Still', and 'Nobody Knows the Trouble I've Seen' musically play across an observed landscape, in which trees, fireflies, the moon, and the river share the narrator's memories of being with 'folk' during such rituals. The 'oracles' who oversee Christmas here are not only priests, but also all who assume divinity during this period: everyone with whom we share our celebrations and the natural world on which we rely. The 'yule moonshine' of line eight is the same 'cold and clear' moon that illuminates Rossetti's faith, even as Shockley's work draws us closer to the emotional than the religious content of the festival. The experience her poem illumes is solitary, private, and lonesome, but it ultimately calls on her reader to identify the familiar and the homely through poetry, the song or 'croon' of the final line.

Shockley's poem directly addresses the relationship between race, gender, and the earth, all subjects of historical and continued violence that the spirituals from which she quotes offer a medium. But the immediate and repeated allusions to trees and evergreens in 'you must walk this lonesome' also remind the reader both of pagan winter holidays celebrated thousands of years before Christianity as well as the 'tree of paradise' noted in medieval mystery plays, laden with apples to represent the forbidden fruit of Genesis, and wafers to invoke the Eucharist and redemption of grace. Pagan and Christian alike, trees remind their onlookers that the end of the year is a hallowed time, their branches reaching out to others, to heaven, and to God. In the modern religio-ecological poem, 'praying // firs \\ attenuate', Peter Larkin observes neglected and industrial woodlands that reveal a God who is entangled within his created world, now broken and ruined by pollution, chemical waste, and Earth's devastated biodiversity. Larkin begins his seven-part poem by locating the firs 'in faith' and 'at praise' (2014: I. ll. 1, 4) before tracing their vertical and horizontal uplift as their branches sweep up and out:

> what is upright is gift—
> apparent but not as prayer
> a sample of transparency
> so that green shoots
> in season don't inhibit
> the stubbed proclivity
> of horizon   (2014: I. ll. 41–8)

The firs' fractal movement towards the sky 'is gift' because their roots, boughs, and springs are channels and shelters for multiple life forms, including themselves (as branches extend and flourish, they fragment and splinter into undergrowth and brushwood in which other species thrive). Their gift is not apparently or obviously prayer specifically because their being is transparently always already an act of givenness, grace, and worship for Larkin. The unbounded and enduring nature of their perennial shoots and sprigs open the observer into an infinite time while anchoring her on the ground they regenerate and from which they grow. Larkin's trees never disrupt the horizon we know and recognize, but they also bridge that space between the material and the divine, 'spiritually aphonic' (2014: IV, ll. 117), but embodying a continual prayer for connection and interdependence.

While Larkin's opaquely interwoven poetics sound and feel strikingly distinct from the lyrical but disarranged syntax of e. e. cummings, both poets visually suggest trees as points of connection and heightened perception. cummings' 'little tree' gently invokes the Christmas tree before the reader as that which relates the other-than-human world to the human and the divine. The tree is at once 'like a flower' from 'the green forest' (1991: ll. 4–5), a comforter who invites the 'kiss' and 'hug' (ll. 9–10) of those who meet it, and a sacred presence to whom we sing 'Noel Noel' (l. 28), a song that recalls Christ's birth through its etymological connection to the Latin *natalis* or natal. The narrator's tender affection for the tree unfolds the loving joy of the season sensually as well as affectively. The sweet smell of the tree, its 'cool bark', 'spangles', and 'fluffy' decorations, invite the embrace of a narrator intent on holding the tree with the same warmth he has for his 'little sister' with whom he sings and dances at the end of the poem. Addressing the tree with signature lowercase charm, cummings writes:

> put up your little arms
> and i'll give them all to you to hold
> every finger shall have its ring
> and there won't be a single place dark or unhappy   (1991: ll. 17–20)

The apparent simplicity of these lines holds within it a concise commentary on the awaited birth of Christ, the moment in which 'light is come into the world' even though 'men loved darkness rather than light' (John 3:19). By focusing on the little Christmas tree rather than Mary's little child, cummings creates a bright and sparkling shelter for all readers, believers and non-believers alike, the dance and song on which the poem closes a familial and jubilant one sealed from the 'dark or unhappy'. It is this same affective simplicity that enchants the reader of Robert Frost's 'Christmas Trees', a poem that follows the narrator's bewildered exchange with a stranger from the city who arrives at his rural home to buy 'my Christmas trees; / My woods—the young fir balsams like a place / Where houses all are churches and have spires' (2001: ll. 12–14). The woods with whom he shares his life are sacred and domestic, like homes and churches that might be shared but not sold. The narrator is reluctantly tempted by the buyer, but his discourteous offer, a thousand trees for thirty dollars, makes up his mind:

> But thirty dollars seemed so small beside
> The extent of pasture I should strip, three cents
> (For that was all they figured out apiece) [. . .]
> Worth three cents more to give away than sell,
> As may be shown by a simple calculation.   (2001: ll. 47–9, 56–7)

The stranger's thirty dollars recalls the thirty pieces of silver (Matthew 26:15) with which Judas is paid to betray Jesus, who responds with his own 'simple calculation' regarding his friend's guilt. But Frost's seemingly mundane 'As may be shown by a simple calculation' arouses the same wonder as cummings' glittering tree branches and

Larkin's 'upright' gift, all of which bless the reader by mediating an affection and care that remains unspoken outside of the Christmas season.

Poetry carries these affects where other forms falter, its rhythms and line breaks mediating an intimacy that goes beyond the granting of a warm glow into a compelling call for the overturning of an uneven world in which many are isolated or abused. Martín Espada's poem, 'Imagine the Angels of Bread', for example, finds in Christmas a moment in which power is redistributed, wherein 'squatters evict landlords', 'shawled refugees / deport judges', 'police revolvers, / stove-hot, blister the fingers / of raging cops' and 'darkskinned men / lynched a century ago / return to sip coffee quietly / with the apologizing descendants / of their executioners' (1994: ll. 1, 7, 12–14, 18–22). Toi Derricotte domesticates the experience of power in 'Christmas Eve: My Mother Dressing' by unveiling the repeated abuses of racism, slavery, violence, and labour, black women endure in a portrait that draws us close to its annual cessation. As she prepares herself for Christmas Day, the narrator's mother appears almost uncomfortably restrained by her holiday 'costume' make-up, that which 'seemed to hold her down, to trap her' as 'her poor hands', 'old from scrubbing', pray 'for the scrub bucket and brush to make them useful' (1989: ll. 2, 10, 15, 21). Derricotte's visceral cinematic of an exhausted woman struggling to pull her body into an imagined expectation is beautifully suspended by a closing moment of touch, one that recalls Gabriel's visit to Mary as well as the woman who washes and anoints Jesus with her tears (Luke 7:38):

> But once a year my mother
> rose in her white silk slip,
> not the slave of the house, the woman,
> took the ironed dress from the hanger—
> allowing me to stand on the bed, so that
> my face looked directly into her face,
> and hold the garment away from her
> as she pulled it down.   (1989: ll. 25–32)

The purity and sheen of the white slip prefaces a pause signified by the dash of line twenty-eight in which the narrator's mother is freed into the hope of the day for which she prepares. This apparently rare and tender meeting between mother and daughter is founded on the two being lifted up towards their communion, the mother rising into the slip as the narrator climbs up to stand on the bed. Here is a poetic instant in which two people are momentarily bound in a dynamic and moving love, as if they stand interwoven together at what T. S. Eliot called 'the still point of the turning world' (1943: l. 16), attending to each other in anticipation of the revelation of God incarnate as Jesus Christ.

Eliot's dramatic monologue, *Journey of the Magi*, also focuses on anticipation and barely given resolution. The poem is narrated by an elderly magus recalling being on the way to see the newly born Christ, but his references to Lancelot Andrewes and Matthew Arnold dislocate his narrative to spotlight instead the struggle and anxiety with which his journey is framed. His travels are anguished—the camels, 'galled, sore-footed', lie 'down in the melting snow', and their guides want only 'liquor and women': all are sleep deprived and find animosity in the villages in which they hoped to find shelter (1927: ll. 6–7, 12). Once the group move 'below the snow line', however, all appears changed (l. 22). The weather is more temperate and spring-like, but the 'Birth' they seek feels defamiliarizing and disquieting: 'this Birth was / Hard and bitter agony for us, like Death, our death' (ll. 36–37). Christ's arrival is material and certain, but the new way of thinking, perceiving, and imagining he brings is truly an epiphany in which old gods with whom one might bargain and barter are displaced by an uncertain incarnation (Atkins 2014: 48). This is the same uncertainty on which Rossetti draws in her unspeaking sky, that Angelou lyricizes in the 'whisper', 'tremble', and 'thrill' of 'Amazing Peace' (2006: ll. 26, 33), or that Merwin observes in his mystified three kings. As a necessary preface to the merrymaking of Christmas Day, the wonder of this unknowing confusion is welcomed and revered as a darkness and depth that quietens and settles. Like Langston Hughes' shepherds, who burst with questions even as they so willingly bring their hearts to 'Him. / I will bring my heart / To the Manger' (1995: ll. 30–32), Merwin's kings let go of conviction to privilege being:

> We are breath and human
> And awake have seen
> All birth and burial
> Merge and fall away,
> Seen heaven that extends
> To comfort all the night   (2000: ll. 41–6)

The birth of Jesus is thus transformed into that which marvels rather than reassures or describes. Christopher Smart's rapturous 'The Nativity of Our Lord and Saviour Jesus Christ' illuminates this in his invocation of 'this stupendous stranger' that becomes 'O Most Mighty! O MOST HOLY!' before the witnesses of creation (1990: ll. 1, 5). Like Rossetti's Christ, Smart rejoices in a God who is glorified at Christmas time by all things:

> Nature's decorations glisten
>   Far above their usual trim;
> Birds on box and laurels listen,
>   As so near the cherubs hymn. [. . .]
> Oaks no more are riv'n in splinters
>   By the whirlwind and his host.
> Spinks and ouzels sing sublimely,
>   'We too have a Saviour born'   (1990: ll. 21–4; 27–30)

Smart's classical references convince the reader that the magnitude of former gods is now overwhelmed, not by power, but by birds, oak trees, and angels, joined as they are in a unified creation of which the newly born Christ is also 'a native' (l. 35). The poetic word might shatter our desire for certainty, but it does so with familiar cadences and measures that usher in an intimacy and fellowship with all those who honour the season.

This fellowship is lovingly animated in my final example: Sufjan Stevens' Christmas albums, *Songs for Christmas,* produced between 2001 and 2006, and *Silver and Gold: Songs for Christmas* from 2006 to 2012. Initially comprised of songs written as gifts for friends and family, Stevens' compilations include his own compositions and new versions of traditional ballads and carols in which 'Silent Night', 'Amazing Grace', 'I Saw Three Ships' and 'Joy to the World' are set alongside 'Come On! Let's Boogey to the Elf Dance!', 'Get Behind Me, Santa!', 'The Friendly Beasts', and 'Christmas Unicorn'. While Stevens is recognized as a musician rather than a poet, his work is alive to poetry's affinity for incantation and wonder, and his carols, hymns, and canticles read like songlines through which we navigate the shifting affects, emotions, and moods Christmas carries. A word associated with the invisible dream maps Aboriginal communities nomadically forge through music, the 'songline' manifests Stevens' affectively delicate, otherworldly, and entrancing texts in which muffled lyrics resonate almost out of hearing to amplify atmosphere, spirit, and faith. The soft plink of bells, merry quiver of flutes, and fluctuating waves of electronica make audible Stevens' own still faith, which finds expression in the glimmer of starlight in his song 'Star of Wonder':

> I call you
> From the comet's cradle
> I found you
> Trembling by yourself
> When the night falls   (2006: ll. 1–5)

The repeated refrain, 'When the night falls', gently intimates that while all things fade and recede, their poetic expression continues to resound for those who engage with it on their own terms and in their own neighbourhoods and families: 'I see the stars coming down there / Coming down there to the yard [. . .] Coming down there to my heart' (2006: ll. 22–5). I close by arguing for Stevens as a poet because he conjures the same depth of joy and love reached through submission to divine uncertainty as the other writers discussed here. But his bare and vulnerable words also give form to the wonder that is most difficult for many to feel at Christmas time. The song 'Put the lights on the tree' lightly moves the listener from the warmth of decorating the tree with loved ones and the practicalities of calling a relative to the presence of Jesus:

> Put the lights on the tree
> (Put them on the tree)
>
> Put the ribbon on the wreath
> (Put it on the wreath)
>
> Call your grandma on the phone
> (Call her on the phone)

> If she's living all alone
> (If she's all alone)
> Tell her Jesus Christ is here
> (Tell her He is here)   (2006: ll. 1–5)

Steven's final lines, 'If she's crying on the phone / Tell her you are coming home', embodies the affective challenges of a time that is sometimes accused of correlating to loneliness more than the marvellous (2006: ll. 7–8). Poetry's accommodation of a language, affective, meditative, sacramental, and in which gentle visions of joy and love might be found free of fear or expectation is why readers and poets alike return to its possibilities year after year.

REFERENCES AND FURTHER READING

Angelou, Maya (2006). *Amazing Peace: A Christmas Poem*. Random House: New York.
Armstrong, Isobel (2000). *The Radical Aesthetic*. Oxford: Blackwell.
Armstrong, Isobel (2011). 'Meter and Meaning', in Jason David Hall (ed.), *Meter Matters: Verse Cultures of the Long Nineteenth Century*. Athens, Ohio: Ohio University Press: 26–52.
Atkins, G. Douglas (2014). *T. S. Eliot's Christmas Poems: An Essay in Writing-as-Reading and Other 'Impossible Unions'*. New York: Palgrave.
Berlant, Lauren, and Kathleen Stewart (2019). *The Hundreds*. Durham and London: Duke University Press.
Brennan, Teresa (2004). *The Transmission of Affect*. Ithaca and London: Cornell University Press.
cummings, e. e. (1991). 'little tree', in George James Firmage (ed.), *Tulips and Chimneys* (1922), *e. e. cummings: Complete Poems 1904–1962*. New York: Liveright: 29.
Derricotte, Toi (1989). 'Christmas Eve: My Mother Dressing', in *Captivity*. Pittsburgh, PA: University of Pittsburgh Press: 9.
Eliot, T. S. (1943). 'Burnt Norton', in *Four Quartets*. New York: Harcourt, Brace.
Eliot, T. S. (1927). *Journey of the Magi*. London: Faber and Gwyer.
Espada, Martín (1994). 'Imagine the Angels of Bread', *The Massachusetts Review*. 35, no. 1: 24–5.
Frost, Robert (2001) 'Christmas Trees (A Christmas Circular Letter)', in Edward Connery Lathem (ed.), *Mountain Interval* (1916), *The Poetry of Robert Frost*. London: Vintage: 105–7.
Hamman, Jupiter (1977). 'An Evening Thought: Salvation by Christ with Penitential Cries: Composed by Jupiter Hamman, a Negro belonging to Mr Lloyd, of Queen's-Village, on Long-Island, the 25 of December 1760'. *New York Times*, 25 December: 195.
Helsinger, Elizabeth K. (2015). *Poetry and the Thought of Song in Nineteenth-Century Britain*. Charlottesville and London: University of Virginia Press.
Hollander, John and J. D. McClatchy (1999). *Christmas Poems*. New York: Everyman.
Hopkins, Gerard Manley (2002). 'The Blessed Virgin Compared to the Air We Breathe' (1883), in Catherine Phillips (ed.), *Gerard Manley Hopkins: The Major Works*. Oxford: Oxford University Press: 158.

Hughes, Langston (1995). 'Shepherd's Song at Christmas' (n.d.), in '18 Poems for Children' (1958), in Arnold Rampersad and David Roessel (eds.), *The Collected Poems of Langston Hughes*. New York: Vintage Classics: 610.

Jennings, Elizabeth (2012). 'The Annunciation', in *A Sense of the World* (1958), in Emma Mason (ed.), *Elizabeth Jennings: The Collected Poems*. Manchester: Carcanet.

Larkin, Peter (2014). 'praying // firs \\ attenuate', in *Give Forest Its Next Portent*. Bristol: Shearsman: 160–93.

Mason, Emma (2018). *Christina Rossetti: Poetry, Ecology, Faith*. Oxford: Oxford University Press.

Merwin, W. S. (2000). 'Carol of the Three Kings', in *A Mask for Janus* (1952), in *The First Four Books of Poems*. Washington: Copper Canyon Press: 55.

Moore, Tara (2009). *Victorian Christmas in Print*. New York: Palgrave Macmillan.

Redding, David A. (1965). 'Let Advent Begin', in *If I Could Pray Again*. Millbrae, California: Celestial Arts: 47.

Rossetti, Christina (1979) 'Advent (This Advent moon shines cold and clear)' (1858), in Rebecca Crump (ed.), *The Complete Poems of Christina Rossetti: A Variorum Edition: Volume 1*. Baton Rouge and London: Louisiana State University Press: 68–70.

Rossetti, Christina (1986a). 'Advent (Earth grown old)' (pub. 1885), in Rebecca Crump (ed.), *The Complete Poems of Christina Rossetti: A Variorum Edition: Volume 2*. Baton Rouge and London: Louisiana State University Press: 212.

Rossetti, Christina (1986b). 'Christmas Eve' (pub. 1885), in Rebecca Crump (ed.), *The Complete Poems of Christina Rossetti: A Variorum Edition: Volume 2*. Baton Rouge and London: Louisiana State University Press: 213–214.

Rossetti, Christina (1986c). 'Advent (The End of All Things)' (pub. 1892), in Rebecca Crump (ed.), *The Complete Poems of Christina Rossetti: A Variorum Edition: Volume 2*. Baton Rouge and London: Louisiana State University Press: 247.

Rossetti, Christina (1990). 'Advent ("Come," Thou dost say to Angels)' (1851), in Rebecca Crump (ed.), *The Complete Poems of Christina Rossetti: A Variorum Edition: Volume 3*. Baton Rouge and London: Louisiana State University Press: 199.

Shockley, Evie (2009). 'you must walk this lonesome', in *half-red sea* (2006), in Camille T. Dungy (ed.), *Black Nature: Four Centuries of African American Nature Poetry*. Athens and London: The University of Georgia Press: 42.

Smart, Christopher (1990). 'Hymn 32: The Nativity of Our Lord and Saviour Jesus Christ', in *Hymns and Spiritual Songs for the Fasts and Festivals of the Church of England* (1765), in Karina Williamson and Marcus Walsh (eds.), *Christopher Smart: Selected Poems*. London: Penguin: 192–193.

Stevens, Sufjan (2006). *Songs for Christmas*. New York: Asthmatic Kitty.

Stevens, Sufjan (2012). *Silver and Gold: Songs for Christmas*. New York: Asthmatic Kitty.

Wordsworth, William (2014). 'Preface' (1802) to the *Lyrical Ballads*, in Nicholas Halmi (ed.), *Wordsworth's Poetry and Prose*. New York: Norton.

Yeats, William Butler (1968). 'The Mother of God', in A. Norman Jeffares (ed.), *Words for Music Perhaps and Other Poems* (1932), in *W. B. Yeats: Selected Poetry*. London: Macmillan: 155.

Yousef, Nancy (2013). *Romantic Intimacy*. Stanford: Stanford University Press.

CHAPTER 31

FICTION

NATALIE McKNIGHT

The Men Who Invented Christmas

Charles Dickens has often been referred to as the man who invented Christmas. A book by Les Standiford (2008) and now a major-release film (2017) both make that claim in their titles, as have numerous well-meaning pundits on the subject. The assertion arises, of course, because of the widespread and continuing popularity of Dickens's *A Christmas Carol* (1843), one of the most beloved holiday tales of all time and a story which has come to dominate the local and regional theatre schedules every December. It has also given rise to dozens of film and TV versions, many of which air repeatedly every holiday season. It is the most filmed of all of Dickens's works.

While *A Christmas Carol* probably is the most famous and popular Christmas story after the Gospel narratives of the birth of Jesus, neither it nor Dickens deserve full credit for reinvigorating the celebration of Christmas. Part of the credit must go to Washington Irving, who immortalized characteristics of Santa Claus in numerous references within his *History of New York* (1809), and whose Christmas sketches in *The Sketch Book of Geoffrey Crayon, Gent* (1819–20) provided a richly nostalgic description of Christmas customs at the estate of an English squire who is enamoured of Christmas traditions. Irving's tone in the sketches is nostalgic because traditional Christmas practices were on the wane in both England and the United States. Christmas had come under attack by Puritans because of its roots in pre-Christian festivities, and the boisterous practices associated with Christmas celebrations offended strict religious observers. One such practice, the Feast of Fools, a medieval Christmas custom, included a day where the hierarchy of the Church was inverted and laypersons dressed up like clergy and ridiculed church leaders in skits and pantomimes. Such practices, along with widespread overindulgences in drinking and eating, ran counter to the high seriousness and restraint of Puritans and other strict religious observers. But they weren't the only enemies of the holiday. There was a degree of upper-class prejudice against what was seen as the vulgarities of traditional Christmas festivities, as David Parker points out in 'Dickens and the American Christmas' (Parker 2002: 160–9). According to Parker, 'practices varied, but, broadly speaking, the lower social ranks celebrated [Christmas] more enthusiastically than the higher. Among elite groups, a certain awkwardness about it was prevalent. To say the least, manners inherited from the eighteenth century were not easily reconciled with traditional revelry' (160).

In addition to the restraining effects of fashion and Puritanism, Americans' fascination with newness and progress also fuelled a move away from ancient Christmas traditions in the United States. But not for Washington Irving. As he states in 'The Author's Account of Himself' at the beginning of *The Sketch Book of Geoffrey Crayon, Gent*, he gravitated to travelling in Europe because the United States 'was full of youthful promise: [but] Europe was rich in the accumulated treasures of age' (Irving 1963: 2). Irving's *Sketch Book*, published at first serially in 1819–20, was inspired by his travels and his longing to 'loiter about the ruined castle—to meditate on the falling tower—to escape, in short, from the commonplace realities of the present, and lose myself among the shadowy grandeurs of the past' (2). In *The Sketch Book*, Irving's descriptions of holiday practices at a country estate evoke a nostalgic relishing of all the trappings of a traditional Christmas, with the Yule log, carols, wassail, games (such as blind man's bluff), ghost stories, a special church service, and a hall festooned with mistletoe and holly. Irving offers five sketches that chronicle the narrator's Christmas experiences: 'Christmas', 'The Stage Coach', 'Christmas Eve', 'Christmas Day', and 'The Christmas Dinner'. Throughout these pieces, Irving muses on the passing of the traditions he describes. In the first paragraph of 'Christmas' he says that '[n]othing in England exercises a more delightful spell over my imagination, than the lingerings of the holiday customs and rural games of former times', but he regrets that 'they are daily growing more and more faint, being gradually worn away by time, but still more obliterated by modern fashion. They resemble those picturesque morsels of Gothic architecture, which we see crumbling in various part of the country' (176). 'Society has acquired a more enlightened and elegant tone; but it has lost many of its strong local peculiarities,' he adds a few pages later (179). His nostalgic tone is taken up by Squire Bracebridge, the owner of the estate. Bracebridge laments 'the deplorable decay of the games and amusements which were once prevalent at this season... when the old halls of castles and manor houses were thrown open at daylight; when the tables were covered with brawn and beef, and humming ale; when the harp and the carol resounded all day long, and when rich and poor were alike welcome to enter and make merry' (211). Irving ends the Christmas pieces with the same kind of nostalgia that began them: "I felt an interest in the scene,' he confesses, 'from the consideration that these fleeting customs were posting fast into oblivion, and that this was, perhaps, the only family in England in which the whole of them were still punctiliously observed' (228).

Yet the 'fleeting customs' did *not* pass 'fast into oblivion' as Irving predicted, partly because he wrote about them so memorably and so appealingly that they influenced the practice of Christmas and writings about Christmas for years to come. It is Irving's descriptions that 'live[d] on for many years in Christmas cards, posters, and illustrations' according to Van Wyck Brooks, who wrote the introduction to the 1963 Dent edition of Irving's *Sketch Book* (Irving 1963: vi, v–vi). Brooks adds, 'Generations of children all over the world were to see the "old England" that Irving saw and as he saw it, because he had seen it first' (vii). Irving also strongly influenced contemporary conceptions of Santa Claus in his numerous depictions of St Nicholas in *History of New York*, in which he describes the gift-giving saint as smoking a pipe, 'laying his finger beside his nose' and 'riding over the tops of trees in that self same wagon wherein he brings his yearly presents to children' (Irving 1809: Bk. 2, Ch. 5, 118).

It is ironic, of course, that it took an American—an outsider—to appreciate English customs that were on the wane and to describe them in details compelling enough to inspire subsequent authors, most notably Charles Dickens. Dickens was fond of Irving's sketches, and was no doubt alluding to them with his first published book, *Sketches by Boz*. As Parker points out, Dickens was 'a disciple of Irving' and, in a letter of 1841, Dickens told Irving he had copies of all his books, and had loved them since childhood (Parker 2002: 163). Writing to Irving on April 21, 1841, Dickens alludes to Irving's Christmas sketches when he muses, 'I should like to travel with you outside the last of the coaches down to Bracebridge Hall. It would make my heart glad to compare notes with you...about all those delightful places and people that I used to walk about and dream of in the daytime, when a very small and not over-particularly taken-care-of boy' (Johnson 1952: 311). Dickens's *Sketches by Boz* is a compilation of short essays that had originally been published individually, but then were published (like Irving's sketches) in book form. The influence of Irving can be seen most notably in Dickens's first signed Christmas publication 'Christmas Festivities', which was originally published in *Bell's Life in London* on 27 December 1835 and later reprinted as 'A Christmas Dinner' in *Sketches by Boz*, although Michael Hancher makes a persuasive argument that Dickens's first publication was actually a humorous letter to the editor of the *Athenaeum* entitled '"Merry Christmas to You;" or Wishes Not Horses', which appeared on Saturday, 7 January 1832 (Hancher 2014: 287). 'Christmas Festivities' begins, like Irving's Christmas sketches, by suggesting that there are some who dismiss the celebration of Christmas: 'Christmastime! That man must be a misanthrope indeed, in whose breast something like a jovial feeling is not roused—in whose mind some pleasant associations are not awakened—by the recurrence of Christmas' (Dickens 2003: 1). It is worth noting that the first line of Dickens's first publication on Christmas presents an interesting seed for the creation of Ebenezer Scrooge a few years later (i.e. the 'misanthrope' who has no 'jovial feeling...roused' by Christmas). The similarity between this sketch and the later *Carol* continues in the same paragraph when Dickens states that some people complain about Christmas because it brings to mind their disappointments, which is certainly also true of Scrooge. Other details that emerge in fuller form in *A Christmas Carol* are Dickens's descriptions of mince pies, plum cakes, roast turkey, flaming brandy, churchgoing, blind man's bluff, reconciliations between enemies, the boisterous gathering of a loving family, even the death of a young child.

Dickens drew all of these elements together (and many more) into the rich tapestry of *A Christmas Carol*, which some scholars feel is Dickens's most perfect work of fiction

(Schlicke 1999: 102). The reasons for the *Carol*'s popularity with literary critics and general audiences alike are many. Its core story of Ebenezer Scrooge's redemption, his transformation from pinched and pinching miser to mensch, is deeply appealing to many, for who doesn't hope they can make up for past sins and lost time? That this transformation is brought about through the agency of four ghosts (Scrooge's former partner Marley, and the Ghosts of Christmas Past, Present and Yet-to-Come) adds to the appeal of the transformation, as they bring the mystery of the supernatural—the pleasure of experiencing fear—but in the safety of a narrative. Ghost stories have been a perennially popular form for centuries and were part of traditional Christmas practices, probably dating back to pagan winter solstice celebrations. So Dickens's use of ghosts and his decision to subtitle *A Christmas Carol* 'A Ghost Story of Christmas' were fitting for the occasion. (Dickens also used supernatural elements in another precursor to the *A Christmas Carol*, 'The Goblin Who Stole a Sexton', one of the interpolated tales in his first novel *The Pickwick Papers*.) Connecting the haunting of ghosts with the way memories haunt underscores the compelling psychological dimension of *A Christmas Carol*, which, among other things, explores how essential it is to be in touch with one's own past if one is to live fully in the present; it also traces the way in which people can be their own worst enemies in pursuing what they think they want the most.

Other elements that add to the *Carol*'s success are its five-part structure, which reflects the organization of Five Act plays, with the exposition, rising action, climax, and denouement. The tightness of the plotting along these dramatic lines helps to condense the impact of the tale and no doubt contributes to the *Carol* inspiring so many successful theatrical and film versions. Tightness of plotting is *not* something Dickens tends to be known for, so his success in managing it in this tale is one of the reasons some critics feel this is his best work.

In addition to the successful plot structure, Dickens showers readers with an abundance of detail to capture the beauty and opulence of the season. He devotes an entire page to detailing (and personifying) the produce on display in a shop window:

> There were great round, pot-bellied baskets of chestnuts, shaped like the waistcoats of jolly old gentlemen, looking at the doors, and tumbling out into the street in their apoplectic opulence. There were ruddy, brown-faced broad-girthed Spanish Onions, shrinking in the fatness of their growth like Spanish friars; and winking from their shelves in wanton slyness at the girls as they went by, and glance demurely at the hung-up mistletoe. There were pears and apples, clustered high in blooming pyramids; there were bunches of grapes, made in the shopkeeper's benevolence to dangle from conspicuous hooks, that people's mouths might water gratis as they passed.... (75–6)

He goes on. In passages like this, or in his description of the Cratchit's Christmas dinner of roast goose, stuffing, mashed potatoes, and plum pudding (81), Dickens makes readers relish the details as much as he does. And in doing so, he both records and celebrates Christmas practices for posterity, as Irving did.

Dickens's other Christmas books are less successful: *The Chimes* (1844), *Cricket on the Hearth* (1845), *The Battle of Life* (1846), and *The Haunted Man and the Ghost's Bargain* (1848). While popular at the time they were published, they are not read much now except by Dickens scholars, and they do not deal directly with Christmas per se except for *The Haunted Man*. All of them share the celebration of home and hearth, but none as memorably as the *Carol*. The *Chimes* (subtitled *A Goblin Story of Some Bells that Rang an Old Year Out and New Year In*) depicts reveries inspired by the ringing of church bells and is worth noting for its dire depictions of poverty and its relatively radical politics. *The Haunted Man* (subtitled *A Fancy for Christmas Time*) is also worth noting for its grim portrait of a man cut off from his memories of sorrow and the Romantic refrain that ends the tale, 'Lord, keep my memory green.' The story clearly extends the theme of the importance of memory that is so prominent in the *Carol*. The protagonist of *The Haunted Man*, Redlaw, a chemistry professor, is haunted by painful memories of lost love, and he wishes to be released from them, a wish which is granted on Christmas Eve by a Phantom which Redlaw refers to as the 'Evil spirit of myself' (Dickens 2003: 147). The Phantom's 'gift' extends to everyone Redlaw encounters, who also are freed from their memories of sorrow. But Redlaw soon discovers that to be 'free' of painful memories is to be less than human, to have nothing inside but a 'barren wilderness' (204). He and his friends become surly, mean-spirited and depressed once 'freed' from their sad memories. But Redlaw begins to reclaim his memories and his humanity when distant Christmas music moves him to tears. The scene echoes the passage in the *Carol* in which Scrooge weeps upon seeing himself as a boy abandoned at school at Christmastime, a moment that marks the start of his redemption. Redlaw's reclamation and that of his friends continues through the loving presence of Milly Swidger, the wife of Redlaw's servant, William. Milly has no children of her own, a situation which seems to inspire her to be the mother of all. She alone is not affected by the curse/gift of the Phantom, and only her presence can lift it. The story ends with a large dinner feast in the medieval hall of the college under the gaze of a portrait that bears the motto, 'Lord, keep my memory green' (230).

The success of Dickens's Christmas books led to a host of similar efforts being published by other authors each December, including fiction by William Makepeace Thackeray, Anthony Trollope, Elizabeth Gaskell, and George MacDonald. But none of these offerings matched the popularity of *A Christmas Carol*. Dickens continued the Christmas story tradition for sixteen years after the last Christmas book by issuing special Christmas numbers of *Household Words*, a weekly journal he edited from 1850 to 1859. He then continued the practice in his subsequent journal, *All the Year Round*. Dickens understood that families counted on him to produce a Christmas fiction that they would read aloud around the fire, so his Christmas tales in addition to preserving Christmas traditions became fundamental to new traditions which continue today in the annual proliferation of *Christmas Carol* productions, readings, and film showings.

The only other Christmas production that comes close to matching the ubiquity of Dickens's *Carol*, is Tchaikovsky's ballet, *The Nutcracker*, based on E. T. A. Hoffmann's tale 'Nutcracker and Mouse King' (1816) and Alexander Dumas' adaptation of it, 'The

Tale of the Nutcracker' (1845). Although the story is far better known as a ballet than as a work of prose, it still must be counted as one of the most influential works of Christmas fiction, given the popularity of Tchaikovsky's version (and later adaptations of it). While the fairy tale seems on the surface to be far removed from the religious origins of Christmas, its narrative of a young girl's transformative love (and faith in love), which brings life even to the lifeless, resonates with themes at the core of the Nativity story.

CHRISTMAS ELSEWHERE IN THE NINETEENTH CENTURY

As already mentioned, many authors jumped on the holiday fiction bandwagon in the nineteenth century, and it's impossible to survey them all. Hans Christian Andersen is certainly one of the most memorable and influential of the group. A contemporary and sometime friend of Charles Dickens, Andersen put his distinct stamp on the world of Christmas fiction with the stories 'The Little Match Girl' and 'The Fir Tree'. Both employ the kind of pathos that gives *A Christmas Carol* much of its power, yet neither has the humour or lavish detail of Dickens's masterpiece. In both stories, Christmas features as a key setting, if not the main theme, and Andersen uses the holiday and all the expectations that come with it to create the pathos and painful ironies that make the tales so memorable.

'The Little Match Girl' is the most powerful of the two, and possibly of all Andersen's fiction. It was first published in December 1845 in *Dansk Folkekalender for 1846*, and then republished in 1848, 1849, and 1863. Its popularity and impact are widespread: there are numerous live-action and animated film adaptations, video games, and anime and manga adaptations, musical interpretations, television shows, and poems and novels based on the story. It is, without a doubt, a heart-breaking tale, and certainly it out-Dickens Dickens in its pathos. While the story actually takes place on New Year's Eve not Christmas Eve as is suggested in numerous adaptations, the images throughout are redolent of the Christmas season, with a glowing Christmas tree, a feast with a roast goose, a star that signals an existential event, and the appearance of an angel (in the form of the little match girl's grandmother). The story is very short: on a bitterly cold New Year's Eve, the little match girl has lost her slippers and is freezing, but terrified to return home to her angry father who might beat her because she's failed to sell matches. So she huddles down in a corner between two buildings and lights her remaining matches to stay warm. With each light, she sees a vision—of a glowing Christmas tree, of a feast, and of her grandmother. The grandmother takes the little match girl and flies with her into heaven, and the next morning the girl is discovered frozen to death, but with a smile on her face, with no one knowing about the beautiful visions she had as she died. Andersen ends the tale by saying the girl and her grandmother are now with God, where there is no cold, no hunger, and no fear (Andersen 1980b: 159). While Andersen attempts to shine a positive light on the girl's death with this religious reference, several adaptors have found the ending too grim and have revised the tale so that the girl lives. Andersen capitalizes on the contrast between dreams and expectations of Christmas-time and the stark reality for someone in dire poverty, something Dickens does as well in *A Christmas* Carol, but with a happier outcome.

Andersen draws on a similar contrast in 'The Fir Tree', first published in 1844, but this time from the point of view of a tree who never appreciates the blessings of his current situation but always wishes for something better. When he is out in the woods with larger trees, he wishes to be bigger. When he grows, he wishes he could be cut down to serve as a mast or a Christmas tree, and he never appreciates the bushes and flowers around him until he is finally cut to serve as a Christmas decoration. When he is set up in a beautifully appointed drawing-room, all he can think about is the splendour of the evening to come. But when evening arrives, and he is finally lit up with candles, he trembles so much from excitement he sets himself on fire. When the fire is quickly put out he is uneasy and 'bewildered by all the splendor' (Andersen 1980a: 99). At the end of the evening he promises himself that he won't tremble when they light candles on him the next day—that he will enjoy the splendour to the fullest. But there is no next day—he is carted off to the loft until the spring when he is brought out to be chopped into pieces. Andersen makes the moral of the story quite clear: in the words of the fir tree, 'If I had only enjoyed myself while I could? It's over, it's all over!' (103).

Like Dickens, Andersen uses the setting of Christmas to highlight the pathos of the story, but the holiday itself is not the main topic or theme. Andersen admired Dickens greatly and dedicated his *Christmas Greetings to My English Friends* to him (Cronin 2002: 4). The admiration was mutual, at least at first, although Dickens seems to have influenced Andersen more than Andersen, Dickens. When Andersen followed up on their initial meeting by staying five weeks at Dickens's Gad's Hill Place in 1857, he wore out the patience of the entire household. Dickens's daughters Mamey and Katey called him a 'boney bore' (Johnson 1952: 874), and Dickens himself put up a sign in the room where Andersen had stayed, reading, 'Hans Christian Andersen slept in this room for five weeks which seemed to the family ages' (875).

Louisa May Alcott was also influenced considerably by Dickens. While her much-loved *Little Women* (1868) is not primarily concerned with Christmas, the holiday plays a pivotal structural and thematic role in the novel, serving as a rich and warm backdrop to some of the most memorable scenes. The first sentence of the novel deals with Christmas; indeed, 'Christmas' is the novel's first word and it gets repeated twice in the first line: ' "Christmas won't be Christmas without any presents," grumbled Jo, lying on the rug' (Alcott 2004: 11). The opening chapter introduces and distinguishes the four March sisters—Jo, Meg, Amy, and Beth—by showing their varying reactions to their mother's decision not to have presents on Christmas because of the suffering of soldiers in the Civil War. As Meg puts it, 'she thinks we ought not to spend money for pleasure, when our men are suffering so in the army' (11). Alcott effectively uses the holiday and its tradition of present-giving to establish Jo's love of books, Amy's love of art, Beth's love of music, Meg's comparative maturity, and their united devotion to their mother (Marmee) and father. While the girls' grumbling about not getting presents opens the chapter, it ends with Marmee reading a letter from the girls' father in which he reminds them to be loving and dutiful and to 'conquer themselves' so that when he returns he will be 'prouder than ever of my little women' (17). The letter brings them all to tears and to a renewed sense of selflessness, which they'd already begun to show by taking what little money they had and buying small Christmas presents for their mother. In chapter 2, entitled 'A Merry Christmas', their selflessness is strengthened on Christmas morning when they each receive a specially bound copy of the New Testament, 'that beautiful old story of the best life ever lived', as Alcott writes (19). They put their resolution into action when they take their own holiday breakfast to a neighbouring German woman with six hungry children and no food or fuel. The scene not only establishes the March family's selfless nature, it introduces the connection with the German family that will lead to Beth's illness and eventual death as she will later contract scarlet fever from the family's baby. The women's charitable actions leave them merrier than anyone in town on Christmas morning, much like Scrooge creating his happiest moments on Christmas morning by numerous acts of generosity. In the evening the 'little women' participate in raucous and imaginative theatricals in their living room, which culminate in slap-stick episodes, including a stage-tower toppling and the cot bed which seats the audience closing up suddenly, which 'extinguishe[s] the enthusiastic audience' (25). The mix of comedy and pathos in the first two chapters and throughout the novel mirrors the variations in tone that Dickens used in his novels in order to keep readers emotionally engaged. Alcott was clearly influenced by Dickens, not only in her writing style, but also in names and other references throughout *Little Women*: the sisters have formed their own 'Pickwick Club', named after Dickens's first novel, and they produce a weekly newspaper, 'The Pickwick Portfolio'. Their pet bird is named 'Pip', after the protagonist of *Great Expectations*, and the moving death of Beth draws from Dickens's famous sentimental portrayals of children's deaths (e.g. Little Nell in *Old Curiosity Shop*, Paul Dombey in *Dombey and Son*, and Jo in *Bleak House*).

Christmas makes two other significant appearances in *Little Women*, and each marks a stage in Jo's maturation. In chapter 22, 'Pleasant Meadows', the penultimate chapter of the first volume, Christmas has come around again, and the selflessness demonstrated in the opening chapters has grown, by necessity. Marmee has left to nurse her seriously ill husband in Washington DC, Beth is recovering slowly from her long illness, and Jo and Laurie make a snowman for her to enjoy from the window, topped with a Christmas carol that the two have written just for her. Beth says that all she needs to make her happiness complete is for their father to be home, and that night, they all get their wish (173). The tearful homecoming of Mr March is one of the most memorable scenes in the book (and numerous film versions), and it hints at *A Christmas Carol*, with the contented and grateful family all together enjoying a holiday dinner of stuffed foul and plum pudding, and with the frail Beth reminding all of what they have to be grateful for, much as Tiny Tim does in *A Christmas Carol*. Jo's focus in this chapter is clearly more on Beth and her father than on herself, which demonstrates her maturity and growth in selflessness compared to her complaints about no presents in chapter 1.

The last Christmas described in the novel occurs when Jo is in New York; she writes home thanking everyone for 'The Christmas bundle' they have sent (270), and in her descriptions of her life in the boarding house, one can see her increased maturity, independence, and the beginnings of her love for Professor Bhaer. In the last paragraph of the chapter, she writes home to say that she'd had a very happy holiday and felt 'as if I was getting on a little in spite of my many failures, for I'm cheerful all the time now, work with a will, and take more interest in other people than I used to, which is satisfactory' (272). The novel ends, not with Christmas, but with a chapter entitled 'Harvest Time', in which the extended family, with spouses and new children, gather for apple picking and to express gratitude for all their blessings; even though the setting is not Christmas, the scene is reminiscent of the Cratchit family counting their blessings at their Christmas dinner in *A Christmas Carol*.

Alcott turns to Christmastime again in *Jo's Boys, And How They Turned Out*, the last book of the Little Women trilogy, which follows the stories of Jo's sons and some of the other boys from the school she and Professor Bhaer run at Plumfield. Two key chapters in this novel use the holiday season as a poignant backdrop to depressing situations: the chapter 'Dan's Christmas' describes the experience of one Plumfield orphan as he spends Christmas in jail for involuntary manslaughter; the other, 'Nat's New Year' chronicles another Plumfield orphan as he comes to terms with his profligate behaviour as a music student in Germany. In both cases, the dolefulness of the men's situations is heightened by the contrast with the festivities and expectations of the Christmas season, and their warm memories of Plumfield.

Alcott turned to Christmas in shorter works of fiction, as well, some of which anticipate *Little Women*, such as 'Tilly's Christmas', first published in the children's magazine *Merry's Museum* (1868). As the editors of the Norton critical edition of *Little Women* point out, 'Tilly's Christmas' is a clear 'precursor to the opening Christmas scenes in *Little Women*' (Alcott 2004: 537) as it revolves around children contemplating Christmas presents, with 'Tilly' being the poorest and expecting none. But she gets a present in the form of a wounded bird that she takes home and nurses, and her eagerness to help the bird—to love her neighbour as herself, as she tells her friends—leads to many blessings both tangible and intangible on Christmas Day. Another story from *Merry's Magazine* also served as a precursor to *Little Women*: in 'Merry's Monthly Chat with His Friends', also published in 1868, Alcott tells the 'true story' of a family giving away their New Year's Day breakfast to a starving German family nearby, clearly the origins of the story of the March family helping the Hummels on Christmas Day (541).

Of course, one of the most famous nineteenth-century Christmas stories is actually a narrative poem: 'A Visit from St. Nicholas', also known as "Twas the Night Before Christmas', written by Clement Clarke Moore and first published in 1823 (although some argue that the author is actually Henry Beekman Livingston, Jr). Moore's depiction of jolly old Saint Nicholas, or Santa Claus, was influenced by the historical figure of St Nicholas as well as Washington Irving's references to St Nicholas in *The History of New York*, but Moore added details such as Santa driving a sleigh pulled by reindeer. These details as well as specifics about St Nicholas's appearance (rotund, rosy cheeked) continue to shape secular depictions of Christmas to this day. But since this work is actually a poem, it will be addressed elsewhere in this volume.

Turning a Strange Corner: Twentieth-Century Fictional Christmases

Many twentieth-century works of fiction that feature Christmas work both with and against the grain of the traditions established in the nineteenth century. They play on the nostalgia associated with remembrances of the holiday, and they often use the expectations about Christmas—of presents, cheerful gatherings, festive surroundings— to create a painful contrast with the realities of the present time of the story. As many twentieth-century authors strove to distinguish themselves from past literary traditions, so did many try to distinguish their Christmas depictions from those defined by Washington Irving, Charles Dickens, and others.

O. Henry's much-loved 'The Gift of the Magi' (1905) definitely has one foot in the nineteenth century in its portrait of a young couple each of whom sells the thing they value the most to buy the other a Christmas present. Their mutual sacrifice rings strongly of Dickens and nineteenth-century sentiment in general, particularly in the last lines when the narrator compares the couple to the original Magi, the Wise Men of the Nativity story, and proclaims of the husband and wife, 'Of all who give and receive gifts, such as they are wisest' (214). Yet the crux of the story pivots as much on irony as sentiment: the wife has sold her hair to buy her husband a watch chain, while the husband has sold his watch to buy his wife a hair comb. The terseness of the story (it's just a few pages long) adds to the impact of the ironic ending and helps to create a tone that is more modern than the works so far described in this chapter.

James Joyce harnesses the tension between the traditions of the past and the realities of the present in 'The Dead', the final story in *The Dubliners* (1914). The story takes place on a snowy evening at an annual holiday dance party at the home of the elderly Miss Morkan sisters. Joyce paints a rich, nostalgic portrait of family and friends enjoying a gathering that may not continue for much longer. 'The Dead' isn't about Christmas, but it takes place at Christmastime as Joyce emphasizes in the opening paragraphs, when Gabriel, the protagonist, offers a tip to the maid Lily, saying, 'It's Christmastime, isn't it?' When Lily resists, Gabriel encourages her by repeating the reference to the holiday, 'Christmas-time! Christmas-time!' (Joyce 2006: 155). As in

Little Women, the early repetition of the word makes it hard not to notice the holiday setting and underscores that Christmas plays a thematic role in the narrative. But the glow of nostalgia, and then Gabriel's warm feelings toward his wife at the end of the evening, are undercut by his wife's revelation that her thoughts that evening have been turning to a boy who died of love for her when she was a young woman. Gabriel's nostalgia turns to anger and alienation but then to compassion as he watches his wife sleep while the snow falls 'all over Ireland' (194). The final sentences are expansive and elegiac, and they evoke a sense of the universal experience of an old world passing. The lines are some of the most beautiful in English literature, and deserve being quoted in full:

> Yes, the newspapers were right: snow was general all over Ireland. It was falling on every part of the dark central plain, on the treeless hills, falling softly upon the Bog of Allen and, farther westward, softly falling into the dark mutinous Shannon waves. It was falling, too, upon every part of the lonely churchyard on the hill where Michael Furey lay buried. It lay thickly drifted on the crooked crosses and headstones, on the spears of the little gate, on the barren thorns. His soul swooned slowly as he heard the snow falling faintly through the universe and faintly falling, like the descent of their last end, upon all the living and the dead. (194)

The final paragraph reads more like a prose poem than fiction. The image of the snow, often interpreted as representing the mortality that unites 'the living and the dead' or as an image of communion brought about by the passing of time, transcends any one reading in these evocative lines. Yet it seems clear that Gabriel experiences an epiphany of some sort at the end of 'The Dead'—one that forces him to see beyond his narrow self-interest and self-involvement—a revelation befitting the Christmas season, particularly as the last day of the traditional twelve days of Christmas *is* Epiphany (January 6).

William Burrough's 'The Junky's Christmas' is without a doubt one of the most non-traditional Christmas stories in the history of the genre. Originally published in 1990 in *Interzone*, a collection of short stories and other short writings, the story follows heroin addict Danny the Car Wiper as he tries to score a fix on Christmas Day. When he finally persuades a doctor to give him a small amount of morphine, he returns to his rented room and prepares to inject it but is disturbed by a man moaning in the next room. He checks on the man who is suffering from kidney stones and can't find a doctor to treat him because they think he's an addict faking illness to get drugs. Danny injects the man with the dope he'd struggled to find for himself, and when he returns to his room he suddenly and miraculously feels as if he has injected himself too. 'The immaculate fix' he calls it as he falls into a peaceful stupor. The story was recorded by Burroughs and Kurt Cobain in 1993, with Burroughs narrating and Cobain playing dissonant versions of 'Silent Night' and the tune to the United States national anthem in the background; they entitled the collaboration 'The "Priest" They Called Him'. It was also adapted as a clay-mation animated video in 1993, produced by Francis Ford Coppola. While the protagonist is a junkie, and the bulk of the short story is devoted to the details of Danny trying to get a fix on Christmas, the theme of giving, particularly giving the thing that one most values, and the peace that Danny experiences because of his selflessness, clearly resonate with themes typical of more traditional works of Christmas fiction, and indeed key elements of the original Christmas story.

Christmas has come to play such a dominant role in Western culture that it even emerges as a strong presence in fantasy worlds, such as C. S. Lewis's Narnia and the world of wizards in J. K. Rowling's *Harry Potter* series. As in non-fantasy fiction, Christmas provides a rich and evocative emotional and sensory setting that heightens the impact of particular scenes and plotlines. In the first book of Lewis's Narnia series, *The Lion, the Witch, and the Wardrobe* (1950), the plot revolves around the Pevensie children trying to free Narnia from the grips of the White Witch who has cursed the land with a permanent winter in which there is no Christmas. Father Christmas makes an appearance at a crucial point in the narrative and gives Christmas presents to the children which become their signature tools in fighting the Witch: a sword for Peter, a horn for Susan, and a vial of potent medicine for Lucy. While Father Christmas is a secular figure, Lewis uses the war against the Witch in Narnia as an allegory of the war between good and evil in Christianity, with the lion Aslan serving as a Christ figure in his willing sacrifice of himself to save others. So Father Christmas's presents have religious significance since they play such key roles in the battle for good.

Unlike C. S. Lewis, J. R. R. Tolkien, a friend of Lewis's, did not import Christmas into the fantasy world of Middle Earth in *The Hobbit* or *The Lord of the Rings* trilogy, at least not overtly. And yet the Christian holiday—and its counterpart of Easter—play an understated role in the fantasy trilogy, if one examines the chronology of events that Tolkien appends to the final book in the series, *The Return of the King*. In Appendix B of that book, Tolkien provides a timeline of the chief events of the narrative, indicating that the Fellowship sets off on its quest to destroy the ring of power on 25 December (Tolkien 1994: 1066). The ring then gets destroyed in the Cracks of Doom on 25 March (1069). Tolkien, who plotted out every aspect of his tale meticulously, including the thousands of years of back story that give *Lord of the Rings* such a rich history and three-dimensionality, surely must have made a conscious choice to begin the quest on Christmas Day and end it shortly after the vernal equinox which is the date Easter is based on. Tolkien's story of a hobbit from humble origins who saves a world by ultimately sacrificing himself—a pattern that mirrors the story of Jesus's life—is projected against the two main celebrations of the Christian calendar.

A lesser known work of fantasy, John Masefield's *The Box of Delights* (1935), places Christmas right at the forefront of a tale of a schoolboy returning home for the holidays and getting involved in adventures that include time travel, crooks, and folkloric heroes as part of the action. The approach of Christmas Day adds urgency to the action, and Christmas decorations, carol-singing, and other festivities add atmosphere, but the story has never transcended its intended audience of children, as has Lewis's Narnia series or Tolkien's tales of Middle Earth. Similarly, L. Frank Baum's *The Life and Adventures of Santa Claus* (1902), has not become standard reading fare, although elements of the tales have influenced numerous animated film adaptations.

J. K. Rowling's *Harry Potter* series clearly *has* transcended its original young adult audience to become not just a series of novels, but a cultural phenomenon, with wildly popular films based on each book (two films for the last), and Harry Potter theme parks in Orlando and Los Angeles, as well as a Harry Potter tour at Warner Brothers Studio in London. Each book in the series of seven includes memorable Christmas scenes that are showcased in the film versions as well. In general, the religious aspects of Christmas take a back seat to a secular focus on decorations, mountains of holiday foods, and festivities, with rich descriptions of the great hall at Hogwarts School festooned with holly and mistletoe, multiple Christmas trees, and magical snow (Rowling 1998: 196, 200–3). But the descriptions serve for more than just atmosphere; the gifts Harry receives on his first Christmas at Hogwarts play important roles in plot and character development throughout the series. One of his gifts is the invisibility cloak, which aids him in his struggle against the evil Lord Voldemort right up until their last confrontation (Rowling 1998: 201). He also receives his first handknit sweater from his friend Ron Weasley's mother, a gift that shows she now considers him part of their family (200). The Weasleys become more of a family to Harry than his own aunt and uncle who raised him ever were, and his relationship with them provides some of the most emotionally satisfying scenes in the series.

The Christmas scenes in the first four Harry Potter books all take place at Hogwarts, but in the fifth book, *Harry Potter and the Order of the Phoenix*, the scene shifts to the darker and more cramped confines of 12 Grimmauld Place, the headquarters of the wizards allied in the war against Voldemort. While there are still decorations, a feast, and friends and family gathered to celebrate, the mood is far more sombre, which is typical of the last books of the series as the war with Voldemort and his followers intensifies. In the last book, *Harry Potter and the Deathly Hallows*, the holiday season is anything but festive: Harry and Hermione visit the grave site of Harry's parents on Christmas Eve, and Hermione makes a wreath of Christmas roses to adorn their tombstone (328–9). This is the only Christmas scene in the series with overt religious references, as Harry and Hermione overhear carols being sung in the small church next to the graveyard. It is fitting that Rowling refers to a religious celebration of Christmas at this point because at the end of the book (and series) Harry chooses a Christ-like sacrifice of himself in order to rid the world of Voldemort.

While secular references to Christmas predominate in Christmas fiction, religious references still persist even in tales of junkies and hobbits and wizards. The story of Jesus of Nazareth has been called the greatest story ever told, and in the persistence of its themes in such wildly diverse narratives, there is evidence to support that claim.

References and Further Reading

Alcott, Louisa May (2004). *Little Women; Or, May, Jo, Beth and Amy*. Ed. Anne K. Phillips and George Eiselein. New York: Norton.
Andersen, Hans Christian (1980a). 'The Fir Tree', in *Tales and Stories by Hans Christian Andersen*, transl. with an Introduction by Patricia L. Conroy and Sven H. Rossel. Seattle: University of Washington Press: 95–104.

Andersen, Hans Christian (1980b). 'The Little Match Girl' in *Tales and Stories by Hans Christian Andersen*. Trans. and Introduction by Patricia L. Conroy and Sven H. Rossel. Seattle: University of Washington Press. 157–9.

Baum, L. Frank (2015) *The Life and Adventures of Santa Claus*. New York: Penguin.

Burroughs, William (1990) 'The Junky's Christmas', in *Interzone*. New York: Penguin.

Cronin, Mark (2002). '"Curses on all Fairies": The Christmas Books of Dickens and Thackeray'. *Presented at the Dickens Symposium*. Oxford, England.

Dickens, Charles (2003). *A Christmas Carol and Other Christmas Writings*. Intro. and notes by Michael Slater. New York: Penguin.

Dumas, Alexandre (2007). *The Tale of the Nutcracker*, trans. Joachim Neugroschel. Intro. by Jack Zipes. New York: Penguin.

Hancher, Michael (2014). 'Dickens's First Effusion', *Dickens Quarterly*, 31, no. 4: 285–97.

Henry, O. (2017). 'The Gift of the Magi', in *A Christmas Treasury*. New York: Barnes and Noble: 207–14.

Hoffmann, E. T. A. (2007). *Nutcracker and Mouse King*, trans. Joachim Neugroschel. Intro. by Jack Zipes. New York: Penguin.

Irving, Washington (1809). *History of New York*. New York: Inskeep & Bradford.

Irving, Washington (1963). *The Sketch Book of Geoffrey Crayon*. Ed. and intro. Van Wyck Brooks. London: Dent.

Johnson, Edgar (1952). *Charles Dickens: His Tragedy and Triumph*. New York: Simon and Schuster.

Joyce, James (2006). *The Dubliners*. Ed. Margot Norris. Text ed. Hans Walter Gabler and Walter Hettche. New York: Norton.

Larsen, Timothy (2018). *George MacDonald in the Age of Miracles: Incarnation, Doubt, and Reenchantment*. Downers Grove, Illinois: IVP Academic.

Lewis, C. S. (2000). *The Lion, The Witch and the Wardrobe*. New York: HarperCollins.

Masefield, John (2014). *The Box of Delights*. London: Egmont.

Moore, Clement Clark (1823). "Twas the Night Before Christmas'. Available at https://www.teachervision.com/twas-night-christmas-full-text/ (accessed 23 March 2020).

Parker, David (2002). 'Dickens and the American Christmas', *Dickens Quarterly*, 19, no. 3: 160–9.

Rowling, J. K. (1998). *Harry Potter and the Sorcerer's Stone*. New York: Scholastic Inc.

Rowling, J. K. (2004). *Harry Potter and the Order of the Phoenix*. New York: Scholastic Inc.

Rowling, J. K. (2007). *Harry Potter and the Deathly Hallows*. New York: Scholastic Inc.

Schlicke, Paul (ed.) (1999). *Oxford Reader's Companion to Dickens*. New York: Oxford University Press.

Standiford, Les (2008). *The Man Who Invented Christmas: How Charles Dickens's A Christmas Carol Rescued His Career and Revived Our Holiday Spirit*. New York: Crown.

Tolkien, J. R. R. (1994). *The Return of the King*. Vol. III of *The Lord of the Rings*. Boston: Houghton Mifflin.

Trollope, Anthony (2014). *Christmas at Thompson Hall & Other Christmas Stories*. New York: Penguin.

CHAPTER 32

FILM AND TELEVISION

MARK CONNELLY

During the course of the twentieth century Christmas was adopted by cinema and television. The two visual media allowed the key nineteenth-century tenets of Christmas, particularly those encapsulated in Dickens's *A Christmas Carol* (1843), to become a global language, and have ensured that the festival has penetrated non-Christian cultures. The idea of Christmas most commonly explored in cinema and television, whether as celebration or critique, is largely based upon the vision that evolved in the nineteenth century. The Victorians took up Christmas and all its trappings and used them to celebrate home, family, and charity. These values were picked up by cinema, and once Hollywood adopted Christmas, an American-centric concept of the season quickly grew in strength and pervasiveness. Although individual nations maintained their own native interpretations of Christmas in film and television, the American version became ubiquitous and a touchstone for the perceived values of the season globally. So potent did the visual and aural language of the film and television Christmas become that the festival quickly evolved into a useful *mise-en-scène* device for screenplay writers and directors: short glimpses of Christmas decorations and fragments of carols or Christmas tunes provide the ability to set an emotional atmosphere and register for an entire production within moments regardless of the wider theme or focus of the piece.

Christmas was such an all-pervasive part of European (but particularly English) and North American life by the late nineteenth century it is hardly surprising that cinema took to it from the start. Silent versions of *A Christmas Carol* proliferated: three were produced by 1914, and a further two in the 1920s. Alongside these, all manner of Christmas films were produced, such as *The Old Folks Christmas* (1913), *Christmas Day in the Workhouse* (1914), and *One Winter's Night* (1914). There was a relative paucity of direct Christmas films in the 1920s and 1930s, which possibly reflected the way the new medium of radio dominated the festival and encouraged its domestic consumption. However, two sound versions of *A Christmas Carol* were produced: a British version in 1935, followed by a Hollywood production in 1938. In the British film, the national preoccupation with the search for consensus in a period of economic slump and the rising threat of fascist aggression is apparent in the focus on rich and poor celebrating the same festival. For MGM, the story reflected American values as its version of *A Christmas Carol* turned Fred and Bob Cratchit into friends, thus ignoring the class difference between them in the original tale. By this stage, the Christmas scene was also beginning to emerge, and the costume drama found such scenes particularly useful. David Selznick's 1936 *A Tale of Two Cities* had a Christmas scene inserted. Christmas provided the crucial underlining of the family values of the Manettes and Darnays, as recognized by Sydney Carton, who then decides to sacrifice himself for love and righteousness. At the same time, it also revealed the depth of the association between Dickens and Christmas: an audience almost expected any Dickens adaptation to have a Christmas scene in it somewhere.

During the Second World War the format of the modern Christmas film began to emerge, forged from the peculiar circumstances created by a global conflict. First, the dislocation of millions of people heightened a sense of family associations; this intertwined with an intense desire for entertainment which saw cinema attendance increase significantly. Thus, for Hollywood, the Christmas season itself became even more important economically, being a time of year in which people went to the cinema, and as a festival it could be harnessed to support and reflect the values the allies were fighting for. During the course of the conflict, Hollywood produced *Remember the Night* and *The Man Who Came to Dinner* (both 1940), *Holiday Inn* (1942), *Meet Me in St. Louis*, *I'll Be Seeing You* (both 1944), and *Christmas in Connecticut* (1945). In all materialism, ego, and selfishness are exposed and found hollow, and are replaced with genuine relationships, unity, and love. Lonely, homesick GIs and female factory workers were presented with a dream of home and values they could recognize and live by.

By contrast, British cinema used Christmas to face up to the immediate realities of war. The Crown Film Unit produced *Christmas Under Fire* in the winter of 1940 to show the world, but particularly Americans, how the British were desperately holding on to their Christian traditions in the face of the darkness of Nazism. In 1942, *In Which We Serve*, a naval drama produced and directed by Noël Coward and David Lean, compared and contrasted the Christmases of the upper-class officers, the middle-class petty officers, and the working-class sailors. All were linked by their devotion to the navy and its traditions, their monarch, and their wholehearted support of decency and freedom.

For a short period in the immediate aftermath of war, when it appeared that the dreams of many Americans for a stable and prosperous future might not appear, Hollywood changed tack. This fear can be detected in the most important Christmas film of the late 1940s, *It's a Wonderful Life* (1946). Frank Capra's classic movie is sometimes considered overly sentimental, and yet this ignores its almost *film noir* darkness. The world inhabited by the hero, George Bailey (played by James Stewart), is one of doubts, malaise, and unfulfilled dreams and hopes. Spiritually lost, Bailey prepares for suicide, but is saved by an angel, Clarence (played by Henry Travers), who gives Bailey a different way of assessing and understanding his life by revealing an alternative world in which he had never lived. Redeemed and restored, Bailey returns to his loving family, thankful for his immense blessings. Despite the wonder of the ending, the sheer darkness of Bailey's journey reveals *It's a Wonderful Life* to be a very sophisticated movie, and possibly a coded warning that America had not yet achieved homes—and Christmases—fit for heroes, but had at least recognized that fact. *It's a Wonderful Life* also reintroduced the supernatural element to Christmas films. The wartime Christmases of British and American movies had avoided this angle, preferring the vision of reality and a homely dream respectively. The intervention of Clarence, the angel, in *It's a Wonderful Life* was soon imitated in such films as *The Bishop's Wife* (1947), in which Cary Grant descends to Earth in order to bring human warmth and Christmas cheer to a rather dour bishop (played by David Niven), and *Tenth Avenue Angel* (1948).

In 1951, perhaps the finest adaptation of *A Christmas Carol* was produced. Retitled *Scrooge*, the film was driven by Alastair Sims's bravura performance in the title role, which many regard as definitive. However, this did not deter others from interpreting the story. In 1970 a big budget Technicolor-Panavision version of Leslie Bricusse's musical was released; fourteen years later an equally lavish version (originally made for US television) was produced. Clive Donner's *A Christmas Carol* starred George C. Scott, who played Scrooge as a rather sardonic and ironic character, but one who retained his business savvy, which was perhaps an ideal way to criticize the materialistic values of the eighties. Even harsher, but far more anarchic, was Richard Donner's *Scrooged* (1988) starring Bill Murray. Then, in 1992 came *The Muppet Christmas Carol*; by turns irreverent, and yet keen to ensure period detail, Jim Henson's version saw Michael Caine produce a deliberate caricature of the filmic image of Scrooge.

A remarkably late arrival to the cinematic Christmas was the figure of Father Christmas/Santa Claus himself. Significantly, he emerged as an important screen figure once America truly became an acquisitive and mass-consumerist nation, making his real screen debut in *Miracle on 34th Street* (1947). A feature of most Santa Claus films is that he is both the symbol, and critique of, materialist values. He often performs this role against the backdrop of broken families whom he helps heal and find solutions to their problems, as seen in *Miracle on 34th Street* and five decades later in *The Santa Clause* (1994), which was so successful it spawned two sequels. In *Miracle on 34th Street* he is the magical figure who creates what all children want deep down: a solid family life with happy parents. At the start of the film young Susan (played by Natalie Wood) is seen to be lonely and somewhat ill at ease despite having a loving mother, Doris (played by Maureen O'Hara). It is not made clear what happened to Susan's father, but there are subtle hints at divorce. By shrouding the whole thing in ambiguity the film reflects the sensitivities and morals of the time, and also reveals its status as a film made in the immediate aftermath of the Second World War. Doris's marriage may have been strained to breaking point by the war, perhaps due to long separation from her husband. At the same time, the ambiguity also makes her something akin to a war widow. When charming, handsome Fred Gailey (played by John Payne) comes into their lives, Susan perks up, especially when she sees the flickerings of a deep relationship between him and her mother. Through the agency of Kris Kringle (played by Edmund Gwenn), a seemingly eccentric old man playing Santa Claus in Macy's department store, Susan's mother and Fred are brought more closely together. And, the vehicle that brings them all together is the gradually emerging fact that Kris really is Santa Claus. As all accept that dreams and fairy tales can come true, Susan, her mother, and Fred come together and the three can start a true family life engineered by their faith in Santa Claus. The film also manages some interesting sleights of hand regarding the true nature of Christmas. On the one hand, the greatest gift that can be given is love. But, on the other, there is a free advert for Macy's (and indeed virtually every other Manhattan department store, as Bloomingdale's, Gimbel's, Hearn's, and Stern's all get a positive mention), although it seems all great captains of retail are, deep down, Roosevelt-like figures who believe in one-nation Americanism.

If the original *Miracle on 34th Street* reflected its time, then the Tim Allen vehicle, *The Santa Clause* (1994), very firmly highlighted issues affecting late twentieth-century America. Once again there is a broken family, but this time it is not as a result of war, it is a divorce, seemingly marked by acrimony and leaving a legacy of bitterness. Charlie's mum has found a new partner, Neil, a psychoanalyst, and as Charlie finds, he can never treat any issue in simple, old-fashioned family terms. Instead, everything has to be analysed rationally in order to get to the root of the problem. Thus, no problem, or indeed opportunity, can ever be simply explained or easily solved. Rather, everything has to be dissected for hidden meanings, agendas, and issues. Liberation comes for Charlie when his father, Scott (played by Tim Allen), accidentally kills Santa Claus on Christmas Eve! At first Scott simply refuses to believe what is happening but, with the innocence of youth, Charlie does so immediately. He eventually persuades his father to stand-in for Santa Claus. Stripping him of his iconic livery, Scott dons Santa's clothes, gets into the sleigh with his son, and then they set off together for a stunning adventure. Father and son are united more strongly than ever, and the bond isn't broken by finding that in taking on the role, Scott has accepted the Santa Clause of the title, and is now the full-time incumbent. Charlie finds great new pride in his dad, and knows he shares him with every child in the world.

As Western, and more particularly American, consumer society has matured, its Christmas-time cinematic rendering has added elements of violence and built on the long-standing association of the season with the supernatural. Films such as *You Better Watch Out* (1980) show how middle-class Christmases can descend into hellish adventures, while *Silent Night, Deadly Night* (1984) turns Santa Claus into a Herod-like character who is more intent on killing children than giving them presents. At the same time, irony emerged in films such as *Lethal Weapon* (1987) which deliberately mixed Christmas and violence in a tongue-in-cheek approach to the action movie genre. Setting Christmas in a Los Angeles December also neatly inverted all the traditional expectations of the seasons. Similar ironies can be detected in *Die Hard* (1987). Bruce Willis plays John McClane that most clichéd of cinematic (and television) characters, the hard-bitten cop, who deep down is desperately hoping something of his old idealism might be resurrected. Visiting Los Angeles in an attempt to revive his marriage and family life with his daughter, he becomes involved in a high-energy, high-thrills adventure in order to save her and her work colleagues from a group of hijackers who invade their Christmas Eve party. Having achieved good box-office business, a sequel was produced, also set at Christmas, with an equally improbable plot.

Home Alone (1990) also made Christmas an extremely violent time. However, in this offering, young Kevin (the role that turned Macaulay Caulkin into a star) is accidentally left behind by his family when they set off for their Christmas holidays. Stuck in his wealthy Chicago suburb, a setting beloved of the director, John Hughes, Kevin realizes his house has become the target of a pair of burglars. Resorting to his well of boy's-own cunning and inventiveness, he sees off every break-in attempt with a range of tricks and sabotage operations. The degree of slapstick violence is very high, sharing much with Laurel and Hardy and cartoons, and in its broad lampooning of stereotypes has much of the British pantomime tradition about it. Of course, though his actions would be regarded as extremely reprehensible in different circumstances, here they became laudable. In its own way *Home Alone* therefore represents the lingering pagan Saturnalia aspect of Christmas. It is a period in which usual social norms and codes can be transgressed without fear of sanction.

A similar theme of seemingly unruly children being given the opportunity to express themselves fully can be detected in *Nativity* (2009). This small-budget British film was a great box-office success on its first release, and has become a fixture of Christmas BBC television scheduling. The film tells the story of a failing primary school suddenly energized when it is rumoured that a major Hollywood director is coming to see their Nativity play. Children who were once thought misfits or outcasts are galvanized to such an extent that they don't mind that the promise of Hollywood proves to be a rumour. Instead, they throw themselves into producing the best Nativity play ever, redeeming their reputations and that of the school in the process. When a real Hollywood producer does arrive just in time to see the climax of the play, it is merely the icing on the Christmas cake. The real success had already been achieved: the children had shown the world they had great potential and were well-meaning members of the community. Two spin-off versions have been produced to date, *Nativity 2: Danger in the Manger* (2012) and *Nativity 3: Dude, Where's My Donkey?* (2014), and for Christmas 2018 there was *Nativity Rocks*. Despite mixed reviews for the sequels, the films have tended to do well as families find them useful ways of entertaining children during the Christmas holidays.

Given the huge interest cinema has taken in Christmas, the actual Nativity itself has not been of great interest to filmmakers. The birth of Christ has been seen on the screen, but it is usually incidental to other tales. There is a traditional Nativity scene in *Ben Hur* (1959) made all the more powerful by Miklós Rósza's stunning score, and a more sober one in Pasolini's *Il Vangelo Secondo Matteo—The Gospel According to St Matthew* (1964) in which there is a particularly brutal Slaughter of the Innocents. But the stark truth is that Christmas films, like much of the modern Christmas itself, are often not directly interested in the birth of Christ.

The Idea of Christmas and Cinema

As noted earlier, Christmas has also developed into emotional shorthand for many film-makers, which has made a Christmas scene, or a lingering Christmas backdrop, a perennial cinematic technique. For example, Barry Levinson's *Diner* (1982) starts on Christmas night 1959 and concerns events running up to New Year. The trappings of Christmas are everywhere: decorations and songs heard in the diner, a Nativity display outside a church, and chilly mid-winter weather. However, Christmas itself is not at the heart of the film as it explores the life of a mixture of characters, some explicitly Jewish. However, it is a film about relationships, problems between older and younger family members, and about establishing a place within society, and thus Christmas and its associations create an appropriate emotional milieu.

Norman Jewison's comedy-romance *Moonstruck* (1987) also used Christmas as a vital backdrop to its plot. Loretta's (Cher) and Ronny's (Nicolas Cage) unlikely courtship is played out against frosty New York and Brooklyn nights and shop windows framed by twinkling Christmas lights. A tipping point in their relationship is a night at the Metropolitan Opera where they meet to see a performance of *La Bohème*, the plot of which commences with a chance Christmas Eve meeting. A similar use of New York Christmases can be seen in Rob Reiner's *When Harry Met Sally* (1989). The great bulk of the action takes place during a succession of New York autumns and winters, with the run-up to Christmas being particularly important. At one point Harry (Billy Crystal) states: 'Boy, the holidays are tough. Every year I just try to get from the day before Thanksgiving to the day after New Year's.' The film is unashamedly emotional and nostalgic with music being particularly important to the creation of mood through a succession of fifties brat pack and Bing Crosby hits. This combines with the cinematography, which alternates between russet-sepia tints and cold whiteness to keep the entire film in an autumn-into-winter mode. We therefore see Central Park covered in snow, accompanied by the strains of *Winter Wonderland*, and a huge Christmas tree is taken home to Bing Crosby singing *Have Yourself a Merry Little Christmas*. The film is sentimental, and so Christmas is vital to it. Both *Moonstruck* and *When Harry Met Sally* also reflect the American obsession with the fifties, a cultural phenomenon that was triggered by *American Graffiti* (1973) and reached new heights in the eighties. Christmas was, no doubt, more like Christmas in the fifties. The degree of nostalgia for those mythical days of the real Christmas was self-reflexively parodied by Bob Clark in *A Christmas Story* (1983). Set in the late forties, the film takes the viewpoint of two young brothers from a lower middle-class, Middle American family, and their Christmas rituals in a well-observed comedy mixing clever jokes with slapstick. Dreaming of the world of Christmas adverts, Ralphie and his brother are instead trapped in all the everyday problems and stresses of a family trying to prepare for Christmas. The film very finely balances itself between sending up the clichés of Christmas as never, ever real, whilst being deeply nostalgic for a bygone age in which everything was genuinely better.

The Christmas backdrop and straight comedy was also used by John Landis in his *Trading Places* (1983). The film is a variant on the Prince and Pauper theme, but this time involving involuntary swapping of roles, and mistaken identities, a theme enhanced by constant musical references to *The Marriage of Figaro*. The entire landscape of the film is dominated by Christmas, which in turn also ensured the juxtapositions of the poor man's Christmas with that of the rich, as also seen in *A Christmas Carol*. Woody Allen also used Christmas as an aid to comic effect in *Annie Hall* (1977). Allen's character, Alvy Singer, flies from New York to spend Christmas with his former writing partner, Rob (Tony Roberts). Rob drives Alvy to a Christmas party in Hollywood in his open top Rolls Royce. As they drive along Los Angeles boulevards in glorious sunshine they pass gardens decorated with large reindeer, and at the party there is a frost-effect Christmas tree. Allen uses the incongruities of the scene to expose the seemingly fake and empty world of Hollywood in which a veneer of reality disguises the truth. 'Real Christmas' is one of snow, frost, and cutting winds, which, ironically, is largely a cinematic construction.

Through Hollywood, Thanksgiving has also been presented to the wider world, and doubtless its appeal to producers lies in the fact that it can be depicted as a mini-Christmas in its own right, and thus makes it translatable to the rest of the world. As noted, *When Harry Met Sally* overtly creates a seamless, long mid-winter festival stretching from Thanksgiving to New Year (and now massively reinforced by the phenomenal success of the Black Friday Christmas shopping spree immediately following Thanksgiving). John Hughes's *Planes, Trains and Automobiles* (1987) embeds the road movie genre, heavy hints at Laurel and Hardy, as well as flashes of *The Odd Couple* (1968), into a festive comedy in which two completely different personalities, Neil Paige (Steve Martin), a highly-strung, somewhat impatient, but successful advertising executive, and Del Griffith (John Candy), a good-natured, exuberant shower-curtain-ring salesman, are forced to collaborate in order to get home for Thanksgiving. All of the elements of the festive film are present in the form of a desire to be home with an adored wife and family for the big day, misunderstandings as to what the true festive spirit actually is and represents, and how the trappings of the season can only obtain true meaning if they are felt in the heart. For a non-North American audience, the whole thing is almost indistinguishable from Christmas: snow is piled up through the Midwest states, a vast turkey is basted, the extended family gathers, and a special event is put on at the local school. And the whole thing ends on a typical Christmas film resolution. Paige recognizes the essential humanity of Griffiths and invites him to share Thanksgiving in his house. Griffiths, who has lost his wife, is overwhelmed to be accepted by Paige and his extended family.

Embedding the cinematic image of Christmas into audiences was given a massive boost by television. Television broadcasters were very quick to recognize the potential of the season, and as most had their roots in radio broadcasting they transferred that knowledge to the new medium. Christmas specials of soap operas and popular comedies were soon being made, as were specifically commissioned dramas, as well as versions of traditional seasonal entertainments such as circuses. Much of this scheduling was anchored around big budget films, many of which were originally released in the Christmas season to maximize box office potential. Christmas Day 'blockbuster' movies were soon a staple of television. Often these films had absolutely nothing to do with Christmas, but were chosen for their spectacle, action, or family appeal such as *The Sound of Music* (1965), *Mary Poppins* (1964), *Raiders of the Lost Ark* (1981), or a James Bond title. Around these centrepieces would be the Christmas specials and the films in which Christmas is a major theme.

In the United States, the *Andy Williams Christmas Show* became a fixture of NBC's Christmas Eve between 1962 and 1974. It was rivalled by ABC's *Bing Crosby Show*, which had commenced a year earlier. Crosby's final Christmas show was recorded shortly before his death in 1977, but was broadcast at the express wish of his widow. Interestingly, the programme revealed the depth of American sentimentality for the Dickensian English Christmas, as the plot revolved around Bing receiving a letter from his long-lost English relative, Sir Percival Bing, inviting him to his country home for the festivities. On arrival, Bing finds a house somewhere between an Agatha Christie mystery and *Upstairs, Downstairs*, both highly popular genres in the US television market. While browsing the library he encounters the ghost of Scrooge, and a Dickensian pageant of characters ensues. But, it is perhaps most famous now for creating arguably the strangest singing duo ever as Crosby joined forces with David Bowie to sing 'Peace on Earth/The Little Drummer Boy'. The incongruity was a deliberate ploy to appeal to a broad demographic, and with it ensure contented advertisers and sponsors.

The instrumentalizing of Christmas—and the feelings it inspires—for commercial purposes through television is encapsulated by the Hallmark Channel. Already a giant in the greetings' cards market, and therefore possessing an undisputed stake in the significance of Christmas, Hallmark turned to broadcasting in the 1990s. After taking various formats and names, in 2001 it adopted the Hallmark Channel label and continued as a producer of its own films, underpinned by lavish budgets. In 2009 it introduced its 'Countdown to Christmas', which marked the start of a major campaign to colonize Christmas television broadcasting. At the same time, the Channel has been a significant force in pushing the start date of the season back into autumn, as 'Countdown to Christmas' begins in the last weekend of October, and thus ensures a baton-exchange between Halloween and the winter festivals of Thanksgiving, Christmas, and New Year. And at the same time, Hallmark has also sought to push the season as a component of a non-denominational, universal desire to mark winter by the addition of the term 'Winterfest', and its associated programming, in 2016, which is dedicated to New Year celebrations.

By working to the commercial demand of creating a very broad time frame in which to celebrate Christmas, the next step was to drag it into a completely different season. In 2012 Hallmark Channel launched the high summer, 'Christmas in July'. Deliberately using the exact same title as Preston Sturges's 1940 comedy, Hallmark cleverly attached itself to Hollywood's golden era and the associations it forged with Christmas. 'Christmas in July' then serves as an opportunity to repeat films while also flagging up its forthcoming seasonal lines in cards, decorations, ornaments, and mementoes. The Hallmark Channel therefore represents the most determined attempt to promote Christmas as a dominant feature of the year, while at the same time using it as a platform for sales.

As might be expected, the channel's home-produced Christmas films follow very similar plot lines and approaches, which border on cliché as summed up in the titles. The top ten in terms of viewing figures includes *Christmas Under Wraps* (2014), *My Christmas Love* (2016), and *My Christmas Dream* (2016). The well-understood concept of the special trip home for Christmas, as reflected in Chris Rea's 1986 seasonal hit, *Driving Home for Christmas*, has also been implied in many Hallmark titles: *The Christmas Train* (2017), *A Christmas Detour* (2015), and *Journey Back to Christmas* (2016). Connected with the special journey home is the concept of reunions, especially if there has been estrangement. In *Switched for Christmas* (2017) twin sisters who are envious of each other's lives manage to change places leading both, of course, to find deeper understanding of their sibling and gratitude for what they actually have. Hints of the snowed in, with its resonances of *Holiday Inn*, were provided by *The Christmas Cottage* in 2017. The film is about a young woman who realizes she doesn't actually love her boyfriend, but finds real (romantic) love with her friend's brother whilst snowed into the remote Christmas Cottage of the title. The search for love *and marriage* reflects middle-class family values, and is a constant theme of the Hallmark Christmas films (and thus also segues nicely into Valentine's Day products). *My Christmas Love* is a romantic comedy in which Cynthia (Meredith Hagner) is wooed by Liam (Booby Campo), who leaves presents at her door for each of the twelve days of Christmas as a very romantic wooing, no doubt perceived to be a reflection of a simpler and better past. In *Christmas Under Wraps*, Candace Cameron Bure plays a doctor in an Alaskan town (what better almost all-year-round Christmas setting?), who discovers romance. In 2017 all of the elements of a Christmas fairy tale were brought together in *A Royal Christmas Ball*, complete with the long-lost relatives of its very own Prince Charming, the mythical King Charles of Baltamia.

The endurance of the Christmas romance is equalled in the continuing association of the season with the supernatural. During the 1970s the BBC produced its critically acclaimed *A Ghost Story for Christmas* dramas. Broadcast every Christmas season between 1971 and 1978, the BBC produced a set of highly effective and atmospheric adaptations of ghost story classics, mainly by M. R. James, but including Dickens's *The Signalman*, with much of the effect created by the use of film (as opposed to the increasingly popular, and cheap, video format) and location shooting. Abandoned in the eighties, the BBC has returned to this genre over the last few years, and now often mixes new material with repeat broadcasts of the originals. As a public broadcaster funded through a unique licence system, the BBC created a role for itself as interpreter and impresario of the British national Christmas. Determined to create high-quality family entertainment, the BBC provided significant budgets for its biggest comedy stars, Eric Morecambe and Ernie Wise, throughout the sixties and seventies. Nine high budget Christmas specials were produced between 1968 and 1977. The duo then transferred to independent television making six more seasonal specials. Very much modelled on American formats of celebrity guests joining the anchors for songs and sketches (and building on a BBC favourite of the 1950s and 1960s, *Christmas Night With The Stars*), the shows were a huge hit with British audiences. The BBC replaced the stars with another comedy duo, Ronnie Barker and Ronnie Corbett. *The Two Ronnies Christmas Specials* of 1982, 1984, and 1987 proved equally great successes.

As with cinema, television could also make arch comments about the season, and produce clever variants on its expected trappings. Two notable examples are the 'Twas the Episode Before Christmas' (1985) instalment of the *Moonlighting* series (1985–89), which was extremely popular on both sides of the Atlantic, and the special of the BBC historical comedy, *Blackadder's Christmas Carol* (1988). The very title 'Twas the Episode Before Christmas' summed up the arch, tongue-in-cheek style of the entire series, and in this particular episode made a point of playing on Christmas clichés and including a very clever twist on the Slaughter of the Innocents, as a woman named Mary is forced to abandon a newborn baby after having witnessed the murder of her husband. In *Blackadder's Christmas Carol* the Dickens story is played backwards as Edmund Blackadder, 'the kindest and loveliest man in all England', is turned into a selfish money-grabber by witnessing the fate of his meek ancestors conjured up the Spirit of Christmas.

Cinema and television forged a deep association with Christmas. It is too early to state exactly what effect the relatively recent advent of multi-media, multi-platform, and multi-format broadcasting will have on the season, but the association is likely to continue given its crucial importance as both a holiday period and one intimately connected with mass consumption.

REFERENCES AND FURTHER READING

Connelly, Mark (ed.) (2000). *Christmas at the Movies. Images of Christmas in American, British and European Cinema*. London: I.B. Tauris.

Davis, Paul (1990). *The Lives and Times of Ebenezer Scrooge*. New Haven and London: Yale University Press.

Restad, Penne (1995). *Christmas in America: A History*. New York: Oxford University Press.

PART VII
AROUND THE WORLD

CHAPTER 33

BETHLEHEM AND THE MIDDLE EAST

ELIZABETH MONIER

WHERE IT ALL BEGAN

ALTHOUGH the Christmas story could be said to have begun at any number of points or places, it was Bethlehem that became the stage for the birth of Jesus. Today, Bethlehem is recreated in village halls, school auditoriums, and churches all over the world for the annual ritual of the Nativity play. The imagery of the humble stable, lit up by a star, with the shepherds and wise men converging upon it, is familiar from the greetings cards we send. At Christmas carol concerts we sing 'O little town of Bethlehem'. Somehow this often remains disconnected from our imagining of Christmas, which, in the West, is so heavily tied up with traditions formed in the Victorian period in England and in America and so is removed geographically and temporally from Bethlehem at the time of Jesus.

Our Christmas cards focus on two distinct themes: the snowy scenes and cosy fires of Europe and North America, and the depictions of the Middle East with camels, people in Eastern dress and a donkey beating a dusty path to Bethlehem. While both these aspects are entwined, the Eastern scenery is present mainly as the backdrop. It represents a distant time and ancient land. What is glossed over is that Christians live and worship and celebrate Christmas in the Middle East still (Sennot 2003: 14). For many Christians in the Middle East, and especially those from the Holy Land, there is a sense that they are overlooked, despite the ancient roots of their communities. The Revd Dr Mitri Raheb, a Palestinian Christian and pastor in the Lutheran Church has described in many of his publications and talks how he has encountered surprise that there are Christians in Palestine on numerous occasions (Raheb 2002).

In actuality, there have been Christians in the Middle East continuously since the birth of the Christian faith. Christmas is therefore widely celebrated throughout the region and its diverse Christian communities proudly celebrate their links to the earliest Christians. Bethlehem was a village at the time of Jesus's birth. Today it has a population of approximately 25,000 and is a focus of religious life for Palestinian Christians. The district of Bethlehem includes Bethlehem itself, as well as the towns of Beit Jala and Beit Sahour. Approximately half of Palestinian Christians live in this district. Prior to the Arab–Israeli war of 1948, Christians made up the majority of the population of Bethlehem, but they are now the minority. Marsh (2005) notes a number of reasons why Christians are emigrating in disproportionate numbers compared to their Muslim counterparts, including historical, social, economic, and political factors.

Despite this, Palestinian Christians emphasize their rootedness in the region and in Christian faith and history by referring to themselves as the 'living stones' (*al-Hijara al-Haya*), an expression drawn from the Bible (1 Peter 2:5). This chain linking modern Christians in the Middle East with the first Christians is important in many different denominations and other national communities. The tradition of the flight of the Holy Family to Egypt is important to Egyptian Christians, as is the tradition that the Coptic Orthodox Church was founded by St Mark. For Antiochian Orthodox Christians, Acts 11:26 is a key verse as it reads, 'The disciples were called Christians first at Antioch' (Monier 2018). Other Christians, such as those belonging to the Syriac churches (including the Church of the East, the Chaldean Catholic Church, Syriac Orthodox Church, and the Syriac Catholic Church) emphasize the fact that they still use a dialect of Aramaic, the language spoken by Jesus. Clearly, Christianity is not foreign to, nor removed from, the modern Middle East.

This demonstrates that Bethlehem is more than a clichéd image for Christmas cards or backdrop for school Nativity plays. It is also more than a site for foreign Christian pilgrims to visit. Despite the politics and conflicts that persist in the region, Bethlehem also remains home to a Palestinian Christian community and a focal point for Christians within the Middle East. This chapter locates Christmas in this region. It considers how Western versions of Christmas celebrations interact with local traditions and also what Christmas means for both Christians and non-Christians in the Middle East. This is particularly important in the face of the decline of Christian populations in the region and concerns about its disappearance altogether in the wake of the violence unleashed by the terrorist group the Islamic State (IS). This context gives the celebration of Christmas in Bethlehem and the Middle East today more significance, not less.

Celebrating Christmas in the East

Bethlehem, and the Middle East in general, are not just a historical backdrop to the first Christmas. Christians continue to inhabit the region and the link between their local roots and Christian heritage remains integral to their identity and culture. The next question might be: are they permitted to celebrate Christmas or other Christian festivals openly? In general, the answer is yes. Apart from in Saudi Arabia, Christians are normally able to practise their faith. Qatar had also discouraged public worship of religions other than Islam, but in 2008 the first official church building was constructed. This has been followed by further buildings that together form 'church city' just outside the capital, Doha. Political circumstances do have an impact on expressions of Christian faith, however. Therefore, the way Christmas is celebrated varies across the region due to the different local contexts and also the diversity and number of different denominations and traditions that exist in the region.

Beginning with Bethlehem, celebrations naturally focus on the Church of the Nativity. This is set in Manger Square, which was renovated for the millennium celebrations and is lined by shops selling local traditional crafts, such as crosses carved from olive wood. Tourism is of major importance to Bethlehem, and Christmas is the highlight for pilgrims and tourists. The numbers visiting can vary according to the political climate. Celebrations were scaled back in 2017, for example, in the wake of the decision of the American president to move the American Embassy from Tel Aviv to Jerusalem. Nevertheless, visitor numbers to the Church of the Nativity are increasing overall. Visiting in 1999, I had the grotto that marks the spot where Jesus was born, denoted by a silver star on the ground, all to myself. In 2017, there were reports that church authorities were considering developing an app to help book and plan visits to the grotto to improve the problem of overcrowding.

The church was first built on the site identified by Christian tradition as the birthplace of Jesus in AD 339. The local tradition pictures the place as a cave rather than a stable. The original church was later replaced after a fire in the sixth century. In 2012, it was added to the UNESCO list of world heritage sites and attracts visitors from all over the world, and naturally there is particular interest in visiting at Christmas time. Christmas celebrations spill out into Manger Square where crowds gather to listen to music and watch the parade of bagpipe-playing scouts, a legacy from the British Mandate period in the early twentieth century. The square is decorated with lights and a Christmas tree, in a way that is familiar in towns across the world. These celebrations take place on 24 and 25 December, yet many Palestinian Christians celebrate Christmas on 6 and 7 January instead. This is not peculiar to Palestine or to the Middle East; the Russian Orthodox, Serbian Orthodox, Coptic Orthodox, and Armenian Orthodox, for example, also celebrate Christmas Day on 7 January. Still most foreign visitors expect to celebrate on the 25 December, and the Palestinian Christians of other denominations, such as the Catholics and Anglicans share this date. Christmas in Jesus' place of birth then represents a mixing of international expectations and local traditions.

If Christmas in Bethlehem demonstrates a mixing of local traditions and foreign influences, Egypt has been less influenced by foreign traditions. Although Egypt has its tradition of the exile of the Holy Family, it is not a Christmas 'destination' like Bethlehem. The majority of Christians in Egypt belong to the Coptic Orthodox Church, which celebrates in January rather than December. Like in much of the East, Christmas is not celebrated with as much pomp when compared to Easter; the opposite of the situation in much of the Western world. Western traditions have filtered into the accoutrements associated with Christmas, however. Christmas trees and Baba Noel

(Father Christmas) figures are widely available and have become part of the Christmas rituals in Egypt to some extent, but this is mainly in urban areas and middle-class families because these are linked more to culture than to Christian worship.

For most Egyptian Christians, Christmas means the end of *Sowm al-Milad*, the Nativity Fast, which lasts for the forty days before Christmas. Christians follow a diet that excludes most animal products during this fast and when it is broken on Christmas day, normally after attending a long liturgy on Christmas Eve, food is central to the celebration. Food is often where local differences withstand the Hollywood version of Christmas. For Egyptians, there are many food traditions associated with Easter but less so for Christmas, reflecting the relatively greater importance of Easter for Copts. In general, beef or lamb is what is eaten on special occasions and so for Christmas, dishes such as kofta or kebab are often the centrepiece. Traditionally, it is common to eat meat with rice and fried liver after the Christmas Eve service, and Christians dress in new clothes to mark the occasion. Visits are made to friends and family and greetings are exchanged. Celebrations are not usually extravagant, however, as Christmas falls within the school term and in fact it coincides with an important exam period. Consequently, even though Christmas Day is a national holiday in Egypt, Coptic children usually spend it revising for exams the day after.

Christmas, celebrated on 25 December, is also a national holiday in Lebanon. This is to be expected because Lebanon has the largest Christian population proportionally in the Middle East. The last official census carried out in 1932 shows that Christians then formed the majority of the population (Maktabi 1999). Although Christians are now only thought to make up approximately 35 per cent of population, they retain their influence to a large extent. The Lebanese president must always be a Maronite Christian according to the Lebanese constitution and Christianity is conspicuously visible in the public space (Monier 2018). The visible imagery is not restricted to neutral symbols but crosses and icons are common in the areas of the country where Christians have traditionally been dominant. Statues of the Virgin Mary are also very popular due to the Catholic heritage.

The largest Christian denomination is the Maronite Church, an Eastern Catholic church in communion with Rome. This link to Europe through the connection to Rome, and also a longstanding historical relationship with France, bolstered the Lebanese Christian influence (Gheorghiu 1979: 147–52). The Maronite Church played a significant role in the formation of Lebanon as an independent country after World War I and has maintained strong political, social, and cultural influence ever since. For the Maronite Church, Lebanon was intended to act as a de facto Christian state in the region and the 9 February is a national holiday in Lebanon to celebrate St Maroun, the Maronite's founder. Due to this clear dominance of the Christian heritage of Lebanon, Christmas traditions have developed and been maintained to varying degrees.

Traditionally, it has been the crib and the Nativity scene that have been at the centre of Christmas decorations and displays, rather than Christmas trees, though the latter are now very common. The famous ABC mall in Achrafiyeh, a Christian district in Beirut, always houses a large Christmas decoration display that normally includes a

Nativity scene, also known as a *crèche* due to the strong French influence. The Lebanese Nativity scene is usually set in a cave (*me'ghara*) rather than a stable, reflecting the more common Middle Eastern imagining of the scene of Jesus' birth. This forms the focal point in homes for prayer over the Christmas period. Traditionally, the Lebanese add sprouted seeds such as chickpeas, broad beans, wheat, oats, and lentils to the Nativity scene, though this is not as common as it was a generation or two ago before the civil war. Mixed with these local traditions is of course the adoption of Western traditions. Baba Noel, along with Christmas trees are the most obvious additions. The French influence has also added the chocolate log (buche de noel) to the Christmas menu, although the traditional Lebanese Christmas desert *Meghli* remains popular. This is a rice pudding flavoured with anis, cinnamon, and caraway and topped with almonds, pistachios, walnuts, and coconut flakes. It is served to celebrate the birth of a baby and so it is eaten at Christmas to celebrate the birth of Christ. Families come together to celebrate after Mass with these desserts and Levantine dishes such as Kebbeh, and may dance the *debkeh*, the Levantine folk dance, together.

Before Lebanon became an independent country, it was a region of Syria or *Bilad al-Sham*. Syria also has a relatively large and important Christian population, though it differs from Lebanon as the majority of Christians in Syria belong to the Greek Orthodox Church rather than the Maronite Church. Although they do not have the proportionally large size of population or influence that Christians in Lebanon have, they do have a relatively strong position within Syria. Syrian Christians tend to be fiercely proud of the fact that Islam is not the official religion of the state, as it is in the majority of the states of the Middle East. Furthermore, while Islam is a source of law in Syria, it is not the principal source of law. As a result, Syrian Christians are often intensely loyal to the state (Rabo 2012). Christmas is celebrated openly and the Nativity scene, *al-Me'ghara*, is as central to Christmas displays as it is in Lebanon. In Syria the scene is left without adding baby Jesus until after the celebration of Midnight Mass on Christmas Eve. Families return home after the service to begin celebrating with a meal of meat and local dishes such as Kebbeh, and gifts are exchanged.

Bethlehem as the birthplace of Jesus, Egypt which boasts the largest Christian population in the region, Lebanon where Christians have the most political and cultural influence in the Middle East, and Syria which features frequently in the Bible, are four obvious places where Christmas is celebrated. However, Christmas is also celebrated in more unexpected places in the region. The Arabian Peninsula is not commonly linked with Christianity or celebrations of Christmas and, of course, in the Kingdom of Saudi Arabia the practice of Christianity is prohibited. However, in most of the rest of the states of the Arab Peninsula, Christianity is practised. The Arabian Peninsula does actually have an ancient Christian heritage, and monasteries and bishoprics were established mainly during the fourth to seventh centuries. Archaeologists have found evidence of churches across the region.

In modern times there is also a large Christian population in the region, as a result of the waves of migration to the oil-rich states of the Peninsula since the second half of the twentieth century (Monier 2020). As a result, Christianity has become the second-largest religion after Islam in a number of Arab states in the Gulf region. These Christians come from incredibly diverse backgrounds in terms of nationality, language, and Christian denomination. The celebration of Christmas in the states of the Gulf, such as Kuwait, Bahrain, the UAE, and so on, reflect this. It also encapsulates the globalization of Christmas. Shopping malls and supermarkets sell Christmas trees and decorations, and public spaces are decorated with Christmas trees and lights. When viewing these decorated spaces, it can often be hard to tell where in the world you are. Dubai has a delivery service for real 'Canadian fir' Christmas trees, while there is a Facebook group called 'Christmas in Kuwait', which is followed by almost 6,000 people. In these ways the globalization of Christmas through migration and its commercialization have disconnected aspects of the festival from its religious meaning, but at the same time it has allowed Christians and non-Christians to participate in a public celebration of Christmas in regions where it would not otherwise be visible or perhaps even permissible to celebrate.

THE POLITICS OF CHRISTMAS IN THE MIDDLE EAST

Although Christmas can be celebrated without significant hindrance throughout much of the Middle East, this is within certain boundaries. It can also be a political tool or a political challenge in some places, so Christmas attracts its share of politics in the Middle East. Each year in the run-up to Christian festivals including Christmas, there is the perennial question of whether Muslims are permitted to greet Christians during their religious holidays. For some conservative Muslims it is wrong to wish Christians a happy Christmas, although Egypt's *Dar al-Ifta*, the official body for religious rulings or fatwas, has said that it is permissible.[1] Holidays such as Christmas can also lead to heightened security measures amid fears that Christians and churches could be targeted by terrorists. For example, in 2010, seven people were shot outside a church in southern Egypt at the end of Christmas Eve Mass, while in December 2017, a church was bombed in the run-up to Coptic Christmas and disrupted celebrations, with metal detectors having to be installed at church entrances. This is not the case in Egypt only. Security is usually increased around churches in the Gulf due to fear of attack. In 2013, a Baghdad church was attacked as worshippers were leaving after Christmas Mass.

Iraq, of course, witnessed further brutal violence after this, leading to a further decline in the Christian population of Iraq. IS captured Mosul, one of Iraq's major Christian cities, in 2014. Christians, along with Yezidis and others were killed or displaced from their homes, and churches and homes were destroyed. After Iraq

---

[1] Dar al-Ifat al-Missriyah, *Congratulating Christians on the occasion of Christmas*. Available at http://www.dar-alifta.org/Foreign/ViewFatwa.aspx?ID=6815/ (accessed 24 March 2020).

eventually expelled IS from Mosul in 2017, there was a lot of symbolism surrounding the reinstitution of Christmas services that year. Services were held in the recaptured areas, often in partially destroyed churches. This was important as a form of resistance and an important part of reclaiming the areas of northern Iraq, which have traditionally been inhabited by Christians. Other Iraqis dressed up as Father Christmas and toured the devastated towns to hand out gifts to children, a bright spot amidst trauma. Christmas trees and Nativity scenes were also erected amidst the rubble and in refugee camps hosting displaced Christians.

Christmas that year featured heavily in state propaganda in an effort to show that they were protecting their Christian citizens and that displaced people could return home and exercise their faith once more. When the patriarch of the Chaldean Catholic Church, the largest denomination in Iraq, requested that the government make Christmas a public holiday in Iraq in 2018, the government granted the request. The Iraqi government tweeted on 24 December 2018 to announce the news and to wish "Happy Christmas to our Christian citizens, all Iraqis and to all who are celebrating around the world."[2] The process of return has of course been slow and complicated with many fearing to return. Nevertheless, the act of celebrating Christmas after the ousting of IS, whether back in the vandalized churches of Mosul, in refugee camps, or new homes abroad, was symbolically important to Christians from Iraq struggling to defy attempts to destroy their community, culture, and faith.

Christmas 2018 in Syria was also celebrated with gusto and pride despite the years of civil war and conflict with IS. Christmas trees were lit up and music and celebrations held in the streets and squares, calling to mind similar celebrations of Christmas light switch-on parties elsewhere in the world. The enthusiasm which was in evidence that year was partly as a reaction to the horror witnessed in the country after years of civil war and then occupation under IS. It was also partly to emphasize Syrian Christian support for Bashar al-Assad, and the message that Christians have religious freedom under his regime (Farha and Mousa 2015). Like in Iraq, processions and singing in the streets were important to reclaim Christians' place in their homelands and their determination to maintain their faith and culture. The celebration of Christmas acts in this way as an affirmation of Eastern Christian identity and of the right and ability of Christians to exercise their faith and religious traditions in their historical homelands.

In Egypt also, Christmas has become a symbolic occasion for the relationship between the government and Christian citizens. Former president Mohammed Hosni Mubarak had already made Christmas a national holiday in 2002. In the wake of 9/11, this was likely a political gesture, first to send a message to Egypt's Western allies that Egypt was an important partner in the Middle East and Mubarak a secular leader. Second this was a gesture for the Coptic Orthodox Church, which gave the Mubarak regime consistent and public political support. Under President Abdul Fattah al-Sisi, Christmas has taken on further political value. Sisi was the first Egyptian president to

---

[2] Twitter, Government of Iraq @IraqiGovt online. Available at https://twitter.com/IraqiGovt/status/1077213857586782208?s=20/ (accessed 24 March 2020).

appear at the Coptic Christmas Eve Mass, which is broadcast on Egyptian television. This was considered to be a dramatic and significant gesture, which he used to emphasize unity among Egyptians. Since then he has made an appearance each year and given a brief address, which has gained him appreciation among many Christians.

While politics has in some ways supported public celebrations of Christmas in Egypt and used Christmas as a point of reconciliation in Iraq, the political complications in Bethlehem are entrenched. In 2002, Israeli Defence Forces (IDF) occupied Bethlehem as part of Operation Defensive Shield. During this period, Palestinian militants took refuge in The Church of the Nativity, thereby attracting the focus of the world. Normal Palestinian citizens also took refuge inside the church, thinking that they would be safe and that Western countries would not permit a siege in the place of Christ's birth (Audeh 2002: 29). A number of priests were also inside the church and surrounding buildings (Cristal 2003). However, despite the importance of the site and the impact of the siege on international politics, the siege lasted well over a month before it was resolved.

This wasn't the only dramatic event in Bethlehem that year. In 2002 the segregation wall was erected, extending over 80 kilometres in the Bethlehem Governorate and surrounding the city on three sides. Consequently, the church marking the place where Christ was born is separated from the church that marks the place where he is thought to have died by checkpoints and roadblocks, even though the distance between them is less than 10 kilometres.[3] As a result of this wall it is more difficult for Palestinian Christians from other areas to visit Bethlehem for Christmas and it restricts movement between Bethlehem, which is under Palestinian control, and Jerusalem in Israel. Before politics made it difficult, it had been common for Christians to move between the two holy sites during celebrations such as Christmas (Sabella 2018: 145–6). There is no doubt then that the celebration of Christmas in its region of origin is subject to the complications of politics and history. In some cases, politics can lead to greater visibility and acceptance for the celebration of Christmas; in others it hampers celebrations or even targets Christmas to maximize the impact of violence.

Christmas in the Middle East: Local, Global, or Globalized?

Christmas in the Middle East, as elsewhere is also subject to the pressures of globalization and commercialization. This has negative aspects in that the globalization and commercialization of Christmas overshadow local traditions and overlook the religious aspect of Christmas. In the Middle East in countries that have long celebrated

---

[3] Visualising Palestine. Available at https://www.visualizingpalestine.org/visuals/bethlehem-besieged/ (accessed 24 March 2020).

Christmas, this encroachment of inauthentic practices has eroded attention given to longstanding traditions. At the same time, where Christmas has been a less important occasion and not developed strong associated traditions, the universal Christmas traditions have been at least partially adopted and augment the celebration of Christmas, especially for younger generations. For Christians who live in Muslim-majority societies, adopting international aspects of Christmas, such as wearing Santa hats or Christmas jumpers and singing about dashing through the snow, gives them a sense of solidarity with the global Christian community and for some this is a brief escape from their culturally and religiously minoritized status.

This exposure to Western Christmas celebrations does not always necessarily undermine the religious message either. An example is the way that Western Christmas carols have been translated into Arabic and used as part of the celebrations. Due to the lyrics, these songs do preserve the religious aspect of Christmas. The Arabic version of 'Silent Night', *Laylatan,* sung by Majida al-Roumi, was broadcast on Lebanese TV and in Egypt to Protestant Christians in particular, but middle-class urban Christians from other traditions will also listen to the Better Life Band singing *Fi Mizwad al-Ba'ar,* to the music of 'Away in a Manger'. Christmas celebrations are undergoing a process of change as different traditions come into contact with each other, which is quite natural.

It is not only the Middle East that is experiencing the move of Christmas celebrations to a more commercialized and globalized occasion. But while in traditionally Christian countries this can be seen as diminishing the message of Christmas, in non-Christian countries this process could ironically allow the Christmas message to gain greater exposure. In countries that previously had no, or very small, Christian communities such as in the Arabian Peninsula, the celebration of Christmas is familiar to most today. The universal message of peace on earth and goodwill to all mankind has spread further, though at a cost. While trees and the jolly figure of Santa dressed in red and white proliferate, Jesus and his religious message is edged further out of the picture. Christmas does represent common ground in the Middle East from an interfaith perspective because Muslims also believe that Jesus was born of the Virgin Mary. This Nativity story, albeit with many differences, is included in the Qur'an.

Additionally, most people find joy in the birth of a baby and see birth as a reason to celebrate. In Arabic, Christmas is called *Eid al-Milad,* the festival of *the* birth. The disagreements arise over who Jesus was and is and what happened to him; Muslims believe Jesus was a prophet but not the son of God and they do not believe he was crucified. The birth of Jesus then is less problematic a celebration than his resurrection and this perhaps partly accounts for the greater proliferation of Christmas celebrations in the public space in the Middle East, despite its lesser importance for Christians, especially in the East. This explains why the common manifestations of Christmas celebrations in the region include those that are most neutral; Father Christmas and Christmas trees, lights and decorations, are those most widely available and on public display. This is helped along by the dominant place that Christmas has in the Western imagination and culture and which is then transferred globally.

In these ways, the secular culture that has grown up around the 'holidays' in the West has globalized Christmas celebrations and facilitated the acceptance of Christmas celebrations in regions of the Middle East where Christmas would not have been openly celebrated previously. Despite this, Eastern Christians have a great awareness of their own origins in the region and strong connections with the Christmas story and biblical history in general. This is why, despite declining numbers and political instability, Christians in the Middle East will continue to celebrate Christmas in their traditional homelands, many wearing red Santa hats.

REFERENCES AND FURTHER READING

Audeh, I. (2002). 'Narratives of Siege: Eye-Witness Testimonies from Jenin, Bethlehem and Nablus', *Journal of Palestine Studies*, 31, no. 4, Summer: 13–34.

Cristal, M. (2003). 'Negotiating under the Cross: The Story of the Forty Day Siege of the Church of Nativity', *International Negotiation*, 8: 549–76.

Farha, M. and Mousa, S (2015). 'Secular Autocracy vs. Sectarian Democracy? Weighing Reasons for Christian Support for Regime Transition in Syria and Egypt', *Mediterranean Politics*, 20, no. 2: 178–97.

Gheorghiu, V. (1979). *Christ au Liban*. Paris: Plon.

Maktabi, R. (1999). 'The Lebanese Census of 1932 Revisited. Who are the Lebanese?', *British Journal of Middle Eastern Studies*, 26, no. 2: 219–41.

Marsh, L. (2005). 'Palestinian Christianity—A Study in Religion and Politics', *International Journal for the Study of the Christian Church*, 5, no. 2: 147–66.

Monier, Elizabeth (2018). 'Faith and Culture', in Ross, K., Tadros, M., and Johnson, Todd (eds), *Christianity in North Africa and West Asia*. Edinburgh: Edinburgh University Press: 303–12.

Monier, Elizabeth (forthcoming 2020). 'The Gulf States: Bahrain, Kuwait, Oman, Qatar, United Arab Emirates and Yemen', in Mitri Raheb, Meredith L. D. Riedel, and Mark A. Lamport (eds.), *Christianity in the Middle East: Historical Sketches and Contemporary Practices*. New York, London: Rowman & Littlefield.

Rabo, A. (2012). '"We are Christians and We are Equal Citizens": Perspectives on Particularity and Pluralism in Contemporary Syria', *Islam and Christian–Muslim Relations*, 23, no. 1: 79–93.

Raheb, M. (2002). 'Sailing Through Troubled Waters: Palestinian Christians in the Holy Land', *Dialog: A Journal of Theology*, 41, no. 2, Summer: 97–102.

Ross, K., Tadros, M., and, Johnson, Todd (2018). *Christianity in North Africa and West Asia*. Edinburgh: Edinburgh University Press.

Sabella, B. (2018). 'Palestine', in K. Ross, M. Tadros, and Todd Johnson (eds), *Christianity in North Africa and West Asia*. Edinburgh: Edinburgh University Press: 140–51.

Sennot, C. (2003). *The Body and the Blood: The Middle East's Vanishing Christians and the Possibility for Peace*. New York: Public Affairs.

CHAPTER 34

CATHOLIC EUROPE

NADINE CRETIN

At Christmas, European Catholics celebrate the Nativity, Jesus's birth in Bethlehem. But for almost all Europeans, believers or not, Christmas is the occasion of a family celebration. Sacred and secular customs are both present and intermingle: these traditions include ancient ones arising from the winter solstice, which is indicated by their permanency in the whole of Europe; others, which are more recent than that, have nevertheless a traditional reputation. By syncretism, all aspects of the festival have added to its overall meaning, creating the Christmas celebration as it is known today. Some facets have a Christian origin, including the very name 'Christmas', the date of 25 December fixed by the Roman Church around 330, the Midnight Mass, the Nativity scene, Christmas carols, and the Advent wreath with its candles. Other facets belong to the Twelve Days, a season that was more explicit in the past, namely, the period going from Christmas to Epiphany (6 January). During this *Janusian* period—from *Janus Bifrons*, a Roman god who looks at the past year and at the new one at the same time—comes the New Year, since the days begin to lengthen in the northern hemisphere at that time of year (Fabre 1992: 25). This gave rise to customs of hope where people, especially peasants, sought to predict a coming year full of prosperity, fruitfulness, and happiness. 'To the coming Year! If we are not more numerous, let's hope that we shall not be less', the families would say in Provence in front of the Yule log. It was a genuine prayer. In observing the height of the sparks in the fire, the cracklings sounds and so on, they would question the future regarding a promising year ahead for their families and livestock, and for a favourable climate and harvests. The *blé de la Sainte-Barbe*, wheat seeds put in little cups on 4 December to sprout, must have grown straight up on 24 December. During the two solstices of the year, the heavens were supposed to be opened, making the distance closer to those in the hereafter, as it was at Samain and Belteine for the Celts on the eve of their new seasons, cold or warm. Christmas is still a difficult period for those who have lost a member of their family, or those who are sick or alone.

Today, European society has a great deal of religious diversity, but Christianity—the largest religion in Europe—has had a major influence on its culture, as Christmas traditions demonstrate. According to the Vatican's *Agenzia Fides* statistics for 2018 of the Roman Catholic Church, and also the material in the latest Church book published in 2016, the number of Catholics around the world is increasing. In 2019, the number of Catholics is increasing again. However, in Europe, there has been a decline for the third consecutive year. Catholicism represents 39.76 per cent of the population of the continent of Europe (718,018,000 inhabitants). (see www.fides.org/en/stats/.) Catholicism is the majority religion in Austria, Belgium, the Czech Republic, France, Hungary, Ireland, Italy, Luxembourg, Malta, Poland, Portugal, Slovakia, Slovenia, and Spain. Christmas (which is, in practice, the largest feast, despite the Church's official position that Easter, Christ's Resurrection's day, is the pre-eminent one) is sometimes held over two days. It includes the evening of 24 December, and may go up to St Stephen's Day, 26 December. 'The Feasts' (*les Fêtes* in French) include the week from Christmas to New Year's Day. Many people prefer not to work during that week, and these days are also part of the school holidays. Epiphany or 'Kings' day' is on 6 January and it is a public holiday in some places such as Spain, Italy, and Poland. Alternatively, since the council of Vatican II (1965), Epiphany is sometimes observed on the first Sunday after 1 January.

In order to explore Christmas in Catholic Europe further, this chapter will consider how it is celebrated in three different arenas: at church, at home, and in public places.

Christmas at Church

Like the English Christmas (the Mass of the Christ), the different names for this feast in Europe indicate its Christian origin: Weihnachten in German (sacred nights), Noël in French (from the Latin Nativitas), Navidad in Spanish, Natal in Portuguese, and Natale in Italian.

Neither of the two Gospels that recount Christ's birth (Matthew and Luke), specify the day of the year when this event took place. Several dates were eventually suggested, based on various calculations. December 25 was fixed as the date to observe Christ's Nativity in the West by around 330. It appears for the first time in the Philocalian Calendar (354). From the late fourth century, there exist representations of the Nativity already on marble sarcophagi in Italy and in the south of France. They depict the Virgin Mary, the ox and ass near the crib, and the Magi with their gifts, dressed in Persian costumes and Phrygian caps. St Joseph, however, is not included.

Christmas is celebrated by several Masses in Catholic Europe. From the time of Pope Gregory I († 604), the Church in Rome observed three: at night in Santa Maria Maggiore (where there exists today a replica of 'the cave of the Nativity' as well as a relic venerated as part of the original manger), at dawn in Saint Anastasia of Sirmium (whose feast day is also 25 December), and in the morning in Saint Peter. These Masses are preceded by a Vigil on Christmas Eve. In France and in Italy, the Mass during the night is called 'Midnight Mass', because of *The Book of Wisdom* (18:14–15): 'For while all things were in quiet silence and the night was in the midst of her course, Thy almighty word leapt down from heaven from thy royal throne.' In Spain, the Midnight

Mass is called *Missa del Gallo*, and in Portugal *Missa do Gallo*—these names are derived for the third moment of the night in ancient Rome: *ad galli cantum*. It was common for people to wish to attend all three Masses, as can be seen in Alphonse Daudet's comic Provencal tale, *The Three Low Masses* (1873). In some regions such as Lorraine in France, a magical value was given to this feat: it was claimed that attending all three Masses would protect one 'from death from water, or fire, or iron'. Today, the 'Midnight' Mass—now usually observed earlier in the evening—is still very popular, even with people who do not regularly attend church. They often sing by heart the Christmas carols that made an indelible impression on them during their childhood: *Adeste Fideles*, *Les Anges dans nos campagnes*, *Gesù Bambino*. The Austrian carol famous all over the world, *Stille Nacht, Heilige Nacht*, is a lullaby written by the Catholic priest, Joseph Mohr, and put to music on guitar by the organist Franz Gruber at the last moment for the Christmas Eve service, 1818.

Indicating how popular these feasts had become by the medieval period, Christmas and Epiphany were frequent themes of illuminations in liturgical books. They also inspired many painters such as Giotto, Botticelli, and Mantegna in Italy, Zurbaran in Spain, and Nicolas Poussin, Philippe de Champaigne, and Georges de La Tour in France. Liturgical plays, developed at various shrines in Europe during the Middle Ages, allowed the Mass to solemnize the special nature of the occasion through performances: the shepherds or Magi's happiness or surprise (there was a parallel at Easter, with the recreating of Mary's astonishment finding the tomb empty). In their early years, these plays were discreet. That was the case, for instance, with the Italian, Francis of Assisi who, in 1223, had the idea of celebrating the Midnight Mass in a cave in Greccio, where the Nativity scene would be evoked with the aid of a manger and a real ox and an ass. Starting in the eleven and twelfth centuries, at various shrines in Western Europe, the festive celebrations in the days following Christmas included elections of pretend prelates: a 'bishop' was chosen on 26 December from among the deacons, on the 27th from among the priests, and on the 28th (the Feast of the Holy Innocents), for among the choirboys. Wearing episcopal robes, one child was allowed to take the bishop's place for twenty-four hours. From the end of the twelfth century, the Feast of Fools, for subdeacons (who were students), was celebrated on Circumcision Day (1 January), or Epiphany, or on its octave. These noisy and mocking plays became larger and wilder until they came to be considered indecent. Their lasting reputation has been harmed by the fact that they were incorrectly represented in clerical judgments in the seventeenth century. (Dahhaoui 2013: 373) Therefore, by the fifteenth century, these liturgical dramas were disappearing. They were replaced by quieter and more decorous traditions such as Nativity scenes and Christmas carols interspersed with dialogues. Out in the open air, there were also the Mystery Plays, which flourished between the fourteenth and the sixteen centuries in France, Belgium, England, Italy, and Spain. Spectators were often delighted by the special effects.

Christmas is preceded by Advent, a liturgical season that includes four Sundays. The first one marks the beginning of the liturgical year. Nativity scenes are set up in churches and they stay up until the Sunday following Epiphany, or even, in Provence, all the way to Candlemas (2 February). These dramatic representations made with mobile statues began to appear in churches during the Catholic Reformation in the sixteenth century. The first such Nativity scenes were in Prague (1562), and in Piccolomini Castle in Celano (Abruzzo) around 1567 (Gockerell 1998: 13). In France, devotion to the Christ Child spread through the influence of the Carmelites, who helped to make Nativity scenes widespread. Bavarian and Austrian convents also appreciated their pedagogic character, as did several religious orders in Central Europe, in Provence, and in the Iberian Peninsula.

Some other dramatic additions also sometimes take place during the Mass, such as in France where a real lamb is offered to the priest. In many places, Christmas was the patron feast for shepherds as they were first to be told by the angels of the Nativity. The *pastrage* (this presentation of a newborn lamb to the priest) in Les-Baux-de-Provence is famous. It was revived at the beginning of the twentieth century through the *Félibrige* movement (founded in 1854 by Frédéric Mistral), which promotes the continuation of old traditions. Similarly, enactments involving the Magi, including exotic processions with camels and the distribution of gifts, have been revived in Spain. These are polysemous events which are both accessible in a poetic manner to nonbelievers, while also serving to reinforce the faith of believers. Live Nativity scenes, usually played by children, are still popular in many churches today.

Christmas at Home

Since Christmas is also a family celebration, domestic rituals are important as well. At the beginning of Advent, even young children notice that 'the house is changing'. This period lasts for more than a month, from the end of November until mid-January—and even all the way to the beginning of February in some regions. The countdown to Christmas is marked with Advent calendars. Children love them since many of these calendars contain chocolates: a little window is opened every day, from 1 to 24 December. From an idea that existed in some German families already in the nineteenth century, the first Advent calendars were printed at the beginning of the twentieth century. In 1908, in Munich, Gerhard Lang decided to turn them into a commercial product. These calendars were illustrated with religious scenes with the twenty-fourth picture being the Nativity. During the 1970s secularized version first began to appear which are still popular. These often depict Santa Claus, Christmas trees, and gifts. Some Advent calendars are for grown-ups, with cosmetic products or beers. Sometimes there are even ones for pets that offer treats for dogs or cats!

Like the calendar, the Advent wreath, with its count down through four candles, also marks the time to Christmas. On the first Sunday of Advent one candle is lit, on the second Sunday two candles, and so on. Known in some regions of Germany since the end of the nineteenth century, and well known in other European countries after the 1960s, this custom derives from a Protestant practice (as did the Advent calendar). Around 1840, Johann Heinrich Wichern, founder of the Inner Mission of the Evangelical Church near Hamburg, would gather the pupils near the organ during Advent for prayer whilst each day a new candle of a cartwheel would be lit. According to an Anglo-Saxon tradition, Christmas wreaths hang on front doors. During the winter solstice period, to put greenery in the house is an expression of hope, as most of the trees are bare in the northern hemisphere at that time. Already in the beginning of the third century in Roman North Africa, the apologist Tertullian deplored the fact that Christians would put laurels and candles in their houses during this season in the manner of the pagans. Known in German public buildings already in the fifteenth century, and in Alsace in the sixteenth (such as in Selestat in 1521), *mays* (evergreen trees) were cut in forests to appear in houses at Christmastide. The little trees would decorate the centre of the living-room table or they would be hung from the ceiling. Red apples, nuts, sweets, and candles were hooked onto them, symbolizing hope for immortality, prosperity, and fecundity. Some paper flowers and unconsecrated hosts represented heaven. With the rise of the bourgeoisie, the tree was more and more popular in the second half of the nineteenth century, first in urban areas, then in the countryside as well. Originally a Protestant custom, the Christmas tree has been for a long time in competition with the Nativity scene, the Catholic custom derived from Italy. Nowadays, the fir tree is an obligatory Christmas decoration in most European homes. It is now decorated with baubles instead of apples: the glassworkers in Meisenthal (Lorraine) are supposed first to have had this idea around 1850 in response to a scarcity of apples. Illuminations are also a response to the darkness of this period. By the end of the nineteenth century, electric strings of lights had started to replace candles. These garlands of electric lights also decorate balconies, the exteriors of houses, and gardens. In the nineteenth century, German farmers from Erzebirge created wooden Christmas pyramids that turn with the heat of candles that people would put in their living rooms. Scandinavian angel chimes are made of brass: created in the 1900s, they became popular everywhere in Europe during the 1960s.

A Nativity scene is set up in Catholic families at the beginning of Advent. Looking outside for stones and moss, children like to help to set it up, in the same way that they enjoy helping to decorate the Christmas tree. Arising among aristocratic families in the seventeenth century, Neapolitan crèches are rare and exquisite works of art. They depict scenes such as the search for an inn at Bethlehem, the Nativity set in a ruined temple (symbolizing the end of paganism), the announcement to the shepherds, and the exotic procession of the Magi with musicians. In these baroque representations, angels are numerous, and they became a common decoration for the tree, as is the Bethlehem star at the top. The Provencal Nativity scenes appeared in families there at the end of the eighteenth century. The various inhabitants of a village bring to Jesus a gift having to do with their trade—fish, flour, wood, and so on. The *ravi*, who is innocent, is welcoming Jesus with his open arms. Moulded in clay, the *santons*, small painted figures from usually 2.5 to 3.5 inches tall, are wearing suits from the French Restoration period (1830). Their name comes from *santoun,* 'little saint' in the Provencal language. If they are taller (5 to 8 inches), they are dressed with real fabrics. These developed in the nineteenth century. People say that, while the churches were closed during the French Revolution of 1789, the inhabitants, sad not to see the Nativity scene, decided to make one at home instead. The mystery of Christmas is particularly prodigal in its rural and popular representations: for example, in Catalonia, there is the *caganer,* a surprising figure who is crouching to relieve himself (Soler i Amigó 2007: 148).

In the kitchen, the children are fond of helping to bake spiced biscuits. These baked goods are distinct from the desserts for the Christmas dinner. Instead, they are for decorating the tree or giving to children who come to the house carolling. Some have an anthropomorphic shape. Some have a pointed shape once used to protect against witchcraft: fir-trees, stars, hearts, crescent moons, and so on. This shape, which is also the form of holly leaves, is supposed to bring good fortune. All the senses are catered to at this time of year. Songs and music are essential. In addition to the sacred ones, since the nineteenth century, many secular songs also evoke Christmas happiness or hope, such as *O Tannenbaum* (1824), *Jingle Bells* (1857), or *Petit Papa Noël* (1946) of Tino Rossi. The TV programmes join in. Today, in a more secular climate, the sacred songs make way for *Jingle Bells*, as well as new secularized content in French advertisements that is often presented in English.

Advent includes the feasts of generous saints, such as St Nicholas (Santa Claus's most famous ancestor) on 6 December, and St Lucy on 13 December, a Sicilian young girl tortured to death at the end of the third century, who brings light and baked goods in Swedish families on her feast day. St Nicholas's day is still very important in some Catholic and Protestant Rhine countries, including Belgium, Luxembourg, the Netherlands, and some regions in Germany, Austria, Switzerland, in the north and in the east of France (especially in Lorraine), as well as in Slovakia, the Czech Republic, and Hungary. St Nicholas was a bishop of Myra (Asia Minor, now Turkey) in the late third and fourth century, and he became the patron saint of sailors, of scholars, and of children because of the stories of miracles and good deeds that he was said to have wrought. He saved some sailors in a storm, delivered three unfairly condemned officers, and offered some money to three girls whose impoverished father was tempted to prostitute them. According to *The Golden Legend* of Jacques de Voragine (from the thirteenth century), in order to help the young girls, the bishop came at three different times and threw some money anonymously in a cloth through the window: it is like a Christmas gift fallen from heaven! The miracle of the three children St Nicholas brought back to life from the salting pot could be a corrupted version of the tale of the three prisoners emerging from their tower. Developed by the Norman poet Wace around 1150, the story first appeared in the eleventh century, in Godehard of Hildesheim's work. The cult of St Nicholas grew in Europe after the translation of his relics to Bari (Italy) in 1087. Because of a relic of one finger brought to Port, he went on to become the patron saint of Lorraine (Méchin 1978; Vincent et al. 2015). As his fame spread in new regions, St Nicholas took on some of the traits of German gods, such as Wotan or the Wild Hunter, well known in Europe under different names and guises, including, for instance, the faculty of going from rooftop to rooftop on a flying steed. This generous distributor of gifts comes with a frightful Bogeyman threatening with his rods who goes by various names: *Père Fouettard, Hans Trapp, Knecht Ruprecht,*

Krampus, Mikulas, Schmuzli, Hóseker, and *Zwarte Piet*. Although there are concerns today, especially in the Netherlands, that this is a racist trope, the origins of this dark creature were not based in depictions of ethnicity. The partnership between the two contrasting figures derives from an ancient New Year's tradition where the generous people—with beautiful suits like the *Gilles* of Binche, distributing fruits—come side-by-side with ugly and frightening ones, covered with straw or dark furs. Both are still present in some masquerades in January, as in the Appenzell in Switzerland, or in February in German and Austrian carnivals. Symbolizing prosperity and life, the nice ones are accompanied by the ugly ones, who represent death, sterility, and winter. More than just cruelty, they personify the hereafter: a fearsome, unknown and uncivilized world, which is obscure, as were the forests in the Middle Ages (Ueltschli 2012: 71). Today, St Nicholas is the nice one who has been Christianized, and he sometimes still comes with the shaggy Bogeyman. Like Santa, all the gift distributors keep this same ambiguous balance, keeping in play what is fair and right.

Arriving with the winter, Santa Claus is now a universal figure: with his stuffed red suit and his long white beard, he is today the main gift distributor. He comes with his reindeers from a wintery place, the North Pole, as the Wild Hunter was supposed to wander with his steeds during the winter solstice period. Reimagined as St Nicholas or St Nick, he lost his austerity in the United States, where he became 'a right jolly old elf', and gained 'a broad face and a little round belly' in Clement C. Moore's 1822 poem. In 1855, the French writer George Sand mentioned '*le petit Père Noël*', a tiny creature who came during the night through the fireplace to distribute his gifts. After World War II, Santa came to Europe in full force, where he was already known, usually as a hieratic person called *Saint Nicolas, Bonhomme Noël, Père Janvier, Père Chalande, Knecht Ruprecht*, or *Weihnachtsmann*. In the 1950s, the gap widened between pagan Christmas and Christian Christmas: well accepted before, Father Christmas was supposed to be Jesus' loyal messenger. In December 1951, at the gate of the cathedral of Dijon (France), some priests set his effigy on fire in front of many children, denouncing him as a usurper and heretical. Promoted by reading an article in *France-Soir* about this event, the anthropologist Claude Lévi-Strauss theorized belief in Santa as a rite of passage, and saw a connection between the gifts given to the children and offerings to ancestors in the past: 'the Christmas gifts are a real sacrifice to the sweetness of the art of living, which consists first of not dying' (Lévi-Strauss 1952: 1572). As time went on, Santa Claus's life was made even more concrete: he would live in the Arctic Circle, in Rovaniemi in Finland, for instance, with a wife and several elves to help him in his work.

In Europe, some other gift distributors are also famous. In Catholic families, *le Petit Jésus* is often mentioned, which allows there to be a connection between the gifts and the Nativity. After the Reformation in the sixteenth century, the cult of St Nicolas was sometimes forbidden in Protestant regions and replaced by the *Christkindel*, a young girl in a long white dress and wearing a crown, who acts as Jesus' messenger. Also named *Christmas Angel* or *Dame de Noël*, she is still popular in some regions of Germany, Austria, Switzerland, and Alsace. In Spain, on the eve of Kings' Day, the distributors of gifts are the *Santos Reyes* (the Holy Kings), who, according to Matthew's Gospel, went to Bethlehem following the star, to honour Jesus with precious gifts.

Tradition called these three Magi, Melchior, Caspar, and Balthazar, and made them kings. In Italy, the mysterious *Befana* comes on the same night to give her presents. The disobedient children are supposed to receive some coal from this witch riding her broom in the air. She is worrying and dangerous to those who do not respect her invisibility (Cattabiani, 1994: 113).

Gifts for the New Year, the *étrennes*, were known in ancient Rome, as the Latin poet Ovid describes them in *Fasti*. Given on the Kalends of January, their sweetness was supposed to announce a sweet year ahead: honey, figs, and dates served for this purpose. Ovid already perceived that many people would prefer to receive money, because of the general 'thirst for profit'! Until the beginning of the twentieth century, items of food such as sweets, biscuits, and oranges were the main Christmas gifts. Already established in wealthy families, the toys came later, in parallel with the growth of the bourgeoisie and of department stores in the nineteenth century (Perrot 2013: 19). Today, the *étrennes* are no longer Christmas gifts, but gratuities for the New Year, usually in the form of money, given to those in the service sector including door attendants, firefighters, and postal workers.

The chimney and fireplace, through which the gifts are supposed to fall from heaven, is an important part of Christmas in people's imaginations. Next to it, symbolizing the person himself or herself in an intimate way, the shined shoe or stocking is like an outstretched hand. The letter to Santa is another prominent Advent undertaking. Children would sometimes cut out a picture from a toy catalogue and include it in order to make their request quite clear. There are special post offices for letters to Santa such as those in Libourne (France) and in Rovaniemi (Finland). In Swiss Romandie, children shouted their wishes to the *Père Chalande* through the fireplace. In Germany, they would leave a letter with some sugar on the envelope on the windowsill for the *Christkind*. In France, since 1962, children can receive a response from Santa: the first model was written by the famous French pediatrician Françoise Dolto (Cretin 2010: 106).

Even if the family does not attend Midnight Mass, Christmas Eve can still have a reverent tone. In Germany and Austria, the children discover the lit tree and the gifts. With their parents, they sing *O Tannenbaum* when they enter the living room. This ritual resembles a prayer; one's own childhood is recalled, and ancestors are remembered. In France (Auvergne, Provence), even as late as the beginning of the twentieth century, families would leave out some plates of the Christmas dinner for their departed relatives to find during the night. As with the fire of the Yule log, this spiritual presence makes one realize that Christmas is also linked to Samain (which became Halloween), at the beginning of the Celtic year, a time out of time. Known in several European countries, the Yule log, like a sacred 'new fire', is attested in 1184 in Germany. In the thirteenth century, the Norman vassals had to offer one to their lord as a fee. In most families, it was lit with ceremony, as the Provencal writer Frédéric Mistral described in 1906 in his *Memories*. Placed with care by the oldest and youngest members of the family, the log was blessed: some wine or olive oil was poured on it, in the hope that the New Year would be prosperous, productive, and healthy. In Brittany, people would kneel in front of it. A brand was put aside, which would be burnt again in stormy weather. Often replaced by stoves or woodburners, the fireplaces disappeared and along with them the use of the log. Today, the French *bûche de Noël* is a dessert for Christmas in the form of a Yule log. Several pastry chefs had the idea for it at the end of the nineteenth century.

In ancient Rome, large, domestic meals would take place on Saturnalia, at the winter solstice period, and on the eve of the Kalends of January: this *tabula fortunata,* which was supposed to comfort and bring good fortune for the New Year, is attested in the fourth century (Monfrin 2003: 110). Abundance promises abundance. The big meal on Christmas Eve, with the family, and on New Year's Eve, usually with friends, have the same meaning. Many people prefer Christmas dinner on 25 December rather than Christmas Eve—or on a day close by if it is more convenient. In Alsace, the typical menu included representatives of water (fish), earth (pork), and air (poultry). Until the 1950s, European farmers would kill a pig before Christmas, as indicated already in the French *Roman de Renart* (twelfth century). Now paired with fine wines, the quintessential French menu includes oysters, smoked salmon, foie gras, stuffed poultry, and a *bûche* for dessert. Always abundant in spices, marzipan, and dried fruits—like the German *Stollen,* the Italian *Panetone,* and the English pudding—the Christmas desserts can be counted on as part of the feast as well. According to a 'tradition' now unchangeable, the thirteen desserts are famous in Provence. They used to be more variable but their number was fixed at thirteen in the 1920s (Brégeon-Poli 1995: 145). They are made with fresh, candied, or dried fruits, white and black nougats, and a *pompe à l'huile* or a *gibassié,* kinds of fougasse. The dried fruits are called *les quatre mendiants,* 'the four beggars' (since they have the same colour as the monks' cowl of the mendicant orders) and include plums, dried grapes, almonds, and other nuts. Thirteen was the number of the 'calendric breads' eaten at this time of year in seventeenth-century Provence: twelve small breads around a big one, like Jesus with his twelve apostles.

The Twelve Days are famous for divination regarding the weather: each day would announce the fate of one of the months to come in the new year. They still occasion cards games on New Year's Eve, and cakes like *la galette des Rois* on Kings' Day where a bean is hidden inside (a China fève since 1875 in Saxony). The ritualized distribution of the cake, called *Le Roi boit,* was already known in 1311 in Amiens (France). The youngest of the company would go under the table to designate to whom the piece of cake would go. The nomination of this 'king' is reminiscent of the ancient election with dice of a fancy king on the Roman Saturnalia. Still in the 1950s, on the farms the animals had an extra portion of food on Christmas Eve, in memory of Bethlehem. During the night, the animals were reputed to speak, but it was forbidden to listen to them, otherwise misfortune would happen!

CHRISTMAS IN PUBLIC PLACES

Even before the decoration of the houses, the towns are already garnished with greenery and special lights in November. A Christmas sightseeing tour by bus or boat allows people to witness this beautiful but short-lived sight. In the big cities, avenues are officially lit around 20 November by a leading figure (such as a comedian or singer), a notable example being the Champs-Elysées since 1982. This, in turn, was modelled on Regent Street in London, which was already known for its Christmas lights in the 1950s. A tall Christmas tree is erected on a central square in places such as Strasbourg, Paris, and the Vatican. The stores are decorated. Twenty-four windows of some town halls are lit up, like a gigantic Advent calendar, in Augsburg (Germany), for instance, since 1977.

The Nativity scene, the traditional representation of Jesus' birth, is accepted in public places almost everywhere: there is even one every year in the hall of the European Parliament at Brussels. In Cracow (Poland), next to Adam Mickiewicz's statue, a famous competition of Nativity scenes, *Szopki*, has taken place every first Thursday of December since 1937. In France, however, because of secularism and freethinking, the presence of the crèche is contested if it is set up at town halls, hospitals, or railway stations, on the grounds that it is a 'conspicuous religious sign'. Some of these quarrels have led to judicial rulings. In October 2015, two court decisions were absolutely opposed. In Nantes, the Administrative Tribunal accepted the presence of a Nativity scene since it belongs to a popular Christmas tradition, while two days later, the Melun Court of Appeal prohibited it. On 7 April 2019, Pope Francis insisted that such prohibitions were unacceptable.

With the desire to be generous that is awakened during the Christmas period, it has become an important period for commercial activity. The French ethnologist Martine Segalen explains the necessary 'ceremonial waste' well known in the related case of weddings: the lavish expenses serve as a sign predicting future prosperity and abundance. Set in central public squares, Christmas markets or *Christkindelmarkts* have existed since the late Middle Ages. The one at Strasbourg can be traced back at least to 1570. All sorts of Christmas decorations and pastries are sold there; the hot wine is well appreciated in this cold period. Parts of some Christmas markets, like Strasbourg's or the famous one in Nüremberg (from 1653), are exported now to cities including New York and Tokyo. Distinct from the markets, the Provencal fairs called *foires aux santons* have existed since 1803 (the one at Marseille being the oldest) at Christmastide.

Since the 1950s, department stores have constructed highly popular Santa's workshops, where the children can meet the gift giver. The window displays are famous: the first one in Paris, in 1909 in *Le Bon Marché*, depicted the discovery of the North Pole by Robert Peary with automatons. Modern technology has made many advances on how these displays are contrived, and these windows are now the highlight of Parisian Christmas sightseeing.

Best wishes and Christmas carols used to be sung by groups of young children going door to door. Everywhere in Europe such ritual visits might occur from around 21 December until Epiphany, but this tradition largely disappeared over the course of the twentieth century. The version with three children disguised as Magi, and a fourth holding a star, however, is still well known in Austria, Germany, and Switzerland. The children sometimes write with chalk near the front door the initials of the Magi and the year. It is important to give treats or money to these young visitors, in order to receive the good wishes they bring, since they are the guardians of the future. Those who give nothing or will not open their door are supposed to have a bad year, and the children speak forebodingly about what is ahead for them. This element of blessing and cursing also adds to the magical aura of these visits. Sometimes, adults will go door to door with children to show a small, wooden Nativity scene, such as in Hungary or in Slovakia. In Austria, near Salzburg, the tour of 'Wearing the Lady' (the Virgin Mary) is given during the nine days before Christmas. In Romania, the 'Herods' are an occasion for young boys to go and visit neighbours in the role of the Magi: they begin their tour by visiting the nicest girls!

Ovid explained that 'good words must be spoken' on the Kalends of January. In the same way, wishes are usually written on cards sent during Advent or later in January. Christmas cards became well known during the second half of the nineteenth century, but there are examples from the fifteenth century in Alsace, with Baby Jesus on them. The cards are often sold for humanitarian causes, such as UNICEF since 1949. Christmas good cheer makes the wallets as open as the hearts! Especially since the Victorian age, with the tales of England's Charles Dickens, Denmark's Hans Christian Andersen, and France's François Coppée, people are particularly receptive to the distress of the poor at this time of year. Many charity fundraisers and television campaigns for those suffering from diseases and disabilities, such as the *Téléthon* in France, happen in December. Meals are organized for the lonely, and unused toys are collected in many places to give to needy children.

Young carollers are in the streets. During the Christmas holidays, entertainment is all the rage. Many people go to circuses, theatres, concerts, or the opera. There are special puppets shows like *Tchantchès* adventures in Liège (Belgium), or Barbizier's ones in the *Crèche Bisontine* in Besançon (France). In Provence, the *pastorales* are acted in theatres: Bethlehem is no more than a pretext to a comic show where the faults of some villagers are mocked. The first one was in Marseille, the *Pastorale Maurel* (1844). Some street parades take place, like the St Nicholas and his Bogeyman's one in Lorraine, or the Magi's exotic one with camels in Spain, or in Aix-en-Provence.

These Christmas 'traditions'—a word which shows their desired unchanging nature, even for the new ones—are still alive in Catholic Europe, even if its inhabitants are believing less. People are glad to observe the family customs. An evolution can be observed with social changes and stepfamilies: some children are invited to five or six Christmases. Secularism will not succeed in eliminating this feast to which so many families are so deeply committed.

References and Further Reading

Brégeon-Poli, Brigitte (1995). 'Va pour treize!' *Terrain*, 24: 45–152.
Cabantous, Alain and Walter, François (2016). *Noël. Une si longue histoire*....Paris: Payot et Rivages.
Cattabiani, Alfredo (1994). *Calendario*. Milano: Rusconi Libri.

Cretin, Nadine (2010). *Histoire du Père Noël*. Toulouse: Le Pérégrinateur.
Cretin Nadine (2013). *Noëls des Provinces de France*. Toulouse: Le Pérégrinateur.
Dahhaoui, Yann (2013). 'L'évêque de Paris, le légat et la fête des fous à Notre-Dame. Histoire de l'interprétation d'une ordonnance (1198)', in *Notre-Dame de Paris, 1163-2013*, Turnhout: Brepols: 367-83.
Dorival Gilles and Boyer Jean-Paul (ed.) (2003). *La Nativité et le temps de Noël. Antiquité et Moyen-Âge*. Vol. 1. Bertrand, Régis (ed.) (2003). *La Nativité et le temps de Noël. XVIIe-XXe siècle*. vol. 2, Aix-en-Provence: PUP (Publications de l'Université de Provence).
Fabre, Daniel (1992). Carnaval *ou la fête à l'envers*. Paris: Gallimard.
Gockerell, Nina (1998). *Krippen. Nativity scenes. Crèches*. Bayerisches Nationalmuseum, Münich: Taschen.
Gockerell, Nina hrsg (2000). *Weihnachtszeit, Feste zwischen Advent und Neujahr in* Süddeutschland und Österreich, *1840-1940*. München: Prestel.
Lautman, Françoise (1986). *Crèches et traditions de Noël*. Paris: RMN.
Leser, Gérard (1989). *Noël-Wihnachte en Alsace: Rites, coutumes, croyances*. Mulhouse: Ed. du Rhin.
Levi-Strauss, Claude (1952). 'Le Père Noël supplicié', *Les Temps modernes, 77*. Paris: Julliard: 1572-90.
Mallé, Marie-Pascale (2006). *Faire la crèche en Europe*. Paris: RMN.
Méchin, Colette (1978). *Saint Nicolas. Fête et traditions populaires*. Paris: Berger-Levrault.
Monfrin, Françoise (2003). 'La fête des Calendes de Janvier entre Noël et Epiphanie', in Dorival and Boyer (eds.), *La Nativité et le temps de Noël: Antiquité et Moyen-Âge*. Aix-en-Provence: Publications de l'Université de Provence: 95-119.
Perrot, Martyne (2000). *Ethnologie de Noël: Une fête paradoxale*. Paris: Grasset.
Perrot, Martyne (2013). *Le cadeau de Noël: Histoire d'une invention*. Paris: Editions Autrement, Paris.
Soler y Amigó, Joan (2007). *Tradicionari del Nadal Català*. Barcelona: Ed. Joan Soler Amigó.
Ueltschli, Karin (2012). *Histoire véridique du Père Noël. Du traîneau à la hotte*. Paris: Imago.
Vincent, Catherine et al. (2015). *En Orient et en Occident le culte de saint Nicolas en Europe. Xe-XXIe siècle*. Paris: Ed. du Cerf.

CHAPTER 35

GERMANY AND SCANDINAVIA

JOE PERRY

Outside observers have long recognized that Germans and Scandinavians feel intense connections to Christmas.[1] 'The great festival of the year in Norway, as among all Germanic nations, is Christmas', wrote one observer in 1876. 'The preparations for the Yule-tide...would for American eyes, look perfectly enormous' (Anon. 1876: 2). As this comment and many like it suggest, the peoples of northern Europe created an impressive reservoir of holiday observances. This chapter explores their history across the nineteenth and twentieth centuries, when today's holiday took shape. Proceeding across themes, in chronologically organized sections, the chapter opens with the nineteenth-century fascination with pre-Christian 'Nordic' solstice rituals and their relationship to the contemporary holiday, and then examines the 'new' family Christmas, a celebration of middle-class values consolidated by 1900. The chapter then turns to the impact of consumer culture and evolving mass media and the nationalization and politicization of this supposedly private family festival in the twentieth century.

Christmas observances in northern Europe repeatedly crossed boundaries normally kept separate: between the sacred and the secular, the public and the private, the personal and the political, the commercial and the authentic. From the start, such syncretism generated concern. Critics carped that waning piety, excessive commercialization, or drunken frivolity threatened the 'true meaning' of the holiday. Customs did evolve, but this chapter argues that such changes were both inventive and productive. Annual festivities were guided by common observances that brought people together, but they also encouraged improvisation and conflict. Christmas in Germany and Scandinavia (and elsewhere) was never static, but was a mutable set of ritualized practices, which opened space for the contestation, clarification, and reproduction of changing ideals of religious faith, family affection, and community belonging.

[1] This chapter is dedicated to the memory of my late mother Frances, whose unbounded love for Swedish Christmas inspired my own.

'Pagan Survivals': Myths and Origins

The pagan symbols and rites that underlie today's Christmas have long exerted a pull on the scholarly and popular imaginations. The historic roots of the Christmas tree, for example, reportedly grew out of celebrations of the pre-Christian Germanic tribes. Countless popular accounts suggest that the forebears of the decorated tree or the mischievous Scandinavian Christmas *tomten* (house gnome) lie 'in the pagan celebration of the passing of the seasons in the darkest days of winter' (Perabo 2015: 1), and that the ancient Nordic word 'jul' indeed persists, in the Yule Log and the use of *jul* as the name for Christmas across Scandinavia. Historian Gerry Bowler, however, casts doubts on these ties to times primordial: 'Most of these pagan connections are grossly exaggerated', he writes, 'and anthropologists have pointed out that many ceremonies that supposedly date to an animist past are of comparatively recent origins' (Bowler 2000: 170).

If scholars today approach the supposed links between pagan and modern customs with some reserve, nineteenth-century folklorists and theologians did not. They obsessively claimed that the history of Christmas revealed the ancient traces of the national people or 'folk', and their accounts are richly revealing about the way what we might now call 'invented traditions' were fabricated and popularized (Hobsbawm and Ranger 1983). The Nordic-German holiday had particular resonance, concluded numerous scholars, because northern European customs connected the Christian and the pagan. 'Christmas with us has both a national and religious meaning,' wrote Swedish linguist Carl Ekbohrn in 1854. 'Upon the ruins of the old heathen festival grew the new', he explained, 'but it gained an even more sacred significance as it was now celebrated in memory of the birth of our Savior' (Ekbohrn 1854: 1, 2). German scholars were even more eager to uncover the 'Teutonic' origins of the Christian holiday. By the end of the century, books such as such as Alexander Tille's *Geschichte der Deutschen Weihnacht* (History of German Christmas, 1893) or Gustav Bilfinger's *Das germanische Julfest* (The Germanic Yule Fest, 1901) confidently assured readers that Christmas spanned historical time, linking the German '*Volk*' (people) to their national pre-Christian ancestors.

Popular literature spread such notions to wide audiences. In his 1878 *Golden Christmas Book*, Professor Hugo Elm explained that the 'mysterious magic' of the German holiday derived from the 'pagan-German worldview' and winter solstice rites of our 'Nordic-Germanic forefathers' (Elm 1878: 1, 19–20). Such proud assertions became familiar clichés. By 1885 a Frankfurt reporter could ironically remark that the connections made between the holiday and 'ancient Germanic sacrificial festivals and other holy pagan customs' were 'the typical subjects in the conventional Christmas articles of many newspapers' (Perry 2010: 56). By 1912 explanations of what folklorist Clement Miles called 'pagan survivals' filled almost 200 pages of his now-classic account of the holiday's history (Miles 1976: 159–356).

Although the pagan foundations of the Nordic holiday continued to inspire fascination, the holiday observed today had more obvious precursors, which date to the early modern period. Established Christian observances, including saint's days, Advent, and the Nativity provided the holiday's annual backbone. The timing of agricultural cycles undergirded an annual festival season conducive to feasting and celebration, as peasants (and city dwellers) consumed stores of grain or livestock that would not survive the winter (Nissenbaum 1996: 5). Sometime around 1800, the common aristocratic practice of ringing in the New Year by sharing modest gifts was moved to Christmas Eve. On another level, the most fundamental Christmas scene—deep countryside bedecked with snow, green pines casting scent into the night, twinkling starlight—was unthinkable without the forests and ever-shorter days that heralded the arrival of deep winter in northern Europe. Such visions remain embedded in our current celebrations, with their insistence on a 'White Christmas' and snow-filled Nativity scenes, no matter what the region.

'CHRISTMAS TURNED OUT TO BE MOST BEAUTIFUL': INVENTING MIDDLE-CLASS TRADITIONS

Early modern traditions and landscapes thus informed the nineteenth-century holiday. They took shape in the urban homes of the upper bourgeoisie, moved down social hierarchies to the middling classes, and travelled from big cities to smaller towns. E. T. A Hoffmann's *Nutcracker and the Mouse King*, first published in German in 1816 and translated into Swedish in 1848 and Danish in 1856, represented an initial step in the process. This famous fairy tale about a young girl's struggles in a magic land was an early example of prescriptive literature about how to observe a 'proper' holiday, in ways that preserved but also transformed older observances.

The story was set in the sort of wealthy bourgeois household that would first experiment with the new Christmas traditions; the father is a state physician, and the cosmopolitan parents can afford an elaborately decorated tree and sumptuous gifts. With talking mice and animate objects, the tale draws on but reworks peasant superstitions about animals that spoke on Christmas Eve. The narrative's one gesture toward an otherwise entirely jettisoned religious faith is seen in the children's belief that the '*Christkind*' (Christ Child, pictured in German and Scandinavian sources as a young boy or girl with angel wings) delivered their gifts, before flying away on a cloud to visit other happy youngsters. The use of a remade baby Jesus as the holiday's gift-bringer was an early example of the potent melding of the sacred and secular that came increasingly to define the nineteenth-century holiday. The story was also an early example of a turn towards bourgeois domesticity. The *Nutcracker* depicted an idealized, loving family Christmas and the rich sensual and emotional world evoked by opening gifts around a beautiful tree, wrapped up in childlike expressions of innocence and nostalgia for a 'better' Christmas past. This was perhaps the most forward-looking aspect of the tale.

Hoffmann's bedtime story captured many of the features that would eventually make Christmas 'Christmas', but it took time for such features to crystallize into what we recognize today as the German or Scandinavian holiday, elements of which penetrated British, North American, and other national traditions. On one hand, this was a story of loss. The early nineteenth-century Christmas was still 'so permeated by specific local customs that it presents a picture of quite spectacular herterogeneity' (Miller 2017: 414), and many of these observances have vanished. Yet this was also a story of remarkable invention and productivity. Across the second half of the nineteenth century, Christmas changed in ways that reflected the values and lifestyles, the moral economy as it were, of the ever-growing middle classes. Christmas celebrated Christian faith, to be sure, but also private life and domesticity, material abundance, social status and stability, and national belonging.

The Christmas tree, perhaps the key holiday symbol, exemplified this evolution: its spread took decades. The tree has deep but obscure roots, and the widely held notion that it was 'made in Germany' deserves some qualification; it seems to have emerged across the Nordic world at about the same time. In 1741, Countess Cristina Wrede-Sparre recorded the first mention of a tree in Sweden, a tall fir surrounded by gifts and decorated with candles, apples, and saffron buns. Danish Countess Wilhelmine Holstein observed Christmas around a Christmas tree with her daughter in 1808. Caroline von Humboldt, wife of the famous philosopher Wilhelm, celebrated a holiday in Berlin in 1815 with two trees, much like that described in the *Nutcracker*. 'Christmas has turned out to be most beautiful', Humboldt wrote her husband, it brought 'so much joy' (Perry 2010: 13–14).

As these 'first' reports show, the tree and holiday festivities were organized by women, and the gendered trope of 'the good mother with children', celebrated at its most appealing around the Christmas tree, would be one of the foundations of the middle-class lifestyles that would dominate the nineteenth century. The actual shape of the tree was still in flux. Early illustrations from elite households show that it was usually small and installed on a tabletop, could be hung from the ceiling, or might take the form of a pyramid-shaped candleholder. The Franco-Prussian War (1870–1871) helped spread and nationalize the custom in Germany. However idealized, pictures of and stories about proud German soldiers celebrating Christmas around a tree 'in enemy territory' were staples of wartime reports and postwar veteran's memoirs (Perry 2010: 97–103). After German unification in 1871, holiday imagery invariably included trees decorated with the national flag and children playing with toys deemed to be gender-appropriate: boys riding rocking horses wearing 'pickle-sticker' helmets and brandishing sabres, and girls playing with dolls.

Contemporaries acknowledged that the tree was a German import, but as it grew increasingly common in Sweden, Denmark, and Norway, it was nationalized there as well, in part by simply adding the national flag to its decorative scheme. One of the most popular Danish Christmas songs, *Højt fra træets grønne top* (From High Upon the Green Tree's Top), written in 1848 during a territorial war with Prussia, showcased the decorated tree and the Danish flag, but never mentioned the baby Jesus—a nationalist appropriation of both sacred and secular family observances (Warburg 2017: 137). The tree's popularity overcame alternate traditions. As the '*julgran*' (Christmas tree) penetrated Swedish observances in the 1850s and 60s, for example, it pushed aside the widely used '*julträd*', an elaborately carved wooden candleholder. Two or three feet tall, the *julträd* held numerous candles, but also had spikes for decoration with apples, which children could 'plunder' on Christmas Eve (Bringéus 1991: 108). By 1900, new and now-national customs served a more visible role in both preserving and helping to forge an evolving sense of identity beyond national borders. Whether expressed through the treasured lutefish or lamb ribs that Norwegian immigrants ate for Christmas dinner in the United States or the ersatz trees that German settlers decorated in the African colonies, Christmas evoked the homeland in faraway places (Stokker 2001: 76–8; Perry 2010: 62).

The standardization of the holiday's gift-bringer also turned older traditions into now-familiar observances that celebrated middle-class lifestyles. The German Weihnachtsmann (Father Christmas) was not only a distant relative of St Nicholas, he also represented 'the last of the wild men' (Siefker 2006)—the evil, child-threatening trolls, devils, and spooks, who abounded in early modern European folk tales. The kindly Father Christmas, who emerged around 1850, was a sanitized version of these frightening beast-men; he still punished the bad but rewarded the good. In many ways Father Christmas's visit also replaced early modern mumming rituals, in which groups of masked artisans spent evenings in the holiday season drinking and carousing through villages or towns demanding symbolic handouts from their social superiors (Gunnell 2007). Class-based demands made by masked strangers for 'presents' now became family gifts, tokens of parental affection, as the holiday was moved inside and cleaned up at the cost of more diverse folk traditions. Newly invented family rituals accompanied Father Christmas's Christmas Eve visit. He read the names of good and bad children from his golden book, and demanded proof of a child's industry by asking him or her to recite from memory a prayer, poem, or song. Such tests had a serious side. They required diligent study and afforded parents a means to discipline children throughout the year ('he knows if you've been bad or good'). Waiting until Christmas Eve to open gifts, and 'paying' for them through recitation reinforced the middle-class values of education and delayed gratification; this 'cultural organization of anticipation' furthermore regulated excessive material desires, a key lesson for those growing up in an emerging consumer society (Löfgren 1993: 219).

Father Christmas became wildly popular in the nineteenth century, yet children (and adults) in Germany and Scandinavia enjoyed (and still enjoy) the ministrations of a wide variety of other magical gift-bringers. In Germany, the Weihnachtsmann and the Christkind were sometimes accompanied by a more ominous figure who had various names—Krampus, say, or Pelznichol—a furred, horned beast who might beat or carry away 'bad' children in a burlap sack; Krampus and his ilk have enjoyed something of a recent revival in Austria and southern Germany (Basu and Little 2014). In Norway, remnants of mumming traditions survived in the semi-menacing *julebukken* (Christmas goat), dressed in a furry goatskin with devilish horns, who with his followers visited families on Christmas Eve (Hodne 1982: 37).

By the end of the nineteenth century, most Scandinavian children received their gifts from the *jultomten* (Swedish) or *julenisse* (Danish/Norwegian), a white-bearded house gnome or goblin wearing a bright red cap who lived outdoors, typically in the stables or perhaps in a nearby forest. The house *tomten*, another so-called 'pagan survival' (really a nineteenth-century invention), could be grumpy and might work some sort of mischief if he did not receive a treat, perhaps porridge with cream, on Christmas Eve. In the end, though, he was a good-natured trickster, often accompanied by a goat pulling a sled full of presents. Straw goats of various sizes, held together by straps of red ribbon, are still a favourite Swedish holiday decoration.

The cast of holiday players in Scandinavia included St Lucia, a Christian virgin originally martyred in third-century Sicily, who by the nineteenth century sometimes visited Swedish families on the morning of 13 December. The Scandinavian Lucia appears as a girl or young woman dressed in a white gown and a crown with candles in her hair. She typically presents a tray of coffee and saffron buns to her parents, while singing the mid-nineteenth-century Italian song 'Santa Lucia'—which has different sets of lyrics about night, cold, and light in the different Scandinavian countries. Was St Lucia some Scandinavian version of the German Christkind? Was she related to the early modern witches and monsters who welcomed long December nights with increased activity? The sources do not answer, but it is clear that she was first mentioned in late eighteenth-century Swedish texts. Her feast day corresponded to the solstice season, which helped her household rites become a symbol of the return of light and spring that combined religious, nationalist, and familial elements (Bringéus 1999: 119). Although Lucia masqueraded as an age-old tradition, she was actually a much more recent phenomenon: her rituals only took off in Stockholm in the 1920s, made their way to other Scandinavian countries, and then to public institutions such as schools, factories, and senior centres—another example of the bourgeoisification, feminization, and nationalization of Christian, and perhaps even pagan, traditions. (Löfgren 1993: 220).

As the history of the evolving Lucia carol suggests, songs were key to the holiday season. In part, this was because learning to perform music was central to the ideal of self-cultivation that flourished in nineteenth-century bourgeois homes, and carols were an important part of the repertoire (Weber-Kellermann 1994: 199). Each country had its own treasured songs, which ranged across topical–emotional spectrums from pious hymns to jovial children's ditties about presents and Father Christmas. The German-language carol and international 'hit' 'Silent Night' (1818) expressed the holy peace brought to Earth by the Saviour's birth, while 'O Christmas Tree' (1824) captured the beauty of an emerging custom with lyrics that ignore faith all together. The popular, mid-nineteenth-century, Swedish-Danish song 'Nu är det Jul igen' (Now It Is

Christmastime Again) with its sing-song melody and repetitive nonsense lyrics about Christmas and Easter, was typically sung by celebrants as they held hands and danced around the tree. It represented the family fest at its most raucous, just one example of the intimate ways carols, popular piety, middle-class values, and national traditions came together and reinforced one another, as they helped 'reinvent' Christmas during the nineteenth century.

'THE MOST BEAUTIFUL CHRISTMAS TREE': CHRISTMAS STORIES AND NATIONAL TRADITIONS

By the 1870s, stories about the meaning of Christmas and illustrations of domestic festivities in newspapers, family magazines, and Christmas gift books helped popularize and nationalize the customs that took shape in the first half of the century. As we have seen, articles about the meaning of Christmas filled the holiday issues of daily and weekly newspapers. By the 1870s, pictures of decorated trees and family celebrations also adorned the annual Christmas issues of illustrated magazines such as the German *Leipziger Illustrierter Zeitung* (founded in 1843); the Swedish *Ny Illusterad Tidning* (1865); and the Danish *Illustretet Familie-Journal* (1877). Family 'Christmas Books' (e.g. *Weihnachtsbücher* in German or *julbøker* in Norwegian) appeared in increasing numbers in the second half of the nineteenth century. The contents of these sometimes lavish volumes, often cast as Christmas Eve gifts, varied. Some were determinedly Christian, with poems and prayers for children to learn and recite—perhaps attempts to preserve piety in an era of advancing secularization. Others, such as Norwegian folklorist and bishop Jørgan Moe's 1859 *En liden Julegave* (A Little Christmas Gift) were volumes of poetry with minimal holiday content, obviously meant to sharpen reading skills. Yet others, such as Swedish professor Carl Ekbohrn's 1854 *Jul-Bocken: Handbok för Trefnad och Nöje under Julen* (Christmas Goat: Handbook for Coziness and Entertainment) or Elm's *Golden Christmas Book* contained potted histories of the holiday; Christmas stories and poems, some famous some not; instructions for decorating the tree and otherwise observing holiday customs; and games to play during holiday leisure time. Such texts consistently reminded readers of the joys and beauty of proud national–familial traditions.

The popularization of the Swedish gift-bringing *tomten* (and his Danish and Norwegian counterparts) exemplified the way emerging forms of print media contributed to the standardization of holiday practices, even as they helped produce distinct national traditions. The *tomten* gained attention with the publication of romantic author Viktor Rydberg twenty-page 1871 children's book *Lille Viggs äventyr på julafton* (Little Vigg's Christmas Eve Adventure). Pictures by the 18-year-old artist Jenny

Nyström helped sell the book and marked her debut as a famous Swedish illustrator. Rydberg and Nyström collaborated again in the 1881 poem 'Tomten,' first published in the *Ny Illusterad Tidning*. Rydberg's poem describes the secret visit of a grizzled but hardy *tomten* to a family farm on a cold Christmas Eve, when 'Midwinter's nightly frost is hard' (the first line of the poem). The *tomten* watches carefully over the barn animals, the parents, and the children, but also ruminates on the passing of time and the riddles of human mortality. Nyström's accompanying picture portrayed a lonely *tomten* at his most dwarfish standing guard on the farmhouse's porch; poem and picture reminded readers of the spiritual depths of the holiday season and gave voice to a powerful romantic–nationalist nostalgia for vanishing rural life, common throughout Scandinavia.

Rydberg's works would become Swedish holiday standards, while Nyström's ability to draw beautiful *tomten* in any number of sentimental guises and situations turned her into a national treasure. Nyström's *tomten* evolved. By the 1890s, the dwarf-like figure had sometimes grown taller and donned a red cloak with white fur trimmings; he could look a lot like the German Father Christmas. The unparalleled beauty of his ever-mutable image as pictured by Nyström, and by other Swedish illustrators such as John Bauer (and by Danes and Norwegians as well), was captured in the covers of and pictures in the children's illustrated magazine *Jultomten*, a holiday annual with stories, songs, poems, and games published from 1891 to 1935. Influenced by folk stories and the art nouveau movement, and then later by the sharper lines of modernism, Nyström's widely copied illustrations remain Christmas card and advent calendar standards to the present day (see the online archives at Rydquist 2014 and Jultomten 2019; Neumuller 2009).

Famous Christmas stories, reprinted time and again in newspapers, magazines, and Christmas books, contributed to the emergence of national canons; many first appeared in the 1830s and 1840s. German readers returned again and again to Hoffmann's *Nutcracker*, romantic poet Ludwig Tieck's 1835 'Weihnacht-Abend' (Christmas Eve), or the overtly nationalist 'Unter dem Tannenbaum' (Around the Christmas Tree), written by Theodor Storm in 1862, in which the narrator reminisces about holiday traditions in the lost territories of Schleswig-Holstein, ceded to Denmark in 1851. Already in 1843 Norwegians could imagine Christmases past in folklorist Peter Asbjørnson's 1843 classic 'En gammeldags Juleafton' (An Old-Fashioned Christmas Eve). Danes could point to Hans Christian Andersen's rather gloomy 'Grantræt' (The Fir Tree) of 1844 which tells the story of a naïve yet striving young fir tree, used for a family Christmas and then cast out on the rubbish pile (English translations of Asbjørnson and Andersen in Rossel and Elbrønd-Bek 1996).

Many famous (and not so famous) Christmas stories offered their middle-class readers ways to think about one of the thorniest issues of the nineteenth century: the 'social question'. Tales about the holiday interactions between rich and poor typically portrayed utopian visions of social harmony, in which small acts of bourgeois charity alleviated harsh social inequalities or impious workers found God and pulled themselves up by their bootstraps (Perry 2010: 48–53). In Tieck's 'Christmas Eve', for an early example, a destitute mother and daughter find a God-given silver taler in the

Christmas market and have a happy holiday after all. Ryberg's poor, orphaned Little Vigg, who helps the Christmas *tomten* deliver presents, has to renounce his envy after seeing the grand gifts given to his social superiors.

In some stories, death offered the ultimate resolution to the thorny issues of social inequality. In Andersen's well-known 'Little Match Girl' (1845), the most famous of many similar tales, a shivering urchin dies peacefully after warming herself with a vision of 'the most beautiful Christmas tree' illuminated with thousands of candles and a fine Christmas dinner—a roast goose that, in her fantasy, waddles towards her with a knife and fork in its breast, ready for eating. Some few authors pushed such tales in critical ways. In Norwegian naturalist Amalie Skram's 1885 story 'Karens Jul' (Karen's Christmas), a policeman cares for the impoverished title character and her baby but fails to visit them on Christmas Eve. He finds them on Christmas Day:

> They were both stone-dead. The baby lay up against its mother, in death still holding her breast in its mouth. Down its cheek had trickled from her nipple some drops of blood.... She was terribly emaciated, but on her face there was something like a quiet smile. (Rossel and Elbrønd-Bek 1996: 24)

Such sombre images might have saddened—or titillated—middle-class readers, but they hardly undermined the festivity of the Christmas season. Indeed, nineteenth-century literature ensured that Germans and Scandinavians would celebrate well-scripted holidays. The festivities began with the first Advent Sunday, when many families across northern Europe recognized the coming anniversary of the Nativity by lighting a candle on a special wreath or holder; a new candle was lit on subsequent Advents. A ritual house cleaning, especially in Scandinavia, accompanied other preparations such as shopping for gifts and foods and decorating the home; simple tree ornaments shaped like hearts, stars, birds, or goats—typically made of straw or wood—were (and are) typical Scandinavian household decorations. Feasting and partying with family and friends meant engaging national (but overlapping) traditions that specified distinct holiday foods. Roast goose or duck and red cabbage was particularly German but also popular across the region. Scandinavians might eat lutefisk as part of a traditional meal; other favourites might include roast pork or ham, blood pudding, and any variety of cookies. Designing and maintaining one's personal festive traditions built up an archive of family history across generations, even as it enlisted individuals in the imagined national community.

Christmas Eve—the season's highpoint—combined the sacred and the secular, with gifting rituals around the tree, often seen by children for the first time on the 24th, but also an evening Christmas service at a local church. Following the church calendar, the season extended until Epiphany (6 January), including New Year's festivities; in Sweden the holiday might stretch until Knut's Day (13 January), when the tree was finally taken down and decorations stored for the following year. Fictional accounts that capture the solemnities and pleasures of the late-nineteenth-century bourgeois Christmas Eve can be found in Thomas Mann's *Buddenbrooks* (1909) or more recently in the idealized frolic captured with such loving care by Ingmar Bergman in *Fanny and Alexander* (1982).

As even this short description suggests, observing a 'proper' Christmas was explicitly Christian, exactingly prepared, and expensive, which meant that some groups had problems with the holiday. German Jews were forced into a variety of compromises vis-à-vis Christmas, in ways that reflected the broad diversity of the Jewish community, which was not technically included in the national imaginary constructed around the holiday. Orthodox Jews and Zionists might entirely reject the Christian holiday, while more liberal and acculturated families celebrate what was sometimes called 'Weihnukka'—a syncretic combination of Christmas (Weihnachten) and Hanukkah that included a decorated tree and Christmas Eve gifts. Such celebrations were welcomed by the Jewish children who learned about and observed Christian holiday customs at school, but were regarded with some scepticism by Jewish traditionalists and community organizations (Embacher 1997: 288–90; Perry 2010: 68–76).

Christmas could exacerbate class as well as religious tensions. Despite the visions of social harmony presented in middle-class stories, workers and poorer folk often struggled to celebrate what was still a rather elite holiday simply because of the expense. The Christmas books discussed earlier, for example, were far too expensive for those at the bottom. Working-class memoirs include recollections of cheap handmade gifts, scrawny Christmas trees, and fathers who spent their Christmas bonuses on liquor and passed out at home before they could observe even a modest holiday. For live-in domestic servants serving wealthy families—one of the most common jobs for young working-class women around 1900—Christmas meant undertaking extra work as demanded by the household mistress, not the tender family festival so often described in the prescriptive literature (Perry 2010: 84–92). Although class differences undermined holiday harmony, the modernization of Christmas after 1900 would standardize and popularize mainstream observances, and make them accessible across the social spectrum.

'Commercial at its Very Core': Modernizing Christmas

Starting around 1900 and continuing through the twentieth century, the Christmas shaped by nineteenth-century middle classes was transformed and 'modernized' to meet the needs and address the values of a highly industrialized society. These processes could be seen at work in relatively banal changes, such as the growing use of electric lights to replace candles on the tree or the emergence of a thriving gift-wrap paper industry in Sweden in the 1920s (Bringéus 1999: 141). Father Christmas and the *tomten* could be portrayed, say, talking on the telephone around 1900, flying an aeroplane some twenty-five years later, and taking a rocket to the moon in the 1970s.

As these relatively minor examples suggest, changing traditions were invariably entangled in two main processes dating back to the 1800s: the growth of the mass media and the consolidation of consumer society. As ever, stories about the holiday in newspapers and magazines, and then on the radio, in movies, and on television, aided the ongoing diffusion of customs across classes and regions. And although the increasingly unavoidable commercialization of the holiday remained a consistent focus of cultural critics, it brought joys to many. As historian Stephen Nissenbaum convincingly argues, Christmas was 'commercial from its earliest stages, commercial at its very core...itself a force in the spread of consumer capitalism' (Nissenbaum 1996: xii, 318). The modernization of the holiday democratized and standardized holiday customs, and opened new areas for invention and creativity.

One way to track the history of commercialization is to explore the evolution of the Christmas market, popular across Scandinavia and Germany, and the rise of its competitor, the department store. In early modern Europe, the Christmas market was just one annual street fair of many, an important site of exchange where farmers, artisans, and skilled craftspeople brought their goods to market. After 1800 the holiday market helped anchor changing rituals. Vendors came to sell holiday-related foods, gifts, trinkets, and Christmas trees, and a visit to the market became an indispensable holiday observance.

Yet the Christmas market had a troubled history. By the late nineteenth century, in Berlin, Munich, and elsewhere, city authorities had come to see it as a tawdry nuisance, where the indigent stole, begged or, at best, hawked shabby wares; worse, the market kept holiday shoppers away from the new commercial districts that had grown up around the emerging department stores. In Berlin and Munich the market was forced out of the city centre to working-class suburbs. In an ironic twist, in both cities National Socialist mayors revitalized the downtown fairs in the 1930s in an effort to revive deep 'folk' traditions (see below). After the Second World War, the Christmas market grew ever more popular across northern Europe. It has become an indispensable aspect of the holiday season, a 'time-out-of-time' when revellers enjoy a moment of beauty and nostalgia as they browse through stalls selling mulled wine and handicrafts; in 2007, Germany alone could boast a national total of over 2,100 markets (Lorenz 1987; Perry 2010: 156).

By 1900, however, the newly emerged department store had overtaken the Christmas market as the locus of real economic exchange in the holiday season. Lavishly decorated store windows, with all manner of mobile puppets, snowy landscapes, Christmas trees, and other products, lured shoppers to the new stores, which opened across Scandinavia and Germany in the late-nineteenth century. Those living in rural areas could join the rush by ordering gifts from holiday mail-order catalogues, which evoked but also controlled consumer desires. Sweden's Åhlen & Holms's catalogue, for example, advertised over thirty-two different kinds of pocketknives in 1912 and helped turn them into a popular boy's gift (Löfgren 1991: 84–5).

This was no mistake. Already in the 1890s the December issues of trade journals targeting marketing professionals—a brand new profession—included instructions for full-blown holiday sales campaigns. Interested business owners could purchase model Christmas advertisements, featuring elves and angels, trees, and shining stars, with blank spaces where they could insert their own sales pitch (Perry 2010: 146–50; Hodne 1982: 61–3). Changing forms of commercialization encroached directly on religious time, as city authorities relaxed sumptuary laws and allowed stores to stay open on the Advent Sundays preceding Christmas Eve. Germans called these days 'Golden Sundays' but the Swedish term 'Syltsöndag' (Display-Window-Sunday), which first appeared in the Swedish Academy Dictionary in 1895, reflected more of the truth (Löfgren 1991: 84–6).

Changes in shopping and advertising were thoroughly entangled in emerging forms of mass media that made the Christmas books read by the nineteenth-century bourgeoisie look quaint. Across northern Europe, radio, film, and then television offered novel ways to observe familiar holiday traditions even as they transformed them. By the middle of the 1920s, radio broadcasts had restructured holiday time around daylong holiday shows. In 1928, in north-west Germany, for example, the Christmas Day special began at 6:00 a.m. with the broadcast of a local Christmas Mass, and continued with various Christmas-themed programmes and hours and hours of holiday music. An evening 'Christmas Concert' featured popular dance music until 1:00 a.m., a 'gift' to those who sought holiday revelry (Perry 2010: 178). As in Germany, radio broadcasts in Sweden encouraged listeners to 'feel that they were joining a national event', bringing compatriots together in a 'mass-mediated "we", celebrating Christmas together' (Löfgren 1993: 222).

Film and then television likewise brought national audiences together in changing modes of celebration, which, while novel, played on familiar traditions. Cinema newsreels in the 1920s and 1930s could cover quaint rural customs and bustling city shoppers, famous church choirs and explanations of cherished symbols, in a single reel. The list of classic Christmas feature films, from Norway, Sweden, Denmark, and Germany, is far too long to explore here. But they extended back into the golden age of cinema, when movies such as the 1934 Danish film, *Nøddebo Præstegård* (Nøddebo Parsonage), offered audiences a holiday love story set in the 1860s, about students visiting a parsonage not far from Copenhagen. After the Second World War the pace of production picked up, as holiday standards—dubbed or subtitled—crossed national borders. Bergmann's *Fanny and Alexander* perhaps represents *the* Scandinavian Christmas movie, so much that Swedes (and others) can long for 'a real Fanny-and-Alexander-Christmas' (Löfgren 1991: 87).

The arrival of television in the 1960s brought ever larger national audiences together, further democratizing holiday practices. By the late 1950s, building on a radio tradition, televised 'Advent calendars', short holiday-themed episodes broadcast each day in the weeks leading up to Christmas, were popular across Sweden and Denmark. From 1964 on, St Lucia shows became an annual staple on Swedish TV (Bringéus 1999: 108, 115). On Christmas Eve in 1962, a record-breaking 11.5 million West Germans watched the holiday special *The Little Lord* (Perry 2010: 273). Television also shaped brand new observances. Since 1959, a 'traditional' Swedish Christmas Eve has included watching a selection of about a dozen classic Walt Disney cartoons, centred not on Christmas but on Kalle Anka (Donald Duck). Attempts to take the show off the air were met with public protest, and between 40 and 50 per cent of Swedes tune in to the annual show (Stahl 2009: 2–3).

The ability to record one's own Christmas favourites on tape or video, and the arrival of the Internet in the 1990s (trends that go beyond the scope of this chapter), no doubt fractured national audiences, but also made it easier to curate one's own collection of holiday standards. A recent survey from Germany underscores the impact technological change has had on Christmas. In 2018, sweets (or confectionaries) topped the list of favourite presents, but these were followed closely by gift-coupons and cash, and—for men especially—CDs, DVDs, and electronic games (Deloitte 2018).

'THE MOST GERMAN OF HOLIDAYS': NATIONALISM AND POLITICS

By the early twentieth century, northern Europeans could cherish their distinct national Christmas traditions, from the 'Teutonic' roots of the Christmas tree to the Scandinavian *tomten*, which epitomized the country's late-nineteenth-century romantic nationalism. The political appropriation of Christmas in Germany, however, stands apart. Germany's late unification brought an urgent search for viable ways to develop broad feelings of national cohesion among a diverse population, and as numerous studies have shown, Germany's politicians aggressively harnessed the holiday to serve communal ideological goals (Foitzik 1997; Faber and Gajek 1997; Perry 2010). Although radicals in Scandinavia also appropriated Christmas, scholarly work on the topic is relatively spotty. Yet the politicization of Christmas deserves attention, and the German case was quintessential.

By the 1890s, the German Social Democratic Party (SPD) had already invented a 'worker's' Christmas that challenged the mainstream holiday. For the SPD, myths of Christmas 'joy' underscored the vast gaps between the rich and the poor; the words to the 'Worker's Silent Night' (same melody) epitomized the message: 'silent night, sorrowful night / working people rise up and fight' (Foitzik 1997: 43). SPD propagandists cast Jesus as 'the first socialist', eager to 'smash the rule of Rome', even as they reworked the holiday's fabled origins in pagan sun worship. Just as the ancient Germans celebrated the 'return of light' that followed the solstice, so workers should welcome the 'new society' that would follow the socialist revolution (Perry 2010: 77–8).

The First World War further nationalized 'German Christmas'. The 1914 Christmas Truce—when British and German troops briefly fraternized on the Western Front—has received much attention (e.g. Weintraub 2001). Yet when Germans spoke of 'Kriegsweihnachten' (War Christmas), they referred to a vastly different set of experiences. Between 1914 and 1918, official voices insisted that Christmas unified Germany and that the family ties animated by the holiday were worth defending. During the war, as charity groups organized gift drives for 'the beloved defenders' at the front, descriptions of soldiers' modest but fervent celebrations in the trenches filled the pages of the national press and appeared on countless picture postcards. The message of loving community was inescapable and should be taken seriously. Charity drives, frontline parties, and 'field post' served as a form of 'mobilization from below', when proud assertions of protecting the homeland shared space with tender expressions of love and longing in the letters written home by ordinary soldiers (Perry 2010: 121).

In the 1920s, the German Communist Party (founded in 1918) at times argued that the holiday was so corrupt it should be entirely abolished. The number of party officials who made such claims in public meetings and then went home to celebrate around the tree remains unrecorded. Scandinavian leftists also portrayed Christmas as a capitalist myth or a revolutionary solstice celebration. The 1921 Christmas cover of the Norwegian magazine *Klassenkamp* (Class Struggle), for example, showed a powerful worker ringing a bell above a red star bearing the hammer and sickle, while a priest, a policeman, and a top-hat capitalist run off in fright (Hodne 1982: 9, 104–5).

Christmas's association with family and national unity made it a particularly appealing target for National Socialists determined to build a fascist '*Volksgemeinschaft*' (People's Community) in the Third Reich. Borrowing from the SPD, Nazi propagandists championed the holiday's connections to ancient Teutonic solstice rituals and the deep history of the national 'Volk'—just as the changing season brought the return of light, so Nazi political victory would lead to revolutionary social transformation. Christmas played into racial policies as well. Articles and ugly cartoons repeatedly admonished readers not to spend holiday budgets at department stores owned by German Jews, whom they said used the season to cheat German workers out of hard-earned wages. Group celebrations sponsored by Nazi mass organizations or district party offices brought these politicized messages to growing numbers of party members.

National Socialist propagandists worked tirelessly to "nazify' public celebrations of what propaganda minister Joseph Goebbels called 'the most German of holidays'. Newspapers, radio broadcasts, and newsreels invariably included reports on the pagan-Germanic aspects of the holiday, the parties sponsored by Nazi organizations or celebrity politicians, and the deep feelings of community supposedly engendered by such practices. Millions of Germans participated in the Nazi-organized Christmas charity drives of the official Winter Aid, either as volunteers or recipients of 'gifts', one of the more successful examples of nazification. Propagandists also tried to transform private observances, urging families to celebrate a 'racially correct' holiday by including Norse runes, swastikas, and revised 'nazified' carols in their domestic festivities. It is difficult to gauge how ordinary people reacted to all of this. What the Nazis called 'Volksweihnachten' (People's Christmas) did bring tangible benefits, including Winter Aid handouts and feelings of community. Yet the encroachment on Christmas traditions generated grumbling and discontent, especially among more pious German Christians (Perry 2016).

With the start of the Second World War, Nazi propagandists revised 'War Christmas' observances familiar from 1914–1918 with even greater ferocity. Such efforts hardly hid the costs of the war, a fact brought home by the German defeat at Stalingrad during the holiday season. Annual issues of the Danish Nazi party's magazine *Jul i Norden* (Christmas in the North) suggest that Scandinavian propagandists copied German attempts to colonize Christmas; the relative unpopularity of fascism in Scandinavia suggests the limits to such attempts (Lauridsen 1993: 150). Norwegians appear to have been more open to Christmas cards that brazenly portrayed *tomten* raising the (outlawed) national flag or King Haakon's anti-Nazi Christmas speeches, broadcast from exile in London on Christmas Eve from 1940 to 1944. After the war, the royal speech became an annual event (Stokker 2001: 48; Hovland 2000: 29).

With 'East' and 'West' variants, German Christmas played a role in the Cold War as well. East German Communists dusted off approaches to the holiday familiar from the 1920s. Good citizens celebrated an anti-fascist 'Friedensweihnacht' (Peace Christmas), employed solstice rituals and symbols, and turned their backs on Christian observance (Foitzik 1997: 168–90). Cold War West Germans, for their part, celebrated capitalist consumer abundance, but also Christian values and a return to 'normalcy' in family life. As historian Doris Foitzik reminds us, this 'traditional Christmas', with its roots in the conservative family cultures of the nineteenth century, advanced values that supported liberal capitalism even though it was cast as the 'normal'—and thus apolitical—version of the holiday (Foitzik 1997: 252–3). And even though this mainstream festival predominates across northern Europe today, what Stephen Nissenbaum called 'the battle for Christmas'—the contest to define the holiday's meaning and observances—is far from over (Nissenbaum 1998).

'Mary and Joseph were also Refugees': Conclusion

Gerry Bowler writes that 'Christmas looms far too large in our moral, religious, economic, and social landscapes for one to expect a tranquil uniformity of position' and the holiday's recent history in northern Europe confirms this conclusion (Bowler 2016: 243). Christmas remains a powerful celebration of family, faith, and community, but it is also a time to grapple with social conflict. It should not be too surprising, then, that beyond long-familiar conflicts between the material and the spiritual, northern Europeans use Christmas to grapple some of the most hotly contested issues of today: national identity, Islam, and immigration policies.

There are many examples. In Germany, the holiday has been 'weaponized' in the struggle over community belonging. On the right, attempts to observe a 'multicultural' holiday season that includes space for Muslim holidays are seen as examples of political correctness and 'creeping Islamicization' wrought by unwanted immigrants (Scheer

2019: 25). More liberal Germans argue that the message of Christmas is to embrace 'the foreigner'. As a priest delivering a Christmas sermon in a small Bavarian town explained, 'Mary and Joseph were also refugees' (Klassen and Scheer 2019a: 3–4). In a Danish example from 2012, a scandal in a suburb north of Copenhagen ensued when a Muslim-majority housing association voted against a years-old tradition and refused to install a Christmas tree on the premises of its apartment block. After more than 650 articles in the national press, and the intervention of four government ministers, the association leadership was replaced and the tree went up (Warburg 2017). The failed Tunisian asylum seeker who—with encouragement from the Islamic State—hijacked a truck and drove into the crowd at a Berlin Christmas market in 2016, killing twelve people, must have realized that his attack pinpointed these conflicts. He targeted a major Christian institution and a cherished secularized custom, as well as the immigration policies of contemporary Germany.

Despite familiar appeals to supposedly age-old, unchanging traditions, the world's most popular holiday remains mutable and contested. Unlike Dickens's ghost, it is difficult for us to project out from current trends to the future of Christmas with precision. Its history, however, suggests that the holiday will be a time and place where heartfelt values associated with faith, family, and belonging will remain at once reinforced, challenged, and transformed.

References and Further Reading

Anon. (1876). 'Christmas in Norway', *The Messenger*, December: 2.

Basu, Tanya and Little, Becky (2014). 'Krampus the Christmas Devil Is Coming to More Towns. So Where's He From?' *National Geographic*, 22 December. Available at https://www.nationalgeographic.com/news/2014/12/141222-krampus-christmas-devil-demon-krampusnacht/ (accessed 6 April 2020).

Bilfinger, Gustav (1901). *Untersuchungen über die Zeitrechnung der alten Germanen II: Das germanische Julfest*. Stuttgart: Hofbuchdruckerei Carl Liebich.

Bowler, Gerry (2000). *The World Encyclopedia of Christmas*. Toronto: McClelland & Stewart.

Bowler, Gerry (2016). *Christmas in the Crosshairs: Two Thousand Years of Denouncing and Defending the World's Most Celebrated Holiday*. New York: Oxford University Press.

Bringéus, Nils-Arvid (1999). *Årets Festdagar*. Stockholm: Carlssons.

Deloitte Christmas Survey (2018). 'Einkaufsverhalten der Deutschen zu Weihnachten 2018', October 2018. Available at https://www2.deloitte.com/de/de/pages/consumer-business/articles/christmas-survey.html. (accessed 6 April 2020).

Ekbohrn, Carl Magnus (1854). *Jul-bocken: Handbok för trefnan och nöje under julen*. Stockholm: P. A. Huldberg. Available at https://weburn.kb.se/metadata/299/EOD_2731299.htm/ (accessed 22 August 2019)

Elm, Hugo (1878). *Das goldene Weihnachtsbuch*. Halle: Schwetschke. Available at http://www.digibib.tu-bs.de/?docid=00000332/ (accessed 6 April 2020).

Faber, Richard and Gajek, Esther (eds.) (1997). *Politische Weihnacht in Antike und Moderne: Zur ideologischen Durchdringung des Fests der Feste*. Würzburg: Königshausen & Neumann.

Foitzik, Doris (1997). *Rote Sterne, braune Runen: Politische Weihnachten zwischen 1870 und 1970*. Münster: Waxmann.

Gunnell, Terry, (ed.), (2007). *Masks and Mumming in the Nordic Area*. Uppsala: Kungliga Gustav Adolfs Akademien för Svensk Folkkultur.

Hobsbawm, Eric, and Ranger, Terrence (eds.) (1983). *The Invention of Tradition*. Cambridge: Cambridge University Press.

Hodne, Bjarne (1982). *Glædelig Jul! Glimt fra Julefeiringens Historie*. Oslo: Universitetsforlaget.

Hodne, Ørnulf (2000). *Jul i Norge: Gamle og Nye Tradisjoner*. Oslo: J.W. Cappelens.

Hovland, Brit Marie (2000). *Kongelege Jule- og Nyttårstalar som Nasjonale Ritual: Tre Skandinaviske Eksempel*. Copenhagen: Nordisk Ministerråd.

Jultomten (2019): Wikimedia Commons, https://commons.wikimedia.org/wiki/Category:Jultomten/ (accessed 6 April 2020).

Klassen, Pamela E. and Scheer, Monique (eds.) (2019). *The Public Work of Christmas: Difference and Belonging in Multicultural Societies*. Montreal: McGill-Queen's University Press.

Klassen, Pamela E. and Scheer, Monique (2019a). 'The Difference that Christmas Makes: Thoughts on Christian Affordances in Multicultural Societies', in Klassen and Scheer (2019): 3–16.

Lauridsen, John T (1993). '"Nu Gjalder Luren!": Fortiden i DNSAP's Tjeneste', *Fund og Forskning*, 32: 144–84.

Löfgren, Orvar (1991). "Drömmen om den perfekta julen: Stora julgrälet och andra traditioner', in Jonas Frykman and Orvar Löfgren (eds), *Svenska Vanor och Ovanor*. Stockholm: Natur och Kultur: 79–100.

Löfgren, Orvar (1993). 'The Great Christmas Quarrel and Other Swedish Traditions', trans. Alan Crozier, in Daniel Miller (ed), *Unwrapping Christmas*. Oxford: Clarendon Press: 193–234.

Lorenz, Christa (1987). *Berliner Weihnachtsmarkt: Bilder und Geschichten aus 5 Jahrhunderten*. Berlin (East): Berlin-Information.

Miles, Clement (1976). *Christmas Traditions and Customs: Their History and Significance*. New York: Dover (reprint of 1912 edition).

Miller, Daniel (2017). 'Christmas: An Anthropological Lens', *HAU: Journal of Ethnographic Theory*, 7, no. 3: 409–42.

Moe, Jørgen (1859). *En liden Julegave: Gammelt og Nyt*. Christiania: P. F. Steenshalle. Available at https://www.nb.no/nbsok/nb/502b5fd7f59c96e133ac49256d1a22e7?index=5#0/ (accessed 6 April 2020).

Neumuller, Anders (2009). *God Jul: A Swedish Christmas*. New York: Skyhorse.

Nissenbaum, Stephen (1996). *The Battle for Christmas*. New York: Alfred A. Knopf.

Perabo, Lyonel (2015). 'Jul, a Nordic Christmas pt. 2: A Miscellany of Remarkable Traditions', *BIVROST stories*. Available at https://www.bivrost.com/jul-a-nordic-christmas-pt-2-a-miscellany-of-remarkable-traditions/ (accessed 6 April 2020).

Perry, Joe (2010). *Christmas in Germany: A Cultural History*. Chapel Hill: University of North Carolina Press.

Perry, Joe (2016). 'Christmas as Nazi Holiday: Colonising the Christmas Mood', in Lisa Pine, (ed.), *Life and Times in Nazi Germany*. New York: Bloomsbury: 263–89.

Rossel, Sven H. and Elbrønd-Bek, Bo (eds) (1996). *Christmas in Scandinavia*. Lincoln: University of Nebraska Press.

Rydquist, Melissa (2014). 'Månadens Dokument December 2014: Tomtar i Arkivet', TAM-Arkiv. Available at http://www.tam-arkiv.se/node/1498/ (accessed 6 April 2020).

Scheer, Monique (2019). 'Tense Holidays: Approaching Christmas through Conflict', in Klassen and Scheer (2019): 17–35.

Siefker, Phyllis (2006): *Santa Claus, Last of the Wild Men: The Origins and Evolution of Saint Nicholas, Spanning 50,000 Years*. Jefferson, NC: McFarland & Company.

Stahl, Jeremy (2009). 'Nordic Quack: Sweden's Bizarre Tradition of Watching Donald Duck Cartoons on Christmas Eve'. *Slate.com*. Available at https://slate.com/culture/2009/12/sweden-s-bizarre-tradition-of-watching-donald-duck-kalle-anka-cartoons-on-christmas-eve.html/ (accessed 6 April 2020).

Stokker, Kathleen (2001). *Keeping Christmas: Yuletide Traditions in Norway and the New Land*. St. Paul: Minnesota Historical Society Press.

Tille, Alexander (2015). *Die Geschichte der Deutschen Weihnacht*. Dresden: Fachbuchverlag (reprint of 1893 edition).

Warburg, Margit (2017). 'Much Ado about a Christmas Tree: A Conflict Involving Danish Civil Religion', *Implicit Religion* 20, no. 2: 127–48.

Weber-Kellermann, Ingeborg (1994). *Das Buch der Weihnachtslieder*. Mainz: Piper Schott.

Weintraub, Stanley 2001: *Silent Night: The Story of the World War I Christmas Truce*. New York: Free Press.

CHAPTER 36

RUSSIA

FRANCESCA SILANO

The Orthodox liturgy on the Feast of the Nativity emphasizes the intersection of the timeless God with time and ponders the image of the cavern as the birthplace of Christ. On this day, the Church sings, 'Today, the Virgin gives birth to the Transcendent One, and the earth offers a cave to the Unapproachable One. Angels, with shepherds, glorify Him!...Since for our sake the Eternal God is born as a little child' (Hopko 1981). The Christmas liturgy reflects understandings of time, human nature, and the purpose of history that were incorporated into Russian Orthodox life with the arrival of Christianity in the tenth century.

Long before 1917, when the Communist Bolshevik Party came to power and sought to abolish Christianity and every holiday associated with it, the Christmas holiday had become a contested site. An investigation into the ways Russians imagined, discussed, and celebrated Christmas throughout their history reveals how processes that have affected much of the world, such as urbanization, modernization, and secularization were reflected in, developed through, and challenged by way of Christmas. A study of Russia's Christmas can provide a rich source for comparison with other countries and empires in the world.

Liturgy and the Rhythms of Life in Rural Russia

Orthodoxy became the official religion of the lands that would come to make up the Russian Empire in the year AD 988. The 'Primary Chronicle', one of the earliest written accounts of Russian history, claims that Vladimir, the Prince of Kiev, then the political centre of the lands of Rus', sent emissaries to Jewish, Muslim, and Western and Eastern Christian communities. Those who visited Constantinople returned wonderstruck, exclaiming, '[W]e knew not whether we were in heaven or on earth....We only know that God dwells there among men, and their service is fairer than the ceremonies of other nations' (Cross and Sherbowitz-Wetzor 1953: 111). The notion that to be Orthodox was to be devoted to both liturgy and beauty was one that shaped the development of Orthodoxy in the Russian lands.

It is crucial to conceive of Russian Orthodox life as liturgical life, one where the Church's yearly, weekly, and daily liturgical cycles determined the rhythm of life for most people in the empire, up until the Revolution of 1917. According to the last imperial census, taken in 1897, almost 70 per cent of imperial subjects were Orthodox (Werth 2014: 37). And although the Russian Empire was a vast multi-ethnic and multi-religious one, the civil calendar largely mirrored the Orthodox one (Shevzov 2004: 131). The vast majority of imperial subjects were, moreover, either peasants or merchants living in rural areas whose lives were determined by the liturgical and agricultural calendars, both of which, in turn, influenced each other and the way Christmas was experienced.

The Nativity of Christ (25 December—in the Julian calendar, thus 7 January in the West) and the Baptism of Christ or Theophany (6 January in the Julian calendar) bookend the 'Christmas Season'. Preparations for Nativity begin on November 15, the day after the feast of St Philip the Apostle, when Orthodox believers undertake a forty-day period of fasting that lasts until the Eve of the Nativity. Fasting, in the words of Sergei Bulgakov (1859–1932) is 'a means of promoting the elevation of the spirit over the flesh, the domination of spiritual and moral aspirations over the sensual' (Bulgakov 1993: 446). The Nativity Fast coincides with the beginning of the Church year and the close of the agricultural year.

In the prerevolutionary village, fasting was never an individual exercise. Rather, Vera Shevzov explains, 'individuals understood themselves as participating in an entire rhythm of sacred time and as participating thorough fasting alongside others involved in the same journey' (Shevzov 2004: 135–6). Those who chose not to fast were often chided by fellow villagers and sometimes even forbidden from participating in village assemblies (Ibid: 136). The preparation for feasts such as the Nativity was therefore a means of formation of individual and collective identity in rural Russia.

In the case of the Nativity, fasting and liturgical services were all structured towards the preparation of the soul, the village community, and the Church for the birth of Christ. Throughout the Orthodox Church's history in the Russian lands, priests have given homilies on the Nativity that have aimed to shock the listeners into contemplating the contrast between the limitless richness of God and the poverty of the birth of Christ. In a nineteenth-century homily, Saint Theophan the Recluse (1815–1894) compared the coming of Christ to a king giving freedom to a prisoner who had been awaiting his arrival for years and to the appearance of the most skilled doctor to a sick man 'covered with wounds and paralyzed in all his members'. 'Bring these examples closer to yourself,' Theophan adjured his listeners, 'and you will see our whole history in them.' The believer was induced by the liturgy to read his or her life within the sacred history of the Church and the historical accounts of the birth of Jesus, and to address contemporary problems through the prism of the feast.

Theophan continued his homily with a reproach to listeners, warning them against falling into debauchery while celebrating the Nativity. He insisted that

> [m]any of our social festivities are really pagan abominations[.] ... And it is purposely contrived for such festivities to appear in great quantities during the Feasts of Nativity and [Easter]. By getting caught up in them we give the prince of this world—our tormentor, the enemy of God—an excuse to say to God, 'Look what You've done for me with Your Nativity and Resurrection! They're all coming to me!
> (Theophan 2010)

Warnings of this sort were not untypical in Orthodox Russia. They reveal the tension between pre-Christian and Christian practices that especially characterized the major feasts of the liturgical year (Rock 2007). In the Western Russian Empire, Nativity festivities superseded and absorbed the Yuletide holidays of the pre-Christian Slavs known as *Koliada*. The name refers to the pre-Christian Greco-Roman celebrations of *kalanda* (Greek) or *calandae* (Latin), and probably also to the Slavic Deity Koliada or Koleda, the God of the winter sun being reborn after the solstice (Sokolov 1950: 174–183). Aspects of pre-Christian Yuletide festivities that celebrated the lengthening days and sought to guarantee a good agricultural year became integral parts of Nativity celebrations in many rural areas. Nativity carols, known as 'koliadki', reflected this blending of pre- and post-Christian traditions. Villagers would go from house to house, singing about *koliada*, a bountiful harvest, and, sometimes, God, and threatening to damage property if they were not met with hearty holiday fare (Alexander 1975: 29–36).

A series of ethnographic reports from Russian villages from the end of the nineteenth century recounts many practices from the Christmas season. Since the season coincided with a quiet period in agricultural life, rural inhabitants counted on the days of Nativity to meet and pair off with inhabitants of neighbouring villages. Sometimes, mummers played a role in matchmaking, selecting women and men to be partnered off and dance together (Ibid. 53; 94–6; 174–82; 272; 282; 325–6) Thus, the necessities of agricultural, social, and religious life were not experienced by rural-dwellers as being separate, but as deeply intertwined. These practices seemed to have little or nothing to do with the birth of Jesus: the presence of mummers; fake funerals that sometimes involved mocking the person pretending to be dead; and divination (especially for young women who wanted to know if they would marry in the coming year). As people dabbled in these practices, stories circulated about the appearance of the devil on Christmas Eve, and also of means by which to ward him off (Grusman 2004: 98). *The Night Before Christmas* by the famous satirist Nikolai Gogol (1809–1852) depicts the devil's wanderings on Christmas Eve and the hero's success in thwarting him (Gogol 2011).

Villagers indeed appeared to be practising pagan rituals; but always present within these activities was the sense that they risked transgressing Christian norms, and that they must make an effort to repair these transgressions. What's more, these practices often coexisted easily in the minds of believers with their own attendance at Nativity liturgies. In fact, rural dwellers mostly considered themselves to be members of the body of the Church, which included its hierarchy. Bishops like Theophan (cited earlier), considered it their responsibility to observe and pass judgment on villagers' practices. Sometimes, their warnings were heeded, and other times they were simply dismissed by locals. But rarely would clerics have considered their flock to be outside the bounds of the Church, and neither would the lay people have conceived of themselves as existing separately from their local priest, church, or perhaps even bishop. (Rock 2007: 150–7; Shevzov, 2004: 10).

Vera Shevzov has noted, moreover, that rural dwellers 'often assimilated established feasts in a way that made sense in their local worlds' (Shevzov 2004: 131). Thus, the Christmas season was marked in different ways in different regions. In some villages, the feast of Epiphany was more important than that of the Nativity. Celebrated on 6 January, the Epiphany does not celebrate, as it does in the Western Church, the appearance of the Magi in Bethlehem. Rather, it coincides with the Feast of the Baptism of the Lord and commemorates the threefold manifestation of God as Father, Son, and Holy Spirit, as recorded in the Gospels of Matthew, Mark, and Luke. The feast expresses the Church's belief in the Holy Trinity, and in the necessity of baptism for its members. The eve of the feast is marked by the Great Blessing of Water either in the church building, or at a natural source of water (Hopko 1981).

In pre-revolutionary rural Russia, the blessing of the water would have been more easily experienced as immanent to daily existence. In the volost' (self-governed unit of peasant villages) of Ilinsko-Khovanskaia, villagers brought some of the water home and sprinkled it on their houses, livestock, and any other buildings and drew a cross in chalk on their doors so as to protect their families from 'misfortune and adversity'. At midnight, inhabitants often went to drink from a pond or another source of water because it was believed that at that time, 'it is as if the water was swaying in remembrance of the Baptism of the Lord' (Grusman 2006: 247). In another village, the same water was kept on hand all year and sprinkled on the cows during the spring when they were sent out to pasture (Ibid: 417). Clearly, events that took place during the Nativity season continued to influence the daily lives of rural-dwellers long after the close of the season itself. This intricate balance between rural and liturgical life began to shift with the introduction of industrialization and its counterpart, urbanization, in the mid-nineteenth century. With these events came changes in the experience of time, space, and the trajectory of human life that were reflected in the celebration of Christmas.

CHANGING THE RHYTHMS OF LIFE: CHRISTMAS IN THE CITY

In the first half of the nineteenth century, Russian intellectuals began to fervently debate the course of the empire's future. Those known as 'Westernizers' believed that Russia, with its overwhelmingly Orthodox and rural population, was hopelessly backward, and that Russia's economic, social, and cultural development would be guaranteed only through a wholehearted embrace of Western European ways. In the empire's capital, St Petersburg, intellectuals and members of high society alike embraced, among other things, German customs and ideas. It was in this context that the Christmas tree or *elka* was introduced into Russian life.

The Christmas tree came to St Petersburg with an influx of German immigrants at the beginning of the nineteenth century, and, over the next sixty years became—with the help of journalism, children's stories, and the market—a staple of urban Christmas. Fascination with the *elka* grew in the 1840s alongside elite fascination with Western culture. The tree, however, did not just become a new ornament attached to old traditions; rather, it brought a whole new experience and narrative of Christmas itself. The Eve of Nativity became, as in Germany, an evening for children: gifts were given to children, and the tree came to represent, among other things, an understanding of community that was now centred around the family (Dushechkina 2002: 93–118).

As the *elka* grew in popularity, so too, did Christmas in the city take on the character of a children's feast. In 1840, 'The Nutcracker,' by E. T. A. Hoffmann—which would become the basis of Tchaikovsky's 1892 ballet—was translated into Russian and published in a special edition for children, with pictures of Christmas trees included (Hoffmann 1840). By the 1870s, authors of pedagogical manuals theorized about the value of Christmas for children. In one, *The Christmas Tree in Live Pictures, Scenes, Songs and Games: For Schools and Families* (1887), the author, D. D. Semenov, explained to parents how they should involve their children in the preparation of the tree, claiming that the tree itself was 'a symbol of the Christian love of the old towards the young'. In schools, the tree was supposed to communicate, even to those children whose parents could not afford trees, that they, too, could enjoy the holiday. 'Organized like this,' Semenov concluded, 'the *elka* takes on less an amusing than an educational and social character' (Dushechkina 2002: 297–99). By the late nineteenth-century, then, Christmas was being portrayed not as a feast of the Incarnation of God, but as a pedagogical opportunity.

The practice of giving gifts was encouraged by St Petersburg merchants. Pastry shop owners played a crucial role in the dissemination of the *elka* as they began selling pre-decorated trees complete with hanging lanterns and gifts and a variety of baked goods (Dushechkina 2002: 108–9) The Petersburg elite was enchanted by the introduction of these Western traditions. On Christmas Eve, 1897, Olga Aleksandrovna, the youngest child of Tsar Alexander III and sister of the last tsar, Nicholas II, wrote, in her diary, '*Elka*! *Elka* today! Hurrah! Hurrah! Hurrah!' (GARF 1897: l. 108) She fleetingly described her visit to church, but what dominated her entries from these days and those of the next year was the practice of gift-giving, the preparation of stockings, and the eating of plum pudding (Ibid; GARF 1898: l. 90–2).[1] Participation in English and German traditions was now clearly a marker of elite status. Christmas cards entered the

---

[1] I thank Alison Smith for generously sharing these diaries with me.

empire and were reproduced with Russian texts, though they depicted scenes that seemed more appropriate to Victorian England than Tsarist Russia: families gathered around a hearth; children in sleighs; and, increasingly, a bearded figure bearing gifts.

How this figure, known as *Ded Moroz* (Grandfather Frost) came to occupy a central place in Russia's Christmas tradition reflects the complexity of Russia's sense of identity. *Ded Moroz* has roots in Slavic mythology, where the god of the frost, Moroz, was known as a figure capable of great cruelty and great kindness. In his 1864 narrative poem, 'Red-Nosed Frost' (*Moroz, Krasnyi Nos*), the poet Nikolai Nekrasov (1821–1878) depicted the death and funeral of a peasant, followed by his widow Dar'ia's freezing to death in the woods as she gathers wood for the cold house after the funeral. The cold, personified as *Ded Moroz*, speaks to Dar'ia, boasting of his power to both terrify men and to assist them through the freezing of water to make bridges over which merchants can pass (Nekrasov 1887). Critics have debated the meaning of the poem, but most agree that the work represents in some way the Russian national character.

Over the nineteenth century, however, the same Moroz, who was seen to represent something uniquely Russian, slowly came to be associated with the commercial feast of urban Christmas. Elena Dushechkina sees the association of Moroz with Christmas as being primarily the result of children demanding to know just *who* was bringing the Christmas tree and its gifts. St Nicholas, although an extremely popular saint in Russia, did not have a reputation as a giver of gifts (Dushechkina 585–609). Perhaps Ded Moroz, who was increasingly depicted in children's stories by the late-century, allowed for Russians to co-opt the Western tradition of Santa Claus while insisting on a mythical agelessness and national uniqueness of the figure himself. *Ded Moroz* is a bearded old man who comes bearing gifts; but, unlike Santa Claus, he lives in the forest, and often wears sandals and a blue fur coat.

If Christmas in Russia's major cities had become a Westernized commercial feast, it also became an opportunity for Russians to reflect upon Westernization, urbanization, and commercial culture. The peasants whose lives had been determined by the rhythms of the countryside with its church bells and agricultural calendar were now shocked into a new time cycle governed by the factory or the employers of domestic servants. As they streamed into Russia's cities in the latter half of the nineteenth century to find work, these peasants found themselves in much the same poverty and squalor as the poor of Dickensian London. It is perhaps not surprising, then, that the great admirer of Dickens, Fyodor Dostoevsky (1821–1881), was among the first writers to contribute to a new motif of Russian literature, that of the 'frozen child'. 'The Boy at Christ's Christmas Party' (1876), depicts a young boy, 'on Christmas Eve in a *certain* [read St Petersburg] huge city during a terrible cold spell'. The child's mother lies dying on a thin bed of straw, destroyed by the conditions of urban life.

The young boy, unaware that his mother is in fact dead, sets out in search of something to eat and relief from the cold. Dazed, he walks through the oppressive maze of urban streets, and stares at the tantalizing displays of Christmas abundance that beckon to him through the shop windows. The boy takes shelter beside a woodpile and suddenly finds himself at a glorious Christmas party, complete with a *elka*. There, he sees his mother and a joyous group of children who explain, 'this is Christ's Christmas tree....On this day Christ always has a Christmas party for those little children who have no Christmas tree of their own.' The children are all those who have been ravaged by the city, those who had 'frozen to death in the baskets in which they had been abandoned on the doorsteps of Petersburg officials', or who 'suffocated from the fumes in third-class railway carriages' (Dostoevsky 2009: 93–7). If Russian Christmas had been transformed by city life, Christmas had also become a means of critiquing that life.

Such stories (and parodies of them) became a staple of Russian newspapers and literary journals in the late-nineteenth and early-twentieth centuries (Stroud 2006: 114; 124–7). The Christmas story soon became an essential part of Russian authors' canons (*A Very Russian Christmas* 2016). In general, by the 1890s, newspapers were running special Christmas Day issues. But the feast increasingly became a means of reflecting on Russia's social and political life. During the tumultuous years of the Russo-Japanese War (1904–1905) and the 1905 Revolution, Christmas Day editorialists and authors behaved in much the same way as the Orthodox priests did with their homilies: they evaluated and judged contemporary events by reflecting on Christmas and the values associated with it. Liberal authors who deplored the oppressive practices of the tsarist government used the holidays to 'show the disparity between the ideals celebrated during the holiday and everyday Russian reality'. Conservatives, seeing the upheaval wrought by revolutionary ideals in Russia, referred to the holiday 'to underscore the message that the current situation in Russia was a violation of everything the nation had held sacred' (Baran 1994: 213).

As Russians debated their national identity, then, Christmas became a means of reflecting on Russia's 'eternal questions': What is Russia? What is to be done? And Who is to blame? The Bolshevik Revolution of 1917 appeared to resolve these questions definitively: Russia was to be the harbinger of the international Communist revolution. The task was to bring about the revolution; and to blame were the ruling classes who, in the Russian Empire, were said to have been buttressed by the Church. It would seem that any reflection on Christmas or its meaning for Russia should have ceased with the revolution. Not so.

Soviet Christmas: A New Battle for Time

When the Bolshevik Communists led by Vladimir Lenin (1870–1924) took over the government of Russia in October of 1917, they promised to remake Russia in the image of the revolution, thus establishing the first Communist government in the world. The Bolsheviks were not simply a new political party: they had the confidence of those who knew the course of history and the truth about human nature. They not only wanted to liberate humanity, but to create a New Man, who would be severed from any reference to the transcendent. With such a conception of time and human nature, it is no wonder that the Bolsheviks identified the Orthodox Church as one of their first enemies to be destroyed. Where the Church proclaimed the Incarnation of God in time as the source of salvation for humanity, the Bolsheviks claimed the liberation from God as being essential for the realization of paradise on Earth (Shevzov, forthcoming).

The Bolsheviks made it a priority to undermine the Orthodox Church and, eventually, all religions. They did this not only through violence, the destruction of Church property, and the legal prosecution of Orthodox clergy and lay people, but also through propaganda and efforts to destroy the connection between sacred and civil life. Thus, in January 1918, the new government issued a decree officially separating church and state, nationalizing Church property, and declaring religious education illegal (Miliakova 2016: 131–2). This decree coincided with the government's decision to change from the Julian to the Gregorian Calendar. The shift signalled that Russia's time would now coincide with Western time. Meanwhile, the Orthodox Church remained on the Julian Calendar (approximately 13 days behind the Gregorian). All the seasons and days of the year that marked the rhythms by which people lived had now shifted: thus, Christmas would now have to be celebrated on 7 January (25 December on the Julian Calendar).

The Bolsheviks were also keenly aware of the power of holidays to shape people's sense of themselves and of the meaning of their lives. In December 1918, the government published a decree on holidays by which Sunday would no longer be a day of rest for all workers; it also established six new official holidays. The decree eliminated the Christmas holiday and organized state holidays on 1 January (New Year's) and 22 January (Day of Commemoration of the 1905 Revolution) (*Dekrety* 1957: 122–4). Thus, the Bolsheviks attempted to wrest the Christmas season from the hands of Christians and invest it with new meaning.

The new government also sought to undermine the old holidays. From 25 December 1922 to 6 January 1923, the Communist Youth League (Komsomol) organized 'Red Christmases' to mock the Church and its Nativity celebrations. In that year, the Komsomol organized 184 similar carnivals, and 417 anti-Christmas events throughout Soviet Russia (Husband 1998: 99–100). Organizers emphasized the pagan traditions that preceded Nativity celebrations, and tried to demonstrate the relativity of all religions by having participants dress up as Allah, Buddha, Osiris, and Orthodox priests (Tirado 1992: 105). The desired didactic function of the festivities was likely overshadowed by the aggressive antireligious activities that marked them: the burning of icons, religious books, and pictures of Jesus and the saints (Ibid: 106). So offensive did many people find these activities that they were quickly abandoned; the question of how to conquer Christmas, however, remained.

In the late 1920s, the government gave up on trying to invest those days with new meaning and simply suppressed the holiday season. Whereas Lenin had not been opposed to the continuation of *elka* celebrations as long as they were divorced from

Christian themes, even the Christmas tree fell victim to Joseph Stalin's (1878–1953) campaign to revolutionize Soviet society in the late 1920s and early 1930s. These years were characterized by a radical effort to transform society, culture, and the economy through crude and violent efforts from above. On the one hand, Stalin sought to create a Soviet paradise that could rival Western countries economically and socially. On the other, he wanted to gain internal control of the peasantry and the countryside through the collectivization of all farmland into large, state-run, farms. This project of internal colonization also entailed an attempt to rid the peasants of the Orthodox religion to which many of them continued to cling (Viola 1996: 38–44).

Thus, in 1928, the *elka* was labelled a symbol of bourgeois Western excess, and *Ded Moroz* himself was 'unmasked as an ally of the priest and the *kulak* [rich peasant]' (Stites 1989: 230; Petrone 2000: 86). For seven years, no public symbols of anything once associated with Christmas were seen in Soviet Russia. Meanwhile, the government transformed New Year's into a didactic holiday for workers. The initial purpose of the holiday was to ridicule inefficiency, waste, and lack of productivity (Petrone 2000: 86). Yet, this rather drab manner of ushering in the New Year did not last for long. By 1935, Pavel Postyshev, a member of the Politburo, proposed the resurrection of the *elka* and the festivities surrounding it.

In an editorial from 28 December 1935 in *Pravda*, the official organ of the Bolshevik Party, Postyshev wondered how the children of the prerevolutionary 'bourgeoisie and bureaucrats' could have been allowed to enjoy the joys of a *elka* while the privilege had been withheld from children of the workers of Soviet Russia. Postyshev spoke of the *elka* as if it had only and ever been attached to New Year's festivities, claiming that the tree was the 'purest example of a seasonal holiday of Winter—New Year's. It is a holiday of beauty and joy for children of all ages....For the one who feels the *elka* no explanation of the significance of this holiday is necessary' (Flerina and Bazykin 1936: 3–4). With this vague ideological justification, Postyshev was successful in reintroducing *elka* celebrations into Soviet life.

In a 1936 volume titled *Elka*, Soviet pedagogues, like their nineteenth-century predecessors, outlined a series of *Elka* activities for children of all ages, and even advised bringing back mummers for children of a certain age (Ibid: 9–22). The book contained an anecdote from Vladimir Bonch-Bruevich (1873–1955), one of the central figures in the anti-religious campaigns of the early Soviet period, about an evening he had spent with Lenin and children around the *elka*. The year was 1919, and Russia was in the midst of its bloody Civil War, but that did not stop Lenin from asking Bonch-Bruevich to join him in celebrating the *elka* with schoolchildren in Sokolniki, a district on the outskirts of Moscow. Bonch-Bruevich claimed the children had surrounded the Bolshevik leader as he sang songs, played games, and prepared their tea, watching over the children, 'as if they were all his family' (Ibid: 5–8). The story was soon adapted for children and became a central myth of Soviet New Year's in a volume complete with socialist realist drawings of Lenin and young children around the *elka* (Kononov 1954). Whereas in Dostoevsky's story Jesus had come as the saviour of cold and starving children, Lenin was now being introduced as the friend of children in troubled times.

In 1937, the year in which the infamous Great Terror began, the Moscow Trade Unions Council organized *elka* celebrations involving nearly 27,000 children and 8,000 adults. *Ded Moroz* was reintroduced as the New Year's gift-giver, this time with his young granddaughter, *Snegurochka* (the Snow Maiden), who would thereafter become a staple of Soviet New Year's celebrations (Dushechkina 2002: 654-67). The children gathered together to sing songs celebrating their joy as Soviet citizens and their love of Stalin, such as one titled 'Thanks to Stalin for our miraculous days' (Petrone 2000: 96). The miracle of the Incarnation was being supplanted through these new carols by the miracle of Stalinism.

By the late 1930s, the state was presenting New Year's to adults as a day of festiveness, rather than a feast for accounting or efficiency. Carnivals and dances were arranged at Palaces of Culture across the Union. At a festival for the Stakhanovites, the highest-producing workers in the Union, attendees were encouraged to abandon any sadness at the door, celebrate, and meet members of the opposite sex. The organizers of these carnivals reintroduced the practice of fortune telling, an essential aspect of peasant Nativity celebrations (Ibid: 100-05). In the name of fun and leisure, even the insistence that the Soviet Union was a strictly scientific and rational state was put aside. Such a concession, Karen Petrone argues, signifies how New Year's itself became a site of negotiation during the most violent period of Soviet history. The festival, unlike most of the others in the Soviet calendar, did not commemorate any significant event in revolutionary history: it was simply a day of revelry, from which people could expect a moment of respite (Ibid: 100-09). It is perhaps for this reason that New Year's quickly became the most popular holiday in the Soviet Union, and continued to be so until the time of its collapse.

Yet, even as Christmas seemed to have been erased by the revolution, Orthodox believers clung stubbornly to the feast. Homilists continued to reflect on the birth of Jesus to make sense of contemporary events. In a homily from Orthodox Christmas in 1919, the same year of Lenin's legendary visit to the children of Sokolniki, Patriarch Tikhon (Bellavin) (1865-1925) recalled wistfully how the birth of Jesus had carried a promise of peace on Earth. Tikhon had been elected to lead the Church when it restored the position of the patriarchate, shortly after the Bolshevik Revolution. The patriarch claimed that civil war and famine were destroying the country 'because Christ was not born in our hearts.' Christ had come to accomplish 'the great work of redemption and the salvation of the human race,' Tikhon continued, a task that no human being, nor 'the whole of humanity' could accomplish. But 'God does not save man without man.' Orthodox Christians had to decide to convert their hearts towards Christ and the Church. This conversion would be manifested in love for their brethren and, by extension, would save Russia from the 'hostility, anger and hatred' into which it had been plunged. Then and only then,' concluded the patriarch, 'will the long-desired peace upon earth draw near, and will there be good will among men' (Tikhon 2009: 216-19).

Through the feast of the Nativity, the leader of Russia's Orthodox Christians was not only calling his people to conversion, but also *re*-calling them to the anthropology of the Church—an anthropology that was diametrically opposed to the Bolshevik one.

The human person was not the New Man, free of all connection to God and, therefore, free to create a utopia. The true image of the human person was, instead, reflected in the baptized Orthodox Christian whose transformation in Christ allowed him or her to transform the world. What was at stake in the celebration of New Year's as opposed to the Nativity were conceptions of the nature of the human person, of humanity as a whole, and of the best way to save it. These conceptions were, in turn, reflected in the conceptions of time that were proposed by the celebrants of these respective feasts.

* * * *

The first week of January is now designated as a holiday week for all Russians, and it contains within itself the contested nature of Christmas in Russia. Since the collapse of the Soviet Union, the Orthodox Church and Christmas have been reintroduced into Russian society, and it is celebrated on 7 January, since the Church remains on the Julian Calendar. Sources of water are again being blessed at Epiphany. But New Year's remains the most popular holiday in the country, and Soviet customs have not disappeared. The *elka*, *Ded Moroz*, and *Snegurochka* continue to be features of this season, but the holiday with which they are associated depends on the celebrant. Christmas, it seems, will always reflect something of Russians' competing senses of the meaning of time, and of human life.

REFERENCES AND FURTHER READING

A Very Russian Christmas: The Greatest Russian Holiday Stories of All Time (2016). New York: New Vessel Press.
Alexander, Alex E. (1975). *Russian Folklore: An Anthology in English Translation*. Belmont: Nordland Publishing Company.
Baran, Henryk (1994). 'The Tradition of Religious Holiday Literature and Russian Modernism', in Robert P. Hughes and Irina Paperno (eds.), *Christianity and the Eastern Slavs. Vol. 2: Russian Culture in Modern Times*. Berkeley: University of California Press: 201–44.
Bulgakov, S.V. (1993). *Nastol'naia kniga dlia sviashchenno-tserkovno-sluzhitelei (Sbornik svedenii, kasaiushchikhsia otechestvennago dukhovenstva)*. Moscow: Izdatel'skii otdel Moskovskogo Patriarkhata. Available at https://azbyka.ru/otechnik/Pravoslavnoe_Bogosluzhenie/nastolnaja-kniga-svjashennosluzhitelja/ (accessed 25 March 2020).
Cross, Samuel Hazzard and Sherbowitz-Wetzor, Olgerd P. (eds. and trans.) (1953). *The Russian Primary Chronicle: Laurentian Text*. Cambridge, MA: The Mediaeval Academy of America.
Dekrety Sovetskoi vlasti. T. IV. 10 noiabria 1918 g.—31 marta 1919 g. (1957). Moscow: Politizdat.
Dostoevsky, Fyodor (2009). *A Writer's Diary (Abridged Edition)*. Ed. Gary Saul Morson. Trans. Kenneth Lantz. Evanston: Northwestern University Press.
Dushechkina, E.V. (2002). *Russkaia elka: istoriia, mifologia, literatura*. Saint Petersburg: Evropeiskii universitet v Sankt-Peterburge (Apple Books edition).
Flerina, E. A. and Bazykin, C. C. (eds.) (1936). *Elka: Sbornik statei o provedenii elki*. Moscow: Gosudarstvennoe uchebno-pedagogicheskoe izdatel'stvo.

GARF (State Archive of the Russian Federation) 1897–1899. Fond 643, Opis 1, Dela 7–9.
Gogol, Nikolai (2011). *The Night Before Christmas*. Trans. Constance Garnett. New York: New Directions.
Grusman, V. M. (ed.) (2004). *Russkie krest'iane. Zhizn'. Byt. Nravy. Materialy "Etnograficheskogo biuro" kniazia V.N. Tenisheva. Tom 1: Kostromskaia i Tverskaia gubernii*. Saint Petersburg: Navigator.
Grusman, V. M. (ed.) (2006). *Russkie krest'iane. Zhizn'. Byt. Nravy. Materialy "Etnograficheskogo biuro" kniazia V.N. Tenisheva. Tom 2: Iaroslavskaia guberniya. Chast' 2: Danilovskii, Liubimskii, Romanovo-Borisoglebskii, Rostovskii i Iaroslavskii uezdy*. Saint Petersburg: Navigator.
Hoffmann, E. T. A. (1840). *Podarok na novyi god. Dve skazki Gofmana dlia bol'shikh i malen'kikh detei*. Saint Petersburg: Tip. A. Sycheva.
Hopko, Thomas (1981). *The Orthodox Faith, Volume 2: Worship*. Yonkers: St. Vladimir's Seminary Press [Kindle Version].
Husband, William (1998). 'Soviet Atheism and Russian Orthodox Strategies of Resistance, 1917–1932', *The Journal of Modern History*, 70, no. 1: 74–107.
Kononov, A. (1954). *New Year's in Sokolniki*. Moscow: Foreign Languages Publishing House.
Tikhon (Bellavin) (2009). *"V godinu gneva Bozhia...": Poslaniia, slova i rechi sv. Patriarkha. Tikhona*. Ed. N. A. Kriovosheeva. Moscow: PSTGU.
Miliakova, L.V. (ed.) (2016). *Otdelenie Tserkvi ot gosudarstva i shkoly ot Tserkvi v Sovetskoi Rossii. Oktiabr' 1917–1918 g.: Sbornik dokumentov*. Moscow: PSTGU.
Nekrasov, N. A. (1887). *Moroz Krasnyi Nos/Red-Nosed Frost*. Trans. W. R. S. Ralston. Boston: Ticknor and Company.
Petrone, Karen (2000). *Life Has Become More Joyous, Comrades: Celebrations in the Time of Stalin*. Bloomington: Indiana University Press.
Rock, Stella (2007). *Popular Religion in Russia: 'Double Belief' and the Making of an Academic Myth*. London: Routledge.
Shevzov, Vera (2004). *Russian Orthodoxy on the Eve of Revolution*. New York: Oxford University Press.
Shevzov, Vera (forthcoming). 'The Orthodox Church and Religion in Revolutionary Russia, 1894–1924', in Randall Poole, Caryl Emerson, and George Pattison (eds.), *Oxford Handbook of Russian Religious Thought*. Oxford: Oxford University Press.
Sokolov, Y. M. (1950). *Russian Folklore*. Trans. Catherine Ruth Smith. New York: Macmillan.
St. Theophan the Recluse (2010). 'The Nativity of Christ', in *Thoughts for Each Day of the Year According to the Daily Church Readings from the Word of God*. Ed. Nun Cornelia. Trans. Lisa Marie Baranov. St. Herman of Alaska Press. Available at http://orthochristian.com/50827.html/ (accessed 25 March 2020).
Stites, Richard (1989). *Revolutionary Dreams: Utopian Vision and Experimental Life in the Russian Revolution*. New York: Oxford University Press.
Stroud, Gregory (2006). 'Retrospective Revolution: A History of Time and Memory in Urban Russia, 1903–1923'. PhD thesis, University of Illinois at Urbana-Champaign.
Tirado, Isabel (1992). 'The Revolution, Young Peasants, and the Komsomol's Antireligious Campaigns (1920–1928)', *Canadian-American Slavic Studies*, 25, nos. 1–3: 97–117.
Viola, Lynne (1996). *Peasant Rebels Under Stalin: Collectivization and the Culture of Peasant Resistance*. New York: Oxford University Press.
Werth, Paul (2014). *The Tsar's Foreign Faiths: Toleration and the Fate of Religious Freedom in Imperial Russia*. New York: Oxford University Press.

CHAPTER 37

THE UNITED KINGDOM

MARTIN JOHNES

Christmas in Modern British Culture

The importance of Christmas in British culture was evident by the celebrations in 1914. Despite the war, pantomimes, charitable dinners, and distributions to the poor, sick, and elderly all took place. Some even thought that more effort than normal was going into giving children treats. Oranges, holly, and mistletoe were all scarcer than normal but there was still turkey and beef on sale for Christmas dinner, albeit at more expensive prices than usual. Father Christmas could be found in department stores and all manner of goods were being advertised as presents. Appeals were made for troops to be remembered in Christmas prayers and for donations of mufflers, mittens, socks, and shirts that could be sent as presents to those in the forces. At the front itself, there was a desire to celebrate. Much of the fighting came to an unofficial halt and there was carol singing, good spirits, and even some fraternization. Senior commanders did not approve, and back home too a few objected to festivities at a time of war. Some local authorities turned down the many requests for extensions to licensing hours on Christmas Eve and Boxing Day. In Burnley, a mill manager tried to stop the Christmas Eve tradition of stopping work for a while for 'a little jollification'. The result was that one of his workers punched him (Johnes, 2016: xii–xiii).

Ultimately, Christmas carried on during the conflict because of how embedded it had become in British culture during the Victorian and Edwardian periods. Drawing on older traditions and an emphasis on fellowship, the modern British Christmas was reinvented from the 1840s onwards, with the development of a modern shopping culture, a cult of Santa Claus, and a festival more focused on the home and family than the traditional communal public celebrations. While Armstrong (2010) and Hutton (1996), quite rightly stress the continuities from previous generations in the nature of the Victorian Christmas, Golby and Purdie (1984: 4) argue it was 'so extensively refurbished and reinterpreted that it amounts to an invented tradition'. Connelly

(1999), in contrast, argues that the idea of the Victorian Christmas being an invention is too strong and thus instead talks of the 'inflation' of Christmas.

As Armstrong (2010) maintained, even if the idea of the Victorian Christmas being an invented tradition is useful, it does not explain how and why the festival developed. In the popular imagination much credit is given to specific individuals. This is not entirely misplaced. Charles Dickens played a part, but he was knocking at an open door because of the existing popularity of the festival, and the success of *A Christmas Carol* was rooted in how it represented values and changes that were already in place and process (Rowell 1993). Another specific influence was Prince Albert's introduction of Christmas trees into the Royal household. He was not the first royal to do this, but the publicity given to his tree and the mid-Victorian mania for aping the habits of people's social superiors certainly meant Albert can claim some influence on the spread of this particular ritual (Lalumia 2001). The influence of America was important too and the ritual of hanging stockings brought together the American Santa (who himself owed much to immigrant Dutch traditions) and the older English tradition of Father Christmas.

Central to the growth of the Victorian Christmas was its social and cultural functions. These extended far beyond a day to simply enjoying oneself in the depths of winter. It was a festival that celebrated the bedrocks of Victorian and Edwardian respectable society: religion, commerce, and domesticity. Shopkeepers were often seen as the primary promoters of Christmas but, first and foremost, it was a religious celebration, not just of Christ but of the values of charity and goodwill that were deemed to be integral to true Christianity (Pimlott 1978). One form that goodwill took was present-giving and this freed what could be a frenzy of Christmas shopping from the guilt or vulgarity of normal consumption and spending. The festival also brought families together and soothed the consciences of those who shut their children away in nurseries and at boarding schools, and lived with plenty when there was poverty and misery all around. Yet that poverty meant not everyone could enjoy the Christmas ideal. While the middle classes ate, drank, and were merry, the workers were more limited to a few simple presents for the children and a modest celebratory meal. Ironically, middle-class charity meant those in institutions such as hospitals and workhouses probably enjoyed a better Christmas than the better off members of their class. Christmas was thus as much an illustrator of social divides as something that crossed them. Nor was the Victorian and Edwardian Christmas free from conflict and doubt. Commercialization was a matter of some concern, even though that was what had created much of Christmas culture in the first place. The middle classes also worried about gluttony, drunkenness, begging, and a lack of propriety and Christian feeling. But these concerns were clearly outweighed by the social good that was seen in Christmas (see Armstrong 2010 for the fullest exploration of how the Victorian Christmas was related to wider trends).

In Victorian and Edwardian Britain, the festival was also viewed as an expression of the antiquity of the nation and its civilized, good natured, and tight social bonds. It was a celebration of tradition and the idea of a simple, 'merrie' England in an industrial world of change and complexity. Celebrating Christmas was thus seen as a way of maintaining British heritage. But not all traditions were British and, during the First World War, aspects of the festival, most notably Christmas trees and Santa Claus, were occasionally attacked for their real or imagined Germanic links. In the interwar period, patriotism emerged as a strong theme in Christmas shopping and customers were continually exhorted to buy British, a concept which then included the whole Empire (O'Connor 2009). Indeed, colonials across the Empire consciously followed the traditions of home as a means of expressing their national identity, even if it meant eating heavy winter food in the tropical heat (Clarke 2007; Donaldson 2004). Over the course of the twentieth century, the idea of Christmas as a British festival fell away. This was partly rooted in the growing importance of the festival across the Western world and beyond. It also owed something to how clear American influences on the festival were becoming. Increasingly the festival was viewed not as a symbol of national identity but of globalization (Moore 2014). Of course, national identity was never a primary driver of Christmas and such symbolism was not as important to adherents as the fun, family, and sacred character of the festival.

Nonetheless, historian Mark Connelly (1999: ch. 4) has argued that Christmas epitomized Englishness. The same might be said of Britishness, and the concepts of Englishness and Britishness were always inseparable and interchangeable for many. Christmas was part of a British popular culture that over the twentieth century became more homogenous because of technological developments, the growth of a mass media, rising affluence, and global influences. Indeed, as this chapter explores, after the First World War, Christmas may have been spoken about less often as a symbol of national identity but it remained a powerful integrative experience that drew together national, regional, and local communities in the United Kingdom. It gave form to the abstract 'imagined community' that the nation was, by providing people with common cultural reference points and shared experiences. Yet, as had always been the case, ideas of a unified national culture obscured the significant variations that existed with that culture. This did not mean that Christmas' role as a symbol of and agent in national unity was not real. All nations are diverse entities at one level or another. Their unity is imagined rather than actual, and that imagination draws upon cultural ideas, habits, and symbols that are often banal and taken for granted, underpinned by and embedded in shared everyday practices (Edensor 2002). Christmas was one such practice and one of the most far reaching.

Towards Uniformity

The Victorian and Edwardian middle class may have predominantly celebrated at home but for the working class, whose residences were often uncomfortable, overcrowded, and unappealing, a rare day free from work was reason to take to the streets, not to relax at home. Between the wars too, there were sporting events, pantomimes, cinema showings, folk rituals, and informal gatherings on Christmas Day. But these communal entertainments were by then clearly on the decline as the festival took greater root in the home. Public entertainments, shops, and transport services all began to shut down between the wars. In 1937, *The Economist* (25 December 1937), pointing to how Christmas was slowly becoming more private than public, argued that there was 'no time of the year when the average citizen withdraws more completely and gratefully to his domestic hearth'. In itself, this was a reflection of wider processes. As homes got more comfortable and new estates were built, people were able to live more domestic lives, anchoring themselves in their wider family rather than neighbourhood.

The growing focus of Christmas on the home had a profound impact on the plethora of local and regional festive customs that had helped define local communities, giving them a sense of their own past and identity. Before the First World War, these practices had given something of a local flavour to Christmas. Many were surviving forms of medieval or even older customs centred on ancient superstitions and beliefs. One of the most common was burning a Yule log or bundle of sticks in order to bring good luck or deter ill fortune. There were also a host of visiting customs that combined carnival and community, where people went from house to house or pub to pub, often in fancy dress, offering some form of performance in return for drink or money. Many were based on the 24th or 25th of December, but others—notably wassailing, where people either visited homes with songs and a bowl of drink, or drank and sang around fruit trees to ensure a good crop—centred on Twelfth Night, the end of the Christmas season but also regarded as 'old Christmas Day' by those who kept up the popular memory of pre-reform calendars.

In 1938 one writer remarked that 'all kinds of quaint, picturesque, and amusing' Christmas customs could be found across rural Britain (Owens 1938). But the reality was that many were in decline or had already ceased altogether. This owed something to the emergence of a mass culture where local and regional variations were being subsumed by the uniformity of a mass media, growing urbanization, and perhaps rising class consciousness. In this context, some interwar festive practices were being kept up as part of a conscious attempt to maintain local traditions in the face of modernization and what was perceived as a homogenization of British culture. They helped define local communities, giving them a sense of their own past and identity. Even wishing people a merry Christmas using some form of local dialect could fulfil this role. Where traditions had fallen away but were still within living memory, there were attempts to revive the practices. The first such revivals dated back into the interwar years, a period when there was a growing interest in traditional rural culture and newspaper discussions of the origins of old customs. The local and national publicity given to such events fuelled the desire of others to follow suit and by the 1950s and 60s some were even televised (Johnes 2016: 146–54).

Seeing the decline of local festive traditions, one writer argued in 1951, 'There is a standard Christmas on its way, as there is to be a standard speech and standard dress and a standard wage and a standard goodness-knows-what else' (Harrison 1951: 226). That standardized Christmas grew stronger in the immediate postwar years, as affluence gave people options and an ability to enjoy themselves. It was one where most families ate a similar meal, decorated their home with a tree and some combination of manufactured and natural goods, exchanged wrapped presents, and sent cards to friends and family. They spent the day socializing and engaging with a national media. It was a day of rest, fun, and worship. People did this in their own way and they might miss out some traditions, but it was a day when most people were doing something quite similar (Johnes 2016: chs 2 and 3). *The Times* (24 December 1960) claimed that at Christmas 'the whole nation becomes one kith and kin'. That was a romantic exaggeration, but it summed up how over the twentieth century the festival of the Victorian middle classes became one that belonged to everyone, erasing some ancient regionalized rituals in the process and undermining some of the diversity of the United Kingdom.

Uniting the Imagined Community

Christmas might have become more focused on the home over the course of the twentieth century, but the idea of the festival as a time for local community remained significant. Churchgoing and charitable-giving remained important throughout the period and were often seen as activities that brought people together and reaffirmed social bonds. Carol singing, although sometimes perceived as begging or a nuisance when carried out by children, was infused with a sense of community. Newcomers could integrate themselves through taking part, while the receivers had an opportunity to demonstrate their commitment to the community, especially given how many groups gave the money they raised to charity. Indeed, generous giving was often expected of the richer members of a community. Inevitably, the practice could sometimes get entangled with local divisions and rivalries but that was not what caused its gradually decline in the last third or so of the twentieth century. This was perhaps a product of growing secularization, but it also owed something to how parents were less likely to let their children wander the streets unaccompanied. Whatever the cause, the result was the near disappearance of a ritual that connected people to their communities, even if some had never really appreciated that in the first place. Like the decline of organized religion itself, the falling away of carol-singing was sometimes seen as another symbol of the (misplaced) perception that community feeling was in its death throes in post-war Britain (Johnes 2016: 150–3).

Community was not dying but it was changing. The nature of people's relationships with their neighbours might not have been as intimate as they once were but those relationships rarely disappeared altogether. Some festive practices that were often looked down upon as vulgar were actually about community and connections with others. People who put extravagant lighting displays on the outside of their homes had a strong sense that in doing so they were giving something to the community, even if not all their neighbours and passers-by agreed. Organizations also tried to raise spirits with public decorations. Even before the Second World War, public places such as offices and pubs had their 'festoons of paper flowers and silver bells cut out of card' (Collins 1945: 12). Public trees in villages, towns, and communal places such as railway stations began in the 1930s. This new custom was given a boost in the 1940s when, to much media coverage, a tree was erected in London's Trafalgar Square, an annual gift from the people of Oslo in gratitude for the help rendered during the war. Enjoying such trees and public decorations was part of the way that Christmas created a common experience, even in the era when it was becoming more and more focused on the home. People may have celebrated as individuals, but they did so at the same time and it was a topic of conversation and shared concern.

Churchgoing, charity, and public decorations were rooted in local communities, but Christmas was also increasingly a national event. Above all, it was the media, in all its forms, that created a new shared festive experience that made the rhetoric of a national event something resembling a reality. The radio, with its mix of humour, festive stories, religion and carols, quickly embedded itself in the routine of Christmas Day, especially as the day was simultaneously becoming more focussed on the home. The BBC was very conscious of its role in national culture and took Christmas very seriously. In 1952 the *Radio Times* (19 December 1952) argued that broadcasting was widening the 'great British family' and 'at the same time drawing it closer together'. Like all the British establishment, its vision of Britain was an imperial one. In the 1930s the BBC tried to tighten imperial bonds through Christmas broadcasts from across the Empire, but this programming increasingly seemed outdated in the context of decolonization in the 1950s. Having lost its novelty and its emotional resonances, it was finally dropped in 1965 (Connelly 1999: ch. 5; Johnes 2016: 157).

Whatever the BBC was trying to do to unify Britain and the Empire, the primary appeal of listening on Christmas Day was entertainment. The same was true of television as well. Festive programming was not seen by the BBC as a tool of national integration, but over the course of that period watching television became embedded in people's expectations of the day and it marked the biggest transformation in the twentieth-century Christmas. People watched for fun, because there was little else to do, and sometimes because it avoided arguments. For many, festive programming was something of an event in itself. Broadcasters saw it as the year's highlight and their choice of content over the holidays was a matter for comment at work, home, and in the press. People scanned the listings to plan what to watch, focussing in particular on what films were on because, before video recorders became widespread in the 1980s, Christmas was a rare opportunity to see a recent blockbuster or a classic movie that was not on cinema release. For the most popular broadcasts, half the population could be watching and this represented a very real national experience. There have been few other moments in British history when so many people were doing exactly the same thing. As the technology changed, first with videos and then multiple channels and then streaming, the mass audiences that peaked in the 1970s and 80s fragmented. Audience figures were still huge numbers compared to any activity outside the home, but they marked how specific television programmes were no longer the same kind of shared experience that they once were. Television itself remained a Christmas habit but what, when, and how people watched had fragmented (Johnes 2016: 163–7).

Key to how the festive media became a shared national experience was the Royal broadcast. It first went out in 1932, but was disrupted by changes to the monarchy and George VI's dislike of doing it, and so it did not become an annual affair until 1939. At first, the speech had a strong imperial theme and was intended to unite the Empire and Commonwealth making them seem both more intimate and together. This was something that the speeches repeatedly played upon, mixing up and conflating the ideas of the families of home, nation, and empire. Historian David Cannadine (1983: 142) has thus argued that they 'enhanced the image of the monarch as the father-figure of his people'. This intended intimacy was enhanced from 1957 when the broadcast was televised. Listeners and viewers, however, had their own minds. Some were certainly impressed, but others were cynical or indifferent. Viewing figures fell significantly in the 1990s, as the monarchy itself lost something of its gloss and popular deference. Even the act of consciously not watching lost its power as an act of rebellion as the significance of the tradition faded (Johnes 2016: 158–62).

Alongside the wireless and television was a shared canon of Christmas songs and films that were widely known, adding to the role of the festival in the construction and maintenance of the nation. Christmas pop music was nostalgic in evocation, if not actually in lyrics; it often conjured up simpler times (Whiteley 2008). That was often down to the songs' whimsical or romantic feel, but it was also simply because of the frequency they were played. During December they were inescapable because they were not just heard on the radio but in public places such as shopping centres too. Christmas also dominated television and film in December and the images that people saw on the small and big screen were part of the standardization of Christmas, helping create a shared understanding of what the festival should look like and what people should do on the day. Many of the festive films and television programmes were widely repeated and sometimes remade, becoming traditions in themselves. Whether they were produced in the UK or not, the outputs of cinema and television provided memories and stories that people grew familiar with. They replaced the traditions of local communities and the street, both literally in terms of providing seasonal entertainments, and in their social role in uniting people. They provided talking points within families and between friends and even strangers. They reinforced Christmas' position as a cornerstone of British culture and acted as a bridge that united the individualized experiences of celebrating at home. Christmas music, television, and films may not have hit the standards of high culture, but you did not have to like a story to know it.

Christmas in the media, film, and fiction began as resolutely romantic, sentimental, or comic in tone, capturing and reinforcing people's perception of the season. This has led Connelly (1999, 2000) to describe Christmas films as embodiments and transmitters of Christmas spirit. The genre did evolve to satirize and paint a more complex picture of Christmas that in its own way was just as much a cliché as what it was lampooning. Jokes about annoying relatives, bad presents, and overeating and drinking became staples of Christmas television that everyone recognized and empathized with but were only part of the actual festive experience. Such outputs did not replace the more saccharine genre and there were thus now films, songs, and stories that appealed to all tastes. This variety of Christmas popular culture lessened the chances of people being alienated by the festival and reinforced it as a shared experience and marker of British culture. Christmas—and all its songs, programmes, films, jokes, and tropes—was part of what people understood as British life. It was part of the mundane and banal markers of nationhood and recognizing and relating to it was part of national belonging (Johnes 2016: ch.5).

A Divided Kingdom

Beneath the veneer of a shared national culture was a more diverse picture. This was hardly surprising since the United Kingdom itself was made up by four different nations, making it 'a country of countries, a nation of nations' (Edgerton 2019: xxxiv). Some, of course, denied that the UK was a nation at all. This was clearest in Northern Ireland where such questions could sometimes be a matter of life or death. Political and religious tensions in Northern Ireland inevitably sometimes impacted on Christmas. In the wake of civil war in 1922, for example, the government refused to lift a curfew to allow Catholics to hold their normal Christmas Eve Midnight Mass. When the Cardinal of Armagh announced he would hold one anyway, he was told that the police would surround the cathedral and not let anyone out until morning. In 1971, a Civil Rights Association in Newry campaigned against Christmas as a symbolic gesture against British policy in Northern Ireland. It advised people not to buy British toys for their children and to display candles and black flags instead of Christmas trees. The press claimed that a high proportion of the population was following the instruction that there should be 'no external signs of joy'. To avoid trouble, the army declined invitations for soldiers to have Christmas lunch in local homes and the chamber of commerce decided not to erect its annual town-centre tree. However, the festival could also be a moment of respite from such wider tensions whether that was through soldiers wearing Santa hats or the Christmas truces called by the IRA in 1972, 1974, and 1990 (Johnes 2016: 142, 205, 206).

In nineteenth- and twentieth-century Wales, many of the celebrations took place through the medium of Welsh because that was many people's mother tongue. This did not mean any significant difference in the form of celebrations, but it is a reminder of how misleading the idea of a single British culture could be. Indeed, although Welsh co-existed and was entwined with British culture, the power of the latter, and especially the English language, could create a defensiveness in Wales. In 1914 a Welsh-language newspaper referred to Father Christmas as belonging to the English, although he could be found at Welsh parties and stores (*Dinesydd Cymreig*, 23 December 1914). In 1919, another Welsh-language newspaper was urging readers not to reject him because he had an English name (*Y Cymro*, 24 December 1919). Such was the allure of Christmas that such arguments fell away and Santa became as much a feature of Welsh life as he was in England. This can be seen as part of a wider process of cultural assimilation. Over the course of the twentieth century, the cultural distinctiveness of Wales subsided as the number of Welsh speakers fell and the Nonconformist sects that had been so influential in promoting Welsh identity went into retreat. This led to efforts to reinforce and protect Welsh culture. One example of this was giving Santa, probably in the 1950s, his Welsh name, Siôn Corn (John Chimney). Thus while Christmas was helping integrate the diverse cultures of the United Kingdom, this did not mean or require the subsuming of their different identities. Britishness was a plural experience.

The distinction from mainstream British festive culture was strongest in Scotland. This was rooted in the nation's different religious and sectarian history. Christmas had Catholic undertones that Presbyterians disapproved of. They also complained that it was associated with debauchery, had no real scriptural basis, and painted Christ as a child rather than a saviour. Thus, in the nineteenth century, it was Hogmanay, the Scottish New Year, that was the main winter celebration, while Christmas was a normal working day. In 1871 Christmas Day was made a bank holiday in Scotland. While many places of work stayed open on the 25th, or at least in the morning, the rituals of present shopping and giving were becoming more common in late Victorian Scotland. In 1885, an Aberdeen newspaper remarked how even Presbyterians were being 'weaned over to the customs of our English brethren' and that Christmas was 'speedily overcoming our Scotch prejudice' (*Aberdeen Evening Express*, 25 December 1885). In 1902 the *Dundee Courier* (24 December 1902) suggested that 'Something of the same spirit of mirth and revelry is beginning to creep into the Scottish Christmas as in the English, and the customs in North and South Britain are practically the same'. Yet, in 1904, a Falkirk newspaper (*Falkirk Herald*, 31 December 1904) maintained that beyond the decorations in shop windows and the pressure at the Post Office, the 'event passed without too much to mark its approach'.

Into the 1950s, Christmas in Scotland remained a mixed affair, varying from place to place according to local holiday customs and religious influences, although comments on its increased observance continued. Gift exchange and a special meal became very widely practised, even in homes that were not decorated or where the father had to work in the morning. Yet the whole event seems to have lacked some of the excitement and vigour that it had in other parts of the United Kingdom, and Hogmanay remained the real occasion for celebration, mirth, and joy. Some families continued to consciously not celebrate Christmas, believing it a Catholic or heathen affair (Weightman and Humphries 1987). But, as the indulgence of children gathered strength as a cultural norm in the twentieth century, the pressure to celebrate Christmas in such homes increased too. Parents did not want their children to feel left out if their friends were receiving visits from Santa Claus. War, advertising, consumerism, cinema, and radio were other forces for the cultural integration of Scotland and all were vehicles for the Scots to learn about Christmas.

Of course, there were still limitations to what was happening and in 1948 the MP for Perth claimed that Christmas was practically unobserved in Scotland. That was plainly untrue and by the 1950s the distinct Scottish experience of Christmas was very much in decline, something only too evident in the falling number of workplaces open on Christmas morning. Depictions of Anglo-American feasts and celebrations on television sped up the process of creating festive expectations and aspirations that newsreels, films, and radio had begun before the Second World War. Nonetheless, it was not until 1974 that Boxing Day was made a bank holiday in Scotland, thus expanding the time people had at home to celebrate. Even in the 1980s, there were urban Baptist churches choosing not to hold Christmas Day services, but it was in the Highlands and Islands that the old Presbyterian values lasted longest. The spread of the traditional Christmas to Scotland was a marker of growing cultural and political integration within the UK and of the growing secularization the far north was holding out against. But the growth of Christmas in Scotland was also about a simpler sociological truth. As anyone watching on screen realized—Christmas was fun (Johnes 2016: 169–73).

While Scotland and Wales were losing something of their individual cultural distinctiveness, British culture was becoming more diverse through rising immigration from the Commonwealth after the Second World War. Many migrants were Christian and brought their own Christmas traditions with them, adding a little more variation to British festive practices. But Christmas, with all its associations of home, family, and nostalgia, could be a difficult time for some migrants: it was a reminder of how they often felt and were treated as outsiders within Britain. In the 1960s, rising immigration from the Indian subcontinent created new dynamics since many of these migrants were not from Christian backgrounds. As with Jewish Britons before them, the ubiquity of the festival forced non-Christians to make a conscious decision as to whether they wanted to celebrate or not. Moreover, both family members and onlookers often perceived celebrating Christmas as a signal of integration. The desires of their children certainly encouraged some non-Christian families to celebrate Christmas, and this was made easier by the growing secular nature of the festival. Nonetheless, the explicit and implicit pressure on migrants, their families, and those of different faiths to celebrate could create tensions, resentment, and feelings of alienation. Right-wing commentators, meanwhile, had the opposite fear and some argued that politically correct pressures not to offend minorities were undermining the festival. Stories were told of offices and councils that banned decorations or changed the title of the festival to something not involving the word Christ. At the roots of such complaints was the same nostalgic reverence for the comfort of tradition that helped underpin Christmas itself. But it was also paranoid nonsense, infused with more than a touch of racism (Johnes 2016: 173–7).

Another complication to the idea of a British Christmas was the growing international dimensions of the festival. It was, after all, celebrated across much of the globe and its Christian message was about the fellowship of man not nations. Even Santa was an international figure rather than the benefactor of any one country. Thus, when Scotland fell into line, it was not just integrating into a British culture but a global tradition. One anthropologist has even suggested that festive rituals repeated across the globe created 'a relationship between the celebrant and the world at large' (Miller 1993:

31). Here, once again, the media was central. Images of Christmas in other parts of world were staples of newsreels, newspaper reports, and television and radio broadcasts. The songs and films that made up so much of festive popular culture were often from the United States. Indeed, Christmas demonstrated how so much of what was taken as the globalization of popular culture was really about the Americanization of the world. This was not just a product of the post-1945 world. 'Jingle Bells' was an American song penned in 1856. The holly wreaths on front doors and public trees that began to become popular in inter-war Britain were imitations of American fashions. Santa Claus himself was an American import, even when he went by his more British name of Father Christmas. That name was often used very self-consciously as part of a wider distrust of American influences on post-1945 culture. Similarly, some rejected the term 'Xmas' as a crass Americanization, despite its much older Christian roots. The antipathy towards Americanization of Christmas was also somewhat misplaced because it was far from a complete process. There were, for example, traditions such as civic parades and the expression 'happy holidays' that never found a home on the British side of the Atlantic despite being depicted in widely watched American films. For Christmas, like all aspects of culture, globalization was always an uneven and partial process.

Wherever it came from and whatever it represented, the place of Christmas in national culture was also undermined by the fact that not everyone could afford to take part. For the Victorian and Edwardian working class, celebrations had been limited to a better than normal meal and fruit or a homemade present for the children. For those in work, material conditions improved between the wars and the working class saved all year to ensure they had a bit of spare money to indulge themselves and their family. This mattered to them because the ability to spend so freely and indulgently was so rare. However, unemployment also rose significantly between the wars, and Christmas was a miserable time for those out of work precisely because it was meant to be a time of excess and fun. The 1950s saw the spread of a genuine affluence to the masses and the excesses became more common, as parents tried to give their children what they had so often not had themselves. Thus, although the commercial nature of Christmas was often blamed on retailers, it was also rooted in fulfilling people's desire to spend, especially amongst those who were not always able to do so. This continued to fuel high levels of spending amongst the less well off into the twenty-first century. Christmas also remained a time of the year when the isolation of those unable to spend much, or share the festival with friends or family, was often most keenly felt because of the inescapable plethora of images in the shops, media, and on the streets of others having fun (Johnes 2016: ch. 1).

As affluence gave people options, families made efforts to mark their individuality and taste through Christmas. They developed their own personal rituals that cemented their sense of family identity and united the generations. These personalized traditions might be marking the start of the holiday by always watching the same film, reusing decorations passed down through the generations, or having certain rules for the choice, presentation, and distribution of presents. Even in the 1930s and 40s, there were families with their own customs such as piling presents in the bath or giving 'daft' gifts such as a potato wrapped in Christmas paper or an apple, nut, or sweet wrapped in multiple layers to make a large parcel. Such very individualized traditions were self-conscious symbols of the collective personality of a family, a ritual that displayed their humour or tastes within a mass culture that could seem rather monolithic. Indeed, all Christmas rituals were chosen and shaped by people's aspirations and tastes. Christmas gave people an opportunity to say something about themselves, whether that was through a virtuous wait for presents, stylish decorations, ironic kitsch, carefree extravagance, or anything that showed one had a sense of humour or was able to put aside sartorial concerns for the enjoyment of the children (Johnes 2016: ch.3; Mason and Muir 2013).

Yet no matter how personal they were to someone, rituals were always a blend of personal preference and a wider cultural heritage. Like all forms of consumerism, Christmas may have given people the opportunity to define their own personality—to mark themselves out from the crowd—but they were doing so in a way that mirrored hundreds of thousands of other people. Those people using Christmas rituals to demonstrate their taste, even if this meant opting out altogether, were still operating within a broad culture of conformity. The variations were just that—variations within a theme—and most people still adhered to the general rules and traditions of sending cards, playing along with Santa, erecting a tree or decorations, and having a substantial meal. This broad conformity might seem trivial but it says something very significant about Britain. It shows how strong the nation's cultural unity was; it shows how a majority went along with traditions and established ways of doing things, consciously or otherwise. Conforming to these rituals was not always everyone's choice and those with children were particularly vulnerable to peer pressure. But that did not change the fact that there was a remarkable degree of conformity in people's festive behaviour. However fractured Britain was in terms of its social and economic structure, Christmas was at least an indicator that its cultural web was intact.

Conclusion

Christmas was an integrative experience. It brought people closer to their family, friends, neighbours, community, compatriots and, occasionally, the poor and suffering. It crossed any notional boundaries between the private and public spheres and helped maintain a common way of life in a society divided by class, ethnicity, and taste. Sometimes this integration was literal and physical. Sometimes it was through the medium of a shared media or even just the fact that it was something everyone encountered. The vast majority of people did celebrate Christmas and partook in its key rituals of feasting, gift-giving, and the shopping required for both. Even those who did not celebrate, or tried to keep their adherence as minimal as possible, could not escape Christmas unless they literally shut themselves away for the whole of December, never leaving the house, turning on a television, or reading a newspaper. While all this made Christmas an integral part of British culture, individuals still had freedom to celebrate in their own way, to manipulate and recast its rituals, to put their own stamp of personality and status on it. Without that flexibility, Christmas could never have had the powerful integrative role it did.

Christmas was, thus, simultaneously a symbol of family, local, national, and global cultures. But beneath the facade of unity were diverse communities. Not everyone took part in local traditions or welcomed the calling of neighbours and children. Just because people were watching the same programme did not mean they were thinking the same thing or watching in the same conditions. Even family celebrations concealed strong gendered aspects to shared experiences. Throughout the century, women had to shoulder very disproportionate shares of the cooking and shopping, meaning the festival was as much a time of slog as fun for them (Johnes 2016: 55–62). For a few, Christmas was actually an exclusionary experience. So powerful was Christmas as a cultural norm that when people, through choice or circumstance, did not celebrate, it could leave them feeling outside or removed from the mainstream.

Unity may have been an illusionary concept but it was a powerful one nonetheless. Christmas was part of a British way of life. This was more than just rhetoric. The United Kingdom may have been divided by wealth, region, gender, and ethnicity, but history and culture gave most of the people within them a sense that they all belonged to the same country and Christmas was part of the shared culture that engendered the sense of togetherness. It may not have been celebrated much as a sign of national culture after 1945, but it was still part of the array of habits and routines that defined British society, an example of what Michael Billig (1995) called 'banal nationalism'. It produced a widely known canon of traditions, music, films, and stories that were part of the cultural web that bound people together. One did not have to like or consume these for them to produce a national community; it was enough to know that they existed. There may not have been that much about Christmas and its cultural canon that was peculiarly British but that did not make Christmas any less something that the British shared and, by sharing in it, in whatever guise they wanted, people reaffirmed their place in British culture.

References and Further Reading

Armstrong, Neil (2010). *Christmas in Nineteenth Century England*. Manchester: Manchester University Press.
Billig, Michael (1995), *Banal Nationalism*. London: Sage.
Cannadine, David, (1983). 'The Context, Performance and Meaning of Ritual: The British Monarchy, and the "Invention of Tradition", c.1820–1977', in Eric Hobsbawm and Terence Ranger (eds.), *The Invention of Tradition*. Cambridge: Cambridge University Press: 101–64.
Clarke, Alison (2007). *Holiday Seasons: Christmas, New Year and Easter in Nineteenth-Century New Zealand*. Auckland: Auckland University Press.

Collins, Norman (1945). *London Belongs to Me*. London: Collins.
Connelly, Mark (1999). *Christmas: A Social History*. London: IB Tauris.
Connelly, Mark (ed.) (2000). *Christmas at the Movies: Images of Christmas in American, British and European Cinema*. London: IB Tauris.
Donaldson, Rhiannon (2004). 'Revisiting a "Well-Worn Theme": The Duality of the Australian Christmas Pudding 1850–1950'. *Eras Journal*, 6. Available at http://www.arts.monash.edu.au/publications/eras/edition-6/donaldsonarticle.php/ (accessed 26 March 2020).
Edgerton, David (2019), *The Rise and Fall of the British Nation: A Twentieth-Century History*. London: Penguin.
Edensor, Tim (2002). *National Identity, Popular Culture and Everyday Life*. Oxford: Berg.
Golby J. M. and Purdue, A. W. (1986). *The Making of Modern Christmas*. London: B. T. Batsford.
Harrison, Michael (1951). *The Story of Christmas: Its Growth and Development from the Earliest Times*. London: Odhams.
Hutton, Ronald (1996). *Stations of the Sun: A History of the Ritual Year in Britain*. Oxford: Oxford University Press.
Johnes, Martin (2016). *Christmas and the British: A Modern History*. London: Bloomsbury Academic.
Lalumia, Christine (2001). 'Scrooge and Albert', *History Today*, 51, no. 12: 23–30.
Mason, Jennifer and Stewart Muir (2013). 'Conjuring up Traditions: Atmospheres, Eras and Family Christmases', *Sociological Review*, 61, no. 3: 607–29.
Miller, Daniel (1993). 'A Theory of Christmas', in Daniel Miller (ed), *Unwrapping Christmas*. Oxford: Oxford University Press: 3–37.
Moore, Tara (2014). *Christmas: The Sacred to Santa*. London: Reaktion Books.
O'Connor, Kaori (2009). 'The King's Christmas Pudding: Globalization, Recipes, and the Commodities of Empire', *Journal of Global History* 4, no. 1: 127–55.
Owens, W. H. (1938). 'Christmas Customs around Britain', *Chamber's Journal*, December: 979–81.
Pimlott, J. A. R. (1978). *The Englishman's Christmas: A Social History*. Hassocks: Harvester.
Rowell, Geoffrey (1993). 'Dickens and the Construction of Christmas'. *History Today*, 43: 17–24.
Weightman, Gavin and Humphries, Steve (1987). *Christmas Past*. London: Sidgwick & Jackson.
Whiteley, Sheila (2008). 'Christmas Songs—Sentiments and Subjectivities', in Sheila Whiteley (ed), *Christmas, Ideology and Popular Culture*. Edinburgh: Edinburgh University Press: 98–112.

CHAPTER 38

THE UNITED STATES

DANIEL VACA

WHAT is Christmas about? In a way, the answer is obvious. The purpose of the holiday even appears in its name, which literally denotes a Christian Mass in honour of Jesus Christ. And yet that etymological answer does not account for the scale and scope of contemporary Christmas celebrations in the United States. According to a survey conducted in 2017, approximately 90 per cent of American adults reported celebrating Christmas, but only 55 per cent reported celebrating Christmas for what they understood as religious reasons. As many as 85 per cent of people who claim no religious affiliation also celebrate Christmas.

Recognizing that Christmas is not simply about Christianity, some observers have presented this fact as a recent development. Analyzing the results of the 2017 survey, a number of popular media outlets highlighted what appeared to be a discernible decline in the proportion of American adults who see Christmas as a religious phenomenon. Reports noted that 3 per cent more adults associated Christmas with religion in 2013 (Pew 2017). For advocates of the ongoing campaign to 'put Christ back in Christmas', this statistical decline could serve as evidence that they should amplify their efforts. But another interpretation simply acknowledges that the celebration always has found its centre in something other than Christology. For centuries, the time surrounding Christmas perennially has been a season in which individuals, families, and communities have sought to envision and enact particular social aspirations. As this chapter illustrates through a variety of examples, Christmas has served this purpose throughout the history of the United States.

In serving this purpose, Christmas has spanned the two major categories that scholars have used to understand the function of particular holidays. One set of holidays focus on 'tension management'. They cultivate social cohesion by 'releasing tension that results from conformity to societal beliefs and the behavioral prescriptions they entail' (Etzioni 2004: 12). Examples include holidays known for debauchery, such as Mardi Gras and New Year's Eve, as well as holidays known for relaxation, such as Memorial Day and Labor Day. Today no less than in earlier centuries of American history, Christmas has served as a time to relieve tension through practices of giving and consuming. But a second and especially significant feature of Christmas has involved a focus on 'recommitment'. Including examples such as Easter and the Fourth of July, recommitment holidays ask celebrants to ritually pledge themselves to particular issues or identities (Etzioni 2004: 11–13). Through a wide array of ritual practices and cultural productions, Christmas has become a time to cultivate recommitment to varied social aspirations, including but not limited to particular visions of self, family, community, and nation.

INDULGENCE AND INVERSION

As contemporary Christmas celebrations developed over the course of the nineteenth century, they often involved practices that temporarily manifested alternate ways of seeing and being in the world. The seasonal celebrations that swirled around Christmas had this effect by enabling celebrants to temporarily flout ordinary social conventions and conditions. Examples included prevailing class disparities, accepted standards of propriety, and generational hierarchies.

Many of these practices derived from ancient traditions of winter celebration. The historian Joseph Kelly points out that the 'non-religious festive element' of winter celebrations 'probably went a long way toward making the religious festival a popular one' (Kelly 2004: 128–9). Long before Christians began treating Christmas as a major religious festival during the fourth century, the month of December and the beginning of the New Year had been a time of relaxation and indulgence for northern European agricultural societies. Having completed the fall harvest and made preparations for winter, people in societies throughout Europe found themselves able to enjoy minimal work as well as a relatively large stock of grain, meat, beer, and wine. Encouraging indulgence, winter celebrations manifested a sense of idyllic abundance. Those celebrations became associated with Christmas in European societies and colonies later dominated by Christians.

In British America, the Christmas season paired a spirit of indulgence together with a spirit of 'misrule'. Despite the objections of Protestants who condemned Christmas for its supposed vulgarity as well as its lack of biblical justification, traditions of misrule remained popular because they allowed working-class celebrants to disregard and even overturn the standards of deference between social classes that typically oriented public behaviour. As the historian Stephen Nissenbaum explains, social hierarchies were 'symbolically turned upside down, in a gesture that inverted designated roles of gender, age, and class'. In the seventeenth and eighteenth centuries, wealthy members of the propertied class often welcomed peasants, servants, and apprentices into their homes and offered food, drink, entertainment, and even gifts. This practice provided guests with an experience of material abundance, while hosts enjoyed the notion that this gesture might abate class resentment enough to prevent social tension from transforming into outright conflict. It functioned as a 'safety valve that contained class resentments within clearly defined limits' (Nissenbaum 1997: 51).

The need for this sort of wintertime safety valve became more pronounced in the nineteenth century, as the rise of wage labour and industrial production not only created starker contrasts between the wealthy and working classes but also transformed December into a quiet time in the annual schedule of factory production. With many of the waterways in the north-eastern United States iced over, urban factories often were forced to slow production or shut down. Workers accordingly sought relief from the unemployment and want that the wintertime brought, and one method of seeking relief involved taking advantage of traditions that allowed them to make demands of the more prosperous and propertied classes (Nissenbaum 1997: 8–11, 50–2).

But as new modes of economic production made traditions of misrule more pronounced, members of the wealthier classes sought to reimagine practices that they increasingly viewed not as aspirational glimpses of social harmony but rather as menacing threats. Reimagining the social inversion that misrule involved, some members of the propertied classes sought to portray children as the proper recipients of Christmas charity. With young children generally occupying lower rungs of household hierarchies, the act of showing them deference and offering them gifts not only allowed children to symbolically stand in for the working class but also encouraged anyone with children to invert their own households. This focus on the home and its own stratifications complemented a more general cultural focus on the ideal of domesticity as a tonic in an age of dramatic economic and demographic change.

The mythology of St Nicholas and Santa Claus served this transformation. Portrayed in the early nineteenth century as a genteel Christian cleric, St Nicholas initially was known as an authoritative figure that dispensed punishments as well as rewards. Beginning in the 1820s, however, authors such as Clement Clarke Moore cultivated St Nicholas's emergence as what the historian Gerry Bowler describes as a 'nonsectarian, genial avatar of grandfatherly benevolence' (Bowler 2016: 53). In 'A Visit from St. Nicholas', Moore describes the story's titular figure as someone who 'looked like a peddler'. With Christmas traditions having prioritized displays of charity and deference toward working-class dependents by their propertied patrons, Moore's plebeian St Nicholas complemented the notion that working-class people shared an obligation to show charity and deference toward others—and especially towards children. Whereas Christmas traditions of misrule had drawn on the notion that an inversion of class hierarchies relieved class conflict, Moore's St Nicholas encouraged households to focus on internal rather than external disparities. In addition to helping domesticate Christmas, the popularity of St Nicholas and his itinerant gift-giving helped shift the holiday's celebration earlier in the calendar, with the season of celebration reaching its peak on Christmas Day rather than New Year's Day (Schmidt 1995: 108).

With the figure of Santa Claus manifesting a spirit of family-focused inversion, the practice of lying to children about that figure's existence has served as a way for parents to commit to that spirit and instil it in their children. Through seemingly harmless dishonesty, children are taught to imagine and commit themselves to alternate ways of seeing and being in the world. Those alternate worlds feature abundance, indulgence, and magic. As some critics of this ritualized dishonesty have noted, the fantasy conflicts with the harsh conditions of many children's lives. For children facing poverty and violence, alternate worlds can be difficult to imagine or realize even temporarily. But the persistence of the practice nevertheless testifies to the way that envisioning and enacting social aspirations have proven central to the idea and practice of Christmas in the United States (Gill and Papatheodorou 1999: 200).

Charity and Giving

Even as generational inversions and practices of showing charitable deference to children became increasingly prominent features of Christmas, the season's emphasis on enacting particular social aspirations allowed charitable giving to remain a prominent practice. Drawing together ideals of family and charity, popular Christmas stories and practices focused especially on temporarily rescuing women and children from poverty (Restad 1995: 135). As these stories illustrate, however, practices of giving often have served not just as efforts to enhance the lives of others, but especially as expressions of givers' aspirations for their own lives. At Christmas, people have given—in part—because it became recognized as a time for people to perform ideal versions of their charitable, generous, and prosperous selves.

The paradigmatic example of giving as an expression of givers' seasonal aspirations long has been Charles Dickens's *A Christmas Carol*. Published in 1843 and extraordinarily popular among American readers, the story focuses on the wealthy moneylender Ebenezer Scrooge's decision to repent of his penuriousness. After spirits help him see that his lack of regard for others would consign him to a miserable and lonely life, he awakens on Christmas Day and sets out to ameliorate the crushing poverty of the family of an employee, Bob Cratchit, by raising his wages and sending his family a turkey. Still today, this story seems to typify an ideal of Christmas charity that prioritizes the practice of giving gifts or money to those in need. But as a variety of commentators have pointed out, Scrooge's gift does not radically transform the structural conditions of Cratchit's work life. Arguing that Cratchit ultimately gives Scrooge more than he gets, the historian Penne Restad remarks: 'the story's real patron proved to be Cratchit, and the wealthy, miserable Scrooge, the recipient' (Restad 1995: 139). The story focuses above all on how giving transformed Scrooge's own life.

To be sure, givers cannot avoid reaping some benefit from their gifts. As the sociologist Marcel Mauss explained in his famous treatise *The Gift*, generosity and self-interest 'are linked in giving', insofar as people often give due to their self-interested desire to respect perceived social obligations (Mauss 2002: 87). By acknowledging this insight, examinations of self-interested motivations for giving can reveal the obligations that people have responded to through their gifts and contributions.

In many cases, people have given in order to secure access to an idealized status, including but not limited to particular class and national identities. Well into the eighteenth century, wealthy elites and aristocrats throughout Europe and the British Empire often exchanged valuable and precious gifts around the New Year. Participants used these exchanges to display their current and aspired status in elite hierarchies (Schmidt 1995: 111). Noting that 'charity and gift-giving are integral parts of the Christmas holiday season', the historian Joshua Plaut recounts how American Jews turned to charity in the nineteenth century as 'an opportunity to be part of a new American tradition'. Jewish welfare societies provided aid to soldiers during the Civil War, gathered donations for families, and supported an array of non-Jewish causes. Some charitable efforts even focused on relieving non-Jews from work obligations at Christmas, so that celebrants could spend the holiday with their families. Those work obligations included performing in costume as Santa Claus. Although these acts of charity and service express a spirit of generosity, they also have served as a method of investing American Jews with a sense of status and civic responsibility (Plaut 2012: 42, 115–24, 133).

Alongside their charitable activities, many American Jews came to see gift-giving at Christmas as means of conjuring ideal Jewish and American identities. As cultures of Christmas and consumerism began to flourish during the second half of the nineteenth century, many newly immigrated European Jews treated Christmas celebrations and gifting traditions as opportunities to participate in and assimilate into American society. Due to the popularity of Christmas in Germany—where the Christmas tree originally became a seasonal fixture—Jews from Germany embraced Christmas especially eagerly. Although Jewish leaders in the United States were concerned that Christmas celebrations might dilute Jewish identity, they also worried that simply condemning Christmas might alienate Jews from their own tradition. To address these anxieties, Jewish leaders elaborated upon the relatively minor holiday of Hanukkah and transformed it into a way for Jews to participate in the national festivities surrounding Christmas. Just like Christmas, Hanukkah not only focused on pleasing children and cultivating family-focused domesticity but also featured the purchase and exchange of gifts (Ashton 2013: 98). One legacy of American Jews' ambivalent relationship with Christmas is the phenomenon of interfaith holiday celebrations and an array of Jewish spoofs on Christmas and its cultural expressions. Examples include Jewish interpretations of Santa as well as the invention of hybrid celebrations, such as 'Chrismukkah' (Mehta 2018; Shandler and Weintraub 2007).

For Jewish Americans and others, the impulse to give gifts drew strength from the rise of consumer capitalism. As early as the 1830s, merchants in urban centres such as New York and Philadelphia created what the historian Leigh Schmidt describes as a robust 'Christmas bazaar', which provided middle-class consumers with 'a world of faith, freedom, and contentment that revolved around the plentiful choices of the marketplace' (Schmidt 1995: 129). This marketplace not only enhanced the variety and quantity of gifts that consumers could purchase but also allowed those gifts and the process of selecting them to amass more social significance. The activity known as shopping emerged as a leisure activity through which consumers performed particular class identities and aspirations.

For women in particular, Christmas shopping became a way of recommitting self and family to an ideal version of middle-class domesticity (Schmidt 1995: 153). Shopping had this effect because it is what the historian James Farrell describes as 'an *imaginative* activity', which transformed the practice of searching for and acquiring commodities into a way for people to attempt to locate and acquire 'a whole way of life that would be better than ours' (Farrell 1998: 154–7). To be sure, shopping made this aspirational imagining possible any time of the year. But Christmas and Hanukkah elevated shopping's significance by focusing the phenomena on the priority of the family and its welfare. Shopping and gifting have remained focused on this priority since the nineteenth century, and women have continued to feel a disproportionate obligation to take responsibility for procuring gifts (Fischer and Arnold 1990).

Recognizing the invariable self-interest of gift-giving and charity, some commentators have proposed methods for ensuring that givers focus more attention on the interests of the recipients of holiday gifts. The economist Joel Waldfogel, for example, argues that the best gift typically is simply cash. Why? When people purchase consumer goods as gifts, those gifts often draw primary attention to the quality or value of the giver's selection. Because the recipient's desire for the item is secondary, conventional gifts often provide the recipient less value than the giver intended. Transfers of money to individuals or charities solve this problem by allowing recipients to choose their own gifts or by using money otherwise wasted on gift purchases to charitably meet someone's need (Waldfogel 2009). Yet even if Waldfogel's call to selfless giving would allocate resources more efficiently, it struggles to overcome the weight of centuries of traditions that have made the gift about the giver.

Conflict and Unity

Christmas celebrations in the United States have perpetually taken shape around understandings of what communities, families, and individuals could or should be. But those understandings never have been universally shared, and Christmas traditions and their implied commitments have continually generated social conflict. In response to that conflict, however, Christmas celebrations also have inspired new attempts to conjure forms of unity.

In colonial North America, European Christians used Christmas stories and celebrations as resources for converting and socializing indigenous populations. As the historian Kristin Mann has explained, in the seventeenth and eighteenth centuries Franciscan and Jesuit missionaries to New Spain adapted 'Christian liturgy and European folk traditions to the practical realities and local practices of life in frontier mission communities' (Mann 2010: 333). Repurposing techniques developed in Europe of using religious plays and music to transmit Christian instruction, Catholic missionaries in New Spain used the arts—including dramas, folk dances, and music—to engage potential converts. Their attempts at representation and translation often focused on religious festivals, which were seen as effective opportunities for 'integrating Christian devotions into indigenous understandings' (Mann 2010: 338). In Nuevo Mexico, for instance, Franciscans emphasized the coincidence of Christmas and indigenous Puebloan groups' emphasis on the winter solstice as an important time in their own ritual calendars.

Although these missionizing techniques largely succeeded in engaging indigenous populations with Christian teachings, indigenous peoples also resisted colonizers' strategies of subjugation by reinterpreting Christian teachings through and alongside their own cultural practices. Encouraged to perform dances and musical performances as part of Christmas celebrations, for example, Puebloans used those festal occasions to perform their own dances. Otherwise discouraged, those dances could occur in public under the guise of Christian celebration. This process of cultural conflict, dialogue, and mixing not only led Christmas to become a primary feast day in the northern communities of New Spain but also shaped cultural traditions that remain prominent in the region today. Those traditions include *pastorelas*, religious dramas that creatively re-enact the Nativity narrative found in the Gospel according to Luke, using motifs and characters that reflect the geographic and cultural traditions of the borderlands between what is now the United States and Mexico.

As this example illustrates, varied groups recurrently have treated Christmas celebrations as expressions of an aspirational ideal vision for society. In this way, Christmas exemplifies the classic social theory of the sociologist Émile Durkheim, who described rites as 'ways of acting that are born only in the midst of assembled groups and whose purpose is to evoke, maintain, or recreate certain mental states of those groups' (Durkheim 1995: 9). But the examples of Catholic missionaries and indigenous populations also highlight the way in which rites evoke the 'mental states' of some groups more than others, and rites can reveal social divisions by serving as vehicles for groups to attempt to enforce and enshrine their own power.

Consider, for example, the United States Supreme Court case of *Lynch v. Donnelley*. Decided in 1984, the case involved an annual Christmas display in the downtown shopping district of Pawtucket, Rhode Island, that included a Nativity scene, which featured such explicitly Christian figures as Jesus, Mary, and Joseph. Although the display was located on private land, it was purchased and maintained with public funds. Claiming that the display had the effect of publicly endorsing particular religious perspectives, a city resident sued the city on the grounds that this Nativity scene's use of public funds amounted to an unconstitutional establishment of religion. Writing for the court's majority, Warren Burger did not disagree with the claim that the Nativity scene was religious; instead, Burger argued that the scene's religious content was so firmly established as part of the history of the United States and so essential to American society that the city's display could be seen as having a 'secular purpose'. Notwithstanding the 'special meaning' of the Nativity scene for Christians, Burger insisted that it 'engenders a friendly community spirit of goodwill in keeping with the season' (Lynch v. Donnelly 1984). Because Burger not only viewed Christian symbols as inextricable aspects of Christmas but also understood Christmas rites and their symbols as essential features of American society, he sought to secure the public prominence of Christianity.

While the Supreme Court ultimately repressed the conflict that Pawtucket's Nativity scene engendered, other instances of opposition to majoritarian visions of Christmas unity have proven more difficult to ignore. As a rite that enshrines particular social ideals and aspirations, for example, Christmas historically has manifested concepts of racial identity that people of colour have viewed as exclusionary. In the early twentieth century, the Ku Klux Klan treated Christmas as a time to celebrate the ideal of a society dominated by white supremacy. To do so, they donated money to a variety of charitable causes, including donations to former slaves and immigrants in order to underline their patronizing benevolence. During the late 1960s, civil rights leaders responded to a similar spirit of racial division at Christmas. Recognizing that consumer spending had become essential to maintaining social stability during the Christmas season, civil rights leaders launched 'Black Christmas' movements across the South. Those movements sought to raise awareness about the campaign for rights and reallocated consumers' money to initiatives such as the Montgomery Improvement Association (Bowler 2016: 155–6).

In addition to inspiring acts of opposition, majoritarian social visions associated with Christmas have generated entirely new holidays. Although a reaction to Christmas animated Jewish leaders' transformation of Hanukkah from a minor Jewish celebration into a much more prominent Jewish holiday, no holiday exemplifies this reaction against Christmas better than Kwanzaa. Founded by the black nationalist Maulana Karenga, the holiday of Kwanzaa began in 1966 in the wake of riots in Watts, a black neighbourhood of Los Angeles. The riots took shape out of frustration with police brutality and an array of inequities. Viewing the creation of an independent black nation as a social ideal, Karenga believed that the first step in a longer process of independence would be the creation of an independent black culture. To work toward cultural liberation, Karenga encouraged supporters to learn the common language of Swahili and embrace a philosophy that combined black nationalism, pan-Africanism, and anti-capitalist ideology. That philosophy became the heart of Kwanzaa, which dedicated seven days to celebrating seven principles that included unity, self-determination, collective work and responsibility, and cooperative economics (Pleck 2001: 79).

But Kwanzaa did not achieve prominence until the 1980s, when it was embraced by the black middle class. That embrace became possible as it was reinterpreted as a celebration that supplemented Christmas rather than competed with it. African American magazines encouraged and detailed Kwanzaa celebrations, and publishing firms began developing Kwanzaa cookbooks for mass audiences. According to the historian Elizabeth Pleck, these popular depictions transformed Kwanzaa into a celebration that 'served the important function of affirming racial and familial identity within the black middle class' (Pleck 2001: 15). Both as a black nationalist celebration and a celebration of 'the black version of the idea of family values', the essence of the celebration lay in its function as an expression of what its celebrants believed society could and should look like. In this way, Kwanzaa can be seen as more than a reaction against or a supplement to Christmas; Kwanzaa fundamentally shared Christmas's preoccupation with imagining and enacting an ideal world.

Among all of the examples of individuals and groups who have used the season and celebration of Christmas to articulate and perform their visions for society, few examples have done this more starkly than avowed conservatives who annually have bemoaned a supposed 'War on Christmas'. Around the turn of the twenty-first century, this war became associated above all with the cable news network Fox News Channel, whose contributors regularly chronicled what they saw as efforts to drive Christmas and Christianity from public view. 'The war on Christmas is worse than I thought—and perhaps than you thought,' the former Fox News host John Gibson explained in 2005, 'because it's really a war on Christianity.' Gibson surmised that 'secular humanist hostility to Christianity is not merely a joking bumper sticker demonstrating a willingness to be outrageous, but a deeply felt hostility toward Christians that wouldn't be tolerated against other world religions' (Gibson 2005: 160, 163). Here, Gibson described Christmas as a synecdoche for Christianity itself.

Yet as this chapter has shown, Christmas never has been solely about Christianity, and arguments to the contrary ultimately reveal less about Christmas than about the Christians who see themselves under attack. Remember that Christians always have possessed a disproportionate amount of social prominence and privilege in the United States. Remember also that 'Christianity' encompasses a wide range of Christians. Taking these two reminders together, complaints about the 'war on Christmas' appear as an attempt by some Christians to lament what they perceive as a loss of prominence and privilege.

The concept of Christmas serves as a useful instrument for this purpose, not simply because its ambiguous religiosity allows it to serve as an index of religion in the public sphere but also because it always has distilled the social ideals and aspirations of those who celebrate it. This latter quality makes it an object of nostalgia for forms of society that people imagine in the past and hope for in the present. All of this helps explain why Donald Trump insisted repeatedly as a presidential candidate and president that 'we are going to say "Merry Christmas" again' (Stack 2016). For Trump, this vow was not about Christianity: it was an extension of his promise to revive an earlier era and ideal of American society.

Conclusion

Writing about Christmas films, the scholar of religion Christopher Deacy has claimed that they 'act as a barometer of how we might want to live and how we see and measure ourselves' (Deacy 2016: 167). I suggest that the same could be said about virtually all aspects of Christmas's celebration. From shopping to gift-giving to family rituals to fighting, the Christmas season serves in the United States as a moment not only to imagine ideal selves and communities but also to practise recommitment to those ideals through varied rituals. Christmas has had this function for centuries, among a wide range of communities, ethnic groups, and socio-economic classes.

Yet even though I have claimed in this chapter that Christmas is about more than Christianity, that does mean that Christmas does not remain a holiday that Christians hold especially dear. How could it be otherwise? Beyond the title of the holiday itself, Christians possess a wide range of theological principles that have defined and continue to capture the spirit of the season. The story of the Incarnation and its theological interpretations, after all, find their centre in the notion of a divine creator who renews the world by inhabiting it. It is, fundamentally, a story about divine recommitment to a vision of an ideal world. That is the story of Christmas—in the United States, and beyond.

REFERENCES AND FURTHER READING

Ashton, Dianne (2013). *Hanukkah in America: A History*. Goldstein-Goren Series in American Jewish History. New York: NYU Press.

Deacy, Christopher (2016). *Christmas as Religion: The Relationship Between Sacred and Secular*. New York: Oxford University Press.

Durkheim, Émile (1995). *The Elementary Forms of Religious Life*, trans. Karen E Fields. New York: Free Press.

Etzioni, Amitai (2004). 'Holidays and Rituals: Neglected Seedbeds of Virtue', in Amitai Etzioni and Jared Bloom (eds.), *We Are What We Celebrate: Understanding Holidays and Rituals*. New York: NYU Press: 3–40.

Farrell, James J. (1998). 'Shopping: The Moral Ecology of Consumption', *American Studies* 39, no. 3: 153–73.

Fischer, Eileen, and Arnold, Stephen J. (1990). 'More Than a Labor of Love: Gender Roles and Christmas Gift Shopping', *Journal of Consumer Research* 17, no. 3: 333–345.

Gibson, John (2005). *The War on Christmas: How the Liberal Plot to Ban the Sacred Christian Holiday Is Worse Than You Thought*. New York: Sentinel Trade.

Gill, Janet, and Papatheodorou, Theodora (1999). 'Perpetuating the Father Christmas Story: A Justifiable Lie?', *International Journal of Children's Spirituality* 4, no. 2: 195–205.

Kelly, Joseph F. (2004). *The Origins of Christmas*. Collegeville, Minn: Liturgical Press.

Lynch v. Donnelly. 1984. U.S. Supreme Court.

Mann, Kristin Dutcher (2010). 'Christmas in the Missions of Northern New Spain.' *The Americas*, 66, no. 3: 331–351.

Mauss, Marcel (2002). *The Gift: The Form and Reason for Exchange in Archaic Societies*. London: Routledge.

Mehta, Samira K. (2018). *Beyond Chrismukkah: The Christian-Jewish Interfaith Family in the United States*. New York: NYU Press.

Nissenbaum, Stephen (1997). *The Battle for Christmas*. New York: Alfred A. Knopf.

Pew Research Center (2017). 'Americans Say Religious Aspects of Christmas Are Declining in Public Life'. Available at https://www.pewforum.org/2017/12/12/americans-say-religious-aspects-of-christmas-are-declining-in-public-life/ (accessed 26 March 2020).

Plaut, Joshua Eli (2012). *A Kosher Christmas: 'tis the Season to Be Jewish*. New Brunswick, NJ: Rutgers University Press.

Pleck, Elizabeth (2001). 'Kwanzaa: The Making of a Black Nationalist Tradition, 1966–1990', *Journal of American Ethnic History*, 20, no. 4: 3–28.

Restad, Penne L. (1995). *Christmas in America: A History*. New York: Oxford University Press.

Schmidt, Leigh Eric (1995). *Consumer Rites: The Buying and Selling of American Holidays*. Princeton: Princeton University Press.

Shandler, Jeffrey, and Weintraub, Aviva (2007). '"Santa, Shmanta": Greeting Cards for the December Dilemma', *Material Religion* 3, no. 3: 380–403.

Stack, Liam (2016). 'How the "War on Christmas" Controversy Was Created', *The New York Times* (19 December).

Waldfogel, Joel (2009). *Scroogenomics: Why You Shouldn't Buy Presents for the Holidays*. Princeton, NJ: Princeton University Press.

CHAPTER 39

AFRICA

JOEL CABRITA

This chapter considers the question of Christmas in Africa by focusing on Southern Africa and by examining three Christmas 'moments'—what I'll call 'snapshots'—from the twentieth century and the dawn of the twenty-first century. The overarching argument is simple: the celebration of Christmas in Southern Africa can only be understood in relation to the region's unique social make-up; in particular, Christmas has been profoundly shaped by the overwhelming importance of gold in Southern Africa, and by the seasonal culture of labour and leisure that accompanied the extraction of the mineral from the earth. The discovery of gold on the Witwatersrand in 1886 initiated the creation of a cosmopolitan workforce centred in Johannesburg, the rise of a middle-class urban African sensibility resistant to racist segregation, and the forging of urban–rural linkages, as city-dwelling gold miners continued to invest in kin and family 'back home'. The labour patterns of the Witwatersrand, furthermore, were cyclical, structured around a regular pattern of work and rest. Other than Sundays, the most important leisure period for this vast international labour force—which numbered 200,000 at its peak—was the Christmas holiday (Delius 2017).

From a very early date, then, the celebration of Christmas in Southern Africa both reflected and helped shape popular debates around these topics: leisure and work, the consumption of alcohol and the abstention from it (seasonal dipsomania has long characterized Christmas in Southern Africa), industrialization, urbanization, and what it meant to be a 'modern' African man or woman, freed from a 'heathen' past yet still subject to the racist strictures of the colonial and later apartheid states. The celebration of Christmas was also intimately connected to contemporary arguments about masculinity and femininity; it was around Christmas time that new ideas emerged about what constituted a modern African woman, marked by their discernment as shoppers of gifts during the festive season, or a modern man, characterized by their ability to act as a provider to families in the rural areas, particularly in December when they returned home for the holidays. Thus alongside the creation of these urban African selves, Christmas also came to signify the continued importance of a home in the countryside. And it was also an occasion when practitioners of traditional religion asserted their belief in gods of old; rather than the birth of Christ, in many rural areas it was familial ancestors who were celebrated and venerated during this holiday.

In sum, the Christmas period in Southern Africa is a particularly rich window into understanding how the key concerns of twentieth-century Africa—gender, modernity, work, leisure, consumption and wealth, rural–urban networks, the repressive white state, the significance of Christianity and the persistence of traditional religion—were expressed, codified, and contested. And while my examples are solely drawn from South Africa and its neighbouring countries, the social transformations set into motion by industrialization, urbanization, and colonialism were occurring across the entire African continent during the period under discussion. While offering insight into goldmining Witwatersrand, Johannesburg's culture of Christmastide celebration can also indirectly shed light on comparable social processes occurring in other parts of the continent. So let us now turn to the first of our three Christmas snapshots.

CHRISTMAS 1909: A DEATH

On Christmas Eve 1909 in the gold-mining metropolis of Johannesburg, one James Faulkner, a 38-year-old bricklayer, withdrew £15 from his bank and claimed a further £8 in pay due to him from his employers. With these riches in his pocket, he bought a new suit and hat and—in the words of Johannesburg's daily newspaper the *Rand Daily Mail*—proceeded to spend Christmas Eve and the whole Yuletide holiday 'painting the locality red'. And after having 'gone the rounds of many public houses,' the *Daily Mail* continued, 'his fighting propensities came uppermost... [he] spent Christmas in wild style, drunk most of the time.' But for Faulkner, this Christmas would end in the worst possible way. Four days later, on the evening of 29 December, Faulkner was discovered motionless and cold in his bed in his small rented room at the 'Progress Beer Hall' (a residential hostel for single working men in the city located at the corner of Marshall and Smal Streets). His cause of death was undetermined—perhaps due to fatal injuries sustained during his rambunctious fighting (his 'left eye blackened by a punch, his ear bruised in a way to suggest a heavy blow') or perhaps just poisoned by a stupendous excess of alcohol (30 December 1909).

James Faulkner was one of tens of thousands of unattached young men of all races in early twentieth-century Johannesburg who spent the Christmas season of 1909 inebriated, fighting, engaging in petty and violent crime, and carousing in the streets. The discovery of gold on the Witwatersrand in 1886 had catapulted a dusty stretch of Transvaal grassland—known as the *veld* in Afrikaans, the language spoken by the Dutch-descended white settlers who farmed this area—into a booming industrialized city, certainly the largest such concentration of labour in the African continent (Van Onselen 1982). Men—and to a far lesser extent, women—from across the world streamed into Johannesburg, from Cornish tin mines, Chinese cities and towns, and Californian and Australian gold fields, as well as both African and European labour from across southern and central Africa: from the east coast of Gazaland, a Portuguese colony, to as far north as Nyasaland, present-day Malawi (Hyslop 1999: 404). By 1914, there were approximately a quarter of a million workers and residents of the gold fields of the Rand, many domiciled in racially mixed working-class compounds, suburbs and slums centred around areas like Brickfields and Vrededorp (Van Onselen 198: 145). Even at this early stage, and belying the cosmopolitanism of the racially mixed slum yards, African labour tended to be concentrated in formally established residential compounds policed by mine officials (Moroney 1982: 259).

A distinct culture of working-class urban men of all races, largely unattached and without families (the stratospheric cost of living in the new city prohibited many migrants from settling with families), and heavily centred around alcohol and prostitution came to characterize the first few decades of Johannesburg's life. This was despite the fact that alcohol—especially for African mine workers—was severely discouraged by mining officials. In fact, complete prohibition on African consumption of alcohol—except for low-alcohol beer served in the compounds twice a week—had been in effect since 1897 (Van Onselen 1982: 15). But amongst Africans a vibrant culture of procuring and consuming alcohol arose, one which included weak officially issued beer surreptitiously buried underground to ferment it further as well as illegal drinking spots known as shebeens in the nearby urban townships. Drinking became a key means through which working-class mine labourers of all races consolidated new friendships in the alien milieu of the mines. For African workers, especially, confined to the demoralizing and unsanitary conditions of the mining compounds, drinking networks tended to centre around friends and kin from the same rural area, providing a forum for sociability, conviviality, and a greater sense of 'feeling at home' (Moodie 1994: 161). Prostitution, unsurprisingly for a largely male, single population, was another route by which men in the city found companionship (Van Onselen 1982: 104).

Time off—which included Sundays but which also meant the much-anticipated several-day holiday during the Christmas period—became a focal cultural point for this heavy-drinking, male community. Christmas Day was typically suffused with alcohol, leading one journalist to comment of 1909's Christmas Eve that 'the number of gentlemen whose addiction to and affliction by the bottle is a matter of periodical concern was markedly great last night...a large number of people were ordered to be removed to hospital [and] found to be suffering from alcoholic poisoning' (27 December 1909). Alongside heavy drinking, favourite Christmas-time activities of the city's male population included betting upon horses at the races, watching vaudeville shows, and taking the train to the nearby Portuguese-speaking coastal city of Lourenco Marques, renowned for its flowing supply of alcohol and other narcotics, and favoured as a destination for prostitution and seaside fun (24 December 1908). Drinking and carousing were invariably accompanied by violence and crime: reports of thefts, fights, and attacks filled the pages of newspapers around this time of year. A report of 27 December 1910 noted:

[T]he Christmas season this year has been remarkable for a series of amalaita [armed gangs of young men] outrages... at 5:30pm on Christmas Day, a gang of amalaita assaulted a native with sticks and battle axes and injured him so seriously he had to be removed to hospital.

Amongst African workers in the compounds, in particular, Christmas became the occasion for massive so-called 'faction fights', alcohol-fuelled armed clashes between migrant workers usually organized according to ethnic affiliation and rural networks. Christmas 1910 saw 'native quarrels' between the 'Zulus and the Xosa, several hundred being involved... a body of two hundred Zulus sallied forth to attack the natives in adjoining location' (28 December 1910).

But while for many, perhaps even most, mayhem and alcohol were the order of the day, there was nonetheless a sizeable church-going minority who attempted to infuse different meaning into the holiday season. A small coterie of evangelically minded temperance organizations was active in Johannesburg, espousing a 'muscular Christianity' marked by healthy living and abstention from alcohol and attempting to pioneer new definitions of urban masculinity. As one commentator of 1903 put it, 'Johannesburg is not supposed to be a religious town, people do not come here for religion. And yet it has religion, of a strong and virile type' (*Rand Daily Mail*, 27 January 1903). Organizations like the Salvation Army, the YMCA, and early Pentecostal and faith-healing churches such as the Zionist Church and the Apostolic Faith Mission pushed back against Johannesburg's dominant culture of libation and bachelorhood by stressing clean living and family values (Cabrita 2018: 120). Christmas—with all its contemporary associations of licentiousness—became a particularly potent occasion for these organizations to mount their battle for the soul of the city. In contrast to the drunken debauchery that characterized much of the city on Christmas Day, these organizations put on elaborate programmes aimed at reclaiming the holiday for the service of their holy-living agenda. The Salvation Army provided a free Christmas dinner for working men of the city (*RDM*, 23 December 1907), while the YMCA organized lectures in its meeting rooms on Christmas Day as well as wholesome evening 'entertainments' for young single men (*RDM*, 2 December 1907). For the Zionist Church, Christmas season was the occasion for loud, curbside religious meetings, more often than not culminating in prayerful protest outside a saloonkeeper's establishment (*RDM*, 19 December 1905).

CHRISTMAS 1937: A PICNIC

From 1909, we now turn to the Christmas season of 1937. Rather than alcohol, vice, and prostitution, for this festive season our gaze falls upon the entirely different matter of a staid and leisurely afternoon picnic in the summer sunshine—which was hailed by the *Bantu World* newspaper as 'the greatest open-air Picnic planned in the Province by the Transvaal African Picnic Party'. Attendees—largely families—had purchased tickets for six shillings from the Bantu Men's Social Center, an institution frequented by Johannesburg's small-yet-growing African middle classes. This fee—by no means inconsiderable for many of the city's working classes—transported attendees to the spectacular water-filled Sterkfontein Caves, where they would celebrate Christmas Day by decorously viewing the caves, engaging in frivolous games, eating, and consuming (non-alcoholic) drinks. No less than twenty buses were engaged, leaving from Alexandra and Orlando Townships, two important residential hubs for the new black middle class. If inebriation and fighting marked James Faulkner's Christmas of 1909, this year's Christmas was all about decorum and the display of civilized progress by those leisurely strolling around the Sterkfontein Caves (25 December 1937).

The thirty years since James Faulkner had died drunk and bruised in his bed had seen significant cultural and social transformations take place in Johannesburg. Broadly speaking, the shift was one from a town renowned for its licentiousness and godlessness (one commentator of the day dubbed Johannesburg the new 'Nineveh and Babylon' [Van Onselen 1982: Preface]) and populated largely by unattached working-class men, to a city characterized by a permanently urbanized population, the emergence of a more settled family culture and the rise of a small black African middle-class predominantly identified with the values of 'civilized society'. Education was key to this class, many having attended schools run by European and North American missionaries, and who prized themselves on their possession of literacy, their frequenting of the few libraries for Africans established on the Rand, and their subscription to newspapers and magazines (Phillips 1938: 306). Christianity and church attendance were a further defining value of this class, with the Anglican church being an especially well-frequented institution. In the 1930s, the Western Townships of Johannesburg saw some 700–800 African worshippers at a typical Sunday service at the local Anglican mission (Goodhew 2002: 247).

By the 1930s, the Christmas season had become a particularly important moment for this small black elite, both in defining and displaying their progressive values as well as marking out their distance from their less 'enlightened' African compatriots. Church attendance was an important part of this. Most people's Christmas Day would begin with a service at their local church (in December 1925, the most prominent Christmas services for elite Africans could be found at the Anglican and Catholic churches, St Peters in Rosettenville, and St Mary Magdalen in Sophiatown) (*Umteteli wa Bantu*, 19 December 1925). But church was only one component—and by no means the most important—of the Yuletide celebrations of the black middle classes. Selecting, buying, and bestowing an appropriate present was a crucial marker of their new consumer power and their 'progressive' taste. Advertisements in the popular newspaper, *Bantu World*, give a sense of what was at stake in the selection of a good Christmas gift: the Women's Supplement of 21 November 1935 advised the discerning 'shopper' that although 'men always present the most difficult part of the Christmas present problem', the solution always lay in a good 'reading lamp, an object of delight, both decorative and practical'. For women, 'dainty socks, coat hangers, shoe trees, evening bags, diamante ornaments' were all suitable gifts for the modern African female who cultivated an attractive appearance and bought smart new clothes. Indeed, for women, Christmas in the city was a particularly important time, for it was upon them that fell the responsibilities of cleaning, cooking, and hosting parties for the family. *Bantu World's* pages were full of recipes for fruit cakes, Christmas mincemeat, and Christmas puddings, while also offering handy hints for 'etiquette for Christmas entertainment', including sending party invitation cards with the 'wording "Dance" or "music" in the corner' and remembering as a hostess not 'to be stiff and formal', but 'gay and bright' (23 December 1935).

Implicit in this redefinition of Christmas as a showcase for consumption, taste, and class was this group's critique of the seasonal licentiousness of working-class Africans, many domiciled in the barracks of the mining compounds. Writers and contributors to the black press bemoaned the alcohol-fuelled excesses that still characterized the way many celebrated the holiday. On 21 December 1935, one E. J. Tilo wrote to *Bantu World* to remind readers in advance of the festive season that 'prisons, hospitals, divorce courts are tenanted by people with the alcoholic mind...we must curtail unproductive expenditure which impedes the rapid advancement of our social and moral prosperity.' Making clear the connections many drew between alcoholism, violence, and a deficit of 'progressive' values, one *Bantu World* columnist angrily ranted at widespread Christmas drunkenness: 'this is the time of year when people who are uncooked and half-baked in the fire of civilization think they can do what they like to others...when savagery in its jungle form goes abroad unabashed' (26 December 1942). Responding to the news of a 'faction fight' in one of the mines, R. V. Selope Thema, the editor of the leading weekly paper, *Umteteli wa Bantu*, angrily asked, 'Is Christmas a time of killing and stabbing, or revelry and wickedness, or a time of peace and goodwill?' (2 January 1926).

It was for this reason that many middle-class Africans collaborated closely with Johannesburg's authorities in an attempt to redefine the meaning of Christmas for their less elevated compatriots. White officials in the city had long been engaged in a strategy of providing 'wholesome' entertainment for Africans from the mines: cinema screenings and athletics were both thought to provide healthy distraction from the bottle and 'faction fights' and thus render labourers more productive. Indeed, it was none other than the Bantu Men's Social Center (where picnic tickets for Christmas 1937 were on sale) that led the way in this regard. Led by a committee of the cream of Johannesburg's black society, the BMSC and its affiliate organization, the Bantu Sports Club, ensured a new Christmas Day experience was on offer for ordinary people. Christmas Eve 1934 saw a 'grand concert and dance' at the BMSC by the 'Choral and Dramatic Society of Mafeking' (largely composed of teachers) (*BW*, 15 December 1934), while Christmas Day 1926 saw cinema screenings of 'From the Manger to the Cross', followed by 'Ladies' Day on the Tennis Court at the Center and tea served at 4 o'clock' (*UWB*, 19 December 1926). When the supply of respectable Christmas Day activities failed, African residents of middle-class townships such as Orlando took other steps to curb violent crime. In the early 1940s, leading community members formed 'Christmas

Watchmen' groups to patrol their streets throughout the holidays; evidence suggests they were highly effective in reducing crime at this unusually violent time of year (Goodhew 1993: 456).

Yet for all the aspirational hopes of this class of Africans, this was in fact a highly precarious group. Numerically tiny, they were beset by financial problems, with Africans earning far less than a European would in a comparable position. Racist job protection for Europeans meant scarce work opportunities for even the best-educated African (Phillips 1938: 14–15). Often teachers, nurses, clerks, and social workers lived in the most atrocious slums of the city, making it clear how poignant their critique of the 'savage' masses 'unbaked in the fire of civilization': were they, after all, so very different? Educated Africans were still subject to the harsh pass laws that demanded any African stopped by a policeman had to present their pass document as evidence that they were legally allowed within the city's precincts. Failure to do so meant being bundled into a humiliating 'pick up van', transported to the nearest police station and spending the night in prison (Phillips 1938: 200). Amidst this painful mismatch between aspiration and reality, middle-class Africans lent upon Christmas as an opportunity to criticize the state's racist policies and to argue for equal rights for all. Throughout the 1920s and 1930s, R. V. Selope Thema and others wrote Christmas editorials in which they meditated upon the true meaning of 'the spirit of Christ and the message of Christmas' and the lessons it held for the powers-that-be in South Africa. For Selope Thema, Christ came to 'proclaim peace and goodwill to all men', yet in present-day South Africa

> are the oppressed and slaves unknown to this world? Is the gulf between the races bridged? White South Africa has received a Christmas present of freedom...it is hoped that this will not be confined to the European population. 'What has been given freely to you,' says Christ, 'you must give freely to others.'
> (*UWB*, 25 December 1926).

CHRISTMAS 2000: A DANCE

Our final Christmas Day snapshot moves from the city to the country. The year is 2000 and we are in the small rural town of Keates' Drift in Msinga, an arid hilly district within the Zulu-speaking province of KwaZulu-Natal. Like many other similar rural outposts across South Africa, Msinga's male population has been decimated through the exodus of its menfolk to Johannesburg and other industrial hubs (Rogan et al. 2009: 38). The occasion today is a dance called ngoma, an aesthetic form born in migrants' experience of life in Johannesburg. As is the case for many other rural Zulu communities, its performance is the highlight of the Christmas festivities. On Christmas Day, family, friends, and neighbours gather around a dusty space in the heat of the summer afternoon. The ngoma dance team—made up of men newly returned home for the festive season from Johannesburg and other industrial hubs—files into the centre of the arena. They begin singing call-and-response melodies and then start dancing in unison, supported by two deep bass drums. The event moves on to its competitive stage: individual male dancers break away from the troupe and engage in spectacular solo displays of talent, kicking legs into the air and bringing them down on the earth with a heavy thud. Singing still accompanies this phase of the ngoma performance; many of the lyrics are reflections on men's experience of life and work in the city, the joy and excitement of returning to families and friends at Christmas, and the keenly felt pressure of bringing home presents and money for loved ones. A typical lyric might be one such as this humorous song about the ritual of Yuletide gift-giving, performed by Siyazi during Christmas Day 2000: 'Darling, you will get all the promises... Hurry back home in the afternoon, darling, I'm going to get things set up for you/You'll get your stove this afternoon/Not a coal one, darling, but a gas one, the temperature setting will be just right' (Meintjes 2004: 173).

Our Christmas-time jump from urban Johannesburg to rural Msinga is not as awkward as one might suppose. The everyday reality of labour migrants in Johannesburg was—as with other cities of the African continent—a constant perambulation between city and countryside, a cyclical rotation between the mining compounds of the Witwatersrand where contract work was found for several months of the year, and small rural outposts such as Keates' Drift to families and wider kinship networks. Being the time of year when so many migrants returned home, the Christmas holidays—lasting for about two weeks from 20 December to 2 January—were a particularly important time for both migrants and their rural communities. As one account from the 1980s put it: 'at Msinga men are strangers, Christmas visitors who pour into the valleys in a flash flood of taxis and buses' (Alcock 1984: 7). This annual influx of men represented a time of intense financial expectation; all the extended family were waiting for urban migrants to return laden with presents and for the latter, the shame of failing to procure Christmas gifts would be intense. Small villages such as Keates' Draft were seasonally flooded by a range of material goods usually absent during the course of the year; as anthropologist Zolani Ngwane puts it 'straightening hair and dyeing products, skin lightening creams, new clothing styles, plastic Christmas trees, furniture, Primus stoves, new dance styles and new music genres' were all gifts born back by migrants to their home villages (Ngwane 2003: 684). For male workers in particular, Christmas was thus an opportunity to display their prowess as responsible and respectable earners and underscore their potential as romantic partners. The holiday became a potent season of courtship, sexual intimacy, and marriage; many migrants would spend earnings on new clothes and the latest smart phone, buying copious drinks for others, and competing for the attention of their chosen romantic partner (Manamere 2014: 102). The Ngoma dance celebration should also be understood in this light; prize dancers from the city were especially attractive to young women as exemplars of virility, strength, and urban street-smarts (Meintjes 2004: 188).

Christmas in the countryside was not just about consumption and courtship. The festive season, as was the case in Johannesburg, continued to be linked in many people's minds with criminality and violence. This was especially true for a rural area such as Msinga which since the early twentieth century had been devastated by violence precipitated by intense competition between neighbouring communities over land and resources for livelihood; in addition to being scarce, land in Msinga was also amongst the country's worst arable territory with frequent droughts and famine (Clegg 1981: 178). Msinga had also been subject to chronic underdevelopment by the apartheid state, meaning it lacked roads, schools, electricity, and running water well into the 1990s (Meintjes 2017: 39). Much of the violence occurred between the Mchunu and Thembu people, and the worst period was the Christmas season when large numbers of young men flooded the villages and alcohol flowed copiously. In 1986, for example, the Christmas period in Msinga saw three separate conflicts which left twenty-seven Mchunu dead (Church Agricultural Project Report August 1986). Christmas 1987 saw a small-scale civil war amongst two groups within the Mchunu; in the first few months of the year, forty-one Mchunus had died in the fighting (CAP Report June 1987). Christmastime Ngoma dancers—with their ritualistic displays of valour and athleticism—were sometimes selected as prominent fighters in such vendettas. Sometimes this had tragic consequences, as was the case with one of Keates' Drift's best-known dancers who was murdered in an inter-ethnic faction fight during Christmas 1992 (Meintjes 2004: 193).

But the meaning of Christmas in rural areas like Msinga went far beyond warfare. Christmas could also be infused with intense spiritual significance. Sometimes this bore little resemblance to the way in which Christmas was celebrated in historically Christian Europe and North America. Christmas, for example, became a moment when—due to a critical mass of men returning home—rural communities were able to affirm important traditional religious practices, rituals that depended in large part upon key (male) members of the community being present. One such ceremony was ukubuyisa ('bringing back the body'), a ritual that marked the one-year anniversary of a family member's death, and when ancestral spirits were supplicated to accept the deceased peacefully into their fold. Initiation rites and circumcision for young boys and girls were, and are, commonly performed during the Christmas season, as were negotiations between families for bridal wealth and rituals designed at purifying and strengthening homesteads (Ngwane 2003: 696). In the Eastern Cape in the 1970s, there was a common ritual known as a ukufafa isikhonkwane ('to hammer in a nail') which annually took place at Christmas and in which migrants solicited the blessings of their ancestors as they were leaving home after the holidays to return to work in the city (Ngwane 2003: 697). The manner in which Christmas was historically 're-purposed' by rural communities across Southern Africa is evident in the neighbouring country of Swaziland's December celebration of the Incwala—a rain-making ceremony aimed at strengthening the Swazi monarch's potency, and which similarly relied upon a critical mass of men returning home from the mines. Broadly known as the 'Christmas of the heathens', one Incwala participant of the 1940s agreed with this assessment: 'Yes, it is our Christmas, the Christmas of our king, the beginning of the new year' (Kuper 1944: 241).

So far Christianity itself has been absent in this discussion of Christmas celebrations in rural South Africa. What of the many churches with large rural followings, and in what ways have they encouraged believers to celebrate this season? The most popular churches in rural South Africa fall under the umbrella of the 'African Independent Churches', a broadly Christian movement stemming from early North American Pentecostal and faith-healing groups in South Africa and which have since characterized themselves by their African leadership and autonomy from European control. Many of these churches deal with Christmas only tangentially, often sidestepping the holiday in favour of vast Easter celebrations. There is, for example, the well-known Zion Christian Church, with a membership of six million, and whose headquarters is in the small town of Moria, an hour north of the city of Polokwane. The ZCC is famous for its vast annual Easter pilgrimage, during which millions of believers from South Africa and neighbouring countries travel to Moria for several days of prayer, sermons, testimonies, and song. Christmas, by contrast, goes almost unrecognized within the church (Muller 2015: 183).

On the other hand, some churches create entirely new liturgical events around the time of December–January, intentionally superseding the place of Christmas. The large Zulu-speaking 'Church of the Nazaretha', outside of the city of Durban in KwaZulu-Natal and founded by charismatic prophet Isaiah Shembe in the 1910s, has successfully crafted a rival event to Christmas, occurring a week or so after 25 December. This is its annual pilgrimage to nearby Mount Nhlangakazi, undertaken on foot by some 20,000 Nazaretha. Once atop the mountain, they will spend two to three weeks in prayer, fasting, religious dancing, and contemplation (Cabrita 2014: 105). According to Isaiah Shembe's grandson, Londa Shembe, Isaiah discontinued Christmas celebrations because he felt the holiday ran counter to his message of black empowerment; this, it must be remembered, was a day that typically involved African women chained to domestic service for the large lunches of wealthy white families in Durban's suburbs (Oosthuizen 1993: xxiii). For African Independent Churches devising new indigenous interpretations of Christianity, Christmas was perhaps too loaded with associations to a white-dominated colonial Christianity. Furthermore, the season's widespread connotation of drunkenness, violence, and crime (and increasingly, widespread carnage on South Africa's roads) may also have disposed these churches against the holiday. Over the past century, Christmas for Southern Africans, it turns out, has meant many things in addition to and alongside the birth of Christ. It has also acted as a fulcrum for emerging ideas and debates around black autonomy, an indigenous African Christianity, modern femininity and masculinity, gainful employment, and the correct deployment of leisure time.

REFERENCES AND FURTHER READING

Alcock, Creina (1984).'Msinga', in *Afra Newsletter* 1984. Ed. Sheila Meintjies.
Cabrita, Joel (2014). *Text and Authority in the South African Nazaretha Church*. Cambridge: Cambridge University Press.

Cabrita, Joel (2018). *The People's Zion: Southern Africa, the United States and a Transatlantic Faith-Healing Movement*. Cambridge, MA: Harvard University Press.

Clegg, Jonathan (1981). 'Ukubuyisa isidumbu – "Bringing Back the Body" – An Examination into the Ideology of Vengeance in the Msinga and Mpofana Rural Locations, 1882–1944', in P. Bonner (ed), *Working Papers in Southern African Studies*. Johannesburg: Ravan Press: 178.

Delius, Peter (2017). 'The History of Migrant Labour in South Africa, 1800–2014', *Oxford Research Encyclopedia of African History*, Online Publication Date May 2017. Available at https://oxfordre.com/africanhistory/view/10.1093/acrefore/9780190277734.001.0001/acrefore-9780190277734-e-93?rskey=xa43HE&result=6/ (accessed 6 April 2020).

Goodhew, David (1993). 'The People's Police-Force: Communal Policing Initiatives in the Western Areas of Johannesburg, 1930–62', *Journal of Southern Africa Studies*, 19, no. 3: 447–470.

Goodhew, David (2002). 'Working Class Respectability: The Example of the Western Areas of Johannesburg, 1930–1955', *Journal of African History*, 41, no. 2: 241–66.

Hyslop, Jonathan (1999). 'The Imperial Working Class Makes itself "White": White Labourism in Britain, Australia and South Africa before the First World War', *Journal of Historical Sociology*, 12, no. 4: 398–421.

Kuper, Hilda (1944). 'A Ritual of Kingship Among the Swazi', *Africa: Journal of the International African Institute*, 14, no. 5: 230–57.

Manamere, Kundai Tichagwa (2014). 'Majoni-joni: Wayward Criminals or a Good Catch? Labour Migrancy, Masculinity and Marriage in Rural South Eastern Zimbabwe', *African Diaspora*, 7: 89–113.

Meintjes, Louise (2004). 'Shoot the Sergeant, Shatter the Mountain: The Production of Masculinity in Zulu Ngoma Song and Dance in Post-Apartheid South Africa', *Ethnomusicology Forum*, 13, no. 2: 173–201.

Meintjes, Louise (2017). *Dust of the Zulus: Ngoma Aesthetics after Apartheid*. Durham, NC: Duke University Press.

Moodie, Dunbar (1994). *Going for Gold: Men, Mines and Migration*. Berkeley: University of California Press.

Moroney, Sean (1982). 'Mine Married Quarters – the Differential Stabilisation of the Witwatersrand Workforce 1900–1920', in S. Marks and R. Rathbone (eds.), *Industrialization and Social Change in South Africa*. London: Longmans: 259–69.

Muller, Retief (2015). 'The Zion Christian Church and Global Christianity', *Religion*, 45, no. 2: 174–190.

Ngwane, Zolani (2003). 'Christmas Time and the Struggle for the Household in the Countryside: Rethinking the Cultural Geography of Migrant Labour in South Africa', *Journal of Southern African Studies*, 29, no. 3: 681–99.

Oosthuizen, G. C. (1994). 'Theology of the AmaNazarites', in Irving Hexham (ed.), *The Scriptures of the amaNazaretha of Ekuphakameni*. Calgary, Alberta: University of Calgary Press.

Phillips, Ray (1938). *The Bantu in the City*. Lovedale, SA: Lovedale Press.

Rogen, Michael, Lebani, Likhani, and Nzimande, Nompumelelo (2009). *Internal Migration and Poverty in KwaZulu-Natal*. Working Paper Series No. 30. Southern Africa Labour and Development Research Unit, University of Cape Town.

Van Onselen, Charles (1982). *Studies in the Social and Economic History of the Witwatersrand, 1886–1914*, Volumes I & II. London: Longman.

CHAPTER 40

ASIA

JOSEPH TSE-HEI LEE

The widespread acceptance of Christmas as a celebratory event, both religious and secular, in Asia hinges on several factors, such as the adoption of the Gregorian calendar, the influence of Christian missionary evangelization and local churches, relatively stable church–state relations, and the integration of host societies into a global consumer economy. Following a chronological approach, this chapter explores how Western missionaries and Asian converts indigenized the ritual of Christmas celebrations and remembrance from the nineteenth century on, and how the spread of Christmas took place in an environment different from Europe and America, where most people self-identified as Christians and had observed Christmas for generations. The nineteenth century, the era of missionary expansion and colonialism, witnessed a regionally diverse pattern of localizing Christmas. By the early twentieth century, the spread of nationalistic sentiments led to public attacks on Christmas as a symbol of imperialism. From the late twentieth century to the present, Christmas celebrations have been commercialized worldwide as a result of consumerism. A distinction between sacred and secular components is hard to draw because Christmas has become a magnet, not just for missionaries, pilgrims, and evangelists concerned about spiritual reflection, but also for merchants and consumers intent on commercial activities.

CHRISTMAS AS PART OF EVANGELIZING AND 'CIVILIZING' EFFORTS

The intermingling of Christianity and Western civilization through proselytizing and 'civilizing' activities, shaped the transmission and reception of Christmas in Asia. With the global missionary expansion in the eighteenth and nineteenth centuries, many pioneering missionaries incorporated Christmas as an integral part of evangelization. Attracting the attention of curious crowds was the key purpose of worship services at Christmas, widely called *Shengdan jie* (literally, the Holy Birth Festival) in Chinese.

Chapels were usually crowded, as the festival decorations, singing, and a chance to listen to the Nativity story attracted people from all cross-sections of society (Selles 2011: 80). On Christmas Day in 1891, Wang Tsong-Ih, an ex-military officer dismissed for opium addiction, attended a congregation run by the China Inland Mission in Paoning, Sichuan Province, where he met Cecil Polhill-Turner of the 'Cambridge Seven' missionary band. Deeply moved by a convert who destroyed his tobacco-pipe publicly and by other congregants who abstained from alcohol, Wang joined the church and was baptized on Christmas Day of the following year (Cassels 1898). Similar stories of Christmas conversions take on a deeper spiritual meaning in the missionary literature. Eleanor van Lierop, who arrived in Korea in 1949 and subsequently founded the first shelter for single mothers and Amerasian children, recalled the hardships of a poor, war-torn society: 'It was even difficult to decorate for Christmas because Korean stores stocked no decorations. So we made do with our own inventions: brightly painted pine cones, amber balls wrapped in tinsel saved from a year's supply of chewing gum, strings of popcorn and streamers of interlocking paper circlets with burned-out flash bulbs painted red, green, yellow and blue' (Driskill 2002: 25). On Christmas Eve, she led her congregants in a visit to a church-run orphanage, where young children carolled and dramatized the Nativity story. After the performance, a street prostitute named Sun Ok knelt on her knees before the Christ Child, crying: 'I no money, I no things. I nothing to give Jesus. I give me! I work hard for you. I good worker, I work hard for Jesus'. She converted on the spot and received training to be a Bible woman (Driskill 2002: 29–30). Because of the potential to convert newcomers, missionaries made proselytization a top priority and native churches often prepared a communal feast for visitors after the Christmas service.

In areas where Christianity exerted significant influence, local business leaders and government officials exchanged Christmas cards with foreign missionaries, and decorated their homes for the festival. To create a celebratory atmosphere, 'the general token of mutual remembrance' among Chinese Christians was the circulation of postcard greetings. Some municipal post offices admitted the pressure of handling the heavy load of holiday mails (Wernecke 1959: 138). Baptist communities in China's Guilin City adapted exquisite samples of Chinese art to depict the Holy Family in Christmas cards from the 1930s (Wernecke 1959: 140). In Japan's North Star School (Hokusei Gakuen), founded in Sapporo, Hokkaido, in 1887 by Sarah Clara Smith of the United Presbyterian Church of North America, Japanese Christians sent handmade cards decorated with original drawings, which read: 'Please come to our homeroom Christmas party' (Driskill 2002: 40). The embrace of Christmas by local Christians solidified their shared faith identity and trust, and allowed them to take part in a globalizing festival. In Korea, Christian artist Kim Ki-Chang received an old Christmas card with an image of the baby Jesus. The image stirred his mind. After the Korean War, when he made a series of Christian paintings, he represented Mary as a humble Korean girl, operating the spinning wheel; a Korean cowshed instead of a stable as the location of Jesus' birth; and portrayed the three wise men as Confucian scholars (Anonymous 1978: 27, 29, 31).

As an official holiday in the British Empire, Christmas allowed Christians of different castes, ethnicities, and localities to nurture their ecclesiastic ties, and to show their attachment to the colonial order. In Singapore, Christians of the four ethnic groups—Tamils, Chinese, Siamese, and Malays—celebrated the Christmas service with British colonialists in English and their respective mother tongues. Yet, Protestant pietism was infused with the norms of patriarchy and gender segregation, and in these Singaporean churches, 'girls of twelve or thirteen, being too old to appear in public, had little remembrances sent to them' (Waterbury 1897: 468). In the multi-ethnic frontier of Burma, Christmas was 'a polyglot celebration, English, Karen, and Burmese rejoicing together'. Members of these Baptist churches exchanged gift bags, 'made of the bark of the plantain tree', and filled with 'tea, sugar, cocoanut, and a handkerchief' (Waterbury 1897: 468). One Karen Baptist believer even gave a bag of cigars to the American missionaries.

Wherever Catholics and Protestants were the minority of the population, institutional space and mechanisms were needed to promote Christmas as the zenith of the annual church festivities. Mission schools and hospitals were cross-cultural comfort zones where the early generations of Christians experimented, indigenized, and advanced various modes of Christmas remembrance. Though not an official holiday in East Asian countries, no classes were held in the mission schools at Christmas, and children of different linguistic, kinship, class, and ethnic groupings prepared for the celebrations. Carolling and role-playing were unique pedagogies through which educational missionaries taught students sacred and secular ideas, allowing them to appreciate the Virgin Birth of Christ, the imagery of angels, and the Star of Bethlehem as miraculous symbols for Christians. Rehearsing the Nativity drama was a popular extra-curriculum activity for boys and girls of the sex-segregated schools to socialize, cooperate, and entertain each other on stage. Missionaries invented artefacts, images, words, and body movements to create a tangible reality for students to practise the collective ritual of remembering Jesus' birth at a specific place and time. Born out of the European Reformation, Protestant missionary movements had disenchanted the world through a rationalistic approach towards human destiny, but new mission churches in rural Asia re-enchanted the world by recognizing the interdependence between the material and cosmological universe. Growing up with strong beliefs in a powerful world of gods, ghosts, and ancestors, Chinese students in the Baptist and Presbyterian schools in Shantou, Guangdong Province, often treated deities with fear and awe. When they read and re-enacted the biblical account of the Archangel Gabriel's Annunciation to Mary, they were fascinated by the concept of divine intervention in the human domain. Apart from understanding the cosmological meaning of what was being performed, they sometimes began to reject their subordinate relationship with popular deities and ancestral spirits in Chinese traditional religions.

In British India, the development of indigenous hymnody was a key to local church growth. Many Indian hymns, including carols, developed out of their popularity in worship. In 1877, Christians in Amritsar, Punjab, were awakened by carols sung by mission-school choirs (Cox 2002: 110). In Madras, the Telugu Baptist school choir sang a carol and greeted American missionary Lucy W. Waterbury, with 'Merry Kismis' (Waterbury 1897: 465). Christmas also provided an important link between urban and rural churches. In the 1880s, Baptist congregants from Baraut walked 60 kilometres to attend city-wide celebrations in Delhi (Cox 2002: 111). In 1896, the Methodists in Lucknow, the 'City of Roses,' organized a Sunday-school picnic at Christmas, bringing two thousand Sunday schoolers to the city park and rewarding outstanding students with elephant rides (Waterbury 1897: 467).

These same elaborate celebrations continued on in the Catholic and Protestant schools of the former British colony of Hong Kong. Throughout the 1970s and 1980s, students of the Cantonese-speaking Anglican, Baptist, Catholic, Lutheran, and Rhenish schools decorated their classrooms, exchanged home-made greeting cards, learnt Chinese carols, and rehearsed the Nativity play. Since the performances were popular with parents and grandparents, the mission schools partnered with their respective churches to carry out this evangelistic outreach. The story of the Nativity fit in with the old strategy of making Christmas intelligible to the people. Unless local audiences experienced something visual and tangible, they found it hard to comprehend the spiritual significance of Christmas. The performative mode of Christmas celebrations appeals to Evangelical churches in Asia today. Founded by the American Baptists and English Presbyterians, the fast-growing Chaozhou-speaking churches in coastal Shantou, China, blend the annual Christmas worship with local cultural practices. On Christmas Eve of 2016, they performed the parable of the Prodigal Son and the Nativity in the style of a traditional Chaozhou-language opera, and had Rev. Youngman Chan, a popular pastor of Chaozhou descent in Hong Kong, to preach the next day, encouraging newcomers to accept the faith.[1]

The popularization of Christmas is often reflected through the prism of Christian charity. In Chinese mission centres, the crowning moment at Christmas was to reach out to non-Christian children:

> The chapel was packed with a motley crowd of the great unwashed. Expectation was on tiptoe, for they [non-Christian children] had been told that, if they came regularly, they would receive on Christmas day a nice card, and when in addition, each boy and girl was given a package, with the strict injunction not to open it until out of the chapel.... The little girls with their dirty faces, partially concealed by paint, would caressingly hold their packages against their cheeks, smoothing them gently, and rock them back and forth crooning, "I believe it's a doll", while listening to the sermon.   (Waterbury 1897: 469)

Gertrude Jenness Rinden recalled that Christian nurses lit a pair of tall red candles next to the Bible. Although the children had only heard the Nativity story for the first time, they used their imagination to make red Christmas paper-cuttings of the stars of

---

[1] Joseph Tse-Hei Lee recalls these stories from his upbringing in British Hong Kong during the 1970s and 1980s, and his observation of the Christmas celebrations in Shantou in 2016.

Bethlehem, chains, and pagodas (Wernecke 1963: 30). At the Hunan-Yale Hospital in Changsha, Hunan Province, nurses woke up patients with carols at dawn on Christmas (Anon. 1922: 173). A doctor impersonated Santa Claus, distributing gifts among patients, and the chaplain preached. A special evangelistic session was prepared for neighbourhood children, who received from Santa Claus 'a package containing a toy, another containing a cake of soap and face cloth (a most highly prized gift, as soap is rare and expensive), and some candy' (Anon. 1922: 174). At the end of the day, a Chinese Christmas feast was prepared for 'medical staff and patients—not turkey and cranberry sauce, but what those people would like much better—bird's nest soup, buried eggs, and eight-precious rice, a pudding of glutinous rice and preserved fruits, and sugar—altogether eight ingredients' (Anon. 1922: 173). It was a collective effort to organize this indigenized Christmas celebration.

Christmas was full of entertainment at the mission hospital in Guntur, South India. Visitors of various castes came in 'gala dress, bringing with them gifts of fruits, sweets and money. There were many very wealthy friends, former patients, who never forget to return with their gifts'. A traditional Christmas service was held in the hospital chapel for patients and, at the end, an upper caste Hindu stood up to offer greetings to the missionaries (Anon. 1922: 170). At the Presbyterian-run Severance Hospital in Seoul, Korea, Edna Lawrence observed that Korean culture was preserved in the mission compound, with a fusion of Western and Korean festivities. Nursing students made rag dolls and created bright red bags in the shape of the Korean peninsula as a silent resistance against Japanese colonialism. They filled the bags with 'candy, nuts, a white handkerchief, and one of the gospels' (Anon. 1922: 170). At 5 a.m. on Christmas Day, nurses gathered outside the home of the missionaries, singing 'Joy to the World' in Korean. At 9 a.m., they distributed gifts to patients. Unfortunately, the joyful celebrations were overshadowed by the executions of several Korean independence fighters, including many prominent pastors and mission-school students.

CHRISTMAS AS A SYMBOL OF IMPERIALISM AND A SIGN OF SOLIDARY IN WARTIME

Modern missionary movements took place in an imperialist context where the Bible and the gun were intertwined on many levels. In late nineteenth-century Kobe, Japan, American missionaries socialized kindergarten children with the rituals of carolling, reciting biblical verses, decorating a Christmas tree, sharing gifts, and eating 'bean paste, sugar storks, and [rice] cakes' (Waterbury 1897: 470). Meanwhile, Japanese Christians strove to reconcile their faith with an attachment to their rising empire. They made the American and Japanese national flags out of chrysanthemums, and placed them on both sides of the Christmas scrolls for decoration (Waterbury 1897: 469). In the age of rising nationalism, Christmas was perceived as a symbol of Western cultural imperialism. When anti-foreign, anti-Christian sentiments spread in China during the mid-1920s, the nascent Chinese Communist Party was determined to combat church communities at Christmas in 1924–1926. As graduates of the mission schools, the Communist leaders appropriated many evangelistic tools in mass mobilization. They organized student and labour activists to distribute anti-Christian Christmas cards, sing revolutionary songs, and give political speeches outside Catholic and Protestant mission institutions in Hong Kong, Guangzhou, Shantou, Fuzhou, Xiamen, and Shanghai (Ashmore 1925). In 1926, the Christian Reformed Church mission in Rugao, Jiangsu Province, was disrupted by student protesters on Christmas Day. Seeing the angry crowd outside the church, the missionaries blocked the entrance, 'having heard of how students in Wuhan had once burst into a church and had shouted blasphemies from the pulpit'. The students hurled projectiles of turnips and onions into the chapel, injuring two missionaries' heads. After shouting, 'Down with the church', they handed out yellow placards and urged people to boycott the celebrations (Selles 2011: 93).

Besides revolutionary protests, the tragic memories of total war shaped the ways in which surviving Asian Christians associated Christmas with war commemoration. During the Japanese occupation of China's Nanjing (or Nanking) in December 1937, Christmas was remembered as a day of hell. Dozens of courageous missionaries stayed behind to look after civilians. On Christmas Eve, five Japanese soldiers joined in the service the Chinese Methodist pastor conducted at the women's Bible School, but on Christmas Day, Ernest H. Foster of the American Church Mission had to perform 'police duty' during the service, 'keeping unauthorized soldiers out' (Zhang 2001: 121). The missionaries could not protect everyone, as when some male Christians were taken by the soldiers as forced labourers. Medical missionary Robert O. Wilson sat 'in a small X-ray room to keep Japanese soldiers from looting' the hospital (Zhang 2001: 398). Minnie Vautrin, head of the Ginling Women's College, shielded women from being sexually assaulted by soldiers. She reflected on the life of Christians under occupation:

> At Christmas, although we were in a period of great danger and we did not know what each day would bring forth, we had a number of special Christmas services—one for Mrs. Tsen's grandchildren whom we have learned to love and who have helped to keep us normal; one for the adults who have been helping carry the burdens of the work and we included their families; one for the college servants; one for the neighborhood women, and still one other for the young people who acted as scouts in those early days of the invasion.   (Zhang 2001: 341)

The Nanjing Christians set up 'an altar with a Cross, a little Christmas tree with colored lights, a great bouquet of Heavenly bamboo with bright red berries, several large pots of poinsettias, the red Christmas cuts and the Christmas scrolls'. They hung 'a heavy green curtain for the one window' and 'a thick cloth over the transom' for soundproof purposes. They lowered their voice when carolling to avoid the soldiers' attention (Zhang 2001: 341). Each carol carried a meaning as they 'eagerly accept the comfort and strength it gives' in these darkest hours (Zhang 2001: 345).

Shortly after the Pearl Harbor attack on December 7, 1941, Japan invaded the Philippines. American Presbyterian missionaries, Paul and Clara Lindholm, left with their four children for the mountains of Negros Island. The Christian islanders organized a Christmas performance for sojourners who had fled the war:

> A long-time unused lantern was brought out to light up the simple drama depicting the Nativity story. The eager and appreciative congregation looked on as the drama coach led the actors through their paces... As one scene led to the next, the coach would ask one or another in the audience to loan a coat or a shawl needed for an upcoming part. Even though it was a bit impromptu, everyone thoroughly enjoyed this dramatization of the story of Jesus' birth.   (Driskill 2002: 41)

Missionaries and congregants carolled together in the midst of an escalating war. Thelma Appleton remembers that with the end of the Second World War, two Christmas traditions were adapted to the heat and humidity of the Philippines. Christians hung 'a big paper-covered star in the front of their doorway', and called it a *parol*. 'The star is made of split bamboo put together like a knife', and '*parols* are covered with bright-colored paper to make them beautiful'. The second adaptation were 'the roving musical bands, called *comparsas* that visited all the homes in town to play Filipino folk songs and carols' in exchange for a modest monetary gift (Driskill 2002: 52–3). At a different place in a different time, when US President Richard Nixon implemented a policy of Vietnamization designed to bring American troops home in 1972, he unleashed deadly bombing raids against North Vietnam's largest cities, Hanoi and Haiphong, on Christmas Day. The Christmas bombings caused unprecedented casualties and forced Nixon to switch to a negotiation strategy (Agius 2008: 147).

CHRISTMAS AS KEY TO COMMUNITY BUILDING

Observing the calendrical rituals of Christmas is central to native churches. The communal element of Christmas celebration manifests itself among Asian Christians who have experienced an incremental transition to urban modernity. In Little Rome, a Hakka-speaking Catholic settlement in Guangdong Province, Christmas reinforces the shared identity of parishioners with no agnatic relationships in the same way as ancestral worship strengthens the kinship bonds among non-Christians (Lozada 1999: 122). After the outbreak of the Korean War, Christian refugees from the North adhered to the collective celebration of Christmas. On Christmas Eve, each home hung paper lanterns, decorated with red crosses, at the gateposts. Many mission institutions and Christian businesses decorated their entrances with lanterns, which could be seen for blocks. In the evening, Christians paraded in the streets, carolling, before a two-hour worship service. Afterwards, they shared a supper, serving Duck Kook, a soup laded with pieces of duck or bread, *kimchi* rice, rice cakes, fruits, and ginger candy (Wernecke 1963: 54). On Christmas Day, congregants attended a morning service. While the missionaries feared that American commercialism had spread to Korea, poor Koreans embraced the practice of gift exchange, offering dolls, brassware, and live chickens to the missionaries.

In the Muslim world where Christians have existed for centuries, Christmas is a major festival. In Iran, Christmas is celebrated as the Little Feast, and Easter, the Great Feast. The first twenty-one days of December is a time of fasting and spiritual reflection. The fast ends on Christmas Eve with a feast (Wernecke 1963: 67). In Iraq, on Christmas Eve, children read the Nativity story from an Arabic Bible, and other members hold candles. They light a bonfire in the courtyard and sing a psalm. When the fire is reduced to ashes, they jump over the ashes three times and make a wish. On Christmas Day, there is a bonfire of thorns burnt in the churchyard and while the fire burns, male congregants chant a hymn. The bishop and church officials lead a public procession, carrying an image of the infant Jesus upon a scarlet cushion (Wernecke 1963: 40). In Buddhist Thailand, Christians utilize the opportunity to make their presence felt. The high point is when young congregants take part in all-night carolling, walking from house to house, honouring Christians and non-Christians, families, and elected officials alike (Wernecke 1963: 72).

COMMERCIALIZATION OF CHRISTMAS

The globalization of Christmas has been made possible by an internationally integrated economy. American Presbyterians in India recall buying decorative items from around the world:

> Christmas was universal, or at least international, for us in another respect. Our tree came from Germany, the ornaments from America, the lights from Japan, the stand from India, cards from Japan, Germany, England, Ceylon, Iraq, Pakistan, the Persian Gulf, India, and America, . . . a wooden crèche from Italy, another from Jerusalem, a book from Greece, and even caviar from Russia. (Wernecke 1963: 38)

A major change occurred in modern Asia when Christmas worship gave way to consumerism. The commercialization of Christmas has been linked to the growth of an urban, industrial, and consumer economy. Christmas Eve has become a long night of consumption and entertainment, across urban Asia, where discos, nightclubs, bars, hotels, and restaurants hold parties for young students and professionals. China makes this a global 'foreign festival' (*yangjie*) a crucial business event in the cycles of advertisement and consumption. Young Chinese with limited consumption power visit Walmart on Christmas Day 'to enjoy the Christmas decorations and displays and the general atmosphere of hustle and bustle' (Sigley 2007: 97). Some Communist officials see Christmas, in its secular form, as an irresistible attraction, without which no city can claim to be modern. Unlike Chinese Lunar New Year, Christmas is not a family affair, but is a social celebration among friends and colleagues, with a focus on 'the individual sense of pleasure' through consumption (Sigley 2007: 99). It is even regarded as a 'democratic festival' that implies freedom to pursue individual pleasures and avoid the family obligations associated with traditional ceremonies. The visibility of Christmas festivities suggests that the Chinese Communist state has lost its monopoly over public space. Despite 'an uneasy political alliance between the ever-changing ideology of the party-state and the further penetration of global capitalism', Christmas cannot be detached from its Christian roots (Sigley 2007: 92).

Faith and politics are symbiotically interconnected in multifarious manners, and Christmas in China embodies competing voices that cannot be fit neatly into the East-West dichotomy. Christmas is always 'a time of heightened government restrictions on Chinese church activities', partly because both Catholics and Protestants envision a potential for mass conversions (Colijn 2019: 207), and partly because in this sacred moment and space of celebrations, the state-controlled patriotic and house churches confess their loyalty to God as the highest order of the world. In December 1989, a few months after the Communist government's brutal crackdown on pro-democracy demonstrators in Beijing's Tiananmen Square on 4 June, seminarians of the state-run Nanjing Theological Seminary debated with their professors whether Nanjing churches should open their doors to the public on Christmas Eve. Eventually, the churches welcomed everyone to Christmas services, providing a rare opportunity for people to gather in a politically tense environment. Known for his faith-based activism, Wang Yi of the Early Rain Covenant Church in Chengdu converted on Christmas Day in 2005. After becoming a pastor, Wang launched evangelistic outreach programmes every Christmas. He usually rented out a hotel's ballroom, but the hotel manager sometimes backed out due to government pressure (Johnson 2017: 60, 331). The act of Christmas worship is symbolically subversive in an authoritarian country, where churches set the Christian God apart from the secular authorities, and even subject the latter to the spiritual judgment of God. This explains why the Communist state has cracked down on Christian religious celebrations and symbols in major cities since 2018.

In the countryside with high concentrations of Christian families, Christmas celebrations involve large numbers of choirs and dance groups, creating an excitingly 'hot and noisy' atmosphere, rivalling temple festivals, and advancing a positive image of Christianity (Colijn 2019: 212). In Linyi, Chinese Christians put together a 'rich and colorful Christmas show over a few weeks' for non-Christian relatives and friends (Kang 2016: 216). Practising a 'strategy of relational evangelization' (*guanxi chuandaofa*), they prepare 'a richly organized gala consisting of various performances, such as drama, dance, music and comedy', and the event concludes with a 'movingly persuasive sermon' (Kang 2016: 217). Unlike the Western emphasis on the solemnity and sanctity of the occasion, Linyi congregants infuse the colourful and noisy entertainment with relevant spiritual messages. In the multi-ethnic regions of Yunnan and

Tibet, Christian minorities seldom share in the Han Chinese Communist discourse that dismisses Christmas as a secular economic event. The ethnic churches carry on the celebratory rituals learnt from the missionary era. Tibetan Catholics hold overnight prayers and Mass on Christmas Eve, followed by baptisms on Christmas Day, and Miao Protestants in Dali, Yunnan Province, often combine celebrations with leadership training sessions (Galipeau 2018).

As with the ethnic churches in China, the famous Wanchin Basilica of the Immaculate Conception, outside Kaohsiung, Taiwan, partners with township authorities to enmesh Christmas into a deeply commercialized environment. Convinced that Christmas should be more than a party-oriented event for young people to experience a foreign culture, Taiwanese Catholics have reinvented Christmas as a cultural as well as a religious moment. They welcome non-Christian visitors, mostly extended family, to the Basilica to learn about the local church history and heritage. On Christmas Eve, they put together a '3D laser display' of the Christmas story to provide an artistic experience to visitors (Wang 215). Similarly, in Macau the most creative mode of Catholic civic engagement is to present religious pilgrimage services for non-Catholic tourists. Offering 'spiritual education in the guise of cultural heritage tours' has become an important outreach to tourists from China, Hong Kong, Taiwan, and South East Asia, and to Korean, Japanese, Philippine, and Vietnamese Catholic pilgrims. Enhancing the global and local linkages of Macau's Catholics, this faith-based heritage tour renews the laity's interest in religious services and bulwarks against the corrosive effects of casino liberalization and excessive consumerism.

Conclusion

In Asia, the indigenization of Christmas, as both a sacred and secular event, has never taken place in a cultural vacuum, and should be contextualized in specific temporal and spatial settings. Ever since the era of Christianization and colonialism, Christmas has transformed itself from an obscure religious festival into a globally recognized celebration, and has shaped the ways in which people in the Confucian, Buddhist, Hindu, and Muslim cultural zones have encountered and responded to, willingly or not, the challenges of Christianity and Western modernity. Today, Christmas has been embedded into Asian Christians' experience of the sacred and has merged with the pre-existing material concerns and cultural practices of the host societies.

References and Further Reading

Agius, Christine (2008). 'Christmas and War', in Sheila Whiteley (ed.), *Christmas, Ideology and Popular Culture*. Edinburgh: Edinburgh University Press: 137–48.

Anon. (1922). 'Christmas in Other Lands', *American Journal of Nursing*, 23, no. 3: 169–94.

Anon. (1978). *The Life of Jesus: Collection of Sacred Paintings by Kim Ki-Chang*. Seoul: Kyong-Mi Publishing Co.

Anon. (2002). *Christmas Stories from China: Living Faith on the Front Lines*. Reading, PA: Open Doors International.

Ashmore, Lida Scott (1925). 'Extracts on Church'. Box 15, Folder 15, The Ashmore Family Papers, Ax 564, Special Collections and University Archives, University of Oregon Libraries, Eugene, Oregon.

Cassels, W. W. (1898). *Wang: A Chinese Christian*. London: Morgan & Scott, and China Inland Mission.

Colijn, Bram (2019). 'Christmas Reverberations in Xiamen: Insights from a Grand Religious Festival in Contemporary China', in Chris White (ed.), *Protestantism in Xiamen: Then and Now*. New York: Palgrave Macmillan: 193–221.

Cox, Jeffrey (2002). *Imperial Fault Lines: Christianity and Colonial Power in India*. Stanford, CA: Stanford University Press.

Driskill, J. Lawrence (ed.) (2002). *Christmas Stories From Around the World: Honoring Jesus in Many Lands*. Pasadena, CA: Hope Publishing House.

Galipeau, Brendan A. (2018). 'A Tibetan Catholic Christmas in China: Ethnic Identity and Encounters with Ritual and Revitalization', *Asian Ethnology* 77, nos. 1 and 2: 353–70.

Guinness, Mary Geraldine (1900). *One of China's Scholars: The Culture and Conversion of a Confucianist*. London: Morgan and Scott.

Johnson, Ian (2017). *The Souls of China: The Return of Religion After Mao*. New York: Vintage.

Kang, Jie (2016). *House Church Christianity in China: From Rural Preachers to City Pastors*. New York: Palgrave Macmillan.

Lozada, Jr, Eriberto P (1999). *God Aboveground: Catholic Church, Postsocialist State and Transnational Processes in a Chinese Village*. Stanford, CA: Stanford University Press.

Selles, Kurt D. (2011). *A New Way of Belonging: Covenant Theology, China, and the Christian Reformed Church, 1921–1951*. Grand Rapids, MI: Eerdmans.

Sigley, Gary (2007). 'A Chinese Christmas Story', in Xu Shi (ed.), *Discourse as Cultural Struggle*. Hong Kong: Hong Kong University Press: 91–104.

Wang, Chiao-li (2018). 'Wanjin's Basilica: Church Evangelization Encountering Government's Tourism', in Francis H. K. So, Beatrice K. F. Leung, and Mary Ellen Mylod (eds.) *The Catholic Church in Taiwan: Birth, Growth and Development*. New York: Palgrave Macmillan: 201–31.

Waterbury, Lucy W. (1897). 'Christmas in Heathen Lands', *The Biblical World* 10, no. 6: 464–72.

Wernecke, Herbert H. (1959). *Christmas Customs Around the World*. Philadelphia, PA: Westminster Press.

Wernecke, Herbert H. (1963). *Celebrating Christmas Around the World*. Philadelphia, PA: Westminster Press.

Zhang, Kaiyuan (ed.) (2001). *Eyewitness Accounts of the Nanjing Massacre: American Missionaries Bear Witness to Japanese Atrocities*. Armonk, NY: M. E. Sharpe.

CHAPTER 41

LATIN AMERICA AND THE CARIBBEAN

DAVID THOMAS ORIQUE, O.P.

On Christmas Day night in 1492, the flagship of Christopher Columbus's three-bark fleet ran ashore off the northern coast of the island of Hispaniola, which today is part of Haiti (Casas 1992: Vol. 14, p. 125; Davies 1953: 854–65). As recorded in the Genoese mariner's log, after celebrating the birth of Christ, the *Santa María*'s experienced crew slept and left an inexperienced boy at the helm. The consequent collision of the Christian world on that Christmas Day into the Indigenous world seems a fitting metaphor for the crashing of Christianity into what would become America. Moreover, as a result of the scuttling of the largest of the three ships, thirty-nine members of Columbus's crew remained on the island. Using salvaged materials and supplies from the *Santa Maria* and with the help of local Tainos, they constructed the first fortified European settlement, which Columbus denominated *Navidad*—a significant toponymy because 'Nativity' means 'birth' and, indeed, on 25 December, Christians celebrate the birth of Jesus Christ.

This initial nautical collision between two mutually unknown lands and peoples generated subsequent geographic disorientation and disastrous demographic decline as well as painful cultural conflict. (Forebodingly, upon returning nearly a year later, Columbus found *Navidad* and the surrounding Indian villages completely destroyed, and all of the marooned crew—whom Columbus had instructed to look for gold—were dead.) In keeping with the trajectory of centuries-long inculturation of Christianity as, for example, in language, art, clothing, food, music, and so on, Iberian-European Christmas commemorations brought to America would also be inculturated over time in complex ways—first by Indigenous people and later by Africans (Bensusan and Carlisle 1978: 155–60).

However, the fundamental Christian theological understanding of the meaning of Christmas as a celebration of the birth of Christ—of God Incarnate—remained unchanged. As a central axis of the Christian tradition, the Incarnation addresses the birth of the eternal God—God–human, Jesus Christ—into human history. As such, any discussion of the Christian celebration of the Nativity must be canopied with the meaning and message of the eternal and boundless God born in space and time in human form. How this birth is celebrated in Christmas festivities, such as with the Mass or extra-liturgical activities, depends on the culture in which it is embedded and on the nature of the cultural adaptations reflected in the celebrations ('Inculturation' 2018). Accordingly, while the theological meaning of the Incarnation is perennial and universal, the celebration of this central axis of Christianity is variant and particular in its adaptation to different cultures, places, and times.

Arguably, this is true theologically because, according to Christian belief, humans are the same insofar as they are all created in the image and likeness of the One unchanging and eternal God; yet, while humans collectively share in divine ontological unity, women and men express and celebrate the Incarnation in a pluriformity of ways. Accordingly, the Catholic Christian celebrations of Christmas in Spanish and Portuguese colonial America (including the Caribbean)[1] manifested both continuity and change: continuity, by the commemoration of the birth of Christ as an honoured universal reality in the central ritual of the Mass as a liturgical act of worship; change, in the various inculturated extra-liturgical components from Indigenous, African, and European traditions, which enhanced liturgical worship as well as the extra-liturgical commemorations of Christ's birth.

Cultural accommodations in Latin American Christmas celebrations were not unusual or aberrant: they were part of the continued unfolding of celebration of the Nativity that were constitutive of an ongoing retelling of the earliest Incarnation narratives. Because of the tremendous theological diversity of expression within Latin America, examining the complexity and sophistication of the Christmas tradition for the entire region is too vast and complex to present in one short chapter, or even to explore in numerous scholarly tomes (see Orique et al. 2019; Garrad-Burnett et al. 2016). As such, this essay examines selected Latin American Catholic Christmas celebrations, including the Mass and extra-liturgical observances that manifest the influence and blending of aspects from the three distinct cultural traditions: European—principally Spanish and Portuguese—as well as the diverse and complex Indigenous and African expressions.[2]

To contextualize these Latin American observances of the birth of Christ, this chapter first presents some of the earliest known instances of the celebration of the Mass in America—those during the celebratory Christmas season, which in Roman Catholicism begins with First Vespers on Christmas Eve and ends with the Feast of the Baptism of the Lord, and those during the preparatory-penitential four-week period of Advent, which commences on the Sunday nearest the 30 November feast of St Andrew the Apostle and concludes on Christmas Eve. Thus, Catholic Christians prepare for the

---

[1] Henceforth these three areas of the region are referred to as Latin America.
[2] The writer acknowledges the many non-Catholic Christian Christmas celebrations as well as pre-contact Indigenous-inspired and African-imbued belief systems; yet, this discussion focuses on Iberian Catholicism as initially brought to and eventually changed in Latin America (Lynch 2012: xv).

Nativity of Jesus with both liturgical and extra-liturgical activities during Advent (with most ending with fasting and prayer on 24 December) and culminating in the midnight Mass, which liturgy marks the beginning of the Christmas season.

In 1494, the first recorded Mass during the Christmas season in Latin America was celebrated in the Caribbean on the 6 January feast of the Epiphany. Among those disembarking from Columbus's second expedition were five priests: the Jeronymite Ramón Pané, three Franciscan missionary clerics, and the Benedictine monk, Bernardo Buil (or Boyl), who was the first apostolic vicar in the New World. In a temporary shelter on Hispaniola, in a service for the mariners and Spanish settlers, Buil presided at this Mass commemorating the Magi's arrival (Schwaller 2011: 37; Jesse 1965: 62–71; Poole 1974: 194–95; Vigneras 1977: 83).

In 1500 in Brazil, where on 22 April, Pedro Álvares Cabral's Portuguese expedition to India accidentally encountered the South American mainland, Franciscan friar Henrique Soares de Coimbra (1465–1532) celebrated the first-known Mass there four days later on Easter Sunday at Coroa Vermelha on the beach, which was watched at a distance by a group of curious autochthonous peoples (Schwaller 2011: 67–8; Caminha 2000). While sporadic Portuguese settlement continued after the initial encounter, not until 1549 did the Portuguese pursue consistent colonization when Jesuits arrived to Christianize the Indians; as such, presumably after this date the first Advent and Christmas seasons and the Christmas Mass liturgy were celebrated (Legend 2002: 12–13; Prien 2012: 42).

In 1511, another event on the same Western Antillean island, nineteen years after Columbus's initial arrival in America, invites speculation about the Advent season as a preparation to celebrating the birth of Christ. At Mass on 21 December, the fourth Sunday of Advent, Dominican friar Antonio de Montesinos delivered an impassioned sermon to Spaniards that condemned their tyrannical and cruel abuse of the Taino Indians. Bartolomé de las Casas recorded that Montesinos, 'having finished with the introduction and having said something which had to do with the subject of the time of Advent', went on to say: 'What concern do you have for them? You do not teach them so that they might know their God and creator, might be baptised, go to Mass, celebrate feast days and Sundays' (Casas 1998: vol. 5: 1761–2). In spite of Spanish protests, the following Sunday, 28 December, Friar Antonio repeated his denunciatory message, which in the pre-Trent Dominican liturgy was the Sunday within the Octave of the Christmas season (Catholic Church 1849).

In 1525 or 1526 in Mesoamerica, after the fall of the Mexica (Aztec) capital in 1521, which was precipitated in part by Cortez's pursuit of wealth, Franciscan Friar Pedro de Gante deliberately sought to include Indigenous people in the celebration of the Christmas Mass by inviting those living within twenty leagues of Mexico City to attend (Sabido 2014: 21; Mann 2010: 336–8; Torre 2016: 90–116). The first Christmas Mass was likely celebrated after the fall of Tenochtitlan (13 August 1521), as Cortez had a Christmas Day meal in 1523, and clergy accompanied him during the siege on the Mexica capital (Restall 2018: 172; Burns 1937: 5).

In 1530 in Panama, Pizarro and members of his third expedition to Peru celebrated a Christmas-season Mass on 27 December before departing. William H. Prescott writes:

> On St. John the Evangelist's day, the banners of the company and the royal standard were consecrated in the cathedral church of Panama; a sermon was preached before the little army by Fray Juan de Vargas, one of the Dominicans selected by the government for the Peruvian mission; and mass was performed, and the sacrament administered to every soldier...Having thus solemnly invoked the blessing of Heaven on the enterprise, Pizarro and his followers went on board their vessels...early in January, 1531, sallied forth on his third and last expedition for the conquest of Peru. (Prescott 2018)

After capturing the Inca ruler, Atahualpa, at Cajamarca on 16 November 1532, these conquistadores attended the first-known Masses in the Andean region before travelling to the Inca capital of Cuzco. Indeed, Pizzaro also

> employed his men in making Caxamalca a more suitable residencefor a Christian host, by erecting a church, or, perhaps, appropriating some Indian edifice to this use, in which mass was regularly performed by the Dominican fathers, with great solemnity...Atahualpa discovered, amidst all the show of religious zeal..., a lurking appetite more potent in most of their bosoms than either religion or ambition. This was the love of gold. He determined to avail himself of it to procure his own freedom. (Prescott 2018)

In late 1532 and early 1533, arguably, these greedy Spaniards celebrated the first Advent and Christmas seasons in the Andean area, as well as hunted for riches as did Columbus's marooned crew forty years earlier in Natividad and Pizarro's cousin Cortez in Mexico (MacCormack 1993: 72).

Eventually, in Latin America, Christmas Eve (rather than Christmas Day) became generally celebrated as the time of Christ's birth. This night is customarily called *La Buena Noche*—meaning 'the good night', and is alternatively known as *La Noche Buena* or *La Navidad*; in Portuguese, Christmas Eve is denominated *Véspera de Natal*, seemingly in keeping with the European tradition of reciting Vespers on Christmas Eve. Christmas Mass, however, is predominantly referred to as *La Misa del Gallo* (The Mass of the Rooster), a term arising from an old European tale about a crowing rooster being the first to herald the birth of Christ. Whatever the names given to Christmas Masses, this liturgical ritual is usually celebrated at midnight; yet, this too is flexible; for example, in Peru, the 'midnight' Mass—the '*Misa del Gallo*'—is at 10 p.m. on Christmas Eve (see Pozo 2009: 677–8; Marchant 1941: 1375).

These sometimes differently titled Christmas Masses echo the ancient Church custom initiated in Jerusalem to celebrate three liturgies: one at midnight and heralded by angels, which honours the time of Christ's birth into a world of spiritual darkness; one at dawn as the Light of Christ was revealed to the shepherds and gradually dispelled the darkness of sin and death; and one in the fullness of daylight to signify that the promised Messiah was revealed to the whole world. While this custom of celebrating three distinct Christmas Masses is not a specifically Latin American tradition, the region's extra-liturgical celebrations do focus on angels, shepherds, and Christ's kingship (Crump 2013: 114–15; Wernecke 1959). As such, the liturgical components of Christmas Masses in Latin America generally reflect the symbolic and progressive manifestation of Christ from a shining star and adoring angels to a humble manger where Mary and Joseph, shepherds and kings, worshipped.

Adherence to these theological components in the particular celebrations of the Mass demonstrates the ubiquity and primacy of the Christmas Mass in Latin America. However, although the Christmas liturgy of the Mass is prescribed, ample fluidity is expressed in extra-liturgical activities, which range from preparations for the Christmas celebration to various extra-liturgical ways of commemorating the Incarnation—including in extra-ecclesial spaces such as streets, neighbourhoods, and homes until, as well as usually concluding with, the feast of the Epiphany.

Selected discernible components in Latin American Christmas commemorations are now presented to demonstrate both the presence of cultural blending as well as the pervasiveness of cultural accommodations that began early in the region's Catholic Christianity. These inculturated commemorations of Christ's birth and related celebrations prior to and following the Christmas Mass further demonstrate how Indigenous and Afro-Latin American religiously inspired cultural components were incorporated into European Catholic Christian celebrations (Lynch 2012: 38; Silva 2014: 222–3).

In Latin America (and elsewhere), preparations for the celebration of Christmas during Advent vary in when they begin, in how long they continue, and in what they consist. For example, in Panama, preparations begin on 2 December; in Nicaragua, on 7 December; in Argentina and Brazil, on 8 December—the feast of the Immaculate Conception; and in Mexico, on 12 December, the feast of Our Lady of Guadalupe—a celebration that combines Catholic sensibilities, pre-contact cosmology, and Mexican nationalism (Brading 2003). However, in Nicaragua, a special observance prefaced Advent that honours Mary as 'La Purissima' from late November to 7 December and culminated with a jubilant *gritería*.

Nicaraguans and other Latin Americans also extend the Christmas season beyond 25 December—some to the feast of the Holy Innocents or to the Epiphany as did the *Folia de Reis* celebrations in rural Brazil (Passos 2011: 255, 257ff.). Some embrace a forty-day cycle that commemorates the Nativity and the circumcision of Jesus, the visit of the Magi, and the purification of the Virgin Mother.

However, throughout most of the region, Advent preparations for Christmas consisted of two types of novenas. In early colonial New Spain, the first type consisted of nine days of special Masses celebrated in the early morning hours before dawn. The first day's Mass was dedicated to the Annunciation; the second, to the visit of the Virgin Mary to her cousin Elizabeth; the third, to the journey to Bethlehem; the fourth, to the Nativity; the fifth, to the shepherds; the sixth, to the Magi; the seventh, to the flight into

Egypt; the eighth, to the boy Jesus in the Temple with the scholars; the ninth, to the boy Jesus' return to Nazareth. This novena of Masses introduced participants to Scriptures about John the Baptist, a biblical figure who called people to 'prepare the way of the Lord' as well as to repentance and conversion (Crump 2013: 64b).

These special Masses also promoted cultural blending. Since a novena Mass is a 'Low Mass'—a *Misa rezada* without the gloria, credo, or collect, missionaries seemingly promoted music at these liturgies with a genre of Indigenous music known as *aguinaldos*. (*Aguinaldo* has two usages: one means 'gift' (of Christ to the world and the world to Christ) as well as the gift of an employer of one year's salary to an employee; the other refers to singing 'carols'.) By using Indigenous melodies (but with Christian words to evangelize), the *Misa de aguinaldos* became extremely popular and attendance soared. However, over time, as a *gran ruido* (great noise) akin to that on a 'battle ground' characterized the people's participation in these Masses, some Church authorities deemed the song renditions and instrumental music as inappropriate for a sacred liturgy. Consequently in 1585 to halt the perceived 'abuse', the Third Provincial Council of Mexico and the Mexican hierarchy forbade the celebration of Masses after sunset and before sunrise. In response, few conformed. Subsequently in 1586, Augustinian Fray Diego de Soria appealed to Sixtus VI who granted papal permission to celebrate Masses outdoors, which along with related festivities, became very popular—due in part to the pope's granting a perpetual indulgence for those attending the nine *Misas de aguinaldo* (Solana 1965: 15; Pozo 2009: 679-78).

The second type of novenas consisted of special prayers offered on nine successive days prior to Christmas—as the Jesuit founder Ignatius Loyola suggested and promoted. Other exposure to Christianity consisted of nightly processions re-enacting Mary and Joseph's journey to Bethlehem and their wandering in search of a *posada* (lodging); another pertained to the enactment of *pastorales* (theatrical performances) about the shepherds' arrival at the manger to worship the Christ Child. In the mid-1500s and in accord with the genre of European folk dramas, *posadas*, and *pastorales*, inspired the production of religious plays as another mechanism beneficial for conversion. One example that has been studied is the adaptation and/or accommodation of Spanish Christianity in Venezuela (Prieto Rodriguez and Suinaga 2013: 256-8).

Besides liturgical celebrations of *Misas de aguinaldos* predominantly in Colombia, Venezuela, and Ecuador, quasi-liturgical Advent celebrations—from prayer novenas to *posadas*, from *pastorales* to religious theatre—arose in various parts of Latin America. For example, *La posada*, imported from Spain, was first popular in Mexico and then expanded to Honduras, Guatemala, El Salvador, Costa Rica, Nicaragua, and Panama. However, the most unifying and common quasi-liturgical component consisted of Nativity scenes (crèches), which in Spanish-speaking countries were varyingly referred to as *nacimientos*, *pesebres*, or *portales*; in Portuguese-speaking Brazil, as *presépio*. The word 'presépio' comes from '*presepium*' meaning the bed of straw on which Jesus first slept after his birth in Bethlehem. This custom is common in parts of north-eastern Brazil (Moreno 2009: 655-74; Vargas 2006: 8-9; León-Portilla and Chávez, 2006: 32-47; and Cantú 2006: 48-57). These manger scenes—a tradition dating to 1223 when Francis of Assisi apparently created the first manger scene in a cave at Greccio—were erected in homes and churches, in plazas, and other public places (Rosenthal 1954: 57–9).

Such celebratory elements in the Advent and Christmas seasons originated in Europe and built on and/or coincided with components of Indigenous and African cultures. For example, in Central Mexico, these festivities were layered on top of Nahua celebrations dedicated to Huitzilopochtli (Mann 2010: 336–8; Jáuregui 2000: 26–7). Augustinian missionaries introduced nine-day *posadas* to replace a portion of the Aztec celebration of *Panquetzaliztli* observed from 17–26 December. This period was both the fifteenth month of the Nahuatl calendar of 365 days and a festival in the Aztec religion that honoured Huitzilopochtli. Each year this sun god's birthday was celebrated in December just as Christians celebrated the birthday of Christ, the God-made-human, in December. Furthermore, the Great Huitzilopochtli festival lasted the entire twenty days of the Aztec ceremonial calendar and, like 24 December—a day of fasting for most Christians, included a preliminary period of fasting. The Huitzilopochtli festival also concluded with consuming small edible images of this Mesoamerican deity—just as Christians believe that consuming the Host at Mass is consuming the body and blood of Christ (Sabido 2014, Durán 1880: 298–300). Finally, the choice of 25 December—the date of Christ's birth according to the Julian calendar—also coincided with winter solstice celebrations.

Another pervasive inculturating component in the celebration of Christmas in Latin America pertains to the enhancement of the liturgy of the Christmas Mass by dance (and, of course, music), even into contemporary times. For example, in central Michoacan, Mexico, a culturally mixed Indigenous community of Chichimecas, Nahuas, and pre-Tarascos, known as the Purepechas, settled near the Lake Patzcuaro region, where they enhanced the celebration of Christmas in Tarímbaro with their Takari (Christmas) festival's four days of special sacred dance. Moreover, they revised their Nativity plays to include the participation of all members of their community, which also served to strengthen group solidarity among its members (Araiza 2014: 163–90). Another small settlement—deep in Copper Canyon in the state of Chihuahua, and one of the oldest surviving Indigenous communities—also honoured their deity as a part of their Christmas liturgical ritual by a special dance called the *matachín* (Robb 1961: 87–100; Rodriguez 2009; López 2004: 252). For these Tarahumaras people, dance was the most sacred form of worship.

In like manner, dances predominated in Afro-rituals and, for some, in Christmas celebrations, and were performed in the Caribbean, in Venezuela, as well as in Argentina, Peru, and Uruguay, and in Brazil. In the Viceroyalty of Río de la Plata region, the African slaves inculturated the celebration of the Magi (Walker 2001: 259, 262, 267). In the Caribbean, African slaves were given one or two days off work at Christmas, during which time they prepared for and performed dances rooted in West Africa. For example, in Jamaica, they created masks and costumes as well as musical instruments, and then elaborately performed one of the oldest dance rituals: the *Jonkonnu* (Fenn 1988: 127–53; Hill 2000: 6; Turner 2008: 599–96). On other Caribbean islands, namely, those of St Vincent, Bermuda, Belize, St Kitts, Antigua (and pre-revolutionary Cuba), they did the same (Bettelheim 1990: 31–3). Another dance also with West African origins, which is featured in the *Jonkonnu* Christmas celebrations, consisted of the *Moko Jumbie*, apparently part of Amerindian Christmas *parrandas* (merrymaking). Another traditional dance in the Dominican Republic was the *Gagá*, which acted out scenarios of death and rebirth—a dance presumably linked theologically to Christ's death and Resurrection (Sloat 2005: 140–1, 26, 273–6; 360).

In Afro-Venezuelan celebrations of Christmas, where Nativity scenes were erected and midnight Mass attended, dance, drumming, and *gaita* (a genre of Christmas folk music) characterized their customary *parrandas* of groups singing gaitan carols as they go from house to house (Moodie 1983). Afro-Uruguayan celebrations paraded their troupe of traditional drummers, whose Candomblé-inspired rhythm evoked ancestral memories, and symbolized their strength and survival during their experiences of slavery. Afro-Peruvian celebrations combined musical elements to create a genre first developed and performed by the initial African slave population at the time the Inca Empire disintegrated. Like the Uruguayans, Afro-Argentinian celebrations in the form of dance formations also survived and constituted an integral part of Afro communities in these countries. Indeed, in time, wherever Afro *cofradías* were permitted ecclesiastically, such as in Venezuela, Uruguay, Peru, and Argentina, Afros were more united and able to assert their cultural agency (Bastide 2007: 54–6).

In Brazil, many Christmas traditions, such as erecting Nativity scenes and attending the shepherds' play (*Os Pastores*), came from Portugal. Other quasi-liturgical celebrations unique to Brazil included lyric theatre, *Reisados* (*Folia de Reis* or *Festa de Santos Reis*), which among its historical and religious themes included a musical play from Maranhão that consisted of killing or stealing a bull followed by the bull's resurrection or reappearance—a religious theme echoing the death and Resurrection of Christ. More universally, in the celebration of the liturgy of the Mass (and other sacraments), African elements of dancing, drumming, music, costumes with bright coloured patterns, and offerings of food gradually emerged. Of these components, music and dance remained a significant central form of worship and the 'beating heart' in the inculturated Afro-Masses and other Christmas celebrations (Gottheim 1988: 41–5, 52; Burdick 2004: 111–30; Silva 2014).

Indeed, great diversity existed in these inculturated celebrations, since in Brazil (and throughout Latin America), enslaved Africans came from different regions. In like manner, the Indigenous Christmas Masses manifested a great diversity of influences drawn from the wide range of pre-contact American hemispheric populations. These Afro and Indigenous diversities resulted from tremendous religio-cultural-linguistic compression as various groups encountered and appropriated Christianity and its celebrations in distinctive ways (Bastide 2007: 54–6; Kiddy 2007: 123–29, 141, 164, 190; Hill 1998: 184–5, 189).

Such was the general process of inculturation of the celebration liturgically and quasi-liturgically of Christmas in Latin America that started after the initial collision of Iberian Christianity with heterogeneous and sophisticated cultures, first Indigenous and later African. With the participation of these various and complex autochthonous and allochthonous peoples in Christmas celebrations (sometimes willingly, other times forced), the ongoing inculturation process consisted of catechizing via *posadas*, *pastorales*, and *confradías*, and of accommodating Indigenous and Afro-Brazilian cultural elements, such as their music and dance, to enhance Christmas liturgical and quasi-liturgical festivities.

Beyond this initial inculturation period of Catholic Christianity in Latin America, today globalization also contributes to religious pluralism as the region's theological landscape has shifted to include growing Protestantism, in particular Pentecostalism, as well as non-Christian religions. In this postmodern environment, many retain traditional inculturated Catholic celebrations—such as those rooted in Afro and Indigenous traditions; some reflect their own emerging subcultures; others choose no religious affiliation. In addition to this expansion of religious options, there are secular choices for the celebration of Christmas: some now embrace Christmas expressions not historically part of Latin American festivities (e.g. Santa Claus, Christmas trees, Black Friday, or, as in Venezuela, roller skating to midnight Mass). Indeed, with advancing secularization and commercialization, many celebrate the Christmas season with little or no effort to engage liturgically or quasi-liturgically in the traditional Christian theological content of the 'holiday'. For example, in colonial Mexico, the piñata referred to the struggle between good and evil; however today, in Latin America, piñatas are constructed in various motifs and filled with small gifts, which upon rupture are distributed to enliven birthday and other celebrations. In contrast and in very recent times, *posadas* have been held at the Mexican border to dramatize the plight of migrants as well as have been performed to assist with efforts to fight poverty and domestic violence, as well as to promote health and safety programmes (Rotella 1994; Langois 2010).

Yet, in spite of (and maybe because of) the processes of globalization, pluralization, secularization, and commercialization that impact Latin America, the celebration of Christmas as an inculturated Christian celebration of the eternal and unchanging divine message of the Incarnation continues to capture the imagination of countless Latin Americans, as they participate in traditional expressions of the theological meaning of the birth of Jesus Christ (Payne 2016: 145–74; Pew Forum 2014).

References and Further Reading

'Afro-Venezuelans—Religion and Expressive Culture'. *Countries and their Culture*. Available at http://www.everyculture.com/South-America/Afro-Venezuelans-Religion-and-Expressive-Culture.html#ixzz5GK9cU3Md/ (accessed 27 March 2020).

Alexander, J. Neil (2013). 'Advent', in Paul F. Bradshaw (ed.), *New SCM Dictionary of Liturgy and Worship*. London: SCM Press: 2.

Araiza, Elizabeth (2014). 'Ritual, teatro y "performance" en un culto al niño Dios y al diablo. Las Pastorelas de la región Purépecha, Michoacán, México', *Journal de la Société des Américanistes*, 100-1: 163–90.

Bastide, Roger (2007). *The African Religions of Brazil: Toward a Sociology of the Interpenetration of Civilizations*. 1st ed. 1960. Baltimore: Johns Hopkins University Press.

Bensusan, Guy and. Carlisle, Charles R. (1978). 'Raices y Ritmos/Roots and Rhythms: Our Heritage of Latin American Music', *Latin American Research Review*, 13, no. 3: 155–60.

Bettelheim, Judith (1990). 'Carnival in Cuba: Another Chapter in the Nationalization of Culture', *Caribbean Quarterly*, 36, no. 3–4: 29–41.

Brading, D. A. (2003). *Mexican Phoenix: Our Lady of Guadalupe: Image and Tradition across Five Centuries*. Cambridge: Cambridge University Press.

Burdick, John (2004). 'The Catholic Afro Mass and the Dance of Eurocentrism in Brazil', in Henry Goldschmidt and Elizabeth McAlister (eds.), *Race, Nation, and Religion in the Americas*. New York: Oxford University Press: 111–30.

Burns, Sarah M. (1937). 'Fray Pedro de Gante and Early Education in New Spain'. Master's thesis, Loyola University.

Caminha, Pêro Vaz de (2000). *Carta de Pêro Vaz de Caminha a El-Rei D. Manuel Sobre o Achamento do Brasil*. Eds. Ana Maria de Azevedo, Maria Paula Caetano, and Neves Aguas, Mem Martins, Portugal: Publicações Europa-América.

Campo del Pozo, Fernando (2009). 'Misas de aguinaldos, posadas y paraduras en Venezuela', in *La Natividad arte, religiosidad y tradiciones populares*. Actas del Simposium. 4-7-5-IX. coord., Francisco Javier Campos de Fernández de Sevilla. San Lorenzo de El Escorial, España: DES: 675–96.

Cantú, Graciela Romandía de (2006). 'Nacimientos, belenes y presepios', *Artes de México*, no. 81, El arte tradicional del Nacimiento, November: 48–57.

Casas, Bartolomé de las (1998). 'Historia de las Indias', in Álvaro Huerga (ed.), *Obras Completas* 14 vols. Madrid: Alianza Editorial.

Catholic Church (1849). *Missale ad consuetudinem fratrum praedicatorum*. In clarissima Parisiorum Academia Johannes Petit.

Chasteen, John Charles (2004). *National Rhythms, African Roots: The Deep History of Latin American Popular Dance*. Albuquerque, NM: University of New Mexico Press.

Chocano Mena, Magdalena (2000). *La América colonial (1492-1763) Cultura y vida cotidiana*. Editorial Síntesis, S. A. Kindle version.

Cirio, Norberto Pablo (2000). 'Antecedentes históricos del culto a San Baltazar en la Argentina: "La Cofradía de San Baltazar y Animas" (1772–1856)', *Latin American Music Review/ Revista de Música Latinoamericana*, 21, no. 2, Autumn–Winter: 190–214.

Comings, Jill Burnet (2005). *Aspects of the Liturgical Year in Cappadocia (325-430)*. Patristic Studies Series. New York: Peter Lang Inc., International Academic Publishers.

Connell, Martin F. (2013). 'Christmas', in Paul F. Bradshaw (ed.), *New SCM Dictionary of Liturgy and Worship*. Norwich: Hymns Ancient and Modern Ltd: 113.

Cross, F. L. and E. A. Livingston (eds.) (2005). 'Advent', *The Oxford Dictionary of the Christian Church*. Oxford: Oxford University Press.

Crump, William D. (2013). 'Advent' and 'Christmas Masses', in *The Christmas Encyclopedia*, 3rd ed. McFarland.

Davies, Arthur (1953). 'The Loss of the *Santa Maria* Christmas Day, 1492', *American Historical Review*, 58, no. 4, 1 July: 854–65.

'Del sueño de la Argentina blanca europea a la realidad de la Argentina americana: la asunción del componente étnico-cultural afro y su (nuestro) patrimonio musical'. Instituto Nacional de Musicología 'Carlos Vega'. Available at https://www.cultura.gob.ar/institucional/organ ismos/museos/instituto-nacional-de musicologia-carlos-vega/

Durán, Diego (1880). *Historia de las Indias de la Nueva España y islas de tierra firme*. Vol. II. MexicoCity: Imprenta de Ignacio Escalante, México.

Edwards, Erika Denise (2008). 'Argentina: Afro-Argentines', in *Encyclopedia of the African Diaspora*. Santa Barbara, Ca: ABC-CLIO.

Fenn, Elizabeth A. (1988). 'A Perfect Equality Seemed to Reign: Slave Society and Jonkonnu', *North Carolina Historical Review*, 65, no. 2, April: 127–53.

Garrard-Burnett, Virginia, Paul Freston, and Stephen C. Dove (2016). *The Cambridge History of Religions in Latin America*. New York: Cambridge University Press.

Gottheim, Vivian I. (1988). 'Bumba-meu-boi, a Musical Play from Maranhão', *The World of Music*, 30, no. 2: 40–68.

Hill, Donald R (1998). 'West African and Haitian Influences on the Ritual and Popular Music of Carriacou, Trinidad, and Cuba', *Black Music Research Journal*, 18, nos. 1/2, Spring–Autumn: 183–201.

Hill, Errol (2000). 'Perspectives in Caribbean Theatre: Ritual, Festival, and Drama', *Caribbean Quarterly*, 46, nos. 3/4, The Sir Philip Sherlock Lectures (September–December): 6.

'Inculturation, Theology of' (2018). *New Catholic Encyclopedia*, Encyclopedia.com. Available at http://www.encyclopedia.com/religion/encyclopedias-almanacs-transcripts-and-maps/inculturation-theology/ (accessed 27 March 2020).

Jáuregui, Carlos A (2000). 'Saturno caníbal: Fronteras, reflejos y paradojas en la narrativa sobre el antropófago', *Revista de Crítica Literaria Latinoamericana*, 26, no. 51: 9–39.

Jesse, C. (1965). 'The Papal Bull Of 1493 Appointing The First Vícar Apostolíc In The New World', *Caribbean Quarterly*, 11, nos 3/4, September and December, 1965: 62–71.

Kiddy, Elizabeth W (2007). *Blacks of the Rosary: Memory and History in Minas Gerais, Brazil*. University Park: Penn State University Press.

Langlois, Ed (2010). 'Event Mixes Christmas Tradition and Charity', *Catholic Sentinel*, 23 December. Available at https://catholicsentinel.org/Content/News/Local/Article/Event-mixes-Christmas-tradition-and-charity/2/35/13755/ (accessed 27 March 2020).

Legend, Cayapo (2002). 'The Origin of Fire', in Robert M. Levine, John Crocitti Robert M. Levine and John Crocitti (eds.), *The Brazil Reader: History, Culture, Politics*, 3rd. ed. Durham, NC: Duke University Press: 12–13.

León-Portilla, Miguel and Para Celia Chávez (2006). 'Cantos navideños en náhuatl', *Artes de México*, 81, El arte tradicional del Nacimiento, November: 32–47.

Library of Congress. 'Exploring the Early Americas'. Available at https://www.loc.gov/exhibits/exploring-the-early-americas/columbus-and-the-taino.html/ (accessed 27 March 2020).

López de la Torre, Carlos Fernando (2016). 'El trabajo misional de fray Pedro de Gante en los inicios de la Nueva España', *Fronteras de la Historia*, 21, no. 1, January–June: 90–116.

Lynch, John (2012). *New Worlds: A Religious History of Latin America*. New Haven, CT: Yale University Press.

Mann, Charles C. (2012). *1493: Uncovering the New World Columbus Created*. New York: Vintage.

Mann, Kristin Dutcher (2010). 'Christmas in the Missions of Northern New Spain', *The Americas*, 66, no. 3, Evangelization as Performance, January: 331–51.

Marchant, Annie D'Armond (1941). 'Christmas in Brazil', *American Journal of Nursing*, 41, no. 12, December: 1375.

Moodie, Sylvia María (1983). 'Survival of Hispanic Religious Songs in Trinidad Folklore', *Caribbean Quarterly*, 29, no. 1, Caribbean Traditional Music (March): 1–31.

Moreno, Félix Carmona, OSA (2009). 'Navidad en Ecuador: Manifestaciones de religiosidad popular en torno al Niño Jesús', in *La Natividad: arte, religiosidad y tradiciones populares*, 655-74.
Nava López, E. Fernando (2004). 'Musical Traditions of the P'urhépecha (Tarascos of Michoacán, Mexico', in Malena Kuss (ed.), *Music in Latin America and the Caribbean: An Encyclopedic History*, vol. 1: 'Performing Beliefs, Indigenous Peoples of South America, Central America, and Mexico'. Austin: University of Texas: 246-60.
Orique, David, OP, Susan Fitzpatrick Behrens, and Virginia Garrard-Burnett (eds.) (2019). *Oxford Handbook of Latin American Christianity*. Oxford: Oxford University Press.
Passos, Mauro (2011). Lá vem a bandeira...os reis e seus atores", *Revista Brasileira de História das Religiões* ANPUH, Ano III, n. 9, January: 253-68.
Payne, William Price (2016). 'Folk Religion and the Pentecostalism Surge in Latin America', *Asbury Journal*, 71/1: 145-74.
Pew Forum and Research Center (2014). 'Religion in Latin America: Widespread Change in a Historically Catholic Region' (13 November). Available at https://www.pewforum.org/2014/11/13/religion-in-latin-america/ (accessed 27 March 2020).
Poole, B. T. F. (1974). 'Case Reopened: An Enquiry into the "Defection" of Fray Bernal Boyl and Mosen Pedro Margarit', *Journal of Latin American Studies*, 6, no. 2, November: 193-210.
Pozo, Fernando Campo del (2009). 'Misas de aguinaldos, posadas y paraduras en Venezuela', in *La Natividad arte, religiosidad y tradiciones populares: Actas del Simposium* (4-7 October). San Lorenzo de El Escorial, Spain: Ed. Escurialenses: 675-96.
Prieto Rodriguez, Adlin de Jesús, and Marina Meza Suinaga (2013). 'Baby Jesus' Standing, Theft and Search—A Traditional Venezuela Christmas Feast', Politeja 24, *Venezuela Studies* : 255-66.
Prescott, William. (2018) *History of the Conquest of Peru*, Project Gutenberg. Available at http://www.gutenberg.org/cache/epub/1209/pg1209-images.html/ (accessed 27 March 2020).
Prien, Hans-Jürgen (2012). *Christianity in Latin America*, rev. ed. Leiden, Netherlands: Brill.
Restall, Matthew (2003). *Seven Myths of the Spanish Conquest*. Oxford: Oxford University Press.
Restall, Matthew (2018). *When Montezuma Met Cortes: The True Story of the Meeting that Changed History*. New York: Ecco.
Robb, J. D. (1961). 'The Matachines Dance: A Ritual Folk Dance', *Western Folklore*, 20, no. 2, April: 87-100.
Rodriguez, Sylvia (2009). *The Matachines Dance: A Ritual Dance of the Indian Pueblos and Mexicano*, rev. ed. Santa Fe: Sunstone Press.
Rosenthal, Erwin (1954). 'The Crib of Greccio and Franciscan Realism', *Art Bulletin*, 36, no. 1, March: 57-9.
Rotella, Sebastian (1994). 'Christmas Story Finds a Place on the Border: Immigration: Activists on Both Sides of the Border Point Up Migrants' Plight with a Mexican *Posada*'. *Los Angeles Times*. 25 Dece La Natividad: arte, religiosidad y tradiciones Populares mber. Available at http://articles.latimes.com/1994-12-25/news/mn-12940_1_illegal immigrants/ (accessed 27 March 2020).
Sabido, Miguel (2014). 'Prólogo', 'La Pastorela', and 'El Calendario Ritual Católico y susrepresentaciones sagradas', in *Teatro sagrado: Los "coloquios" de México*. Siglo XXI: 21.
Schwaller, John Frederick (2011). *The History of the Catholic Church in Latin America: From Conquest to Revolution and Beyond*. New York: NYU Press.

Silva, Vagner Gonçalves da (2014). 'Religion and Black Cultural Identity Roman Catholics, Afro-Brazilians and Neo-Pentecostalism', *vibrant* v. 11 no. 2, July–December: 210–46.

Sloat, Susanna (ed.) (2005). *Caribbean Dance from Abakuá to Zouk: How Movement Shapes Identity*. Gainesville, FL: University Press of Florida.

Solana, Rafael (1965). 'Las Posadas', *Artes de* México, no. 72, Nacimiento, Villancico, y Pastorela: 14–16.

Taylor, Hargus (1990). 'Christmas', in Watson E. Mills and Roger Aubrey Bullard (eds.), *Mercer Dictionary of the Bible*. Macon, Georgia: Mercer University Press. 142–3.

Turner, Grace (2008). 'Junkanoo', in Carole Boyce Davies (ed.), *Encyclopedia of the African Diaspora: Origins, Experiences, and Culture*, vol. 2 (ABC-CLIO), 599–596.

Vargas, Rafael (2006). 'Nacimientos mexicanos, un acto de alegría', *Artes de* México, no. 81, El arte tradicional del Nacimiento, November:

Vigneras, Louis-André (1977). 'Saint Thomas, Apostle of America', *The Hispanic American Historical Review*, 57, no. 1, February: 82–90.

Walker, Sheila S. (ed.) (2001). *African Roots/American Cultures: Africa in the Creation of the Americas*. Lanham, MD: Rowman & Littlefield.

Wernecke, Herbert Henry (1959). *Christmas Customs Around the World*. Louisville, KY: Westminster Press.

Westerfield Tucker, Karen B. (2000). 'Christmas', in Adrian Hastings, Alistair Mason, and Hugh Pyper (eds.), *The Oxford Companion to Christian Thought*. Oxford: Oxford University Press.

PART VIII

THE STATE AND SOCIETY

CHAPTER 42

PUBLIC HOLIDAYS AND THE LAW

RICHARD W. GARNETT
AND JACKSON C. BLAIS

The course of the seasons, too, matures the fruits of the earth necessary for our support, and the succession of years reminds us of the fleeting nature of everything earthly, for our whole life is composed of successive years. Consequently the civilized peoples already in remote antiquity have found a call to the worship of God in the changing seasons and times, and so have introduced sacred seasons. Sacred times and places are common to all religions in general. The change of times, bringing with them corresponding changes in nature, made a religious impression upon mankind. In turn, man sanctified certain times and dedicated them to God, and these days thus consecrated to God became festivals (Kellner 1908: 1–2). Celebrating holidays and making laws appear to be natural for human persons and communities. It is not surprising, then, that laws *about* holidays are ubiquitous in human history and practice, too.

ALTHOUGH '[w]e do not know where or why the first holy day was observed ... we do know that holidays are as old as the [human] race'. These holidays 'may have celebrated the rising sun, the arrival of spring or a bountiful harvest ... [o]r it may have invoked whatever gods there were to dispel the fearful spirits of the dead from the land' (Hutchison and Adams 1951: vii). But the point remains that we have consistently selected specific and recurring days to celebrate important moments together as a community.

The ancient Romans notably made holidays a fixture of public life in the empire. They celebrated *feriae publicae*, that is, 'public holy days' or 'festivals'. The Roman government 'ordained and paid for' *feriae publicae* and mandated that freeborn Romans suspend business, lawsuits, and political transactions for the period of the holiday. Even slaves were required to be given a rest from labour. This abstention from work on *feriae publicae* was taken seriously. Although some work was deemed necessary on these holy days, the government sometimes fined or required a sacrifice of a pig from those who chose to work on *feriae publicae* as though they were normal days. The *feriae publicae* recognized a variety of religious observances, as well as major events such as the emperor's birthday. For religious holidays, the priesthood would hold ceremonies and sacrifices at temples in observance. Visits to the temple were not required, however, and many people took the opportunity for a simple day of rest (Scullard 1981: 39–40).

After the Roman Empire adopted Christianity, it formally abolished the *feriae*, but functionally maintained them by replacing the old celebrations with new Christian holidays. Additionally, the Sabbath became a regular 'public holiday' of sorts, as all political and judicial proceedings halted on Sundays. In practice, then, the observance of *feriae publicae* continued unabated, just with Christianity (*A Dictionary of Greek and Roman Antiquities* 1875: 528–30).

CHRISTMAS AS A FEDERAL HOLIDAY IN THE UNITED STATES

The ebbs and flows of Christmas observances, practices, and regulations in colonial and early America are covered elsewhere in this volume. For the purposes of this chapter, it is enough to say that Christmas and its celebration were consistently addressed and shaped, in many and diverse ways by the civil laws of political communities. By the time of the Founding, the new United States of America had relatively few publicly celebrated holidays in comparison to Europe (Restad 1995: 17). President George Washington proclaimed 26 November 1789 as 'the first official American Thanksgiving', a practice generally followed by later presidents (Epstein 1996: 2113). The federal government did not declare it a national public holiday as we understand the concept today, though. Similarly, local communities celebrated the Fourth of July on their own accord and while the federal government tended to encourage such celebrations, it did not designate or treat it as a *national* public holiday. Indeed, the new nation did not adopt a national calendar at all, opting instead to leave the decision of which holidays to celebrate to the states. This comports with the general understanding of the time that the federal government was one of limited, enumerated powers, with the states in charge of local obligations and affairs, and with health, safety, welfare, and morals. Thus, by the early nineteenth century, many states, cities, and townships celebrated holidays, Christmas included, but there was no uniform understanding of public holidays from the federal government until 1870 (Restad 1995: 21–5).

That all changed, however, in 1870, when, after being lobbied by bankers and businessmen who wanted certain holidays formalized, Congress passed a law declaring four national public holidays (see 41 Cong. Ch. 167, 16 Stat.168 1870). This law established New Year's Day, Christmas, the Fourth of July, and Thanksgiving as holidays for federal employees specifically within the District of Columbia. It is noteworthy that, during the debate over this bill, congressmen had no discussion about whether declaring holidays with certain religious undertones, such as Christmas and Thanksgiving, would violate the Establishment Clause of the First Amendment. In fact, the only major point of debate that resulted in a change was clarifying that the statute applied only to federal employees within the District of Columbia and not the states, as the law was written to 'correspond with similar laws of the States' around Washington DC (Cong. Globe, 41st Cong., 2d Sess. 4529 1870).

This was not unfamiliar for the time period, as the general understanding of the parameters of the Establishment Clause in the nineteenth century was narrower than it is today—'public expression of religion...laws inspired by religion, [and]...governmental endorsements or accommodations of religion' struck no one at the time as unconstitutional actions (Buck 2002: 408). Some congressmen suggested including only the dates of the holiday instead of naming the holidays specifically in the bill, but that proposal failed. Thus, from the moment the federal government began recognizing public holidays in the United States, days of religious significance such as Christmas were included along with important secular holidays such as the Fourth of July. There was never a time when *only* secular or religious holidays were recognized—many people across the country already celebrated these four holidays on their own time, so it appears to have been more a matter of convenience on the government's part in recognizing these first four national holidays than anything else.

Christmas in the Supreme Court of the United States

As already noted, for most of the history of the United States (the country that is the main focus of this chapter), the Establishment Clause, which states that Congress may 'make no law respecting an Establishment of religion', was not widely regarded as a legal basis for challenging the presence of religious symbols and expression in public life. Indeed, the interpretation of the Clause was a question that, for the first century-and-a-half of American constitutional history, almost never arose in litigation. This would change, of course, after World War II. In the landmark Supreme Court case of *Everson v. Board of Education*, Justice Hugo Black announced a new understanding of the Establishment Clause, one that the Court would implement and enforce, even if not always consistently, in the following decades:

> The 'establishment of religion' clause of the First Amendment means at least this: Neither a state nor the Federal Government can set up a church. Neither can pass laws which aid one religion, aid all religions, or prefer one religion over another.

Neither can force nor influence a person to go to or to remain away from church against his will or force him to profess a belief or disbelief in any religion. No person can be punished for entertaining or professing religious beliefs or disbeliefs, for church attendance or non-attendance. No tax in any amount, large or small, can be levied to support any religious activities or institutions, whatever they may be called, or whatever form they may adopt to teach or practice religion. Neither a state nor the Federal Government can, openly or secretly, participate in the affairs of any religious organizations or groups or vice versa. In the words of [Thomas] Jefferson, the clause against the establishment of religion by law was intended to erect a 'wall of separation between Church and state. (*Everson* 1947: 15–16)

This expansive interpretation of the Establishment Clause, along with the citation to Thomas Jefferson's oft-repeated aphorism of a high wall between Church and State, resulted in a notable increase in Establishment Clause challenges, including challenges to traditional practices such as prayer and Bible reading in schools—and the public celebration of Christmas.

For example, there have been several lower-level court opinions challenging the constitutionality of laws declaring certain religious holidays to be public holidays. The cases focus on the two important Christian celebrations, Easter and Christmas. The challengers claimed that the Establishment Clause prohibits the government from recognizing these holidays because of their religious origins and nature. By recognizing and singling out one particular religion's holy days as nationwide holidays, the argument went, the government had unconstitutionally established or 'endorsed' Christianity. An appropriate examination of these cases, however, requires an understanding of how American courts approach and decide Establishment Clause cases generally.

The Supreme Court laid down the test that became the standard tool, at least in theory, for applying the Establishment Clause in *Lemon v. Kurtzmann* (1971). In *Lemon*, a disgruntled taxpayer whose child attended a public school in Pennsylvania challenged a state statute that reimbursed private schools' expenditures for 'teacher's salaries, textbooks', and other instructional materials. Because most of these private schools were Roman Catholic, Lemon claimed that the state statute had the effect of directly funding religious institutions and that this support breached the 'wall of separation' invoked by Justice Black in *Everson*. The Supreme Court agreed, and in so doing, established what became known as the *Lemon* test. For a statute to avoid running afoul of the Establishment Clause, the Court held that the statute: (1) must have a secular legal purpose, (2) must have a principal or primary effect 'that neither advances nor inhibits religion,' and (3) must not create an 'excessive entanglement with religion' (*Lemon* 1971: 612–13, quoting *Walz* 1970: 674). If a statute failed to meet *any* of these three requirements, the Court announced, it violated the Establishment Clause.

Although it has been dutifully invoked and applied by lower courts and law students for decades, the 'test' has long been criticized as unworkable, imprecise, unpredictable, and malleable. The justices have adjusted, refined, and often simply ignored it, especially in cases involving religious symbols, public prayers, God-themed mottos, and the like. After all, an ardent atheist may see it as simple common sense that making Christmas a federal holiday has the principal effect of advancing Christianity and excessively entangles the government with religion. On the other hand, many Christians (and non-Christians) would argue that recognizing Christmas as a national holiday does nothing more than appreciate and accommodate the fact that a majority of the country's citizens celebrate a common religious holiday, and that an easy way to avoid conflicts and confusion is simply to give everyone the day off.

The status of the *Lemon* test has become increasingly unclear, and the justices have become more likely to invoke history, tradition, or their own 'reasoned judgment' in Establishment Clause cases. As the late Justice Antonin Scalia colourfully put it, *Lemon* is '[l]ike some ghoul in a late-night horror movie that repeatedly sits up in its grave...after being repeatedly killed and buried' (*Lamb's Chapel* 1993: 398, Scalia, J., concurring in the judgment). Similarly, Justice Neil Gorsuch recently observed during a Supreme Court oral argument that:

> It's been a long time since [the Supreme Court] has applied *Lemon*...yet the court of appeals continue to cite it and use it. And...reasonable observers process things in all sorts of different ways. And it has resulted in a welter of confusion...by anyone's admission.   (Transcript 2019: 67)

Still, the case has not yet been explicitly overruled, and it continues, for now, to be invoked by litigants and applied by judges in lower courts.

In *Ganulin v. United States*, Richard Ganulin argued that the federal statute establishing Christmas as a federal holiday violated the Establishment Clause (*Ganulin* 1999: 831). The trial court applied the *Lemon* test with a twist: the second prong of the *Lemon* test—that is, whether a law has the principal or primary effect of advancing religion—received a new gloss. Favoured by Justice Sandra Day O'Connor, this 'endorsement test' asked whether a reasonable observer would think that the federal government had endorsed religion by making Christmas a national holiday. The court first determined that the statute declaring Christmas a national holiday met the first prong of *Lemon* because the statute has a secular purpose. The judge noted that no Supreme Court justices had ever suggested that public holidays violated the Establishment Clause and that the winter holidays, Christmas, and Hanukkah had 'become largely secularized' in a way that other well-known religious holidays like Good Friday had not (see *Ganulin* 1999: 832–3, citing *Granzeier* 1999: 580, Moore, J., dissenting). Because the first *Lemon* requirement only requires *a* secular purpose that is not a sham, the judge had no difficulty determining it had been met.

With respect to *Lemon*'s second requirement regarding 'effects', the judge determined that the Christmas holiday statute did not have the primary effect of advancing or endorsing religion. Even though the holiday has religious origins, the court recognized that many of our current practices can be traced to religious beginnings or foundations. For example, the days and months of the year derive their names from

Roman and Norse gods, and 'the year is calculated by reference to events' from Christianity. The judge also cited Supreme Court precedent to support what it saw as a key distinction:

> If the government celebrate[d] Christmas as a religious holiday (for example, by issuing an official proclamation saying 'We rejoice in the glory of Christ's birth!'), it means that the government really is declaring Jesus to be the messiah, a specifically Christian belief. In contrast, confining the government's own celebration of Christmas to the holiday's secular aspects does not favor the religious beliefs of non-Christians over that of Christians. Rather, it simply permits the government to acknowledge the holiday without expressing an allegiance to Christian beliefs, an allegiance that would *truly* favor Christians over non-Christians.

Thus, by recognizing Christmas as a national holiday, the government had only recognized 'the cultural significance of the holiday' and nothing more (*Ganulin* 1999: 833).

Next, the court determined that the Christmas holiday statute created no excessive entanglement between Church and State, dismissing Ganulin's claim that the statute required pervasive governmental monitoring. All the government had to (and indeed, all it *has* done since 1870) is declare 25 December a national public holiday—nothing more. No monitoring or supervising was required—people are free to do as they wish on Christmas Day. Thus, the statute declaring Christmas a national holiday did not violate the Establishment Clause.

Another individual, Kimberly Edelstein, recently sued the state of Ohio in the federal Southern District of Ohio, arguing that the state statute recognizing Christmas as a statewide holiday is unconstitutional. Unlike in *Ganulin*, Ms Edelstein asserted her claim under the Free Exercise Clause. Edelstein argued that the state had functionally granted Christians extra vacation days, whereas she, as a Jewish woman, had to take extra days off on Jewish holidays and risked being terminated for doing so. The court, relying upon *Ganulin*, remained unconvinced and quickly dismissed this line of argument as entirely unsupported by precedent (*Edelstein* 2018: *6–7).

Recently, and after lower courts decided these and similar public-holiday cases, the Supreme Court has noted that the *Lemon* test is particularly ill suited to justifying, among other things, public holidays that have a basis in religion (*Am. Legion* 2019: *13–14, quoting *Van Orden* 2005: 699; Breyer, J., concurring in the judgment). The current Court has identified four reasons that *Lemon* should not apply to Establishment Clause cases that address 'longstanding monuments, symbols, and practices' such as public holidays. First, as already discussed, *Lemon*'s requirement of divining a motivating religious or secular purpose of laws becomes more and more difficult the older the law is. Second, laws developing out of longstanding religious practices like public holidays tend to develop 'multiple purposes' as our country has become 'more and more religiously diverse'—as a society, we have 'preserve[d]' certain practices and symbols as a sign of 'historical significance or...common cultural heritage'. Third, because of these shifting and evolving purposes, so too does the message of a historical practice or symbol change over time into a more secular, historical message. And fourth, as a historical practice becomes more settled and routine in our society's way of life, an act to remove the practice from society ceases to appear neutral—a central commandment of *Lemon*. Thus, a majority of the Supreme Court held that *retaining* religious symbols and practices is 'quite different' from 'adopting new ones', and so courts should presume that these traditional and historical practices are constitutional (*Am. Legion* 2019: *15–21).

The *American Legion* case is very likely not the last word on the matter. In that case, several justices wrote separately to address the status of the beleaguered Establishment Clause test. Both Justices Thomas and Gorsuch separately called for its direct overruling, insisting that '[i]t is our job to say what the law is, and because the *Lemon* test is not good law, we ought to say so'. Justice Kavanaugh appeared to suggest a quiet retirement for *Lemon*; Justice Kagan argued that *Lemon* still remained relevant in part; and Justice Breyer—while not calling for *Lemon*'s overruling—recognized that 'there is no single formula for resolving Establishment Clause challenges'. In any event, as Justice Gorsuch observed, for challenges against public holidays with religious foundations like Christmas, 'not a single Member of the Court' appears to believe that *Lemon* ought to apply.

The Crèche and Tree Cases

Perhaps the most well-known type of Establishment Clause case is the crèche case. The crèche, or Nativity Scene, depicts the birth of Jesus in the manger in Bethlehem. These cases typically appear during the Christmas season during which they are 'found in hundreds of towns or cities across the Nation' (*Lynch* 1984: 671). Take the crèche from *Lynch v. Donnelly*, for example: for over forty years, the city of Pawtucket, Rhode Island had placed a crèche in a park in the municipality's downtown shopping district. The Pawtucket crèche did not stand alone in the park; the city placed, among others: 'a Santa Clause house, reindeer pulling Santa's sleigh, candy-striped poles, a Christmas tree, carolers, cutout figures representing... a clown, an elephant, and a teddy bear, hundreds of colored lights, [and] a large banner that read "SEASONS GREETINGS"'.

A group of Pawtucket citizens sued the city under the theory that the presence of the crèche amounted to an Establishment Clause violation. Writing for a 5–4 majority, Chief Justice Warren Burger held that simply placing a crèche amongst other Christmastime figures and symbols did not amount to an impermissible attempt to advocate on behalf of Christianity. Rather, the crèche display 'depict[ed] the historical traditions of [a] historical event long recognized as a National Holiday'. The Chief Justice concluded the opinion by noting that, considering the Court had recently upheld opening legislative sessions with a prayer, the notion that the 'inclusion of a single symbol of a particular historic religious event, as part of a celebration acknowledged in the Western World for 20 centuries' constitutes a 'real danger' of an establishment of religion is 'far-fetched'.

Justice O'Connor, concurring fully in the majority opinion, added her own twist on the *Lemon* test that would have a major impact on the crèche cases to come. She suggested that the purpose prong of *Lemon* should be reframed as determining whether 'the government intends to convey a message of endorsement or disapproval of religion' (*Lynch* 1984: 691; O'Connor, J., concurring). Justice O'Connor had no problem concluding that the city of Pawtucket did not intend to approve of Christianity here, but rather intended to celebrate the Christmas public holiday, as the crèche was placed amongst a larger display of various secularized Christmas symbols and characters. Of key interest for legal challenges to the existence of public holidays writ large, O'Connor noted that '[c]elebration of public holidays, which have cultural significance even if they also have religious aspects, is a legitimate secular purpose'. Because Christmas has pervaded our society so much, the crèche, which taken alone may be considered religious, did not so overpower the presence of so many other 'purely secular symbols' that Pawtucket had impermissibly endorsed Christianity.

This, of course, did not end the crèche debate. Five years later, the Court decided *County of Allegheny v. American Civil Liberties Union* (1989), which addressed two separate public holiday displays in downtown Pittsburgh. One was a crèche placed on the main staircase of the Allegheny County Courthouse, and the other was the placement of a menorah next to a large Christmas tree and a sign 'bearing the mayor's name...entitled "Salute to Liberty"' (*Cty. of Allegheny* 1989: 582). After reciting the *Lemon* test standard, the Court honed its analysis with Justice O'Connor's endorsement test: the government cannot appear 'to take a position on questions of religious belief or from "making adherence to a religion relevant in any way to a person's standing in the political community"'. In crèche cases, a court must pin down and understand the context within with these religious displays exist—no two cases are the same. According to the Court, the crèche in the grand staircase of the Allegheny County Courthouse lacked any other objects that would 'detract' from the crèche's inherently religious message. Whereas the crèche display in Lynch had a Santa Claus figure, reindeer, and a 'talking wishing well' to accompany it, the courthouse crèche stood alone. The Court further distinguished the crèche from other governmental recognitions of religious holidays. Singling out Christmas, the Court noted that '[t]he government may *acknowledge* Christmas as a cultural phenomenon, but...it may not observe it as a Christian holy day by suggesting that people praise God for the birth of Jesus.'

The menorah display created an even thornier question. Justice Blackmun, who wrote the majority opinion in the case, lost the votes of Justices O'Connor, Brennan, and Stevens in reasoning why the menorah display did not violate the Establishment Clause. Justice Blackmun placed heavy emphasis on the question whether the combined display of the large Christmas tree, the menorah, and the sign saluting to liberty endorsed both Christianity and Judaism in a religious manner. Justice Blackmun argued that the Christmas tree, even more so than Santa Claus, was the quintessential secular Christmas symbol, since many non-practising Christians (and non-Christians) put up Christmas trees in their homes. Its placement next to the menorah suggested that the City had attempted to recognize both Christmas and Hanukkah as important *cultural* holidays and celebrations. The combination of the large (secular) Christmas tree and the 'Salutation to Liberty' sign in conjunction with the menorah convinced Justice Blackmun that the entire display merely recognized cultural diversity in the area. Justice O'Connor on the other hand, pushed back on Justice Blackmun's understanding of the menorah as a secular symbol of Hanukkah—the menorah 'is *the* central religious symbol and ritual object of' Judaism. She instead focused on the sign next to the menorah and Christmas tree which read: 'During this holiday season, the city of Pittsburgh salutes liberty. Let these festive lights remind us that we are the keepers of the flame of liberty and our legacy of freedom.' This sign clearly indicated that the city intended to advocate its pluralism because a reasonable observer could not read the sign and then view the tree and menorah as an endorsement of religion.

Lower courts have applied these two Supreme Court decisions in inconsistent ways and reached inconsistent results, suggesting to many that legal doctrines which rest on judges' aesthetic and design-related intuitions are ineffective legal tools for resolving Establishment Clause disputes. For example, the Court of Appeals for the Second Circuit upheld the constitutionality of a crèche display in a public park not because secular symbols were placed in the crèche's immediate vicinity, but because the surrounding downtown area had been decorated with various Christmas lights and other secular symbols (*Elewski* 1997: 54). Furthermore, the court theorized that a reasonable observer in the city would know that merchants and storeowners in the area encouraged the placement of the crèche display because it attracted more customers.

Similarly, the Third Circuit, in an opinion written by then-Judge Samuel Alito, held that a display of a crèche, menorah, and Christmas tree placed in front of city hall did not violate the Establishment Clause because, in between the start of the lawsuit, the city had added figures of Santa Clause, Frosty the Snowman, a sled, Kwanzaa symbols (on the Christmas tree), and signage that celebrated the city's cultural and ethnic diversity (*Am. Civil Liberties Union of N.J. ex rel Lander* 1999: 96). The court likened the vast arrange of symbols and characters to the display upheld in *Lynch*, and could not find any meaningful facts that would otherwise distinguish the two displays. The Sixth Circuit upheld a similar crèche display as constitutional—this display was only surrounded by four Christmas trees, two large wrapped Christmas presents, and a Santa Claus figure (*Doe v. City of Clawson* 1990: 244–5).

What we might call the 'take-aways' of *Lynch* and *Allegheny County*, as well as subsequent lower-court cases, it is that would-be crèche displayers ought to have a Santa Claus figure on hand. The more 'secular' symbols placed next to a 'religious' display, the more likely that an Establishment Clause violation has not occurred. Although it may sound sardonic to describe the standard this way, advocates of crèche displays have listed out the necessary 'secular' guidelines so that people may set up crèches without fearing Establishment Clause challenges (Outdoor Nativity Store

2016). The Supreme Court has not decided further crèche cases since *Allegheny County*, so the standard remains: states, towns, and municipalities must make the context in which a crèche appears clearly secular. Leaving the crèche on its own to speak for itself risks running afoul of the First Amendment. It remains to be seen whether the Court's emphasis on history, tradition, and longstanding practice in the *American Legion* case, and its recognition that the war-memorial cross at issue in that case may and should be distinguished from an 'establishment of religion', will carry over into cases involving displays and expression connected with recurring religious holidays.

Conclusion

This chapter has focused on the legal and constitutional treatment of Christmas as a public holiday in the United States. Clearly, many other countries recognize Christmas as a public holiday, even if many of those countries' citizens do not identify as Christian (see Glover 2018). On the other hand, some countries have banned the celebration of Christmas because it is considered offensive to their predominant religious traditions (Reuters 2015). The example of the United States illustrates the possibility of a kind of 'middle ground' between a comprehensive secularism, or aggressive *laïcité*, one the one hand, and a pervasively faith-filled public square. As a general matter, the American Constitution's prohibition on official 'establishments' of religion is understood to permit, within limits, the public acknowledgment, accommodation, and even celebration of Christmas. Precisely where those limits should be located, in any particular case on context, continues to be a live question.

References and Further Reading

41 Cong. Ch. 167, 16 Stat.168 (1870).
5 U.S.C. § 6103 (2018).
Am. Civil Liberties Union of N.J. ex rel Lander v. Schundler, 168 F.3d 92 (3d Cir. 1999).
Am. Civil Liberties Union v. City of Florissant, 186 F.3d 1095 (8th Cir. 1999).
Am. Legion v. Am. Humanist Assoc., No. 17–1717 (U.S. June 20, 2019).
Bowler, Gerry (2016). *Christmas in the Crosshairs: Two Thousand Years of Denouncing and Defending the World's Most Celebrated Holiday*. Oxford University Press.
Bridenbaugh v. O'Bannon, 185 F.3d 796 (7th Cir. 1999).
Buck, Stuart (2002). 'The Nineteenth-Century Understanding of the Establishment Clause', 6 Tex. Rev. L. & Pol. 399.
Cahn, Edmond (1962). 'Justice Black and First Amendment "Absolutes": A Public Interview', 37 N.Y.U. L. Rev. 549.
Cammack v. Waihee, 932 F.2d 765 (9th Cir. 1991).
Capitol Square & Review Advisory Bd. v. Pinette, 515 U.S. 753 (1995).

Cong. Globe, 41st Cong., 2d Sess. 4529 (1870).
Cty. of Allegheny v. Am. Civil Liberties Union, 492 U.S. 573 (1989).
Cualcutt, Clea (2014). 'French Court Bans Christmas Nativity Scene', *BBC*, 4 December. Available at https://www.bbc.com/news/world-europe-30326257/ (accessed 27 March 2020).
Display of Nativity Scene by Public Authorities (2016). The Conseil de'Etat (10 November). Available at http://english.conseil-etat.fr/Activities/Press-releases/Display-of-Nativity-scenes-by-public-authorities/ (accessed 27 March 2020).
Doe v. City of Clawson, 915 F.2d 244 (6th Cir. 1990).
Edelstein v. Stephens, No. 1:17-cv-305, 2018 WL 948769 (S.D. Ohio Feb. 16, 2018), *aff'd* No. 1:17-cv-305, 2018 WL 1558868 (S.D. Ohio Mar. 31, 2019).
Elewski v. City of Syracuse, 123 F.3d 51 (2d Cir. 1997).
Empt. Div., Dept' of Hum. Res. of Ore. v. Smith, 494 U.S. 872 (1990).
Epstein, Steven B. (1996). 'Rethinking the Constitutionality of Ceremonial Deism', 96 Colum. L. Rev. 2083.
Everson v. Bd. of Ed. Of Ewing Twp., 330 U.S. 1 (1947).
'Feriae' (1875). *A Dictionary of Greek and Roman Antiquities*. London: John Murray: 528–30. Available at http://penelope.uchicago.edu/Thayer/E/Roman/Texts/secondary/SMIGRA*/Feriae.html/ (accessed 27 March 2020).
Freedom from Religion Found., Inc. v. Thompson, 920 F. Supp. 969 (W.D. Wisc. 1996).
Ganulin v. United States, 238 F.3d 420, 2000 WL 1888594 (6th Cir. 2000) (per curiam).
Ganulin v. United States, 71 F. Supp. 2d 824 (S.D. Ohio 1999).
Glover, Nathan (2018). 'Christmas Day Declared a National Holiday in Iraq', *World Religious News*, 27 December. Available at https://www.worldreligionnews.com/religion-news/christmas-day-declared-national-holiday-iraq/ (accessed 27 March 2020).
Granzeier v. Middleton, 173 F.3d 568 (6th Cir. 1999).
Gunn, T. Jeremy (2004). 'Religious Freedom and Laïcité: A Comparison of United States and France', 2004 B.Y.U. L. Rev. 419 (2004).
'Gunpowder Plot'. *Encyclopaedia Britannica*. Available at http://www.britannica.com/EBchecked/topic/249505/Gunpowder-Plot/ (accessed 20 March 2020).
'Holiday'. *Online Etymology Dictionary*. Available at https://www.etymonline.com/word/holiday/ (accessed 20 March 2020).
Hutchison, Ruth and Adams, Ruth (1951). *Every Day's a Holiday*. New York: Harper & Brothers Publishers.
Kellner, K. A. Heinrich (1908). *Heortology: A History of Christian Festivals and their Origin to the Present Day*. London: Kegan Paul.
Koenick v. Felton, 190 F.3d 259 (4th Cir. 1999).
Lamb's Chapel v. Ctr. Moriches Union Free Schl. Dist., 508 U.S. 384 (1993).
Lemon v. Kurtzman, 403 U.S. 602 (1971).
Lynch v. Donnelly, 465 U.S. 668 (1984).
Metzl v. Lenninger, 57 F.3d 618 (7th Cir. 1995).
Morago, Greg (2019). 'King Cake Flavor is More Popular than Ever—But the Taste has Actually Evolved Over Time', *Hous. Chron.*, 21 January. https://www.houstonchronicle.com/life/food/article/King-Cake-flavor-is-more-popular-than-ever-13549885.php/ (accessed 20 March 2020).
Restad, Penne L. (1995). *Christmas in America*. New York: Oxford University Press.

Reuters (2015). 'Somalia Joins Brunei by Banning Christmas Celebrations "to Protect Islam"', *Telegraph*, 24 December. Available at https://www.telegraph.co.uk/topics/christmas/12067683/Somalia-joins-Brunei-by-banning-Christmas-celebrations-to-protect-Islam.html/ (accessed 20 March 2020).

Reynolds v. United States, 98 U.S. 145 (1878).

'Saudi Arabia Basic Law of Governance' (1 March 1992). http://www.wipo.int/wipolex/en/text.jsp?file_id=200064/ (accessed 20 March 2020).

Scullard, H.H. (1981). *Festivals and Ceremonies of the Roman Republic*. Cornell University Press.

Sommer, Allison Kaplan (2018). 'Do Jewish Israelis Celebrate New Year's Eve? It's Complicated, New Survey Finds', *Haaretz* (30 December). Available at https://www.haaretz.com/israel-news/.premium-do-jewish-israelis-celebrate-new-year-s-eve-1.6790343/ (accessed 27 March 2020).

Straus, Jacob R. (2014). 'Federal Holidays: Evolution and Current Practices', Cong. Research Serv., R41990.

Toland, Bill (2012). 'The Next Page: Meet Belsnickel, the Counter Claus', *Pitt. Post-Gazette* (25 November). Available at https://www.post-gazette.com/life/holidays/2012/11/25/The-Next-Page-Meet-Belsnickel-the-Counter-Claus/stories/201211250132/ (accessed 27 March 2020).

Transcript of Oral Argument at 67, *Am. Legion v. Am. Humanist Assoc.*, No. 17-1717 (Feb. 27, 2019).

U.S. Const. amend I.

United States Department of State (2017). 'International Religious Freedom Report for 2017: United Arab Emirates'. Available at https://www.state.gov/documents/organization/171747.pdf/ (accessed 27 March 2020).

Van Orden v. Perry, 545 U.S. 677 (2005).

Walz v. Tax Comm'n of City of N.Y., 397 U.S. 664 (1970).

'What the Supreme Court Says About Outdoor Nativity Scenes' (2016). Outdoor Nativity Store (30 July). Available at https://outdoornativitystore.com/blog/outdoor-nativity-scenes-and-supreme-court/ (accessed 27 March 2020).

CHAPTER 43

COMMERCIALISM AND CONSUMERISM

JOHN SCHMALZBAUER

COMMERCIALISM and consumerism loom large in both popular and scholarly discourse about Christmas in the United States (the geographical focus of this chapter). Despite Theodor Geisel's reminder that 'Christmas doesn't come from a store' (Geisel 1957), historians and social scientists have focused much of their attention on shopping and consumerism, revealing the deep connections between commerce and the emergence of the modern American version of the holiday. As scholars such as Stephen Nissenbaum (1996), Penne Restad (1995), Leigh Schmidt (1995), and Karal Ann Marling (2000) have painstakingly documented, the modern American Christmas would be unrecognizable without commercialism and consumerism. Though it cannot be reduced to such forces, they have played a significant role in its history. Together with churches, families, and a nascent mass media, commercial forces shaped Christmas in America, transforming a season that was often downplayed (though rarely ignored)—or celebrated very differently—into the holiday we know today. Reflecting this confluence of God and mammon, today's Christmas season marks the annual high-water mark of both church attendance and retail sales, allowing both congregations and department stores to finish the year in the black. When social critics lament the commercialization of Christmas, they critique the way that most Americans have celebrated the holiday since the late nineteenth century. Even critiques of American Christmas celebrations cannot be separated from the topic of commercialization. The deep irony of commercialism and Christmas is that commercialization is responsible for the aspects of the holiday most reviled by critics *and* many elements they cherish and revere.

This ironic storyline intersects with other ironic narratives in the sociology of religion, tales that apply to America and many other modern societies. In *The Protestant Ethic and the Spirit of Capitalism*, Max Weber blames Puritan proto-capitalists for disenchanting the English holidays, not by commercializing their observance, but by eliminating them from the calendar. According to Weber (1958: 168), 'asceticism descended like a frost on the life of "Merrie old England"', adding that the Puritans' 'ferocious hatred of everything which smacked of superstition, of all survivals of magical or sacramental salvation, applied to the Christmas festivities and the May Pole and all spontaneous religious art'. In the Weberian account of modernity, Protestant Christianity (with the help of capitalism) serves as its own gravedigger (Berger 1967: 129), an ironic storyline that he also applies to Christmas. Making similar claims, philosopher Charles Taylor discusses the disenchantment of modern holidays in *A Secular Age*. Before the coming of secular modernity, Taylor argues, European societies participated in 'higher times' that connected time to the sacred in powerful ways. Good Friday, for example, 'was important, not only for the theologically orthodox reason, but because the power it carried made it a good day for planting crops, and enabled hot cross buns to save houses from fire' (Taylor 2007: 438). As such higher times faded from the modern calendar, holidays like Christmas became more like other days, a process that cannot be separated from the rise of both Protestantism and capitalism. For both Weber and Taylor, modern societies disenchanted both Christmas and Easter. For both authors, capitalism and commercialism are at the heart of modern secular societies, transforming both space and time. As Taylor (2007: 483) writes in *A Secular Age*, 'Modern consumer society is inseparable from the construction of spaces of display: topical spaces, palaces of consumption, like the arcades of nineteenth-century Paris.'

Yet a strange thing happened on the way to the modern American Christmas. Rather than secularizing the holidays, commercialization contributed to its growing visibility in American culture, including its religious manifestations (Forbes 2007). During the nineteenth and early twentieth centuries, commercial forces helped shift the locus of the holiday 'from the tavern and street to the kitchen and family fireplace' (Bowler 2017: 53), transforming an adult festival known for alcoholic beverages and folk theatre into a family-oriented season of gift exchanges and home decorations, many of which took on a sacred character (Restad 1995; Nissenbaum 1996; Schmidt 1995). Rather than disenchanting the calendar, modern holidays such as Christmas, Valentine's Day, and Halloween increasingly involved 'devout consumption' (Veblen 1912: 120 quoted in Schmidt 1995: 3) and '[n]ew forms of magic, improvisation, charivari, enchantment, and trickery' (Schmidt 1995: 13). Instead of conceptualizing the commercial and the religious in binary terms, it is more helpful to see them as fused, a site of creative tension and paradox (Schmidt 1995). As historian Richard Callahan (2003: 597) writes, '[S]acred time is increasingly marketed and has become a commodity itself.' It is both sacred and commercial.

Far from peripheral, people of faith have played a central role in the rise of a modern commercial Christmas, popularizing the figure of Santa Claus (see Timothy Larsen's chapter in this volume), adopting new forms of domestic holiday decorations, and serving as a market for seasonal music, literature, and food. Rather than erasing the pre-modern folkloric and religious Christmas described by Weber and Taylor, these new forms of celebration have incorporated some of it into the modern version of the holiday, enchanting the Christmas season. These combinations of sacred and profane mirror what Martin Marty (2003) calls our religio-secular society. They also draw on contributions from religious minorities. Reflecting this diversity, some of America's most visible expressions of Christmas music were written by Jewish Americans, who also struggled with the hegemony of a Christian holiday.

The remainder of this chapter will explore the role of commercialization and consumerism in creating the modern American Christmas. For the most part, it will follow a chronological path, beginning with pre-commercial folk celebrations (and non-celebration), early forms of commercialization and consumption, the emergence of mass-produced Christmas decorations, holidays and the modern department store, and the role of the mass media and popular culture, in fusing the commercial and the religious. It will conclude by discussing contemporary debates about holiday retailing and the ways that commercial Christmas celebrations sacralize secular spaces.

PRE-COMMERCIAL CELEBRATIONS AND NON-CELEBRATIONS OF CHRISTMAS

In *The Battle for Christmas*, historian Stephen Nissenbaum describes the celebration and regulation of Christmas in colonial America, noting it was 'neither a domestic holiday nor a commercial one' (Nissenbaum 1996: 38). Reflecting the religious and ethnic diversity of the colonies, the season was celebrated with door-to-door revelling, gunfire and explosions, feasting, and quiet church services, depending on the locale (Restad 1995: 9). Many of these activities did not rely on items purchased from a store. Describing one family's celebration, Nissenbaum (1996: 30) notes that most of the food consumed at holiday feasts was raised nearby, with only 'the special ingredients that went into making cakes and pies—the sugar, ginger, allspice, and rum—involved a commercial transaction'. Door-to-door mumming, in which working-class gangs donned masks and begged wealthy households for free food and drink, did not depend on retail purchases, but instead featured impromptu plays and carols, gender bending, and an inversion of the social order (Bowler 2017; Nissenbaum 1996). The same was true of the *julebukking* tradition of nineteenth-century Scandinavian immigrants. Like mumming, it involved roving bands of costumed revellers, with the leader dressed as a Yule goat, a practice observed by the brother of sociologist Thorstein Veblen (Stokker 2000: 144–6). Equally raucous traditions prevailed in other parts of the country. Especially popular in the South, the shooting of guns and other explosives was not a commercialized affair. In several states, revellers smashed inflated hog bladders, dubbing them their 'Christmas guns' (Restad 1995; Ownby 1990).

Of course, not all colonial Americans celebrated the Christmas season with such gusto. In Puritan New England, Christmas revelry was briefly outlawed, though never completely eliminated. Between 1659 and 1681, residents of the Commonwealth could be fined five shillings for celebrating the holiday with feasting or refusing to work.

Much of this was a reaction to the bacchanalia of early American Christmas. As Cotton Mather wrote in 1712, '[T]he Feast of Christ's Nativity is spent in Reveling, Dicing, Carding, Masking, and in all Licentious Liberty...by Mad Mirth, by long Eating, by hard Drinking, by lewd Gaming, by rude Reveling' (Nissenbaum 1996: 7). By the mid-1800s, Christmas church services had become more common among Baptists, Congregationalists, and other Protestant dissenters (Nissenbaum 1996). In eighteenth-century America, Anglicans, Lutherans, and Methodists went to church at Christmas. Yet old traditions died hard. At a 1788 Christmas service in Virginia, the circuit-riding Bishop Francis Asbury detected 'an offensive smell of rum among the people' (Asbury 1821: 41).

From the 1600s to the early 1900s, Christmas celebrations in some parts of North America continued to resemble Charles Taylor's 'higher times', linking the dates on the calendar to the events of the Incarnation. From the Maritime Provinces of Canada to the Midwest, some rural people viewed the season as enchanted, reporting that animals 'kneel down and bellow, exactly at midnight, in honor of the birth of Jesus' at 'Old Christmas' (from the Julian calendar) (Tizzard and Widdowson 1979; Randolph 1947: 77). Rooted in folk customs, such beliefs were reinforced by almanacs, which blended astrology with modern publishing, selling millions of copies in the process. Such beliefs persisted into the early twentieth century, overlapping the early years of the Sears catalogue, suggesting that magical and commercial conceptions of Christmas could and did coexist. So did the pre-commercial custom of mumming, which lived on in Newfoundland (Halpert and Story 1969) and in Philadelphia's Mummers' Parade, held on New Year's Day since 1901. As Leigh Schmidt (1995: 145, 147) notes in *Consumer Rites*, department store parades eventually dominated holiday street life, 'colonizing the mummers' world and working-class celebrations with their own spectacles that were eventually staged more for the consumption of television audiences than for the folks in the avenues.' As for loud noises and Christmas guns, fireworks remain a popular holiday diversion in the American South, lighting up the sky and enriching the local economy (Blevins 2006).

THE RISE OF A COMMERCIAL CHRISTMAS

As the previous section suggests, the differences between folk and commercial celebrations were not absolute. Yet the holiday did change. Over the course of the nineteenth and early twentieth centuries, industrialization, urbanization, and modern transportation networks helped create a nationalized version of Christmas. As Penne Restad notes in *Christmas in America*, the commercialization of Christmas was made possible by changes 'in the realms of commerce, communications, and industry', including the proliferation of railroads, the success of the US Postal Service, and the emergence of a middle class (Restad 1995: 29). Describing the middle-classing of Norwegian Americans, Thorsten Veblen's brother wrote that 'eventually Christmas became quite different' (Stokker 2000: 134). The emergence of a nationally mediated popular culture played a role in this transformation, displacing folk cultures with mass culture (Nye 1970), while not entirely eliminating them. As new ways of celebrating Christmas emerged, they were popularized by magazines such as *Godey's Lady Book* and *Harper's Weekly* (Schmidt 1995), as well as nineteenth-century bestsellers such as *A Christmas Carol*. While Charles Dickens did not invent Christmas (see Larsen in this volume for a critique of this hyperbolic claim), he introduced millions of readers to a new version of the holiday through his books and a celebrated American tour. In a similar way, the rise of the department store (Kirk 2018) and national retail chains (Restad 1995) were key steps in the birth of a modern commercial Christmas, influencing home decorations (Marling 2000), gift-giving customs (Schmidt 1995), and holiday music (Forbes 2007).

It did not happen all at once. Unfolding throughout the nineteenth century, the commercialization of Christmas has been plotted on a timeline. In the late nineteenth-century, home-made gifts gave way to cheap gimcracks, notoriously shoddy novelty items exchanged by adults (Waits 1993). These were followed by store-bought Christmas cards and gifts. Reflecting the domestication of the holiday, women played a growing role in gift-giving rituals, a development that can be traced in changing advertisements. In *The Modern Christmas in America*, historian William B. Waits calls it the 'feminization of Christmas'. Centred around hearth and home, rather than raucous street theatre, it was a far cry from the days of mumming male revellers (Waits 1993: 80; Schmidt 1995). Tracing these transformations, much of the literature is preoccupied with marking the decades in which various innovations emerged. In the context of the United States, scholars date the emergence of the Christmas tree to the 1820s and 1830s (Nissenbaum 1996; Restad 1995), printed Christmas cards to the 1840s (Forbes 2007), store-bought ornaments to the 1850s (Bowler 2000), Christmas shopping to the 1830s (Restad 1995), and glass ornaments and electric lights to the 1880s (Forbes 2007).

Santa Claus and Department Stores

The emergence of Santa Claus took place over a much longer timespan. While the story of his creation is told elsewhere in this volume, it is worth pausing to recognize the role of commercial forces in his rise. Though writers such as Washington Irving and Clement Clark Moore emerged out of New York's Knickerbocker elite, their works reached a larger audience because of the rise of print culture and modern publishing. Originally published in 1809, Irving's *Knickerbocker's History of New York* exposed a national audience to the invented tradition of the Dutch St Nicholas, including a gift-bearer who goes down the chimney. According to historian Charles W. Jones (1954: 374), 'Without Irving there would be no Santa Claus.' Moore did even more to popularize the legend. Originally written for his children, Moore's 'A Visit from St. Nicholas' appeared in the *New York Sentinel* in 1823 (Nissenbaum 1996). Since then it has been republished countless times, reaching millions of readers. Thomas Nast's Civil War era drawings in *Harper's Weekly* further developed the modern image of Santa Claus, depicting him in domestic settings as well as on the battlefield (Nast 1978). Like Julia Ward Howe's vision of Jesus in 'The Battle Hymn of the Republic', Nast saw St Nicholas in the watch fires of a hundred circling camps. Thanks to the magazine's large circulation (*Harper's Weekly* reached over 200,000 readers in the early 1860s), Nast's image of Santa Claus became even more famous than his depictions of the Republican Elephant and the Democratic donkey (Seal 2005: 192). The modern version of Santa Claus was further refined by the 1930s' drawings of Coca Cola artist Haddon Sundblom, who also created the Quaker Oats Quaker (Forbes 2007). Shaping the popular imagination, Nast and Sundblom exemplified the close relationship between commercial media and the pre-eminent symbol of American Christmas.

Though the department store Santa is a staple of the holiday season, this tradition took decades to emerge. According to local tradition, the first Kris Kringle (derived from the German Christkindl) appeared in 1841 at J.W. Parkinson's store in Philadelphia, though others may have done it earlier (Schmidt 1995). Founded in 1858, Macy's has featured Christmas window displays from the very beginning. Presbyterian businessman John Wanamaker's namesake store in Philadelphia took things one step further, converting retail spaces into a quasi-ecclesiastical environment, complete with Gothic revival architecture, the world's largest organ, and songbooks with religious Christmas carols. In such settings, it was difficult to tell where the commercial Christmas ended and the religious holiday began. That was exactly the point. In 'Wanamaker's Temple', business was seamlessly combined with Christianity (Kirk 2018; Schmidt 1995). In the Upper Midwest, Dayton's Christmas windows drew large crowds to the chain's flagship store in downtown Minneapolis, employing mechanical animals to dazzle Minnesota shoppers. Unlike Wanamaker's, Dayton's did not include overtly Christian symbolism, distinguishing 'the religious side and the festive side of Christmas' (Marling 2000: 96). In the 1960s, Dayton's brought the show indoors, constructing elaborate themed displays that led visitors straight to the toy department. While avoiding biblical themes, they featured plenty of enchantment, including displays on Dickens' London, Peter Pan, and the Nutcracker (Firestone 2007: 82). During this period, Christmas sales made up 40 per cent of the company's annual profits (Marling 2000: 97).

Pop Music, Hollywood Movies, and Commercial Television

From Wanamaker's organ to 'Frosty the Snowman', popular music played a key role in shaping American celebrations of Christmas. While *Messiah* performances by Boston's Handel and Haydn Society raised the visibility of sacred holiday choral music

(Harrison 2010), a host of commercial songwriters helped to shape the sounds of the season. Many were Jewish, including the composers of 'Let It Snow', 'Rudolph the Red Nose Reindeer', 'The Christmas Song', 'Silver Bells', and 'Rockin' Around the Christmas Tree'. Chronicling these compositions, the Canadian documentary *Dreaming of a Jewish Christmas* explores the tensions songwriters felt between Jewish identity and their work. The companion website provides a helpful timeline of Jewish American holiday songs, calling them the 'soundtrack of Christmas'. The leading exemplar of this genre (Rosen 2002: 68), 'White Christmas', was written by a Russian Jewish immigrant (Irving Berlin), recorded by an Irish Catholic crooner (Bing Crosby), and purchased by millions of Protestants. Featured in the films *Holiday Inn* (1942) and *White Christmas* (1954), it was the top-selling single of all time (Harris 2009). The impressive catalogue of Jewish-American Christmas music reflects the prevalence of 'Yankee Doodle Yiddishkeit' in Tin Pin Alley's songbook (Rosen 2002: 12).

It does not reflect the embrace of Christmas consumerism by Jewish Americans. Chronicling the ambivalence many Jews feel about the season, Rabbi Joshua Eli Plaut describes a variety of responses to the hegemony of Christmas. According to Plaut (2012: 4), at Christmas 'Jews eat in Chinese restaurants, watch movies, and attend concerts and comedy performances'. Like the commercialization of Christmas, resistance to the holiday has involved popular culture, including situation comedy such as *Seinfeld*'s alternative holiday of Festivus ('Festivus for the rest of us'), later made into a Ben and Jerry's ice cream flavour. Reflecting on the ubiquitous presence of Christmas in the American and European marketplace, anthropologists Pamela Klassen and Monique Sheer (2019: 14) write that the 'holiday takes over city streets with both traffic and stillness: busy shoppers, Santa Claus Parades, and profusions of lights mark the city with a Christian ambiance'. After bustling on December 24th, even the mall is closed on Christmas Day.

Impossible to avoid in retail spaces, the Christmas season has also shaped American film and television, industries that cannot be separated from their commercial aspects. Tying together the retail environment with the silver screen, *A Miracle on 34th Street* (1947) both sanctifies and relativizes the relationship between capitalism and Christmas. While employed at Macy's, the film's department store Santa has nice things to say about Gimbel's and Bloomingdale's, questioning the competitive ethos of American retailing (Connelly 2000: 124). In a similar way, *It's a Wonderful Life* questions the hard-nosed capitalism of the film's villainous businessman (played by Lionel Barrymore), casting down the mighty from their upholstered chairs. Directed by the Italian-American filmmaker Frank Capra, it looks at the life of its protagonist (Jimmy Stewart's George Bailey) through the lens of a communitarian Catholic perspective (Lourdeaux 1990; Blake 2000). In the words of Clarence, the movie's angelic visitor, 'Each man's life touches so many other lives' (De Las Carreras Kuntz 2002). Unsuccessful at the box office, *It's a Wonderful Life* has become one of the most watched Christmas movies of all time. It is number one on the American Film Institute's 100 most inspiring films of all time, beating *To Kill a Mockingbird* and *E.T.* (American Film Institute). Immensely popular, Capra's film is hardly secular, beginning with a prayer to 'Joseph, Jesus, and Mary', and concluding with Charles Wesley's 'Hark the Herald Angels Sing'.

Wesley's hymn can also be heard at the conclusion of *A Charlie Brown Christmas*, the 1965 television special that culminates in Linus Van Pelt's reading of St. Luke's Christmas narrative. The script includes a strong critique of commercialization (at one point, Charlie Brown exclaims, 'Oh no, my own dog, gone commercial!'), ironic for a programme sponsored by corporate behemoth Coca Cola, the same company that commissioned Haddon Sundblom's drawings of Santa. While mystifying executives at CBS (who initially said they would not order any more Peanuts specials), the programme attracted over 15 million viewers. The network changed its mind. In the words of creator Charles M. Schulz, a former Church of God lay minister, 'There will always be a market for innocence in this country' (Mendelson 2000: 32–3). Far from standard children's fare, the programme included references to psychoanalysis and real estate. Innocent or not, it showed that overt religious content could penetrate the world of commercial television. While not overtly religious, Theodor Geisel's *How the Grinch Stole Christmas* featured a character who was 'against the commercialization of Christmas' (Geisel quoted in Jones 2019: 264), while earning millions of dollars for its creator. Once again, a work of popular culture was both commercial and anti-commercial, a pattern that recurs in many other Christmas specials (Thompson 2000). More recently, the Hallmark channel's Christmas movies have combined softer inspirational themes with holiday storylines, much like the company's greeting cards. Though references to religion are often muted, the 2018 season included *A Godwink Christmas*, a reference to the ways in which providence 'winks' at human beings (Haven 2018). It is an apt metaphor for the mixture of sacred and secular in popular culture.

Conclusion

The tension between the commercial and the religious is at the heart of the modern American Christmas. Ever since the Massachusetts Bay Colony's prohibition of the holiday, Americans have argued about the proper place of Christmas in the public square. Critiques of commercialization are not new, but go back to nineteenth-century reactions to the spread of holiday retailing. Where do such critiques stand today? As in the past, the relationship between Christmas and commercialization is full of paradoxes and ironies.

At the dawn of the twenty-first century, some Americans are actually demanding the commercialization of Christmas and the sacralization of commerce. Complaining about a 'war on Christmas', they are asking retailers to bring overtly Christian greetings into the commercial sphere by saying 'Merry Christmas', rather than 'Happy Holidays'. Representing a radically different perspective, another group of cultural critics laments the triumph of consumerism and materialism, urging American Christians to separate the holiday from commercial transactions. Dubbed the Advent Conspiracy, this movement urges believers to 'celebrate Christmas humbly, beautifully, and generously' (Advent Conspiracy). Such movements dramatize an ongoing tension between Christmas and commercialization that can be traced back to the early history of the nation (see Bowler 2017 and Forbes 2007 for an overview).

What does this convoluted history say about the place of religion in the modern world? Far from simple, the mutual influence of Christmas and commerce represents what religion scholar Conrad Ostwalt (2003: 77) calls the 'sacralization of secular space', bringing religious meanings and symbols into the public sphere. To be sure, this can result in the trivialization of religious narratives and symbols (a form of secularization), as Christmas becomes just one more marketing gimmick for profit-seeking retailers. Yet this is not the end of the story. Because of the commercialization of Christmas, religious meanings leak into previously secular settings, bringing Gothic church architecture into bustling department stores and the Gospel of Luke into prime time television. Raising the holiday's national profile, modern commercial culture has promoted rather than hindered the celebration of Christmas in the United States. While Christmas did not originally come from a store, it has most certainly invaded the sphere of retailing and commercial culture. As a result of commercialization, Christmas has become more, rather than less, visible over the course of American history.

REFERENCES AND FURTHER READING

Advent Conspiracy (2019). 'About Advent Conspiracy'. Available at https://adventconspiracy.org/about/ (accessed 27 March 2020).

American Film Institute (2006). 'It's a Wonderful Life Tops AFI's List of 100 Most Inspiring Films of All Time'. Press Release. https://web.archive.org/web/20060822172719/https://www.afi.com/Docs/about/press/2006/100inspiring.pdf

Asbury, Francis (2009 [1821]). *The Journal of the Rev. Francis Asbury*. Bedford: Applewood Books.

Berger, Peter (1967). *The Sacred Canopy: Elements of a Sociological Theory of Religion*. New York: Doubleday.

Blake, Richard A. (2000). *AfterImage: The Indelible Catholic Imagination of Six American Filmmakers*. Chicago: Loyola Press.

Blevins, Brooks (2006). 'Fireworking Down South', *Southern Cultures*, 10, no. 1, Spring: 25–49.

Bowler, Gerry (2000). *The World Encyclopedia of Christmas*. New York: Random House.

Bowler, Gerry (2017). *Christmas in the Crosshairs: Two Thousand Years of Denouncing and Defending the World's Most Celebrated Holiday*. New York: Oxford University Press.

Callahan, Richard (2003). 'Sacred Time', in Gary Laderman and Luis León (eds.), *Religion and American Cultures: An Encyclopedia of Traditions, Diversity, and Popular Expressions, Volume II*. Santa Barbara: ABC Clio: 589–98.

Connelly, Mark (2000). 'Santa Claus: The Movie', in Mark Connelly (ed.), *Christmas at the Movies: Images of Christmas in American, British, and European Cinema*. London: I. B. Tauris: 115–34.

De Las Carreras Kuntz, Maria Elena (2002). 'The Catholic Vision of Frank Capra', *Crisis*, 1, February: 38–43.

Dreaming of a Jewish Christmas (2017). Toronto: CBC Television.

Firestone, Mary. (2007). *Dayton's Department Store*. Chicago: Arcadia Publishing.

Forbes, Bruce, David (2007). *Christmas: A Candid History*. Berkeley: University of California Press.

Forbes, Bruce, David (2015). *America's Favorite Holidays: Candid Histories*. Berkeley: California.

Geisel, Theodor (1957). *How the Grinch Stole Christmas*. New York: Random House.

Halpert, Herbert and Story, G. M. (eds.) (1969). *Christmas Mumming in Newfoundland*. Toronto: University of Toronto Press.

Harris, Jr, Roy J. (2009). 'The Best-Selling Record of All', *Wall Street Journal*, 5 December.

Harrison, Leah (2010). 'Handel for the Holidays: American Appropriations of the Hallelujah Chorus', MA Thesis, Florida State University.

Haven, Riely (2018). 'Take a First Look at Hallmark's *A Godwink Christmas*', *Parade*, 18 October. Available at https://parade.com/709876/rielyhaven/take-a-first-look-at-hallmarks-a-godwink-christmas/ (accessed 7 April 2020).

Horsley, Richard and James Tracey (eds.) (2001). *Christmas Unwrapped: Consumerism, Christ, and Culture*. Harrisburg: Trinity Press International.

Irving, Washington (1893 [1809]). *Knickerbocker's History of New York*. New York: Putnam.

Jones, Brian Jay (2019). *Becoming Dr Seuss: Theodor Geisel and the Making of an American Imagination*. New York: Dutton.

Jones, Charles W. (1954). 'Knickerbocker Santa Claus', *The New-York Historical Society Quarterly*, 38, no. 4 (October): 357–83.

Kirk, Nicole (2018). *Wanamaker's Temple: The Business of Religion in an Iconic Department Store*. New York: New York University Press.

Klassen, Pamela and Monique Scheer (2019). 'Introduction', in Pamela Klassen and Monique Scheer (eds.), *The Public Work of Christmas: Difference and Belonging in Multicultural Societies*. Montreal: McGill University Press: 3–16.

Lourdeaux, Lee (1990). *Italian and Irish Filmmakers in America*. Philadelphia: Temple University Press.

Marling, Carol Ann (2000). *Merry Christmas! Celebrating America's Greatest Holiday*. Cambridge: Harvard University Press.

Marty, Martin (2003). 'Our Religio-Secular World', *Daedalus*, 132, no. 3 (Summer): 42–8.

Mendelson, Lee (2000). *A Charlie Brown Christmas: The Making of a Tradition*. New York: HarperCollins.

Nast, Thomas (1978). *Thomas Nast's Christmas Drawings*. New York: Dover Publications.

Nissenbaum, Stephen (1996). *The Battle for Christmas*. New York: Alfred A. Knopf.

Nye, Russel (1970). *The Unembarrassed Muse: The Popular Arts in America*. New York: Dial Press.

Ostwalt, Conrad. (2003). *Secular Steeples: Popular Culture and the Religious Imagination*. Harrisburg: Trinity Press International.

Ownby, Ted (1990). *Subduing Satan: Religion, Recreation, and Manhood in the Rural South, 1865–1920*. Chapel Hill: University of North Carolina Press.

Plaut, Joshua Eli (2012). *A Kosher Christmas: 'Tis the Season to be Jewish*. New Brunswick: Rutgers University Press.

Randolph, Vance (1947). *Ozark Superstitions*. New York: Columbia University Press.

Restad, Penne L. (1995). *Christmas in America: A History*. New York: Oxford University Press.
Rosen, Jody (2002). *White Christmas: The Story of an American Song*. New York: Scribner.
Schmidt, Leigh Eric (1995). *Consumer Rites: The Buying and Selling of American Holidays*. Princeton: Princeton University Press.
Seal, Jeremy (2005). *Nicholas: The Epic Journey from Saint to Santa Claus*. New York: Bloomsbury.
Stokker, Kathleen (2000). *Keeping Christmas: Yuletide Traditions in Norway and the New Land*. St. Paul: Minnesota Historical Society.
Taylor, Charles (2007). *A Secular Age*. New York: Harvard University Press.
Thompson, Robert J. (2000). 'Consecrating Consumer Culture: Christmas Television Specials', in Bruce David Forbes and Jeffrey H. Mahan (eds.), *Religion and Popular Culture in America*. Berkeley: University of California Press: 44–55.
Tizzard, Aubrey M. and John David Allison Widdowson (1979). *On Sloping Ground: Reminiscences of Outport Life in Notre Dame Bay, Newfoundland*. St. John's Newfoundland: Memorial University Press.
Veblen, Thorstein (1912). *The Theory of the Leisure Class: An Economic Study of Institutions*. New York: Macmillan.
Waits, William B. (1993). *The Modern Christmas in America*. New York: New York University Press.
Weber, Max (1958). *The Protestant Ethic and the Spirit of Capitalism*. New York: Scribner's Sons.
Whiteley, Sheila (2008). *Christmas, Ideology, and Popular Culture*. Edinburgh: University of Edinburgh Press.

CHAPTER 44

SECULARITY

DAVID NASH

IT would be scarcely surprising for those who have read many studies on the theme of Christmas to wonder what do atheists and people who consider themselves secular have to do with the holiday? This is quite obviously a fair and reasonable question, since those who find themselves outside of any aspect of mainstream culture constitute a minority whose thoughts and opinions we can choose to investigate and consider, or instead ignore and disregard. The desire to explore this area becomes further hampered by the fact that atheists and the secular seem substantially indifferent to Christmas as a concept. But it is worth remembering that even indifference has a history, and the failure to investigate this phenomenon would leave us with something of an incomplete picture of the Christmas festival. Moreover, it remains interesting to examine the world view of the group of people whose mixture of ideological hostility and indifference to religion has been disseminated (albeit in a highly diluted form) throughout many Western populations. These have written over and decentred the strictly religious aspects of the Christmas festival. This therefore becomes a minor, if still intriguing, episode in the history of the world potentially becoming more secular. But digging deeper, in and around a wider history of Christmas, it becomes a history of individuals seeking to ignore, transcend, or even remodel an aspect of wider popular culture that scarcely has anything like immediate relevance to them.

It might seem natural, or widely expected, for the atheist and the secular to have a natural opposition and animosity to the Christian festival of Christmas. After all, it was an almost compulsory religious celebration that, even in the first quarter of the twenty-first century, still does much to overshadow the secular world for a period of anything up to a fortnight. For the secular it also appears to be an irritating and unnecessary opportunity for organized Christianity to reassert its tenuous hold upon the thoughts and imagination of the populace at large. For those who espouse a secular world view it might seem reasonable to assume they would complain about Christianity's privileged position in taking over the media at a specific time of year. Certainly in Britain and other countries, where organized Christianity has notably declined, it seems to do this by offering a message that appears increasingly incoherent and (if statistics are to be believed) less and less relevant as time passes. This situation, to the neutral observer, should signal that atheist and secular people would consider this incongruous to say the least!

Yet most observations and analyses discover the secular and atheist response to Christmas tends to be largely one of indifference. Substantially, Christmas does not worry, bother, or annoy atheists and the secular. Nor does it provoke protest or significant opposition. Christmas as a festival experiences no boycotts, nor does it provoke retaliatory atheist and secular proselytizing. Nonetheless, in thinking about this we are accidentally reminded of some aspects of the role of Christmas in the Christian religion and, through this, the precise aspects of Christianity that are capable of provoking opposition in the unbeliever. Christmas, whilst central to the Christian religion, is capable of being seen by the outside observer as a significantly inoffensive festival. It celebrates the birthday of Christianity's founder, an individual that atheists have had more time for than the God of the Old Testament, notably parodied by Python in both *Life of Brian* and *Monty Python and the Holy Grail*. This preference has been noticeable since at least the time of D. F. Strauss (1808–74) if not before, and contains a message about the part of the divine which shared human form—even if the truth of this appears to them as often distorted or spurious. Moreover, Christmas does remain a relatively innocent, or comparatively unproblematic, festival for the atheist. It is certainly not as central to the Christian message as Easter. As such, it contains none of the motifs of cruelty (bar Herod's spectacular over-reaction) that are prevalent at Easter. There is no suffering, crucifixion, atonement, or Resurrection to ponder—all those being troublesome ideas that provoke a veritable cluster bomb of anti-theological and moral arguments about the behaviour of the supposed creator of the world. In comparison, Christmas is simply the birth of an individual the churches choose to consider the Son of God and not really much more than this.

For the secular who grew up with forms of Christianity and now reject it, these particular attitudes are not an especially large or significant departure anyway! Both Anglicanism (Episcopalians in the US) and Catholicism saw the Easter story as central, with less attention given to Christmas in the overall religious calendar. It is also overshadowed in these denominations by the sacrament and Christ's eventual passion. For more evangelical groupings, Christmas and its nature as a festival were always likely to be manifestly less important than the preaching of the Word—a message ideally to be sustained for every day of the year and not reserved for a piece of exceptionalism in the shape of Christmas. So for even the lapsed, ex-religious baby boomer—or even the actively apostate one—Christmas had always had much of its message overlaid already by narratives of family, as well as the more insidious messages associated with post-war consumerism. Thus, it seems that anti-religious hostility to the festival of Christmas, at least in recent decades, has scarcely been in the forefront of secular and atheist minds. As Elisabeth Cornwell's post on the website of the Richard Dawkins Foundation suggested: 'While we might make a noise when religion attempts to break through the wall of the separation of church and state, we are not in the habit of kicking Santa in the shins' (Cornwell 2011).

However, this has not always been so. Some radical secularists and atheists have taken aim at Christmas, but it remains noteworthy how infrequently this has been attempted. It is also important that the actual success of such attacks has been marginal, or indeed considerably limited. Christmas as a feast day, and its religious significance, could suffer collateral damage in secular and atheist questioning of the Bible and its message. In some instances, this could result in blasphemous publications. In nineteenth-century England, George William Foote's determination to be prosecuted for blasphemy was only satisfied when he turned his own disdain for the Bible onto the Nativity. After several months of attempting to offend by producing cartoons which ridiculed the logic and questionable morals of biblical events, by the time Christmas 1883 came around Foote turned his attention to the Christmas story itself as inspiration. In the Christmas number of his waspish and forthright weekly paper, *The Freethinker*, Foote published an irreverent cartoon comic strip of the life of Christ. This was deliberately provocative and portrayed a range of episodes in Jesus' ministry. The Nativity appeared in one such cartoon. This showed the baby Jesus lying in a manger that was surrounded by the stable animals looking into the manger. Underneath this Foote placed the caption, 'He is worshipped by the wise ones'. Foote's more obvious assaults on Christianity were reserved for the other cartoons in this life story sequence, centred around the adult activities of the Christ figure. The Nativity episode was merely something of a juvenile joke that the *Life Story* swiftly moved away from to areas that were far more profitable. Ultimately, no lasting offence or assault on doctrine could really be perpetrated by focussing on this episode. Indeed, it was other texts and images from this issue which were explicitly cited in the prosecution (Nash 1999: 107–66; Marsh 1998).

It is also revealing how Monty Python's *Life of Brian* treated its own Nativity scene. The film opens with a display of the heavens and the bright star of Bethlehem moving across the screen. Heavenly music follows in what must clearly be a lampoon of the religious film genre. We then see three riders moving towards the horizon, followed by their entrance into the backstreets of Bethlehem. Upon entering an inauspicious stable Terry Jones (dressed as Brian's mother) questions their motives, believing them to be drunk but, his (her) attitude softens when they indicate they have brought gold, frankincense, and myrrh as gifts. Jones relieves them hurriedly of these gifts and dismisses them, hoping they will return with more riches. The three kings then depart but abruptly reappear to repossess the gifts so that they can take them to the 'real' venue of the Nativity further down the street, where the Bethlehem star has settled. Again, there is little to cause offence, certainly when compared to other scenes in the film as originally shot. But this Nativity scene is also one of only two appearances by the figure of Christ in *Life of Brian*, both of which do not actually mock or blaspheme, nor do they lampoon his character. At most, the Nativity story in *Brian* seems to excite gentle, comparatively mild humour when placed alongside the much wider anti-clerical canon of targets elsewhere in the film.

Beyond the festival of Christmas itself, the secular and atheist have been more readily prepared to take issue with the attitudes of the religious who use Christmas as an opportunity for sermonizing, or actively to undermine secular world views. Such instances have a long history but leave obvious traces in the press. This became a trope from the moment the medium entered into its growth spurt in the last quarter of the nineteenth century, a period when a truly national press was possible for the first time on both sides of the Atlantic.

We can get a flavour of this by following an example generated by the foremost American atheist of this period, Colonel Robert Ingersoll. In 1891 he had produced a 'sermon' on Christmas for the *Evening Telegram* and, as a result, the newspaper came under threat of boycott by its religious constituency. This had been instigated by The Rev. Dr J. M. Buckley who was appalled that the newspaper would actively publish such a sermon, an article which he claimed propounded 'Lies that are Mountainous'. Ingersoll replied with the commonplace nineteenth-century atheist and secularist's view that Christmas in many respects ought to be taken back from Christianity, instead to be given an identity that was simultaneously both old and new. Ingersoll had regularly argued for the antiquity of Christmas, noting that it had been a festival of sun worship that predated all forms of religion, including the Abrahamic ones. It stemmed from natural primeval instincts to somehow banish seasonal darkness (Ingersoll 1889: 431–3). In sketching this pattern of development, a clear purpose was to note the obviously recent nature of religious colonization of this, thereby emphasizing starkly the potentially transitory nature of Christianity's involvement in the winter holiday or festival:

> The good part of Christmas is not always Christian–it is generally Pagan; that is to say, human, natural. Christianity did not come with tidings of great joy, but with a message of eternal grief. It came with the threat of everlasting torture on its lips. It meant war on earth and perdition hereafter.
>
> It taught some good things–the beauty of love and kindness in man. But as a torch-bearer, as a bringer of joy, it has been a failure. It has given infinite consequences to the acts of finite beings, crushing the soul with a responsibility too great for mortals to bear. It has filled the future with fear and flame, and made God the keeper of an eternal penitentiary, destined to be the home of nearly all the sons of men. Not satisfied with that, it has deprived God of the pardoning power.
>
> (Ingersoll 1897, Volume 7: 263)

Thus, this tends to suggest that atheists would only muse upon what Christmas had supposedly given the world when provoked. However, it is worth observing how this instance also opened the door for Ingersoll to note the inequalities in the contemporary world which religion's message served to neglect. Christmas, he suggested, only really helped such people by accident:

> It is popular because it is a holiday. Overworked people are glad of days that bring rest and recreation and allow them to meet their families and their friends. They are glad of days when they give and receive gifts—evidences of friendship, of remembrance and love. It is popular because it is really human, and because it is

interwoven with our customs, habits, literature, and thought. For my part I am willing to have two or three a year—the more holidays the better. Many people have an idea that I am opposed to Sunday. I am perfectly willing to have two a week. All I insist on is that these days shall be for the benefit of the people, and that they shall be kept not in a way to make folks miserable or sad or hungry, but in a way to make people happy, and to add a little to the joy of life.   (Ingersoll 1889)

Taken together, many of these attitudes suggest that atheists and secularists have both a residual fondness for Christmas and a fondness for what it has become. On the one hand, its status as a benign celebration of aspects of Christianity reaches back into memories of family and childhood. On the other, it perhaps covertly comforts the atheist as a small snippet of what secularization and the evolution of human attitudes can wreak upon religion and the sacred, if given long enough. A religious festival which had colonized earlier religious festivals could be seen to have lost its central message, or perhaps more correctly discerning populations had sifted through what it had to offer in search of ideas and experiences that pleased them alone. These were increasingly divorced from the doctrinally prescribed religious experience. Thus, Christmas had become a holiday which had a range of residual messages attached to it. Many were cut-down remnants from deeper and more complex ideas, many were created by the canon of classic seasonal literature (increasingly overlaid by more modern works, often cinematic, straining to attain similar classic status). These were all smothered in the deeply significant cultural wrapping paper of the past. In its way, this was an embodiment of one of the religious lightbulb jokes pertaining to Anglicanism. The recipient of the joke learns that it takes many Anglicans/Episcopalians to change a light bulb because one changes the bulb and an inordinate number in attendance reminisce about 'how good the old one had been'.

Interestingly, if Christmas for this reason genuinely pleases the atheist and secularist, then this shows a future that will be different from that contemplated by more organized secular movements in the nineteenth century and first years of the twentieth. In fighting against religion that had a greater cultural and psychological foothold upon the consciousness of the population, secularists and atheists were conditioned to believe they were perpetually engaged in forms of struggle. In such circumstances, the urge for the secularist and atheist minority to achieve the rights of citizenship was paramount to their cause. But, in describing and evaluating the apparent 'damage' they believed religion perpetrated upon society, they came to believe in one of two stances. These were described as Eliminationist (seeking completely to eradicate religion from human culture) or Substitutionist (which sought to 'replace' religion with a better alternative). What emerges from how the eventual history played out is that seeking rights alongside seeking the end of Christianity were incompatible.

What striving for rights produced was not a mainstream secularist and atheist opponent culture to Christianity, but one that avowedly espoused the powerful principle of free choice and the ability to exercise this. The situation has a reasonably close analogy. From a belief that atheists and secularists could produce a culture of death and dying that would eventually snuff out the Christian versions, the reality turned out somewhat differently. This nonetheless provided opportunities for the imagining and eventual realization of a slightly different secular culture of choice. From a defence of rational death at the start of the twentieth century, the end of this same century witnessed secular and Humanist burial services that offered the ultimate in choice for populations at large. This very important element of choice became central in these services as representing what Humanist and secular services could offer to those who were now detached from the mainstream religious culture. This could appeal to atheists and sceptics but also could appeal to the growing generations of 'nones' who had not known the original message of Christianity. In this, atheism, secularism, and Humanism had found a natural and lucrative niche within a wider 'marketplace of comfort' (Nash 2018). Such a niche followed demand and provided not so much a secular experience of death and burial, but a personalized one.

The atheist approach to Christmas has conceivably developed in the same way. There has not been anything like an orthodox atheist and secularist doctrinal 'line' on Christmas and how to regard it. Instead, it is possible to see small strands of atheist and rational thinking influencing personal approaches to the feast of Christmas. Interestingly, they can sometimes seem diametrically opposed to one another, but they further destabilize the idea of there being one atheist and secular mindset concerning how to engage with Christmas.

One atheist might well decide that they wish to turn their back upon the consumerist levels of indulgence that so frequently characterize the Christmas period. They may deliberately choose to have a notably more austere Christmas than friends and relatives around them. They may eschew gift-giving in favour of donating such funds they would have used purchasing these gifts to charity. This attitude may equally persuade them that Christmas is a holiday at which they should devote their time to helping human beings less fortunate than themselves. This might lead them to fundraise over the Christmas period, or perhaps to volunteer to visit or work with people in hospital, or to spend time with those alone during the festive season, or with the homeless in similar circumstances. This species of activism remains a legacy of past times when atheists were chided for having no moral impulses to engage in charitable work or giving. Such ideas claimed that Christianity was essential to instil the charitable impulse. But within austere approaches to the festive season are some inherent criticisms of modern cultures of consumption. At least some of these attitudes seemed to be evident in the mind of the *Huffpost* blogger Arthur Peirce who noted that secular Christmas could enable many of America's poorest to avoid the crippling levels of personal debt that the commercialization of Christmas had led many into:

> This consumerism which is sold to children first and foremost has become accepted. This can be said to be an insidious mutation of the beautiful tradition of gift-giving designed to wholly benefit corporations, more than those receiving the gifts. (Peirce 2016)

The attitude of the individual just described can be contrasted with a different atheist more obviously interested in the sensual pleasures of consumption. For this individual there is no puritanical sense of guilt preventing the enjoyment of giving and receiving lavish presents. Nor does there seem to be any need to somehow 'answer' potential Christian detractors who might label this a form of vapid consumerism. A hybrid of the atheist sensualist approach is to note that atheism and secularism do have a philosophical and psychological link to Epicureanism. This world view saw (and sees) considerable validity in the simple enjoyment of sensual pleasures within this life, as one of our few human certainties. Such pleasures, in the contemporary world, have come to be, for many, centred upon sensual consumption. This may legitimately be seen by this atheist as signalling a holiday period when time for rest can be augmented by the opportunity to enjoy the pleasures of seasonal food, or particularly luxurious versions of everyday fare. The same might also be said for the consumption of alcohol which may increase in volume or quality as the festive season arrives.

Whilst these are deliberate stances which reach back to atheism and secularism's philosophical past, there are other attempts to create a very personal blend of responses to Christmas. Many approaches consider the importance of the family and how an individual's atheism might collide, or conflict, with the beliefs and wishes of others. In his article, *What do Atheists do During Christmas?*, Austin Cline indicated the multifaceted pressures that potentially loomed for the atheist in the association of family with Christmas, and many associated religious traditions:

> Holidays can serve to form a connection to the past and can form and reinforce connections with the friends and family with whom you celebrate. As it is during most religious holidays, at Christmas it's customary to attend church services. Often, people attend services as a family as part of a long-running tradition, and even those who rarely attend religious services are moved to attend during the Christmas season. (Cline 2019)

This was also evident in Elisabeth Cornwell's discourse upon Christmas, posted on the webpage of the Richard Dawkins Foundation, when she suggested: 'I feel no sense of hypocrisy because I enjoy the many threads of my familial past' (Cornwell 2011). Cline also asked if it were appropriate for an atheist to go to church or chapel with their family during the Christmas period. Noting how the element of free choice had clearly entered the equation in the contemporary world, he stated:

> That's a matter of personal choice, but many prefer not to, to avoid misrepresenting themselves and their beliefs. Some may choose to attend in order to continue a family tradition, especially if it's one which the atheist may have participated in when they were younger and still a believer. (Cline 2019)

This indicates also that Christmas and its momentary re-association with religion might serve as a meeting point between family and ritual. It had also been noted that overall church attendance in Britain continues to be in a considerable state of decline, whilst attendance at religious services during the Christmas period is actually increasing (*New Statesman* 2017). This had already been noted by one sociologist in another context when she argued that one manifestation of forms of secularization might be to have turned religion into a practice which evoked and manifested a 'Chain of Memory'. This meant residual references to religion in people's lives were motivated by tradition and the personal history of cultural practices. (Hervieu-Léger 2001) Others have gone further to suggest that Christmas may be an essential site where religion gets to inhabit the secular. Here it becomes a repository of the sacred; indeed, it may even have gone beyond its religious origins to somehow become a religion in itself. This is a conclusion which is capable of dealing a potentially crushing blow to cruder elements of the secularization thesis (Deacy 2016).

Some other atheists may seek to keep a 'Chain of Memory' alive in other ways. One website advertised *An Atheist Christmas Album* which offered to give 'kids' and other listeners a 'Christmas without the Christ'. This offered many of the traditional carols, but altered their titles and internal lyrics or sometimes both, in order to move beyond religious messages at Christmas. 'God Rest Ye Merry, Gentlemen' became 'Oh Rest Ye Merry, Gentlemen' and internal changes were made to 'Silent Night'. There was a concession to non-Christian customs in the inclusion of 'Here we come A-wassailing' and the seasonal if not religious 'Auld Lang Syne', itself inadvertently carrying a secular message about fellowship. As the advert stated: 'At Atheist Christmas, we believe in raising children in an environment that supports rational thinking and reason. As an atheist living in a Christian culture, this can be challenging all year long, but it can be especially tricky during Christmas' (AtheistChristmas 2019). This compromise seemed appropriate because *The Atheist Christmas Album* represented 'a desire to pass on the best traditional music with new, family-orientated lyrics' (AtheistChristmas 2019).

Drawing on Christmas' long standing association with family has led some to consider that Christmas might be the appropriate time to openly declare their atheism. However, this clearly requires careful consideration. Austin Cline noted the potential ambivalence of the situation:

> If you think your family would appreciate knowing so they don't unintentionally make you feel uncomfortable, it may be a good idea to 'come out' as an atheist. But weigh your personal needs with the potential disruption to family harmony, because there's likely to be confusion and hurt feelings at first.   (Cline 2019)

Again, invoking the 'Chain of Memory', Cline also discussed the issue of atheists attending church with their families by noting that Christmas brings people together. But it also allows them to dust off long lapsed religious habits—meaning that togetherness at this time, even if it resulted in a visit to church, was by no means necessarily a bad thing: 'holidays can serve to form a connection to the past and can form and reinforce connections with the friends and family with whom you celebrate' (Cline 2019). Balancing personal needs with family harmony was considered extremely important to Cline, who scarcely wanted atheists to become killjoys, selfish individuals responsible for the end of long-standing and cherished family traditions. This seemed calculated to ensure atheism moved away, at least in the minds of its opponents, from a spirit of dogmatic austerity and joylessness.

Alongside this, Austin Cline noted that atheists might well have a need to tell themselves why they might be prepared to celebrate the festive season alongside Christians, or Jews celebrating Hanukkah. These included noting its proximity to the winter solstice which has been celebrated by many cultures, a point also made in the Vox article, *In Defense of Secular Christmas* (Vox 2015). However, he did recognize that many atheists would shy away from aligning themselves with pagan beliefs which could be construed as theist (Cline 2019). An alternative route might be for an atheist to appreciate the psychological function of such rituals, thereby sidestepping their apparent theological importance. As Cline suggests:

> If you can't find meaning in the usual traditions and rituals, and especially religious or holiday traditions, then make your own traditions where you can. Even small ones have value and while they may not seem like much at first, you'll come to appreciate them eventually. Traditions and rituals serve important roles in binding us together socially, psychologically, and emotionally. (Cline 2019)

Elisabeth Cornwell also suggested Christmas was a time to focus the atheist mind upon memories (Cornwell 2011). Celebrating departed loved ones and their Christmas traditions remained a way of invoking them. This added a new way to repurpose Christmas, and perhaps ultimately stretch the 'Chain of Memory' away from religious practices altogether.

In the end, Christmas essentially sparks the individualism in most atheists and secularists into life. This does not substantially push them into protesting or opposing the religious festival of Christmas but, as with other rites of passage, it does persuade of the need to find ingenious ways to repurpose and rebrand it. It is, most of the time, not enough simply to try and ignore it, since Western civilization is so deeply coloured by its existence. Instead, new styles of thinking have produced myriad ways of relating to this festival and contributing still further to its evolution. All of this is perhaps best summed up by the parting shot of Elisabeth Cornwell who emphasizes most clearly how the atheist and secularist has adapted and processed Christmas, enabling them to come out the other side totally unscathed:

> Christmas belongs to anyone who wants it, and just because I gave up believing in a god doesn't mean I gave up believing in the love and joy of family. I did not give up the joy of celebration with my abandonment of the absurd. So to my religious and non-religious friends, I wish them all a Merry Christmas or a Happy Hanukkah from the heart and I hope they take it with the true spirit with which I give it—that of the spirt of humanity—something we can all celebrate. (Cornwell 2011)

REFERENCES AND FURTHER READING

AtheistChristmas (2019). Available at https://www.atheistchristmas.com/ (accessed 28 March 2020).

Cline, Austin (2019). 'What do Atheists Do During Christmas Holidays?' *Learn Religions*. 25 June 2019. Available at learnreligions.com/what-do-atheists-do-during-christmas-249571/ (accessed 28 March 2020).

Cornwell, R. Elisabeth (2011). 'A Very Atheist Christmas', *Washington Post*. Now available at the Richard Dawkins Foundation page https://www.richarddawkins.net/2012/12/a-very-atheist-christmas/ (accessed 28 March 2020).

Deacy Christopher (2016). *Christmas as Religion: Rethinking Santa, the Secular and the Sacred*. Oxford: Oxford University Press.

Hervieu-Léger, Danièle (2001). *Religion as a Chain of Memory*. New Brunswick, New Jersey: Rutgers University Press.

Ingersoll, Robert (1889). 'Essay on Christmas,' *Tribune* (New York), in Clinton P. Farrell (ed.), *The Works of Robert Ingersoll*, 12 vols. New York: Dresden Publishing, 1903, 2: 431–3.

Ingersoll, Robert (1891). 'Christmas Sermon,' *Evening Telegram* 19 December 1891, in Clinton P. Farrell (ed.), *The Works of Robert Ingersoll*, 12 vols. New York: Dresden Publishing, 1903, 7: 263.

Marsh, Joss Lutz (1998). *Word Crimes: Blasphemy, Culture and Literature in Nineteenth Century England*. Chicago: Chicago University Press

Nash, David (1999). *Blasphemy in Britain 1789 to the Present*. Aldershot: Ashgate.

Nash, David (2018). 'Negotiating the Marketplace of Comfort: Secularists Confront New Paradigms of Death and Dying in Twentieth-Century Britain', *Revue Belge de Philologie et d'Histoire*, 95: 327–52.

New Statesman (2017). 'Christmas Without Christians: How Do We Celebrate in a Secular Age?' (14 December). Available at https://www.newstatesman.com/politics/religion/2017/12/christmas-without-christians-how-do-we-celebrate-secular-age/ (accessed 28 March 2020).

Peirce, Arthur (2016). *Benefits of a Secular Christmas. Huffpost* (9 December). Available at https://www.huffingtonpost.co.uk/arthur-peirce/secular-christmas_b_13480004.html/ (accessed 28 March 2020).

Vox (2015). 'In Defense of Secular Christmas'. Available at https://www.vox.com/2015/12/25/10663946/in-defense-of-secular-christmas (accessed 28 March 2020).

CHAPTER 45

CULTURE WARS

GERRY BOWLER

It is a sad fact, that in some places and times, Christmas can be and has been an occasion for social division, rather than a celebration of peace on earth and good will. In the United States this clash is often portrayed as a shallow bickering over the use of 'Merry Christmas' as a greeting in commercial outlets, but much more profound disagreements surface around the world in late December.

The first blast fired in this war in twentieth-century America came in 1905 in New York City when Jewish families objected to the religious component of Christmas observances in the public-school system. After some bewilderment by the authorities, who had assumed that programmes designed for Protestant children would be universally acceptable—and outright opposition by nativists such as Henry Ford—schools began to be more sensitive about the content of their end-of-term celebrations (Plaut 2012: 28). But it was a series of court cases after the Second World War where the real battle over how much religion could be allowed in public spaces took place. Turning to the constitution's First Amendment, which says in part: 'Congress shall make no law respecting an establishment of religion, or prohibiting the free exercise thereof', a 1947 ruling by Justice Hugo Black of the US Supreme Court seemed definitive: there was to be a 'wall of separation...high and impregnable' between Church and State.

That wall was soon to be eroded. In the 1971 *Lemon v. Kurtzman* case, it was decided that three conditions would prevent a Church–State association from being ruled unconstitutional. First, the statute must not result in an 'excessive government entanglement' with religious affairs. (This came to be known as the Entanglement Prong). Second, the statute must neither advance nor inhibit religious practice (the Effect Prong), and last, the statute must have a secular legislative purpose (the Purpose Prong) (Menendez 1993:111). To this so-called 'Lemon test' were added the 'Reindeer rules' emerging from *Lynch V. Donnelly* (1986) in which the American Civil Liberties Union objected to a Nativity scene in front of the Allegheny County courthouse in Pittsburgh. Emerging from that decision was the impression that a religious Christmas element, such as a crèche, could be acceptable on public property if its Christian content were diluted by the nearby presence of a menorah, some candy canes, or other symbols of a secular nature. These rulings were so vague and ad hoc that decades of litigation, 'lawfare' as it came to be called, followed. Secularizers such as the ACLU, the Freedom from Religion Foundation, and Americans United sued to have offending Christmas displays removed, and groups such as the Becket Fund for Religious Liberty, the American Center for Law and Justice, and the Alliance Defence Fund countered to keep public space open for religious expression at Christmas time.

Schools became the chief battleground for these conflicting approaches, with often bizarre results. In Port St. Lucie, Florida, the school presentation of *A Penguin Christmas* was deemed to be tainted by religious content and the principal pulled it from the holiday programme. Though the little play contained nothing of a sectarian nature, the use of the word 'Christmas' and a Santa Claus character were found worrisome, baffling one parent who complained: 'What do penguins have to do with the gospel? I don't even think penguins could survive in Nazareth.' In the San Joaquin valley, a school board's decision to change the names of winter and spring breaks to 'Christmas' and 'Easter' vacation caused one irate citizen to set himself and a Christmas tree on fire in protest. In Newport Beach, California, Christmas enthusiasts were told to pull down strings of coloured lights they had put up at a local elementary school in December. While most seemed to find the display only a harmless holiday custom, others were convinced of a more sinister purpose. 'It's a provocative act to put the lights up—it disenfranchises and marginalizes non-Christian students who are attending the public school,' said Rabbi Mark Miller. Christmas carols are a landmine for school administrators who have resorted to denuding the songs of religious content, replacing the offending words with meaningless sounds as in 'Silent Night, mmm, mmm, mmm, / All is calm, all is bright, mmm, mmm, mmm,' and so on. Even a non-religious holiday song like 'Silver Bells' can be dangerous unless the C-word is excised; thus: 'Ring-a-ling, hear them sing; Soon it will be a festive day.'

The Christmas tree, a tradition that grew from the medieval custom of bringing greenery indoors during winter months, is in no way a religious symbol, but it causes no end of offence to the easily offended. In Bellevue, Washington, parents and children had decided to help the less fortunate by setting up a tree decorated with mittens and bearing the wishes of gift recipients. Already attuned to potential grumbling, they did not call this a 'Christmas' tree but a 'Giving Tree'. All in vain. A complainant quickly alerted the principal to the fact that the tree (a coil of silver topped by a star) 'represents some part of Christianity'. So the Giving Tree had to go, to be replaced by the 'Giving Counter', on which the mittens could be inoffensively placed. Perhaps warned by the venom engendered by the term 'Giving Tree', another high school changed its donation tree to a 'Giving Snowman', only to find that this expression was sexist, necessitating a change to 'Giving Snowperson'.

Even universities are not immune to such seasonal brouhahas. An administrator at the University of Maine warned staff: 'Just wanted to remind everyone that Auxiliary Services is not to decorate any public areas with Christmas or any other religious themed decorations. Winter holiday decorations are fine but we need to not display any decoration that could be perceived as religious.' Banned items included 'xmas trees, wreaths, xmas presents, menorahs, candy canes, etc.' Permitted symbols included 'snowmen, plain trees without presents underneath, decorative lights, but not on trees, snowflakes, etc. If you are unsure, best to not use or ask me for clarification.' At Cornell University, the 'Guidelines for the Display of Religious Symbols' allowed snowflakes to be used. Trees could be decorated with snowflakes but no religious decorations were permissible. Caution (in the form a 'dialogue within unit or living area') was urged for the display of trees decorated with bows, garlands, and lights; wreaths with bows; holly; or a combination of snowflakes, Santa Claus figure, and dreidel (a toy top associated with Hanukkah). Banned were any Nativity scene, menorah, angel, star at the top of a tree, cross, Star of David, or mistletoe. The 'Inclusive Holiday Practices' of Ohio State University went so far as to discourage the use of red or green bows in decorating.

'When is a Christmas tree not a Christmas tree?' In order to get around the use of that dangerous word 'Christmas', officials of various sorts have presented it as a 'Holiday Tree'. Or a 'Care Tree'. A 'Multicultural Tree'. A 'Tree of Lights'. A 'Community Tree'. A 'Winter Solstice Tree'. A 'Grand Tree'. A 'Special Tree'. A 'Family Tree'. The 'Annual Tree'. A 'Festive Bush'. A 'Unity Tree'. A 'Culture Tree'. A 'Seasonal Conifer'. A 'Giving Tree'. A 'Tree of Celebration'. A 'Magical Tree'. 'The Finals Tree'. This is a particularly touchy subject when it comes to trees in front of government buildings; politicians are forced to see which way the wind of voter sentiment is blowing before pronouncing on this charged subject. The best example of the sort of kerfuffle arose in Boston in 2005. In gratitude to the people of New England for their aid to the city of Halifax after it had been devastated by a huge explosion in 1917, the province of Nova Scotia has for decades annually sent an enormous Christmas tree to Boston to be lit on Boston Common. In 2005, press releases referred to the gift as a 'Holiday tree', a term that caused an enormous ruckus back in Canada. The logger who had chosen and cut the tree down said that if he had known what they were going to call it, he would have run it through the woodchipper. The premier of Nova Scotia noted pointedly that when it had left his domain it was still a 'Christmas tree'. Fortunately for international goodwill, Boston mayor Thomas Menino announced that in his estimation the tree was, and always had been, a Christmas tree (Drummond 2005).

The growing social acceptability of atheism, as witnessed by the appearance of best-sellers such as Richard Dawkins's *The God Delusion* and Christopher Hitchens's *God Is Not Great*, emboldened the godless into frequent attacks on Christmas celebrations, in order to discredit Christianity and to undermine the supernatural claims of the feast. Atheist carols appeared, with lyrics such as 'Faith just makes us hateful and small, / We'll start growing strong by knowing / God isn't great at all!' Atheist groups demanded space in parks and government buildings for their anti-religious manifestoes and paid for ads in subways and on buses proclaiming, 'Who needs Christ at Christmas? Nobody', or 'Why believe in a god? Be good for goodness' sake', or 'Reason's Greetings'. Atheists avow that they have no desire to ban Christmas as the Puritan Parliament had once done in the 1640s, only to privatize it. As Christopher Hitchens said:

No believer in the First Amendment could go that far. But there are millions of well-appointed buildings all across the United States, most of them tax-exempt and some of them receiving state subventions, where anyone can go at any time and celebrate miraculous births and pregnant virgins all day and all night if they so desire. These places are known as 'churches,' and they can also force passersby to look at the displays and billboards they erect and to give ear to the bells that they ring. In addition, they can count on numberless radio and TV stations to beam their stuff all through the ether. If this is not sufficient, then god damn them. God damn them everyone.   (Hitchens 2005)

Perhaps surprisingly, there were Christians who objected to Christmas too. These were the spiritual descendants of Puritans, ultra-Calvinists for whom all man-made ceremonial was idolatry. They wrote earnest tracts denouncing Christmas as un-Christian and wrote anti-Christmas carols of their own, such as 'I'm Dreaming There Will Be No Christmas' or 'Banish Christmas', sung to the tune of Mel Tormé's 'Christmas Song', where instead of roasting chestnuts we have the heretical Michael Servetus, executed in John Calvin's Geneva in 1553:

> Servetus roasting in an open fire,
> John Knox preaching where he can.
> Calvin teaching against every sin.
> The folk all look so Puritan.

Santa Claus was a particular target of these fundamentalists who were quick to point out that his name was an anagram of Satan, and to hang him in effigy. The most offensive proponents of this critique were the followers of Fred Phelps, leader of the Westboro Baptist Church in Topeka, Kansas. Once a prominent politician and civil-rights lawyer. Phelps became convinced that tolerance of homosexuality was leading to the downfall of America. In order to make this point Phelps and his family picketed the funerals of children and soldiers claiming that their deaths were God's punishment for gay sin. Among the other objects of Phelp's hate were the Catholic Church, Princess Diana, Mormons, Mr Rogers, Billy Graham, and Christmas. The Phelps clan has a large supply of parody Christmas songs: 'Doom to the World' replaces 'Joy to the World'; 'This Might Be Your Final Christmas' is based on 'We Wish You a Merry Christmas'; and this ditty replaces 'Santa Claus Is Coming to Town':

> You better watch out,
> get ready to cry.
> You better go hide I'm telling you why,
> 'cuz Santa Claus will take you to Hell.
> He is your favorite idol,
> You worship at his feet,
> But when you stand before your God,
> He won't help you take the heat.

> So get this fact straight,
> You're feeling God's hate;
> Santa's to blame for the economy's fate;
> Santa Claus will take you to hell.   (Westboro Baptist 2010)

Other Christian groups, uneasy about Christmas because of its association with capitalism and consumerism, sought to make the public aware of their concerns and to emphasize that there was more to the season than buying gifts. The rallying cry 'Put Christ Back in Christmas' was first uttered in 1949 in Milwaukee by an organization of Catholic mothers; it was soon taken up by Protestant churches as well. The United Church of Canada, launched a 'Christ in Christmas' initiative—a series of billboard, radio, and television ads that aimed at reducing consumerism and alcohol consumption during the holidays. In 1992, a coalition of American religious leaders embarked on 'A Campaign to Take Commercialism out of Christmas'. Activist Bill McKibben began a 'Hundred Dollar Holiday' movement, stating 'Christmas is a school for consumerism—in it we learn to equate delight with materialism. We celebrate the birth of One who told us to give everything to the poor by giving each other motorized tie racks' (McKibben 1996: 18). The Alternatives for Simple Living organization produced an influential booklet entitled 'Whose Birthday is it Anyway?', suggesting tips for a simpler and more meaningful Christmas. In 2001 a number of Canadian Mennonites combined anticonsumerism with a Marxist perspective on the economy to produce the 'Buy Nothing Christmas' campaign while in the US, the entertaining provocateur Bill Talen donned the mask of the Reverend Billy of the Church of Stop Shopping, ever ready to exorcise cash registers, sermonize in bank lobbies, and stage 'retail interventions' (Talen 2006: 172).

Naturally, supporters of a public face for Christmas undertook public relations campaigns of their own. Billboards sprang up around America with messages such as 'God Is'; 'You know it's Real. This season celebrate Jesus'; and 'I Miss Hearing You Say "Merry Christmas"—Jesus'. In 2014 the Catholic League for Religious and Civil Rights took aim at the nation's entertainment industry with the message:

> Not All Christian Haters Are Equal:
> Abroad We're Beheaded
> At Home We're Bashed
> The Differences Are Profound;
> So Are the Similarities
> Have a Peaceful and Joyous Christmas

In 2001 the town council of Kensington, Maryland called for the removal of Santa Claus from his usual role in lighting the municipal Christmas tree—apparently two local families had deemed him an avatar of Christianity and thus a violator of Church–State separation. A hurricane of criticism erupted. Social media mercilessly mocked the hapless politicians who had voted for the ban; town officials received more than two thousand hostile e-mails. Volunteers organized a 'Million Santa March'; dozens of men dressed as St Nick marched, rode motorcycles, or waved to the crowds from the backs of pickups. The collective of Clauses sang carols, patted children on the head, and distributed candy canes. Protestors chanted, 'No Santa, No Peace!' Some carried signs proclaiming, 'Grinch for Mayor', 'Mean Spirited Arrogant Santa Hating Liberals', 'Yes, Kensington, There Is a Santa Claus', and 'PC = Stupid'. Peace was restored when town officials agreed to present Santa Claus with a special proclamation, and a local merchants' association planned to give him a key to the city (Bowler 2005: 229).

This war of opposing notions of what a separation of Church and State should mean for Christmas is largely an American affair, the result of that pesky First Amendment; and in Britain, where mass immigration has made civil servants and teachers wary. Other democratic countries manage to accommodate their secular political arrangements with a culture that finds room for seasonal displays of religion. In 2006, a Canadian judge's attempt to remove the Christmas tree from her courthouse ended with her being pilloried by the legal profession, politicians, and members of public—and a stay of execution for the tree. In largely irreligious Scandinavia there are few objections to traditional religious activities in schools during the Christmas season. In Sweden, for example, the December 13 Luciatåg (St Lucy's Day) ceremonies are major events in schools, with processions of girls and boys carrying candles and singing carols. In Norway and Sweden it is also common for students to attend church for Christmas Mass with the support of the government.

In Europe the culture wars over Christmas are largely about 'patrimonialization', the defence of native customs over foreign intruders. The worst of the Christmas intruders, as far as many Europeans are concerned, is Santa Claus, an American invention and a supplanter of native magical Christmas gift-bringers. In Dijon, France, in 1951 two Catholic cardinals superintended an amazing spectacle: before a crowd of young people assembled in front of the Gothic cathedral an over-sized effigy of Santa was strung up and a man in a top hat demanded: 'Does Santa Claus deserve death?' 'Yes, yes!', screamed the mob of children as he was set alight. After the execution, a manifesto was posted on the church door:

> United in all the Christian homes of the parish, 250 children who want to fight against lies have burned Santa Claus. This is not a vaudeville act, but a protest against lies which are incapable of awakening the religious feelings of children and are in no sense a method of education. To a Christian, Christmas is the anniversary of the Savior's birth.   (Bowler 2016: 129)

But who will deliver presents to good little girls and boys if Santa is banished? The authentic native gift-bringers of choice are St Nicholas, the Three Kings, and the baby Jesus, who operates in Europe under a number of names: *le petit Jésus, das Christkindl, Ježíšek, Dzieciątko, Jézuska,* and so on. Vigorous local efforts are made by such groups as the German Pro-Christkind Association to alert folk to the Santa menace; their motto is *Wir glauben ans Christkind. Gebt dem Weihnachtsmann keine Chance*—'We believe in the Christ Child. Don't Give Santa A Chance.' In some towns in the

Netherlands it is illegal for anyone dressed as the American gift-bringer to appear before St Nicholas has had his turn in the spotlight and departed after his feast day, December 6. In that country, St Nicholas's dark-skinned helper Zwarte Piet has been attacked as a racist hangover by well-meaning reformers who have suggested a rainbow-coloured or (in Gouda) a cheese-coloured sidekick, but most Dutch people seem to want to keep the traditional version (Seward et al. 2016: 117).

But it is not just Santa Claus who was despised as an interloper. The Soviet occupation of eastern Europe after 1945 brought with it an emphasis on New Year's festivities and a Russian secular figure, Ded Moroz, or Grandfather Frost, that was meant to replace Christmas observances and religious gift-bringers. With the fall of the USSR, countries once behind the Iron Curtain made sure Grandfather Frost accompanied the departing Red Army. In the Czech Republic, a comic pseudo-documentary portrayed Santa presenting his American citizenship in a police office and being declared an undesirable alien. He ends up on a stairway drinking his blues away with a bottle of cheap vodka proffered by a slovenly Ded Moroz figure (Antisantaczech 2012).

Sometimes defenders of local culture have attempted to introduce well-meaning synthetic replacements for Santa Claus, with humorous and short-lived results. In the 1930s the Brazilian government tried to displace *Papai Noel*, the local version of Santa, with *Vovo Indio*, or 'Grandfather Indian', meant to be an alternative to Euro-American gift-bringers and thus inflate Brazilian patriotic sentiments. About the same time, Mexican authorities tried to boost nationalism and assert Mexican independence of American and Spanish cultural figures, by replacing Santa Claus and the Three Kings with a pre-Columbian pagan deity, the Aztec god Quetzalcóatl. Before Fidel Castro banned the public celebration of Christmas in 1969, there was a brief attempt to create a Cuban-style holiday free of Yankee influences, with Don Feliciano, 'Mr Happiness', a straw-hat wearing, bearded peasant as a Santa replacement. None of these Latin American inventions had any lasting effect (Bowler 2016: 141).

In non-Christian countries the culture wars surrounding Christmas have taken on a grimmer hue. In Turkey in 2010, students at an Istanbul university paraded with an inflatable Santa Claus and delivered a tirade against Christmas as a phenomenon that estranged Muslims from the true religion and seduced them with a corrupt Western imperialism. In front of the effigy were strewn beer cans, a syringe, and a cross to show the danger of allowing Christmas into Turkish homes. Santa came in for worse treatment in Tajikistan in 2012 where a mob of Muslim extremists set upon a man dressed as the Russian Grandfather Frost. Crying 'You infidel!' they beat him and stabbed him to death. In Indonesia's Aceh province where sharia law is the rule, the Islamic clergy have instructed its Muslim community not to celebrate Christmas and New Year's. Instead, they want authorities strictly to enforce Islamic law by severely punishing anyone who violates it; for example, Christian ceremonies must not disturb or cause problems for Muslims at work, at home, or even when they are staying in hotels, which are already prohibited from holding holiday celebrations.

Similarly in India, the Vishwa Hindu Parishad (VHP), a right-wing nationalist organization dedicated to defending the country's religious heritage against foreign influences, fears that Christmas customs pose a danger to the Hindu majority. When a Santa Claus at Christian schools in Chhattisargh distributed chocolates to children during the 2014 Christmas season, the VHP demanded that Santa was to stop trying to convert kids to Christianity through the use of sweets or cash bribes, Catholic priests were no longer to be called 'Father', and the schools must put up pictures of Hindu deities (India Times 2014).

Authorities in China seem equally bent on preserving their nation from 'Western spiritual pollution'. In 2014, the Modern College of Northwest University in Xi'an hung banners around campus exhorting its students, 'Strive to be outstanding sons and daughters of China, oppose kitsch Western holidays', and 'Resist the expansion of Western culture'. Officials locked its gates to prevent any participation in Christmas activities and instead made students attend a three-hour course of cultural propaganda focusing attention on Confucius. In Hunan, students held anti-Christmas demonstrations, carrying signs reading 'Resist Christmas'. The Department of Education in Wenzhou banned any Christmas activities from being held in schools or kindergartens. These government actions seemed motivated by a combination of national pride and fear of the growth of Christianity in China—Wang Zuo'an, the director of the State Administration for Religious Affairs, visited a Beijing church on Christmas Eve but used the occasion to call for a 'firm determination against any foreign influence through Christianity' (Fang 2014).

One final aspect of the Christmas cultural wars which deserves attention is the appropriation of the holiday by groups seeking to use the season's many positive meanings to advance their own causes. African-American activists in the United States have used the phrase 'Black Christmas' in a number of campaigns, such as a 1967 drive for fair housing laws in Milwaukee, or a 1968 campaign in Durham, North Carolina, to protest changes in welfare and minority unemployment. In Chicago in 1969, Jesse Jackson denounced the white Santa Claus as irrelevant to the city's black population and introduced 'Soul Santa' who came not from the Arctic but from the southerly 'Soul Pole'. Soul Santa was 'young, gifted and black', clad in a dashiki of traditional African colours and travelled in a horse-drawn wagon; his message was to boycott white businesses and to buy Christmas gifts from black businesses. Though Kwanzaa, a tradition established in the 1960s, has now achieved a kind of middle-class respectability, it originally included anti-capitalist and black nationalist elements which called for the death of Santa Claus and an end to African Americans celebrating Christmas. The equation of Christmas with white exploitation continues to be an emphasis of Black Muslim leader Louis Farrakhan who in 2015 renewed the trope, saying: 'We intend to boycott Christmas, but not Jesus. We think that they have taken advantage of us and our consumer dollars by materializing the respect and honor of Jesus and making it a bonanza for white business.... So on Black Friday, we won't be there. We choose not to spend dollars on Black Friday, Black Saturday, Black Sunday, Black Monday. We are not going to spend our money for the rest of that year with those that we have traditionally spent our money on' (Farrakhan: 2018).

'Black Christmas' can also take on violent meanings. The South African uprisings in the urban townships of the 1970s and 1980s saw gangs of dissident youth enforcing joyless Christmases on their communities, letting the inhabitants and the world know that as long as racial segregation and inequality continued there would be no celebrations of the Nativity. Though there was resistance at first to this movement, as time went on many came to see the significance of the phenomenon. One supporter said:

> The civic society demand for a 'black Christmas' without any kind of celebration initially proved a difficulty for many of us for whom Christmas was a time of celebration. Celebrating the religious significance of the event without forgetting the many who suffered, however, did not prove as difficult as originally expected. We simply reminded ourselves that Jesus was born into poverty and oppression, that he became a refugee, an exile from his own land, and proclaimed peace in a world not too far removed from our own in terms of oppressive violence. (Spong 2006: 283)

On Christmas Eve 2013, a gay anarchist group in Bristol, England, glued shut the doors of the city's Catholic cathedral, smashed stained glass windows and painted anti-religious graffiti on the building. This was in aid of a protest against 'subservience and patriarchy'. A message posted on the Internet boasted:

> Early morning mass was blackened this Christmas Eve. Overnight we glued locks on their doors, spray-painted 'without God', 'without law', and anarchy symbols on the grand exterior and signed 'queers x'. We hate the many forms of churches and priests who work to instill subservience and patriarchy with their wretched morals, when not still with the whip.

Those many social groups who wish during the year to correct our incorrect behaviour find Christmas time a splendid moment for making their point. Thus, an anti-smoking zealot publishes a version of 'The Night Before Christmas' in which St Nick is deprived of his pipe. Environmental groups predicting a climate apocalypse produce a video of a dishevelled Santa Claus pleading for action:

> Dear children. Regrettably, I bring bad tidings. For some time now melting ice here at the North Pole has made our operations and our day to day life intolerable and impossible and there may be no alternative but to cancel Christmas...

> My home in the Arctic is fast disappearing and unless we all act urgently then I have to warn you of the possibility of empty stockings for evermore. Please help me.
> (Greenpeace 2013)

The annual seasonal holocaust suffered by our fine-feathered friends has brought forth pleas to end 'The Carvery', and a singing turkey warbling: 'What is wrong with a great tofu? / Plenty of protein and good for you / My drum sticks are meant to run.'

If Christmas means love, reconciliation, family and mass social participation, it must, therefore equal respectability. Marginalized groups are quick to use Christmas to shed a second-hand gloss on their issues. If they can claim a place at the Christmas table, who can then deny them the larger social attention that they demand? And so we see pagans stepping forward in December to insist that their primeval forbears were the real inventors of midwinter mirth; gay advocates producing LBGTQ versions of *A Christmas Carol*; bare-breasted *FEMEN* activists attempting to steal the image of the Baby Jesus from the Nativity scene erected by the pope in front of St Peter's Basilica; Palestinian crèches pointedly constructed with a wall down the middle; and German anti-immigration protesters singing Christmas carols on their marches. Anti-militarism groups take aim at war toys; IRA militants send cards reminding the Irish people of interned prisoners; supporters of increased immigration display images of the Holy Family as refugees; conceptual artists erect images of crucified Santas on their lawns; and anti-capitalists erect billboards proclaiming 'Santa Gives More To Rich Kids Than Poor Kids'. Terrorist groups around the world have also used the season to gain publicity, as can be seen in attacks staged in Mexico, Chile, Italy, Argentina, and Greece which targeted not only economic targets owned by the oppressive ruling classes but also Christmas trees and Nativity scenes.

Is there a war on Christmas? Of course, there is. The holiday is simply too important not to use for one's own ideological purposes and argue about. As long as Christmas has so many powerful tugs on the heart strings and purse strings of the world, there will be contests to control its meanings.

References and Further Reading

Antisantaczech (2012). 'Santa Claus je nežádoucí!' Available at https://www.youtube.com/watch?v=-60MNolZY9c/ (accessed 28 March 2020).

Bowler, Gerry (2005). *Santa Claus: A Biography.* Toronto: McClelland and Stewart.

Bowler, Gerry (2016). *Christmas in the Crosshairs: Two Thousand Years of Denouncing and Defending the World's Most Celebrated Holiday.* New York: Oxford University Press.

Drummond, Charles R. (2005). 'Boston's "Holiday Tree" Sparks Controversy'. *Harvard Crimson*, 28 November 28. Available at https://www.thecrimson.com/article/2005/11/28/bostons-holiday-tree-sparks-controversy-last/ (accessed 28 March 2020).

Fang, Frank (2014). 'Santa Suppressed in China, but Regime Head Likes Him'. *Epoch Times* (29 December). Available at https://www.theepochtimes.com/santa-suppressed-in-china-but-regime-head-likes-him_1168462.html/ (accessed 28 March 2020).

Farrakhan, Louis (2018). 'Why We Are Calling on You to Boycott Christmas'. *The Final Call* (10 December). Available at https://www.finalcall.com/artman/publish/Minister_Louis_Farrakhan_9/Why-We-are-Calling-You-to-Boycott-Christmas.shtml/ (accessed 28 March 2020).

Greenpeace (2013). *Radio Times* (2 December). Available at https://www.radiotimes.com/news/2013-12-02/downton-abbeys-carson-is-father-christmas-in-new-greenpeace-campaign/ (accessed 28 March 2020).

Hitchens, Christopher (2005). 'The Horror of Christmas in a One-Party State', *Slate* (20 December). Available at http://www.slate.com/id/2132806/?nav=ais/ (accessed 28 March 2020).

India Times (2014). 'Sorry Kids, But VHP Just Told Santa Not to Give You Chocolates!', *India Times* (26 November 26). Available at http://www.indiatimes.com/news/india/sorry-kids-but-the-vhp-just-told-santa-claus-not-to-give-you-chocolates-this-christmas-228620.html/ (accessed 28 March 2020).

McKibben, Bill (1996). 'Christmas Unplugged', *Christianity Today* (9 December): 18–23.

Menendez, Albert (1993). *The December Wars: Religious Symbols and Ceremonies in the Public Square*. Buffalo: Prometheus Books.

Plaut, Joshua Eli (2012). *A Kosher Christmas: 'Tis the Season to be Jewish*. New Brunswick NJ: Rutgers University Press.

Seward, Pat, et al. (2016) *The Netherlands*. London: Cavendish Square Publishing.

Spong, Bernard (2006). *Sticking Around*. Pietermaritzburg: Cluster Publications.

Talen, Bill (2006). *What Would Jesus Buy: Fabulous Prayers in the Face of the Shopacalypse*, New York: Public Affairs.

Westboro Baptist Church (2010). 'Santa Claus Will Take You to Hell'. Available at https://www.youtube.com/watch?v=o-l8iqevaoU/ (accessed 28 March 2020).

EPILOGUE

The Many True Meanings of Christmas

TIMOTHY LARSEN

In the spirit of Christmas (or, if you prefer, the holiday season), all that is left for me to do is attempt to spread some peace and goodwill. While the *season* of Christmas often brings out the best in people, somehow the *subject* of Christmas does not. Indeed, this highly influential holiday too often elicits a snide tone, a dictatorial streak, or a taunting tendency. Christmas studies—as well as popular discussions about the holiday—are particularly rife with the genetic fallacy. The supposed origins of things are being continually weaponized in order to insist that they somehow discredit or contradict a person's stated beliefs, practices, and sentiments. People have a strange tendency to insist that Christmas does not or cannot mean to you what, in fact, it does mean to you. Religious people are told that Christmas is really secular, and secular people are told it is really religious. Christians are told it is inescapably pagan, and pagans are told it is inescapably Christian. Protestants are told it is inherently tainted by Catholicism, and Catholics are told that the modern celebration of Christmas is inherently tainted by Protestantism. Somehow the poor Christmas tree gets all these charges heaped upon it—it is, by turns, too religious, too secular, too Christian, too pagan, and too Protestant. The same goes with Santa Claus, who also even gets to be too Catholic or Orthodox (given his St Nicholas side), as well as too Protestant. Moreover, given the fact that some people trace the Christmas tree to the Tree of Life in medieval sacred plays, I suspect some polemicists have deemed it too Catholic as well.

The genetic fallacy is even more tendentious than usual in this context because so many aspects of the celebration of Christmas are what the anthropologist Mary Douglas referred to as 'natural symbols'—connections that are so obvious to make that they are likely to occur to many different cultures independently. No one has a copyright, for instance, on the symbolic significance of light coming into the darkness—it belongs to Jews celebrating Hanukkah, pagans celebrating the winter solstice, Hindus celebrating Diwali, African Americans celebrating Kwanzaa, Catholics at Midnight Mass, Protestants at a Christmas Eve carol service, and innumerable others as well. Cultures across the globe and the centuries have marked time by the course of the sun and the moon. Jewish festivals are often tied to solar and lunar cycles (Passover, for instance, to the Spring equinox). The Hebrew Scriptures even declare that the

Almighty created the sun and the moon in order 'to mark out the sacred seasons' (Genesis 1:14). Solstices have marked time for peoples across the planet from time immemorial, however much their religions and cultures have differed from each other. Likewise, no one has proprietary claims over the religious, ritual, or cultural significance of the display of evergreen trees and plant decorations during winter—these are natural symbols. A common way to celebrate across the centuries and the globe has likewise been with feasting and gift-giving.

Furthermore, even when a new religion or ideology or way of life emerges, it inevitably expresses itself through the cultural resources to hand, which are therefore derived from pre-existing ones. This is so self-evident it is hard even to imagine what the alternative might be. In other words, a clear, direct case of cultural borrowing does not necessarily tell us anything about something's meaning in its new context. Take, for instance, a holiday observed in the United States of America: Independence Day (the Fourth of July). An informed observer could notice innumerable cultural borrowings. For example, the use of red, white, and blue as the national colours is obviously simply adopted from Great Britain. Hearing the song 'America (My Country, 'Tis of Thee)', one would immediately recognize the melody as that of the British national anthem ('God Save the Queen'). The fireworks might remind one of celebrations of the British monarchy, famously evoked just a couple of decades before the American War of Independence in Handel's Music for the Royal Fireworks (1749). Our observer might be baffled by the claim that serving apple pie—a very common, traditional English dish—is somehow distinctively American ('as American as apple pie'). Again, what all this goes to show is that Great Britain preceded the United States and that new cultures arise by using the resources that are available to them. It would be absurd, however, to use these facts to claim that in their Fourth of July celebrations Americans are somehow *really* honouring the British monarchy and expressing their loyalty to the British nation and that if they want to be *truly* American they therefore must forsake the red, white, and blue, and the apple pie, and all the rest. Yet people routinely claim that when an elderly Lutheran woman puts up a Christmas tree in her home she is *really* doing something pagan or when a secular teenager gives his friends candy canes he is *really* endorsing Christianity, and endless other such misguided and mischievous assertions along these lines.

The bullying or taunting aspect of all these notions is illustrated by the fact that people who are otherwise quick to make so much of origins never seem to notice the ways that Christmas draws upon Judaism. Yet, the sacred narrative of the Nativity of Christ in the New Testament is clearly influenced by the miraculous birth accounts of certain major figures in the Hebrew Scriptures. Indeed, the parallels between Hannah giving birth to Samuel and Mary giving birth to Jesus extend all the way to the songs of the two mothers—Mary's *Magnificat* being noticeably influenced by Hannah's prayer (1 Samuel 2:1–10; Luke 1:46–55). As has been noted already, Christians continued the Jewish practice of dating their major religious feasts based on the stations of the sun and the phases of the moon. Even some of the seemingly merely cultural (as opposed to overtly religious) aspects of Christmas likewise can be seen as directly derived from ancient Israel's approach to a sacred day: 'a holiday; that they should make them days of feasting and gladness, days for sending gifts of food to one another and gifts to the poor' (Esther 9:22). Because Christians are generally quite comfortable with the Jewish roots of their faith, these connections somehow become not worth pointing out. (By contrast, bullies can and do try to discredit the Jewish faithful by arguing that their modern celebration of Hanukkah has been influenced by the Christian Christmas.)

So many of the words and phrases that are used to describe the Christmas season are wielded as indictments. Consumerism and commercialism are obvious examples. Those words can express real critiques of real problems. Gift-giving, however, is a way of fostering social bonds that has always existed across all human cultures, and thus it is bizarre indeed to try to make people who do wish to give presents feel ashamed simply for engaging in a beneficial and universal custom of social life. As I say in my chapter in this volume, nostalgia is another case in point. Of course, there is a nostalgic element in how many people approach Christmas. Nevertheless, other realities are often misguidedly subsumed under this label. True nostalgia is rooted in the belief that the past was better than the present. Its purest form is a wish to be living in former times. The evocation of Christmas past, however, can be rooted in a human delight in tradition, in a desire to be reassured that change is tempered by continuity, in antiquarian enthusiasms, and in a longing to make connections across time. The more discontinuity one is currently experiencing, the more meaningful traditions can become. Hence the ideal of having 'an old-fashioned' Christmas. Out on an extreme sledging expedition in the Antarctic on Christmas 1902, Ernest Shackleton triumphantly produced a Christmas pudding he had hid away in a sock. Every Christmas has such moments when a connection with what endures over time makes the present more endurable.

Another much-abused catchphrase is 'the invention of tradition'. At its best, this is an illuminating bit of scholarly analysis. Too often, however, invented tradition becomes a charge which is intended to discredit. All traditions were invented at some point: the fact that one is not as old as people generally assume—or that it is the product of a deliberate effort—does not affect how significant it is for the people practising it. An invented tradition is not *ipso facto* an illegitimate one. A custom is legitimate if you find it meaningful; someone labelling it an invented tradition does not imply that somehow you are no longer allowed to find it meaningful. Furthermore, the cavilling spirit in which these claims are sometimes made is highlighted when one places the 'pagan' and 'invented tradition' critiques side-by-side: essentially, one is challenging the appropriateness of a Christmas tradition by saying it is too old, and the other is challenging the appropriateness of other traditions by saying that they are too young, thereby arbitrarily dictating that 'valid' traditions must have arisen within a carefully proscribed window of time. (Although it is also true that the latter claim is sometimes used to repel the former when allegedly ancient, pagan customs are exposed as more recent, invented ones.) Finally, 'sentimentality' is another such word. Of course, there is a valid version and application of that critique. Too often, however, it just seems to be a way to sneer at the genuine emotional lives and responses of ordinary people.

The theme of this little epilogue is simply that no one should bully you by insisting that Christmas somehow does not mean to you what it in fact does mean to you or that what it means to you is somehow illegitimate. Christmas, for you, is what you decide it will be—religious or secular; pagan or Christian; communal or domestic; commercial or part of the Buy Nothing movement; Catholic, Orthodox, or Protestant. There are many true meanings of Christmas. And there are many other celebrations during the holiday season that one can choose to observe along with or instead of Christmas: winter solstice, Hanukkah, Kwanzaa, Hogmanay/New Year's, and more. They too cannot have their significance dictated to you by others. May whatever holidays you celebrate enrich your life and the lives of those around you. As an expression of my Christian faith, I will always cherish Christmas above all other winter festivals. And, for me, Christmas will always primarily be a celebration of God becoming incarnate in Jesus Christ: 'But the angel said to them, "Do not be afraid. I bring you good news of great joy that will be for all the people. Today in the town of David a Saviour has been born to you; he is the Messiah, the Lord. This will be a sign to you: You will find a baby wrapped in cloths and lying in a manger"' (Luke 2:10–12).

Dear reader, you have tarried long and now have reached the end. The hour is late and you deserve your rest. Peace and goodwill to all—and to all a good night.

Index

Note: Figures and Tables are indicated by an italic '*f*', '*t*' following the page number.

'364 Days to Go' 338

A
Abraham
  angels and 194
  Gospel of John 85
  Gospel of Luke 104
  Old Testament 68, 71, 75, 192, 196, 197
Abram 196
Acts of the Apostles
  angels 193
  Antiochian Orthodox Christianity 424
  on census 208, 210, 211
  on Davidic lineage 86
  on Magi 214
  omission of Christmas story 84
  on Romans 204, 206, 207
  St. Stephen 152
  on Virgin Mary 103, 105
Acts of Thomas 6
Act to Restrain Abuses of Players 374
Adam 17, 67–8, 71, 74, 80, 266, 363
Adelhausen, Abbey of 20
Adenauer, Konrad 57
Advent
  Anglicanism 153
  bells 344
  Book of Revelation 87
  candles and lights 241, 273
  carols and music 314, 315, 319, 323, 329, 353
  Catholic Europe 435–8
  children 290–1, 294–5, 440
  fasting 305
  feasts of saints 438
  food and drink 299, 305
  Germany 245, 305, 453, 456
  Latin America 523, 524–8
  Letters of St Paul 86
  Lutheranism 142, 143, 150–1
  Magi 316
  Mass 117, 314
  middle Ages 15, 16, 22
  nineteenth century 40
  plays 22
  poetry and 386, 388
  Scandinavia 453, 456
  Wesley 174
  wreath 141, 151, 291, 433, 436, 453
Advent calendars 142, 151, 436, 452
Advent Conspiracy, US 556–7
advertising
  Christmas trees 271
  commercialization 518
  cultural differences 60
  gifts 278, 282–3, 455–6, 504–5, 553
  music 322, 324, 340
  Santa Claus 260–1
  secular 438
Aeo 4
Africa 500–9
  Catholicism 120–1
  colonialism 53, 54, 449
  culture 248
  gender roles 500
  growth of Christianity 288
  Magi 219, 361
  North Africa 9, 10, 11, 361, 437
  slavery 243, 522, 523, 528–30
Agenzia Fides 433–4
Age of Atonement 41
agriculture 267, 277, 447, 464–5, 490

Ahab 194
Ahaz 69
Alan of Farfa 17
Albert, Prince 27, 32, 43, 268, 271, 476
Alcock, Creina 507
alcohol 171, 299, 500–3, 505, 508, 566, 574
Alcott, Louisa May 44
   Jo's Boys, And How They Turned Out 405
   Little Women 46, 279–80, 403–5
   'Merry's Monthly Chat with His
      Friends' 405
   'Tilly's Christmas' 405
Aleksandrovna, Olga 467
Alexander of Alexandria 106
Alexandria 4, 97, 218
Alito, Judge Samuel 545
Allen, Woody 417
almanacs 323, 552
Alsace 267, 437, 439, 441, 443
Alta Vista, Mexico 240
Alternatives for Simple Living 574
'Amahl and the Night Visitors' (opera)
   (Menotti) 213–14
Ambeli, Evia (Euboea), Greece 135, 136–7
Ambrose, Bishop of Milan 7, 197, 230
   De virginitate 11
   Illuminans Altissimus 11
   Veni redemptor gentium 313
Amenemhet I 4
America, early 30–1
American Church Mission 516
American Civil Liberties Union 544, 570
American Civil War 279, 403, 493, 554
American Sunday School Union 270
Amerigo (horse) 254
Amoris Laetitia (apostolic exhortation) 191
Amsterdam 351, 355, 357, 359
Amun, Temple of 240
Anastasia, St. 117, 434
Andersen, Hans Christian 43–4
   *Christmas Greetings to My English
      Friends* 403
   'The Fir Tree' 402, 403, 452
   'Little Match Girl' 402–3, 453
Andrewes, Launcelot 156, 392
Andrews Sisters 331*t*, 338
Andriake, port of Myra 254, 257

angel chimes 437
Angelou, Maya 386, 393
angels 192–4
   in Andersen 402
   in art 346, 347, 351, 353, 357, 367
   carols 312, 313, 314, 315, 317
   Catholicism 114
   Christmas Angel 439
   Christmas Mass 525–6
   and Cold War 57
   in decoration 437
   Dickson on 173
   Eastern Orthodox Church 132, 134
   fear and 196
   in film 275, 412–13, 555
   Holy Family and 185, 186, 188, 203
   in Luke 7, 12, 81–3, 116, 118, 129, 224, 228,
      231, 232, 584
   Lutheranism 143–5, 146
   and Magi 214, 221–2
   in Matthew 80, 186, 203
   naming 194–5
   Old Testament 68, 193–4, 361
   in plays 373
   Russian Orthodox Church 463
   see also Gabriel
Angels' Hymn 312, 313, 314
Anglican Communion 156
Anglican Convocation 31
Anglicanism 153–65
   Advent 153
   Catholic turn 175
   centrality of Easter 561
   Christmas worship 39, 40
   cultural adaptation 160–2
   Evangelical 154–5, 162
   focus on the Incarnation 156
   'Midnight Mass' 153
Anglo-Catholicism 40, 41, 162
animal masks 22
animals
   in art 233–4
   Feast of Fools 21
   nativity scene 18, 134, 224–5, 227, 233, 291
   rural beliefs 552
   Scandinavia 450, 551
   speaking 20, 28, 441, 447

Annunciation, The 185
  in Acts 105
  in art 102, 200, 346-7
  Asian response 513
  Catholicism 118
  in Luke 83-4, 103-4
  Mass 526
  poetry and 386-7
Anschütz, Ernst 267
Anslem of Canterbury 219
Antioch 12, 86
Antiochian Orthodox Church 424
Antwerp 351, 359
Apostles' Creed 147, 316
Appleton, Thelma 517
Arabian Peninsula 427-8
Archelaus 203, 208, 209
Argentina 257, 306, 526, 528, 579
Arianism 12, 99, 106
Aries, Philippe 93
Aristobulus II 208
Arius 105-6, 255
Arkwright, Sir Richard 177
Armenian Church 12
Armstrong, Isobel 385
Armstrong, Neil 268, 271, 475, 476
art 346-69
  'Adoration of the Magi' (Bosch) 213, 219
  The Adoration of the Magi (Rubens) 359-61
  The Adoration of the Shepherds (La Tour) 353-5
  animals in 233-4
  Annunciation 102, 200, 346-7
  Annunciation (Fra Filippo Lippi) 346-7
  Catholicism and 435
  The Census at Bethlehem (Brueghel) 348, 350f-1
  Chinese 512
  The Circumcision of Christ (van Oostsanen) 355-7
  The Counsel of Salvation and the Visitation (Witz) 348, 349f
  Early Christian 81, 87, 234
  Eastern Orthodox Church 134
  Ghent Altarpiece (Van Eyck brothers) 200
  The Holy Family with the infant St John the Baptist (Murillo) 367-9
  Icon of the Nativity of Christ (Onufri) 133f
  iconography 91, 126, 132, 192, 240, 245-6, 355
  'Intercession Altarpiece' (Witz) 348, 349f
  infant Jesus 93, 234
  Joseph's Dream about the Flight into Egypt (Crespi) 361-3
  Korean 512
  Magi in 217
  The Nativity of Christ (Campin) 351-3
  Nativity scene 225, 227, 233-4
  Rest during the Flight into Egypt (Patinir) 363-5
  The Return from Egypt (Poussin) 365-7
  Santa Claus and 260, 554
  Simeon in the Temple (van den Eeckhout) 357-9
  St. Joseph 189
  St. Nicholas 253, 254-5, 256-8
  Virgin Mary 110
  Vita Christi (Ludolph of Saxony) 365
Asbjørnson, Peter 452
Asbury, Bishop Francis 552
Asia 511-20
  Catholicism 120
  colonialism 53
  commercialization 518-20
  community building 517-18
  growth of Christianity 288
  imperialism 515-16
  Magi 219, 359
  proselytizing 511-15
  rural 519-20
  Shengdan jie 511
  war 516-17
Asia Minor 5
al-Assad, Bashar 429
Assumption of Mary 106, 107, 109
astronomical events 220-1
Atahualpa 525
Athanasius 98-9
atheism 57-8, 560-8, 572-3
Atheist Christmas (organization) 567
Attridge, Harold W. 6
Augustine of Hippo 10, 11, 17, 106, 196
Aurelian, Emperor 8
Auschwitz 56

Australia 54, 257, 306
Austria
    Catholicism 32, 33, 434, 439, 440,
        442–3
    Christmas songs 323–4
    Krampus 262, 450
authoritarianism 519
Autry, Gene 261, 332t, 338–339
Aztec people 528, 576

B

Baba Noel 425–6, 427
Babylonia 244
Bach, Johann Sebastian 141
    Christmas Oratorio 33, 142, 319–20
    Magnificat 142
Baghdad 428
Bailey, Edward 163
Baily, Michael 228
Balaam 23, 72, 215, 217
Banksy 376
Bantu Men's Social Center *see* BMSC
baptism of Christ
    in Acts 84
    Catholicism 114
    children's celebrations 290
    dating of 3–4, 5–7, 12
    Eastern Orthodox Church 127, 128,
        136, 214
    Latin America 523
    Lutheranism 150, 152
    Russian Orthodox Church 464, 466
Baptist Church
    Asia 512–14
    and Christmas 37, 38, 175, 176, 325,
        484, 552
    Santa Claus 573–4
Baran, Henryk 469
Barbarossa, Frederick 218
Barcelona 190
Barker, Ronnie 420
Barnett, James H. 62
Barth, Karl 94
Basel, Council of 23
Basil, St. 136, 137
Basilica of the Hagia Sophia,
    Istanbul 217

Basilica of the National Shrine of the
    Immaculate Conception, Washington,
    DC 108
Basilica of the Nativity, Bethlehem 87, 227
Basilica Sant'Apollinare (Nuovo),
    Ravenna 218–19
Basilidian sect 4
Basilieus catacomb 215
'Battle Hymn of the Republic, The' 554
Baum, L. Frank 408
BBC (British Broadcasting Corporation)
    157, 163, 374, 415, 419–20, 480
Beauvais, France 21, 23, 316, 377
Bede 123, 159, 197, 200, 219, 230
Beecher, Henry Ward 302
Beeton, Isabella 301
Beijing, Tiananmen Square 519
Beirut 426–7
Beleth, Johannes 16, 20
Belk, Russell 35
Bellows, John 37
bells 314, 336, 337, 343–4, 401
Belteine 433
Benedictional of St. Æthelwold 217
Benedict XV, Pope 190
Benedict XVI, Pope 85, 122
Benson, Bishop Edward 45, 157
Benton, Brook 341
Bergman, Ingmar 454, 456
Berlin 55, 455, 460
Berlin, Irving 56, 331t, 335–7,
    343, 555
Berlin Wall 57, 273
Bernard, St. 17, 121–2, 188, 200
Bernardine, St. 189
Bethel 193
Bethlehem 425
    in art 348, 350f–1, 355, 361
    Catholicism and 114, 117, 119, 122,
        437, 441, 443
    cave 227, 233
    and census 203–11, 348
    Eastern Orthodox Church 12, 129–30
    Economy 91
    evidence 6–7
    Hebrew 74
    Las Posadas, Mexico 190

Latin America 526–7
in Luke 87
Lutheranism 147, 149, 152
in Matthew 75, 213
in Micah 3, 70, 80, 232
plays 376
politics 430
in Samuel 80
secularity 562
St. Francis and 18
symbolism 229
Bethlehem, Pennsylvania 269
Better Life Band 431
bible moralisée 74
Birgitta of Sweden 19, 234, 351
Bishop's Wars 169
Black, Charlene Villaseñor 189
Black, Justice Hugo 539–40, 570
'Black Christmas' 496, 577–8
Black Friday 61, 248, 329, 417
Black Madonna 108
Black Power 284
Blackmun, Justice Harry 544–5
Blanchard, Jonathan 37
blasphemy 562
blé de la Sainte-Barbe 433
Bleuler, Eugen 154
BMSC (Bantu Men's Social Center) 505
Bohemia 320
Bok, Edward 283
Bolshevik Party 57, 463, 469–72
Bonaventure 20, 188, 200
Bonch-Bruevich, Vladimir 471
Boniface, St 266
Book of Common Prayer, The 154
Bosch, Hieronymus 213, 219
Boston 40, 324–5, 544, 572
Botte, Bernard 4, 9
bourgeoisie
 charity 278, 279–80, 282, 283, 285
 Christmas trees 437
 Germany and Scandinavia 447–51, 452, 453–4, 456
 Soviet Union 471
Bourges Cathedral 21
Bourne, Reverend Henry 161
Bowie, David 418

Bowler, Gerry 28, 54–5, 58, 179, 258, 262, 446, 459, 491, 550, 575
Boy Bishop 20–1, 316
Boyd, Jimmy 339
Boynton, Susan 21
Bozzuti-Jones, Revd Dr Mark Francisco 110
Bradford, William 28
Branson, Missouri 261
Brazil 243, 524, 526, 527, 528, 529, 576
Bread of Life 85, 229
Bridelius, Fridrich 320
Bright, John 37–8
bris milah (covenant of circumcision) 355, 357
Bristol, England 578
Britain 475–87
 charity 280
 child labour 294
 church attendance 560, 567
 colonialism 477, 500, 501, 509, 513, 551
 decline of Christianity 560–1
 Father Christmas 262
 films 411–12, 415
 food and drink 62, 297, 298, 299, 300–2, 303, 306
 imperialism 31, 54, 156, 173, 477, 480, 493, 513–14
 mumming 161
 opposition to Christmas 155, 168
 Santa Claus 42–3
 sporting events 45
 St. Nicholas 256
 television 419–20
 Theatres Act 374
 world wars 55–6, 457
Brooks, Phillips 38
Brooks, Van Wyck 399
Brown, Charles 340–1
Brown, David 163–4
Brown, Raymond 219, 226
Brown University, Providence, Rhode Island 157
Brueghel, Jan the Elder 234
Brueghel, Pieter the Elder 348, 350*f*–1
Brunner, Bernd 57, 59, 275
Bublé, Michael 331*t*, 332*t*, 333
bûche de Noël (cake) 302, 305–6, 427, 441

Buck, Stuart 539
Buckley, Rev. Dr J. M. 563
Buddhism 518
Buil (Boyl), Bernardo 524
Built of Living Stones (United States Catholic Conference) 119
Bulgakov, Sergei 464
Bunraku (Japanese puppet theatre) 379
Burger, Chief Justice Warren 495–6, 543–4
Burma 513
Burroughs, William 407–8
Bushnell, Horace 97
Bynum, Caroline 97
Byzantine Empire 117, 126, 127, 131, 132, 134, 136, 233
Byzantium 16

C
Cabral, Pedro Álvares 524
Caelius Sedulius 314, 319
Caesar Augustus
   dating of Christmas 3, 9, 100, 146, 217, 366
   census 204, 205–8, 210, 211
   prohibition on child slavery 253
Calculation (or Computation) hypothesis 5, 8, 9–10
Calderwood, David 169
Caldwell, Mary Channen 316
Callahan, Richard 550
Calvin, John 28, 196, 197, 218
Calvinism 28, 36, 158, 169, 179, 299, 573
Campbell, Mark 56–7
Campin, Robert 351–3
Cana, miracle at 5, 11, 12, 186
Canada
   Catholicism 189–90
   Christmas trees 428, 572, 575
   commercialization 574
   food and drink 62, 303
   mumming 161
   rural 552
   St. Nicholas 257
   Thanksgiving 246, 303
Candlemas 161, 435
candles
   in art 351, 352
   Asia 514, 518

Catholicism 118, 436–7
children 290, 291–2
Christingle 154
Eastern Orthodox Church 135, 136
in fiction 403
Irish diaspora 54
Luciatåg 575
Lutheranism 32, 151
Middle Ages 17
in plays 378
tree decorations 142, 266, 268, 269, 273, 448–9, 453
winter solstice 240–1, 245, 248
Cannadine, David 481
Canterbury Cathedral 18, 374
canticles 83, 87, 104, 131, 314, 357
capitalism
   Anglicanism and 155, 162
   Asia 519
   charity and 280
   Christmas trees and 274
   Cold War and 459
   democratization 455
   in film 555
   Holy days and 172
   Leftism and 458
   rejection of 574
   United States 493–4
   Weber on 549–50
Caplow, Theodore 282
Cappadocia 7, 12
Capra, Frank 412, 555–6
Carey, Mariah 332t, 333, 341
Caribbean, The 243, 523, 524, 528–9
Carlyle, Jane 48
Carlyle, Thomas 48
Carmelites 217, 436
carnivalesque revelry 15, 20, 23, 244, 299
Carolina 31
carols and music 311–27, 329–30, 333–5
   A solis ortus cardine 314, 319
   Agincourt Carol 318
   'Angels from the realms of glory' 174
   Anglicanism 154, 163–4
   Ave maris stella 75
   Asia 513–17
   'In the Bleak Midwinter' 293

'Boar's Head Carol' 318
Catholicism 435, 442–3
children 290, 292, 293
Christmas Oratorio (Bach) 33, 142, 319–20
Christmas trees 267, 268
'Christum wir sollen loben schon' 319
Cold War 247
cultural conflict 571, 573
'In dulci jubilo' 317, 319
early modern period 32–3
'From Heaven Above to Earth I Come' 143–5, 290
Germany and Scandinavia 450–1
'Good King Wenceslas' 319, 323
'Hark! The Herald Angels Sing' 174, 322
Intende qui regis Israel 11
'Joy to the World' 174, 320, 331t, 515
Latin America 529
Lutheranism 143–5
Magnificat (Bach) 142
Middle East 431
National Socialism and 458
Nativity scenes 292
nineteenth century 45, 52
nova cantica 316
'Nun komm, der Heiden Heiland' 319
'O Christmas Tree' 450
'O du fröhliche' 321
origins 313–18
Piæ Cantiones 319
printing 318–19
Russian Orthodox Church 465
'Santa Lucia' 450
secular 567, 572
'Sei uns willkommen, Herre Christ' 316
sense of community 479
'Silent Night' 45, 322, 334, 407, 431, 435, 450, 457
'To Shepherds as They Watched by Night' 143
'Tu Scendi dalle Stelle' 321
Veni redemptor gentium 313, 319
'W żłobie leży' 317
'While Shepherds Watched Their Flocks' 320, 321
world wars 55, 56
Carrier, James 280, 282

Casas, Bartolomé de las 524
Cashdollar, C.D. 178
Cassel, Paulus 265
Casti Connubi (papal encyclical) 190–1
Catholicism
adherence to 434
Advent 435–8
carols and music 320
centrality of Easter 561
Christmas trees 266
early modern 27, 29, 30–3
and Epiphany 243
Europe 433–43
feast days 158
food and drink 299, 304, 305, 438, 441
Holy Family 189–91
home 436–41
immigration US 299
Latin America and Caribbean 523–4, 526
Lumen Gentium 106
and Lutheranism 149–50
Marian devotion 107–9
Middle East 426
missionaries 494–5
music and carols 33
nineteenth century 40
paintings 363
public places 441–3
St. Nicholas 438
trees and decorations 269
Yule logs 440–1
Catholic League for Religious and Civil Rights 574
Catholics & Cultures 118
Cave of Treasures 217, 218
Celestine, Pope 11
Celts 433, 440
Certayne goodly carowles to be songe to the glory of God 319
Çevik, Professor Nevzat 257
'Chain of Memory' 567–8
Chaldean Catholic Church 429
Chalcedon, Council of 97, 99, 100, 105–6, 126
Chalcedonian Creed or Definition 98
Chambers, E. K. 376–7
Chan, Rev. Youngman 514
Chanukah 284

charity 277–85
  Anglicanism 162
  Asia 514
  Britain 479–80
  Calvinism 36
  Catholicism 443
  children 294
  Christmas trees and 270, 274, 275
  in Dickens 47
  in fiction 404
  Germany and Scandinavia 452–3, 458
  Lutheranism 148
  Middle Ages 16
  Presbyterianism 173, 176–7
  Salvation Army 178
  secularity and 565
  United States 491, 492–4, 496
  Victorian 476
Charity Navigator 284
Charlemagne 115
Charles I, King 168–9
Charles II, King 29
Charlotte, Queen 268
Chaucer, Geoffrey 318
child labour 36, 294
children 93, 288–96
  in art 351, 369
  Asia 512, 513, 514–15, 518
  angels and 193, 197
  carol singing 479
  carols and music 152, 324, 325–6, 336–7, 338–9, 435
  Catholicism 118–19, 436, 437–40, 442, 443
  charity to 279–80, 292–4, 491–2
  Christingle 153–4
  Christmas trees 268, 269–71, 448
  commercialization and 178, 260–1, 282–3, 485–6, 565
  in fiction 399, 404–5, 408
  in film 413, 415
  food and drink 303
  gifts 29, 31–2, 58, 62–3, 160, 162, 241, 245, 248, 253–4, 258, 278, 284, 429, 442, 447, 448–50, 476
  Holy Family 187
  Lutheranism 143, 151
  meaning of Christmas 294–5

  Nativity plays 191, 376, 439
  nineteenth century 43–5, 92
  participation and agency 290–2
  'patrimonialization' 575
  in plays 379, 380, 381
  in poetry 386, 451
  Scotland 483
  Soviet Union 471–2
  stories 452, 467–9
  see also Sunday schools
chimneys
  Catholicism 440
  Santa Claus 41–2, 63, 326
  St. Nicholas 253, 260, 553
  stockings 245
  Zwarte Piet 263
China
  Catholicism 120
  commercialization 518–20
  cultural conflict 577
  evangelization 511–15
  gifts 284
  Santa Claus 262
  St. Nicholas 257
  Western imperialism 516
China Inland Mission 512
Chiquart, Master 298
chorales 319
Chorus novae Ierusalem (Easter hymn) 67–8
Christianity, global adherence to 288–9, 560–1
Christian Socialism 41
Christingle 153–4
Christkind 260, 277, 284, 440, 447, 449
Christkindel 439
Christmas books 271, 301–2, 401–2, 446, 451–4
Christmas cards
  Asia 512
  commercialization 61, 553
  Germany 467–8
  as gifts 284
  origins 46, 260–1, 443
  Norway 459
  themes of 423, 424
Christmas crackers 45–6

Christmas Eve
    Africa 501, 502, 505
    Anglicanism 153
    Asia 514, 516, 517–20, 577
    Britain 475
    carols and music 334, 338, 344
    Catholicism 118, 119, 269, 434, 435, 440–1
    children 291–2
    Christmas trees 268, 269, 270
    Eastern Orthodox Church 128, 129, 130, 131, 135, 137
    feast day for Adam and Eve 266
    in fiction 401, 409, 468
    in film and television 416, 418
    food and drink 297, 298, 300, 305
    Germany and Scandinavia 447, 449–54, 456, 465
    gifts 32, 54, 142, 277, 278, 281, 284, 447
    Italian fascism 247
    Japan 60
    Latin America 523, 525
    Lutheranism 142, 151
    Middle Ages 20
    Middle East 426, 427, 428, 430
    nineteenth century 45
    Northern Ireland 482
    in plays 378
    in poetry 389
    Russia 467
    social activism 578
    speaking animals 20, 28, 441, 447
    St. Nicholas 260
    Yule log 59
Christmas Eve Mass 427, 428, 430, 482, 520
Christmas markets 52, 151, 277, 284–5, 442, 455, 460
Christmas Mass
    Catholicism 115–18, 119, 120, 315
    Ethiopian Orthodox Church 290
    Latin America 524, 525–6, 528, 529
    Lutheranism 142, 151, 152
    Middle East 428
    Nativity scene 18
    and state 575
'Christmas mood' (*Weihnachtsstimmung*) 52
Christmas trees 265–75
    Berlin Wall 57, 273
    charity and 270
    children 268, 269–71, 448
    cultural conflict 571–2
    decorations and traditions 272–3
    domestication of Christmas 266–7, 270
    early 32
    Europe 267–9
    in fiction 403
    Germany 269–72, 437, 448–9
    Lutheranism 142
    Middle East 425, 427, 428
    nineteenth century 43
    origins 32, 446
    in plays 379
    political aspects 274
    Prince Albert and 476
    public 273–4
    rejected as German 58
    Russia 467, 468, 469
    Scandinavia 448–9
    Soviet Union 58, 471–2
    United States 54, 553
    wars 55, 56, 273
Christmas Truce (1914) 56–7, 273, 457
Christmas Vigil 16, 20, 22, 115, 117–19, 153, 434
Chromatius, Bishop of Aquileia 7
Chronicles, Book of 206
Chronograph of 354 (Philocalian Martyrology) 114
Chrysostom, John 9, 12, 74–5, 196, 197
Church, Francis P. 42, 261
Churchill, Clementine 55
Churchill, Winston 55
Church of England
    accessibility 157, 164
    carols and music 322
    Catholic turn 175
    Christingle 153–4
    commerce 172
    Evangelicalism 154–5, 173
Church of the Nativity, Bethlehem 425, 430
'Church of the Nazaretha,' Durban 509
Church of the Resurrection (Anastasis), Jerusalem 128
Cioffari, Gerardo 255
Clare of Assisi 18

Clark, David H. 221
Clarke, Alison 39
Clement of Alexandria 3
Cline, Austin 566, 567–8
Cluny, Abbey of 20
Cobain, Kurt 407
Coca-Cola Co. 53, 261, 554, 556
Codex Egberti 218
Coimbra, Henrique Soares de 524
Colossians, Epistle to 86, 193
Cold War 53, 57–8, 247, 273, 459
Cole, Henry 46
Coleridge, Samuel Taylor 44, 268
Colijn, Bram 519
Collins, Norman 480
Colombia 527
colonialism
　British 477, 500, 501, 509, 513, 551
　European 53, 54, 244
　Japanese 515
　Portuguese 523
　Spanish 109, 189, 306, 376, 494, 523, 526, 530
Columbus, Christopher 256, 522
commercialism 549–57
　Asia 518
　Black Power and 284
　Calvinism 179
　Eastern Orthodox Church 135
　modern 61
　United States 340, 574
commercialization 60–1
　Asia 511, 518–20
　Christmas trees and 271
　domestication and 260
　Latin America 530
　Middle East 428, 430–1
　nineteenth century 174
　Northern Europe 445, 455, 456
　United Kingdom 476
　United States 178, 299, 549–53, 556–7, 565
communal traditions 44–5, 248, 277, 279, 477–8, 512, 517
Communism
　China 516, 518–20
　East Germany 273, 459
　Germany 458
　Joseph as alternative 190
　Soviet Union 57–8, 262, 463, 469–72
compagnies de jeunesse 22
Cone, James 375
Cong. Globe 539
Congregationalism 37–40, 42, 552
Connell, Martin F. 7, 10, 11–12
Connelly, Mark 45, 162–3, 475–6, 477, 481
conservationism 246
Constantine, Emperor 105, 206, 217, 227, 253, 254–5
Constantinople
　Catholicism 117
　dating of Christmas and 7, 12
　Eastern Orthodox Church 127
　Magi 218
　Russian Orthodox Church 463
　Virgin Mary and 97
Constantinople, Second Council of 98
consumerism 549–57
　Asia 511, 518, 520
　Anglicanism and 155
　children and 294–5, 449
　Japan 60
　Northern Europe 455
　rejection of 574
　secularity and 561, 565–6
　United States 61, 156, 241, 413, 486, 493–4
Conzelmann, Hans 205
Coolidge, Calvin 273
Cooper, Thomas 47
Coptic Orthodox Church 424, 425–6, 429
Corbett, Ronnie 420
Corinthians, Letter to 76, 86, 377, 388
Cornell University 572
Cornwell, Elisabeth 561, 566, 568
Coroa Vermelha, Brazil 524
Cortez, Hernán 524, 525
Coventry, *Corpus Christi* cycle 317
Coventry Carol 317–18
Coward, Noël 412
Cozens, Samuel 175
Cracow, Poland 442
Crawford, Richard 330
crèches *see* Nativity scenes
Crespi, Daniele 361–3
Croix, St. 30

Cromwell, Oliver 155, 320
Cromwell, Richard 155, 320
Crosby, Bing 330–1t, 333, 335–6, 338, 341, 343, 416, 418, 555
Cross, Samuel Hazzard and Sherbowitz-Wetzor, Olgerd P. 463–4
Crump, William D. 527
Cuba 243, 274, 529
cultural imperialism 516
cultural issues 570–9, 581–2
  Africa 502, 504
  Anglicanism 160–2, 163, 164
  Asia 514, 515, 520
  Britain 477, 478, 480, 481–7
  Catholicism 120–1, 123
  childhood 289
  Christmas trees 269–70, 467
  feminism 97
  food and drink 298, 306
  Gabriel 198
  globalization 54–5
  Holy Family 191
  immigration 53
  Judaism 240, 493
  Latin America 522–3, 526–30
  Lutheranism 151
  nationalism 52
  nostalgia 59, 564
  Santa Claus 262
  secularism 60
  totalitarianism 58
  United States 31, 491, 495, 496, 542, 544–5, 553, 555
  winter festivals 241, 242, 243, 247, 248, 568
cummings, e. e. 391
Cyprian of Carthage 9, 293
Cyril 91, 97–8, 100
Czech Republic 262, 434, 438, 576

D

Dale, R. W. 38, 41
Dana, Daniel 37
Daniel, Book of 23, 193–6, 198, 214–15
Dannhauer, Dr Johann 32, 267
dating of Christmas 3–5, 11–12
Daudet, Alphonse 435

David, King 69–70, 79–80, 83–4, 86, 198–9, 204–5, 226–7
Davies, C. M. 39
Davies, Gilbert 312
Davies, Horton 168
Dawkins, Richard 572
dawn mass 16, 17, 115, 117, 434, 525
Day of the Innocents 152
de la Halle, Adam 317
De Pascha computes (anon) 9
de Sales, Francis 121, 189
De solstitiis et aequinoctiis (anon) 9
Deacy, Christopher 160, 497
Dead Sea Scrolls 83
debauchery 30, 161, 465, 483, 489
Deborah 104
December liberty 22
decolonization 480
Ded Moroz (Grandfather Frost) 262, 468, 471, 472, 576
Denha (feast) 6
Denmark 448, 449, 451, 452, 456, 459, 460
department stores
  commercialization and 260, 261, 455, 552–3
  employment in 283
  Evangelicalism and 178
  gifts 241, 440
  parades 552
  Santa Claus 414, 442, 553–4, 555
Derrett, J. Duncan M. 227, 228
Derricotte, Toi 392
Deuteronomy, Book of 193, 293
devil 20, 67, 68, 134, 262, 465
Dickens, Charles
  The Chimes 401
  A Christmas Carol 27, 35, 36, 47–8, 160–1, 277, 279, 294, 300–1, 302, 312, 379, 397, 399–401, 402, 403, 404, 405, 411–13, 417, 476, 492, 553
  All the Year Round 401
  'Christmas Festivities' (later 'A Christmas Dinner') 399
  A Christmas Tree 43, 269
  Christmas trees 45
  The Haunted Man and the Ghost's Bargain 401
  The Pickwick Papers 36
  Sketches by Boz 399

Dickson, William Steel 173
Dies natalis Solis Invicti (festival) 8
Dijon 575
Dijon Cathedral 439
Dio Cassius 209
Directory for Masses with Children 119
Dittenberger, Wilhelm 206
divine Economy 90–1
Doğan, Professor Sema 257
Dobson, James 179
Dolto, Françoise 440
domestic service 454
domestication of Christmas
  charity 279
  children 245
  Christmas trees 270
  commercialization 260
  gender roles 553
  Germany 44, 278
  nineteenth century 45–6, 48, 324
  St. Nicholas 260–1, 491
  United Kingdom 478
  United States 44, 162, 491
Dominicanism 20, 317, 524, 525
Dominican Republic 529
Dorcas Society, York 270
Dorr, Rheta Childe 283
Dostoevsky, Fyodor 468–9
Douglas, Mary 581
Dowley, Tim 291
Dr Seuss 271
Dresden 305
Driskill, J. Lawrence 512, 517
du Boulay, Juliet 128, 135, 136–7
Dublin 40, 278
Duchesne, Louis 5
Dukes, Mark 110
Dumas, Alexander 401–2
Durandus, William 16–17
Durkheim, Émile 495
Dushechkina, E.V. 467, 468
Dutch Netherlands 262
Dzon, Mary 17, 18

E

Eastern Orthodox Church 126–37
  Community celebrations 135–7
  Epiphany 242
  fasting 128
  gifts 126, 135
  hymns 129–31, 132
  iconography 132–5
  and monastic practice 126
  theology and liturgy 127–32
  vigil 153
Easter
  Africa 509
  Anglicanism 163
  Asia 518
  Catholicism 434, 435
  date of 8, 150, 155
  food and drink 426
  Latin America 524
  music 314, 315
  nineteenth century 41
  as *sacramentum* 11
  secularity and 561
East Germany 57, 273, 459
Ecuador 527
Edelstein, Kimberly 542
Edgerton, David 482
Edinburgh 245
Edmund, St. 217
Edward the Confessor, St. 217
Edwards, James R. 206, 208
Egeria 6, 87
Egypt 4–5, 240, 424, 425–6, 428–30
Ekbohrn, Carl 446, 451
Eldridge, Adam and Pappalepore, Ilaria 285
Eli 226
Elijah 197, 204, 355, 367
Eliminationism 564
Eliot, T. S. 156, 271, 392–3
Elizabeth
  art 348, 349f, 367
  Gabriel and 196–9
  Luke 82–4, 204
  Virgin Mary and 9, 104, 186
Elizabeth I, Queen 31
Elizabethan Settlement 156
elka (Russian Christmas tree) 57, 58, 467, 469, 470–2
Elm, Hugo 446, 451
El Salvador 122, 527

Emerson, Ellen Tucker 283
Emerson, Lidian 280-1
Emerson, Ralph Waldo 277, 280-2
Engberding, Hieronymous 9
England
　blasphemy 562
　carnival 22
　carols 33, 318-23
　Christmas trees 268, 270
　Feast of Fools 21
　nineteenth century 35, 38
　nostalgia 398-9, 476
　Parliament 28
　Protestantism 31
　Puritanism 28-9, 168, 550
　Reformation 28
　revelry 161
　religious tolerance 159
　traditions 20, 32, 59, 63, 164, 277
'English Christmas' 35, 52, 298, 300, 306, 418
English Civil War 158-9, 320
English Hymnal 67-8
Enlightenment 172, 173
Enoch, Book of 195
environmentalism 246, 578
Ephesians, Letter to 11
Ephesus, Council of 105-6, 117
Ephrem 5
Epicureanism 566
Epiphanius of Salamis 4-5
Epiphany
　Byzantium 16
　carols and music 315
　Catholicism 114, 434, 435
　dating of Christmas 4, 5, 8, 11, 12
　drama 23
　Eastern Orthodox Church 128
　gifts 284
　Latin America 524, 526
　Letters 86
　loss of importance 299
　Lutheranism 150, 152
　Magi 214
　Middle Ages 23
　Old Testament 72-3
　Russia 466, 473

　spread of 5-7
　winter celebrations 242-3
Episcopalianism 37, 41, 42, 160, 167, 302, 324-5, 561
Epstein, Steven B. 538
Espada, Martín 392
Esther, Book of 583
Ethiopia 291
Ethiopian Orthodox Church 290
Etzioni, Amitai 489
Eucharist
　Anglicanism 153
　Catholicism 117, 121, 123
　Christmas tree and 45, 266, 272
　imagery 33, 229, 233, 234, 353, 355, 365, 390
　Jerusalem 6-7
　Lutheranism 150, 152
　nineteenth century 39
　Old Testament 74
Eucharistic Prayer 115-16, 359, 361
Euripides 231
Eusebius 206, 210
Evangelicalism
　Anglicanism 154, 162
　carols and music 322
　Magi and 218
　nineteenth century 41, 42
　Protestantism 173-4, 175, 177, 178
evangelization 511-15, 516, 519
Eve 67-8, 71, 74-5, 106, 147, 266, 363
evergreens 40, 142, 241-2, 245, 266-7, 269-71, 390, 437
Excerpta et Collectanea 218-19
Excerpta Latina Barbari 218
Exodus, Book of 75, 121, 192, 193, 199, 355
Ezekiel, Book of 192, 195, 230-1, 232

F

Factory Act 36
Fallows, David 318
Familiaris Consortio (papal encyclical) 191
family 61-3
Fang, Frank 577
Fanthorpe, U. A. 156
Farkasfalvy, Denis M. 187
Farrakhan, Louis 577

Farrell, James 494
fascism 247, 248, 412, 458
Fassler, Margot 21, 23
fasting
　Africa 509
　Asia 518
　Eastern Orthodox Church 128
　Egypt 426
　Ethiopian Orthodox Church 290
　food and drink 305
　Iran 518
　Latin America 524, 528
　Middle Ages 15, 16
　Russian Orthodox Church 464
Father Christmas
　Britain 43, 262, 284, 475, 476, 482, 485
　Catholicism and 439
　in fiction 408
　in films 413
　Germany 449
　Middle East 429, 431
　Sweden 454
Fatima, Portugal 109
Faulkner, James 501, 504
Feast of Fools 21–3, 316, 376–7, 397, 435
Feast of Innocents 31
Feast of Stephen 380
Feast of St. Lucy (Santa Lucia) 151, 245, 438
Feast of St. Philip the Apostle 464
Feast of the Ass 21, 316
Feast of the Baptism of the Lord 114, 466, 523
Feast of the Circumcision 313, 316
Feast of the Holy Family 114, 190
Feast of the Holy Innocents 152, 313, 315, 435, 526
Feast of the Seven Fishes 297
Feast of St. Anastasia 117
Feast of St. Andrew 16
Feast of St. Martin 29
Feast of St. Nicholas 245
Feast of the Staff 21
Feast of the Three Kings 272
feasts, early modern period 31, 32, 36, 37
Félibrige movement 436
feminism 97, 109–10, 246–7
Ferris, Kate 247
Fertig, Theresa Kryst 119

fertility rites 33
Festa di Bari 257
Festal Menaion 128–9, 131
Festival of the Incarnation 90, 92
Festivus 249, 555
fiction 397–409
　All the Year Round (Dickens) 401
　The Box of Delights (Masefield) 408
　'The Boy at Christ's Christmas Party' (Dostoevsky) 468–9
　Buddenbrooks (Mann) 453
　The Chimes (Dickens) 401
　A Christmas Carol (Dickens) 27, 35, 36, 47–8, 160–1, 277, 279, 294, 300–1, 302, 312, 379, 397, 399–401, 402, 403, 404, 405, 411–13, 417, 476, 492, 553
　'Christmas Festivities' (later 'A Christmas Dinner') (Dickens) 399
　Christmas Greetings to My English Friends (Andersen) 403
　A Christmas Tree (Dickens) 43, 269
　'The Dead' (Joyce) 406–7
　The Dubliners (Joyce) 406–7
　'En gammeldags Juleafton' (Asbjørnson) 452
　'The Gift of the Magi' (Henry) 406
　'The Fir Tree' (Andersen) 402, 403, 452
　Harry Potter series (Rowling) 408–9
　The Haunted Man and the Ghost's Bargain (Dickens) 401
　He That Should Come (Sayers) 374, 375
　The Hobbit/ Lord of the Rings (Tolkien) 408
　How the Grinch Stole Christmas (Dr Seuss) 271
　Jo's Boys, And How They Turned Out (Alcott) 405
　'The Junky's Christmas' (Burroughs) 407–8
　'Karens Jul' (Skram) 453
　Knickerbocker's History of New York (Irving) 160, 258, 397, 399, 406, 553–4
　The *Life and Adventures of Santa Claus* (Baum) 408
　The Lion, the Witch, and the Wardrobe (Lewis) 408
　'Little Match Girl' (Andersen) 402–3, 453

Little Women (Alcott) 46, 279–80, 403–5
'Merry's Monthly Chat with His Friends' (Alcott) 405
'My Uncle Peter' (MacDonald) 42–3
The Night Before Christmas (Gogol) 465
The Nutcracker and the Mouse-King (Hoffman) 43, 268, 278, 401, 447–8, 452, 467
The Pickwick Papers (Dickens) 36
The Sketch Book of Geoffrey Crayon, Gent (Irving) 36, 46, 397–9
Sketches by Boz (Dickens) 399
'The Tale of the Nutcracker' (Dumas) 401–2
'Tilly's Christmas' (Alcott) 405
'Unter dem Tannenbaum' (Storm) 452
Filastrius of Brescia 11
films 411–20, 481–2, 555–6
   2012 247
   American Graffiti 416
   Annie Hall 417
   Ben Hur 415
   The Bishop's Wife 413
   Blue Skies 336
   Christmas in Connecticut 412
   'Christmas in Dixie' 337
   'Christmas in July' 418–19
   'Christmas Island' 337
   A Christmas Story 416
   Christmas Under Fire 412
   Die Hard 414–15
   Diner 416
   Fanny and Alexander 454, 456
   Elf 261, 272
   A Ghost Story for Christmas 419
   Holiday Inn 335–6, 343, 412, 555
   Home Alone 415
   I'll Be Seeing You 412
   Il Vangelo Secondo Matteo—The Gospel According to St Matthew 415
   In Which We Serve 412
   It's a Wonderful Life 275, 412–13, 555–6
   Lethal Weapon 414
   Life of Brian 561, 562
   Love Actually 372–3
   The Man Who Came to Dinner 412
   The Man Who Invented Christmas 35
   Meet Me in St. Louis 412
   A Miracle on 34th Street 413–4, 555
   Monty Python and the Holy Grail 561
   The Muppet Christmas Carol 413
   Nativity 415
   The Nativity Story 185
   Neptune's Daughter 342
   White Christmas 56, 336, 555
   Nøddebo Præstegård 456
   Peanuts 273
   Planes, Trains and Automobiles 417
   Remember the Night 412
   The Santa Clause 413, 414
   Scrooge 413
   Scrooged 413
   Silent Night, Deadly Night 414
   Tenth Avenue Angel 413
   Trading Places 417
   When Harry Met Sally 416, 417
   World War II 412
Finland 151, 152, 241, 292, 439, 440
Finne, Jaakko 319
fireplaces 59, 136, 245, 253, 258, 306, 439, 440
fireworks 45–6, 120, 552, 582
First World War 43, 55–6, 157, 273, 457–8, 475, 477–8
Fischer, David Hackett 158–9
Five Articles of Perth 31, 169, 377
Flanders, Judith 260
Flerina, E. A. and Bazykin, C. C. 471
Fletcher, Alexander 39
Foitzik, Doris 457, 459
Follen, Charles 44, 270
food and drink 297–307
   Britain 47, 297, 300–2
   baked goods 242, 245, 438, 467
   Catholic Europe 441
   and commercialization 551
   confectionery 298, 299, 440
   and Epiphany 242, 243
   France 305–6
   Germany 304, 305, 453
   immigration 306–7
   medieval aura 297–8
   Middle East 426, 427
   turkey 298, 300–1, 303

food and drink (*cont.*)
    'Twelfth Cakes' 299
    United States 297, 302–5, 337
Foote, George William 562
Forbes, Bruce David 54, 60
Forsyth, Hannah 244
Foster, Don 258–60
Foster, Ernest H. 516
Foster, Laura 280
Fowles, Jib 155–6
France
    Carmelites 436
    carols and music 33, 317, 321, 353, 355
    Catholicism 434–5, 439, 440, 442–3
    Christmas trees 269
    food and drink 33, 305–6
    Lourdes 108–9
    Middle Ages 21–2
    Middle East 427
    Midnight Mass 434
    Père Noël 262, 284
    Revolution 33, 173, 321, 438
    Santa Claus 575
    secularism 442
    St. Nicholas 256, 262
    Virgin Mary 108
Francis, Naila 57
Francis, Pope 122, 191
Francis of Assisi, St. 18, 33, 119, 188, 291–2, 435, 528
Franciscans 19, 291–2, 317, 494, 495, 524
Franco, Francisco 58
Franco-Prussian War 448
Freberg, Stan 340
Freeman, Margaret B. 219
French Revolution 33, 173, 321, 438
Frost, Robert 391
Frosty the Snowman 339
Fulda sacramentary, The 217
'fulfilment quotations' 80
Fuller, Margaret 270
Fulson, Lowell 341

G

Gabriel 192–201
    in art 102, 346
    China and 513
    in fiction 406–7
    in Islam 193
    in Luke 82–4, 104, 132, 203, 204, 207, 392
    Middle Ages 19
    Old Testament 75
    in poetry 386–7
Gagá (dance) 529
Galatians, Letter to 68, 86, 193
Ganna (Ethiopian Christmas Day) 290, 291
Gante, Pedro de 524
Ganulin, Richard 541–2
GARF (State Archive of the Russian Federation) 467
Gaudet, Marcia 243
Gay, John 301
gay rights 573, 578, 579
Geisel, Theodor 549, 556
gender
    Africa 500, 509
    Asia 513
    Christmas trees 448
    gifts 281, 553
    God's covenant with women 193
    Serbia 136
    spirituality 97
    United Kingdom 487
    United States 62, 494
    Virgin Mary 109
Genesis 67–8, 71, 75, 80, 127, 129, 192, 193–4, 195, 196, 197, 266, 293, 355, 582
Gentiles 19, 68, 71, 207, 215, 217, 357
George VI, King 481
Georgian calendar 290
Germantown, Pennsylvania 43
Germany
    Advent 245, 436–7, 456
    American tourism 270
    carols and music 33, 316, 317, 319–20, 321, 450–1
    Catholicism 32
    Christmas cards 46
    Christmas markets 277, 455
    Christmas trees 32, 43, 265–9, 272–3
    Communist Party 458
    domestication of Christmas 44, 278
    emigration to United States 31
    film and television 456

food and drink 304, 305, 453
'German Christmas' 52
gift-giving 282, 284, 457
'Golden Sundays' 456
Herod games 23
Judaism 454, 458
Lutheranism 32
middle-class traditions 447–51
modernization and
  commercialization 454–7
Moravian Church 154
nationalism 457–60
National Socialism 247, 455
Pro-Christkind Association 575–6
Protestantism 31–2
Reformation 28
right wing 459
SPD (Social Democratic Party) 457
stories and national traditions 451–4
unification 52
world wars 55–7
Gerson, Jean 189
Giblin, Charles H. 228, 229
Gibson, James M. 373
Gibson, John 497
gifts and charity 277–85
Gilbert, Adrian G. 217
Giotto 200, 234
globalization 53, 428, 430–2, 477, 485, 512, 518, 530
Globe theatre, London 376
Glorious Revolution 171
Glossa Ordinaria 219
Godehard of Hildesheim 438
Godey's Lady's Book (magazine) 246, 271, 282, 551
Goebbels, Joseph 458
Goethe, Johann Wolfgang von 267–8, 273
Gogol, Nikolai 465
Golby, J. M. and Purdie, A. W. 35, 475
gold, frankincense, and myrrh 213, 214, 277, 353, 562
Golgotha 91, 365
Good Friday 36, 41, 155, 550
Goodland, Katharine 374
Gorsuch, Justice Neil 541, 543
Gospel of Pseudo-Matthew 129

Gosse, Edmund 175
Grandfather Frost see *Ded Moroz*
Greccio, Italy 18, 291, 435
Greece 59, 135, 137
Greek Orthodox Church 137, 427
Greenland 256
Greenpeace 578
Gregory I, Pope 159, 434
Gregory the Great, St. 7, 12, 115, 127, 128, 131, 220, 230
Groton School (Massachusetts) 157
Gruber, Franz 322, 435
Grusman, V. M. 466
Guaraldi, Vince 343
Guerric of Igny 122
guilds 266

H

Haakon, King of Norway 459
Habakkuk 131–2, 233
Hagar 192, 196
Haggai, Book of 73, 146
Haiphong, North Vietnam 517
Hale, Sarah 246, 271, 279
Hall, George and his Orchestra 331t, 338
Hallmark Channel 418–19, 556
Hamlin, David 278
Hamman, Jupiter 389
Hancher, Michael 399
Han Chinese Communism 520
Hannah 200, 226, 582
Hanoi, North Vietnam 517
Hanukkah 240–1, 454, 493–4, 496, 541, 545, 583
Hardy, John 163
Harris, Max 21, 377
Harrison, Michael 478
Hart, Joseph 174
Hastie, W. 92–3
Hayes, David 244–5
Hebrew Bible 71–2, 80, 83, 104
Hebrews, Letter to 86, 116, 129, 194
Hegelianism 41, 95, 385
Helen of Mecklenburg 269
Henry, O. 406
Henry V, King 318
Henry VIII, King 31

Herder, Johann Gottfried 321
Herod, King
   census 203, 208–11
   Coventry Carol 318
   Holy Family 187
   in Matthew 75, 81, 103, 213
   in play 373–4
Herod Archelaus 203, 208, 209
Herod games 23
Herodotus 214
Hesiod 231
High-Priestly Prayer 85
Hijmans, Steven 10
Hilary of Poitiers 219
Hildegard of Bingen 122
Hilton, Boyd 41
Himmler, Heinrich 56
Hinduism 378, 515, 576–7
Hippolytus 9, 10
Hispaniola 522, 524
Historia trium regum (John of Hildesheim) 217, 219
History of Joseph the Carpenter, The 188
History of Religions hypothesis 4–5, 8, 9–10
Hitchens, Christopher 572–3
Hoffman, Ernst T. A. 43, 268, 278, 401, 447–8, 452, 467
Hogmanay 36, 171, 244–5, 483
Hollander, John and McClatchy, J. D. 384
holly
   in Dickens 279, 300
   early modern 32
   medieval 47, 266
   nineteenth century 36, 178
   Scotland 38
   United Kingdom 485
   United States 269
Hollywood Christmas Parade 338
Holstein, Countess Wilhelmine 448
Holy Cross community 108
'Holy Days' 174
'holy exchange' 115–16
Holy Family 185–91
Holy Spirit
   in art 346, 355
   Catholicism 118, 122, 388
   Eastern Orthodox Church 131

   Gabriel 197, 199
   New Testament 80, 81, 82, 83, 203
Homer 79, 231, 365
Hone, William 312
Hong Kong 514, 516
Hooper, Van B. 51–2, 54, 57, 58–9, 60, 61
Hopkins, Gerard Manley 387–8
Hopko, Thomas 463
Horsley, J. C. 46
Horsley, Richard and Tracy, James 161, 162
Hosea 80, 81
Hospinian, Rudolph 29
Howard, Charles W. 261
Hughes, Langston 375–6
Hughes, Shirley 63
Huitzilopochtli 528
Humanism 497, 565
Humboldt, Caroline von 278, 448
Hutchison, Ruth and Adams, Ruth 537
Hutton, Ronald 35, 169, 171, 475
Hyrcanus II 208

I

Ibsen, Henrik 377–8
Iceland 151
Iconoclasm 134
IDF (Israeli Defence Forces) 430
Ignatius 189, 220
Immaculate Conception 107–8, 110
imperialism 53, 464, 480, 481
Incarnation 90–100
   Anglicanism 156, 164–5, 175
   Annunciation 104
   carols and music 324
   Catholicism 113, 116, 117, 119, 120, 122, 123
   Eastern Orthodox Church 127, 131, 134
   Latin America 522–3, 526
   Lutheranism 141
   Middle Ages 17, 19
   nineteenth century 41
   New Testament 86, 230
   plays 371–2
   poetry 386
   Protestant Dissent 173
India 142, 513–15, 518, 576–7
indigenous people 241, 494–5, 509, 513, 522–4, 526–30

Indonesia 576
industrialization
    Christmas trees and 271, 272
    commercialization 454, 552
    effect of 44, 47
    family unit and 190
    gifts 278
    Russia 466
    Southern Africa 500
    spread of Christmas practices 53
Industrial Revolution 160
Ineffabilis Deus (papal encyclical) 107–8
Infancy Gospel of James 221
Infancy Gospel of Thomas 87
Ingersoll, Colonel Robert 563–4
inn 225–7, 348, 351, 375
Innocent III, Pope 15
Inuit people 241
Ion 231
Iran 518
Iraq 428–9, 518, 530
Irenaeus, St. 75, 87
Irving, Washington 41, 44, 278, 302
    Knickerbocker's History of New York 160, 258, 397, 399, 406, 553–4
    The Sketch Book of Geoffrey Crayon, Gent 36, 46, 397–9
Irwin, Kevin W. 117, 119
Isaac 68, 193, 195, 196
Isaiah, Book of 16, 17, 18, 67, 68–9, 70–4, 80, 83, 105, 116, 117, 118, 192, 196, 200, 227, 228, 229, 233, 293, 348, 353, 361
Ishmael 192, 193
Isidore of Seville 17
IS (Islamic State) 424, 428–9, 460
Islam
    Europe 459–60
    Indonesia 576
    Middle East 427, 428, 431, 518
    Q'ran 193
    United States 577
Israeli Defence Forces *see* IDF
Italy
    arrival of Christmas 11
    carols and music 317, 321
    fascism 247
    food and drink 306

Herod games 23
Midnight Mass 434
Nativity scenes 33
Renaissance 233
Santa Lucia 151
Itinerarium Egeriae 6

J

Jackson, Jesse 577
Jacob 194
Jacobus de Voragine 19, 114, 255, 438
Jael 104
Jakubowski, Scott 121
Jamaica 528
James VI of Scotland/ I of England 31, 156, 169, 377
Japan 53, 60, 284, 300, 300, 512, 515–17
Jefferson, Thomas 42, 540
Jenkins, Philip 194
Jennings, Elizabeth 387
Jeremiah, Book of 23, 75, 80, 197, 214, 226, 227, 374
Jerome 187, 228
Jerusalem
    dating of Christmas 12
    Eastern Orthodox Church 128
    Epiphany 6–7
    in Jeremiah 226
    in Luke 207–8
    Masses 525–6
    star 220
Jerusalem Temple 82–3, 241, 357
Jervis, Frank L. 311–12
Jesse 69, 73, 131
Jesuits 494, 524, 527
Job, Book of 194, 228, 230, 233
Johann, Archduke of Austria 269
Johannes de Caulibus 19
Johannesburg 500–6, 507
John, Gospel of 5, 13, 17, 67, 78, 79, 85–6, 86, 87, 90–1, 95, 103, 115, 116, 157, 210, 277, 367, 391
John of Damascus 131
John of Hildesheim 217
John Paul II, Pope 123, 191, 274
John the Apostle, St. 152
John the Baptist 3, 9, 82, 193, 197, 203

John the Evangelist 20
John III, Pope 117
Johnes, Martin 55, 61, 62–3
Johnson, Edgar 403
Johnston, Brian 379
Jones, Brian Jay 556
Jones, Charles W. 41, 260, 553
Jonkonnu (dance) 528–9
Jonson, Ben 31, 377
Joseph, brother of Jesus 78
Joseph, husband of Mary 187–8
   in art 347, 348, 351, 353, 355, 357, 359, 361–3, 365, 367, 369
   Catholicism and 191
   census 203, 205–6, 208–9, 211
   Coptic tradition 188
   Eastern Orthodox Church 134
   importance of 188–91
   Middle Ages 19, 23, 189–90
   Nativity 225, 227, 230
   New Testament 78–9, 80, 81, 83, 103, 104, 185–6
   nineteenth century 190
   in plays 376
Josephus 208–10, 220
Joyce, James 406–7
Jubilees, Book of 195–6
Judaism
   angels 193–4, 195, 201
   in art 355
   census 208, 210, 211
   Eastern Orthodox Church 131
   Germany 454
   gift-giving 284
   Hanukkah 240–1, 496
   Magi 220–1
   Middle Ages 19
   Nazism 56, 458
   New Testament 80, 82, 83, 84, 103, 204–5, 225, 226
   Old Testament 71–2
   religious feasts 581–2
   United States 493, 542, 544–5, 551, 555, 570
Judas the Galilean 208, 209
Judges, Book of 104, 194, 197
Judith 104

julebukken (Christmas goat) 450, 551
Julian, Emperor 10
Julian calendar 5, 8, 127, 244, 290, 470, 528
jultomten (*julenisse*) (house goblin) 450
Justin Martyr 6, 87, 216, 227
Justinian 217

K

Kagan, Justice Elena 543
Kalends 21, 22–3, 440, 441, 443
Kallenbach, Ulla 378
Kaltenbach, Chris 248
Kang, Jie 519
Karenga, Maulana 248, 496
Karnak, temple of 240
Kaufman, Cathy 304
Keates' Drift 506–8
Keble, John 40
Kelly, Joseph 490
Kempis, Thomas à 106
Kenney, Theresa 18
Kensington, Maryland 574–5
Kepler, Johanes 220–1
Keyte, Hugh and Parrot, Andrew 317
Kierkegaard, Søren 96, 97
Kim Ki-Chang 512
King's College, Cambridge 53, 54, 67, 71, 156–7
Kirkland, Caroline 282
Kitt, Eartha 339
Klassen, Pamela and Sheer, Monica 460, 555
Knock, Ireland 109
Knox, John 28
Knut's Day, Sweden 453
Kobe, Japan 515
Koester, Helmut 206, 207
Koliada (festival) 465
Komsomol 470
Kontakion on the Nativity 130
Korea 512, 515, 517–18
Kosmas the Melodist 127, 131–2
Krampus 449–50
'Kriegsweihnachten' (War Christmas) 457, 459
Krimmel, John Lewis 269
Kris Kringle 260, 414, 554
Kristkindl 32

Ku Klux Klan 496
Kuper, Hilda 508
Kwanzaa 248, 284, 496–7, 577

L

Lagueux, Robert 312, 315
Laine, Frankie 341
Lane, Christel 58
Lang, Gerhard 436
Laon Cathedral 21, 22–3, 315–16
Lapland 241
Larkin, Peter 390
Last Supper, The 226
Latimer, Hugh 30
Latin America 522–30
  Advent 526–7
  Afro-Latin American 526
  dance and music 528–9
  fasting 528
  Holy Family 190
  indigenous people 527, 528, 529–30
  Nativity scenes 527–8
  slavery 528–9
  Mass 523–4
  religious pluralism 530
la Tour, George de 353–5
Laval, Francois 189–90
Lawrence, Edna 515
Lebanon 426–7
Lebrun, Françoise 29
Lee, Brenda 272, 332t, 333
Lee, Robert 176
Lenin, Vladimir 57, 469, 470, 471, 472
Leo I, Pope 11, 121, 122, 216, 219
Le Puy 316
Les-Baux-de-Provence 436
Lévi-Strauss, Claude 439
Lewis, C. S. 408
Liberius, Bishop of Rome 11
light 581
  in art 234, 353, 367
  Asia 516, 517, 518
  baptism and 6, 7
  Catholicism and 118, 121, 122, 437, 441–2
  Christmas trees 43, 56, 63, 266, 273, 274
  Eastern Orthodox Church 128, 132, 134–5
  electric 53, 273, 454

Feast of St. Lucy 245, 438
  in fiction 402–3
  Lutheranism 32, 141–2, 151
  Middle Ages 17
  Middle East 425, 429
  music 338
  Northern Europe 450, 453, 457
  Old Testament 73
  poetry 391, 394
  star 220, 221
  United States 545, 555, 571–2
  winter festivals 155, 240–1, 245, 247, 248, 305
Liguori, Alphonsus 321
Lindholm, Paul and Clara 517
Linyi, China 519–20
Lippi, Fra Filippo 346–7
Liszt, Franz 269
Liturgy of the Hours 114–15
Livingston, Henry 258–9
Llewellyn, R. S. 316
Löfgren, Orvar 449, 456
Lord Chamberlain 374
'Lord of Misrule' 161, 244
Lot 192
Louisiana 243, 304
Lourdes 108–9
Loyola, Ignatius 363, 527
Lucia, St. 54, 151, 245, 292, 299, 450, 456, 575
ludi (games) 22–3
Ludolph of Saxony 365
Luke, Gospel of 3, 7, 11, 12, 67, 72, 77–8, 79, 81–5, 87, 103–5, 116–19, 129, 132, 143, 145, 173, 185–7, 193, 194, 195–201, 203–11, 225–34, 312, 348, 357, 361, 582, 584
Luther, Martin 141–2, 143–50
  Christmas trees 32, 266
  gifts 277
  hymns 290, 319
  Magi 218, 220
  Virgin Mary 107
Lutheranism 141–52
  Advent 150–1
  children 294
  Christmas tree 43
  Evangelicalism 150

Lutheranism (*cont.*)
  gifts 32, 142
  light 141–2
  'Midnight Mass' 153
  music 141, 319
Lux Mundi 41
Luz, Ulrich 220

M

Macau 520
MacDonald, George 42–3
MacQuarrie, John 92
Macy's 216, 414, 554, 555
Magdalen College School, England 157
Magi 213–22
  in art 19, 61, 434
  carols and music 312, 315, 319
  Catholicism and 437, 440, 443, 443
  dating of Christmas 5, 7, 11, 12
  drama 23, 436
  Eastern Orthodox Church 129, 134
  Epiphany 242
  fiction 406
  gifts 277
  New Testament 80–1, 224
  Latin America 528
  in poetry 392–3
Maine, University of 571
de Mal Lara, Juan 363
Malachi, Book of 197, 365
manger 227–9
  in art 233–4, 361
  carols and music 317
  Catholicism and 33, 117, 119, 269
  Eastern Orthodox Church 132
  Latin America 527–8
  in Luke 72, 81, 82, 87, 225
  Lutheranism 149
  Middle Ages 17–18, 23
  Old Testament 230, 233
  relic of 434
Manifest Destiny 246
Mann, Kristin 494–5
Mann, Thomas 453
Manoah 196, 197
Mansbridge, Joanna 381
Maori people 45

Marbach, Johannes 265
Marcus, Leah 377
Marie of Oignies 19
Mark, Gospel of 78–9, 80, 85, 88, 102–3, 204, 226
Marks, Johnny 261, 338
Marling, Karal Ann 271, 279, 280, 282, 283, 554
Maronite Church 426
Maroun, St. 426
Marseille 33, 443
Marsh, L. 424
Martineau, Harriet 270
Martineau, James 173
Martinique 243
Marty, Martin 551
Marxism 574
Mary, Queen of Scots 169
Mary, Virgin *see* Virgin Mary
Maryland 30
Mary Magdalene 103
Mary, Our Lady of Guadalupe 108
Masefield, John 374–5, 408
Massachusetts 28–9, 158, 170
Massachusetts Bay Colony 556
mass media 241, 271, 329, 335, 455, 456, 478, 549
Mass of the Boy Bishop 20–1
matachín dance 528
Mather, Cotton 30, 161, 171, 552
Mather, Increase 30, 161, 171
Matthew, Gospel of 3, 5, 7, 23, 42, 67, 70, 72, 74, 75, 77–81, 103–4, 118, 119, 129, 185, 186, 188, 193, 203, 204, 206, 209, 213–22, 232, 277, 315, 361, 368, 373–4, 391, 439
Matthews, John 240, 241
Maurice, F. D. 48
Mauss, Marcel 492
May, Robert L. 261, 338
Mayan Long Count calendar 247–8
McCartney, Paul 344
McCook, Nebraska 311
McKee, Joseph 177
McKibben, Bill 574
McMillan, William 169
McVey, Kathleen E. 6
Meditationes Vitae Christi 19

Medjugorje, Bosnia and Herzegovina 109
Meintjes, Louise 507
Meisenthal, France 437
Mendelson, Lee 556
Menino, Thomas 572
Mennonites 574
Merwin, W. S. 386, 393
Methodism 153, 173–4, 282, 325, 514, 516, 552
Mexico
    art 189
    festivals 190, 526, 528, 530
    gifts 284
    Masses 527
    nationalism 576
Micah, Book of 3, 67, 70, 71, 80, 205–6, 215, 232
Micaiah 194
Michael the Archimandrite 252–3
Michels, Thomas 11
Middle East 423–32
Midnight Mass 16–18, 30, 39, 153, 434–5, 482, 524
Mikkonen, Ilona and Baide, Domen 249
Milan 7, 11
Miles, Clement 30, 32, 265–6, 267, 446
Miller, Daniel 60, 61, 448, 484
Miller, Jon 329
Miller, Rabbi Mark 571
Miller, Samuel 175
Milner-White, Eric 157
miracles, Christmas as time of 19–20
Misa de aguinaldos 527
Misa de Gallo 116, 435, 525
missionaries 156, 159, 174, 494–5, 504, 511–18, 520, 527–8
Mistral, Frédéric 436, 440
Mitchell, Nathan 107
Moe, Jørgan 451
Moeran, Brian and Skov, Lise 60
Mohr, Josef 45, 435
Moko Jumbie (feast) 529
Molanus, Johannes 189
Monophysitism 106
Montesinos, Antonio de 524
Montgomery, James 174
Montini, Giovanni Battista (later Pope Paul VI) 123

Moody, Dwight L. 176–7
Moore, Clement Clark 41–2, 160, 245, 258–9, 265–6, 269, 326, 338, 384, 405, 439, 446, 491, 553
Moore, Tara 385
Moravian Church 154, 269
Morecambe, Eric and Wise, Ernie 419–20
Morley, Janet 164
Morris, Desmond 164
Moses 80, 131, 193, 196
Mosul, Iraq 428–9
Mount Nhlangakazi 509
Mrs Beeton's Christmas Book 301–2
Mubarak, Mohammed Hosni 429
Muhammed 193
mumming 22, 161, 377, 449–50, 551–2
Murillo, Bartolomé Estéban 368–9
Mussolini, Benito 58
Myra 252, 254, 256–7
Mystery Plays 266, 351, 390, 435
mythology, classical 87, 231, 232, 367

N

Nahua people, Mexico 528
Nanjing (Nanking) 516, 519
Naples 33
Nast, Thomas 260, 554
National Socialism *see* Nazism
nationalism 52–3
    Asia 515
    carols and music 318, 321
    Mexico 576
    nineteenth century 58
    Northern Europe 265, 449, 452, 457
National Socialism *see* Nazism
Nativity plays 22, 154, 191, 290, 372–6, 415, 528
Nativity scenes (crèches) 224–34
    Anglicanism 164
    animals 233, 234
    Catholicism 119, 435–6, 437–8, 442, 443
    children 291–2
    cultural issues 572, 579
    fabricated 33
    in film 415, 562
    inn 225–7
    Latin America 525, 529

Nativity scenes (crèches) (cont.)
  manger 227-9
  Middle Ages 188
  Middle East 426-7, 429
  plays 373
  Shepherds 231-3
  St Francis 18
  Supreme Court ruling 274, 495-6, 543-6, 570
  swaddling cloths 229-31
  symbolism 191
Navidad 522
Nazareth 70, 78, 80, 205, 346
Nazism (National Socialism) 58, 247, 284, 412, 455, 458-9
Neale, John Mason 319, 323
Nebuchadnezzar, King 214-15
Nehemiah, Book of 194
Nekrasov, Nikolai 468
Nelson, Elizabeth White 282
Neopaganism 246-7
Nestorius 91, 97-8, 106
Netherlands 262, 351, 359, 439, 576
New England
  Christmas trees 270, 572
  music 33, 174
  prohibition of Christmas 28-9, 155, 158, 170-1, 299, 551
Newfoundland, Canada 552
Newgrange, Ireland 240
Newman, John Henry 40
New Orleans 30, 243, 244, 304
New Spain 494-5, 526-7
New Year
  Eastern Orthodox Church 126
  Europe 439, 440, 441
  fiction 402, 405
  gifts 126, 278, 440, 447, 493
  Lutheranism 152
  Middle Ages 21
  nineteenth century 46
  Scotland 171, 483
  Soviet Union 57-8, 274, 471-3, 576
  winter festivals 244-5
New York 41, 279
New York Historical Society 257-8
New Zealand 37, 44, 45

Ngwane, Zolani 507
Nicaea, Council of 8, 99, 105, 255
Nicaragua 526
Nicene Creed 99, 118, 255
Nicholas, St. 252-7
  in art 253, 254-5, 256, 257-8
  Council of Nicaea 255
  cultural issues 575-6
  domestication of Christmas 260-1, 491
  in fiction 160, 406
  gifts 41-2, 253-4, 260, 277
  popularity 255-7
  praxis de stratelatis 254-5
  relics 257
  Russia 468
  to Santa Claus 252-63
  United States 553-4
Nicholson, Steve 374
Nikodemos the Hagiorite 131, 132
Nîmes, France 22
Nine Lessons and Carols, service of 53, 54, 55, 67-8, 156-7
Nissenbaum, Stephen 30, 44, 45, 160, 161, 245, 258-9, 270, 278, 279, 280, 455, 459, 490, 491, 551, 552
Nixon, President Richard 517
Noah 219
Nocent, Adrien 117
non-Trinitarianism 52
North Africa 9, 10, 11, 361, 437
Northern Ireland 482
North Vietnam 517
Norway 43, 54, 307, 445, 449, 450, 459, 575
nostalgia 583
  Anglicanism 154, 155
  Christmas tree 267, 448
  fiction 397-8, 406-7
  film 416
  gifts 284
  music 336, 481
  Northern Europe 452, 455
  United Kingdom 484
  United States 497
Notre-Dame, Paris 315
Nova Scotia, Canada 572
Nuevo Mexico 495
Numbers, Book of 72, 196, 199, 215, 217

Nunc Dimittis 83, 357, 361
Nutcracker, The (ballet) 343, 401–2
Nyström, Jenny 452

O

O'Connor, Justice Sandra Day 541, 544–5
Octavian (later Caesar Augustus) 204, 205
Odo of Sully 21
Old Testament, messianic significance
    of 67–76
Onufri 133*f*
Optatus, Bishop of Milevis 11
Orientibus partibus 21
Origen 4, 87, 216, 219–20, 221, 227, 228
Ostwalt, Conrad 557
otherness 375
Our Lady of Ferguson 110
Ovid 241, 361, 440, 443
Owens, W. H. 478
Oxford Movement 40, 270, 322, 323

P

Padua 20, 23
paganism
    amalgamation of festivals 4–5, 8, 10, 136,
        155, 159, 164, 170, 446–7, 450
    art 234, 361, 365
    and dating of Christmas 30
    light 141, 155, 437
    Magi and 216, 217
    Nazism 457, 458
    Russia 465, 470
    Sol Invictus 8, 10, 128
    Teutonic 265
    winter festivals 242, 246–7, 390, 400, 563
Pageant of the Shearmen and Tailors,
    Coventry 317
Pakistan 241
Palestine 423–5, 430, 579
Palestinian Targum 215
Palmer, George 30
Panama 525, 526, 527
Pané, Ramón 524
Panquetzaliztli (festival) 528
Paradise Tree 266
Paravisini-Gebert, Lizbeth 243
Paris 21, 22, 442

Parker, David 398, 399
Parousia *see* Advent
Pascha 12
paschal tables 8
Passion, foreshadowing of 18, 91, 230, 355
Passover 5, 8, 45, 83, 155, 196
Pastorale Maurel 443
Pastorelas (religious dramas) 443, 495, 527
pastrage 436
Patara 252
Patinir, Joachim 363–365
'patrimonialization' 575–6
Patristics 9, 17, 74, 90–1, 93, 99, 131, 197, 225
Paul, St. 68, 71, 75–6, 84, 86, 88, 204, 207
Paul VI, Pope 118, 123
Paulding, James K. 258
Pawle, Gerald 55
Pawtucket, Rhode Island 274, 495–6, 543
Pax Romana 204
Pearl Harbor 336, 517
Pearson, Joanne and Pike, Sarah M. 247
Peirce, Arthur 565
Peirce, James 172
Pensom, John 153
Pentecostalism 355, 509, 530
Perabo, Lyonel 446
Perry, Joe 52, 56, 57, 247, 266, 282, 284,
    446, 448
'Personal or Hypostatic Union' 99
Peru 525, 528, 529
Peter, First Epistle of 84, 86, 424
Peter Chrysologus 214
Peter Damian 17
Petri, Theodoric 319, 323
Petrone, Karen 472
Petrus de Natalibus 255
Phelps, Fred 573–4
Philippians, Letter to 18, 91
Philippines 119, 376, 517
Philo 215, 232
Philocalian Calendar 7–8, 114, 434
Piccolomini Castle, Celano 436
Pierce, Franklin 273
Pilcher, Carmel 121
Pimlott, J. A. R. 169
Pintard, John 257–8
Pittsburgh 544–5, 570

Pius IX, Pope 107–8, 190
Pius XI, Pope 191
Pizarro, Francisco 525
Plato 220, 232
Plaut, Rabbi Joshua 493, 555
plays 371–81
   celebration and performance 376–9
   Black Nativity (Hughes) 375–6
   Christmas as gathering time 379–81
   Christmas, His Masque (Jonson) 31, 377
   The Coming of Christ (Masefield) 374–5
   Danielis Ludus 23, 377
   A Doll's House (Ibsen) 378–9
   Double Nora 378–9
   Gijsbrecht van Amstel (van den Vondel) 359
   Interfectio puerorum 23
   Love (Zeldin) 381
   The Long Christmas Dinner (Thornton) 380–1
   The Long Christmas Ride Home (Vogel) 379–80
   liturgical 15, 18, 22–3, 435
   non-Western contexts 378
   N-Town Plays 373–4
   Officii Stellae 23
   Officium pastorum 22
   Ordo Joseph 23
   Ordo Prophetarum 22, 315
   Ordo Rachelis 23
   Ordo Stellae 315–16
   representations of Christ 374
   Second Shepherds' Play 373
   Towneley plays 373
   Twelfth Night (Shakespeare) 377
Pleck, Elizabeth 278, 496
Plymouth, Massachusetts 246
Plymouth Brethren 175
poetry 384–95
   'Advent (Earth grown old)' (Rossetti) 388
   'The Annunciation' (Jennings) 387
   'The Blessed Virgin compared to the Air we breathe' (Hopkins) 387–8
   'Carol of the Three Kings' (Merwin) 386, 393
   'A Christmas Carol' (Rossetti) 293
   'Christmas Eve' (Rossetti) 389
   'Christmas Eve: My Mother Dressing' (Derricotte) 392
   'Christmas Trees' (Frost) 391
   'An Evening Thought: Salvation by Christ with Penitential Cries' (Hamman) 389
   'Imagine the Angels of Bread' (Espada) 392
   Journey of the Magi (Eliot) 392–3
   'little tree' (cummings) 391
   'Love came down at Christmas' (Rossetti) 90–1
   'The Mother of God' (Yeats) 386, 387
   'The Nativity of Our Lord and Saviour Jesus Christ' (Smart) 393–4
   'The Night Before Christmas' (anon) 258–60
   'praying // firs \\ attenuate' (Larkin) 390
   'Red-Nosed Frost' (Nekrasov) 468
   'Tomten' (Rydberg and Nyström) 452
   'A Visit from St. Nicholas' (Moore) 41, 245, 326, 338, 405, 406, 491, 553–4
   'Weihnacht-Abend' (Tieck) 452–3
   'you must walk this lonesome' (Shockley) 389–90
Poland 56, 317, 434
Polhill-Turner, Cecil 512
polyphony 315, 318, 320
Pompey 208
Pomykalski, Wanda 55
popular songs
   'All I Want for Christmas is You' 333, 341
   'Baby, It's Cold Outside' 332t, 342
   'Blue Christmas' 340
   'The Chipmunk Song' 339–40
   'The Christmas Song' 337
   'The Christmas Waltz' 337
   'Christmas Time is Here' 343–4
   'Do They Know It's Christmas?' 340
   'Do You Hear What I Hear?' 334
   '(Everybody's Waiting for) The Man with the Bag' 339
   'Feliz Navidad' 337
   'Green Chritma' 340
   'Have Yourself a Merry Little Christmas' 336
   'Here Comes Santa Claus (Right Down Santa Claus Lane' 338
   Højt fra træets grønne top 449

'A Holly Jolly Christmas' 332t, 337
'I'll Be Home for Christmas' 336
'I Saw Mommy Kissing Santa Claus' 339
'It's Beginning to Look a Lot Like Christmas' 339, 343
'It's the Most Wonderful Time of the Year' 337
'I've Got My Love to Keep Me Warm' 342
'Jingle Bell Rock' 337
'Jingle Bells' 337
'Jolly Old Saint Nicholas' 338
'Last Christmas' 342
'Let It Snow! Let It Snow! Let It Snow!' 342
'The Little Drummer Boy' 293, 334
'Mary's Boy Child' 334
'Merry Christmas Baby' 341
'Merry Christmas Darling' 340
'Mrs. Fogarty's Christmas Cake' 303–4
'Nu är det Jul igen' 450–1
'Nuttin' for Christmas' 339
'O Tannenbaum' 267, 440
'Rockin' around the Christmas Tree' 272
'Rudolph the Red-Nosed Reindeer' 332t, 338–9
'Santa Baby' 339
'Santa Claus is Coming to Town' 338
'Silver Bells' 332t, 339
'Star of Wonder' 394
'Up on the Housetop' 338
'White Christmas' 330, 333, 335–7, 340, 343, 555
'Winter Wonderland' 337, 342
'Wonderful Christmas Time' 344
'Yankee Doodle Yiddishkeit' 555
'You're All I Want for Christmas' 341
Portugal 434, 435, 523–4, 525, 529
Posada, La (celebration) 527, 528
Postyshev, Pavel 471
Poussin, Nicolas 365–7
Powell, Mark A. 215
Prague 436
praxis de stratelatis 254–5
Presbyterianism
  carols and music 324
  dissent 167–8, 169, 171–3, 175–7
  mainstream 483–4
  nineteenth century 36, 37, 40, 42

Prescott, William H. 525
Presley, Elvis 332t, 340
Priene inscription 206
'Primary Chronicle' 463–4
print media
  magazines 59, 60, 246, 271, 278, 282, 303, 405, 451–2, 485, 496, 553, 554
  newspapers 35–6, 37, 241, 248, 261, 278, 280, 282, 303, 311, 322–7, 374, 446, 455, 458, 469, 482–3, 563
Protestantism 27–34
  in art 351, 363
  carols and music 329
  and Catholic practice 40, 436–7, 439, 574, 581
  Christmas trees 43, 265, 266, 268, 270
  commercialization and 549–50, 552, 555
  feminization of Christ 97
  food and drink 305
  Latin America and Caribbean 530
  Middle East 431
  music 33, 320
  Reformed and Dissenting 37–40, 42, 45, 48, 155–6, 167–79, 322, 324
  Virgin Mary and 105, 106–7, 110
Protevangelium of James 84, 87, 129, 130, 134, 199, 227, 230
Provence 306, 433, 435–6, 440, 441, 442
Proverbs, Book of 99, 228, 233
Prudentius 313–14
Prynne, William 168–9
Psalmes, or Songs of Sion 320
Psalms 33, 73, 193, 194, 199, 217
Pseudo-Bonaventure 367
public holidays and the law 537–46
  Christmas as federal holiday 538–43
  crèche and tree cases, US 543–6
Puerto Rico 284
Purification of Mary 16
Puritan Commonwealth 28, 31, 299, 320
Puritanism
  commercialization and 549–50
  opposition to Christmas 28–32, 158–9, 161, 168–71, 244, 302, 397, 551

Q

Qatar 424–5
Q'ran 193

Quakerism 37, 159
Quebec 189–90
Queen's College, Oxford 298
Quintilius 208–9
Quirinius 208–211
Qumran 83, 195

R

Rachel 23, 80, 315–16
racism 262–3, 392, 439, 484, 500, 506
Raheb, Revd Dr Mitri 423
Rampersad, Arnold 375
Randolph, Vance 552
Rathey, Markus 319
Rätsch, Christian and Müller-Ebelin, Claudia 242
Ratzeburg, Germany 44, 268
Read, Daniel 321
'Red Christmases' 470, 514, 516
Redding, David A. 386
Redemptoris Custos (apostolic exhortation) 191
Reformation 27–34
    carols and music 318–19
    celebrations 159
    gifts 142
    liturgy 150–1
    missionaries 513
    Nativity scenes 436
    Rosary 107
    St. Nicholas 439
Regan, Patrick 114
Regulation of Mills and Factories report 172
regulative principle 168
relics 18, 159, 218, 438
religious scandals 189
Restad, Penne 46, 260, 492, 552
Restoration 28–9, 171, 299, 320
Resurrection 37, 77, 86, 103, 134, 149, 230, 434, 529
Revelation, Book of 87, 88, 106, 192, 193, 194, 348, 388
revelry
    Anglicanism and 161–2
    Epiphany as end of 242–3
    in fiction 398
    Middle Ages 15, 313

Proestant Dissent and 175
Puritanism and 28, 30, 158
reversals 20, 104, 155, 161, 244, 316, 377
Rhoads, John H. 209–10
Richard II, King 217
Richards, Katharine Lambert 40, 175–6
Rinden, Gertrude Jenness 514
Río de la Plata 528
Rist, John M. 208–9
ritualism
    Africa 508
    Anglicanism 40, 174–5
    Christmas trees 268, 275
    food 441
    swaddling 229
    winter festivals 240–1, 247–9, 445
Robinson, Benjamin 172
Rockford, Illinois 40
Roll, Susan K. 11
Roman de Renart 441
Roman Empire
    census 205–8
    children and 292–3
    and Christianity 254
    festivals 29, 175, 241, 299, 415, 441
    Kalends 21, 22–3, 440, 441, 443
    in Luke 204
    North Africa 437
    public holidays 537–8
    Saturnalia 29, 175, 241, 299, 415, 441
Romania 247
Roman Missal 114, 115–16
Romanos the Melodist 130–2
Romans, Letter to 68, 75, 207
Romanticism 270, 298, 322, 457
Rome 7–8, 12
Romero, Óscar 122
Roosevelt, President Franklin 248
Rosary 107
Roscoe, Edmund S. 38
Rossel, Sven H. and Elbrønd-Bek, Bo 453
Rossetti, Christina 90–1, 100, 293, 388–90, 393
Rouen 315, 373
Rousseau, Jean-Jacques 321
Rowling, J. K. 408–9
Royalists 158–9, 169, 302

Rubens, Peter Paul 359–61
Rudolf the Red Nosed Reindeer 261
Rumbaugh, Melinda L. R. 59
Russell, Conrad 168
Russia 57, 463–73
   Baptism of Christ 464, 466
   Bolshevik Revolution 469–70
   Christmas cards 467–8
   Christmas Eve 467
   Christmas in city 466–9
   elka (Christmas tree) 57, 58, 467, 469, 470–2
   Epiphany 466
   fasting 464
   German immigration 467
   gifts 467
   Great Blessing of Water 466
   industrialization 466
   Nativity 464–6
   newspapers 469
   pre-Christian Slavs 465
   Revolution 1905 469
   Revolution 1917 464
   rural 463–6
   urbanization 466, 468
   'Westernizers' 466–7
Russian Orthodox Church 463–6, 470–3
Russo-Japanese War 469
Ruth 68, 115
Rydberg, Viktor 451–2

S

Sabbath 29, 168, 170, 172, 229, 538
Sabinus 209–10
'Sacramental Principle' 92
Saint Augustine, Florida 30
St. Peter's, Rome 434
Sales, Francis de 121, 189
Salome 353
Salvation Army 42, 177–8, 503
Salve Regina 353
Samain 433, 440
Samson 196, 197, 198
Samuel, Book of 80, 200, 206, 215, 226, 582
Sand, George 439
Sandblom, Haddon 53
Sandys, William 312, 313, 323

San Francisco 270
San Nicolò al Lido, Venice 257
Sansom, Ian 302
Santa Claus 257–60
   American representation 53
   Anglicanism 160
   charity 41–3, 245, 493
   cultural issues 573, 574–5
   department stores, USA 553–4
   domestication 44, 162
   family-focused 491–2
   and Father Christmas 476
   in film 261
   gifts 241, 282, 439
   international 262–3
   letters to 261, 440
   'patrimonialization' 575–7
Santa Claus, Indiana 261
Santa Claus Society 43
Santa Lucia 151
Santa Maria Maggiore, Rome 18, 434
Santiago de Compostela, Spain 21
Sarah 197, 204
Satan 67–8, 206, 207
Saturnalia 29, 175, 241, 299, 415, 441
Saudi Arabia 427
Saussure, César de 301
Sayers, Dorothy L. 371, 374, 375
Scalia, Justice Antonin 541
Scaliger, Joseph 294
Scandinavia 445–60
   food and drink 453
   carols and music 450–1
   Christmas Eve 453–4
   Christmas markets 455
   commercialization 454–7
   education 575
   film and television 456
   food and drink 306–7, 453
   gifts 449–50
   mass media 455
   middle-class traditions 447–51
   national traditions 451–4
   politicization of Christmas 458
   St. Lucia 54, 151, 245, 292, 299, 450, 456, 575
Schillebeeckx, Edward 92

Schleiermacher, Friedrich 44, 45, 47, 92–7
Schmidt, L.E. 167, 172, 178, 278, 493, 550, 552
Schmidt, Thomas C. 10
Schöch, Immanuel 284
Schulz, Charles M. 556
Scotland 483–4
  First Book of Discipline 28
  Hogmanay 244–5
  James VI and 31
  national holiday 178
  newspapers 36
  nineteenth century 38
  outlawing of carols 320
  Presbyterianism 167, 169, 176
  Reformation 169
Second Coming 16, 19, 40, 386
Second Helvetic Confession 28, 169
Second Temple period 83, 192, 195, 241
Second Vatican Council 106
Second World War 55–8, 60, 109, 157, 335–6, 412, 459, 480, 484
secularity 560–8
  Anglicanism and 154, 155–6, 163, 164
  Asia 519, 520
  charity 279
  children 289
  Christmas trees and 274
  commercialization 550–1, 557
  festivals 21
  fiction and 408, 409
  food and drink 303
  France 438, 442
  Germany 436
  gifts 284
  and Incarnation 94
  Latin America 530
  music 316, 327, 438
  nineteenth century 45, 52
  poetry and 385, 388
  popular songs 330–44
  Reformed and Dissenting Protestantism 167, 168, 169, 171, 175
  twentieth century 57, 60–1
  United Kingdom 484
  United States 495, 497, 539, 540, 541–6, 570–1, 575

Sedgwick, Catherine 270
Segalen, Martine 442
Selaiha, Nehad 378
Selles, Kurt D. 516
Selope Thema, R. V. 505, 506
Selznick, David 412
Semenov, D. D. 467
Senn, Frank C. 292
Sens Cathedral, France 21
Seoul, Korea 515
Septuagint 226, 227, 228, 231, 233
Septuagint of Daniel 198
Serbia 135–6, 137
Servetus, Michael 573
Seuse, Heinrich 317
Shackleton, Ernest 47, 583
Shakespeare, William 377
Shantou, China 513, 514, 516
Sheba 73, 74
Shembe, Isaiah 509
shepherds
  in art 234, 252, 353–5, 367
  carols and music 312, 315, 321
  Eastern Orthodox Church 128
  feast for 436
  Latin America 526, 527, 529
  in Luke 7, 82, 116, 117, 194, 224–5, 228, 231–3, 361
  Nativity plays 22
  plays 373, 375, 435, 529
Sherman, James 39
Shevzov, Vera 464, 466
Shockley, Evie 389–90
Siefker, Phyllis 449
Sigillaria (end of Saturnalia) 241
Sigley, Gary 518, 519
Silent Night (opera) 56–7
Simeon 82, 83, 84, 357–9
Simon bar Kosiba 72
Simon from Samaria 214
Singapore 513
Sinterklaas 260, 262
Sioux Falls, South Dakota 42, 280
al-Sisi, President Abdul Fattah 429–30
Sitler, Robert 247–8
Sixtus III, Pope 116
Sixtus VI, Pope 527

Skram, Amalie 453
slavery 243, 253, 277–8, 302, 375–6, 522, 523, 528–30
Slayter, William 320
Smaill, Adele Margaret 318
Smart, Christopher 393–4
Smith, John 30
Smith, Mark D. 208–9
Smith, Sarah Clara 512
smudging 242
Snegurochka (Snow Maiden) 472
snow motif 244–5, 336–7
Snyder, Grace 283
Snyder, Phillip 267, 268
social exchange theory 163
Society for the Prevention of Useless Giving *see* SPUG
social hierarchies, inversion of 243–4, 302, 490–2, 551
Society of Friends *see* Quakerism
Society of Mary 103
Sol Invictus 8, 10, 128
Solemn League and Covenant 169–70
Solomon, King 226, 231
Soranus 230
Soria, Fray Diego de 527
Sorin, Edward 108
Soubirous, Bernadette 108
South Africa 506, 509, 578
Southern Africa 500–9
Soviet Union 57–8, 274, 469–73, 576
Sowm al-Milad (Nativity Fast) 426
Spain
    Catholicism 434
    colonialism 109, 189, 306, 376, 494, 523, 526, 530
    commercialization 299
    food and drink 298, 304
    gifts 242, 284, 299, 436, 439
    Midnight Mass 116, 434–5
    Nativity scenes 436
    visions 108
Spong, Bernard 578
Spotify 329–30, 333
spring equinox 9
Springsteen, Bruce 338
Sproul, R.C. 179

SPUG (Society for the Prevention of Useless Giving) 283
Spurgeon, C. H. 40, 45, 176
St-Denis, Royal Abbey of, Paris 314–15
St. Michael's Abbey, Antwerp 359
St. Stephen's Day 152
Stalin, Joseph 471, 472
Stalingrad, Battle of 56, 459
Standiford, Les 35, 397
Stark, Rodney 159
Star of Bethlehem 224, 247, 273, 513
Starr, Kay 339
Stein, Blair 240, 241
Stephen, St. 20
Stephen the protomartyr 114
Stevens, Justice John Paul 274
Stevens, Patricia Bunning 30
Stevens, Sufjan 394–5
Stille Omgang (walk) 357
'Stir Up Sunday' 154
St. Mary Magdalen, Johannesburg 504
St. Mary Magdalene's, Paddington 39
St. Mary Major, Rome 12, 119
St. Nicholas Day 32, 126, 142, 258, 438–9
Stokker, Kathleen 552–3
Stone, Lawrence 158
Stonehenge 239–40, 249
Storm, Theodor 452
Stowe, Harriet Beecher 38, 40
St. Patrick's Catholic Cathedral, Auckland 39
St. Petersburg 466–7
St. Peters, Rosettenville, Johannesburg 504
St. Sergius, Cairo 188
Strabo 365
Strasbourg 32, 267, 272, 442
Strauss, D. F. 561
Streisand, Barbra 334
Strobel, August 5
Stuart monarchy 31, 168–9
Stubbes, Philip 30
St. Victor, Paris 21
Substitutionism 564
Sunday schools 38–9, 42, 44, 175
Sundblom, Haddon 261, 554
Supplement to the New Version of the Psalms 320
Surrey Chapel, London 39

swaddling cloths 225, 228, 229–31, 234
Swaziland 508
Sweden
  gift-wrap paper industry 454
  printing 319
  St. Lucia 54, 151, 245, 292, 299, 450, 456, 575
  'Syltsöndag' (Display-Window-Sunday) 456
  television 456–7
Switzerland 28
Sydney, Australia 244
symbolic number systems 5, 9
Symeon Metaphrastes 252
Syria 5–6, 9, 146, 208–10, 218, 424, 427, 429

T

Ta Phota (festival) 7
tabula fortunata 441
Taino Indians 522, 524
Talen, Bill 574
Talley, Thomas J. 5, 10
Talmud 192, 195
Tanner, Henry Ossawa 102
Tanner, Norman P. 105
Tarahumaras people 528
Tarímbaro, Mexico 528
Tate, Nahum 320, 321
Taylor, Charles 550, 552
Tchaikovsky, Pyotr Ilyich 401–2
technology 294–5
television 411, 417–20
  Andy Williams Christmas Show 418
  Bing Crosby Show 418
  Blackadder's Christmas Carol 420
  carols and music 53, 291
  charity campaigns 443
  A Charlie Brown Christmas 337, 556
  Christmas Night With The Stars 420
  'Countdown to Christmas' 418
  films 415
  Germany and Scandinavia 456–7
  A Godwink Christmas 556
  popular music 261, 337, 339
  Seinfeld 249
  The Two Ronnies Christmas Specials 420
  United Kingdom 480–2, 484
  United States 552, 555–6
Temple, William 92
Teresa of Avila, St. 189
terrorism 424, 428, 579
Tertullian 208–9, 216, 437
Teutonic solstice rituals 458
Texas 30
Thailand 518
Thanksgiving 156, 246, 248–9, 261, 303, 304, 417, 538–9
Theophan the Recluse, St. 464–5
Theophany 4, 12, 127, 136, 214, 464
'Walled Off Hotel, The' Bethlehem 376
Thomas, Carla 341
Thomas, Judge Clarence 543
Thomas Aquinas 106
Thomas of Celano 291
Thompson, Tommy 280
Tiberius Caesar 3
Tibet 520
Tieck, Ludwig 452–3
Tikhon, Patriarch 472
Tille, Alexander 265
Tilo, E. J. 505
Timkat (festival) 290
Timothy, Letters to 86
Titus, Letter to 7, 117
Tizzard, Aubrey M. and Widdowson, John David Allison 552
Todd, Margot 171–2
Tolkien, J. R. R. 408
Tomten (gnomes) 446, 450, 451–3, 459
Torah 193, 232
'totalitarian' regimes 58
Toulmin, Joshua 172–3
Tractarianism 40, 270
Tracts for the Times 40
Transfiguration 200
Trapp Family Singers 334
Tree of Knowledge 266, 365
Trent, Council of 363, 524
Trinitarianism 172
tripudia 20
Troeltsch, Ernst 96
Trollope, Anthony 39
Trump, Donald 497

Truro Cathedral 67, 157
Tudor Court 31
Turkey 576
Tusser, Thomas 300-1
Tuttle, Norman 258, 259
Twelfth Night 243-4, 298-9, 304, 478
typology 74-6, 127, 130-2
Tysdale, John 318-19

U

Ulm 305
Unitarianism 173, 179
United Church of Canada 574
United Kingdom 475-87
  commercialization 476
  domestication of Christmas 478
  imagined community 479-82
  media 480-1
  standardized Christmas 477-9, 481
  television 480-1
United Nations Convention on the Rights of the Child 289
United States 489-98
  African-American population 248, 375-6, 577
  'Black Christmas' movements 496
  charity and giving 492-4
  Christmas cards 46
  Christmas Eve 298-9
  Christmas trees 43, 44, 273-4
  closure of stores 61
  Cold War 57
  commercialization 53, 156, 493-4, 549-57
  domestication of Christmas 44, 162, 491
  First Amendment 539-46, 570
  fiction 397-9
  food and drink 297, 302-5, 307
  gender 62
  gifts 277-8
  Great Depression 280
  immigration 54, 303, 552-3
  Independence Day 582
  indigenous people 494-5
  influence of 476
  inversion 490-2
  Judaism 493
  media 497
  'National Christmas Tree' 54
  Nativity scenes 543-6
  Presbyterianism 176
  public holidays and the law 302, 538-43
  race 496
  Santa Claus 337-40
  slavery 302, 375-6
  St Nicholas 256-260
  Thanksgiving 246
  'War on Christmas' 54
  world wars 53, 56, 284
United States Supreme Court
  Am. Civil Liberties Union of N.J. ex rel Lander 545
  American Legion 543, 546
  County of Allegheny v. American Civil Liberties Union 191, 544, 545
  SC *Doe v. City of Clawson* 545
  Everson v. Board of Education 539-40
  Ganulin v. United States 541
  Lemon v. Kurtzman 540-4, 570
  Lynch v. Donnelly 274, 495-6, 543-5, 570
Universal Norms 113
University of Maine 571-2
urbanization 44, 160, 190, 278, 466, 478, 504
Uruguay 528
Usener, Hermann 4, 5

V

van den Eeckhout, Gerbrand 357-9
van den Vondel, Joost 359
Van Eyck brothers 200
van Lierop, Eleanor 512
Van Onselen, Charles 504
van Oostsanen, Jacob Cornelisz 355-7
Vance, Vince and the Valiants 341
Van Rensselaer, Cortlandt 37
Varietates Legitimae 120
Vatican II, council of 434
Vautrin, Minnie 516
Veblen, Thorstein 550, 551
Venezuela 527, 528
verbum infans 17
Verona 'Sacramentary' 116
Victoria, Queen 27, 32, 43, 46, 268
Vietnam 119
vigil Mass 115, 117, 119

virgin birth 4, 16, 72, 74, 87, 132, 147, 186
Virginia 30, 45, 158–9
Virgin Mary 102–10
  and Advent 16
  Assumption 106, 107, 109
  biblical sources 102–5
  biblical witness 185
  Catholicism and 39, 107–9
  census 205–6
  Christology 97–98, 100
  Council of Ephesus 105–6
  devotion and dogma 107–9
  Eastern Orthodox Church 131–2
  feminism 109–10
  Gabriel 193, 196, 198–200, 207
  historical 187
  identification with Eve 106
  John the Baptist and 197
  'La Purissima' 526
  in Luke 203
  Luther and 143, 146–7, 148, 149
  Magnificat 21, 84, 104, 110, 204, 207, 314, 348, 361, 582
  in Mark 78–9
  in Matthew 80, 81, 82–4, 186
  'mediatrix' 106
  medieval period 19, 106–7
  Old Testament 70, 74–5
  Pope Sixtus III and 116–17
  Protestantism 110
  race 109–10
  theotokos 97, 106, 107, 116
visions 19, 20, 192–5, 196, 234, 254, 351, 402
Visitation 185–6, 348, 349f, 386–7
Vita Moysis 215
Vladimir, Prince of Kiev 463
Vogel, Paula 379–80
'Volksgemeinschaft' 458
'Volksweihnachten' 458
Vondel, Joost van den 359
von der Pfalz, Lisolette 267

W

Wace 438
Wachelder, Joseph 278
Wagner, Anna and Richard 59
Waits, William B. 279, 284, 553
Waldfogel, Joel 285, 494
Wales 482–3
Wanamaker, John 178, 554
Wanchin Basilica of the Immaculate Conception, Taiwan 520
Wang Tsong-Ih 512
Wang Yi 519
Wang Zuo'an 577
Warmstry, Thomas 320
Washington, George 538
wassailing 31, 161, 478
Waterbeach, Cambridge 40
Waterbury, Lucy W. 513, 514, 515
Watt, James 177
Watts, Los Angeles 496
Watts, Isaac 174, 320
Weber, Max 549–50
Weihnachtsmann (Christmas Man) 282, 284, 449
'Weihnukka' 454
Wernecke, Herbert H. 518
Wesley, Charles 174, 322
Wesleyan reform movement 321
Westboro Baptist Church, Topeka, Kansas 573–4
Weston, Anthony 246
Wheaton College, Illinois 37
Wheeler, C. B. 283
Whitburn, Joel 330
White House, National Christmas Tree 273
Wicca 247
Wichern, Johann Heinrich 436–7
Wilde, Anna Day 248
Wilder, Thornton 380–1
Wildflower, Benjamin 110
William, Bishop of Auxerre 22
Williams, David 173
Williams, Frank 4
Wilson, Robert O. 516
Wilson Diptych 217
Winkler, Gabriele 6
Winston, Diane 177–8
Winter Aid 458
winter solstice 239–49
  dating of Christmas and 4–5, 8, 9
  festival 15, 17, 128, 137, 292, 305, 437, 439, 441, 446, 495, 568

Wisdom, Book of 116, 231, 434
Witwatersrand 500–1
Witz, Konrad 348, 349f
Woodforde, Reverend James 32, 159
Woodward, Hezekiah 30
Worde, Wynken de 318
Wordsworth, William 385
Wrede-Sparre, Countess Cristina 448
Wright, N. T. 210, 211

Y
Yeats, W. B. 386, 387
Yousef, Nancy 385
Yule log 33, 59, 240, 305, 433, 440–1, 446, 478
Yunnan, China 519–20

Z
Zachariah 198, 361
Zacharias 193, 196–8, 348
Zahn, Matthew 269
Zarnack, August 267
ZCC (Zion Christian Church) 509
Zechariah 73, 82–3, 203, 204, 205, 207
Zeldin, Alexander 381
Zeno 218
Zhang, Kaiyuan 516
Zimmerman, Mary Ann 109
Zionism 454
Zionist Church 503
Zwarte Piet 262–3, 576
Zwingli, Ulrich 28